AMERICAN JUSTICE

AMERICAN JUSTICE

Volume III
Pullman strike – Zoning

A Magill Book
from the **Editors of Salem Press**

Consulting Editor
Joseph M. Bessette
Claremont McKenna College

Salem Press, Inc.
Pasadena, California   Englewood Cliffs, New Jersey

Editor in Chief: Dawn P. Dawson

Consulting Editor: Joseph M. Bessette   *Project Editors:* McCrea Adams and R. Kent Rasmussen

Research Supervisor: Jeff Jensen   *Photograph Editor:* Valerie Krein

Proofreading Supervisor: Yasmine A. Cordoba   *Production Editor:* Janet Long

Layout: James Hutson   *Maps:* Moritz Design

Library of Congress Cataloging-in-Publication Data

American Justice / from the editors of Salem Press, consulting editor, Joseph M. Bessette
    p. cm. — (Ready reference)
"A Magill Book"
Includes bibliographical references and index.
    ISBN 0-89356-761-2 (set : alk. paper). — ISBN 0-89356-764-7 (vol. 3 : alk. paper).
    1. Law—United States—Encyclopedias. 2. Justice, Administration of—United States—Encyclopedias. I. Bessette, Joseph M. II. Series.
KF154.A44   1996
349.73—dc20
[347.3]   95-51529
    CIP

Third Printing

CONTENTS

ALPHABETICAL LIST OF ENTRIES

Volume I

Volume II

Volume III

AMERICAN JUSTICE

Pullman strike

DATE: 1894

PLACE: Chicago, Illinois

SIGNIFICANCE: A consequence of the mounting frustration of workers during the severe depression of the mid-1890's, the Pullman strike marked increasingly violent conflict between the federal government and organized labor

One of the most important strikes during the United States' industrial revolution occurred in 1894, after workers at the Pullman rail coach factory (which manufactured railroad cars) had experienced five wage cuts in one year. The strike soon drew in the Pullman workers' parent union, the American Railway Union, and virtually halted the movement of Pullman-equipped trains on most railroads in the western United States. Acting on a request of the railroad owners, U.S. attorney general Richard Olney secured an injunction against the strike on the grounds that it was obstructing the delivery of mail. On July 4, 1894, the arrival of two thousand U.S. troops in Chicago to enforce the injunction triggered riots and looting. By the time peace was restored, the strike had been broken.

A number of union officials were convicted of contempt for disobeying the injunction. One such official was Eugene V. Debs, who a few years later would become one of the most influential leaders of American socialism. The success of the U.S. attorney general in securing an injunction against the union and the U.S. Supreme Court's subsequent upholding of the convictions gave official sanction to the use of injunctions in labor disputes.

See also Debs, Eugene V.; Injunction; Labor law; Labor unions; Sherman Antitrust Act.

Punishment

DEFINITION: Penalties imposed for wrongdoing

SIGNIFICANCE: To declare a particular action offensive without imposing consequences for the offense would be meaningless, but what constitutes reasonable punishment for any given offense has been the subject of debate for centuries

If a society were to declare a particular action wrong or offensive without imposing any consequences for that action, the declaration would not carry much weight. Moreover, if the consequences were exceptionally grave for a light offense, the popular notion of natural justice would be so violated that the punishment would rarely be imposed by a jury. On the other hand, if the penalties were light for a serious offense, one would expect that the offense would occur more frequently. In the United States, both the severity of the wrong and whether the wrong is private (civil) or public (criminal) affect the kind of punishment imposed.

Punishments have been inflicted on wrongdoers for as long as there have been societies with rules to be broken. Nevertheless, punishment raises a number of philosophical, moral, and practical issues. The oldest rationale for punishment is that wrongdoers should "pay" for the wrongs they have done to others; they deserve to be punished. This is essentially the notion of retributive justice—that criminals should get their "just deserts." Retribution provides satisfaction to those who have been wronged and sometimes to society at large, but the question remains how society can justify inflicting harm on individuals. One argument is that punishment acts as a deterrent to crime through its threat that wrongdoers, if caught, will be punished. Whether punishment is effective as a deterrent to crime has been heatedly debated. Another reason for punishment is that prison sentences can prevent offenders from committing further crimes simply by locking them up ("incapacitating" them).

Private Wrongs. Modern societies typically distinguish between private wrongs (torts) and public wrongs (crimes). The American court system deals with private wrongs between individuals because it recognizes that a private wrong that is not resolved through an orderly legal procedure can lead to grievances that may produce violence. The courts are therefore open to private individuals to mediate or redress private wrongs. Penalties for those convicted of private wrongs are typically civil damages—either reparations or restitutions.

Restitution is an amount paid for damages that can be calculated directly; reparation is an amount paid for intangible damages. When a private wrong, such as an automobile accident, takes place without injuries, the typical result is that the person judged negligent (or responsible for the action) will be required to pay the monetary cost for repairing the damage, thereby making restitution. If there are injuries associated with the accident, the negligent party may be asked to pay for intangible damages such as "pain and suffering," a reparation, in addition to making restitution for repairs and medical costs. In some cases, fines—a societal attempt to redress grievances—can also be imposed for private wrongs.

Although crimes are generally considered more serious than private wrongdoings, the cost of civil damages, whether reparations or restitutions, may exceed the cost imposed for criminal activity. One who is judged negligent in an automobile accident, for example, might well prefer to have been found guilty of breaking a traffic law and been required to pay a modest fine rather than facing the high damages, legal fees, and perhaps increased insurance payments that the private wrong may entail. Civil law also allows for punitive damages, a kind of reparation, in cases in which the private wrong is so close to a grievous criminal wrong that it is thought that the perpetrator must pay an additional sum to discourage that behavior in the future.

Crimes. Criminal punishments occur when society has judged an action or behavior sufficiently offensive to society as a whole that general public laws must declare it a crime and provide the public with a role in the punishment. Crimes are classified generally according to their severity as misdemeanors or felonies, with misdemeanors being less serious and felonies more serious. Generally, misdemeanors are punishable by fines or by incarceration that does not exceed one year in prison. There are exceptions, however; some serious misdemeanors can carry heavier penalties than some felonies.

Felonies are serious criminal wrongs for which the penalties, as written in statutes, exceed one year in prison. Punishment for felonies may also include the loss of certain political

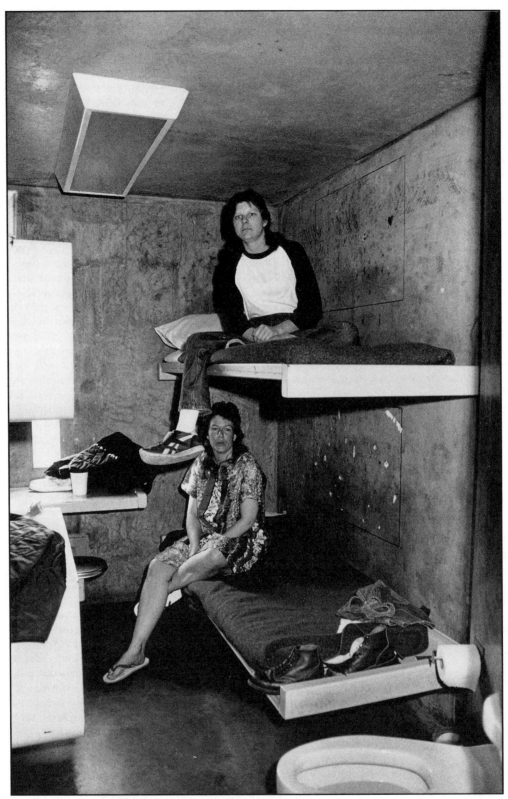

Retribution—the belief that people should "pay" for their misdeeds—is the oldest rationale for punishment of crime. (Ben Klaffke)

or civil rights, such as the right to vote or the license to practice in a certain profession. Some felonies also carry monetary fines. Fines and confinement (incarceration) are widely used in the U.S. judicial system. Corporal punishment (physical punishment such as whipping or beating), which was once common, is no longer practiced in the United States. For the most serious offenses, a sentence of execution (capital punishment) may be imposed. Capital punishment is typically invoked only for murder; it remains quite controversial. Criminal penalties vary in proportion to the crime's severity, with high fines, long prison terms, or execution being imposed on those convicted of the most serious crimes.

Concepts of Punishment. Through most of history, the primary reason for punishment has been retribution for wrongdoing. The Old Testament injunction that one should take "an eye for an eye, a tooth for a tooth" conveys this idea; it also implies that punishment should be proportional to the crime. Modern societies have questioned the benefit of retribution, and retribution has declined somewhat as a justification for punishment. It has been supplemented with ideas such as rehabilitation and reparation.

The relative deterrent effects of harsh punishment compared with efforts to rehabilitate the offender have been debated. The concept of rehabilitation arose as modern societies discovered that an individual may be more likely to commit a crime after release from prison than before incarceration. For one thing, the period of incarceration may have caused the person to lose a means of livelihood. For another, prison may expose first-time offenders to the criminal culture—the way of life of the career criminal.

A still more recent concept of punishment is that the person who has committed the wrong should be required to pay reparations to the victim of the crime. Victims may suffer not simply from the initial action but from a continuing loss; someone wounded by a gunshot, for example, may be disabled for life. Under reparations programs, the perpetrator is released to hold a productive job and required to make long-term payments to the victim. Both the victim and society at large may benefit.

The idea of time off for good behavior (or "good time") occupies an important place in modern ideas about punishment. If a wrongdoer is incarcerated with a long-term sentence, there may be no incentive to stop engaging in criminal behavior while in prison. The provision of good time gives a person an incentive to behave well while in prison and has therefore been popular with corrections officials. Another concept, probation, is sometimes confused with time off for good behavior, although its underlying rationale is different. Probation is generally granted on the notion that the prisoner has been rehabilitated and can safely be returned to society. It is connected to good behavior in that good behavior is sometimes taken as evidence of rehabilitation (thereby justifying probation).

There has been some concern that prisoners may take advantage of provisions such as good time and probation, behaving well in prison and appearing to be rehabilitated; then, upon obtaining release, they may simply return to a life of crime. Accordingly, many states have begun to impose what are called "determinate sentences," seeking to remove probation from the options that the judge may consider for some crimes. Time off for good behavior is normally still granted as an incentive to reduce criminal behavior among prison populations.

Punishment and the Constitution. The idea that punishment should be proportional to the offense has been inherent in the American criminal justice system since the founding of the nation. Only two years after the adoption of the U.S. Constitution in 1789, the Bill of Rights was added. Its Eighth Amendment states that excessive fines shall not be imposed and that cruel and unusual punishments are prohibited. The very words "excessive fines" imply the concept of proportionality. While proportionality is also implied by the phrase "cruel and unusual punishment," this phrase was intended to ban certain kinds of punishment considered so cruel, painful, or unusual as to have no justification other than retribution. The framers of the Constitution realized that pure retribution or revenge was inadequate as a justification for punishment. Tortures, such as mutilation or drawing and quartering, were therefore prohibited by this phrase.

A number of once common punishments, such as public humiliation, public whippings, and public executions, are no longer used because they are regarded as cruel and unusual. Corporal punishment is no longer imposed because of the physical pain it inflicts and the possibility of long-term injury. Corporal punishment is generally held to be purely retributive.

Cases charging that capital punishment in the modern United States constitutes cruel and unusual punishment have reached the Supreme Court, but the Court has not upheld this interpretation. Nevertheless, capital punishment is extremely controversial. Many legal scholars and a significant segment of the general public believe that execution is not an effective deterrent, that retribution is an inadequate justification for capital punishment, and that the danger of executing an innocent person is too great to justify its use. Some legal scholars, including some Supreme Court justices, believe that public sensibilities have changed enough in modern times that capital punishment should be regarded as a cruel and unusual punishment, but this view does not represent majority opinion. In many European nations and in fifteen American states, capital punishment is no longer used even in the most severe crimes.

Punishment and the States. The American criminal justice system is primarily a state-based system. Most serious crimes are state offenses, and most incarcerations are in state prison facilities. The individual states decide how severe penalties should be, and penalties vary widely. Indeed, some observers have thought it irrational that a crime might have a one-year penalty in one state and a twenty-year penalty—or more—in another. Despite the inequity implied by this diversity, support for federalism remains, and the variations are tolerated.

In the latter part of the twentieth century, Congress duplicated many state criminal statutes with federal statutes. One reason for this is that the passage of such legislation offerred an easy, low-cost way for federal legislators to demonstrate their "toughness" on crime and devotion to law and order.

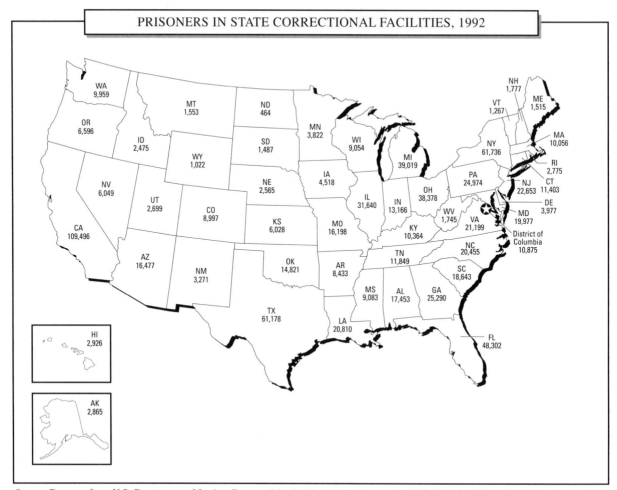

PRISONERS IN STATE CORRECTIONAL FACILITIES, 1992

Source: Data are from U.S. Department of Justice, Bureau of Justice Statistics, *Prisoners in 1992* (bulletin NCJ-141784). Washington, D.C.: U.S. Government Printing Office, 1993.

Note: The five states with the highest incarceration rates, as opposed to total numbers of prisoners, were, in descending order, Louisiana, South Carolina, Oklahoma, Nevada, and Arizona.

Practical and Economic Considerations. A problem in the criminal justice system has been rapidly growing prison populations, partly because of the large number of people convicted and sentenced to prison terms for violating drug laws. The rapidly growing prison population and the extremely high cost of providing adequate prison facilities have led some to recommend legalizing drugs, although no consensus has emerged on this question. Although some drug use (primarily marijuana) has been decriminalized in some states, most drug use will almost certainly remain illegal in the United States. The cost of building and maintaining prisons has also increased as the federal courts have found some state facilities to be inadequate or inhumane and therefore in violation of the Constitution's cruel and unusual punishment provision.

One result of prison crowding is a growing use of probation, community service, house arrest, and technological restraints on movements (such as bracelets with electronic beepers to control criminals sentenced to house arrest). These electronic devices allow convicted offenders to hold down jobs during business hours but confine them to their homes after work. Prison populations are reduced, and offenders can make restitution or reparation to their victims.

All these developments have led to the idea of evaluating penalties from an economic perspective. Cost-benefit analyses of incarceration have increasingly played a role in the evaluation of penalties and, by implication, in the justification for punishment. Some crimes can have dollar values attached to them, allowing cost-benefit analyses comparing the cost of the crime with that of punishment. When applied to drug offenses, for example, analyses indicate to some experts that incarcerating people for these crimes may not be cost effective to society as a whole. *—Richard L. Wilson*

See also Bill of Rights, U.S.; Capital punishment; Criminal justice system; Cruel and unusual punishment; Discretion;

Incapacitation; Just deserts; Mandatory sentencing laws; Model Penal Code; Prison and jail systems; Prisons, Bureau of; Sentencing; Sentencing guidelines, U.S.

BIBLIOGRAPHY

One of the most talked about philosophical treatments of punishment in the twentieth century is Michel Foucault's *Discipline and Punish: The Birth of the Prison* (New York: Random House, 1979). Other overviews of philosophical and practical concerns include David Garland, *Punishment and Modern Society: A Study in Social Theory* (Chicago: University of Chicago Press, 1990); Ernest van den Haag, *Punishing Criminals: Concerning a Very Old and Painful Question* (Lanham, Md.: University Press of America, 1991); and Herbert L. Packer, *The Limits of the Criminal Sanction* (Stanford, Calif.: Stanford University Press, 1968). An excellent summary of the history of law and justice in the United States is *Law and Justice* by Howard Abadinsky (Chicago, Ill.: Nelson-Hall, 1988). Herbert Jacob's *Justice in America* (4th ed. Boston, Mass.: Little, Brown, 1984) is becoming a classic in the study of criminal justice.

Punitive damages

DEFINITION: Damage awards over and above the amount assigned for restitution of loss that are intended to punish a defendant rather than to provide victims with compensation

SIGNIFICANCE: Punitive damages, sometimes called exemplary damages because they seek to make an example of a wrongdoer, punish an offender for extreme wrongdoing, notably in cases involving gross negligence, fraud, violence, or malice

A system was developed in England in the thirteenth century in which monetary penalties, called amercements, were awarded by the courts in civil cases. The awards became frequent and often excessive. As a result, the Magna Carta included provisions limiting amercements and attempted to allow only amounts reasonable for the wrongdoing.

Similarly, the Eighth Amendment to the U.S. Constitution reads, "Excessive bail shall not be required, nor excessive fines imposed, nor cruel and unusual punishment inflicted." There have been several constitutional challenges to the legality of punitive damages, among them *Bankers Life & Casualty Co. v. Crenshaw* (1988) and *Pacific Mutual Life Insurance Co. v. Haslip* (1991). Nevertheless, these awards have become more frequent since the 1960's—so much so that many insurance policies now exclude payment of loss for punitive damages. There have been awards of more than one million dollars when actual damages were relatively small.

See also Bill of Rights, U.S.; Civil law; Civil procedure; Compensatory damages; Litigation; Suit.

Pure Food and Drug Act

DATE: Became law January 1, 1907

DEFINITION: One of the earliest laws regulating the food and drug industries

SIGNIFICANCE: This law prohibited the adulteration or mislabeling of specified food and drug products shipped in interstate or international commerce

The challenge posed by tainted and mislabeled food and drugs was a long-standing concern by the early twentieth century. Certain business interests and advocates of laissez-faire government, however, had stymied efforts at federal legislation. State and local attempts at regulation proved inadequate. Then, in 1906, Upton Sinclair's *The Jungle* focused attention on unsavory conditions at the Chicago stockyards. President Theodore Roosevelt used the resulting popular outcry to push a reluctant Senate to support the Meat Inspection Act, followed by the Pure Food and Drug Act, which took effect on January 1, 1907.

Relying upon the U.S. Constitution's commerce clause, it prohibited the misbranding and adulteration of food and drugs which were shipped between the states or to and from foreign nations. The law has been amended many times, and since 1907 the federal courts have increased the scope of the federal government's regulatory powers. The Pure Food and Drug Act remains one of the most notable laws in American history, both because of the circumstances of its passing—a muckraking novel and a popular president—and because it expanded the federal government's responsibility for the public's welfare.

See also Commerce clause; Food and Drug Administration (FDA); Progressivism; Sinclair, Upton.

Race riots, twentieth century

DEFINITION: Conflict between races, or disorder brought on by racial conflict, that results in widespread illegal activities, including looting, arson, violence, and murder

SIGNIFICANCE: Race riots both threaten the stability of society and, by their very occurrence, call into question the fundamental fairness of society

Referring to racial violence in the United States as "race riots" is often misleading. Many race riots were actually one-sided white massacres of blacks; this was particularly true of those prior to 1921. Nineteenth century race riots were often called "slave revolts" or "slave insurrections." These slave revolts were most frequent in the areas of the South where blacks constituted at least 40 percent of the population. Fearing that slave revolts in one part of the South would trigger similar revolts throughout the South, slaveholders quelled such rebellions quickly and viciously.

Twentieth century race riots differ from nineteenth century riots in both motive and location. Whereas nineteenth century riots were primarily concerned with maintaining the institution of slavery, twentieth century riots—particularly those in the years before World War II—were often designed to maintain white supremacy over urban blacks. Also, where nineteenth century race riots were almost exclusively a southern phenomenon, twentieth century race riots took place in almost every major urban area of America.

1900-1945. Race riots prior to World War II often followed a consistent pattern. In almost all cases, the riots were initiated by whites against blacks. In only two of the major riots—Harlem in 1935 and again in 1943—did African Americans initiate the riots. Second, most riots were caused by a white fear of blacks competing for jobs that previously were held by whites. The rapid movement of blacks from the South to the urban industrial areas of the North contributed to this fear. Third, most riots took place during the hot and humid summer months when young people were out of school. Finally, the riots were often fueled by rumors—allegations of police brutality against blacks or allegations of black violence against whites heightened racial tensions.

One of the major race riots during this period occurred in East St. Louis, Illinois, in 1917. An automobile occupied by four whites drove through black areas firing shots. When a

The race riots that occurred in Detroit in 1943 were initiated by whites; here a mob chases a black man in one of the city's main streets. (AP/Wide World Photos)

similar car was seen, blacks opened fire and killed two occupants, both of whom were police officers. Whites invaded the black community, burning three hundred homes and killing fifty blacks. The summer of 1919 saw twenty riots in communities such as Charleston, South Carolina; Washington, D.C.; Knoxville, Tennessee; and Chicago. The riots of 1919 were so bloody that the period was called the "Red Summer."

Post-World War II Riots. While post-World War II riots were fueled by rumor and also took place during the summer months, they differed from pre-World War II riots in two important ways. First, a majority of the riots were initiated by blacks, not whites. Second, many of the post-World War II riots were not confined to the black community. In several cases, whites were singled out as victims of black violence.

The race riots of the 1960's threatened to destroy the fabric of American society. The 1964 Harlem riot in New York City and the 1965 Watts riot in Los Angeles were both triggered by police incidents. The Watts riot lasted six days and resulted in thirty-four deaths and four thousand arrests. "Burn, baby, burn" became a battle cry in black ghettos throughout the United States.

The year 1967 brought major riots to Newark, New Jersey, and to Tampa, Cincinnati, Atlanta, and Detroit. Newark's riot was the most severe, resulting in twenty-six deaths and $30 million in property damage. The assassination of Martin Luther King, Jr., on April 4, 1968, triggered racial violence in more than one hundred cities. In response to the urban racial violence, President Lyndon Johnson appointed the National Advisory Commission on Civil Disorders, better known as the Kerner Commission. After investigating the causes of the rioting the commission presented a series of recommendations. According to the Kerner Commission, the most important grievances of the black community were police practices, lack of employment opportunities, and inadequate housing. The ominous conclusion of the Kerner Commission was that unless the causes of urban violence were addressed, the United States would continue to become two societies, one black, one white—separate and unequal.

1980's and 1990's. Although there was a lull in race riots during the 1970's, the Miami riots in May of 1980 signaled a renewal of urban racial unrest. On December 17, 1979, a black insurance agent, Arthur McDuffie, was stopped by Miami police officers after a high-speed chase. A fight ensued, and McDuffie was beaten to death. The police officers engaged in a cover-up and reported that McDuffie died as a result of a motorcycle crash. When the cover-up unraveled, five Miami police officers were arrested. Four were charged with manslaughter, and one was charged with tampering with evidence. After deliberating less than three hours, an all-white jury found all defendants not guilty. Within hours of the verdict, the Liberty City section of Miami exploded in violence. Before order was restored three days later, eighteen people were dead, including eight whites who had the misfortune to be driving through Liberty City when the riot began.

The riot that took place in Los Angeles in May of 1992 was triggered by a similar event. Almost immediately after four white police officers were acquitted of assault in the videotaped beating of Rodney King, a black man, one of the most violent race riots in American history broke out. Before it was over, more than sixty people had died, more than four thousand fires had been set, and Los Angeles had suffered property damage totaling more than a billion dollars.

Although the patterns of racial violence may have altered over the decades, the fact remains that race riots continue to occur. Once a southern phenomenon, they have become a national problem in search of a solution.   —*Darryl Paulson*

See also Black Power movement; Civil Rights movement; Commission on Civil Rights; King, Rodney, case and aftermath; Miami riots; National Advisory Commission on Civil Disorders; Racial and ethnic discrimination.

BIBLIOGRAPHY
See James W. Button, *Black Violence: Political Impact of the 1960's Riots* (Princeton, N.J.: Princeton University Press, 1978); Robert Connery, ed., *Urban Riots* (New York: Vintage Books, 1969); Bruce Porter and Marvin Dunn, *The Miami Riot of 1980* (Lexington, Mass.: Lexington Books, 1984); *Report of the National Advisory Commission on Civil Disorders* (New York: Bantam Books, 1968); and Elliott Rudwick, *Race Riot at East St. Louis* (New York: Atheneum, 1972).

Racial and ethnic discrimination

DEFINITION: The act of treating people differently on the basis of race, ethnicity, or cultural heritage; discrimination may be practiced by private individuals or by a government

SIGNIFICANCE: Responding to racial and ethnic discrimination and conflict has been particularly challenging for the United States government, given the immigrant nature of United States society and the longstanding commitment to the principle of equality before the law in the country's political culture

Within the founding documents of the United States are contradictory statements on equality and freedom—and hence on people's right not to be discriminated against. The Declaration of Independence calls it self-evident that "all men are created equal" and have "unalienable rights." Yet the Constitution upholds the institution of slavery, notably in a provision that fugitive slaves must be returned to their owners. Any new country proclaiming equality while allowing slavery and thinking of an entire race as inferior is founded on an impossible contradiction, one that many of the founders undoubtedly realized would have to be faced in the future. Until the mid-twentieth century, however, the federal government generally avoided becoming involved in attempts to legislate against discrimination, allowing the states to establish their own policies. Many of the states, being closer to the people and their prejudices than the federal government was, were inclined to condone discrimination and even actively encourage it through legislation.

Discrimination existed in many different areas of life, including education, employment, housing, and voting rights. Two major pieces of legislation of the 1960's were designed to attack discrimination in these areas: the Civil Rights Act of

1964 and the Voting Rights Act of 1965. The primary avenue for fighting discrimination is through the courts, a fact which causes problems of its own. The Equal Employment Opportunity Commission (EEOC), for example, has the power to bring lawsuits involving employment discrimination; however, a huge number of charges of discrimination are brought before the agency. For that reason, as of the mid-1990's it had a backlog of many thousands of cases awaiting its attention. In discrimination cases the courts have sometimes applied a standard of discriminatory intent and sometimes relied on a standard of discriminatory impact.

Some types of discrimination are easier to see and to rectify than others. A number of activists and legal experts had shifted their attention by the 1980's to a type of discrimination generally known as "institutional discrimination." Institutional discrimination refers to discrimination that is built into social or political institutions, frequently in nearly invisible ways. Institutional discrimination is sometimes not even intentional.

Development of the American Nation. The framework for the development of the United States and its treatment of ethnic minorities was established during the first half century of the nation's history. When the American Revolution ended in 1783, there were few people in the thirteen colonies who considered themselves "Americans," as opposed to Virginians, Pennsylvanians, New Yorkers, and so on. Nevertheless, the people who joined under the Articles of Confederation had much in common. They shared a common language, ethnic stock, and history as well as a philosophy of government that stressed individual rights over group rights. Given time and interaction, one would expect these former colonials to develop a common sense of national identity.

To a substantial extent, that integration occurred during the nineteenth century via such common endeavors as the successful wars against the Spanish in Florida, against Britain in 1812, and against various Indian tribes. As people moved westward to the frontier, the conquest of the continent itself also became a unifying national purpose.

Yet a major challenge to the development of this emerging sense of national identity also arose during the nineteenth century. Between 1830 and 1910, while the country was absorbing new territory, approximately forty-four million immigrants entered the United States, mostly Europeans with backgrounds differing from the white Anglo-Saxon prototype of the founders. Moreover, the Civil War resulted in the freeing of millions of African American slaves, who suddenly became American citizens. There was also a trickle of immigrants arriving from Asia. Finally, there were Jewish immigrants, primarily in the Northeast, and Hispanics, primarily in the Southwest. The country's citizenry was becoming multiethnic and multiracial.

The federal government has historically pursued policy in three broad areas that have related to discrimination: "Indian policy" concerned with Native Americans, immigration policies designed to structure American society, and inclusion policies aimed at ensuring equality before the law for all citizens. The first of these to evolve was the government's policy toward Native Americans, who were the only minority given explicit attention at the constitutional convention in Philadelphia.

Native Americans. Adopted in 1789, the U.S. Constitution made Native Americans wards of the federal government. Treaties with the tribes, like all treaties, were to be federal affairs, and the Supreme Court has repeatedly affirmed the exclusive nature of this power of Congress (*Cherokee Nation v. Georgia*, 1831; *The New York Indians*, 1867). The Supreme Court has also repeatedly upheld the federal government's right to rescind—by ordinary legislation or the admission of new states to the union—those rights accorded the tribes by prior treaties (the *Cherokee Tobacco* case, 1871; *United States v. Winans*, 1905). Even the rationale for the guardian-ward relationship existing between the federal government and the tribes has been elucidated in the opinions of the Court. Essentially, it involves three elements: the weakness and helplessness of Native Americans, the degree to which their condition can be traced to their prior dealings with the federal government, and the government's resultant obligation to protect them. Few of the federal policies adopted before World War II, however, can be described as protective or even benign toward Native Americans.

Policies toward Native Americans traditionally built on the pattern of relations with the tribes established by Europeans prior to the ratification of the Constitution. For hundreds of years, the French, Portuguese, Spanish, English, and Dutch subdued the tribes they encountered, denigrated their cultures, and confiscated their lands and wealth. Early U.S. actions continued the pattern, especially where tribes physically hindered western expansion. During the 1830's, the concept of Indian Territory (land for the Native Americans territorially removed from European settlers) gained favor among European Americans.

When even the most remote of areas were eventually opened to European immigrants, the Indian Territory policy was abandoned in favor of a reservation policy: relocating and settling tribes within contained borders. Meanwhile, contact with European diseases, combined with the increasingly harsh life forced on Native Americans, had devastating effects on the tribes in terms of disrupting their societies and dramatically reducing their numbers. Beginning in the 1880's, reservation policies were frequently augmented by forced assimilation policies: Many young Native Americans were taken from their reservations and sent to distant boarding schools. There, tribal wear and ways were ridiculed, and speaking native languages in class could mean beatings. Only with World War I did these policies soften.

Significant changes in government attitudes toward Native Americans did not come until the "Indian New Deal" instituted by reform-minded commissioner of Indian affairs John Collier in the 1930's. In the late 1960's, another chapter began as Indians began to demand their own civil rights in the wake of the predominantly African American Civil Rights movement. More enlightened federal policies toward Native Americans began to emerge, and since the 1960's considerable legislation has appeared, including the 1968 American Indian Civil Rights Act and the 1975 Indian Self-Determination and Education Assistance Act. A number of factors have worked against Native Americans in advancing their own cause, among them the small number of Native Americans (less than 1 percent of the American population), the assimilation of their most educated members into the general population, and the fact that Native Americans generally think of themselves not as "Indians" but as members of a specific tribe.

Discrimination in Immigration Policy. Fulfillment of the United States' self-determined "manifest destiny" to spread from the Atlantic to the Pacific oceans required people, and early in the nineteenth century the government opened its doors wide to immigrants from Europe.

Yet even during this period, the door was open to few beyond Europe. Hispanic immigrants could enter the country fairly easily across its southern border, but American memories of Texas' war with Mexico made the country inhospitable toward them. More conspicuously, immigration policy was anti-Asian by design. The Chinese Exclusion Act, for example, passed in 1882, prohibited unskilled Chinese laborers from entering the U.S. Later amendments made it even more restrictive and forced Chinese people living in the United States to carry identification papers. The law was not repealed until 1943. Beginning with the exclusion laws of the 1880's, quotas, literacy tests, and ancestry requirements were used individually and in combination to exclude Asian groups. Indeed, even after the efforts during the 1950's to make the immigration process less overtly discriminatory, preferences accorded to the kin of ex-

The fear that American culture would be "swallowed by foreigners" helped fuel discrimination in the latter part of the nineteenth century. This rather grotesque cartoon of the period caricatures Irish and Chinese immigrants. (Library of Congress)

isting citizens continued to skew the system in favor of European and—to a lesser extent—African immigrants.

Meanwhile, Asians who succeeded in entering the country often became the targets of such discriminatory state legislation as California's 1913 Alien Land Bill, which responded to the influx of Japanese in California by limiting their right to lease land and denying them the right to leave any land already owned to the next generation. The most overtly discriminatory act against Asian immigrants or Asian Americans was perpetrated by the federal government, however, which under the color of wartime exigencies relocated tens of thousands of U.S.-born Japanese Americans living on the West Coast to detention camps during World War II. The Supreme Court upheld the relocation program in *Korematsu v. United States* (1944).

It was not until the 1960's and 1970's, during and following the Vietnam War and the collapse of a series of United States-supported governments and revolutionary movements in Asia and Latin America, that the United States opened its doors to large numbers of immigrants and refugees from Asia and the Hispanic world. The government went so far as to accord citizenship to children born of foreigners illegally living in the country.

African Americans. Nineteenth century European immigrants generally were able to make the transition to American citizenship effectively. The urban political machines found jobs for them and recruited them into the political process as voters who, in turn, supported the machines. The prosperity of the country, manifested in the land rushes of the nineteenth century, the industrial revolution, and the postwar economic booms of the twentieth century, enabled the vast majority of these immigrants to achieve upward mobility and a share of the good life.

The citizens who were unable to fit into this pattern, apart from the reservation-bound American Indian tribes, were the African Americans. Enslaved in thirteen states prior to the Civil War and kept in subservience by state laws and various extralegal arrangements for generations afterward, African Americans remained a social, economic, and political underclass with little expectation of progress until nearly eighty years after the Civil War Amendments were added to the Constitution to free and empower them.

The Thirteenth Amendment abolished slavery, the Fourteenth Amendment was designed to prevent states from interfering with the rights of former slaves, and the Fifteenth Amendment constitutionally enfranchised African Americans. By the end of the nineteenth century, however, Supreme Court opinions and state action had combined to minimize the impact of these amendments. In the *Slaughterhouse Cases* (1873), the Supreme Court crippled the Fourteenth Amendment. The Court's decision limited the amendment's privileges and immunities clause only to those rights a citizen has by virtue of national

Overt racial discrimination was sanctioned by law throughout the South until Supreme Court decisions and, finally, the 1964 Civil Rights Act made it illegal. (Library of Congress)

citizenship, not state citizenship. Second, it interpreted the due process clause as a restraint only on *how* a state may act, not on *what* it can do. Only the equal protection clause of the Fourteenth Amendment, which the Court limited to issues of race, continued to offer protection to the newly freed slaves, and in two subsequent cases even that protection was substantially reduced.

First, in the *Civil Rights Cases* of 1883, the Supreme Court ruled that the equal protection clause applies only to state action, not to private discrimination. Then, in the pivotal case *Plessy v. Ferguson* (1896), the Court held that states could satisfy the requirements of the equal protection clause by providing "separate but equal" facilities for blacks and whites. In the meantime, the states began to employ literacy tests, poll taxes, and other devices and arrangements to restrict the ability of African Americans to vote.

Inclusion Policies. Between 1896 and 1936, not only did the separate but equal doctrine legitimize racial discrimination, but also the Supreme Court persistently sustained separation schemes as long as facilities of some kind were provided to a state's black citizens—even if the facilities were woefully inferior to those provided to the white community. In the mid-1930's, however, responding to cases being appealed by the National Association for the Advancement of Colored People (NAACP), the Supreme Court began to shift direction. Between 1936 and 1954, it began to demand that states provide equal facilities to both races and to adopt more demanding tests for measuring the equality of segregated facilities. A Texas system providing separate law schools for blacks and whites, for example, was ruled unconstitutional in 1950 in *Sweatt v. Painter* because the black law school lacked the "intangibles" (such as reputation and successful alumni) that confer "greatness" on a law school and hence was unequal to the long-established school of law for white students at the University of Texas. Likewise, during the same period the Supreme Court began to remove some of the state-imposed obstacles to African Americans voting in the South and to limit the use of state machinery to enforce private acts of discrimination. The separate but equal test itself was finally abandoned in 1954, when, in the landmark case *Brown v. Board of Education*, the Supreme Court ruled that segregated facilities are inherently unequal in public education.

The *Brown* decision led to a decade-long effort by southern states to avoid compliance with desegregation orders. With the Supreme Court providing a moral voice against segregated public facilities, however, these state efforts failed when challenged in court. Moreover, a powerful multiracial Civil Rights movement emerged to demand justice for African Americans in other areas as well. In response, Congress enacted such landmark legislation as the 1964 Civil Rights Act (outlawing discrimination in employment and in places of private accommodation), the 1965 Voting Rights Act, and a series of affirmative action laws designed to benefit groups traditionally discriminated against in American society.

As a result of these laws, the profile of the United States as a multiracial society was irrevocably altered. This change oc-

curred almost entirely as a result of action within the country's legal and constitutional channels. To be sure, prejudice cannot be legislated away even though discrimination can be made illegal. In the mid-1990's, most American cities continued to possess a large African American underclass even as affirmative action and Head Start programs were becoming controversial and being canceled. On the other hand, the policies that had been adopted during the 1950's and 1960's enabled a sizable African American middle and professional class to develop, and many American cities had elected African Americans to govern them by the 1990's. Indeed, it has been argued that the growing prosperity of a subgroup of the African American community undercut the power of the Civil Rights movement. By the 1990's, a number of successful and affluent African American leaders, such as Supreme Court Justice Clarence Thomas, were themselves opposing further affirmative action plans as well as further efforts to finance welfare programs perceived as primarily benefiting a heavily minority urban underclass.   *—Joseph R. Rudolph, Jr., and McCrea Adams*

See also Affirmative action; American Indians; Anti-Defamation League (ADL); Black Power movement; *Brown v. Board of Education*; *Civil Rights Cases*; Civil Rights movement; Equal Employment Opportunity Commission (EEOC); Equal protection of the law; *Griggs v. Duke Power Co.*; *Heart of Atlanta Motel v. United States*; Immigration laws; Jim Crow laws; *Jones v. Alfred H. Mayer Co.*; King, Martin Luther, Jr.; *Korematsu v. United States*; National Association for the Advancement of Colored People (NAACP); *Plessy v. Ferguson*; Race riots, twentieth century; Sex discrimination; *Swann v. Charlotte-Mecklenburg Board of Education*; *Sweatt v. Painter*; *Wards Cove Packing Co. v. Atonio*.

BIBLIOGRAPHY

For good short discussions of government policies toward Native Americans, see Edward H. Spicer, *The American Indians* (Cambridge, Mass.: Belknap Press of Harvard University Press, 1980), and Francis Paul Prucha, *Indian Policy in the United States: Historical Essays* (Lincoln: University of Nebraska Press, 1981). Immigration and discrimination is well treated in Nathan Glazer, ed., *Clamor at the Gates: The New American Immigration* (San Francisco: Institute for Contemporary Studies, 1985); Ronald Takaki, ed., *From Different Shores: Perspectives on Race and Ethnicity in America* (2d ed. New York: Oxford University Press, 1994); Richard J. Meister, ed., *Race and Ethnicity in Modern America* (Lexington, Mass.: Heath, 1974); and Nathan Glazer and Daniel Patrick Moynihan's classic, *Beyond the Melting Pot: The Negroes, Puerto Ricans, Jews, Italians, and Irish of New York City* (2d ed. Cambridge, Mass.: MIT Press, 1970). Interesting works within the vast literature on the Civil Rights movement include Leon Friedman, *The Civil Rights Reader: Basic Documents of the Civil Rights Movement* (New York: Walker, 1968); Anna Kosof, *The Civil Rights Movement and Its Legacy* (New York: Watts, 1989); and Dennis Chong, *Collective Action and the Civil Rights Movement* (Chicago: University of Chicago Press, 1991).

Racketeer Influenced and Corrupt Organizations Act (RICO)

DATE: Became law October 15, 1970

DEFINITION: A federal statute that provides both criminal and civil remedies against persons who commit a variety of common-law and statutory crimes

SIGNIFICANCE: RICO is the primary statutory weapon used by federal prosecutors against organized crime

After twenty years of study and debate, Congress enacted the Racketeer Influenced and Corrupt Organizations Act (RICO) as part of the Organized Crime Control Act of 1970. The statute's primary purpose is to provide an effective means for government prosecutors to act against organized crime. RICO lay dormant for a decade, however, until its architect, G. Robert Blakey of Notre Dame Law School, convinced federal prosecutors to use it against the Mafia.

The Statutory Scheme. The general scheme of RICO is relatively simple. It applies to a defendant who, through a pattern of racketeering activity, has indirectly or directly participated in an enterprise whose activities affect interstate commerce. The critical phrases "person," "enterprise," and "pattern of racketeering activity" are broadly defined in RICO, reflecting a congressional intent to provide for the widest application of the statute in combating organized crime.

The Supreme Court recognized that RICO was to be liberally construed. The term "enterprise" thereby includes "legitimate enterprises" which have committed the requisite illegal acts. RICO prohibits four specific activities: using income derived from a pattern of racketeering activity to acquire an interest in an enterprise, acquiring or maintaining an interest in an enterprise through a pattern of racketeering activity, conducting the affairs of an enterprise through a pattern of racketeering activity, and conspiring to commit any of these offenses.

A "person," defined to include any individual or entity capable of holding a legal or beneficial interest in property, must conduct or participate in the conduct of a RICO enterprise through a pattern of racketeering activity, which requires at least two predicate acts within a ten-year period. The statute is thereby directed at conduct (the predicate acts) rather than status (organized crime). RICO therefore applies to anyone who engages in the proscribed conduct, regardless of who the perpetrator is. Federal prosecutors have generally exercised discretion in limiting RICO prosecutions to cases involving organized crime and securities violations.

The critical phrase "racketeering activity" is defined to include specific state and federal felonies. A veritable laundry list of predicate offenses includes murder, kidnapping, gambling, arson, robbery, bribery, extortion, and dealing in narcotics or other dangerous drugs. Also included as predicate acts are a number of federal crimes, including mail fraud, wire fraud, obstruction of justice, and securities fraud. In 1984 Congress added the distribution of obscene materials to the list of predicate offenses. Several other predicate acts reflect common perceptions of organized crime, such as bribery and sports bribery, unlawful transactions with pension or welfare funds, loan-sharking, interstate transportation of wagering paraphernalia, federal bankruptcy fraud, and violation of any law of the United States concerning drug transactions.

RICO is partially intended to strike at illegal activity that operates through formal, legitimate enterprises. An enterprise is defined to include any individual, partnership, corporation, association, or other legal entity, and any union or group of individuals associated in fact even though they do not constitute a legal entity. One of the most significant features of RICO is that members of an unlawful enterprise can be prosecuted for being part of an enterprise that commits a series of predicate offenses. It is no longer necessary to prosecute individual defendants for a specific crime, such as homicide, which may be difficult to prove.

RICO is distinguished from other criminal statutes because it includes in its penalties the forfeiture of illegally acquired gains and the economic bases of misused power. RICO forfeiture can be of any property that is traceable, directly or indirectly, to the RICO violation. Forfeiture is in addition to any other fine or imprisonment imposed. Criminal forfeiture was common in England, but it is not generally incorporated into the criminal laws of the United States. A freeze on a defendant's assets can also be imposed upon the filing of a RICO complaint by the federal prosecutor.

Civil RICO. Without much thought on the floor of Congress, an amendment to the proposed RICO statute was adopted, adding a civil remedy to the statute. RICO's civil remedy provision is the most commonly utilized provision of the statute. Its popularity rests on the fact that a victim may recover treble (triple) damages and costs of litigation, including attorneys' fees. In addition, the statute can be applied against any defendant who has committed the requisite two predicate acts within a ten-year period. It is widely used in cases of securities fraud, consumer fraud, and real estate development fraud. RICO has also become a standard pleading in business disputes. In January, 1994, the Supreme Court held in *National Organization for Women v. Scheidler* that RICO can be applied against antiabortion protesters. The Court held that RICO is not limited to crimes with an economic motive. Courts frequently use the civil and criminal RICO case-law interpretations interchangeably.

RICO's Effects. RICO has been effective in the government's steady war of attrition against traditional organized crime; its record in prosecuting white-collar criminals has been mixed. Both the civil suit provision and the allowability of freezing assets have proved controversial. Plaintiffs seeking relief under RICO pursue its remedies and application to the fullest. They do not exercise the discretion and self-restraint characteristic of governmental prosecutors. Postconviction forfeitures are also receiving detailed scrutiny, although usually in state cases because of abuses in the use of the forfeited property. One final note is that roughly half the states have enacted "little RICO" laws modeled after the federal statute.

—Denis Binder

See also Anti-Racketeering Act; Forfeiture, civil and criminal; Organized crime; Organized Crime Control Act.

BIBLIOGRAPHY

Overviews of RICO and its application can be found in Norman W. Philcox, *An Introduction to Organized Crime* (Springfield, Ill.: Charles C Thomas, 1978); Gregory J. Wallance, "Criminal Justice: Outgunning the Mob," *American Bar Association Journal* 80 (March 1, 1994); and Douglas R. Abrams, *The Law of Civil RICO* (Boston: Little, Brown, 1991). More specialized views include Organized Crime and Racketeering Section, U.S. Department of Justice, *Racketeer Influenced and Corrupt Organizations (RICO): A Manual for Federal Prosecutors* (2d rev. ed. Washington, D.C.: U.S. Government Printing Office, 1988), and Gregory P. Joseph, *Civil RICO: A Definitive Guide* (Chicago: American Bar Association, 1992).

Randolph, A. Philip (Apr. 15, 1889, Crescent City, Fla.—May 16, 1979, New York, N.Y.)

IDENTIFICATION: Labor and civil rights leader

SIGNIFICANCE: Randolph organized the Brotherhood of Sleeping Car Porters, was vice president of the AFL-CIO, and organized two marches on Washington (1941 and 1963)

A. Philip Randolph was the son of an African Methodist Episcopal minister in Jacksonville, Florida. After being graduated from Coleman Institute he moved to Harlem, where he attended the City College of New York. Attracted to the socialism of Eugene V. Debs, he cofounded the *Messenger*, a radical black monthly, in 1917. He came to believe that the great hindrance to human freedom was economic exploitation. Because the socialists spoke for the workers, and since 99 percent of African Americans were workers, he believed that they should become socialists.

After failing in his attempts to organize laundry workers, motion picture operators, and garment workers, Randolph became the first president of the Brotherhood of Sleeping Car Porters in 1925. It took twelve years of struggle until a collective bargaining contract was negotiated with the Pullman Company. In 1941, when defense industries would not hire African Americans, Randolph planned a mass march on Washington as a protest. To avoid this, President Franklin Roosevelt issued the Fair Employment Practices Order. In 1948 Randolph's efforts led President Harry S Truman to sign an order abolishing segregation in the armed forces.

Randolph advanced in the union leadership, and in 1955 he was elected a vice president of the American Federation of Labor-Congress of Industrial Organizations (AFL-CIO) at its merger convention. He used his position to agitate for the rights of African Americans within the movement, often clashing with its leader, George Meany, over the slow pace of integration in the workplace. In 1963, he was one of the organizers of the March on Washington. On the Washington Mall, he spoke to the crowd of 250,000: "We are the advanced guard of a massive moral revolution for jobs and freedom." Randolph has left an unusual legacy. He was a socialist, union leader, and popularizer of the technique of mass civil disobedience. Yet he was a courtly gentleman who resembled a Shakespearean actor more than a labor leader.

See also American Federation of Labor-Congress of Industrial Organizations (AFL-CIO); Civil Rights movement; Debs, Eugene V.; Labor unions.

Rape and sex offenses

DEFINITION: The term "rape" has widely been replaced in statutes by the more general term "sexual assault," which may include any type of sexual activity involving the use or threat of force; sexual conduct with a juvenile is a felony, with or without the use of force and regardless of consent; other crimes involving the injurious use of sex vary in definition and degree from one state to another

SIGNIFICANCE: Sexual assault and child molestation are the two categories of sex offenses that are widely believed to cause the greatest harm to individuals and to society

In the 1970's, the rate of reported sex crimes, notably rape, began to soar. A combination of growing public awareness of the sensitive nature of such crimes and the continuing difficulty of obtaining convictions in these cases led to significant changes in criminal laws concerning sex-related offenses in the mid-1970's. State statutes defining sex-related crimes were amended nationwide to focus less on the mental state of the victim and more on the intent of the perpetrator. By the mid-1980's, jurisdictions all over the United States had implemented or improved programs for investigating and prosecuting sex offenses, especially those committed upon juveniles. The intent was both to make legal casework more uniform and to minimize courtroom trauma to the victims.

Rape. Generally, modern statutes define rape as the act of intercourse (anal or vaginal) with a male or female who is not the spouse of the offender, committed without the person's lawful consent. Some states acknowledge the crime of rape by one spouse upon another. Degrees of rape and consequent penalties are generally specified, according to the type of force threatened or used and the age or mental capacity of the victim. In prosecutions for rape and other sex crimes, the defense of tacit or explicit consent is often raised. This has been particularly true in cases of what has been labeled date rape or acquaintance rape. Despite legislative changes in the language of rape statutes which have sought to focus more on the intent of the perpetrator and less on the personal life of the victim, courts nevertheless have had to struggle with ambiguous language in rape laws.

Illustrative of this dilemma was a 1992 New Jersey case (*State ex rel. M.T.S.*) in which the appellate courts sought to determine what amount of physical force or coercion was necessary in a case of forcible rape. On its first appeal, the defense successfully argued that the absence of force beyond that involved in the act of sexual penetration precluded a finding of second-degree assault. The New Jersey Supreme Court reversed that ruling, however, holding that the statute did not require additional force beyond that needed to accomplish sexual penetration. In so doing, the court examined the legislative history of the statute, which became effective in 1979 and had changed almost two hundred years of rape law.

A high-profile 1992 rape trial involved boxer Mike Tyson, who was convicted of raping a beauty-contest participant. (AP/Wide World Photos)

Under the old law, the state had to prove both that force had been used and that the penetration had been against the victim's will. Force was measured in relation to the response of the victim, which placed the burden of proof on the victim to show that she had actively and affirmatively withdrawn presumed consent. The issue of consent turned on the credibility of the victim as well as a need for evidence of resistance. Legal and cultural attitudes changed in the 1970's, when feminists and other interest groups began arguing that current rape law minimized the violence associated with the crime and that the resistance requirement was unreasonable and dangerous.

Thus, in 1979, New Jersey altered the language of the law from "rape" to "sexual assault," emphasizing the violent nature of the crime. The words "submission" and "resistance" were replaced with "force" and "coercion." The victim was no longer required to resist or express nonconsent, with the force requirement no longer turning on the victim's state of mind or responsive behavior. Many other states also changed the wording of their statutes around the same time.

In cases where sexual violence which falls short of penetration is committed upon a victim, statutes address the crime in terms of "sexual battery" or similar language. The elements of the crime remain the same as rape, without the requirement of penetration, however slight. Sexual battery must be committed with force or under threat of violence in most states. The majority of jurisdictions also specifically provide criminal penalties for the forced use of oral sex upon a victim, usually designated as oral sexual battery, and in varying degrees, depending upon the degree of force or violence used to commit the crime.

Sex Offenses Committed upon Juveniles. All jurisdictions provide specific statutes prohibiting sexual acts with juveniles. The severity of the penalties varies depending on the nature of the act and the amount of duress, coercion, or force used.

Statutory rape, or intercourse with a minor, is often referred to as carnal knowledge of a juvenile. Consent of the victim is not a defense, and the statutory age varies from one state to another.

Inappropriate touching of a juvenile is criminalized in all jurisdictions. Often designated as indecent behavior with a juvenile, the crime is essentially the commission of any lewd or lascivious act upon the person of a minor (usually a person under the age of seventeen) by an adult. Some states specify that the adult must be over age seventeen and that there must be an age difference of at least two years between the parties. In many jurisdictions, indecent behavior with a juvenile committed with force, duress, or coercion, or perpetrated by a person in a position of authority or control of the juvenile is addressed as a separate and more serious offense, carrying considerably heavier penalties. This is often distinguished from indecent behavior as molestation of a juvenile.

Pornography involving juveniles is treated differently than pornography involving only adults; child pornography is actively and aggressively prosecuted by federal as well as state authorities, as, by its very nature, it involves child molestation or statutory rape. Filming, photographing, or otherwise visually reproducing sexual activities involving a minor provide actual documentation of the crime itself. The solicitation, promotion, sale, and possession of such materials are also generally considered the same crime.

Rapists. Numerous studies of rapists have demonstrated that although not all are alike, common characteristics and personality features are frequently found. Rapists are typically young, with 80 percent being under the age of thirty. The psychosexual backgrounds of rapists have included dysfunctional families with special problems relating to women. Most rapes are committed by men who know their victims. Frequently they are unarmed, but if a weapon is used, it is often a knife. They have a history of violence, with one in three having a prior record of a violent crime and 25 percent having a prior charge of rape.

The serial rapist has been a subject of study for behavioral scientists over the years. It has been shown that the serial rapist more often than not comes from an average or advantaged home and as an adult is a well-groomed, intelligent, employed individual who is living with others in a family context. Serial rapists' family histories show poor relationships with either of their parents, some having been exposed to sexual acts or having been sexually abused at an early age. The majority of victims of the serial rapists studied were strangers, and victim selection was largely based upon availability.

The Psychology of Rape. Studies have shown that the need to assert power and the need to vent anger are frequently parts of the psychological makeup of a rapist. Rapists have been classified into at least three types. The power rapist suffers from great personal insecurity, compensating for fear of impotence by controlling others. The power rapist believes that women like to be raped and often dates women prior to raping them.

The anger rapist is attempting to retaliate for an imagined wrong. He experiences some type of internal explosion that causes an (often unplanned) attack upon a randomly selected victim, using sex as the weapon. He may vent his anger by injuring and degrading the victim. He often has a criminal history of violent crimes.

The sadistic rapist seeks revenge and punishment through the use of violence and cruelty. The victim is only a symbol of the source of his anger. He plans each rape with care and caution, and he is often ritualistic in its execution. In many cases he also murders his victims.

Child Molesters. The sex offender who has a sexual preference for children is referred to as a pedophile. Technically, a pedophile has an age preference for prepubescent children. A molester who prefers children who have reached puberty is referred to as a hebephile. Most of the literature on this subject, however, refers to both types as pedophiles. Although the basic etiology of the pedophile is unknown, numerous studies have suggested some factors that may cause a person to become a child molester. It has been found that most come from homes with domineering mothers and passive or absent fathers. Some have deviant arousal patterns, and others use child molestation to act out responses to nonsexual problems.

A pedophile typically employs seduction and secrecy as methods for gaining sexual entry and avoiding discovery. Pedophiles have been classified as situational molesters (for whom availability is the most crucial factor in the occurrence of molestation) and preferential molesters (who chronically seek mass victims from any source).

Typically, pedophiles and hebephiles have a sex preference as well as an age preference regarding their victims. By far, most pedophiles are heterosexual males, and most victims are young girls. Perhaps about 10 percent of pedophiles are homosexual. Adult sexual preference, however, is not always reflected in preference regarding child victims; a relatively small percentage of pedophiles are married heterosexuals who prefer child victims of the same sex. Two other points are important to note. First, not all pedophiles act on their impulses; second, not all child molesters are pedophiles. A significant amount of child molestation occurs within the family unit itself, and some of this occurs for reasons other than what would be considered pedophilia.

Often the pedophile who molests children is a collector who documents his exploitation with photographs and other memorabilia. Preferential pedophiles seek contact with one another, communicating via mail, telephone, and computer, exchanging photographs, videotapes, and names of victims. There are a number of pedophile organizations in the United States, such as the Rene Guyon Society, the North American Man/Boy Love Association (NAMBLA), and the Childhood Sensuality Circle. The investigation and prosecution of these offenders has presented a serious challenge to law enforcement; often the results of prosecution are disappointing.

Special Problems in Obtaining Convictions. In the prosecution of sex offenses, more than any other type of crime, the government's case relies largely upon the testimony of the victim. Often the state has very little, if any, corroborative evidence to present to the jury beyond the victim's account of the event. The focus of the case becomes the credibility of the complainant. Seasoned defense attorneys will maximize the opportunity to place in question the victim's account or motive in order to create reasonable doubt in the minds of the jurors that the crime occurred at all or that the defendant was in fact the perpetrator.

In cases of rape by an unknown assailant, often a victim cannot perfectly and logically recount the details of the crime or physical facts surrounding the occurrence because of the emotionally charged situation. Defense attorneys will seize this failure to reduce the witness' credibility before the jury. In cases of acquaintance rape, the defense of consent is most common. Despite rape shield laws enacted in the majority of jurisdictions, prior relations with the accused may be raised, and the credibility of the victim regarding her withdrawal of consent may be shaken.

Someone considered an unpopular victim—because of her background or lifestyle in general, or because of the particular activity in which she was engaged just prior to the rape—can be expected to elicit biased or negative reactions from the average juror. Rape victims such as prostitutes, runaways, drug and alcohol abusers, and hitchhikers have often had great difficulty convincing a jury of the severity of the crimes committed against them for this reason.

Similarly, juror bias or misconceptions as to what would be viewed as a normal reaction to being the victim of a sex offense can present a problem that must be overcome by the prosecution. Jurors commonly expect hysteria and the seeking of immediate help after a rape. It is incumbent upon the prosecution to demonstrate that delayed reporting of the crime and guarded or calm, controlled responses by the victim are common reactions to a sexual assault.

In cases of sexual abuse of children, the reliability of the child's testimony is also raised by the defense. The government must establish at the outset of the case that the child witness is competent. Most jurisdictions require a hearing on this issue prior to trial. Generally, the test as to whether or not the child is competent to testify in a court of law is determined by the child's ability to distinguish the truth from a lie and understand the meaning of being sworn under oath. In cases of mental or emotional handicap, the issue of how the handicap affects the child's testimony may also be raised.

When a child has been subjected to repetitive questioning concerning the events, recantation is not unusual. The prosecution must notify the defendant of the recantation and decide whether to dismiss the charges or to proceed, including in the trial expert testimony that recantation is commonplace. Furthermore, seldom is the child molestation event identified accurately as to time and date. With a very young victim, the defense tries to make much of the child's inability to provide exact details and distinguish between fantasy and fact on cross-examination.

Consequently, defense attorneys seek every opportunity the system allows to question the victim of a sex offense, seeking eventual contradictory testimony, emotional and physical exhaustion of the witness, and possibly, recantation or withdrawal of the charge. Preliminary hearings, pretrial motion hearings, and grand jury testimony can be used to erode victims' endurance prior to trial, and minor flaws in their testimony can be magnified to undermine their credibility.

Eventually, the criminal justice system began to recognize the secondary trauma inflicted on victims of sex offenses through the court process and instituted special units and programs to address their needs with greater sensitivity and effectiveness. Victim-witness advocates were employed to assist the witnesses throughout the process. Special sexual assault units were developed in prosecutors' offices to handle the cases vertically, allowing a single prosecuting attorney to handle a case from its investigation and charging phase through final disposition.

Since the 1960's, the community at large has also become more aware of the subject of sexual abuse and its ramifications as various victims' rights groups formed throughout the country, urging legislative change to meet the needs of crime victims. Some groups succeeded in establishing specific victims' rights under state constitutions; this occurred in Wisconsin, for example.

Technological advances and increased knowledge of the impact of sex offenses have contributed in great measure to more effective prosecution of such crimes. The use of deoxy-

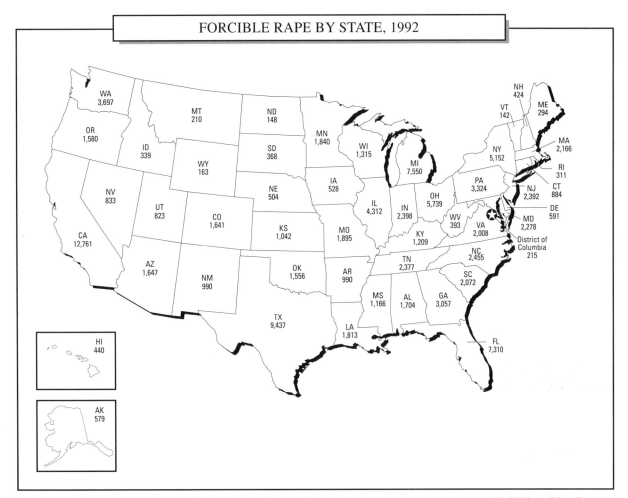

FORCIBLE RAPE BY STATE, 1992

WA 3,697
MT 210
ND 148
MN 1,840
WI 1,315
MI 7,550
NH 424
VT 142
ME 294
OR 1,580
ID 339
SD 368
NY 5,152
MA 2,166
WY 163
IA 528
PA 3,324
RI 311
NV 833
NE 504
IL 4,312
IN 2,398
OH 5,739
NJ 2,392
CT 884
UT 823
CO 1,641
WV 393
VA 2,008
DE 591
CA 12,761
KS 1,042
MO 1,895
KY 1,209
MD 2,278
District of Columbia 215
AZ 1,647
OK 1,556
AR 990
TN 2,377
NC 2,455
NM 990
SC 2,072
MS 1,166
AL 1,704
GA 3,057
TX 9,437
LA 1,813
FL 7,310
HI 440
AK 579

Source: Data are from U.S. Department of Justice, Federal Bureau of Investigation, *Crime in the United States, 1992* (Uniform Crime Reports). Washington, D.C.: U.S. Government Printing Office, 1993.

Note: The five states with the highest rape rates, as opposed to total numbers of rapes, were, in descending order, Alaska, Delaware, Michigan, Washington, and Nevada.

ribonucleic acid (DNA) evidence has been invaluable in rape cases where the identity of the assailant is contested. Expert testimony concerning symptoms consistent with rape trauma syndrome and pedophilia is similarly a powerful tool in cases involving unpopular victims, child abuse, or the victim who does not respond to a shocking event in ways which jurors believe to be appropriate to the crime.

Most significant has been the allowance of videotaped and closed-circuit television testimony in instances of sexual abuse of children. Those jurisdictions which have utilized such methods in presenting the child's statement to the judge or jury have done so in an effort to reduce the trauma of courtroom testimony for young witnesses. Among the issues raised by its use has been the argument that it constitutes denial of the defendant's constitutional right to confront and cross-examine the witness. The U.S. Supreme Court addressed this question in *Coy v. Iowa* (1988), allowing for such testimony to be offered

on a case-by-case basis when the child witness is available for cross-examination. Individual states, however, are still left to struggle with whether the use of such testimony is necessary in each case to preserve the emotional stability of the child witness. *Coy v. Iowa* did not indicate that in every case the child's needs must outweigh the defendant's right to confrontation.

According to the Uniform Crime Reports (UCR), published each year by the Federal Bureau of Investigation, the number of reported rapes and attempted rapes in the United States continued to rise from 1988 through 1992. In 1989 there were a reported 94,504 reported offenses, or 38.1 per 100,000 inhabitants. In 1990, that figure rose to 102,555, in 1991, 106,593, and in 1992, 109,062. The number of reported rapes dropped for the first time in 1993 to 104,806, showing the first decline in the rate since 1987. The number of rapes by force decreased 3 percent in 1993 from the 1992 level, while attempts to rape decreased 12 percent. An estimated 79 of every

100,000 females in the country were reported rape victims, a rate decrease of 6 percent from 1992.

While the data may indicate an encouraging drop in the rate of occurrence of this crime, the quantity of reported incidents remains an imposing one to law enforcement and prosecutors nationwide. The criminal justice system continues to struggle with important unresolved issues concerning the victims' rights and defendants' rights, while striving for effective, uniform prosecutions. —*Kathleen O'Brien*

See also Child molestation; Criminal law; DNA testing; Incest; National Crime Victimization Survey; Pedophilia; Scottsboro cases; Statutory rape; Uniform Crime Reports (UCR).

BIBLIOGRAPHY

A succinct account of the wide variety of sex crimes and those who commit them is Ronald M. Holmes, *Sex Crimes* (Newbury Park, Calif.: Sage Publications, 1991). Kurt Haas and Adelaide Haas, *Understanding Sexuality* (3d ed. St. Louis: Mosby, 1993), offers an in-depth study of sexuality and sexual deviance. One of the most comprehensive and readable studies of the serial rapist can be found in Robert Hazelwood and Janet Warren, "The Serial Rapist: His Characteristics and Victims," *FBI Law Enforcement Bulletin* 58 (February 1, 1989). Robert Hazelwood and Ann Wolbert Burgess, eds., *Practical Aspects of Rape Investigation* (New York: Elsevier, 1987), has a wealth of information on the practical aspects of investigating sex offenses from a law enforcement and behavioral sciences perspective. For a comprehensive study of types of sex offenders, see Paul H. Gebhard et al., *Sex Offenders* (New York: Harper & Row, 1965). Sex offenders who kill their victims are examined in detail in Robert Ressler, Ann Burgess, and John Douglas, *Sexual Homicide: Patterns and Motives* (Lexington, Mass.: Lexington Books, 1988).

R.A.V. v. City of St. Paul

COURT: U.S. Supreme Court

DATE: Decided June 22, 1992

SIGNIFICANCE: This holding, invalidating an ordinance which made it a crime to burn a cross to harass African Americans, demonstrates how the Supreme Court affords a preferred status to First Amendment free speech, even reprehensible speech

During the early morning hours of June 21, 1990, "R.A.V."—an unnamed seventeen-year-old, self-described as a white supremacist—and several other teenagers burned a makeshift wooden cross on the front lawn of the only African American family in their St. Paul, Minnesota, neighborhood. They were prosecuted for disorderly conduct in juvenile court under the city's "bias-motivated crime ordinance," which prohibited cross burning along with other symbolic displays that "one knows" or should know would arouse "anger, alarm or resentment in others on the basis of race, color, creed, religion, or gender."

The state trial court ruled that this ordinance was unconstitutionally overbroad because it indiscriminately prohibited protected First Amendment speech as well as unprotected activity. The Supreme Court of Minnesota reversed the lower court's decision and upheld the ordinance, which it interpreted to prohibit only unprotected "fighting words," face-to-face insults which are likely to cause the person to whom the words are addressed to attack the speaker physically.

The U.S. Supreme Court ruled unanimously in favor of R.A.V. and invalidated the ordinance, but the justices did not agree in their reasoning. Stating that they found the cross burning reprehensible, Justice Antonin Scalia, writing for the majority, nevertheless concluded that the ordinance was unconstitutional because it criminalized only specified "fighting words" based on the content of the hate message and, consequently, the government was choosing sides. He noted that the ordinance would prohibit a sign that attacked Catholics but would not prohibit a second sign that attacked those who displayed such an anti-Catholic bias.

Four justices concurred in the ruling of unconstitutionality, but Justice Byron White's opinion sharply criticized the majority opinion for going too far to protect racist speech. He reasoned that the ordinance was overbroad because it made it a crime to cause another person offense, hurt feelings, or resentment and because these harms could be caused by protected First Amendment speech. Justices Harry Blackmun and John Paul Stevens also wrote separate opinions complaining that hate speech did not deserve constitutional protection.

This holding calls into question numerous similar state laws designed to protect women and minorities from harassment and discrimination. Some of these individuals and groups may still invoke long-standing federal civil rights statutes, however, which carry severe criminal penalties of fines and imprisonment. In 1993, *R.A.V.*'s significance was called into question by the *Wisconsin v. Mitchell* decision upholding a state statute that increased a sentence for a crime of violence if the defendant targeted the victim because of the victim's race or other specified status.

See also Hate crimes; Racial and ethnic discrimination; Speech and press, freedom of; *Wisconsin v. Mitchell*.

Reagan, Ronald (b. Feb. 6, 1911, Tampico, Ill.)

IDENTIFICATION: President of the United States, 1981-1989

SIGNIFICANCE: Reagan improved United States-Soviet relations, promoted supply-side economics, and appointed the first female Supreme Court Justice

Inaugurated in 1981, Republican Ronald Reagan became the oldest president in United States history. Before entering politics, Reagan was an actor, starring in more than fifty films and serving as president of the Screen Actors' Guild (1947-1960). He was outspokenly anticommunist. As governor of California (1967-1975), Reagan decreased state spending, froze hiring, raised taxes, and balanced the budget.

Thwarted in bids for the Republican presidential nomination in the 1968 and 1976 races, he won nomination in 1980 and defeated incumbent president Jimmy Carter in a landslide. Reagan had to deal immediately with runaway national inflation and high unemployment. Following the supply-side theory of

The conservative Republican administration of President Ronald Reagan left a lasting imprint on American government. (Library of Congress)

economics, he reduced taxes, thereby stimulating the economy but creating staggering federal deficits. Reagan's judicial legacy included his appointment of four conservative justices to the U.S. Supreme Court, including Chief Justice William Rehnquist and the first woman justice, Sandra Day O'Connor.

Reagan strengthened the military and increased United States involvement in Central America. The desire of his administration to fund the Contra movement in Nicaragua led to the sales of arms to Iran and the channeling of funds to the Contras, an illegal undertaking that became known as the Iran-Contra scandal. Reagan maintained an uncompromising policy toward the Soviet Union; in 1987, Reagan and Soviet leader Mikhail Gorbachev signed the United States-Soviet arms reduction treaty.

See also Bush, George; Conservatism, modern American; Iran-Contra scandal; Republican Party; Tax Reform Act of 1986.

Real estate law

DEFINITION: The application of general legal principles to the ownership and use of real property

SIGNIFICANCE: Real estate law defines rights in property and then imposes limits on how property can be used or conveyed

Real estate law defines the rights and interests that a person can own in land. Government retains the power to tax, to take property for a public purpose provided just compensation is paid, and to exercise police power to regulate the use to which property is put. Land-use controls such as zoning are an important function of local government.

The greatest amount of ownership an individual may have in property, exclusive of the government's rights, is called a fee simple absolute. An encumbrance or lien, such as a mortgage, may be placed on property. An easement may be granted to a utility company to run electrical power lines on property.

Real estate can be owned in various ways. A husband and wife may own real estate as joint tenants with rights of survivorship, as tenants by the entireties, or as holders of community property, depending on state law. Such laws are primarily designed to guarantee a spouse part of the property in case the other spouse dies. Real estate can also be owned by partnerships, corporations, trusts, and other kinds of businesses.

Contracts for the sale of real estate are governed by ordinary contract law. The Statute of Frauds requires that such contracts be made in writing. Discrimination in the sale of real estate is prohibited by various federal and state statutes governing civil rights and fair housing.

Many people buy real estate with a loan. The lender normally requires a mortgage on the real estate so that it can foreclose on the property if the loan is not repaid. Most mortgage loans are governed by the Truth in Lending Act, which requires uniform disclosure of loan terms so that borrowers can compare loans. The lending policies of financial institutions are governed by civil rights laws, fair credit reporting acts, and fair housing acts. Such statutes require lenders to focus on the borrower's ability to repay a loan without regard to race, sex, or other extraneous circumstances. Lenders must avoid "redlining" (redlining is refusing to provide loans on property in a particular geographic area because residents are of a particular race).

Real estate is subject to taxation by various levels of government. States impose a property tax based on the value of the property. Property is often subject to a special conveyance tax when it is sold. The sale of real estate at a profit will often create an income-tax liability. Most laws reduce taxes on property that is used as a homestead. Income taxes on sales of such property may sometimes be deferred or totally excluded.

Real estate leases present particular problems. Discrimination in leasing is illegal under the civil rights and fair housing laws. Local jurisdictions often define discrimination more broadly in the attempt to ensure that such circumstances as sexual preference are not used to bar people from housing. Landlords are subject to a warranty of habitability, which requires that the premises be in fit condition for living. Most states have enacted landlord-tenant laws that govern residential leases and give tenants more protection than the common law.

See also Capitalism; Commercial law; Contract law; Nuisance; Property rights; Restrictive covenant; Zoning.

Reasonable doubt

DEFINITION: In a criminal case, sufficient doubt that a defendant is guilty to justify a verdict of not guilty

SIGNIFICANCE: The concept of reasonable doubt is intended to ensure that innocent individuals are not found guilty and punished for crimes they did not commit

The requirement that a defendant in a criminal case should be convicted only if a jury is persuaded of the person's guilt beyond a reasonable doubt has a long history in Roman law and common law dating to the fourth century. By the eighteenth century the requirement of proof beyond a reasonable doubt was established in its current form. The requirement of proof beyond reasonable doubt in criminal cases reflects society's judgment that it is better to allow a few guilty defendants to go free than to increase the chance of an innocent defendant being convicted.

In a criminal trial, the prosecution must prove each element of a crime beyond a reasonable doubt, or the defendant is entitled to acquittal. This requirement applies to both state and federal criminal trials, and it is based on the due process clauses of the Fifth and Fourteenth Amendments. Without the benefit of a proper instruction to the jury on the concept of proof beyond a reasonable doubt, a defendant is functionally deprived of the Sixth Amendment right to a trial by jury (*Sullivan v. Louisiana*, 1993).

Some courts and commentators have stated that reasonable doubt is an undefinable term. Others have said either that it is best left undefined or that what constitutes reasonable doubt should be left to the common sense of the jury. The due process clauses of the Fifth and Fourteenth Amendments do not require a court to define reasonable doubt for a jury, but many courts do define it for juries.

What, then, is reasonable doubt? Clearly, reasonable doubt does not exist if the doubt is based only on a hunch or mere suspicion of innocence. Nor can doubts based on imaginary suppositions or fanciful scenarios, or on a wish to avoid making an unpleasant or difficult decision, be considered "reasonable." Reasonable doubt should be based on evidence or lack of evidence. It must be doubt that a reasonable person would entertain in making a serious decision. The reasonable doubt concept does not require a jury to find that the elements of a crime are proved to an absolute or mathematical certainty. Rather, it means that a defendant should be convicted if a reasonable person would find that a strong probability exists— in the light of the evidence presented in the case—that the defendant is guilty.

See also Bill of Rights, U.S.; Burden of proof; Criminal procedure; Due process of law; Jury system; Presumption of innocence; Standards of proof.

Reasonable force

DEFINITION: The amount of physical force that police officers are allowed to use in making an arrest

SIGNIFICANCE: It is understood that police must sometimes use force to arrest a suspect; however, excessive force is sometimes applied, and legal remedies exist for such cases

Police officers are legally allowed to use the amount of force that is reasonably necessary to make an arrest. Courts should not substitute their own judgment for the judgment of the police officer in the field when the latter's discretion is exercised reasonably and in good faith. Nevertheless, the courts examine allegations of excessive force as potential violations of the "due process of law" that is guaranteed under the U.S. and state constitutions. Moreover, excessive force can generate civil liability under tort law and the civil rights laws, and it can itself be a crime.

The standard used for evaluating the use of force is whether an "ordinary, prudent man under the circumstances" would condone the use of force. This is a question of fact for the jury's deliberations. Factors to be considered include the need for force, the relationship between the need and amount of force applied, the extent of injuries caused by the use of force, and whether the force was used in a good faith effort to effect the arrest. In addition, courts consider whether the application of force violates accepted standards of decency. Deadly force may generally be used only against felons, and force used by a police officer to punish (rather than restrain) is strictly prohibited.

See also Arrest; Deadly force, police use of; King, Rodney, case and aftermath; Miami riots; MOVE, Philadelphia police bombing of; Police brutality.

Reconstruction

DATE: 1865-1877

PLACE: The eleven former Confederate States of America

SIGNIFICANCE: One of the most controversial topics in American history, Reconstruction denotes both the period and process after the Civil War in which the Union attempted to solve the problems and restore the status of the southern secessionist states

Soon after the Civil War commenced in 1861, northern leaders began to debate how the Confederate states should be readmitted to the Union and the many attendant problems to be resolved. For example, how should punishment for secession (withdrawing from the Union) be meted out, and against whom? What human and civil rights should be extended to the approximately four million freed slaves, and how could those rights be protected? In 1863 President Abraham Lincoln announced his plan for Reconstruction, but it was countered a year later by a proposal from Congress which touched off a national debate over who should establish Reconstruction policy.

Status of Blacks. After the Civil War ended on April 9, 1865, the status of blacks quickly became the most critical issue of Reconstruction. In January, 1865, Congress had proposed the Thirteenth Amendment to the U.S. Constitution, which called for the abolition of slavery. By March, Congress had created the Freedman's Bureau to protect the rights of southern blacks, most of whom had no private homes, money, or formal education because southern laws had relegated slaves to subhuman status. The Freedman's Bureau obtained jobs and set up hospitals and schools for blacks. In December, 1865, the Thirteenth Amendment was ratified. Most northerners hoped that the United States could be quickly reunited and the rights of blacks protected. Tragically, however, vicious attacks on former slaves increased in 1865 and 1866. Some were accompanied by race riots. Whites murdered about five thousand blacks in the South. By December, 1865, a secret organization called the Ku Klux Klan had been founded in Tennessee. It grew rapidly, spreading terror by murder and intimidation.

Johnson's Plan. After Andrew Johnson became president following Lincoln's assassination in April, 1865, he announced his own Reconstruction plan. It did not offer blacks a role in the process of Reconstruction—a prerogative left to the southern states themselves. During the summer and fall, new state governments were organized under Johnson's plan, but they began passing a series of restrictive laws against blacks called the black codes. These laws did little more than put a new face on the old practices of slavery. As a result, Republicans in Congress, both moderates and radicals, became convinced that President Johnson's plan was a failure and that the rights of both blacks and whites needed greater protection. The radicals also thought that giving blacks the right to vote was the only way to ensure the establishment of southern state governments that would remain loyal to the Union and administer uniform justice.

Civil Rights Legislation. Early in 1866, Congress passed the Civil Rights Act, which guaranteed basic legal rights to former slaves. Though Johnson vetoed the bill because he did

President Andrew Johnson, opposed to sweeping Reconstruction measures, vetoed Congress' 1866 Civil Rights Act, but Congress overrode his veto. (Library of Congress)

not think that the federal government should protect the rights of blacks, Congress overrode the veto, making the 1866 Civil Rights Act the first major law in U.S. history to be passed over the official objection of the president.

In June, 1866, Congress proposed the Fourteenth Amendment to the Constitution, which gave citizenship to blacks and mandated that all federal and state laws apply equally to blacks and whites. Though President Johnson urged the states to reject it (which all the Confederate states except Tennessee did), the Fourteenth Amendment was finally ratified in 1868. A third Reconstruction amendment to the Constitution, the Fifteenth, was proposed in 1869. Ratified by the states in 1870, this amendment made it illegal to deny any citizen the right to vote because of race.

Reconstruction Governments. In 1867, Congress passed a series of laws called the Reconstruction Acts. These enactments abolished the newly formed state governments and placed every secessionist state (excluding Tennessee) into one of five military districts. Federal troops stationed in each district enforced martial law. By 1870 all southern states had been readmitted to the Union, and new state governments were reestablished.

Southern whites (the majority of whom were Democrats) protested the Reconstruction Acts by refusing to vote in elections which established the new state governments. Thousands of blacks (who were Republicans) did vote, and as a result Republicans won control of every new state administration. Most whites in the South refused to support the Reconstruction governments because they could not accept the idea of former slaves voting and holding elected positions. Many whites turned to violence despite military attempts to halt attacks on blacks. Army troops had little success in preventing the Ku Klux Klan and similar groups from terrorizing people and controlling the outcome of elections.

The Legacy of Reconstruction. As white Democrats began regaining control of state governments in the South during the early 1870's, northerners lost interest in Reconstruction. The 1876 presidential election led to the end of Reconstruction when the Republicans agreed to a compromise with three southern states. Their disputed election returns were resolved in favor of Republican candidate Rutherford B. Hayes in exchange for the complete withdrawal of U.S. troops.

Reconstruction produced mixed results. The Union was restored, some rebuilding of the South did occur, and some blacks did get a taste of basic human and civil rights. In the end, however, most things scarcely changed at all. Many blacks remained enslaved by poverty and lack of education. Most continued to pick cotton on land owned by whites. Some scholars have suggested that the most fundamental flaw of Reconstruction was its failure to redistribute land, which would have provided an economic base to support the newly acquired political rights of black citizens.

The most important indicator of the impact of Reconstruction on American justice is the way blacks were treated after 1877. Ending slavery did not, and could not, end discrimination. The southern states continued to violate the rights of blacks for many decades afterward. It was only in the mid-1950's that black Americans inaugurated the intense struggle for complete legal equality known as the Civil Rights movement. This movement was based on the most significant judicial legacy of the Reconstruction period—the Fourteenth and Fifteenth Amendments to the Constitution. Eventually these amendments were used to establish a national system of protecting equality before the law.   —*Andrew C. Skinner*

See also Civil rights; Civil Rights Acts of 1866-1875; Civil War; Civil War Amendments; Jim Crow laws; Ku Klux Klan (KKK); Slavery.

BIBLIOGRAPHY

Of the many books on Reconstruction two are classics. Eric Foner, *Reconstruction: America's Unfinished Revolution, 1863-1877* (New York: Harper & Row, 1988), is the most comprehensive. The abridged version is Eric Foner, *A Short History of Reconstruction, 1863-1877* (New York: Harper & Row, 1990). The other classic is James M. McPherson, *Ordeal by Fire: The Civil War and Reconstruction* (New York: Alfred A. Knopf, 1982). Other important works include Leon F. Litwack, *Been in the Storm So Long: The Aftermath of Slavery* (New York: Alfred A. Knopf, 1979); Richard W. Murphy, *The Nation Reunited: War's Aftermath* (Alexandria, Va.: Time-Life Books, 1987), which is copiously illustrated; and Kenneth M. Stampp, *The Era of Reconstruction, 1865-1877* (New York: Alfred A. Knopf, 1965).

Reed v. Reed

COURT: U.S. Supreme Court

DATE: Decided November 22, 1971

SIGNIFICANCE: Finding for the first time that a state law violated the Fourteenth Amendment because it discriminated against women, the Court insisted that gender classifications must be rationally related to a legitimate state objective

When Richard Reed, a minor, died without a will in Idaho, his separated parents, Cecil Reed and Sally Reed, filed separate petitions in probate court, each seeking appointment to administer the deceased's estate. In a joint hearing, the probate court followed the Idaho Code, which required a preference to the father because he was a male. In applying the statute, the probate judge could give no consideration to the relative capabilities of the two applicants to administer an estate. Sally Reed appealed the judgment with the argument that a mandatory preference to males violated the equal protection clause of the Fourteenth Amendment. After losing the case in the Idaho Supreme Court, she appealed for a review by the U.S. Supreme Court. The Court had earlier indicated that the equal protection clause might forbid some kinds of classifications based on gender, but in contrast to categories of race, the Court had allowed states broad discretion to legislate different treatment for men and women, based on traditional sex roles that had been accepted as reasonable.

Departing from its previous leniency in the matter, the Court unanimously supported Sally Reed's position and ruled that the statute was incompatible with the state's obligation to provide "each person" with the "equal protection of the laws." The case, therefore, was remanded to the Idaho courts for new proceedings consistent with the Court's decision. In writing the official opinion, Chief Justice Warren Burger insisted that classifications of persons must not be arbitrary and must have "a fair and substantial relation to the object of the legislation." Burger conceded that there was some legitimacy for using a gender preference to reduce the workloads of the probate courts, but he found this rationale not sufficient to justify a mandatory preference without a hearing to determine the relative merits of the two petitioners. There was no rational basis to assume that men were always more qualified than women to administer wills.

The *Reed* decision was a landmark case that marked the Court's first use of the equal protection clause to strike down a statute on account of gender discrimination. Based on the history of the clause, Burger declined to consider whether gender is a "suspect" classification requiring strict judicial scrutiny, and his use of the "rational relationship test" would allow states much discretion in making gender distinctions. In later cases such as *Craig v. Boren* (1976), however, the Court would develop a more demanding test with a heightened level of scrutiny.

See also Equal protection of the law; *Frontiero v. Richardson*; *Rostker v. Goldberg*; Sex discrimination.

Regents of the University of California v. Bakke

COURT: U.S. Supreme Court

DATE: Ruling issued June 28, 1978

SIGNIFICANCE: The *Bakke* case established a compromise on the controversial issue of affirmative action in college admissions, deeming numerical quotas based on race to be impermissible but allowing race to be considered as one of several admission criteria

Allan Bakke had applied to the medical school of the University of California at Davis. He was not among the one hundred applicants finally accepted by the school. Pursuant to university policy, sixteen of the hundred slots had been reserved for racial minority students. Bakke, who was white, claimed that since he was better qualified than some of the applicants accepted for the sixteen minority positions, the university had discriminated against him on the basis of race.

The California Supreme Court ruled in favor of Bakke, and the case was appealed to the U.S. Supreme Court. The case drew national attention, attracting a record-breaking number of *amicus curiae* briefs. In June, 1978, the Court, sharply divided, issued its decision in favor of Bakke. In a 5-4 vote, the Court held that University of California at Davis' practice of reserving positions strictly on the basis of race violated Title VI of the Civil Rights Act of 1964. Title VI provides that "[n]o person in the United States shall, on the ground of race, color, or national origin, be excluded from participation in . . . any program or activity receiving Federal financial assistance." Davis did not contest the fact that it was receiving federal

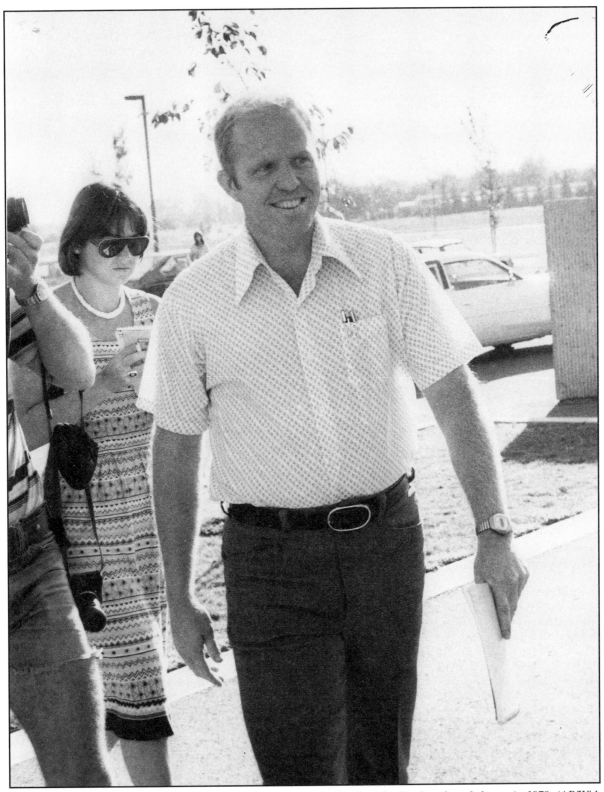

Allan Bakke arriving at the University of California, Davis, medical school for his first day of classes in 1978. (AP/Wide World Photos)

financial assistance. Although the decision was not based on constitutional grounds, Justice Lewis Powell, writing for the majority, noted that the guarantees of Title VI are grounded in principles found in the equal protection clause of the Fourteenth Amendment.

A different 5-4 majority, however, also declared that race could be considered as one of several criteria for admission to a university. One's status as a racial minority presumably could help one secure admission, but only if the position being contested were formally available to all, irrespective of race. The Court thus did not rule out affirmative action programs in general, only those provisions that amount to strict racial quotas. The decision can therefore be seen as a compromise between those who would abolish all forms of affirmative action as reverse discrimination and those who would guarantee outcomes based on race.

The narrowness of *Regents of the University of California v. Bakke* ensured the continuation of affirmative action programs in various forms. Less than a week after the *Bakke* decision, the Court let stand a lower court's ruling that permitted quantitative "goals" for the hiring and promotion of women and minorities. For almost fifteen years after *Bakke* the Court seemed to agree that the lingering effects of slavery, segregation, and blatant discrimination—and perhaps the continuation of more subtle biases—justified some institutionalized efforts to provide special assistance to racial minorities in employment and education. In the mid-1990's, however, those assumptions were challenged anew as affirmative action underwent its most intensive evaluation since it was first applied. The Supreme Court decision in *Adarand Constructors v. Peña* (1995), for example, ruled that a federal policy mandating that a certain percentage of construction projects receiving funding from the Department of Transportation be set aside for minority-owned companies was unconstitutional.

See also *Adarand Constructors v. Peña*; Affirmative action; *Amicus curiae* brief; Civil Rights Act of 1964; Equal protection of the law; Equality of opportunity; Racial and ethnic discrimination.

Regulatory crime

Definition: A crime committed against statutes rather than individuals

Significance: Commission of a regulatory crime is a crime against the law of the land rather than against an individual

Regulatory crimes generally are minor infractions of statutes, or rules, rather than intentional crimes against individuals with the intent to do harm. Regulatory crimes are those acts that are prohibited by law (*malum prohibitum*), such as speeding or littering, but that are not evil in and of themselves, as is murder. They are liability crimes, without fault, and do not require criminal intent. These offenses are usually termed "violations" and result in minimal penalties, such as fines, short jail terms, or community service. They are not characterized as criminal and are generally brought before a magistrate or justice of the peace for disposition.

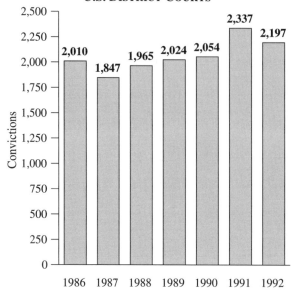

CONVICTIONS FOR REGULATORY CRIMES IN U.S. DISTRICT COURTS

Source: U.S. Department of Justice, Bureau of Justice Statistics, *Sourcebook of Criminal Justice Statistics—1993*. Washington, D.C.: U.S. Government Printing Office, 1994.

See also Criminal intent; *Mala in se* and *mala prohibita*; Misdemeanor; Strict liability.

Rehabilitation

Definition: The reformation of criminal offenders before their return to society; more widely, any restoration of rights, authority, and abilities

Significance: The effectiveness of rehabilitation as a function of the criminal justice system has been widely debated

The term "rehabilitation" most commonly describes the process by which an individual who has served time in prison is returned to society. In this context, rehabilitation is considered by many to be one of the goals of the criminal justice system. In general, the purpose and effectiveness of punishing criminals have been widely discussed and debated. Rehabilitation—along with such other concepts as incapacitation, deterrence, and retribution (or "just deserts")—has figured prominently in that debate. Central among the many questions are which criminal offenders can be rehabilitated and how best to rehabilitate them. The rehabilitation process may include counseling and job training while in prison, time spent in a halfway house (under the supervision of individuals charged with providing help to those returning to society), and help in locating housing, securing a job, or learning a trade. Rehabilitation may also occur under the guidance of a probation officer, to whom a released offender must report regularly and by whom the person is monitored and supervised.

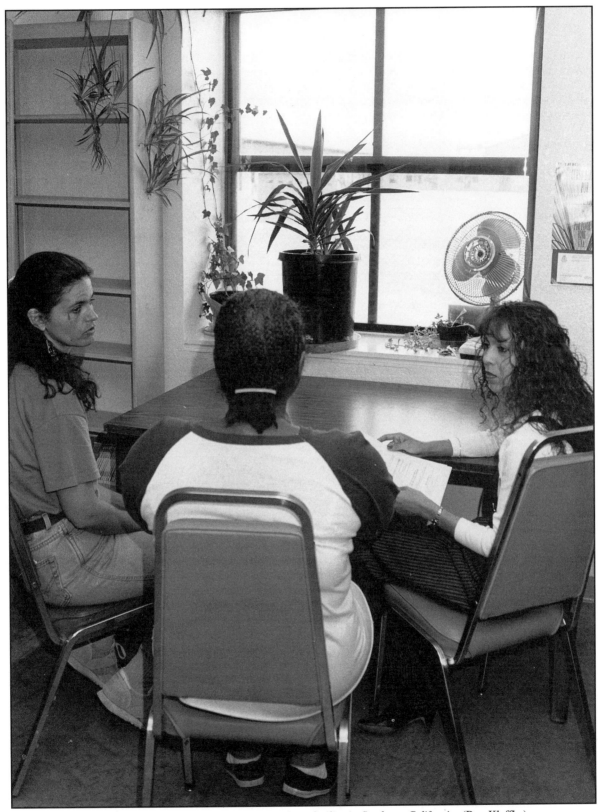

A counselor talks with two inmates at a prison facility in Stockton, California. (Ben Klaffke)

"Rehabilitation" also has other meanings in other legal contexts. For example, it refers to the restoration of the credibility of a witness who has been impeached for false testimony. In the corporate sense, rehabilitation is said to occur when an insolvent corporation attempts to conserve and administer its assets in such a way that the corporation eventually reorganizes and returns to normal corporate operations.

See also Auburn system; Incapacitation; Just deserts; Parole; Prison and jail systems; Probation; Punishment.

Rehnquist, William (b. Oct. 1, 1924, Milwaukee, Wis.)

IDENTIFICATION: Chief justice of the United States, beginning in 1986

SIGNIFICANCE: Committed to conservative values, Rehnquist cogently and consistently defended strict construction of the Constitution, judicial restraint, a dominant role for states, and strong police powers to combat crime

After being graduated first in his class at Stanford Law School, William Hubbs Rehnquist worked for a year as law clerk to Justice Robert Jackson. After practicing law in Arizona, he served as assistant attorney general, Office of Legal Counsel, from 1969 to 1971. President Richard Nixon appointed him associate justice of the Supreme Court in 1971, and on the bench he gained a reputation as a staunch conservative, especially on issues of law and order. President Ronald Reagan's nomination of Rehnquist as chief justice in 1986 was controversial, with critics attacking a pre-*Brown v. Board of Education* (1954) memo he had written for Justice Jackson defending racial segregation. After his confirmation, Rehnquist did not change his views, but he did become more conciliatory in striving toward a broad consensus. The opinions of Rehnquist characteristically show a respect for the literal wording and the historical understanding of the Constitution, while rejecting the idea that the Court should define a "living Constitution." He presented his views in the book *The Supreme Court: How It Was, How It Is* (1987).

See also Conservatism, modern American; Constitutional interpretation; *Lopez, United States v.*; Nixon, Richard M.; Reagan, Ronald; *Roe v. Wade*; *Rummel v. Estelle*; *United Steelworkers of America v. Weber*.

Taking over as chief justice after Warren Burger's retirement, William Rehnquist advocated a strict interpretation of the Constitution. (Supreme Court Historical Society)

Reitman v. Mulkey

COURT: U.S. Supreme Court

DATE: Decided May 29, 1967

SIGNIFICANCE: California's adoption of Proposition 14, which repealed the state's fair housing laws, was struck down by the Supreme Court after the California Supreme Court interpreted the repeal as "authorizing" discrimination

In 1959 and 1963, California established fair housing laws. These statutes banned racial discrimination in the sale or rental of private housing. In 1964, acting under the initiative process, the California electorate passed Proposition 14. This measure amended the state constitution so as to prohibit the state government from denying the right of any person to sell, lease, or refuse to sell or lease his or her property to another at his or her sole discretion. The fair housing laws were effectively repealed. Mr. and Mrs. Lincoln Mulkey sued Neil Reitman in a state court, claiming that he had refused to rent them an apartment because of their race. They claimed that Proposition 14 was invalid because it violated the equal protection clause of the Fourteenth Amendment. If Proposition 14 was unconstitutional, the fair housing laws would still be in force. The Mulkeys won in the California Supreme Court, and Reitman appealed to the Supreme Court of the United States.

Justice Byron White's opinion for the five-justice majority admitted that mere repeal of an antidiscrimination statute would not be unconstitutional. In this case, however, the California Supreme Court had held that the intent of Proposition 14 was to encourage and authorize private racial discrimination. This encouragement amounted to "state action" that violated the equal protection clause of the Fourteenth Amendment.

The four dissenters in the case agreed on an opinion by Justice John M. Harlan. Harlan argued that California's mere repeal of its fair housing laws did not amount to encouraging and authorizing discrimination. If the repeal were to be seen that way, then a state could never rid itself of a statute whose purpose was to protect a constitutional right, whether of racial equality or some other. Harlan also suggested that opponents of antidiscrimination laws would later be able to argue that such laws not be passed because they would be unrepealable. Indeed, several ballot measures which have reversed or repealed civil rights laws protecting gays and lesbians have been struck down on the basis of *Reitman v. Mulkey*.

Reitman v. Mulkey has not had a major effect on American civil rights law. The Supreme Court has not been disposed to expand the "authorization" and "encouragement" strands of constitutional thought. The principle of "state action"—which is all that the Fourteenth Amendment equal protection rules can reach—has not been further broadened. Nevertheless, the precedent remains, with its suggestion that there is an affirmative federal constitutional duty on state government to prevent private racial discrimination.

See also Affirmative action; Equal protection of the law; Racial and ethnic discrimination; *Regents of the University of California v. Bakke*; *Swann v. Charlotte-Mecklenburg Board of Education*.

Religion, establishment of. *See* Establishment of religion

Religion, free exercise of

DEFINITION: The fundamental right of religious liberty protected under the First Amendment of the U.S. Constitution

SIGNIFICANCE: The scope of the free exercise of religion has shifted since the right was first enumerated, with interpretations since 1972 being drawn somewhat more narrowly than in previous periods

The free exercise of religion is considered to be one of the fundamental rights of a free people, and it was included as a basic right protected under the First Amendment to the U.S. Constitution, which also includes a companion prohibition against the official establishment of religion by any government authority.

History. The free exercise and establishment clauses were not originally parts of the Constitution, its framers believing that such rights as those pertaining to religion and speech were already set down by God as "natural" and "inalienable" rights which could not, by their very nature, be granted by human agency. Furthermore, most of the individual states already had made provision for such rights within their own constitutions; thus it was thought that federal action would be redundant. Only pressure from nervous anti-Federalists for a list of basic, fundamental rights as the price for their support of the new Constitution induced James Madison and others to frame the Bill of Rights, including the guarantee of free exercise of religion.

Although the principle of complete and unhindered religious liberty would be thought by most Americans to be indeed an "inalienable" right, the history of the application of the Constitution's free exercise clause and its underlying principle has been decidedly mixed. While the practices of most Christian and Jewish groups have been protected by the "wall of separation" enunciated by Thomas Jefferson, the same could not always be said for groups thought to be outside the Judeo-Christian mainstream. Prerevolutionary America witnessed determined and sometimes violent opposition to Quakers, while black congregations were routinely hindered from establishing their own churches even in "free" states in the years prior to the Civil War. Communitarian groups such as the Oneida Community in the nineteenth century were often harassed by local governments for marriage practices thought to be polygamous. More recently, members of independent sects and people practicing various forms of Satanism have had difficulty in pressing free exercise claims.

Early Test Cases. The issue of "nonstandard" marriage practices brought the Supreme Court into the free exercise debates in *Reynolds v. United States* (1879). The plaintiff, a Mormon, had asserted that his practice of polygamy was an intrinsic part of his religion and was thus protected under the free exercise clause. The Court disagreed, saying that while governments may not interfere with religious beliefs or opinions, the same right does not apply to specific religious practices. This distinction between beliefs and practices would become crucial in subsequent free exercise cases.

In the 1972 case Wisconsin v. Yoder, the Supreme Court held that the state could not require Amish children to attend school beyond the eighth grade. (Pennsylvania Dutch Visitors Bureau)

The Court's major participation in free exercise questions came in the twentieth century. It was just such a question—pertaining to the right of Jehovah's Witnesses to solicit door-to-door without a permit—that led to the application of the First Amendment to individual states through the Fourteenth Amendment (*Cantwell v. Connecticut*, 1940). Jehovah's Witnesses were also the focus of the famous "flag salute" cases: The first, *Minersville School District v. Gobitis* (1940), upheld the expulsion of students who refused to salute the flag for religious reasons. The *Gobitis* decision was overturned three years later in *West Virginia State Board of Education v. Barnette* (1943), when the Court declared that "if there is any fixed star in our constitutional constellation, it is that no official, high or petty, can prescribe what shall be orthodox in politics, nationalism, or religion."

Judicial Principles. The Court, in deciding cases based on free exercise claims, has come to rely on two basic tests: the "compelling interest" test, in which a government authority must show that circumstances warrant intervention which limits the free exercise of religion, and the "alternate means" test, in which a government authority must prove that it did not

have an alternate method of reaching a desired goal outside the limitation of religious free exercise. Examples of "compelling interest" include *Prince v. Commonwealth of Massachusetts* (1944), in which the Court upheld the application of a state child labor law to restrict a Jehovah's Witness from forcing her nine-year-old niece to sell religious literature on the street, and *Goldman v. Weinberger* (1986), which upheld an Air Force uniform regulation that prevented an orthodox Jew from wearing a skullcap while on duty. The "alternate means" test was employed in *Sherbert v. Verner* (1963) to force the state of South Carolina to pay unemployment compensation to a Seventh-day Adventist whose refusal to work on the Sabbath prevented her from accepting available employment and in *Thomas v. Indiana Review Board* (1981), dealing with the case of a Jehovah's Witness whose religion prevented him from working on military armaments.

Prior to 1972, the Supreme Court broadly construed the protection of the free exercise of religion, extending the right to cases involving jury duty (*In re Jennison*, 1963) and compulsory education beyond the eighth grade (*Wisconsin v. Yoder*, 1972). Of particular significance was the application of the free exercise clause to cases of conscientious objection during time of war. Although pre-World War II cases were largely decided in favor of the nation's right to self-defense over individual religious conscience (*United States v. MacIntosh*, 1931), the Vietnam War era saw a change in judicial attitude. The tradition of conscientious objection, which had heretofore been restricted to members of "peace churches," was broadened in *United States v. Seeger* (1965) and *Welsh v. United States* (1970) to include those whose beliefs included "a sincere and meaningful belief which occupies in the life of its possessor a place parallel to that filled by God." For perhaps the first time, free exercise of religion was broadened to include those whose beliefs were not overtly religious in nature.

The 1980's and 1990's. After 1972 the Court adopted a narrower approach. In addition to *Goldman v. Weinberger*, the Court upheld the imposition of minimum-wage laws on religious organizations in *Tony and Susan Alamo Foundation v. Secretary of Labor* (1985), and in two landmark cases it restricted the right of Native American religious groups to press free exercise claims against the government: *Lyng v. Northwest Indian Cemetery Protective Association* (1988) allowed the construction of a logging road through National Forest lands considered sacred to tribes in California, and *Employment Division, Department of Human Resources of Oregon v. Smith* (1990) denied the use of the free exercise clause to avoid compliance with laws forbidding the use of otherwise illegal substances—in this case peyote, which has a central part in the religious ritual of the Native American Church.

Overall the Court, in its adjudication of free exercise questions, has sought to adhere to Jefferson's "wall of separation" between church and state. The thickness of that wall, however, has historically depended on the philosophies of the judges who are sworn to uphold it. —*Robert C. Davis*

See also Bill of Rights, U.S.; *Church of the Lukumi Babalu Aye v. Hialeah*; Constitution, U.S.; *Employment Division, Department of Human Resources of Oregon v. Smith*; Establishment of religion; *Everson v. Board of Education*; Polygamy; *Reynolds v. United States*; School prayer.

BIBLIOGRAPHY

Among the many good sources on this topic are Archibald Cox, *The Court and the Constitution* (Boston: Houghton Mifflin, 1987); Fred Friendly and Martha Elliot, *The Constitution: That Delicate Balance* (New York: Random House, 1984); Paul G. Kauper, *Religion and the Constitution* (Baton Rouge: Louisiana State University Press, 1964); Leonard W. Levy, ed., *Encyclopedia of the American Constitution* (New York: MacMillan, 1986); Leo Pfeffer, *Church, State, and Freedom* (Boston: Beacon Press, 1967); Anson Stokes and Leo Pfeffer, *Church and State in the United States* (New York: Harper & Row, 1965).

Religious sects and cults

DEFINITION: Sects and cults are religious groups that exist in varying degrees of tension or conflict with mainstream society; sects are often unconventional splinter groups of main-

stream denominations, whereas cults are farther from the mainstream and often follow a charismatic leader

SIGNIFICANCE: The treatment of nontraditional religious groups under the law raises major constitutional issues, as even small and unpopular religious groups claim the same First Amendment protection accorded major religions and denominations

The U.S. Constitution guarantees freedom of religion. This freedom is easy for everyone to accept when it is applied to societally accepted, noncontroversial groups. It is more difficult when religious groups that follow codes of conduct which run counter to the behavior or mores of mainstream society also demand the right to practice their religion without interference. In general, the free exercise of religion in the United States is restricted only when a group becomes dangerous to the safety of its members or society at large or when its actions violate laws.

Relatively small religious groups that are not accepted by society are generally deemed cults and sects. To sociologists, the term "cult" means a religion in its early, developing stages. In common usage, however, it usually refers to an unpopular and feared religious group that is led by a charismatic leader and whose members seem to follow the leader's dictates without question. Among the groups since the 1960's that have been regarded with suspicion and animosity are the Unification Church, the Worldwide Church of God, the Rajneeshee Foundation, the Church Universal and Triumphant, and the International Society for Krishna Consciousness (or Hare Krishnas). A sect is sometimes defined as a religious group that exists in tension with mainstream society and does not cooperate with other religions but is not as far from the beliefs and behaviors of mainstream society as a cult is.

Throughout American history, despite the First Amendment's guarantee of the right to religious freedom, the federal and state governments used a variety of tactics to harass unpopular religious groups. The Church of Jesus Christ of Latter-day Saints faced considerable opposition in the nineteenth century, primarily because church members practiced polygamy. In 1890, the government went so far as to attempt to seize the assets of the church. The church ultimately gave in to the pressure and officially renounced the practice of polygamy. Other tactics used against unpopular groups have included denial of tax-exempt status and prosecution for disturbances of the peace.

A few cult groups led by charismatic leaders have left tragic marks, among them the People's Temple, led by Jim Jones, and the Branch Davidians, led by David Koresh. Jim Jones led more than nine hundred people to a mass suicide and murder in November, 1978, in Guyana, South America. Jones was at first an untrained, unordained leader in a Christian ministry associated loosely with the Disciples of Christ. He later declared himself an embodiment of the divine and, following increased public scrutiny and persecution, led his followers to isolation in Guyana, where the group came to a tragic end.

David Koresh, the leader of the Branch Davidians in the 1980's and early 1990's, was a self-proclaimed prophet and messiah. Believing that conflict with the government was necessary to bring in God's kingdom, he stored large amounts of guns and ammunition in preparation for such a conflict. In 1993, agents of the U.S. Bureau of Alcohol, Tobacco, and Firearms (ATF) attacked his compound at Waco, Texas, because of his arms buildup and reports that he was abusing children. This action resulted in the death of four federal agents and, after a fifty-one-day siege, the death of Koresh and the majority of his followers.

Today the Supreme Court affords the same protections to cults and sects that it gives to any other religious group. For example, in a 1982 case involving the Unification Church, *Larson v. Valente*, the Supreme Court held that a Minnesota law was aimed specifically at cults and was therefore unconstitutional. On the other hand, the Court has maintained a fine distinction between the right to freedom of religious thought and the right to freedom of behavior, which has enabled it to uphold the illegality of certain behaviors even though they may be considered central by a religious group (as the Mormons once considered polygamy). To do so, however, the Court must find that the state has a compelling interest in regulating the behavior, and the statute must be carefully written to advance those interests.

See also Branch Davidians, federal raid on; Child abuse; *Church of the Lukumi Babalu Aye v. Hialeah*; Civil liberties; *Employment Division, Department of Human Resources of Oregon v. Smith*; Polygamy; Religion, free exercise of.

Reparations

DEFINITION: Payments for wrongs or injuries suffered

SIGNIFICANCE: Payment of reparations may restore an individual or corporate entity to its original status

Reparations are compensation for wrongs or injuries done to an individual or to a corporate entity. The payment of reparations is designed to restore the individual or entity to its original, preinjury condition. They include the payment to an individual for property or goods that were damaged by another party, or the restoration of property or goods that were taken.

In wartime, vanquished countries may be required to pay reparations to the victor countries for damages inflicted by the armies of the losing countries during the conflict. Reparations have also been granted by governments to individuals for direct or indirect losses suffered as a result of war. The U.S. Congress granted reparations to Japanese Americans, or their families, who lost most of their material possessions while they were held in internment camps in the United States during World War II.

See also Japanese American internment; Punishment; Restitution.

Representation: gerrymandering, malapportionment, and reapportionment

DEFINITION: Political representation is partly determined by the sizes and shapes of electoral districts

SIGNIFICANCE: If electoral districts are designed with an eye to a certain demographic makeup, the outcome of elections can be biased in favor of a particular party or racial group

As of 1995, the citizens of the United States were divided into 435 congressional districts, with each district electing one representative. Every ten years the congressional seats are "reapportioned" through a process of drawing new districts based on the latest census data. In *Wesberry v. Sanders* in 1964, the Supreme Court decreed that congressional representation must be based on the "one person, one vote" principle; that is, districts must be created "as nearly as practicable" with roughly equal numbers of voters. Reapportionment thus is necessary to account for population shifts over each ten-year period. Malapportionment simply describes the situation that results when districts are not fairly drawn.

Simply ensuring roughly equal population does not necessarily ensure that the "one person, one vote" principle is observed. With knowledge of the patterns of party affiliation within a region, a district can be drawn which gives an advantage to one particular political party. This practice is known as "gerrymandering," after Massachusetts governor Elbridge Gerry, who oversaw the creation of contorted districts, one of which was said to resemble a salamander. Gerrymandering has a long tradition in American politics, having been observed in reapportionment efforts since the late eighteenth century. Gerrymandered districts ensured continued control by party "machines" and were blamed for various political ills. In *Davis v. Bandemer* (1986), the U.S. Supreme Court held that gerryman-

A political cartoon satirizing the creation of the monstrous "Gerry-mander" by Massachusetts governor Elbridge Gerry. (Library of Congress)

dering could be considered a violation of the equal protection clause of the Fourteenth Amendment. To avoid charges of gerrymandering, districts must be reasonably and compactly drawn.

More recently the issue of representation has been subjected to another justice claim. Some see the incongruity between the racial makeup of the population and the racial makeup of elected bodies as evidence that racial voting strength has been "diluted." This reasoning implies that (1) racial and ethnic groups have unique, shared interests, (2) those interests can only be represented by a member of the group, (3) the members of such a group tend to vote in the same way, and (4) outsiders will tend not to vote for a member of the group. If all these suppositions are true, then dividing a racial group between two districts may indeed dilute the voting strength of the bloc. Critics, however, claim that this reasoning conflicts with the traditional principles of American liberalism, which place individual interests above group interests and hold ascriptive characteristics such as race to be irrelevant to the awarding of political benefits.

By the early 1990's some districts, such as supervisorial districts in Los Angeles County, had been designed specifically to include a significant proportion of minority citizens, presumably giving those groups more weight in the outcome of an election. The issue remains controversial, however, with some claiming that this government-sanctioned "racial gerrymandering" amounts to creating districts that isolate minority votes. The U.S. Supreme Court supported that charge by holding racially gerrymandered districts unconstitutional in *Shaw v. Reno* in 1993. The Court's 1995 *Miller v. Johnson* decision reaffirmed the unconstitutionality of districts drawn with race as the dominant factor in their design.

See also Democracy; Machine politics; Racial and ethnic discrimination; *Shaw v. Reno*; Voting Rights Act of 1965; *Wesberry v. Sanders*.

Republican Party

DATE: Emerged in the 1850's

SIGNIFICANCE: The Republican Party emerged to oppose slavery in the 1850's; it generally holds conservative positions on racial, social, and criminal justice

The Republican Party emerged in the 1850's as an antislavery party and as a successor to the Federalists and the Whigs. With the election of Abraham Lincoln as president in 1860, the party established itself as the dominant political organization until the 1932 election. Democrats dominated politics for the next half century, until Republicans' victories in 1994 allowed them to regain control of both the House and the Senate for the first time in more than sixty years.

Racial Justice. The Republican Party was formed in opposition to slavery, and the vast majority of African Americans who received the right to vote after the Civil War supported the Republican Party and its candidates. This pattern continued until the 1920's, when black voters began to change their party identification. The switch was completed in 1932 with the election of Democrat Franklin D. Roosevelt as president.

Although Republican President Dwight D. Eisenhower (president from 1953 to 1961) was responsible for the introduction and passage of the 1957 and 1960 Civil Rights acts, later Republican presidential candidates took positions that alienated the party from most minority groups. Barry Goldwater, the Republican nominee in 1964, voted against the 1964 Civil Rights Act on the grounds that it unconstitutionally interfered with the rights of private property owners. In 1968, Richard M. Nixon pursued a "southern strategy" in his successful effort to capture the presidency. This strategy consisted of opposing busing to integrate schools, limiting the federal role in desegregation, and taking a tough stance on law-and-order issues. Subsequently, the presidencies of Ronald Reagan and George Bush provided little comfort to most minorities, who saw these administrations as attempting to turn back the clock on civil rights. Republican administrations contended that they wanted to replace laws requiring racial preference, such as affirmative action, with race-neutral laws.

Social Justice. To a great extent, social justice is concerned with how people treat other individuals and groups in society who are in need of assistance. The role of government, as seen by most Republicans, is to encourage family stability, expand the private sector, and discourage welfare dependency. Republicans see the breakdown of the family as directly related to the issues of welfare and crime. Republicans point to some startling statistics on the issue of social breakdown in the United States. Since 1960, illegitimate births have increased 400 percent. While 5 percent of births were out of wedlock in 1960, by 1990 the figure had risen to 28 percent. Among whites, the illegitimacy rate jumped from 2 percent in 1960 to 21 percent in 1990. By 1990, more than two out of three black births were illegitimate.

Republicans argue that the breakdown of the family has been fostered by government policies that have created a culture of "welfare dependency." Since children from single-parent families are more likely to engage in crime, more likely to lag behind in educational achievement, and more likely to be poor, the key to achieving social justice is to adopt policies that encourage family stability and discourage welfare dependency.

First, Republican welfare-reform proposals seek to impose requirements that recipients work for their benefits. Second, welfare would be limited for unwed teenage mothers. Unmarried teenage mothers should be encouraged to live with their parents and should not be given financial incentives to establish independent households. Third, unwed mothers must identify the father of their child in order to receive public assistance, so that the government can force the father to pay child support; this will reduce the cost of welfare.

Criminal Justice. The Republican Party has carved out a reputation as the "law and order" party. Although both the Republicans and the Democrats see crime as a major political issue, the Republicans place more emphasis on punishment and less on prevention of crime.

For Republicans, the root cause of crime lies in a hard-core group of repeat offenders who commit most of the violent crime.

The Republican Party generally seeks to limit government's role in the areas of racial and social justice, arguing that government action is often both ineffective and too expensive. (AP/Wide World Photos)

Their solution is simple: Sentence repeat offenders to long prison terms, during which they will be unable to prey upon the public. In the 1980's and 1990's, the Republican approach received a favorable response from the public, which was clearly concerned about the high incidence of violent crime.

Republican crime proposals usually stress the following features. First, probation should be prohibited for those convicted of violent crimes such as murder, rape, and armed robbery and for those who have received second felony convictions. Violent offenders should not be freed early, even if more jails and prisons must be built to house them. Second, strict sentencing guidelines must limit the abilities of judges to hand out light sentences. Third, parole and prison furloughs must be abolished. Fourth, prisoners should be required to work. Earnings should be used for victim restitution and to pay the expenses of incarceration. Fifth, reforms are needed in the juvenile justice system. Juveniles account for much of the violent crime in the United States, yet they are usually exempt from criminal penalties until age eighteen. Finally, victims must be assured the right to be heard and to be compensated for the damage they have suffered.

Limiting Government's Role. Republican views on racial, social, and criminal justice are interrelated. Republicans prefer to see government play a minimal role in all areas, and generally they see government programs as contributing to social problems rather than solving them. In the area of racial justice, government should encourage equality under the law by adopting race-neutral laws. In social justice, the government must restore the family and end welfare dependency. Finally, in criminal justice, government must protect society from repeat violent offenders.

—Darryl Paulson

See also Bush, George; Conservatism, modern American; Democratic Party; Eisenhower, Dwight D.; Law Enforcement Assistance Administration (LEAA); Nixon, Richard M.; President's Commission on Law Enforcement and Administration of Justice; Reagan, Ronald.

BIBLIOGRAPHY

On politics and race, see Clint Bolick, *Unfinished Business: A Civil Rights Strategy for America's Third Century* (San Francisco: Pacific Research Institute, 1990); Thomas Edsall and Mary Edsall, *Chain Reaction: The Impact of Race, Rights, and Taxes on American Politics* (New York: W. W. Norton, 1991); and Shelby Steele, *The Content of Their Character: A New Vision of Race in America* (New York: Harper, 1990). On welfare and social justice, see Charles Murray, *Losing Ground: American Social Policy, 1950-1980* (New York: Basic Books, 1984), and Marvin Olasky, ed., *Loving Your Neighbor: A Principled Guide to Personal Charity* (Washington, D.C.: Capital Research Center, 1994).

Restitution

DEFINITION: Restoring or compensating a person for what was wrongly taken away from that person

SIGNIFICANCE: Restitution is one of the oldest forms of justice in the world; although it is now generally considered an unusual sentence in the United States, restitution is receiving renewed attention in the courts

The concept and practice of restitution has its origins in the ancient Semitic civilizations of the fertile crescent. It was part of both the Code of Hammurabi and the Mosaic Code of the Old Testament. In the case of theft, the offender was to restore "ten-fold" what had been stolen. Other crimes involved various forms of compensation; if someone cut another person's hand off, for example, either maliciously or through negligence, compensation had to be paid to cover (to use today's terms) medical expenses, lost wages, and pain and suffering.

This principle, though common in history, generally fell into disuse in the United States. In the American legal system, offenders must go to prison or pay a fine to the state, but victims are usually uncompensated for their losses. (If a person is found guilty in a criminal court, however, the victim can then sue the person in a civil court in an effort to recover monetary damages.) This situation began to change in the 1980's, however, as more laws and courts used the principle of compensation and restitution. In a sense, restitution can be seen as combining the civil law's concern with compensating victims and criminal law's concern with punishing offenders. In one scenario, an offender may be given probation on the condition that he or she make continuing payments to compensate the victim of the crime.

See also Compensatory damages; Equitable remedies; Punishment; Reparations.

Restraining order

DEFINITION: A court order in the nature of an injunction, usually temporary, forbidding a party from doing specified acts

SIGNIFICANCE: This remedy preserves a plaintiff's rights to avoid irreparable injury, pending final determination of the parties' rights; a variant of the restraining order helps protect victims of domestic violence

In the usual course of a civil legal proceeding, the court makes no order affecting either party's substantive rights until the final judgment. In some situations, however, a plaintiff's rights may be irreparably damaged if the defendant continues taking some action. In such a case, the plaintiff may apply to the court for a temporary restraining order (also known as a "temporary injunction").

In order to be granted this extraordinary relief, the party seeking the order must show that immediate and irreparable harm is likely to result from a continuation of the status quo, or that the defendant is acting in a manner that will make any final judgment on the merits ineffectual. The burden is on the plaintiff to show entitlement to the order, and the court is likely to balance the relative inconveniences to the plaintiff and the defendant in determining whether the order should be issued. The temporary restraining order is effective only until a final judgment is issued. If the plaintiff is ultimately successful in the adjudication, the court may replace the temporary restraining order with a permanent injunction.

One special type of restraining order is the domestic violence restraining order. All fifty states have statutes authorizing a court to issue a restraining order against the alleged perpetrator of domestic violence, upon application by the intimate partner or former partner of the alleged perpetrator. Although the law varies among jurisdictions, this type of restraining order typically orders the respondent to refrain from further violence, harassment, or intimidation of the petitioner. It typically orders the respondent to vacate the home and to avoid contact with the petitioner at work, church, and school. The order also usually establishes custody and visitation for minor children, if necessary, and may order child or spousal support.

The typical procedure for obtaining a domestic violence restraining order is for the petitioner to make application for the court in an *ex parte* hearing—a hearing before the court in which only the petitioner is present, not the respondent. If the court finds that the statutory requirements are met, it issues a restraining order, which is then served upon the respondent. The respondent has a period of time (usually twenty-one days) in which to contest the order at a hearing. The restraining order typically is in effect for one year, unless vacated earlier by the court. Violation of the restraining order is punishable by civil or criminal penalties, and the violation itself (such as an assault) is also a separately punishable crime.

See also Domestic violence; Injunction.

Restrictive covenant

DEFINITION: A legal agreement preventing the sale, rental, or leasing of property to any members of an undesired group

SIGNIFICANCE: Restrictive covenants were designed to maintain the "ethnic purity" of neighborhoods and prevent integration

Numerous approaches have been utilized to maintain residential segregation. In the early 1900's, when African Americans were migrating to cities in massive numbers, many communities adopted laws requiring blacks and whites to live in separate neighborhoods. Cities justified such laws as a legitimate exercise of their police powers. In other words, they argued that keeping the races apart would preserve the peace. In *Buchanan v. Warley* (1917) the U.S. Supreme Court struck down the residential segregation law of Louisville, Kentucky. Since the Fourteenth Amendment prohibited state discrimination, and Louisville was an agent of the state, the Louisville law was unconstitutional.

The Fourteenth Amendment prohibits discrimination by states and cities, but discrimination by private individuals is another matter: Is discrimination by one individual against another individual unconstitutional? A restrictive covenant is a form of private discrimination. Private property owners in various neighborhoods inserted clauses in their property deeds preventing the owner from selling the property to African Americans, Jews, or various other groups designated as undesirable.

Early challenges to restrictive covenants were unsuccessful. In *Corrigan v. Buckley* (1926), the National Association for the Advancement of Colored People (NAACP) argued that court enforcement of covenants amounted to state discrimination. The U.S. Supreme Court disagreed with the NAACP and upheld enforcement of the covenant.

It was not until 1948 that the NAACP was successful in persuading the U.S. Supreme Court that restrictive covenants were unconstitutional. In *Shelley v. Kraemer* the Court agreed with the NAACP's contention that judicial enforcement of the covenant constituted state discrimination. The seller was willing to sell and the buyer was willing to buy. Except for the intervention of the courts, the Shelleys "would have been free to occupy the properties in question without restraint."

Twenty years later the U.S. Congress passed the 1968 Civil Rights Act, or "open housing" law, making it illegal to discriminate in the advertising, financing, sale, or rental of housing on the grounds of race, color, religion, or national origin. That same year the U.S. Supreme Court held in *Jones v. Alfred H. Mayer Co.* that all racial discrimination, private or public, in the sale or rental of property, is outlawed by an 1866 act passed under authority of the Thirteenth Amendment.

See also Civil Rights Act of 1968; Equal protection of the law; *Jones v. Alfred H. Mayer Co.*; National Association for the Advancement of Colored People (NAACP); Racial and ethnic discrimination; Segregation, *de facto* and *de jure*; *Shelley v. Kraemer*.

Retroactivity of Supreme Court decisions

DEFINITION: The extent to which new legal rules announced by the Supreme Court apply to cases which arose before the announcement

SIGNIFICANCE: The Supreme Court, though regularly applying its decisions retroactively, has generally declined to do so in cases involving petitions for *habeas corpus* relief, fearing that to hold otherwise would overturn innumerable state criminal convictions and subvert the finality of the criminal process

At common law, a court decision articulating a new rule of law was routinely applied retroactively—that is, to cases which arose before the time the decision was rendered. Prior to 1965, the Supreme Court regularly, if not always, applied its rulings retroactively to cases which had arisen prior to the Court's ruling. This retroactive application of law corresponded to the generally accepted notion that courts find law rather than make it. Having discovered a new principle that had existed all along, the Court might naturally be expected to apply the rule to cases which arose prior to the principle's discovery. This rule of retroactivity also served to further the core value of the "case or controversy" requirement in Article III of the U.S.

Constitution, which precludes the federal courts from issuing advisory opinions. A legal rule with only prospective application might be seen as such an advisory opinion.

Beginning in 1965, the Supreme Court confronted the issue of whether decisions relating to criminal procedure should be given retroactive effect. Criminal cases arrive at the Court both through direct appeals and through petitions for writs of *habeas corpus. Habeas corpus* petitions are collateral attacks on state criminal proceedings made after the conclusion of such proceedings. Were the Supreme Court to apply criminal procedure decisions retroactively, hundreds or even thousands of prisoners might be released as a result of newly determined mistakes in the procedures that yielded their convictions. Eventually the Court determined in 1989 that criminal procedure decisions announcing new constitutional rules would be applied retroactively to cases still on direct appeal to the Court but generally not to petitions for *habeas corpus* relief.

Emphasizing the need for finality in criminal adjudications, the Court determined that retroactive application of new procedural rules to collateral attacks on criminal proceedings would severely undermine this need. The Court has, however, recognized two exceptions to this general rule against retroactivity in the *habeas* context. First, a decision will be applied retroactively to *habeas* petitions when the decision announces that a particular defendant or particular conduct cannot be punished. Second, a decision will be applied retroactively when it recognizes a procedural right which, if not applied, would seriously diminish the accuracy of a criminal conviction.

See also Advisory opinion; Appellate process; *Ex post facto* law; *Habeas corpus*; Supreme Court of the United States.

Reversible error

DEFINITION: An error affecting the rights of parties to an action possibly leading to miscarriage of justice

SIGNIFICANCE: The rights of parties to an action are protected in the case of honest error

The finding of reversible error is limited to appellate review of a lower court's decision, at which time the error becomes apparent. A reversible error justifies reversing a judgment, even if there was no objection to the matter that caused the error in the lower court. The error must be something that would reasonably be expected to prejudice the rights of the party complaining or against whom the error was committed.

Reversible error also includes judicial error, an action committed by the court itself which affects a party's right to a fair trial. Reversible errors include allowing hearsay evidence, allowing unduly damaging evidence that was presented and not objected to during the course of the proceeding, or the failure of a judge to instruct the jury as to the proper limitation of consideration of such testimony, when such instruction was normal and necessary.

See also Civil procedure; Criminal procedure; Evidence, rules of; Harmless error; Hearsay rule; Miscarriage of justice.

Revolutionary war. *See* American Revolution

Reynolds v. Sims

COURT: U.S. Supreme Court
DATE: Decided June 15, 1964
SIGNIFICANCE: For the first time taking action against state legislatures for ignoring constitutionally mandated requirements for redistricting, the Court specifically applied a "one person, one vote" solution to what it deemed to be inaccurate representation

The 1960's witnessed a significant change in the apportionment of state legislative and congressional delegations. For the first time, the U.S. Supreme Court interfered with the apportionment practices of the states. The Court's action was an attempt to rectify what it deemed to be the malapportionment of a great majority of American state legislatures and of state delegations to the national House of Representatives

This situation had developed over the years because predominantly rural state legislatures continually ignored the population shifts that produced the tremendous growth of the country's cities in the twentieth century. In many cases, state legislatures, out of a fear that equitable redistricting would shift the rural-urban balance of power, deliberately ignored the provisions within their own state constitutions for periodic redistricting. The result was a constitutional abnormality that was distorting the democratic political process.

In a series of cases brought before the Court in the 1960's, the malapportionment problems were judicially corrected when the Court applied a "one person, one vote" principle. In 1964, a federal district court ordered the state of Alabama to reapportion but nullified two plans that did not apportion the legislative districts solely on the basis of population. The state appealed to the Supreme Court, which held that the equal protection clause of the Fourteenth Amendment requires that the seats in both houses be equally apportioned. The existing apportionment of the Alabama state legislature was struck down when the Court, in an 8-1 majority, applied the one person, one vote principle in the case. Writing for the majority, Chief Justice Earl Warren declared that restrictions on the right to vote "strike at the heart of representative government." The Court, he added, had "clearly established that the fundamental principle of representative government in this country is one of equal representation for equal numbers of people, without regard to race, sex, economic status, or place of residence within the state." The concept of one person, one vote was virtually a pure and intractable rule.

In his dissent, Justice John M. Harlan argued that the decision had the "effect of placing basic aspects of state political systems under the pervasive overlordship of the federal judiciary." This type of "judicial legislation" frightened not only Harlan but a number of conservatives who did not want to see the Supreme Court become more active in producing equal voting rights.

The legacy of this case is clear: In *Reynolds* and several companion cases decided the same day, the Supreme Court determined that it had an obligation to interfere in the apportionment practices of the states in order to guarantee that no person was deprived of the right to vote. By guaranteeing those individual rights, the legislatures as well as the House of Representatives would more properly reflect the genuine complexion of American society.

See also Equal protection of the law; Representation: gerrymandering, malapportionment, and reapportionment; Vote, right to; *Wesberry v. Sanders*.

Reynolds v. United States

COURT: U.S. Supreme Court
DATE: Decided May 5, 1879
SIGNIFICANCE: Upholding a congressional prohibition of polygamy in the territories, the Court established the principle that the First Amendment protects all religious beliefs but does not protect religiously motivated practices that harm the public interest

George Reynolds, a member of the Mormon church and a resident of the territory of Utah, was tried in a federal territorial court for committing the crime of bigamy, in violation of an 1862 statute. At his trial, Reynolds presented evidence that the accepted doctrine of his church was that every male member had the duty, circumstances permitting, to practice plural marriage and that failure to do so would be punished by "damnation in the life to come." He further argued that the First Amendment prohibited Congress from placing such limitations on the free exercise of religion. The trial judge refused to instruct the jury that the defendant should be exempted from the law for actions motivated by his religious beliefs, and the jury returned a guilty verdict. Reynolds appealed to the U.S. Supreme Court.

The Court unanimously ruled to uphold Reynolds' conviction. Writing the majority opinion, Chief Justice Morrison R. Waite recognized that Congress cannot pass a law that prohibits the free exercise of religion, but he made a distinction between religious beliefs and religious conduct. While beliefs or opinions were fully protected, Congress was free to punish "actions which were in violation of social duties or subversive of good order." An obvious example, Waite pointed out, was the possible practice of human sacrifice. Historically, polygamy had always been punished as a crime in the common law and statutes of Britain, and this tradition had been uniformly followed in every state of the United States. In addition, Waite quoted several respected jurists who argued that polygamy promoted despotic government and had other undesirable consequences. Congress, therefore, possessed legitimate authority to criminalize polygamy in the territories, and there was no obligation to make an exception for those who followed different religious beliefs.

The *Reynolds* decision was the Court's first major consideration of a law that restrained the religious freedom of a minority, and it would become an important precedent because of Waite's formulation of the belief-conduct distinction. Implicitly, the Court acknowledged that Congress could not prohibit a religious practice without a legitimate state interest, but the Court did not try to articulate guidelines for the level of state interest required. In its later decisions, the Court would consistently follow *Reynolds* in its belief-conduct distinction, but the decision would not prove helpful in providing standards to determine what kinds of religious conduct might be protected. The immediate impact of *Reynolds* was limited because the free exercise clause did not then apply to state laws, but the Court would often refer to the case after the clause was made binding on the states in *Cantwell v. Connecticut* (1940).

See also *Church of the Lukumi Babalu Aye v. Hialeah*; *Employment Division, Department of Human Resources of Oregon v. Smith*; Polygamy; Religion, free exercise of; *Sherbert v. Verner*; *Wisconsin v. Yoder*.

Rhodes v. Chapman

COURT: U.S. Supreme Court
DATE: Decided June 15, 1981
SIGNIFICANCE: In this case, the Supreme Court ruled that the "double celling" of inmates at a maximum-security prison in Ohio did not violate constitutional safeguards against cruel and unusual punishment

Rhodes v. Chapman evolved from a class-action suit brought by two inmates at the Southern Ohio Correctional Facility, a maximum-security prison in Lucasville. Cellmates Kelly Chapman and Richard Jaworski, citing a federal statute, maintained that incarcerating two inmates in the same cell violated the protection against cruel and unusual punishment guaranteed by the Eighth and Fourteenth Amendments. The U.S. District Court for the Southern District of Ohio, after an extensive investigation, concurred. Among other supporting reasons for its decision, the court argued that double celling of long-term prisoners aggravated the various problems associated with close confinement. It further noted that the Ohio facility housed a prison population 38 percent larger than its designed capacity and that it failed to provide each inmate with the recommended standard of 50 to 55 square feet of living space. It found, too, that the prison had made double celling a practice rather than a temporary solution to crowded conditions.

After the United States Court of Appeals for the Sixth Circuit upheld the lower court's judgment, the case went to the Supreme Court, which reversed the lower courts' decisions and ruled that double celling did not constitute cruel and unusual punishment. The Court stated that the district court's findings were insupportable and that the data on which it based its judgment were "insufficient to support its constitutional conclusion." The majority opinion, presented by Justice Lewis F. Powell, Jr., held that there was no real evidence that double celling at the Ohio prison facility inflicted undue pain or imposed any hardship that was out of proportion to the crimes warranting the inmates' imprisonment. A concurring opinion, however, cautioned that the Court's decision should not be interpreted as an abrogation of its responsibility to scrutinize prison conditions to ensure that humane but realistic standards are maintained.

The lone dissenter, Justice Thurgood Marshall, argued that prison overcrowding and the double celling of prisoners, unchecked, would eventually have a deleterious effect on the mental and physical health of prisoners, in total disregard of modern standards of human decency. Marshall also expressed concern that the Court's ruling might be construed as an admonition to district courts, enjoining them to adopt a laissez-faire position toward the administration of state prison systems.

For those individuals who believe that hardened felons have been mollycoddled and encouraged to seek legal redress for minor and even frivolous complaints, the *Rhodes* decision has landmark significance. It reflected the rising anger and fear of the nation regarding crime; by the early 1980's, the country was growing increasingly unsympathetic to the rights of prisoners.

See also Bill of Rights, U.S.; *Coker v. Georgia*; Cruel and unusual punishment; *Gregg v. Georgia*; Just deserts; Prison and jail systems; Punishment; *Rummel v. Estelle*.

Richmond v. J. A. Croson Co.

COURT: U.S. Supreme Court
DATE: Decided January 23, 1989
SIGNIFICANCE: *Richmond v. J. A. Croson Co.* made it much more difficult for cities and states to establish race-conscious affirmative action programs

In 1983 the City Council of Richmond, Virginia, adopted a minority set-aside program for city contracting. Under the plan, 30 percent of all city construction subcontracts were to be granted to (or "set aside" for) minority-owned business enterprises. The J. A. Croson Company, a contracting firm which had been the low bidder on a city project, sued the city when its bid was rejected in favor of a larger bid submitted by a minority-owned firm. Croson's position was that the minority set-aside violated the equal protection clause of the Fourteenth Amendment by establishing a racial classification. Richmond argued that the minority set-aside was valid as an attempt to remedy past discriminations. An earlier case, *Fullilove v. Klutznick* (1980), had approved a similar set-aside program for federal government contracts. The city pointed out that only 0.67 percent of its prime construction contracts had gone to minority firms between 1978 and 1983.

By vote of 6 to 3 the Supreme Court decided for the Croson Company. The opinion of the Court was written by Justice Sandra Day O'Connor. Justice O'Connor argued that the earlier federal case was not relevant because the federal government has legislative authority to enforce the Fourteenth Amendment. State governments are limited by it. Race-conscious affirmative action programs are valid only where there is a showing of past discrimination by the state government itself. In the case of the Richmond statute, there was no such showing. It was undeniable that there had been discrimination against minority contractors, but that discrimination was by private firms, not by the city itself. While the city has the power to remedy private discriminations, she argued, it may not do so by setting up a quota system which is itself racially biased.

Justice Thurgood Marshall wrote the major dissenting opinion. He argued that the majority's view of the facts was too narrow. The extraordinary disparity between contracts let to minority and nonminority firms showed that there was systematic and pervasive discrimination which could only be remedied in practice by a set-aside or quota program of the kind passed in Richmond. He pointed out, as he had in earlier cases, the irony of a constitutional rule which forbids racial classifications for benign purposes, given the long history of constitutionally permitted racial classifications for discriminatory purposes. Justice Marshall insisted that the court should not scrutinize racial classifications strictly so long as the purpose of the classification is benign. Justices William Brennan, Jr., and Harry A. Blackmun joined Marshall in his dissent.

Richmond v. J. A. Croson Co. cast doubt on the future of race-conscious programs designed to remedy past discrimination. At the very least it means that racial quotas, however well-meant, are likely to be held unconstitutional.

See also *Adarand Constructors v. Peña*; Affirmative action; Civil War Amendments; *Fullilove v. Klutznick*; *Regents of the University of California v. Bakke*.

Robbery

DEFINITION: The taking of personal property from another person by force or intimidation

SIGNIFICANCE: Robbery is the second most common violent crime in the United States, accounting for close to 35 percent of the nation's violent crimes

Robbery is closely related to larceny (theft), but robbery requires two additional elements. Larceny involves the carrying away of another person's property with the intent permanently to deprive the owner; robbery occurs only when the property is seized in the presence of the owner and is taken using violence or the threat of violence. A theft is normally considered to have occurred in the presence of the owner if the property is taken from the owner's person or if the owner is close enough to the property to attempt to stop the theft. The element of violence occurs if the theft involves the application of any amount of force beyond that which would be necessary to take the property if the victim offered no resistance; intimidation occurs with any action that places the victim in fear of life or limb.

State statutory provisions distinguish between robbery with a weapon and without one. The former is called armed robbery, the latter strong-armed robbery; penalties for armed robbery are consistently much more severe than penalties for strong-armed robbery. In 1993, 38 percent of all U.S. robberies were of the strong-armed variety; 42 percent involved firearms, 10 percent involved knives or cutting instruments, and the remaining 10 percent involved other types of weapons.

Incidence and Distribution of Robberies. Robbery is the second most common violent U.S. crime according to the Uniform Crime Reports (UCR). Aggravated assault is almost twice as common as robbery, but robbery reports to police are more than five times more common than reports of murder and forcible rape combined. In 1993, for example, of 1,772,279 violent crimes known to police, assaults accounted for more than 58 percent, robbery for about 35 percent, and murder and rape for only 6 percent. The Uniform Crime Reports include only crimes reported to police; the National Crime Victimiza-

WEAPONS USED IN ROBBERIES, 1993

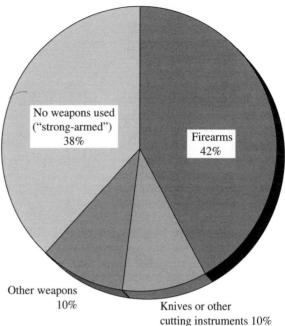

No weapons used ("strong-armed") 38%

Firearms 42%

Other weapons 10%

Knives or other cutting instruments 10%

Source: U.S. Department of Justice, Federal Bureau of Investigation, *Crime in the United States* (Uniform Crime Reports). Washington, D.C.: U.S. Government Printing Office, 1994.

tion Survey (NCVS), a broader crime-reporting system, usually reports robbery rates about twice those reported in the UCR. Moreover, UCR national robbery rates disguise extreme variations from city to city and from state to state.

Streets and highways are the location for more than half of all robberies. Another 22 percent involve commercial or financial establishments, about 10 percent occur at homes, and the remaining 13 percent occur at miscellaneous sites. Although robbery is conventionally associated with banks, only about 2 percent of robberies involve banks. Robberies are more likely to occur at night (54 percent) than during the day (46 percent) and are much more likely to occur in metropolitan areas than in rural areas.

Social Costs. The total estimated losses in U.S. robberies in 1993 were $538 million, based upon an average value of $815 for property stolen in each incident. This figure, however, understates the social loss caused by the crime for several reasons. Not all robberies are reported to police; the costs of investigation, trial, and incarceration are not included in the average; and victims' injuries, both physical and emotional, are left uncalculated. This latter omission is important; in 1993, for example, about one-third of all robberies resulted in injury to the victim, and about 10 percent involved homicides.

Enforcement Effectiveness. Most robberies reported to police go unsolved. In 1993, for example, the arrest rate for robberies in the United States was only 24 percent. Among

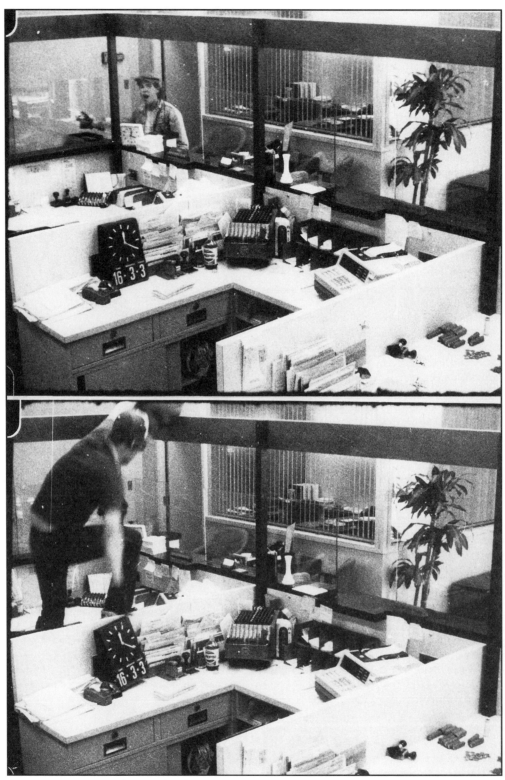

These security camera photographs show a bank robbery in progress in Cambridge, Massachusetts, in 1983. (AP/Wide World Photos)

Types of Robbery by Percentage, 1993

	United States Total	Northeastern States	Midwestern States	Southern States	Western States
Street/highway	54.7%	61.2%	61.2%	50.1%	50.8%
Commercial house	12.5	10.0	10.3	12.7	15.7
Gas or service station	2.3	2.0	2.9	2.3	2.5
Convenience store	5.3	2.4	4.2	7.7	5.6
Residence	10.3	10.2	8.9	12.6	8.0
Bank	1.8	1.4	1.2	1.4	2.9
Miscellaneous	13.1	12.7	11.3	13.1	14.5

Source: U.S. Department of Justice, Federal Bureau of Investigation, *Crime in the United States* (Uniform Crime Reports). Washington, D.C.: U.S. Government Printing Office, 1994.

Note: Because of rounding, percentages may not add to 100 percent exactly.

types of violent crime, this represents the lowest arrest rate. In the same year, 53 percent of forcible rapes, 56 percent of aggravated assaults, and 66 percent of murders resulted in arrest. Rural counties showed the highest robbery arrest rate of 39 percent.

Penalties. The average sentence for persons convicted of robbery in state courts in 1990 was ninety-seven months, or slightly more than eight years. For persons convicted of robbery in federal district courts, the average sentence was 100.7 months. Average sentences, however, do not accurately reflect time served. Average time served for those sentenced by federal district courts in 1990, for example, was 58.6 months, or slightly less than five years.

The Criminals. Persons arrested for robbery in the United States are predominantly male (91 percent) and under the age of twenty-five (62 percent); about 62 percent are African American. About one-third of all offenders are under the age of eighteen, with sixteen to nineteen being the peak period for offenses. Less than 5 percent of robberies are committed by persons forty-five years old or older. Studies of robbery both in the United States and internationally consistently show that perpetrators of robbery are disproportionately drawn from minority and disadvantaged groups.

The Victims. Some approximation of the typical robbery victim can be obtained with survey data such as that compiled by the Roper Center for Public Opinion Research. For more than twenty years, the Roper Center has asked respondents to a national survey to say whether anything had been taken from them by force during the previous year. Based upon the survey's 1991 results, for example, the typical robbery victim is a young, low-income nonprofessional high school graduate of African American descent. The profile of the typical robbery victim, in other words, closely approximates the profile of the typical perpetrator. —*Jerry A. Murtagh*

See also Assault; Burglary; Crime; Crime Index; Criminal law; Felony; National Crime Victimization Survey; Self-defense; Theft; Uniform Crime Reports (UCR).

BIBLIOGRAPHY

Overviews of robbery include Kristen M. Williams and Judith Lucianovic's *Robbery and Burglary: A Study of the*

Characteristics of the Persons Arrested and the Handling of Their Cases in Court (Washington, D.C.: Institute for Law and Social Research, 1979) and Caroline W. Harlow's *Robbery Victims* (Washington, D.C.: U.S. Department of Justice, Bureau of Justice Statistics, 1987). Robbery statistics are summarized in the Federal Bureau of Investigation's annual *Crime in the United States* (Washington, D.C.: U.S. Government Printing Office) and the Bureau of Justice Statistics' *Report to the Nation on Crime and Justice* (2d ed. Washington, D.C.: U.S. Government Printing Office, 1993). Other relevant bureau publications include Jacob Perez's *Patterns of Robbery and Burglary in Nine States, 1984-88* (Washington, D.C.: U.S. Department of Justice, 1992).

Robinson v. California

COURT: U.S. Supreme Court
DATE: Decided June 25, 1962
SIGNIFICANCE: *Robinson v. California* which held that it was cruel and unusual punishment to incarcerate drug addicts simply because of their addictions, was for some critics emblematic of the Warren Court's "softness" on crime

Robinson was convicted under a California statute making it a crime to be a drug addict and was sentenced to ninety days in jail. The statute did not require the state to prove that the accused had either bought or purchased drugs or that he or she possessed them—the mere status of being a drug addict was enough to convict a defendant. Robinson appealed, and the Supreme Court overturned the conviction on grounds that incarceration for ninety days for what amounts to an illness constitutes cruel and unusual punishment.

Because of such rulings as *Mapp v. Ohio* (1961), which extended guarantees against unreasonable search and seizure to state defendants, the Court overseen by Chief Justice Earl Warren was criticized for "coddling" criminals. *Robinson* was doubly controversial because it is based on the assumption that drug addiction is an illness over which the addict has no control. Indeed, six years later the Court declined to follow its own precedent in *Powell v. Texas* (1968), in which it upheld the criminal conviction of a chronic alcoholic, declaring that the state of knowledge regarding alcoholism was inadequate to permit the enunciation of a new constitutional principle.

Still, *Robinson* is important for making the cruel and unusual punishment clause of the Eighth Amendment applicable at the state as well as the federal level. The case was a continuation of the "due process revolution," championed initially by Justice Hugo Black, that reached its high-water mark during Earl Warren's tenure as chief justice. By means of the due process clause of the Fourteenth Amendment, the guarantees of the Bill of Rights limiting federal action were "incorporated" into the Fourteenth Amendment, thus becoming applicable to state governments. The Fourteenth Amendment, passed in the wake of the Civil War, makes all persons born in the United States citizens whose privileges and immunities cannot be restricted and whose rights of due process and equal protection cannot be denied. Some framers of the amendment indicated that the privileges and immunities extended therein included the guarantees of the Bill of Rights, but this point was left ambiguous. In *Palko v. Connecticut* (1937), the Court explicitly addressed the issue for the first time, stating that some of the rights embodied in the first ten amendments to the Constitution were so fundamental that the Fourteenth Amendment obligated states to observe them. Then, writing in dissent in *Adamson v. California* (1947), Justice Black argued that the Fourteenth Amendment obligated states to honor all aspects of the Bill of Rights. The Court has never quite adopted this view, but by the time Earl Warren's leadership ended in 1969, most of the Bill of Rights had been applied to the states.

See also *Adamson v. California*; Cruel and unusual punishment; Drug use and sale, illegal; Due process of law; *Mapp v. Ohio*; *Palko v. Connecticut*.

Roe v. Wade

COURT: U.S. Supreme Court

DATE: Decided January 22, 1973

SIGNIFICANCE: Invalidating nearly all state laws prohibiting abortion within the first three months of pregnancy, this landmark decision led to one of the most emotionally charged and divisive public issues in American history

In the decade prior to the *Roe v. Wade* decision, under pressure from feminist reformers, a few states, including Alaska, Hawaii, New York, and Washington, had modified their existing abortion laws to allow the legal termination of pregnancies not only in cases of rape, incest, or a prenatal prognosis of a threat to the mother's life, but on demand. The most liberal of these was enacted in 1970, in New York, where the legislature passed a law allowing abortions within the first twenty-four weeks of pregnancy, replacing a nineteenth century statute that had predicated the criminality of abortion. In more conservative sections of the United States, however, under growing pressure from antiabortionist factions, many states held firm to their existing laws, and a few even strengthened them.

The Litigants. The specific law addressed in the *Roe v. Wade* case was a Texas law that made it a felony for a person to terminate a pregnancy except as a means of saving the mother's life. "Jane Roe," a pregnant, unmarried woman, brought suit to have the law declared unconstitutional on the grounds that it invaded her personal privacy. The case went before the Supreme Court as a companion case to *Doe v. Bolton*, which was introduced in an attempt to strike down a Georgia statute that prohibited abortions except in cases in which the mother's life was threatened, the pregnancy resulted from rape, or there was a pronounced risk of a serious birth defect.

The Supreme Court's Decision. In delivering the Supreme Court's 7-2 majority opinion, Justice Harry A. Blackmun argued that a woman's right to privacy, implied in the Fourteenth Amendment and in the Ninth Amendment's reservation of rights to the people, "is broad enough to encompass a woman's decision whether or not to terminate her pregnancy." The opinion, however, included a rejection of the idea that a woman was free "to terminate her pregnancy at whatever time, in whatever way, and for whatever reason she alone chooses." It reserved the right of states to regulate abortion to safeguard health, uphold medical standards, and protect potential life, confirming the opinion of several lower courts that a woman's right to an abortion is not absolute. Furthermore, the rights of the woman to decide without medical advice or state sanction were preserved for the first trimester (the first three months of pregnancy) only; thereafter, subject to appropriate medical judgment, states could regulate and even prohibit the termination of pregnancies.

Most important, the Court rejected the argument that a child in embryo has a legal existence and refused to address the issue of when a human life commences. It did argue that a state's "compelling interest" in a pregnancy, which would allow for state regulation, is based on a reasonable need to protect a "potential life," especially by the beginning of the third trimester, when the fetus is capable of surviving outside the mother's womb.

The Ruling Divides the Nation. In the wake of *Roe v. Wade*, as states enacted new statutes either to comply with the ruling or to exploit its potential loopholes, the Supreme Court came under assault from the self-styled "pro-life movement" for having legalized murder. The movement's basic argument was that human life begins, not at birth, but at conception. At times resorting to violence, pro-life advocates carried the struggle to ban abortion from the courts and legislative assemblies into the streets. There, in confrontation with "pro-choice" advocates outside abortion clinics, pro-life activists brought the issue into the public eye.

The pro-choice and pro-life factions have also skirmished on legal battlefields. Pro-life advocates have urged the Supreme Court to reverse the *Roe* decision, and they have pushed for legislation in the form of so-called human-life bills or a constitutional amendment that would protect the rights of an infant *in utero*. While they have not yet achieved either aim, they have vigorously challenged state and federal policies designed to protect a woman's right to an abortion. Partly because of their pressure, and partly because of criticism from various legal scholars who have argued that in *Roe* the Supreme Court usurped legislative authority, the Court—

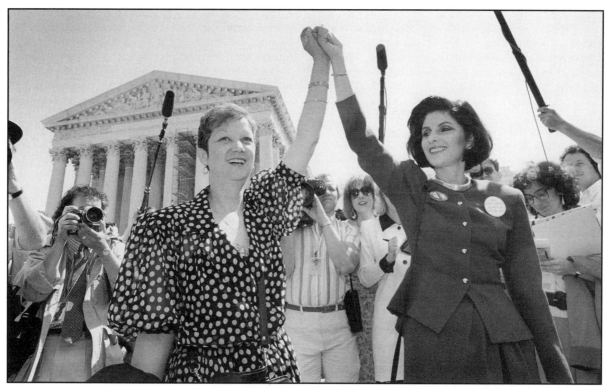

Norma McCorvey ("Jane Roe") in front of the Supreme Court building in 1989 with attorney Gloria Allred. McCorvey was in the capital to observe Supreme Court sessions regarding a Missouri abortion case. (AP/Wide World Photos)

although repeatedly affirming a woman's right to an abortion—has upheld some state laws imposing restrictions on legal abortions either not addressed in *Roe* or based on the relatively vague concept of fetal viability. For example, it has upheld some statutes which require either abortion waiting periods, mandatory "informed consent" after medical consultation, or, in the case of minors, judicial authorization for the abortion.

Although it is conceivable that a more conservative Supreme Court could invalidate *Roe v. Wade*, no court is likely to adjudicate the crux issue of when human life begins. Therefore, unless the pro-life movement succeeds in the court of public opinion and gains passage of a right-to-life law or amendment, a woman's right to an abortion, though qualified, will probably remain guaranteed by the 1973 decision.

—*John W. Fiero*

See also Abortion; Birth control, right to; *Doe v. Bolton*; Feminism; *Griswold v. Connecticut*; *Planned Parenthood of Central Missouri v. Danforth*; *Planned Parenthood v. Casey*; Privacy, right of.

BIBLIOGRAPHY

Studies on abortion, *Roe v. Wade*, and its legal impact include Eva R. Rubin, *Abortion, Politics, and the Courts: Roe v. Wade and Its Aftermath* (Westport, Conn.: Greenwood Press, 1982); R. M. Dworkin, *Life's Dominion: An Argument About Abortion, Euthanasia, and Individual Freedom* (New York: Alfred A. Knopf, 1993); Sidney C. Callahan and Daniel Callahan, eds., *Abortion: Understanding Differences* (New York: Plenum Press, 1984); Marilyn Falik, *Ideology and Abortion Policy Politics* (New York: Praeger, 1983); Paul Sachdev, ed., *Perspectives on Abortion* (Metuchen, N.J.: Scarecrow Press, 1985); Rosalind P. Petchesky, *Abortion and Woman's Choice: The State, Sexuality, and Reproductive Freedom* (New York: Longman, 1984); Laurence H. Tribe, *Abortion: The Clash of Absolutes* (New York: W. W. Norton, 1990); Carol C. Collins and Oliver Trager, eds., *Abortion: The Continuing Controversy* (New York: Facts on File, 1984); and Jay L. Garfield and Patricia Hennessey, *Abortion, Moral and Legal Perspectives* (Amherst: University of Massachusetts Press, 1984).

Roosevelt, Eleanor (Oct. 11, 1884, New York, N.Y.—Nov. 7, 1962, New York, N.Y.)

IDENTIFICATION: First lady and humanitarian

SIGNIFICANCE: A force behind her husband's presidency, Eleanor Roosevelt redefined the role of first lady through her activism while earning respect as an advocate of human rights

One of the most admired women in U.S. history, Eleanor Roosevelt is to many *the* first lady of America. She was instrumental in Franklin Roosevelt's career and presidency, caring for him after he was stricken with polio in 1921 and serving as his trusted political confidant. Through her public speeches, syndicated daily newspaper column "My Day," her radio program, press conferences with women reporters, service as Office of Civilian Defense co-director, and her political activism on behalf of the poor, youth employment, and civil rights for blacks and women, Roosevelt expanded the role of modern first lady.

Prior to Franklin's presidency, Eleanor was active in the League of Women Voters, the Women's Trade Union League, and the women's division of the Democratic Party. She also helped found a furniture factory that benefited the unemployed and was co-owner, vice principal, and history and government teacher at the Todhunter School in New York City.

After her White House years, President Harry Truman appointed her to the U.S. Delegation to the United Nations (1945-1952). As chair of the Commission on Human Rights, she helped draft the U.N. Declaration of Human Rights. President John Kennedy reappointed her to the U.S. Delegation to the United Nations in 1961, and she served until her death. She is the author of *This I Remember* (1949), *On My Own* (1958), and *The Autobiography of Eleanor Roosevelt* (1961).

See also Kennedy, John F.; Roosevelt, Franklin D.; Truman, Harry S.

Roosevelt, Franklin D. (Jan. 30, 1882, Hyde Park, N.Y.—Apr. 12, 1945, Warm Springs, Ga.)

IDENTIFICATION: President of the United States, 1933-1945

SIGNIFICANCE: As president, Roosevelt faced two great challenges: the Great Depression and World War II

Franklin D. Roosevelt belonged to an aristocratic New York family. His Democratic Hyde Park Roosevelts were related to the Republican Oyster Bay Roosevelts, whose most famous representative was President Theodore Roosevelt. In 1905 Franklin married his distant cousin (and Theodore's niece), Eleanor Roosevelt, and he followed Theodore into politics.

Elected to the New York legislature in 1910, in 1913 he became the assistant secretary of the Navy in Woodrow Wilson's administration. In 1920 Roosevelt was selected as the Democratic Party vice presidential candidate, but the Democrats were soundly defeated by Warren G. Harding's Republicans. Struck down by polio in 1921, he courageously battled back, although he was restricted to braces and crutches for the rest of his life. In 1928 he was elected governor of New York. When the Great Depression hit in 1929, Roosevelt was quick to respond with such reforms as unemployment insurance and old age pensions. The Republican president, Herbert Hoover, was popularly held responsible for the economic disaster which had swept the country, and after receiving the Democratic presidential nomination in 1932, Roosevelt was easily elected.

Roosevelt's March, 1933, inaugural address gave the country hope. Claiming that the only thing to fear was fear itself, he promised that he would use his executive powers to the utmost. Congress willingly deferred to his leadership, and the results during the following Hundred Days were unparalleled in American history: The Civilian Conservative Corporation, the Federal Emergency Relief Administration, the Home Owners Loan Corporation, the Agricultural Adjustment Administration, the National Recovery Administration, the Public Works Administration, the Tennessee Valley Authority, and the Federal Deposit Insurance Corporation were all created during this time. These landmark agencies changed the face of governmental

Franklin D. Roosevelt speaking at the site of the Norris Dam, a Tennessee Valley Authority construction project, one of thousands of New Deal projects. (Library of Congress)

responsibility in the United States, and with the later Social Security Administration, National Labor Relations Board, and Works Progress Administration, they made up the New Deal. Relief, recovery, and reform were the aims, and if some of the attempts were more successful than others, no one was left in any doubt that the White House was the center of government.

During the Depression, foreign affairs were largely ignored by Roosevelt in spite of the rise of fascism in Europe and Japanese militarism in Asia. World War II broke out in Europe in 1939, and later in an address to Congress in January, 1941, Roosevelt spoke about the four freedoms he considered crucial for the world: freedom of speech, freedom of religion, freedom from want, and freedom from fear, including fear of military aggression. In August, 1941, Roosevelt and Winston Churchill signed the Atlantic Charter, which was included in the United Nations declaration adopted after the United States entered World War II following the Japanese attack on Pearl Harbor. Roosevelt died in April, 1945, a month before the victory in Europe. Because of his successful leadership in peace and war, against economic oppression and militaristic aggression, Roosevelt is regarded by many scholars as the United States' greatest twentieth century president.

See also Court-packing plan of Franklin D. Roosevelt; New Deal; President of the United States; Roosevelt, Eleanor; Social Security system; Welfare state.

Rosenberg trial and executions

DATE: March 6, 1951-June 19, 1953

SIGNIFICANCE: The Rosenberg espionage case created international debate, pitting national security issues against First Amendment rights, and raised questions about the American justice system's vulnerability to the anticommunist political climate of the Cold War era

The trial of Julius and Ethel Rosenberg and Morton Sobell, a former classmate of Julius, began on March 6, 1951. The Rosenbergs were accused of being part of a communist-inspired spy ring that supplied atomic research data from the Los Alamos project to the Soviet Union. The trial judge was Irving R. Kaufman, and the chief litigator was assistant prosecutor Roy M. Cohn. Emanuel Bloch acted as the Rosenbergs'

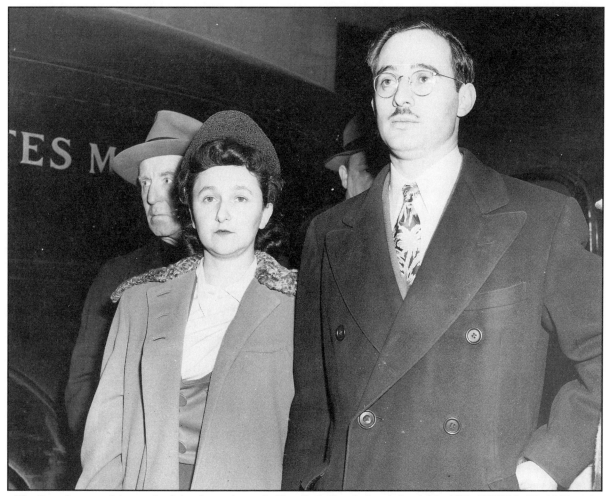

The Rosenbergs arriving at the federal courthouse in New York City during their trial in 1951. (AP/Wide World Photos)

defense attorney. David Greenglass, Ethel Rosenberg's brother, appeared as the government's principal witness. The Rosenbergs insisted on their innocence of all charges throughout the trial and refused to answer questions about their political beliefs and activities. After only two weeks of court time, the trial ended with the conviction of all three defendants. Judge Kaufman found Sobell guilty of espionage not directly linked to atomic research and sentenced him to thirty years in prison. He sentenced both the Rosenbergs to death.

After the convictions, the National Committee to Secure Justice in the Rosenberg Case began to question the proceedings openly. They pointed out that the prosecution's case rested completely on unsubstantiated circumstantial evidence and perjured testimony, that there was no documented evidence, and that references had been made throughout the trial to the Rosenbergs' leftist political beliefs.

Upon public discussion of the trial proceedings, many clergy and some leading scientists, including Albert Einstein, joined the movement asking that clemency be granted to the Rosenbergs. The movement continued to gain momentum and became international in scope. The U.S. Supreme Court, meanwhile, refused to hear an official appeal of the case, and appeals for clemency to presidents Harry S Truman and Dwight D. Eisenhower were unsuccessful.

A stay of execution on a legal point was granted by Justice William O. Douglas but was denied by a vote of the U.S. Supreme Court at large, which reconvened for a special term in order to rule on the case. On June 19, 1953, as thousands of people demonstrated against the executions in cities in the United States and Europe, the Rosenbergs were killed in the electric chair at Sing Sing Prison.

A series of books were written protesting what was perceived as the failure of justice and the misrepresentation of evidence in the case. Most important among them were Walter and Miriam Schneir's 1965 *Invitation to an Inquest* (new edition 1983) and Michael and Robert Meeropol's 1986 *We Are Your Sons*. Documents released through the Freedom of Information Act have revealed that Greenglass devised false evidence that was used against Ethel Rosenberg in the trial and that the government attempted to use its prosecution of Ethel as a tool to force Julius to confess.

In 1995 the decades-old case took another turn when the government released formerly classified documents consisting of decoded transmissions, some of them fragmentary, between Soviet operatives. These messages show that Julius Rosenberg was indeed a Soviet spy and that Ethel was at least aware of his activities, although they do not confirm her active involvement. Although the coded messages portray Julius as the leader of a spy ring, they do not specifically contain corroboration of the charges that he transmitted high-level atomic secrets. Finally, in spite of the confirmation of Julius Rosenberg's espionage activities, it is clear that false evidence was given by government witnesses at the trial.

See also Communist Party, American; Douglas, William O.; Espionage; Freedom of Information Act; McCarthyism.

Rostker v. Goldberg

COURT: U.S. Supreme Court

DATE: Decided June 25, 1981

SIGNIFICANCE: The Supreme Court held that Congress' decision to authorize the president to require registration of males but not females for possible military service did not constitute gender discrimination in violation of the due process clause of the Fifth Amendment

The Military Selective Service Act authorizes the president to require male citizens and male resident aliens between the ages of eighteen and twenty-six to register for the draft. Registration was discontinued in 1975. In 1980, President Jimmy Carter recommended that Congress reactivate the registration process and that Congress amend the act to permit the registration and possible conscription of women. Congress considered the president's recommendations at length and decided to reactivate the registration process but declined to permit the registration of women. A three-judge federal district court ruled that the challenged gender-based distinction violated the due process clause of the Fifth Amendment. By a 6-3 vote, the U.S. Supreme Court reversed that decision on direct appeal.

Justice William H. Rehnquist, joined by Chief Justice Warren Burger and Justices Potter Stewart, Harry Blackmun, Lewis Powell, and John Paul Stevens, wrote the majority opinion. Rehnquist emphasized the Court's traditional deference to Congress in cases involving the national defense and military affairs. Registering women had been "extensively considered" by Congress, and its decision to register only males was not an "accidental by-product of a traditional way of thinking about females." Congress' purpose was to prepare a draft of "combat troops," and since women were ineligible for combat, Congress exempted them. Rehnquist noted that the gender classification was "not invidious." He reasoned that Congress was not choosing arbitrarily to burden one of two similarly situated groups, "such as would be the case with an all-black or all-white, or an all-Catholic or all-Lutheran, or an all-Republican or all-Democratic registration." He found that men and women are not "similarly situated" for purposes of a draft or draft registration "because of the combat restrictions on women."

Justice Byron White, joined by Justice William Brennan, dissented, noting that not all positions in the military must be filled by combat-ready men and that women could be registered to fill noncombat positions "without sacrificing combat-readiness." Justice Thurgood Marshall, joined by Justice Brennan, also dissented on grounds that the government had failed to show that registering women would "seriously impede" its efforts to achieve "a concededly important governmental interest in maintaining an effective defense."

This decision continues to be important because female military personnel who are ineligible for combat find themselves disadvantaged when they compete with combat-eligible male personnel for positions and promotion. In the 1990's, combat restrictions on women were eased. Such developments speak directly to Rehnquist's premise that male-only draft registration is not discriminatory because only males are eligible for combat.

See also Carter, Jimmy; Conscription; Equality of opportunity; *Frontiero v. Richardson*; *Reed v. Reed*; Rehnquist, William; Sex discrimination.

Roth v. United States

COURT: U.S. Supreme Court
DATE: Decided June 24, 1957
SIGNIFICANCE: Ruling that obscene material is not protected by the First Amendment, the Court defined obscenity narrowly and put strict limits on the kinds of obscenity that might be proscribed by law

Samuel Roth conducted a business in New York in the publishing and sale of books, magazines, and photographs. A federal statute made it a crime to send "obscene, lewd, lascivious, or filthy" materials or advertisements through the U.S. mail, and Roth was found guilty in district court for violating four counts of the statute. Contemporary with Roth's conviction, David Alberts was convicted in California of advertising obscenity in violation of the state's penal code. When Roth and Alberts each petitioned the U.S. Supreme Court for review, the Court accepted both cases and consolidated them into one decision. The major issue was whether the federal and state statutes, as interpreted, were consistent with the First Amendment's freedom of speech and press.

Historically, both the federal government and the states had long criminalized most forms of pornography, and in numerous cases the Court had recognized such laws as a reasonable means to promote the state's legitimate interest in "decency." Between 1842 and 1956 the U.S. Congress had enacted twenty antiobscenity laws, and at least six times the Supreme Court had approved prosecutions under these laws. Some American courts continued to follow *Regina v. Hicklin* (1868), which looked at the effects of isolated passages on the most susceptible persons in society. Roth and Alberts had been convicted under a less restrictive standard, endorsed by Judge Learned Hand and many liberals, that considered the work as a whole and its impact on the average adult. Still, given the precedents, few observers considered that the Supreme Court would strike down antiobscenity statutes.

The Court ruled 6 to 3 to uphold Roth's federal conviction and 7 to 2 to uphold Alberts' state convictions. Writing for the majority, Justice William Brennan summarized the Anglo-American tradition of proscribing obscenity, and he concluded that obscenity enjoyed no constitutional protection because it had been historically recognized as "utterly without redeeming social importance." Making a distinction between sex and obscenity, Brennan rejected the *Hicklin* test as "unconstitutionally restrictive." He endorsed the alternative test of "whether to the average person, applying contemporary community standards, the dominant theme of the material taken as a whole appeals to the prurient interest."

Two liberal members of the Court, Justices William O. Douglas and Hugo L. Black, dissented and argued that the First Amendment protected all forms of expression. One member of the Court, John M. Harlan, distinguished between federal and state prosecution of obscenity, allowing the states greater power in the area.

The *Roth* decision was a landmark case because the Court for the first time limited government's prerogative to criminalize obscene material, and because it insisted on a narrow definition of obscenity. While allowing the continuation of antiobscenity laws, *Roth* recognized that all ideas were protected unless they were "utterly without redeeming social importance." Equally important was the explicit rejection of the *Hicklin* test, so that subsequent prosecutions had to be based on the influence of a work in its entirety on an average person of the community. In post-*Roth* cases, the Court would continue to be divided over the definition and protection of obscenity, a controversy that culminated in the three-pronged compromise of *Miller v. California* (1973).

See also *Barnes v. Glen Theatre, Inc.*; Bill of Rights, U.S.; Censorship; Comstock Law; Hand, Learned; *Miller v. California*; *Near v. Minnesota*; *New York v. Ferber*; *Osborne v. Ohio*; Speech and press, freedom of; Victimless crimes.

Rummel v. Estelle

COURT: U.S. Supreme Court
DATE: Decided March 18, 1980
SIGNIFICANCE: The Court found no cruel and unusual punishment in a state's mandatory life-imprisonment statute as applied to a man convicted of three fraudulent offenses involving only $229.11

In 1973, William Rummel was convicted under the Texas recidivist statute, which required a mandatory life sentence after three felony convictions, even for nonviolent offenses. In 1964 Rummel had been convicted of his first felony, the fraudulent use of a credit card to obtain goods worth $80.00. Four years later he had been found guilty of passing a forged check for $28.36. Finally, in 1973 he was charged with a third felony of receiving $120.75 by false pretenses. Rummel might have avoided the life sentence if he had yielded to the state's pressure to accept a plea bargain without a jury trial, but he insisted on a trial. Rummel sought relief in federal court, with the argument that his life sentence was "cruel and unusual" because it was grossly excessive and disproportionate to the penalties for more serious crimes. The district court and court of appeals rejected the argument, and Rummel appealed to the U.S. Supreme Court.

The Court voted 5 to 4 to affirm the constitutionality of Rummel's punishment. Writing for the majority, Justice William H. Rehnquist maintained that the doctrine that the Eighth Amendment prohibited sentences disproportionate to the severity of the crime was relevant only in death-penalty cases, because this penalty was unique in its total irrevocability. Rehnquist found that the Texas statute had two legitimate goals: to deter repeat offenders and to isolate recidivists from society as long as necessary after they had demonstrated their incapacity to obey the law. The states generally had the authority to determine the length of isolation deemed necessary for such recidivists. Rehnquist also made much of the fact that the Texas statute allowed the possibility of parole.

In an important dissent, Justice Lewis F. Powell, Jr., argued that the doctrine of disproportionality also applied to penalties in noncapital cases. He pointed to precedents that could be interpreted as prohibiting grossly excessive penalties, especially *Weems v. United States* (1910) and *Robinson v. California* (1962). Powell observed that in Texas, even those convicted of murder or aggravated kidnapping were not subject to a mandatory life sentence. In addition, he maintained that the possibility of parole should not be considered in assessing whether the penalty was grossly disproportionate.

The *Rummel* decision would prove to be limited and uncertain in its application as a precedent. In 1983, when the Court encountered a life sentence without any chance of parole based on a recidivist statute in *Solem v. Helm*, Justice Powell would write the majority opinion while Rehnquist would write a dissent. While *Solem* did not directly overturn *Rummel*, the *Solem* majority did endorse the idea that a prison sentence might be unconstitutional if it was disproportionate to punishments for other crimes. Yet in upholding a life sentence for the possession of 650 grams of cocaine in *Harmelin v. Michigan* (1991), the Court would indicate its continued reluctance to apply the doctrine of disproportionality in noncapital cases.

See also *Brady v. United States*; *Coker v. Georgia*; Cruel and unusual punishment; *Harmelin v. Michigan*; *Hutto v. Davis*; Mandatory sentencing laws; Plea bargaining; *Robinson v. California*; *Solem v. Helm*.

Runyon v. McCrary

COURT: U.S. Supreme Court

DATE: Decided June 25, 1976

SIGNIFICANCE: In this case, the Supreme Court broadened the meaning of Title 42, section 1981 of the 1866 Civil Rights Act to outlaw discrimination in all contracts

Parents of African American children brought suit in federal court against private schools in Virginia that had denied their children admission. Disregarding the defendant schools' argument that a government-imposed obligation to admit black students to their unintegrated student bodies would violate constitutionally protected rights of free association and privacy, the district and appellate courts both ruled in the parents' favor, enjoining the schools from discriminating on the basis of race.

The parents had based their case on a section of the 1866 Civil Rights Act that was still in effect. In 1968, the Supreme Court had held in *Jones v. Alfred H. Mayer Co.* that section 1982 of the act prohibited racial discrimination among private parties in housing. In *Runyon*, the Court broadened this holding to imply that section 1981, the act's right-to-contract provision, outlawed all discriminatory contracts, whether involving public or private parties—including one between private schools and the parents of student applicants.

In the wake of *Runyon*, lower federal courts employed section 1981 to outlaw racial discrimination in a wide variety of areas, including banking, security deposit regulations, admissions to amusement parks, insurance, and mortuaries. The breadth of the Court's interpretation in *Runyon* of section 1981

also caused it to overlap with Title VII of the Civil Rights Act of 1964, governing employment contracts. This overlap, together with ongoing concern about the extensiveness of the interpretation of section 1981, caused the Court to consider overruling *Runyon* in *Patterson v. McLean Credit Union* (1989). Instead, *Patterson* severely restricted *Runyon* by declaring that section 1981 did not apply to postcontractual employer discrimination. *Patterson* went so far as to declare that although section 1981 protected the right to enter into employment contracts, it did not extend to future breaches of that contract or to the imposition of discriminatory working conditions. Congress in turn overruled this narrow reading of section 1981 in the Civil Rights Act of 1991, which includes explicit language permitting courts to prohibit employment discrimination that takes place after hiring.

The reason for the Court's about-face with regard to section 1981 can be found in its changing political composition. *Runyon* was decided midway through Chief Justice Warren Burger's tenure, when the Court was dominated by justices who occupied the middle of the political spectrum. In 1986, however, one of two dissenters in *Runyon*, Justice William H. Rehnquist, succeeded Burger, carrying with him his conservative agenda. Rehnquist, who had always been outspoken in his criticism of what he regarded as the Court's excess of liberalism under Chief Justice Earl Warren, dissented in *Runyon* on grounds that the Warren-era *Jones* case had been improperly decided. By 1989, when the Court handed down its decision in *Patterson*, Rehnquist had been joined by enough fellow conservative thinkers to overrule *Runyon*'s interpretation of section 1981 by one vote.

See also Arrest; Bail system; Civil Rights Act of 1991; Civil Rights Acts of 1866-1875; Contract, freedom of; Contract law; Criminal justice system; Criminal procedure; Discretion; Due process of law; *Jones v. Alfred H. Mayer Co.*; Presumption of innocence; Prison and jail systems; Racial and ethnic discrimination.

Rush, Benjamin (Jan. 4, 1746, Byberry Township, Pa.— Apr. 19, 1813, Philadelphia, Pa.)

IDENTIFICATION: American physician and a signer of the Declaration of Independence

SIGNIFICANCE: Physician to George Washington's revolutionary army and a prolific essayist, Rush attempted to apply the ideals of the American Revolution to every aspect of American life—particularly education, government, and medicine

Born into a Quaker farming family but reared by his mother as a Presbyterian, Rush was educated at Princeton. On Benjamin Franklin's advice he studied medicine with William Hunter in London and with William Cullen in Edinburgh (1766-1768). He associated with reformers and read the philosophy of John Locke. He became an early member of the Continental Congress and a committed American revolutionary. In his 1787 *Address to the People of the United States*, he proclaimed that "The *American Revolution* . . . requires us to establish and protect our new forms of government; and to prepare the principles, morals and manners of our citizens, for these forms of government." Among the reforms he urged were the abolition of slavery, an end to capital punishment (*On Punishing Murder by Death*, 1792), and the prohibition of "ardent spirits" (*An Inquiry into the Effects of Ardent Spirits upon the Human Body and Mind*, 1805).

See also American Revolution; Declaration of Independence.

Rust v. Sullivan

COURT: U.S. Supreme Court

DATE: Decided May 23, 1991

SIGNIFICANCE: This case is one of a series of decisions dating back to *Maher v. Roe* (1977) authorizing the government to make access to, and information about, abortion dependent on a woman's ability to pay for it

Section 1008 of the Public Health Service Act prohibits the use of federal funds in family planning programs "where abortion is a method of family planning." Prior to 1988, the regulations implementing this provision prohibited family planning programs which received federal funds from performing abortions. In 1988, new regulations also prohibited such programs from abortion counseling and from mentioning abortion when referring pregnant women to other services or facilities. The new regulations were commonly referred to as the "gag rules" because they forbade family planning health care programs to mention abortion and required them, if asked about abortion, to respond only that it was not considered an appropriate method of family planning.

Health care providers that offered family planning services and doctors filed suit, challenging the constitutionality of the gag rules. They raised three arguments. First, they claimed that the Department of Health and Human Services was acting beyond the scope of its authority. Second, they said, the rules violated the free speech rights of family planning programs under the First Amendment. Third, they argued that the rules violated the right to privacy (upheld in *Roe v. Wade*, 1973) of individuals using the services of family planning programs. The Supreme Court, by a 5-4 vote, rejected all three arguments and held that the rules were constitutional.

In an opinion written by William Rehnquist, the Court stated that the statutory language was broad in scope and ambiguous. In such cases the Court defers to the interpretation adopted by the agency charged with administering the statute as long as it reflects a plausible construction of the statute's plain language and does not otherwise conflict with Congress'

expressed intent. Nothing in the language of the statute or its legislative history prohibited the Department of Health and Human Services from adopting a more restrictive view concerning abortion as a method of family planning. The gag rules were supported by a reasoned analysis demonstrating that the new restrictions assure federal funds are spent on only authorized purposes and avoid creating the appearance of governmental support for abortion-related activities.

Second, the Court held that the regulations do not violate the First Amendment free speech rights of family planning programs, their staffs, or their patients. The government may make a value judgment favoring childbirth over abortion and implement that judgment via the allocation of public funds. Such a preference is not discriminating on the basis of viewpoint, but ensuring that government funds are being spent for a chosen activity rather than another which the government has chosen not to support. The gag rules do not force clinic personnel or patients to give up all abortion-related speech. Rather, they require that certain speech must occur outside the government-funded family planning program. When the government chooses to subsidize one activity, nothing in the First Amendment requires it also to subsidize the presentation of an alternative point of view or service.

Third, the Court found that the gag rules do not violate a woman's right to choose whether to terminate her pregnancy. The government has no constitutional duty to subsidize an activity merely because it is constitutionally protected, and it may validly allocate public funds for services relating to childbirth but not to abortion. This allocation, according to the Court, places no insurmountable obstacle in the path of a woman wishing to terminate her pregnancy, and it leaves her with the same choices as if the government had chosen not to fund any family planning programs. The gag rules do not place impermissible restrictions on patient/doctor discussions concerning a woman's right to make an informed and voluntary choice on whether to carry her pregnancy to term, because this information remains available through private health care providers not receiving funds under the Public Health Service Act. The Court decided that the fact that most women participating in family planning programs funded by the act are too poor to obtain private health care services was irrelevant. Such financial constraints on a woman's ability to enjoy the full range of constitutionally protected choices, the Court said, are the product not of governmental restrictions but rather of her personal financial circumstances.

See also Abortion; *Maher v. Roe*; *Roe v. Wade*.

Sacco and Vanzetti trial and executions

DATE: Arrests May 5, 1920; convictions July 14, 1921; executions August 23, 1927

PLACE: Massachusetts

SIGNIFICANCE: The trial of Sacco and Vanzetti took place during the "red scare," one of the most intense periods of political repression in the United States, and became a cause célèbre for those who believed that the pair were wrongly persecuted for their political beliefs

Nicola Sacco and Bartolomeo Vanzetti, two Italian immigrants and anarchists, were arrested in May, 1920, and charged with participating in the April, 1920, robbery and murder of two men who had been carrying a factory payroll in South Braintree, Massachusetts. They were tried in the summer of 1921. Their lawyer was the socialist Fred H. Moore, a prominent defense attorney for the labor movement and the Industrial Workers of the World. Instead of skirting the issue of Sacco and Vanzetti's radicalism, Moore based his defense on the argument that the government was prosecuting the pair because of their beliefs and sought to use the case to help suppress anarchist activism among Italians in the United States.

Vanzetti had also been charged with an earlier robbery attempt and was tried separately on that lesser charge a few months after the pair's arrest. He was convicted in a trial marred by the ethnic prejudice of the jury, which reacted against Italian defense witnesses who either spoke no English or did so as a second language. His conviction set the stage for the harshness of the second trial, which he entered with a criminal record. The Sacco and Vanzetti case had also gained the attention of J. Edgar Hoover, who was then the director of the General Intelligence Division of the Department of Justice.

After a six-week trial emphasizing their radical activities, Sacco and Vanzetti were found guilty of both the robbery and the murder charges. Their conviction set in motion a series of efforts for appeal or a new trial. The defense strategy motivated thousands of people to become active in demonstrations questioning the justice of the trial. Appeal motions cited perjury by prosecution witnesses, illegal proceedings by police and federal agents, misconduct on the part of the judge, Webster Thayer, and evidence pointing to other individuals who may have committed the crimes.

Felix Frankfurter became one of the most outspoken critics of the trial proceedings. He cited the case as a test of the objectivity of American jurisprudence. Public sympathy was also heightened by the articulate dignity with which the two men had reacted to their fate.

In 1924 Moore was replaced by William Thompson, a member of Boston's legal elite. After appeal motions were exhausted and Sacco and Vanzetti were

Sacco and Vanzetti were executed in 1927 despite widespread accusations that prosecutor's emphasis on their radical activities had tainted their trial. (AP/Wide World Photos)

officially sentenced to death on April 9, 1927, an advisory committee headed by Harvard University president A. Lawrence Lowell reviewed the pair's request for executive clemency for Massachusetts governor Alvan T. Fuller. The committee recommended against clemency, and despite the international mass movement that had developed on Sacco and Vanzetti's behalf, the two men were executed on August 23, 1927.

The executions marked an end of idealism for many American intellectuals. The guilt or innocence of the two men remains an issue of debate.

See also Appellate process; Capital punishment; Civil liberties; Frankfurter, Felix; Hoover, J. Edgar; Palmer raids and the "red scare."

Saint Valentine's Day massacre

DATE: February 14, 1928

PLACE: Chicago, Illinois

SIGNIFICANCE: The Prohibition-era gangland murders carried out in this event have made it a symbol of the roaring twenties

On February 14, 1928, members of the Al Capone bootlegging gang in Chicago murdered five members of the rival "Bugs" Moran gang in a garage at the corner of Clark and Wabash. This was the most spectacular and well publicized of the many gang murders carried out in Chicago and other American cities as rivals tried to corner the illegal beer and liquor markets during the Prohibition era. Because the attack occurred on Saint Valentine's Day, it has been dubbed the Saint Valentine's Day massacre. It gave Capone the upper hand in controlling illegal alcohol in South Chicago and enhanced his reputation as the country's most notorious bootlegger. The event has come to symbolize Prohibition-era Chicago as an untamed, mob-controlled city, and Capone has entered American mythology as one of the most legendary outlaws of the twentieth century. The actual killers were hired assassins. Only one of about a half dozen has been definitively identified—Fred Burke, a bank robber and murderer and a fugitive from an Ohio warrant. Capone's rival Moran was not among those killed.

See also Capone, Alphonse (Al); Organized crime; Prohibition; Tax evasion.

Salem witchcraft trials

DATE: 1692

PLACE: Salem Village, Massachusetts

SIGNIFICANCE: The injustice of the Salem witch trials has come to symbolize the terrible results that can come of intolerance and hysteria

Salem, Massachusetts, was settled by English Puritans; the church at Salem was established in 1629 as an independent Protestant church. A belief in witchcraft and the idea that humans could be direct agents of the devil was widespread in Europe at the time, and the Puritans brought the belief with them to New England. The colonial charter had laws against sorcery and witchcraft, and punishment was the death penalty.

The problems in Salem began in February, 1692, when young girls in the home of the church pastor, including the pastor's daughter, began suffering spectacular seizures and speaking incantations. The girls were soon considered bewitched, and they began to implicate people in the community as witches; most of them were middle-aged women. It came to be believed that a servant girl named Tituba, who was said to be familiar with witchcraft practices from her home in the West Indies, and two older women named Sarah Good and Sarah Osborn had influenced the girls. A complaint was filed against them, and warrants were issued for their arrest. Sarah Good was eventually convicted and executed on July 19 of that year. Sarah Osborn died in jail in Boston. In all, over the course of the summer of 1692, twenty people were executed, mostly by hanging, ten more were condemned, and hundreds were accused.

No formal court system existed to handle these trials; they were presided over by governor-appointed commissioners. Concern over the chaotic nature of the Salem antiwitch frenzy spread throughout Massachusetts in the spring and summer of 1692. In October, the new governor of Massachusetts, William Phips, ordered a halt to the trials. He formed a new court in January of 1693 that eventually acquitted all people still accused of witchcraft. It was the questionable reliability of witnesses and evidence (adolescents made the charges and served as the primary witnesses) that led to the discontinuing of the trials. Accusations against the wife of a pastor and other people of seemingly impeccable repute raised considerable doubt as to the validity of the accusations.

Only a few years later the Salem witchcraft trials were seen as a great tragedy. Most prominent people repented of their part in them, and the jurors issued a public statement of regret, saying that they had acted out of ignorance and delusion. The term "witch-hunt" eventually entered the American lexicon as a description of any paranoic, unreasoning attempt to ferret out and punish conspirators; the most famous example was the anticommunist witch-hunts of the late 1940's and 1950's.

See also Due process of law; McCarthyism; Punishment.

San Antonio Independent School District v. Rodriguez

COURT: U.S. Supreme Court

DATE: Decided March 21, 1973

SIGNIFICANCE: The Supreme Court ruled that education was not a fundamental right and that a school finance system that resulted in lower expenditures in school districts inhabited by poor people did not violate the equal protection clause of the Fourteenth Amendment

Texas, like many other states, finances its public schools with both state and local funding. In the 1970's, the state, through its Minimum Foundation School Program, guaranteed a minimum level of education, but individual school districts were permitted to increase the amount spent on education by taxing property within the district. The constitutionality of this method of school financing was challenged by Demetrio Rodriguez, a Mexican American with three children enrolled in the Edgewood School District. The value of property in that district was low, and, though the people of Edgewood taxed themselves at the maximum rate permitted by law, they were able to raise only $26 per child. State funds brought the total expenditure per child up to $356. The Alamo Heights District, inhabited by much wealthier people, taxed itself at a lower rate than Edgewood, but, because of the higher value of the property, was able to raise $333 per child. State funds raised that to $594 per child. Rodriguez believed that such a school finance system discriminated against persons on the basis of wealth. A federal district court agreed and held it unconstitutional. The state of Texas appealed to the Supreme Court.

In a close decision, with the justices divided 5-4, the Supreme Court reversed the district court and upheld the Texas school finance system. The Court recognized the difficulty of measuring the quality of education received and relating it to the amount of money spent. Although Rodriguez had sought to convince the Court that education was a fundamental right because of the close connection between education and the ability to exercise the constitutional right of freedom of speech and the right to vote, the Court conceded only that education was important to the effective exercise of those rights but denied that the Constitution guaranteed their most effective exercise. The Court did not express approval of the challenged school finance system but rather considered that American federalism placed the matter within the states' domain.

State supreme courts did, indeed, respond to inequities in school financing. Several of them held that their states' school finance systems, similar to that of Texas, violated their own state constitutions. The California Supreme Court had rendered such a decision even before the U.S. Supreme Court's decision in the *Rodriguez* case. After the *Rodriguez* decision, other state supreme courts took action. A state may not deny its people federal constitutional rights, but it may certainly accord them greater rights than the federal Constitution. In 1989, the school finance system upheld in the *Rodriguez* case was held to be in violation of the Texas Constitution by the Texas Supreme Court.

See also *Brown v. Board of Education*; Equal protection of the law; Equality of opportunity; Federalism; States' rights.

Sanger, Margaret (Sept. 14, 1879, Corning, N.Y.—Sept. 6, 1966, Tucson, Ariz.)

IDENTIFICATION: American birth control advocate

SIGNIFICANCE: Sanger's challenges to the Comstock Law, banning the dissemination of contraceptive information, helped to legalize birth control in the United States and shaped the course of the reproductive rights movement

A nurse and mother of three, Margaret Sanger devoted her life to securing legal, safe, and available birth control for all women. Sanger initially envisioned the birth control fight as a free speech issue and challenged the Comstock Law, which banned the distribution of birth control information as ob-

scene. In 1914 she edited and published *The Woman Rebel*, a radical journal banned by the post office. After being indicted for violating the Comstock Law, Sanger fled the country, but she first published *Family Limitation*, a more explicit pamphlet containing information about various methods of contraception. On her return, in 1915, all charges against her were dropped for fear that prosecution would make her a martyr to the birth control cause.

While in Europe, Sanger created a new emphasis for the birth control movement: Instead of seeing the issue as one of free speech, she became convinced that birth control required close medical supervision. She shifted her emphasis toward providing medical services modeled on those of Dutch clinics. On October 16, 1916, she opened the first birth control clinic in the United States in the Brownsville section of Brooklyn, New York. The clinic remained open only nine days before it was raided by the police. Sanger, her sister, and a coworker were arrested and tried (*New York v. Sanger, Byrne, and Mindell*). Sanger was convicted and served thirty days in prison, but on appeal the New York State Supreme Court broadened the law to exempt doctors from the restrictions on providing contraceptive information. With this ruling, Sanger could open a legal doctor-staffed clinic in New York (1923). It served as a model for a national network of private birth control providers.

In the 1930's Sanger sought to change the federal Comstock Law and founded the National Committee for Federal Legislation on Birth Control (NCFLBC), which sponsored birth control legislation and aimed to educate the public and Congress about the need for these laws. Despite intense lobbying and national legislative campaigns (1930-1937), Sanger was unable to get any of this legislation passed because of strong opposition from the Catholic church and the social conservatism of many congressmen.

While working toward a legislative victory, Sanger pursued a judicial solution as well. She arranged for a test case in which Hannah Mayer Stone, the medical director of Sanger's clinic, received birth control devices in the mail from Japan. When the U.S. Customs Office seized the devices, Sanger sued the government. Sanger won the case in 1935, and in 1936 the government appealed (*United States v. One Package Containing 120, More or Less, Rubber Pessaries to Prevent Conception*). The case was heard by the Second Circuit Court of Appeals in New York. The appeal decision not only allowed the importation of the devices but also broadly argued that all laws concerning contraception should be reinterpreted, essentially legalizing physician-controlled birth control in the United States.

As one of the United States' most notable and effective propagandists, Sanger developed policies that deeply affected the twentieth century reproductive rights movement. Her legacy can be seen in the close association of reproductive rights with medical services and clinics and in the tendency for activists to seek judicial rather than legislative victories to change existing law. Sanger died in 1966, shortly after the

Margaret Sanger (fourth from left) in 1916; poor mothers brought their families to the courthouse during her trial in a show of support. (Library of Congress)

Supreme Court upheld the right of married couples to practice contraception privately (*Griswold v. Connecticut*, 1965).

See also Birth control, right to; Comstock Law; Feminism; *Griswold v. Connecticut*; Privacy, right of.

Santobello v. New York

COURT: U.S. Supreme Court

DATE: Decided December 20, 1971

SIGNIFICANCE: In this case, which granted the petitioner the right to either a resentencing or a new trial, the Supreme Court confirmed the binding nature of plea-bargaining agreements made by prosecutors with defendants in criminal proceedings

In 1969, in New York, Rudolph Santobello was arraigned on two criminal counts of violating state antigambling statutes. At first, Santobello entered a plea of not guilty, but later, after negotiations with his prosecutors, he changed his plea to guilty to a lesser-included charge, which carried a maximum penalty of one year in prison. Between the entering of the new guilty plea and the sentencing there was a delay of several months, and in the interim Santobello obtained a new defense attorney, who immediately attempted to have the guilty plea removed and certain evidence suppressed. Both motions were denied.

At Santobello's sentencing, a new prosecutor recommended the maximum penalty of one year in prison. The defense quickly objected, using the argument that the petitioner's plea-bargaining agreement had stipulated that the prosecution would make no recommendation regarding sentencing. The judge, rejecting the relevancy of what prosecutors claimed they would do, sentenced Santobello to the full one-year term on the grounds that he was a seasoned and habitual offender. Subsequently, the Appellate Division of the Supreme Court of the State of New York unanimously upheld the conviction.

The U.S. Supreme Court found that the prosecution had breached the plea-bargaining agreement and remanded the case to the state court to determine whether the circumstances required only resentencing before a different judge or whether the petitioner should be allowed to withdraw his guilty plea and be granted a new trial on the two counts as originally charged. The fact that the breach in the plea-bargaining agreement was inadvertent was deemed irrelevant, as was the sentencing judge's claim that he was not influenced by the prosecutor's recommendation. Chief Justice Warren E. Burger, in the Court ruling, argued that the plea-bargaining procedure in criminal justice "must be attended by safeguards to ensure the defendant what is reasonably due in the circumstances." Therefore, any agreement made in the plea-bargaining process, because it is part of the inducement used to encourage a plea of guilty, constitutes "a promise that must be fulfilled."

In its decision in *Santobello*, the Supreme Court both confirmed its formal recognition of plea bargaining, first granted in *Brady v. United States* (1970), and established its binding nature. Although in later decisions it would review and somewhat modify its position, as, for example, in *Mabry v. Johnson* (1984), it established an extremely important principle: that prosecutors and courts could not unilaterally renege on promises made in plea-bargaining agreements. The *Santobello* decision had the effect of encouraging wider use of the plea-bargaining process, an important aid in expediting justice.

See also *Brady v. United States*; Criminal justice system; Criminal procedure; Plea bargaining.

Scales v. United States

COURT: U.S. Supreme Court
DATE: Decided June 5, 1961
SIGNIFICANCE: In this case, the Supreme Court found that laws providing penalties for active membership in organizations advocating overthrow of the government do not necessarily violate the Constitution's guarantees of due process and freedom of speech

Scales, a member of the Communist Party of the United States, was convicted under the membership clause of the Smith Act of 1940, making it a crime knowingly to belong to an organization whose aim is overthrow of the federal government by force or violence. The Smith Act was one of several antisubversive measures Congress passed after the outbreak of World War II. Although its first section addressed attempts to subvert the military, in fact the act was seldom invoked during World War II. Afterward, however, it became one of the government's primary methods of combating domestic communism during the Cold War. In *Dennis v. United States* (1951), the Supreme Court upheld the convictions of eleven Communist Party leaders under the conspiracy provisions of the act, a decision that led to the indictment of 141 state party leaders throughout the country. *Scales v. United States* resulted from those indictments, as did the earlier *Yates v. United States* (1957).

In *Yates*, the Court by a vote of 6 to 1 reversed the convictions of fourteen party leaders involved. The opinion of the Court, written by Justice John M. Harlan and emphasizing the distinction between advocacy of a subversive ideology and advocacy of subversive action, found the conspiracy provisions of the Smith Act defective, thus rendering them worthless. No further prosecutions were undertaken under them.

Between the time the Supreme Court handed down its decision in *Dennis* and that in *Yates*, personnel changes on the Court as well as an easing of Cold War tensions resulted in a reorientation. *Yates* produced a backlash in Congress, however, and by the time the Court decided *Scales*, it had again changed its attitude. Justice Harlan, joined by Justice Felix Frankfurter, changed sides, with the result that Scales's conviction was upheld by a vote of 5 to 4.

In a companion case, *Noto v. United States*, decided the same day as *Scales*, the Court dismissed the conviction of a Communist Party member under the membership clause of the Smith Act. Justice Harlan's opinions in the two cases were careful to distinguish between mere membership in organizations such as the Communist Party and "not only knowing membership, but purposive membership, purposive that is as to the organization's criminal ends." Construed in this fashion, the Smith Act membership clause violated neither the due process clause of the Fifth Amendment nor the free speech guarantee embodied in the First Amendment.

In both *Yates* and *Scales*, the Court interpreted the Smith Act more narrowly than it had in *Dennis*, with the result that finally only twenty-nine of the individuals indicted under the act served time in jail for their convictions.

See also Communist Party, American; *Dennis v. United States*; McCarthyism; Smith Act; Speech and press, freedom of; *Yates v. United States*.

Schall v. Martin

COURT: U.S. Supreme Court
DATE: Decided June 4, 1984
SIGNIFICANCE: In agreeing with a New York State family court in this preventive detention case, the Supreme Court limited the application of the Fourteenth Amendment's due process clause

Schall v. Martin was a preventive detention case involving juveniles. New York State had enacted a Family Court Act pertaining to juvenile delinquents and to juveniles arrested and remanded to the family court prior to trial. If the family court determined that pretrial release of juveniles might result in their disappearance or place them or the general public at risk, it was authorized to detain them. Detention occurred only after notice was given to parents and other authorities, a hearing was held, a statement of facts and reasons was presented, and the "probable cause" that release might be harmful was established.

Juvenile detainees Gregory Martin, Luis Rosario, and Kenneth Morgan (along with thirty-three other juveniles introduced into the case) faced serious charges. Martin had been arrested in 1977, charged with first-degree robbery, second-degree assault, and criminal possession of a gun after he and two others struck another youth on the head with a loaded gun and beat him in order to steal his jacket and sneakers. He was found guilty of these crimes by a family court judge and placed on two years' probation. Martin was fourteen. Rosario, also fourteen, was charged with robbery and second-degree assault for trying to rob two men by putting a gun to their heads and beating them. He previously had been detained for knifing a student. Morgan, fourteen, had four previous arrests and had been charged with attempted robbery, assault, and grand larceny for robbing and threatening to shoot a fourteen-year-old girl and her brother.

Martin and the others brought suit claiming that their detention deprived them of a writ of *habeas corpus* and violated the due process clause of the Fourteenth Amendment. The federal district appeals court agreed that their detention "served as punishment without proof of guilt according to requisite constitutional standards." Gregory Schall, commissioner of the New York City Department of Juvenile Justice, appealed to the Supreme Court. The case reached the Supreme Court at a time when polls showed that crime was a major fear of the American public and when a relatively conservative Court was exercising judicial restraint and limiting the expansion of civil liberties.

Reading the majority 7-2 decision, Justice William Rehnquist acknowledged that the due process clause of the Fourteenth Amendment indeed applied to the pretrial detention of juveniles. He agreed with Schall, however, that when, as in these cases, there was "serious risk" involved to both the juveniles and the public by their release, the New York law was compatible with the "fundamental fairness" demanded by the due process clause.

See also Comprehensive Crime Control Act of 1984; Due process of law; *Habeas corpus*; Juvenile justice system; Preventive detention.

Schenck v. United States

COURT: U.S Supreme Court
DATE: Decided March 3, 1919
SIGNIFICANCE: The Supreme Court promulgated the "clear and present danger" doctrine as a guideline in freedom of speech cases

The Schenck case involved the constitutionality of the Espionage Act. Passed by Congress on June 15, 1917, that wartime measure provided severe penalties for individuals convicted of such treasonable offenses as aiding the enemy, obstructing recruiting, instigating disloyalty among American troops, or mailing seditious material. The passage of the statute reopened the old conflict between military necessity and the Bill of Rights.

Charles T. Schenck, the general secretary of the Socialist Party, strongly opposed American participation in World War I. He expressed his resistance to the "capitalist" war by distributing about fifteen thousand leaflets that urged noncompliance with the 1917 Selective Service Act. He was indicted under the Espionage Act for plotting to obstruct the draft and for using the mails to circulate his leaflets. After a federal court convicted him and sentenced him to prison, Schenck appealed to the U.S. Supreme Court on the grounds that he had been deprived of his freedom of speech and press guaranteed by the First Amendment to the Constitution.

The nation's highest court was thus confronted with the challenge of reconciling the Espionage Act with the First Amendment. After hearing arguments in 1919, the Court upheld the constitutionality of the 1917 law. Justice Oliver Wendell Holmes, Jr., speaking for a unanimous Court, maintained that the First Amendment guarantee of freedom of speech and press is not absolute. "The most stringent protection of Free speech," he said, "would not protect a man in falsely shouting fire in a theater and causing a panic." Freedom of expression is always under restraint, particularly in wartime. In his decision, Holmes formulated the clear and present danger doctrine as a criterion for judging between permissible and illicit speech: "The question . . . is whether the words are used in such circumstances and are of such a nature as to create a clear and present danger that they will bring about the substantive evil that Congress has a right to prevent." Applying the test to Schenck's distribution of antidraft circulars during World War I, Holmes ruled that the defendant's activities did pose an immediate danger to the nation's war effort. Schenck's conviction was upheld.

The major legacy of the case to American justice has been the clear and present danger precept. The test subsequently became an influential yardstick in freedom of speech cases. A version of Holmes's criterion permits advocacy to be punished only if its objective is to incite lawless behavior and if such behavior is likely to occur. If the perceived danger is not imminent or its likelihood is minimal, the government may not restrict freedom of speech.

See also *Abrams v. United States*; *Brandenburg v. Ohio*; Clear and present danger test; *Dennis v. United States*; Espionage Act; *Gitlow v. New York*; *Herndon v. Lowry*; Holmes, Oliver Wendell, Jr.; *Near v. Minnesota*; *New York Times Co. v. United States*; Socialist Party, American.

School law

DEFINITION: Those laws which apply to the realm of public schooling, the rights of public schools, and the rights of individuals attending those schools
SIGNIFICANCE: Many significant rulings and decisions have been made to ensure equal educational opportunities for all individuals and to define the responsibilities of the public schools to society

Historically, issues relating to public education have been left to the authority of individual states. Some federal requirements have been set in place, yet within the boundaries of these federal guidelines, states are free to run public schools as they best see fit.

States have given local school boards authority over local school systems. These boards may institute policies, always in compliance with state and federal laws, which expand upon or interpret the laws for their particular needs. Individuals on these boards may not act alone, but only when meeting together officially as a board.

Compulsory Education. To aid in running the schools, states have passed laws regarding education. One of the most basic laws has to do with compulsory education. Laws have varied from state to state as to how early and how long a child must attend school, but it has been accepted that states have vested interests in seeing that children receive basic skills and training in citizenship. One of the first such laws was established in the 1920's, when the state of Oregon required all school-age children to attend public schools. The law was successfully challenged in 1925 in *Pierce v. Society of Sisters*. The "Pierce Compromise" resulting from this case allowed the state to require children to attend school, but gave parents the right to choose private education for their children, with no state reimbursement.

In certain cases, the Supreme Court has granted exceptions to the compulsory-education requirement. In *Wisconsin v. Yoder* (1972), Wisconsin's compulsory-education law was judged to violate Amish children's free exercise rights under the First Amendment. The Supreme Court decided that requiring these Amish children to complete state-mandated secondary education would significantly infringe upon and harm their religious practices. The Court saw that the sect's own vocational training would, in effect, fulfill the state's interest in the children's schooling.

As time passed, more and more school-related laws were passed. Some of these later laws were passed at the federal level—for example, requiring all states to meet certain standards for education. Also, many lawsuits have been filed over the years, requiring the courts to address issues having to do with school policies and practices.

Free Speech in Schools. Basically, laws pertaining to public education are similar to other legal issues. The rights and responsibilities of students, parents, taxpayers, certified teachers, and staff sometimes clash with the rights of the public school. *Tinker v. Des Moines Independent Community School District* (1969) developed after high school and junior high school students wore black armbands to school in protest of the Vietnam War and were punished by suspension. The case was argued as a freedom of speech issue. In this instance, the wearing of armbands caused no significant disruption of school activities, and the Des Moines schools had previously allowed students to wear or display other symbols of a political nature. Thus, the Court ruled that although the schools

The Supreme Court held in New Jersey v. T.L.O. *(1985) that students are protected against unreasonable searches of their persons, but the Court did not address the issue of searching lockers.* (James L. Shaffer)

have the right to set rules for order and student behavior, students need not "shed their constitutional rights to freedom of speech or expression at the schoolhouse gate."

In *West Virginia State Board of Education v. Barnette* (1943), the Supreme Court overturned a previous decision regarding a law that required students to recite the Pledge of Allegiance and salute the flag. The Court sided with members of the Jehovah's Witnesses, who argued that such a requirement violated their religious beliefs and practices.

Students and teachers need not give up their constitutional right to free speech simply because they operate in a public school setting. Indeed, academic freedom rests on this most basic right of the individual. In *Sweezy v. New Hampshire* (1957), the Court sided with a Marxist professor who had refused to answer state investigators' questions regarding his political beliefs and teaching. The decision affirmed the need for schools to retain an atmosphere of freedom of thought and expression.

Discrimination and the Schools. Students in public schools are entitled to a free, appropriate, and equal education. In one case, *Plyler v. Doe* (1982), the Supreme Court went so far as to require the state of Texas to educate students who were illegal immigrants, since these students were subject to state laws because of their residency within the state's perimeter, legally or not.

There have been many other challenges to the basic right to an education for students. In times past, it was common for schools to be segregated according to race. The courts upheld this custom by stating that separation does not necessarily lead to inequality of educational services.

In 1954, the decision rendered in *Brown v. Board of Education* changed this tradition. The Supreme Court declared that racially segregated schools were inherently unequal, that it would consequently be illegal for public schools to be segregated, and that integration would be required. Title VI of the Civil Rights Act of 1964 prohibited discrimination in any federally funded activity or program based on race, color, or national origin. Unfortunately, many school systems were not quick to comply with the new regulations, so it took a few painful years for the law to become reality in practice.

One outcome of the requirement to desegregate schools was the subsequent need to bus students. In *Swann v. Charlotte-Mecklenburg Board of Education* (1971), the Court ruled that busing was an appropriate means to achieve racial desegregation. Two *Milliken v. Bradley* cases, one in 1974 and one in 1977, also dealt with integration issues. The first case resulted in the decision to limit the lower courts' abilities to impose intersystem desegregation mandates where a school system had not deliberately acted to bring about segregation. The latter case then broadened the allowable mandates of lower courts in requiring schools to comply with measures indirectly related to racial balance.

Pasadena City Board of Education v. Spangler (1976) also dealt with matters of desegregation. In this case, the Supreme Court decided that since the district had not intentionally seg-regated its schools, racially unbalanced student populations would not be subject to annual evaluations and changes. This effectively gave the district more leeway in its remedies to achieve racial integration.

Awareness of educational discrimination against students with disabilities began growing in the 1950's. Section 504 of the Rehabilitation Act of 1973 forbade discrimination based on handicap in any program receiving federal dollars. Although public schools typically receive much more of their funding from the state and local community than from the federal government, they are subject to this regulation. All states have passed their own legislation expanding upon this general guideline for their own school systems.

In 1975, Congress passed the Education for all Handicapped Children Act, renamed the Individuals with Disabilities Education Act (IDEA) in 1990. This act requires that the same programs and services be made available to both disabled and nondisabled individuals. One of the legal requirements of IDEA is inclusion, which calls for handicapped persons to be placed in a regular classroom setting with necessary supplemental services. Only if a child with a disability is better served outside the regular classroom can he or she be removed to a special education environment. IDEA mandates that disabled students be placed in the least restrictive environment for their educational needs to be sufficiently met. Not surprisingly, the need to educate individuals with disabilities equitably has spawned a broad array of legal actions and precedents.

Female students have also taken legal actions against public school systems to ensure that discriminatory practices are eliminated as much as possible. These actions culminated in the passage of Title IX of the Education Amendments of 1972, which holds that any program receiving federal financial assistance cannot legally discriminate against any individual on the basis of gender. Most applications of Title IX requirements in secondary public schools have to do with ensuring that female students have an equal amount of access to appropriate sports and activities as do male students.

Other Educational Issues. Another issue in school law is the relationship between church and state. State institutions, including schools, are not to promote or restrict the exercise of any particular religion. Many misunderstandings have arisen from this seemingly simple assertion, and the applicable laws do differ from state to state. Basically, students are allowed to pray in school silently and individually, and in some states student-led services can be held on school grounds before or after school hours. Many states still allow prayers at school functions such as graduation ceremonies.

Other laws and regulations involving public schools also vary from state to state. These address, for example, the use of corporal punishment, search and seizure matters, and how much freedom students have to express controversial views in school publications. Generally, the core issue involves the right of individual students to act as they wish, set against the need of the school institution to maintain an orderly and safe environment. The law typically sides with the school on these issues, with a view to promoting what is best for the student population as a whole.

Specific laws regarding school liability also vary from one state to another. In general, however, the school is held legally responsible to provide a safe environment for pupils during activities sponsored by the school, even if they take place during noninstructional hours. —*Ruffin G. Stirling*

See also Busing; Due process of law; *In loco parentis*; Little Rock school integration crisis; *Pierce v. Society of Sisters*; *Plyler v. Doe*; School prayer; Segregation, *de facto* and *de jure*; Speech and press, freedom of; *Swann v. Charlotte-Mecklenburg Board of Education*; *Tinker v. Des Moines Independent Community School District*.

BIBLIOGRAPHY

Profiles of school law include E. Edmund Reutter, *Schools and the Law* (4th ed. Dobbs Ferry, N.Y.: Oceana Publications, 1980), and M. Chester Nolte, *Guide to School Law* (West Nyack, N.Y.: Parker, 1969). Efforts at racial integration in schools are discussed in Judith Bentley, *Busing: The Continuing Controversy* (New York: Franklin Watts, 1982); Jennifer L. Hochschild, *The New American Dilemma: Liberal Democracy and School Desegregation* (New Haven, Conn.: Yale University Press, 1984); and Jonathan Kozol, *Savage Inequalities: Children in America's Schools* (New York: Crown, 1991). For treatment of religion in the public schools and other relevant issues, see William O. Douglas, *The Bible and the Schools* (Boston: Little, Brown, 1966), and Nat Hentoff, *American Heroes: In and Out of School* (New York: Delacorte Press, 1987).

School prayer

DEFINITION: The constitutional issue of whether mandatory prayer in public schools is permissible under the First Amendment

SIGNIFICANCE: The debate over school prayer established constitutional boundaries that helped to define the concept of "establishment" of religion in the modern period; the controversy also set the tone for ongoing political debate over the intrusion of government into religious matters

The issue of prayer in the public schools as a point of constitutional contention is unique to the twentieth century, resulting from the application of First Amendment standards to individual states through judicial interpretations of the Fourteenth Amendment. Prior to the latter amendment's application in a 1940 case involving the free exercise of religion, *Cantwell v. Connecticut*, individual states determined the appropriateness of prayer in public schools; some states, such as Massachusetts, made prayer a regular part of the school day, while others, such as California, never chose to include it. Once it was determined that the establishment and free exercise clauses of the First Amendment were binding upon the states, it was inevitable that school prayer would become a constitutional battleground.

The issue was joined before the Supreme Court in 1962 in *Engel v. Vitale*, in which a twenty-two-word prayer composed by the New York State Board of Regents was ruled to be a violation of the establishment clause. The following year saw two more decisions in a similar vein, as recitation of the Lord's Prayer (*Murray v. Curlett*, 1963) and compulsory Bible reading (*Abington School District v. Schempp*, 1963) were also struck down, as was, later, the posting of the Ten Commandments in classrooms (*Stone v. Graham*, 1980).

Central to all three earlier cases was the application of the "law of imitation," as defined by Justice Felix Frankfurter in *McCollum v. Board of Education* (1948). In each instance, provision had been made for children not wishing to take part in religious exercises to refrain from doing so; nonparticipants were also permitted to leave the classroom. The Court, however, noted that children were by nature imitative, and the justices ruled that asking students to refrain in such a noticeable fashion constituted an undue hardship not constitutionally tolerable.

Application was also made of a principle that later came to be known as the "Lemon" test (from its origin in *Lemon v. Kurtzman*, 1971). The principle stated that any government-sponsored activity had to have a secular purpose and could not in any way advance or inhibit religion. The *Schempp* case was interpreted as a prime example of the violation of this standard, and it became an important precedent in the subsequent *Lemon* case.

In 1978, the focus of the debate shifted when Alabama instituted a mandatory "moment of silence" at the beginning of each school day, a move that was echoed by at least twenty-five other states. In 1982, however, the Supreme Court struck down the Alabama provision, basing its ruling primarily on the wording of the statute, which allowed not only for "meditation" but also for "prayer"—thus making the exercise, in the Court's opinion, religious in nature. Some constitutional scholars believe, however, that the Court's opinion leaves room for other "moment of silence" laws, so long as their intent remains entirely secular in nature.

The issue of school prayer has remained on the legislative and political landscape. Amendments to the Constitution have been introduced at various times since the *Engel* decision; Presidents Ronald Reagan, George Bush, and Bill Clinton all expressed support for such an amendment. No such legislation has successfully passed through Congress, however, leaving the Supreme Court's decisions of the 1960's as the decisive word on the question.

See also *Abington School District v. Schempp*; Bill of Rights, U.S.; Constitution, U.S.; *Engel v. Vitale*; Establishment of religion; *Lemon v. Kurtzman*; Religion, free exercise of; School law.

Scopes "monkey" trial

DATE: July, 1925

PLACE: Dayton, Tennessee

SIGNIFICANCE: The Scopes trial had little lasting legal significance, but it created a sensation at the time it was held because of its subject and its famous participants

Intended to be a way of establishing the teaching of the theory of evolution, the Scopes trial was a test case for a state law

The issue of prayer in schools has come before the Supreme Court a number of times; the Court has consistently ruled that prayer in public schools violates the Constitution's provision forbidding any "establishment of religion." (James L. Shaffer)

Members of the Scopes trial jury. The trial created a sensation in 1925. (Library of Congress)

prohibiting the teaching of any theory of creation other than the story of divine creation in the Bible.

The famous and controversial case *State of Tennessee v. John Thomas Scopes* put both religion and freedom of speech on trial. John Scopes, a twenty-four-year-old high school science teacher, was accused of violating Tennessee's 1925 Butler Act, which prohibited the teaching in public schools of any theory that denied the story of divine creation as presented in the Bible.

Two young lawyers from Dayton (the Hicks brothers) and mining engineer George Rappleyea convinced Scopes to be the focus of a case to test the Butler Act. Scopes believed that it was acceptable to teach the theory of Darwinian evolution, which holds that humans evolved over time from simple forms of life and that humans and apes have common ancestors. Dayton was predominantly a Protestant Fundamentalist community, and Rappleyea, both a baptized Christian and a believer in evolution, did not appreciate the Fundamentalist insistence on a literal interpretation of the biblical account of creation. The American Civil Liberties Union aided in the defense of Scopes.

William Jennings Bryan, a nationally known Fundamentalist Presbyterian layman and politician who had tried unsuccessfully for the presidency three times, announced that he would assist the local prosecutor with the case. Another nationally renowned figure, Clarence Darrow, a believer in evolution, volunteered to help defend Scopes. The tiny town of Dayton immediately became the center of national (even international) media attention, as word of the trial—with its twin lures of nationally famous lawyers and a legal showdown between Fundamentalism and science—spread across the country.

The prosecution introduced witnesses who testified that Scopes had taught evolution, thereby violating the law. The defense sought to call a number of scientists as expert witnesses who would testify that there was no conflict between science and religion; they could be reconciled as long as one did not interpret every story in the Bible literally. The judge, however, ruled that such testimony was inadmissible, as the only issue at hand was whether Scopes had broken the law. The trial might have ended there, except that the elderly Bryan insisted on taking the stand as an expert witness on the Bible. Darrow devastated Bryan with his rather sarcastic cross-examination, essentially maneuvering Bryan into admitting that even he did not truly believe every word in the Bible literally. The experience is said to have shattered Bryan, who died in the town of Dayton only five days later. Scopes was found guilty and fined one hundred dollars.

The case was appealed to the Tennessee State Supreme Court, which reversed the judgment because of a technical error in setting the fine. The Butler Act itself remained in effect until 1967, when it was abolished by the state legislature. Today American law dictates that creation as described in the Bible (often called "creation science") may not be taught as a scientific theory in public schools because of its religious bias.

See also American Civil Liberties Union (ACLU); Bryan, William Jennings; Civil liberties; Establishment of religion; Religion, free exercise of; Speech and press, freedom of.

Scott v. Sandford

COURT: U.S. Supreme Court

DATE: Decided March 6-7, 1857

SIGNIFICANCE: In one of the most important decisions in Supreme Court history, the Court decided that a slave could not be considered a citizen, and so invalidated the Missouri

Compromise and all other attempts to exclude slavery from the territories. A major southern victory, it was part of the prelude to the Civil War

In 1857 the nation debated the question of the extension of slavery to new states. Southern congressional extremists argued against any limitations, while their northern counterparts thought that the legislature could bar the institution. Some southern radicals denied the right of the legislature to limit slavery anywhere, while abolitionists wanted to end the practice totally.

It was in this atmosphere that the Supreme Court handed down its verdict in *Scott v. Sandford*. Dred Scott was a slave who had been taken from the slave state of Missouri to the free state of Illinois, and then to the Wisconsin Territory, organized as a free soil area. Scott's owner was an abolitionist who arranged for a test case in which Scott sued for his freedom, arguing that his removal to Illinois ended his servitude, since slavery was not permitted there. The case began in Missouri in 1846 and worked its way up to the Supreme Court in 1856.

At the time, the Court had a decided southern flavor. It had only two members from the North, who were considered opponents of slavery. From the first it appeared certain that there would be a split decision in favor of Sandford, Scott's owner.

As expected, a majority, in separate opinions, decided against Scott, with the northerners for him. Unknown at the time was that Justice John Catron informed President-elect James Buchanan of the temper of the Court, and with this knowledge, Buchanan, who was prosouthern, urged the country to accept whatever verdict was reached.

Speaking for the majority, Chief Justice Roger Brooke Taney declared Scott not a citizen of Missouri, and therefore not entitled to bring suit in a federal court. Had he stopped there, it would have been considered a southern victory, but Taney went further. In an *obiter dictum* (incidental opinion), he went on to say that Congress lacked the power to exclude slavery from the territories: Congress had "only the power coupled with the duty of . . . protecting the owner in his rights." Therefore Scott was property, not a human, and the same was true for all slaves. This implied that states could not bar slavery within their confines. In so stating, Taney provided the southern radicals with a major victory, dismaying the moderates on both sides as well as the northern radicals.

The Dred Scott case exacerbated an already tense situation. Southern supporters of slavery could claim to be defenders of the Constitution, while northern moderates started to drift into the camp of the more radical elements. This decision, along with discussions during the 1856 elections (including the Lincoln-Douglas debates) and John Brown's raid on Harpers Ferry, provided the backdrop for the 1860 election. The polarization of the nation was such that the election of Abraham Lincoln set the stage for southern secession and the Civil War.

See also Abolitionist movement; Citizenship; Civil liberties; Civil War; Slavery; Taney, Roger Brooke.

Scottsboro cases

DATE: March 25, 1931-July, 1937
PLACE: Alabama
SIGNIFICANCE: The Scottsboro cases showed the racist nature of justice in the American South and led to the U.S. Supreme Court's establishment of new rules concerning lawyers and juries

On March 25, 1931, Alabama authorities arrested nine young black men, Olen Montgomery, Clarence Norris, Haywood Patterson, Ozie Powell, Willie Roberson, Charlie Weems, Eugene Williams, and Andrew and Leroy Wright, and charged them with raping two white women, Ruby Bates and Victoria Price. The alleged rape took place on top of a boxcar on a freight train moving rapidly through Jackson County in northeastern Alabama. The "Scottsboro boys," as the nine African Americans were called, denied having seen the girls on the train, but within five days an all-white grand jury indicted them for rape, and a week later, April 6, the first defendants were brought to trial before an all-white jury.

The Initial Trials. After two days of testimony, largely from Price and Bates, the jury found Clarence Norris and Charlie Weems guilty of rape and sentenced them to death. The court-appointed defense attorney, who appeared to be quite drunk during the proceedings, did not bother to cross-examine witnesses and asked few questions of anyone. The next day, another all-white jury convicted Haywood Patterson on the basis of the same testimony and sentenced him to death. He had the same inept lawyer as did the first two defendants. On April 8 and 9, four more of the accused, including fifteen-year-old Eugene Williams, sat in the Scottsboro courthouse and heard similar evidence and the same verdict: death by the electric chair. The final trial took place on the afternoon of April 9 but ended in a mistrial for the thirteen-year-old Leroy Wright. Several members of the jury rejected the prosecution's demand for a life sentence for the youngest of the accused, wanting Leroy to die instead. After the mistrial he was released and not retried. In short, in three days of legal proceedings, eight of the nine defendants were sentenced to death after quick trials before all-white juries and with inadequate legal representation.

The Appeals. The convictions made newspaper headlines across the country and caught the attention of the National Association for the Advancement of Colored People (NAACP). The group quickly sent a team of lawyers to Alabama to appeal the verdicts in state and federal courts. The American Communist Party also dispatched a prominent lawyer, Samuel Leibowitz, to Scottsboro (it hoped to use the case to build its membership in the African American community). The NAACP and the Communist Party fought for months over who would have chief responsibility for the appeals. Finally, Leibowitz took full charge of the case. The Alabama Supreme Court denied the appeals of all the convicted men except Eugene Williams. The court ordered his release because he was a juvenile at the time of his conviction. The appeal to the federal courts had much greater success, however, and in November, 1932, the U.S. Supreme Court ordered new trials for all seven of the "boys" now sitting on death row. The Court ruled in this case, *Powell v. Alabama* (1932), that none of the defendants had been provided with an adequate lawyer, so they had been denied their right to due process under the Fourteenth Amendment.

During a second series of trials in March, 1933, in Decatur, Alabama, a safer distance from the scene of the alleged crime, but also before all-white juries, Haywood Patterson and Clarence Norris were found guilty again and sentenced to death. This happened even though one of the supposed victims, Ruby Bates, reversed her earlier testimony and denied that any rape had taken place. The trial judge, however, in an unusual move, set aside the conviction of Patterson and ordered a third trial for him. At that new trial in December, the jury heard from Price one more time but not from Bates, who by this time was attending Communist Party rallies in the North calling for the immediate release of the Scottsboro boys. The third all-white jury convicted Patterson a third time and ordered his execution. A few days later, at Norris' second trial,

he also was sentenced to the electric chair. Testimony from a farmer who claimed to have witnessed the event from his hayloft about a quarter of a mile away from the fast-moving train helped make the state's case.

In the new round of appeals the Alabama Supreme Court upheld the new convictions, and the prisoners remained on death row. They continued to be abused by vicious guards and wardens. In 1935 the U.S. Supreme Court stepped in once more and reversed the convictions of Norris and Patterson. The Court held in *Norris v. Alabama* (1935) that neither defendant had received a fair trial because of a "long-continued, unvarying and wholesale exclusion of Negroes from jury service" on the part of the state of Alabama. A short time later, the first black man in the state's history was placed on the Jackson County grand jury, and the defendants were quickly reindicted.

In January, 1936, Haywood Patterson stood trial for a fourth time. The same witnesses presented the same testimony, but this time the jury recommended a seventy-five-year sentence

Haywood Patterson in court in 1933; an all-white jury sentenced him to death, but the judge set the verdict aside and ordered yet another trial for him. (National Archives)

SEARCH AND SEIZURE / 705

rather than electrocution, and Patterson was returned to the state prison. The Alabama Supreme Court upheld this conviction, and the U.S. Supreme Court this time found no reason for reversal. In July, 1937, Clarence Norris was tried for a third time, convicted, and sentenced to death. Andy Wright and Charlie Weems got ninety-nine years and seventy-five years respectively. In a major surprise, the state dropped all charges against Eugene Williams, Olen Montgomery, Willie Roberson, and Roy Wright. After six years on death row, they were released.

The Aftermath. A year later, Alabama governor Bibb Graves reduced Norris' death sentence to life imprisonment but denied pardons to the remaining Scottsboro defendants despite promises he had previously made to lawyers for the NAACP. Not until 1943 did a new governor release Charlie Weems, followed the next year by Norris and Andy Wright. Both men immediately violated their paroles by leaving the state. Norris was hunted down and returned to prison in 1944. Two years later he got a second parole; Ozie Powell was also released. Andy Wright was returned by Georgia authorities and sent back to prison. In 1948, Haywood Patterson escaped from Kilby State Prison and headed to Detroit. The FBI tracked him down as a parole violator, but Michigan governor G. Mennen Williams refused to extradite him to Alabama. Patterson died four years later after spending more than seventeen years in prison for a crime he never committed. The last surviving "Scottsboro boy," Clarence Norris, received a pardon from Alabama governor George Wallace in October, 1976. Norris died quietly and in obscurity in 1989.

The Scottsboro cases demonstrated the great biases and inequalities in American law, especially for African Americans in the South. Nine defendants suffered greatly because of biased juries, inadequate lawyers, and the disregard for the basic constitutional rights of black Americans. Still, the United States Supreme Court made two key decisions in the cases which helped affirm these basic rights in the future. *Powell v. Alabama* and *Norris v. Alabama* established the right to effective council in death penalty cases and the guarantee of an unbiased jury. —*Leslie V. Tischauser*

See also Appellate process; Equal protection of the law; Miscarriage of justice; *Powell v. Alabama*; Racial and ethnic discrimination.

BIBLIOGRAPHY

Valuable discussions of the Scottsboro cases include Dan T. Carter, *Scottsboro: A Tragedy of the American South* (Rev. ed. Baton Rouge: Louisiana State University Press, 1979); James E. Goodman, *Stories of Scottsboro* (New York: Pantheon Books, 1994); Loren Miller, *The Petitioners: The Story of the Supreme Court of the United States and the Negro* (New York: Pantheon Books, 1966); Wilson Record, *Race and Radicalism: The NAACP and the Communist Party in Conflict* (Ithaca, N.Y.: Cornell University Press, 1964); National Association for the Advancement of Colored People, *Guide to the Papers of the NAACP, Part 6: The Scottsboro Case, 1931-1950* (Frederick, Md.: University Publications of America, 1986).

Search and seizure

DEFINITION: The law enforcement practice of searching people and places in order to seize evidence or suspects

SIGNIFICANCE: The Fourth Amendment requires an appropriate balance between criminal investigations and protection of people's privacy and possessions

Search and seizure law provides a focal point for the collision of competing objectives within the justice system. On the one hand, police must search for and seize evidence and suspects in order to enforce the criminal laws. On the other hand, the Fourth Amendment's prohibition on "unreasonable" searches and seizures aims to avoid granting too much power to police officials and to preserve people's privacy and liberty. The U.S. Supreme Court has regularly been presented with cases requiring the justices to interpret the Fourth Amendment in a way that satisfies the dual goals of protecting people's rights and simultaneously permitting police officers to conduct effective investigations.

Historical Origins. American search and seizure law can be traced to English origins. Although the roots of search and seizure in English common law are not clear, the English gradually developed the practice of using warrants to justify government intrusions into citizens' homes, usually in a search for stolen goods. Eventually, English kings began to use general warrants justifying unlimited searches. These warrants did not specify the places to be searched or the items being sought. In effect, law enforcement officers could use the general warrants to search as they pleased. For example, warrants came to be used to discover whether people possessed any books or pamphlets that criticized the king. Because of these abusive practices, in the mid-eighteenth century Parliament passed resolutions condemning general warrants, and English courts began to limit the government's use of such warrants.

In the American colonies, people felt victimized by "writs of assistance," general warrants used by British officials to conduct exploratory searches of people's homes and businesses. These searches were frequently used to determine whether all proper taxes and duties had been paid to the king for goods produced, bought, or sold. Disputes about such British tax policies and search and seizure methods contributed to the American Revolution.

After independence from Britain was achieved, the authors of the Bill of Rights had keen memories of their dissatisfaction with British search and seizure practices. As a result, they wrote the Fourth Amendment in order to set explicit limits on the government's ability to conduct searches and undertake seizures. According to the Fourth Amendment, "The right of the people to be secure in their persons, houses, papers, and effects, against unreasonable searches and seizures, shall not be violated, and no warrants shall issue, but upon probable cause, supported by oath or affirmation, and particularly describing the place to be searched, and the persons or things to be seized." The drafters of the Bill of Rights thus sought to prevent unreasonable searches by requiring the use of specific warrants that were to be issued by neutral judges after the presentation of evidence justifying the need for a search.

Legal Doctrines. For most of American history, the Fourth Amendment had little impact on police searches because the Supreme Court paid little attention to such issues. Moreover, the Fourth Amendment was initially applied only against federal law enforcement officials and not against state or local police. Some state judges interpreted their state constitutions to place limits on local enforcement activities, but police officers in many areas searched people and homes with impunity. Such searches were sometimes carried out for purposes of intimidation and harassment of the poor, members of racial minority groups, or political opponents of the local mayor or police chief.

The Supreme Court's development and enforcement of strong search and seizure rules began with the case of *Weeks v. United States* in 1914. Here the Court invalidated federal officers' warrantless search of a home by creating the "exclusionary rule." The Court declared that if any federal searches violate the Fourth Amendment, no evidence discovered during those searches can be used against a defendant in court, even if the evidence demonstrates the defendant's guilt. By making exclusion of evidence the remedy for improper searches and seizures, the Supreme Court effectively declared that it was more important to protect people's rights to privacy and liberty than to make sure that every criminal law was strictly enforced. Advocates of the exclusionary rule assumed that it would deter police from conducting improper searches.

In 1949, the Supreme Court declared that the Fourth Amendment's protections are also applicable against state and local police, although the justices declined to apply the exclusionary rule to such officers (*Wolf v. Colorado*). In 1961, however, the Court began to treat state and local police searches in the same manner as federal searches by applying the exclusionary rule to all law enforcement officers (*Mapp v. Ohio*). The Court's decision generated an outcry from local law enforcement officials, who claimed that the justices were preventing the police from catching guilty criminals. During the 1960's, many politicians criticized the Supreme Court's decisions on this and other cases having to do with the rights of criminal defendants.

One such critic was Richard Nixon, who, after winning the presidency in 1968, used his appointment powers to place on the Supreme Court new justices who believed that the search and seizure rules were too harsh on the police. One Nixon appointee, Chief Justice Warren Burger, wrote an opinion containing strident criticisms of the exclusionary rule and expressed the view that Fourth Amendment rights could be protected without excluding useful evidence found during improper searches (*Bivens v. Six Unknown Named Agents*, 1971). Eventually, the Supreme Court's composition changed to contain a majority of justices who shared Burger's view. Thus, during the 1980's in particular, the Supreme Court issued many new decisions making it easier for law enforcement officers to conduct searches and seize evidence without obtaining proper warrants.

For example, in *United States v. Leon* (1984), the Supreme Court created a "good-faith" exception to the exclusionary rule by permitting police to use evidence seized under a defective warrant that had been based on inadequate justification. Because the error had been made by the judge who issued the warrant rather than by the police officers who conducted the search, the Court permitted the evidence to be used. In another example of relaxed standards, the justices permitted police to search an apartment based on an erroneous belief that the suspect's girlfriend possessed the authority to consent to the search (*Illinois v. Rodriguez*, 1990).

The Supreme Court has identified a variety of situations in which police officers can search and seize people or evidence without any warrant. Such situations include automobile searches, stopping and frisking suspicious persons on the street, searches incident to an arrest, and searches conducted in emergency circumstances. In each of these circumstances, society's need to enforce laws and preserve criminal evidence could be defeated if officers were always required to obtain a warrant before conducting a search. Automobiles, for example, are mobile and could disappear with important evidence if the Supreme Court did not define some circumstances in which warrantless searches are permissible. In defining these circumstances, however, the justices seek to limit the conditions that justify a search in order to withhold from police officers the power to conduct searches on a whim.

A Difficult Balance. American search and seizure laws reflect changing decisions about the most appropriate balance between the need to investigate crimes and the Fourth Amendment's mandated goal of protecting people from governmental intrusions. During the 1960's, when many Americans became keenly aware of the concept of constitutional rights and the existence of harsh and discriminatory law enforcement practices, the Supreme Court gave great emphasis to the protection of rights, even if it meant that some guilty offenders would go free. In the 1970's and 1980's, however, fear of crime became a growing concern for many Americans. The greater attention given to issues of law and order by the public and politicians was reflected in changes in the Supreme Court's composition and, eventually, in changes in legal doctrines affecting search and seizure. By the mid-1990's, the Supreme Court had relaxed many of the restrictions placed on police officers' search and seizure methods during the 1960's.

Although the rearrangement of priorities gave police officers a freer hand in conducting searches and using improperly obtained evidence, the changes did not represent an abandonment of the Fourth Amendment's restrictions on search and seizure. Even the justices who believed that greater emphasis should be placed on crime control still identified some circumstances in which police officers' search and seizure activities went beyond constitutional boundaries. For example, in *Minnesota v. Dickerson* (1993), the Court invalidated the seizure of cocaine from a man's pocket, asserting that police engaged in a warrantless stop-and-frisk search of a suspicious person on the street had erred in extending their inquiry beyond a search for a weapon.

Another factor also helped to protect the Fourth Amendment. By the late twentieth century, police officers and judges had become better trained, more professional, and less connected to and controlled by local patronage politics. Thus these officials had greater legal knowledge and ethical sensitivity than their predecessors and sought on their own to respect citizens' Fourth Amendment rights.

Debates about search and seizure are likely to continue, because of the difficulties involved in achieving a consensus among policy makers, scholars, and judges about the appropriate interpretation of the Fourth Amendment. The inevitable collisions between the social goals of vigorously investigating crimes and protecting citizens from governmental intrusions virtually guarantee that courts will continually be presented with situations in which the Fourth Amendment must be interpreted to strike an appropriate balance between these goals. The most significant conflicts about search and seizure have generally focused on the exclusionary rule. Many scholars and judges believe that the Fourth Amendment is merely an empty promise if police officers are permitted to use improperly obtained evidence, yet the Supreme Court gradually permitted greater use of such evidence during the 1980's. As society's values change and new justices are appointed to the Supreme Court, there are likely to be further developments in search and seizure doctrine. Thus it is difficult to imagine that search and seizure issues will ever disappear from the nation's justice policy agenda. —*Christopher E. Smith*

See also Bill of Rights, U.S.; *Bivens v. Six Unknown Named Agents*; *Chimel v. California*; Evidence, rules of; *Leon, United States v.*; *Mapp v. Ohio*; Probable cause; *Terry v. Ohio*; *Weeks v. United States*; *Wolf v. Colorado*.

BIBLIOGRAPHY

An early comprehensive overview of search and seizure was presented in Edward C. Fisher, *Search and Seizure* (Evanston, Ill.: Northwestern University Press, 1970). A general historical review of criminal defendants' constitutional rights, including search and seizure, can be found in David Bodenhamer, *Fair Trial: Rights of the Accused in American History* (New York: Oxford University Press, 1992). The details of search and seizure legal doctrines are presented in Rolando V. del Carmen, *Criminal Procedure: Law and Practice* (3d ed. Belmont, Calif.: Wadsworth, 1995), and in Charles Whitebread and Christopher Slobogin, *Criminal Procedure: An Analysis of Cases and Concepts* (3d ed. Westbury, N.Y.: Foundation Press, 1993). A historical perspective on the Fourth Amendment is presented in Bradford Wilson, *Enforcing the Fourth Amendment: A Jurisprudential History* (New York: Garland Publishing, 1986).

Secret Service

DATE: Established July 5, 1865

SIGNIFICANCE: Secret Service responsibilities include protecting presidents, former presidents, and their families and enforcing laws involving currency, federal government bonds and checks, and electronic and computer access fraud

On July 5, 1865, Treasury Secretary Hugh McCulloch administered the oath of office to William P. Wood, the first U.S. Secret Service chief. Wood and his operatives (later called special agents) were charged with investigation of counterfeiting. At the beginning of the Civil War, when money was issued by private banks, as much as one-third of paper money in circulation may have been counterfeited. In 1863, the federal government issued the first national currency, and counterfeits flooded the country. If counterfeiting was not stopped, the public's confidence in the new currency could be destroyed. By 1876, Secret Service operatives had arrested some two hundred counterfeiters and foiled a plot to steal the body of former President Abraham Lincoln from its tomb in Springfield, Illinois, and hold it for ransom.

In 1907-1908, Secret Service investigations into illegal exploitation of federal land resulted in prosecution of two U.S. senators, among others. In apparent retaliation, Congress then restricted Secret Service investigations to those specifically involving the Treasury Department. President Theodore Roosevelt, who opposed the restriction, transferred eight agents to the Department of Justice, forming a unit that became the Federal Bureau of Investigation (FBI).

In 1913, however, after three presidential assassinations (Lincoln in 1865, James Garfield in 1881, William McKinley in 1901), the Secret Service was charged with protection of the

A member of the Secret Service reacts during the 1981 attempted assassination of President Ronald Reagan. Behind him the attacker, John Hinckley, is being subdued. (AP/Wide World Photos)

president. In 1914, when World War I began, President Woodrow Wilson charged the agency with investigation of espionage, sabotage, and violations of American neutrality. In 1922, President Calvin Coolidge assigned it to investigate the Teapot Dome scandal; this investigation led to the first prison sentence for a U.S. cabinet member: Albert B. Fall, secretary of the interior.

From 1865 to 1951, the Secret Service gained its authority from annual appropriations from Congress. President Harry S Truman signed permanent authorization in 1951. After the 1963 assassination of President John F. Kennedy, the Secret Service Division (SSD) was reorganized as the United States Secret Service (USSS). Its operations expanded to include the Office of Inspection, the Office of Protective Operations, the Office of Protective Research, the Office of Investigations, and the Office of Administration.

Under titles 3 and 18 of the United States Code, the Secret Service protects presidents, vice presidents, presidents-elect, vice presidents-elect, major presidential and vice presidential candidates, former presidents, and, with some limitations, members of their families. The agency may be assigned to protect visiting foreign officials and official U.S. representatives on special missions abroad. To provide protection, the Office of Protective Research collects and disseminates intelligence information concerning persons considered serious threats. The agency also has power to investigate crimes involving U.S. currency, coins, and securities; the forging of government checks, bonds, and securities; electronic funds transfers; credit and debit card fraud; false identification documents; computer access fraud; and U.S. Department of Agriculture food coupons.

See also Counterfeiting and forgery; Federal Bureau of Investigation (FBI); Fraud; President of the United States; Treasury, U.S. Department of the.

Securities and Exchange Commission (SEC)

DATE: Established 1934

DEFINITION: The agency charged with principal responsibility for the enforcement and administration of the federal securities laws

SIGNIFICANCE: The Securities and Exchange Commission has statutory authority to conduct investigations of alleged violation of federal securities law; this authority includes the power to subpoena witnesses, administer oaths, and obtain books and records anywhere in the United States

The Securities Exchange Act (SEA) of 1934 extended federal regulation to trading in securities which are already issued and outstanding. According to the act, the Securities and Exchange Commission (SEC) consists of five members appointed by the president for five-year terms; one commissioner's term expires each year. No more than three commissioners can be members of the same political party. The SEC generally enjoys a good reputation, noted for the intelligence and integrity of the staff, the flexibility of its procedures, and the avoidance of political and economic pitfalls. The commission is sometimes criticized, however, for its lack of regard to the costs their rules and regulations imposed on corporations.

In order to ensure full disclosure of information, the SEA requires, as a prerequisite for listing on an exchange, that an annual registration statement and periodic reports be filed with the SEC. Corporations must file their periodic financial statements on a 10-K form, significant current developments must be reported on 8-K forms, and unaudited financial statements must be filed quarterly on 10-K forms. The SEA requires all exchanges to (1) register with the SEC, (2) comply with the law, (3) adopt bylaws or rules for expelling or disciplining members of the exchange who do not conduct their activities in a legal and ethical manner, and (4) furnish the SEC with copies of its rules and bylaws and any amendments which are adopted. Within these guidelines the exchanges are free to regulate themselves. The SEC can intervene in the affairs of the exchanges, however; it can alter penalties, expel members of the exchange, or even close the exchange.

The SEC may proceed in a number of different ways if it discovers a violation of the law. If the alleged violator is a broker-dealer or investment adviser, the commission can revoke or suspend the firm's registration. If the case involves an issuer seeking to sell securities, the SEC can suspend the effectiveness of the associated registration statement. These decisions are made by the commission staff after the initial findings of an administrative law judge. If the alleged violator is not registered with the SEC at all, then the commission must go to court. The most common type of proceeding in these cases is an application for an injunction against future violations. A case may also be referred to the Department of Justice for prosecution as a criminal violation of the securities laws. The SEC also obtains insider reports from every insider and owner of more than 10 percent of a listed firm. Insiders are prohibited from making short sales in their firm's stock.

See also Banking law; Capitalism; Commercial law; Insider trading; Justice, U.S. Department of.

Seditious libel

DEFINITION: The criminal act of undermining government by publishing criticism of it or of public officials

SIGNIFICANCE: Reaction against the concept of seditious libel contributed significantly to the growth of a broader concept of freedom of the press

Part of the common-law heritage of American justice, the crime of seditious libel gave way to a more libertarian view of the press's role in American politics.

Origins and Early History. The concept of seditious libel developed as part of English common law and was transplanted to the American colonies. Primarily concerned with the preservation of government, it viewed criticism that tended to lower the respect of the people for government as a criminal "assault." Under the doctrine of seditious libel, it did not matter if the offending words were true; indeed, since damaging words based on truth were likely to be more effective, the law held that "the greater the truth, the greater the libel." In seditious libel trials, the role of the jury was limited to determining the fact of publication. The judge determined whether the words were libelous.

Prosecutions for seditious libel were relatively rare in colonial America, though the concept did give rise to one of the eighteenth century's most famous trials. In 1735, John Peter Zenger, printer of the *New York Weekly Journal*, was charged with seditious libel for his criticisms of the colony's governor. Though Zenger admitted that he had published the offending material, he maintained that it was true and that truth was an adequate defense. Despite the judge's determination that his words were libelous, the jury refused to convict Zenger and found him not guilty. His resultant popularity may well have discouraged other prosecutions.

Seditious Libel and Partisan Politics. Seditious libel was still a crime when the Bill of Rights was adopted in 1791, and contemporary opinion seems to have held that the First Amendment's protection of freedom of the press did not eliminate it. Freedom of the press was held primarily to mean that there should be no censorship before publication, or "prior restraint." After publication, authors and printers could be held accountable for what was published. In the heightened tensions of the nation's first party system in the 1790's, the Federalists and Jeffersonian Republicans criticized each other in the press in terms that ranged from the vigorous to the scurrilous. Fearing that their opponents threatened the very stability of the government, the Federalists persuaded Congress to pass the Sedition Act of 1798. This act made it a crime to bring the president or Congress into disrepute. It also modified the law of seditious libel to allow truth as a defense and to permit juries to determine whether a publication was libelous. The act was employed in a very partisan manner: All those prosecuted under it were Republicans; all the judges were Federalists. Thomas Jefferson and his followers argued that the law was unconstitutional. The act expired in 1800, and after Jefferson's election to the presidency in 1800, Congress repaid the fines of those convicted under the act. The Sedition Act created a strongly negative reaction in public opinion. While the act never came before the Supreme Court and seditious libel was never formally repudiated, the increasingly democratic nature of American politics ensured that any government initiating a seditious libel prosecution would be subject to ridicule. For the next century little was heard of the crime.

Later History of Seditious Libel. Though the common-law crime of seditious libel was seldom used as the basis of prosecutions, the attitude that the federal government needed protection from the writings of subversives surfaced periodically in the twentieth century, particularly during times of crisis. During World War I, the Espionage Act of 1917 made a variety of forms of antigovernment expression illegal, particularly after it was amended by a new sedition act in 1918. During the Cold War, the Smith Act of 1940 was used to prosecute the leaders of the American Communist Party partly on the grounds that the party's publications had seditious purposes. As late as the 1960's, efforts were made by opponents of the Civil Rights

movement to use the law of libel to silence their opponents in the press. The Supreme Court's decision in *New York Times Co. v. Sullivan* (1964), however, established the principal that political figures had to prove "actual malice" rather than mere inaccuracy to sustain a charge of libel.

Though seditious libel has never been declared a dead letter, the absence of its use and the relative rarity of other prosecutions utilizing the concept of sedition are a mirror of the extent to which American government has come to accept the view that vigorous public debate, including strong criticism of the government and its officials, is necessary to the existence of a free society. —*William C. Lowe*

See also *Abrams v. United States*; Alien and Sedition Acts; *Brandenburg v. Ohio*; Censorship; Defamation; Espionage Act; Smith Act; Treason.

BIBLIOGRAPHY

Good sources on libel and seditious libel include Leonard W. Levy, *The Emergence of a Free Press* (New York: Oxford University Press, 1985); Anthony Lewis, *Make No Law: The Sullivan Case and the First Amendment* (New York: Random House, 1991); Norman L. Rosenberg, *Protecting the Best Men: An Interpretive History of the Law of Libel* (Chapel Hill: University of North Carolina Press, 1986); and James Morton Smith, *Freedom's Fetters: The Alien and Sedition Laws and American Civil Liberties* (Ithaca, N.Y.: Cornell University Press, 1956).

Segregation, de facto and de jure

DEFINITION: The separation of people according to such characteristics as race, religion, gender, or social class membership; *de jure* segregation is segregation by law, whereas *de facto* segregation is sanctioned by social custom

SIGNIFICANCE: Both *de jure* and *de facto* segregation are viewed as significant denials of civil rights and social justice in the United States

Segregation is an enduring feature of American social history, although it should be noted that discrimination and segregation are by no means unique to the United States or to the twentieth century. When used in reference to American history, *de jure* segregation (separation of races "by law") most often refers to the system of segregation that existed in the South between the 1870's and the mid-1950's. *De facto* segregation (separation "in fact" or in practice) most often refers to the continuance of segregation after legally mandated segregation was declared unconstitutional in 1954. Yet it is somewhat misleading to pigeonhole segregation with such definitions, as both types may exist simultaneously. Moreover, *de facto* segregation existed before the Jim Crow laws of the late nineteenth century as well as after the end of legal segregation. Both types testify to a refusal to admit various categories of Americans to full membership in American civic culture.

De Jure **Segregation.** Before the Civil War, racial segregation in the South was largely maintained by the institution of slavery. The oppressive nature of the system served both to control the slaves and to intimidate free blacks. In the post-

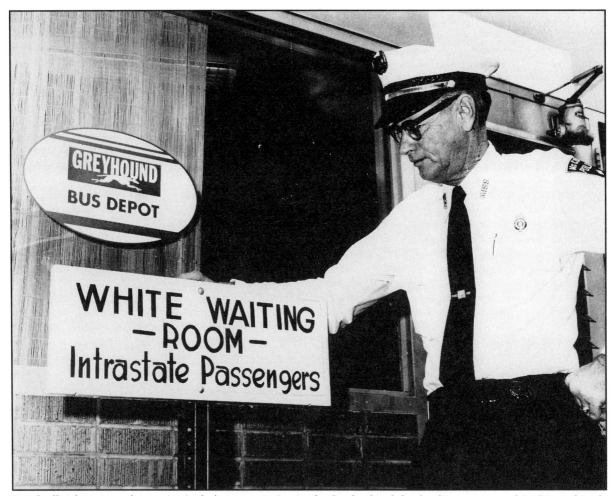

Local officials attempted to maintain de jure *segregation in the South after federal rulings overturned it. Pictured is the McComb, Mississippi, police chief and a sign posted the day after the Interstate Commerce Commission ruled segregation illegal in bus terminals in November, 1961.* (AP/Wide World Photos)

Civil War South, after the abolition of slavery and the passing of the Civil War Amendments to the U.S. Constitution, society was in flux. White leaders needed new ways to ensure continued segregation and white domination. *De facto* segregation was transformed into *de jure* segregation—in this case a system of restrictions and prohibitions known as black codes and Jim Crow laws, enacted at state and local levels. These statutes mandated racial discrimination, requiring blacks to use different public facilities from those used by whites: different schools, theaters, restaurants, and drinking fountains. With the exception of intellectuals such as W. E. B. Du Bois, whose *The Souls of Black Folk* condemned racial separation, many black leaders acquiesced with *de jure* segregation. (Booker T. Washington is a prominent example.) It was not until the middle of the twentieth century that this network of *de jure* segregation laws came undone.

De jure segregation's constitutionality was upheld by the U.S. Supreme Court in *Plessy v. Ferguson* (1896). Declaring

that the Louisiana legislature's 1890 passage of the Separate Car Act decreeing "equal but separate accommodations for the white and colored races" on Louisiana's railroads was constitutional, Justice Henry Billings Brown granted states the right to separate the races physically. Justice John Marshall Harlan was the lone dissenter.

This "separate but equal" doctrine, challenged infrequently in the courts (in *Buchanan v. Warley*, 1917, legally enforced residential segregation was ruled unconstitutional), continued to dominate American race relations through the first half of the twentieth century. During World War I, black Americans served in the military according to segregation policies. Brigaded in all-black units headed by whites, African American servicemen filled noncombative positions, regimental members of the Ninety-third Division excepted. It was not until after World War II that the armed forces were integrated during the Truman Administration. Only with the Supreme Court's unanimous decision in *Brown v. Board of Education*

(1954) did *de jure* segregation end in the United States. The ruling specifically concerned segregated schools, but it spelled the beginning of the end for all forms of legally mandated segregation. Chief Justice Earl Warren reasoned that "separate educational facilities" for black Americans were "inherently unequal." Intangible inequalities of segregation denied African Americans the justice guaranteed in the equal protection clause of the Fourteenth Amendment to the U.S. Constitution. Yet despite the end of *de jure* segregation, various forms of segregation remain facts of American life. *De facto* segregation, especially in the northern United States, has proved extremely resistant to abolition.

De Facto Segregation. *De facto* segregation, in which the physical separation of people is enforced by the dictates of social custom or tradition, has long been a feature of American civic culture. Before the Civil War, white-sponsored segregation policies regarding churches, entertainment, housing, schools, and transportation were partially defeated by successful black protests; segregated schools, however, were unanimously upheld by the Supreme Court in *Roberts v. City of Boston* (1850). One way that northern blacks accommodated to segregation policies in the pre-Civil War period was to form their own churches, such as the African Methodist church, founded in 1816. Largely Protestant, these churches and the "African" schools attached to them became sources for expression of black frustration with segregation. *De facto* segregation in the pre-Civil War South, fueled by the slave rebellions of Gabriel Prosser, Nat Turner, and Denmark Vesey, kept blacks from military service, professional and business life, public accommodations, and voting.

After the Civil War, *de facto* segregation continued in the North, maintained by social and spatial distance, and *de jure* segregation began to rule the South. Following World War I, there was a vast migration of African Americans from the rural South to the urban North; they settled primarily in black areas of large cities. The creation of large urban black communities resulted in outlets for black cultural and political expression, exemplified by the pre-World War II Harlem Renaissance in the arts and by Oscar De Priest's 1928 election to Congress from a black Chicago district. The widespread unemployment and poverty of the ghetto, however, also bred hopelessness, crime, and eventually rage.

Although *Brown v. Board of Education* ruled that *de jure* segregation was unconstitutional, it did not and could not end segregation in the United States. School desegregation, for example, was resisted in many areas until the mid-1960's.

A struggle breaks out as a group attempts to integrate a public beach in St. Augustine, Florida, in 1964. (AP/Wide World Photos)

Even after the passage of the sweeping Civil Rights Act of 1964 and the Voting Rights Act of 1965, *de facto* segregation, most notably by segregated residence patterns, continued. The so-called ghetto rebellions of the 1960's in Detroit, Los Angeles, and Newark focused American attention on the realities of *de facto* urban segregation, including that of inferior schooling. The busing of students to achieve school desegregation (upheld by the Supreme Court in *Swann v. Charlotte-Mecklenburg Board of Education*, 1971) stirred heated controversy and even provoked violence.

Many decades after the *Brown* decision, *de facto* segregation continues to be a fact of life in American schools and in the United States generally. Harvard University sociologist Gary Orfield reported that residential segregation actually increased between 1980 and the early 1990's. A 1993 National School Boards Association study stated that 66 percent of black American children attended schools populated chiefly by minority students. The same study noted that the South, once the center of legally enforced segregation, was the region of the country with the second-largest percentage (39 percent) of black students attending predominantly white schools. The persistence of *de facto* segregation in American cities results from white outmigration from urban areas to suburbs. The "resegregation" of American education, claims Orfield, has also resulted partly from U.S. Supreme Court decisions easing desegregation orders.   —*Malcolm B. Campbell*

See also Black codes; *Brown v. Board of Education*; Civil Rights movement; Jim Crow laws; Ku Klux Klan (KKK); Montgomery bus boycott; *Plessy v. Ferguson*; Reconstruction; Slavery; *Swann v. Charlotte-Mecklenburg Board of Education*; Washington, Booker T.

BIBLIOGRAPHY

Among the texts covering segregation are Gary Orfield, *Must We Bus? Segregated Schools and National Policy* (Washington, D.C.: Brookings Institution, 1978); Charles Spurgeon Johnson, *Backgrounds to Patterns of Negro Segregation* (New York: Crowell, 1970); I. A. Newby, ed., *The Development of Segregationist Thought* (Homewood, Ill.: Dorsey Press, 1968); Jesse Walter Dees, Jr., and James S. Hadley, *Jim Crow* (Westport, Conn.: Negro Universities Press, 1970); Joel Williamson, ed., *The Origins of Segregation* (Boston: D. C. Heath, 1968); C. Vann Woodward, *The Strange Career of Jim Crow* (3d rev. ed. New York: Oxford University Press, 1974); Ceri Peach, Vaughan Robinson, and Susan Smith, eds., *Ethnic Segregation in Cities* (Athens: University of Georgia Press, 1981); and Douglas S. Massey and Nancy A. Denton, *American Apartheid: Segregation and the Making of the Underclass* (Cambridge, Mass.: Harvard University Press, 1993).

Self-defense

DEFINITION: The lawful use of force to defend against an unprovoked, imminent attack when no feasible means of escape exists

SIGNIFICANCE: Self-defense comprises one of the principal affirmative defenses against charges of homicide, assault, and battery; an understanding of the concept is essential to both law enforcement and adjudication

British common law is the source of the doctrine of self-defense in American jurisprudence. John Locke, in his *Second Treatise on Government* (written in the 1680's), observes that the right to defend one's life is a basic principle of natural law. Locke further argues that since property is essential to the preservation of life, natural law is also the source of the right to defend one's property.

Since self-defense is an affirmative defense, the defendant has the initial burden of proof. For a defendant to claim self-defense successfully as a justification for his or her actions, several conditions must be met. The person claiming self-defense must not provoke the attack, the danger must be immediate, the force used in defense must be reasonable and proportionate, and the victim of the attack must have no safe means of escape. In addition to these conditions, certain other limitations are placed on the defense of property.

Provocation. As a general rule, a person who provokes an attack cannot successfully claim self-defense. Two important exceptions to this rule exist, however. First, persons provoking an attack and then withdrawing "in good faith" with no intention of continuing the attack may claim self-defense if they use force against a retaliatory attack. Second, if a person provokes an attack with less than deadly force and the victim responds with deadly force, then the initial aggressor may claim self-defense. A man provoking a fist fight with an evenly matched opponent, for example, may claim self-defense if he kills his opponent after the opponent introduces a gun to the fight. In this case the initial victim of the assault used unlawful deadly force against a less than deadly attack.

Imminent Danger. For a person to claim self-defense, the danger to the person must normally be immediate or imminent. A person may not retaliate for an attack by chasing or searching out an attacker, nor may a person use force to prevent an expected attack that is not imminent.

Some states permit a claim of self-defense when the danger is not immediate but the claimant believes that force is necessary to prevent an attack on the present occasion. When an attacker is leaving to get a weapon, for example, the danger is not immediate, but it is present. Most states, however, still adhere to the rule that the danger must be immediate. A problem arises concerning situations in which a person falsely believes that danger is imminent. The general test is whether a reasonable person confronted with the same set of objective circumstances would believe that danger was imminent.

Reasonable and Proportionate Force. The requirement of reasonable and proportionate force necessitates an evaluation of all the factors surrounding an incident. The relative size, physical condition, and even emotional state of the attacker may all play a role in determining what response to an attack is reasonable and proportionate. An obviously intoxicated football player, for example, might threaten a bartender with death and then jump across the bar to accomplish his plan. The elderly five-foot, two-inch bartender may be justified in reaching for a

SELF-PROTECTIVE MEASURES TAKEN BY VICTIMS OF VIOLENT CRIME, 1992			
	Sex		
Type of Self-Protective Measure	Average of Both Sexes	Male	Female
Attacked offender with weapon	1.3%	1.7%	0.8%
Attacked offender without weapon	11.1	13.8	7.8
Threatened offender with weapon	1.0	1.6	0.2
Threatened offender without weapon	1.6	2.3	0.7
Resisted or captured offender	19.0	21.9	15.4
Scared or warned offender	8.3	6.1	10.8
Persuaded or appeased offender	13.9	14.3	13.4
Ran away or hid	19.6	19.4	19.9
Got help or gave alarm	11.3	7.2	16.3
Screamed from pain or fear	2.5	0.7	4.7
Employed another method	10.6	11.0	10.0
Total number of self-protective measures	7,043,300	3,858,440	3,184,850

Source: U.S. Department of Justice, Bureau of Justice Statistics, *Criminal Victimization in the United States, 1992.* Washington, D.C.: U.S. Department of Justice, 1994.

Note: Victims not taking self-protective measures are not represented in table. Totals may not add to 100% because of rounding.

weapon and using deadly force to prevent the attack. If the situation were reversed, however, with the football player tending bar and the elderly person attacking, the football player may not even be justified in using fists against the attacker.

Retreat. With one notable exception, in most states self-defense is limited to situations in which a safe retreat is not possible. If the attack occurs at one's home, however, the obligation to retreat normally does not exist. Some states have extended this "castle doctrine" to a person's place of business. In cases of domestic violence, when a married couple occupies a home together, each has the obligation to retreat, if possible, from an attack by the spouse. Although some states do not apply the "castle doctrine" to live-in partners, this seems to be changing.

Limitations on Defense of Property. In frontier America the use of deadly force to protect one's property was justifiable under the self-defense doctrine. Theft of horses, cattle, farm equipment, or other necessities could jeopardize survival in that environment, and law enforcement was generally unavailable. As society has developed, various safeguards have arisen so that the loss of property does not threaten physical survival. Consequently, protection of property is now limited to less than deadly force under the doctrine of self-defense in nearly all states. Most states ban the use of "booby traps" designed to maim and possibly kill intruders because of this restriction on resort to deadly force in defense of property.

Defense of Third Parties. Generally a person may claim self-defense when coming to the aid of a third party if that assisted party has a claim to self-defense under the circumstances. A person resisting lawful arrest, for example, cannot claim self-defense; therefore, someone helping that person cannot claim self-defense.

Battered Spouses and Children. Several states permit abused spouses and children to introduce psychological evidence in support of the claim to self-defense. The relative size, age, and physical condition of persons involved in a confrontation is significant in determining whether danger is imminent and what type of force is reasonable or proportionate. It seems to follow that psychological impairments might also be fairly considered in evaluating the immediacy of danger, the possibility of retreat from one's home, and the type of force which a battered child or wife would reasonably employ.

—*Jerry Murtagh*

See also Battered child and battered wife syndromes; Criminal justice system; Manslaughter; Model Penal Code; Murder and homicide; Reasonable force.

BIBLIOGRAPHY

For a good overview of self-defense see Joel Samaha, *Criminal Law* (3d ed. St. Paul, Minn.: West, 1990); for a critical review of deadly force see Henry Kuttner, *Deadly Force: The True Story of How a Badge Can Become a License to Kill* (New York: Morrow, 1983). Another interesting source is George P. Fletcher, *A Crime of Self-Defense: Bernhard Goetz and the Law on Trial* (New York: Free Press, 1988).

Self-incrimination, privilege against

DEFINITION: A privilege found in the Fifth Amendment to the U.S. Constitution that protects persons from being compelled to be witnesses against themselves in state or federal criminal proceedings

SIGNIFICANCE: The privilege against self-incrimination is an important procedural safeguard against the awesome power of the government in the accusatorial system of criminal justice, designed to protect the individual

The privilege against self-incrimination originated in England in the twelfth century, when English subjects were summoned to appear before the ecclesiastical courts, the courts of High Commission, and the infamous Star Chamber to take oaths *ex officio*. Without being informed whether they were being accused of any crime, suspects were obliged to swear that they would answer truthfully any and all questions put to them.

To object, subjects invoked the ancient maxim *nemo tenetur* ("no man is bound to accuse himself"), insisting that they could not be required to accuse themselves of crimes before formal judicial proceedings, and the courts relented. Parliament prohibited administration of oaths *ex officio* and, by the eighteenth century, English courts had extended to defendants and witnesses in criminal trials the right to refuse to testify against themselves. Because the accused was disqualified from testifying at the trial, the privilege became the chief protection against forced confessions.

Fifth Amendment. The privilege was carried over to the American colonies. The fact that twelve of the twenty-three rights in the Bill of Rights (the first ten constitutional amendments, ratified in 1791) deal with criminal procedures is some indication of the importance of balancing individual rights against the government's power to prosecute crime. The Fifth Amendment reads, in part: "No person . . . shall be compelled in any Criminal Case to be a witness against himself." The Fifth Amendment acted as a limitation only on the federal government for a time. Beginning in the 1930's, the Supreme Court relied on the Fourteenth Amendment to reverse state criminal convictions based on confessions that it determined were involuntary under a "totality of the circumstances" evaluation (*Brown v. Mississippi*, 1936). Then, in *Malloy v. Hogan* (1964), the Court decided that the right against self-incrimination itself was so fundamental that it should be applied in state criminal prosecutions, under the so-called incorporation doctrine.

The values underlying the privilege against self-incrimination form the core of the American criminal justice system, which is based on an accusatorial rather than an inquisitorial system of criminal justice. The privilege obliges the government to meet its burden of proving guilt beyond a reasonable doubt without forcing the accused to join the prosecution. The Supreme Court has recognized the premium this system places on individual dignity, even the dignity of those accused of serious crime. The privilege obliges the government to play by the rules: Police and prosecutors may not rely on physical abuse, inhumane techniques, or deceit and trickery. A criminal defendant need not testify at all. The prosecutor may not comment on the failure to testify, and the jury may not take the defendant's silence as any indication of guilt.

The privilege is not without limits. It applies in civil or administrative proceedings only if an answer might tend to be incriminating in a later criminal proceeding. It can be claimed only by individuals and not by corporations, and thus business records usually may be seized. It protects only evidence elicited from the defendant, not incriminating statements of a third party. It is limited to testimonial evidence; a defendant may be obliged to furnish real evidence such as fingerprints or a blood sample. Even a person with a valid claim of privilege may be compelled to testify if the government grants immunity and promises not to use the testimony in any later criminal prosecution.

Interrogations. The Supreme Court first took a Sixth Amendment/right to counsel approach to custodial interrogations and held that an accused had the right to be informed by his lawyer of his privilege against self-incrimination, once an investigation had focused on him (*Escobedo v. Illinois*, 1964). Then in 1966, the Court decided the landmark case *Miranda v. Arizona*, and held that without a waiver, the assistance of counsel during interrogation is necessary to vindicate the right against self-incrimination.

The police must deliver the well-known Miranda warning to the suspect: He has a right to remain silent; anything he says may be used against him in court; he has a right to a lawyer's assistance before and during interrogation; a lawyer will be appointed if he cannot afford one. If the suspect requests a lawyer or invokes the right to remain silent, then the interrogation is supposed to stop. Unless the suspect is expressly and fully afforded this warning and knowingly and voluntarily waives these rights, any confession or statement is not admissible in evidence at trial.

This decision touched off a heated public argument over the advisability of requiring this warning, which was part of a larger debate over the appropriateness of the U.S. Supreme Court elaborating rights for those accused of crime. In numerous subsequent decisions, the Supreme Court has refined the Miranda holding and its exceptions in an apparent effort to accommodate legitimate interests in law enforcement. The central requirement of a formal warning has remained intact.

—Thomas E. Baker

See also Bill of Rights, U.S.; *Brown v. Mississippi*; Counsel, right to; Criminal justice system; Criminal procedure; Due process of law; *Escobedo v. Illinois*; Immunity from prosecution; *Malloy v. Hogan*; *Miranda v. Arizona*.

BIBLIOGRAPHY

The best history is Leonard W. Levy, *Origins of the Fifth Amendment* (New York: Oxford, University Press, 1968). An able summary of Supreme Court cases is Mark Berger, *Taking the Fifth: The Supreme Court and the Privilege Against Self-Incrimination* (Lexington, Mass.: Lexington Books, 1980). Three noteworthy books debate the constitutional values underlying the privilege: Erwin N. Griswold, *The Fifth Amendment Today* (Cambridge, Mass.: Harvard University Press, 1955); Lewis Mayers, *Shall We Amend the Fifth Amendment?* (New York: Harper & Brothers, 1959); and Milton Meltzer, *The Right to Remain Silent* (New York: Harcourt Brace Jovanovich, 1972).

Selma-to-Montgomery civil rights march

DATE: January, 1965

PLACE: Selma to Montgomery, Alabama

SIGNIFICANCE: The civil rights march from Selma to Alabama's capital, Montgomery, hastened the passage of the Voting Rights Act of 1965

During 1964, with civil rights upheavals reaching crisis proportions, leaders in the Southern Christian Leadership Conference (SCLC) realized the urgency of forcing the enactment of a voting rights act to enfranchise southern blacks. The SCLC selected Selma, Alabama, seventy-three miles west of Montgomery, as the place to organize voter registration demonstrations. Early in 1965, Martin Luther King, Jr., announced that the SCLC would lead blacks to the courthouse in Selma to register them to vote. During January, more than two thousand blacks were arrested for trying to register, leading to demonstrations in which blacks and their white supporters, who poured in from across the nation, were also arrested.

King scheduled a march from Selma to Montgomery, culminating in the marchers' handing Governor George Wallace a petition demanding enfranchisement for blacks. State troopers attacked the marchers, beating them with nightsticks and shocking them with cattle prods. This brutality attracted national attention and led President Lyndon B. Johnson to support the Voting Rights Act of 1965, the passage of which, along with Supreme Court decisions upholding the Twenty-fourth Amendment, which outlawed the poll tax in federal elections, enfranchised southern blacks and changed forever the course of politics in the South.

See also Civil Rights movement; King, Martin Luther, Jr.; Poll tax; Southern Christian Leadership Conference (SCLC); Vote, right to; Voting Rights Act of 1965.

Seneca Falls Convention

DATE: July 19-20, 1848
PLACE: Seneca Falls, New York
SIGNIFICANCE: The movement for the equality of women gained both focus and momentum from the Seneca Falls Convention, at which a Declaration of Sentiments lamented existing inequalities and demanded changes

The Seneca Falls Convention was, in the eyes of those who attended, the most important event in the early movement for women's rights. More than one hundred people, both women and men, were present at two days of meetings. The event was planned by Elizabeth Cady Stanton, Lucretia Mott, Martha Wright, Jane Hunt, and Mary Anne McClintock. The women's rights movement was at the time closely allied with the abolitionist cause, and Frederick Douglass spoke on behalf of universal suffrage. Stanton read a prepared Declaration of Sentiments, modeled after the Declaration of Independence, which set out the grievances suffered by women and called for action to remedy them. There followed a series of resolutions aimed at securing equality in the right to vote, in public speaking, and in access to occupations and reform movements. Further meetings and conventions in many locations were held soon afterward. Although much press coverage was critical or condescending toward women agitators, the movement had acquired a momentum and would eventually secure many changes in the status of women in American society.

See also Anthony, Susan B.; Feminism; Stanton, Elizabeth Cady; Vote, right to; Woman's suffrage.

Sentencing

DEFINITION: The process in which a judge imposes punishment on an offender following conviction

SIGNIFICANCE: Judges have considerable leeway in imposing sentences, allowing them to consider mitigating and aggravating circumstances

In some criminal trials, a jury delivers the verdict; in others—in cases in which no jury is involved—the judge does so. The sentencing of a defendant who has been declared guilty, however, is up to the judge (there are situations in which a jury may make recommendations). Judges are expected to have the experience, legal knowledge, and impartiality needed to hand down fair and appropriate sentences. Although various guidelines exist, the judge has a great deal of discretion in how severe a sentence is imposed. Sentencing is arguably the least codified aspect of the criminal justice system, and it is certainly one of the most critical. In general, states have penal codes that set minimum and maximum punishments for various crimes. These punishments represent a combination of the actual damage or injury caused by the crime and society's moral feeling about the crime. Violent crimes are punished most heavily.

For relatively minor crimes, sentencing is often done promptly at the conclusion of a trial. For more serious offenses, sentencing is delayed (usually two or more weeks) and is done at a special hearing. At the hearing, the results of a pre-sentence investigation are presented, generally by a probation officer. The investigation provides information on the defendant's character, background, criminal history, and relevant details of the particular crime; the judge is expected to take the information into account when sentencing. The sentence may be lenient, as in a fine, a suspended sentence (in which no penalty is imposed so long as the offender promises to make restitution or to reform), or the imposition of a period of release into the community under supervision (probation). In other cases it may be severe, involving many years in prison or, in murder cases in some states, the death penalty. Most people tend to equate sentencing with prison sentences. Actually, however, of the 4.5 million offenders who were under some form of correctional custody in 1990, fewer then one million (approximately 25 percent) were in prisons.

There are three broad approaches to imposing sentences involving prison terms. An indeterminate sentence is one in which a judge specifies a maximum and minimum term, which may be reduced by good time (good behavior) in prison or by the granting of parole. A determinate sentence is a fixed term; it also may be reduced. A mandatory sentence, as the term implies, cannot be reduced: The specified time must be served in its entirety. Two other variations come into play if a person is convicted of more than one crime. The person may serve consecutive sentences, in which the sentences for the crimes are added together (with ten years plus five years equaling a fifteen-year sentence), or concurrent terms, in which the terms overlap (a five-year sentence could be considered to be served at the same time as the first half of the ten-year sentence).

Judicial Discretion. The sentencing procedure is purposely designed to give judges considerable discretion, because the circumstances of particular crimes and perpetrators vary widely. This discretion is controversial, however, because it frequently results in criminals convicted of similar crimes being

AVERAGE MONTHS OF STATE COURT FELONY SENTENCES, 1990

| | Maximum Sentence Length for Felons Sentenced to: | | | |
| | Incarceration | | | |
Most Serious Conviction Offense	Total	Prison	Jail	Probation
All offenses	52	75	8	42
Violent offenses	91	119	10	46
Murder	233	243	37	67
Rape	128	160	11	61
Robbery	97	115	12	50
Aggravated assault	52	78	9	43
Other violent	57	85	7	45
Property offenses	47	65	8	44
Burglary	61	80	9	48
Larceny	33	49	7	41
Fraud	40	58	6	43
Drug offenses	44	66	9	42
Possession	30	49	6	39
Trafficking	52	74	10	44
Weapons offenses	34	50	7	34
Other offenses	29	44	9	39

Source: U.S. Department of Justice, Bureau of Justice Statistics, *Sourcebook of Criminal Justice Statistics—1993.* Washington, D.C.: U.S. Government Printing Office, 1994.

given widely different sentences. There are a number of factors involved in sentencing discrepancies. One factor, often termed "bench bias," is simply the differences in individual judges' attitudes regarding the causes of crime (in some respects, whether the judge is a political liberal or conservative) and whether the primary purpose of punishment should be retribution or rehabilitation. Judges who think in terms of rehabilitation tend to be more lenient. There are "hard" and "soft" judges. Other factors involved in the severity of sentencing include the nature of the particular crime, the judge's determination of the criminal's character, public attitudes about crime (or about a particular type of crime) at the time, the criminal's demeanor in court, and whether the case has generated publicity. Moreover, the element of chance comes into play—some judges have admitted that certain sentencing decisions essentially amounted to a "coin toss"—as may, unfortunately, such irrelevant factors as whether the previous case was particularly aggravating, what the judge had for breakfast, or whether the judge is having an argument with his or her spouse.

Goals of Sentencing. In imposing a sentence, judges usually have multiple goals. The most ancient goal is retribution, or "just deserts." The basic concept behind retribution is hurting offenders for the pain they have inflicted by their crimes. This motivation has been modified by the notion that punishment should be equitable and in proportion to the crime committed. A second goal is deterrence: the idea that the threat of punishment will influence individuals not to commit crimes in the future. General deterrence focuses on society and the belief that potential offenders will be deterred because of fear of being punished. Specific deterrence assumes that if the punishment imposed on a specific offender is severe enough, that offender will not commit crimes in the future.

A third goal is rehabilitation. Rehabilitation is based on the notion that offenders can be helped through such programs as psychological counseling and vocational training in such a way as to lessen the probability that they will commit crimes in the future. A final goal is to separate an offender from society by imprisonment. If an offender is imprisoned, the kind of sentence imposed can have a significant impact on other goals of punishment. For example, if the goal of punishment is rehabilitation, an indeterminate sentence will be imposed so that an offender can be paroled early if he or she responds to programming. In the 1980's and 1990's, the philosophy of "just deserts" and tailoring punishment to fit the crime generally prevailed. Under this philosophy, the indeterminate sentence was replaced by a determinate, nonparolable sentence for some crimes.

Two relatively recent developments in sentencing are intermediate punishments and sentencing guidelines. Intermediate punishments refer to community corrections with more stringent conditions than traditional probation, such as house arrest, electronic monitoring, and demands for significant restitution. Sentencing guidelines are designed to control judicial discretion and to reduce disparities in sentencing. Generally, such guidelines require that a judge specifically consider offenders' behavior and risk factors in a consistent manner in setting a sentence. The United States Sentencing Commission, organized in 1985, for example, has developed a system involving the plotting of the specifics of a case and a criminal's background on two axes that is designed to produce consistent sentences in federal courts.

See also Criminal procedure; Discretion; Just deserts; Mandatory sentencing laws; Parole; Prison and jail systems; Probation; Sentencing guidelines, U.S.; United States Sentencing Commission.

Sentencing guidelines, U.S.

DEFINITION: Guidelines created by the U.S. Sentencing Commission, intended to reduce judicial discretion and therefore make sentencing more consistent

SIGNIFICANCE: The use of strict sentencing guidelines implies that the major purpose of imprisonment is punishment rather than rehabilitation and, to a significant degree, takes sentencing out of the hands of a judge

Congress created the United States Sentencing Commission in 1984 as part of a major anticrime package. Critics of the traditional system argued that there was too much discretion in sentencing: People convicted of similar crimes were receiving widely different punishments. Sentencing guidelines had first appeared in California in 1976. Supporters argued that rehabilitating prisoners did not work and that punishment—just deserts—should be the major factor in imprisonment. Longer terms meant more prisoners, and California's convict population jumped by 58 percent in the first five years of mandatory guidelines. Seven states quickly followed California's initiative, reflecting the popular belief that too many criminals were walking free.

The U.S. Sentencing Guidelines went into effect November 1, 1987. They established forty-three categories of federal crime and created a complicated point system that judges were to follow in sentencing convicts. For example, an armed thief might steal $35,000 in jewelry from a hotel room. The "Offense Level" for theft is 17, but because this thief carried a gun, judges would add two more levels, shifting the crime to Offense Level 19. A judge could increase the sentence even more, depending on the amount of money involved in the crime. If a thief stole $10,001 to $50,000, two more levels could be added, and the penalty would be found by consulting Level 21 on a table. If this thief had a prior conviction, that would also mean extra prison time; if his previous sentence had been more than one year and one month, his sentence would go up three more levels. So, after consulting a chart, the judge would find that the sentence for this crime would be between forty-one and fifty-one months. Judges may choose any sentence within this range, and most often they select the middle.

Sentencing tables exist for every level of crime, and judges may go outside the guidelines only in extraordinary cases. If they do, the prosecution can appeal the decision to a higher court. The sentencing guidelines also eliminated parole. Prisoners could have their punishment reduced only because of good behavior, usually counted as one day off for two good days. Elimination of parole greatly increased the prison population.

Critics of the commission warned of overflowing prisons, and the constitutionality of the guidelines was challenged. On January 19, 1989, the Supreme Court rejected the suit and upheld the commission's work. One predicted result of sentencing guidelines did come true: The U.S. prison population increased rapidly. American prisons held 320,000 convicts in 1970. Twenty-five years later they held more than a million. Unless many more prisons are built, prison overcrowding will continue to be a problem as long as strict sentencing is in force and parole is not an option.

See also Discretion; Good time; Just deserts; Mandatory sentencing laws; Model Penal Code; Parole; Probation; Sentencing; United States Sentencing Commission.

Separation of church and state. *See* **Establishment of religion**

Sex discrimination

DEFINITION: Unequal treatment based on a person's sex, such as discharging, refusing to hire, or classifying employees on the basis of sex

SIGNIFICANCE: Laws against sex discrimination make it illegal to make decisions (such as employment decisions) on the basis of sex

Various statutes prohibit discrimination on the basis of sex. Laws prohibiting employment discrimination include Title VII of the Civil Rights Act of 1964, the 1963 Equal Pay Act, Executive Order 11246, and the 1978 Pregnancy Discrimination Act. Under Title VII it is unlawful for an employer to refuse to hire, to discharge, or to discriminate, limit, segregate, or classify employees on the basis of sex. This act applies to federal, state, and local governments, educational institutions, labor unions, and private organizations with fifteen or more employees. Executive Order 11246 prohibits federal contractors with transactions worth more than $10,000 a year from discriminating. A covered organization may be exempt if there is a bona fide occupational qualification (BFOQ) or a business necessity that justifies preferring one sex over the other. It should be noted that these laws are not for the protection of women only—they protect both men and women from being discriminated against on the basis of sex.

As late as the early twentieth century, people were grossly exploited in the workplace; they worked long hours for low wages, and unreasonable work demands were placed on them. To protect workers from exploitation, laws governing employment were enacted. The Fair Labor Standards Act (1938) and its subsequent amendments provided some protection from exploitation. Since women were subject to exploitation, and because women were generally viewed as being more delicate and vulnerable than men, many states enacted additional laws granting special "protection" to women. Such laws typically restricted the weight that women could be asked to lift, the hours that they could work, and so on. Although such laws were intended to protect women, many of them resulted in a loss of employment opportunities for women. When such laws were challenged in court, courts initially upheld the state laws. For example, in *Muller v. Oregon* (1908), the Supreme Court upheld a state law restricting the employment of women to ten-hour shifts. Using such laws, employers could legally keep women out of many desirable jobs.

After Title VII of the Civil Rights Act of 1964 came into effect, court judgments made it illegal to discriminate against women even in situations where state laws allowed such discrimination. State laws in Georgia and California, for example, banned women from jobs in which they would be required to lift weights in excess of 30 and 25 pounds respectively. In the cases *Weeks v. Southern Bell Telephone and Telegraph Co.* (1969) and *Rosenfeld v. Southern Pacific Co.* (1971), the courts held that state laws may not be used to discriminate willfully against women. The courts held that there was no evidence that all or substantially all women would be unable to perform the duties involved safely and effectively. Cases such as this set the precedent for curbing discrimination based on sex.

Defining Discrimination. Although Title VII bans discrimination, it does not define discrimination. The concept of discrimination has, however, been explained by the courts. Courts have defined two types of discrimination: disparate treatment (different standards for different groups) and disparate impact, according to which the results of policies are the key issue. These two types of discrimination differ in terms of intention. In the case of disparate treatment, there is an intent to treat a group differently. In the case of disparate impact, there is no intent to treat any group differently, but the net effect is that one group is favored over another.

Disparate treatment occurs when employers apply different standards to different groups of employees. In proving that disparate treatment exists, intention becomes important. Intent often must be inferred from employer actions. Complicating the analysis of such situations is that disparate treatment may be either illegal and malicious or motivated by legitimate business considerations. Important cases relating to disparate treatment include *McDonnell Douglas v. Green* (1971), *Board of Trustees v. Sweeny* (1978), *Texas v. Burdine* (1981), *U.S. Postal Service v. Aikens (1983), and Price Waterhouse v. Hopkins* (1989).

In disparate impact discrimination, intention is irrelevant. The important thing is to prove that one group was favored over another by policies of the employer. For example, the use of a selection criterion such as the ability to lift a certain amount of weight may result in the selection of a disproportionately large number of men compared with women. If the selection criterion is job related, there is no discrimination; if the selection criterion is not job related, then the employer may be found guilty of discrimination. This is the case even if the

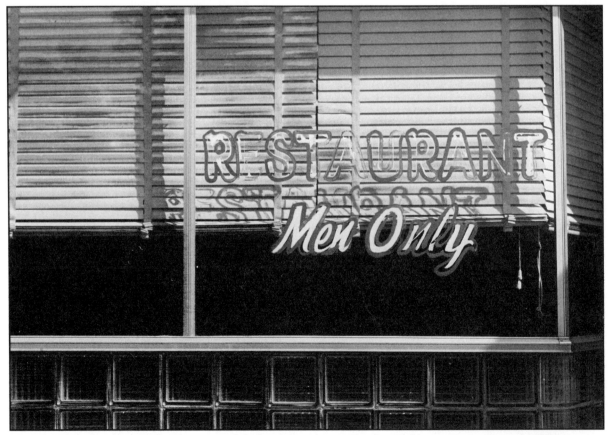

Sex discrimination usually takes more subtle forms than the stated policy of this restaurant. (James L. Shaffer)

selection criterion was common to both men and women and was applied equally. Many tests have been used to prove adverse impact. One is the "four-fifths rule": If the selection rate for a protected group is less than four-fifths of the group with the highest percentage, there is some evidence of adverse impact. The burden of proof then shifts to the employer to defend the selection criterion and show that it is job related. Important cases relating to disparate impact are *Griggs v. Duke Power Co.* (1971), *Albemarle Paper Co. v. Moody* (1975), *Washington v. Davis* (1976), and *Connecticut v. Teal* (1982).

Height and Weight Requirements. Although height and weight requirements may sound neutral, they often have an adverse impact on a certain sex. For example, minimum height requirements may adversely affect women. Based on the Supreme Court ruling in *Dothard v. Rawlinson* (1977), courts have in most cases rejected these requirements. In *Dothard v. Rawlinson*, a state law had imposed a height and weight restriction for law enforcement officials, and it was argued that such standards were necessary because law enforcement duties require strength. The Court ruled, however, that all individuals irrespective of their heights or weights should be given the opportunity to demonstrate their strength. A similar judgment was made in *Horace v. Pontiac* (1980), in which a minimum height requirement of five feet, eight inches for police officers was struck down. In most such cases, courts have ruled that applicants be given an opportunity to show their ability or inability to do a job rather than be judged on arbitrary standards of height or weight.

Sex-Plus Discrimination. Discrimination may also occur when, as a condition of employment, an employer imposes a job requirement on one sex and not the other and then discriminates against members of the affected sex who fail to meet the additional requirement. In this case discrimination is not directly based on sex but on failure to meet a condition imposed on only one sex. This type of situation has been called "sex-plus discrimination." In *Phillips v. Martin Marietta Corp.* (1971), sex-plus discrimination was found when the employer refused to accept applications from women with preschool-age children but accepted applications from men with preschool-age children. On the other hand, courts have rejected the application of sex-plus discrimination to a "short-hair only" rule applicable only to men (*Willingham v. Macon Telegraph Publishing Co.*, 1975). In *Lanigan v. Bartlett & Co.* (1979), the Supreme Court laid down some guidelines for sex-plus discrimination. Sex-plus discrimination involves policies that discriminate on the basis of immutable characteristics, changeable characteristics that involve fundamental rights such as having children or getting married, or characteristics that are changeable but that significantly affect employment opportunities afforded to one sex. In *Carrol v. Tallman Federal Savings and Loan Association* (1979), the Supreme Court held that a policy requiring women to wear uniforms while men did not have to constituted sex-plus discrimination.

Although marital status is not a protected category, job requirements based on marital status may also fall under the category of sex-plus discrimination if policies are applied unequally between the sexes. In *Sprogis v. United Air Lines* (1971), a federal appeals court held that the company's policy requiring female flight attendants to be unmarried while male flight attendants were not so restricted amounted to sex-plus discrimination.

Sexual Harassment. Sex discrimination may also take place when members of a particular sex are harassed. Unwelcome sexual advances, requests for sexual favors, and other unwelcome verbal or physical conduct of a sexual nature are termed sexual harassment. There are two types of sexual harassment possible: *quid pro quo* harassment, in which submission to or rejection of unwelcome sexual advances is used as a basis of employment decisions, and "hostile environment" harassment, which occurs when unwelcome sexual conduct unreasonably interferes with an individual's job performance or creates an intimidating, hostile, or offensive work environment even if there are no tangible or economic consequences. The concept of hostile environment harassment was endorsed by the Supreme Court ruling in *Meritor Savings Bank v. Vinson* (1986). In *Harris v. Forklift Co.* (1993), the Supreme Court added to the guidelines on sexual harassment by stating that the law protecting against sexual harassment comes into play before the victim suffers psychological damage. The Court held that if a "reasonable person" would deem a particular behavior to be offensive, and if the victim found the behavior unwelcome and offensive, then sexual harassment exists. An important issue in sexual harassment cases is the liability of the employer for conduct of its supervisors, workers, and even customers. If an employer knew of harassment and did not take appropriate and timely action—or if the employer should have known but did not care to know—the employer is deemed liable.

Bona Fide Occupational Qualification. Although the law does not support sex discrimination, there are provisions under the law for circumstances under which it may be legal to discriminate on the basis of sex. Under Title VII, an employer may be able to defend discrimination in favor of a particular sex if it can be proved that there is a bona fide occupational qualification or a business necessity. Equal Employment Opportunity Commission (EEOC) guidelines lay down three circumstances, to be narrowly interpreted, for a BFOQ: It may be proved that all or substantially all members of a particular sex will be unable to perform a certain job ("ability to perform"); same-sex persons might be preferred for protection of privacy or for purposes of role modeling; or customers may prefer that a company have employees of a particular sex.

Case law suggests that courts have construed the use of BFOQs very narrowly. In *Weeks v. Southern Bell Telephone and Telegraph Co.*, assumptions about the abilities of women to lift weight beyond a certain amount were found to have no validity unless it could be proved that all or substantially all women would be unable to do so. Further, the court ruled, whenever it is possible to evaluate individual capacities, employers should use individual tests rather than relying on arbitrary standards based on stereotypes of women. Regarding the hiring of same-sex individuals for privacy reasons, the courts have disagreed in the case of prison guards (*Gunther v. Iowa State Men's Reformatory*, 1980; *Torres v. Wisconsin Department of Health and Social Services*, 1989; *United States v. Gregory*, 1984). Outside the prison context, however, same-sex BFOQs based on privacy issues have been upheld in cases involving children's rights to privacy (*City of Philadelphia v. Pennsylvania Human Relations Commission*, 1973), the needs of rape victims (*Moteles v. University of Pennsylvania*, 1984), and reducing stress in potentially life-threatening situations, as in the case of hiring only women for the position of staff nurse in a hospital's labor and delivery room (*EEOC v. Mercy Health Center*, 1982). Same-sex BFOQs have also been upheld for role modeling in some situations (*Chambers v. Omaha Girls Club*, 1986). Customer preference has not been upheld as a BFOQ in the courts. It was rejected in a case of hiring only women despite evidence that customers preferred being attended by women (*Diaz v. American World Airways*, 1971) and in a case in which an expensive restaurant hired only male waiters (*Levendos v. Stern Entertainment*, 1989).

Equal Pay Act. Under the Equal Pay Act of 1963, an amendment to the Fair Labor Standards Act, it is illegal to discriminate on the basis of sex by paying unequal wages for equal work in jobs which require equal skill, effort, and responsibility under similar working conditions. Fringe benefits, pensions, and so on, are all considered wages under the Equal Pay Act. Although there is an overlap between the Equal Pay Act and Title VII of the Civil Rights Act, there are differences between the two. For example, Title VII covers discrimination not covered by the Equal Pay Act. On the other hand, the Equal Pay Act allows for liquidated damages, criminal sanctions, and jury trials not available under Title VII.

The Equal Pay Act requires equal pay for "equal work." This standard does not require that compared jobs be identical, only that they should be substantially equal (*Schultz v. Wheaton Glass Co.*, 1970). It is not the job title but the actual work performed that is relevant for determining if work is equal (*EEOC v. Maricopa County Community College District*, 1984). Also, additional skills and training possessed by one sex cannot justify unequal pay unless these skills are actually used on the job (*Peltier v. City of Fargo*, 1976). In case of an unjustified wage differential, the employer must eliminate the differential by raising the level of wages of the lower-paid employee rather than by reducing the pay of the higher-paid employee. Although the Equal Pay Act prohibits discrimination on the basis of sex, it allows wage differentials on the basis of conditions other than sex, such as merit and seniority.

Another issue related to the Equal Pay Act is "comparable worth." Advocates of comparable worth bring attention to jobs which are dominated by persons of one sex and suggest that pay differentials in these jobs are more a function of the sex of the majority of the workers than of the inherent value of the job's skills or responsibilities. For example, nurses and secretaries have traditionally been women, while construction workers have been men. It has been suggested that nurses and secretaries generally are paid less than construction workers not because their jobs require less effort, skill, or responsibility than construction workers' jobs but because traditionally these have been women's jobs. The concept of comparable worth is an attempt to compare the wages of workers in traditional male and female occupations—that is, in different jobs that have equivalent skills and responsibilities. If two jobs are comparable but pay different wages, then sex discrimination that is covered by Title VII may exist.

In *Washington County v. Gunther* (1981), the Supreme Court held that intentional sex-based discrimination is covered by Title VII without the restriction of the equal work standard applicable to the Equal Pay Act. No guidelines for comparable worth were provided, however, since in that case Washington County had itself established an evaluation system which showed that wage rates for females were very low. Although intentional sex discrimination in wages is subject to Title VII, the courts have not accepted the theory of comparable worth.

Pregnancy Discrimination Act. The Pregnancy Discrimination Act of 1978 amended Title VII by inserting section 701(k) into Title VII. Under this act, it is illegal for an employer to discriminate in any way based on pregnancy. Employers may not terminate, refuse to hire, or refuse to promote a woman solely because she is pregnant. The act also bans mandatory leave for pregnant women that is not based on their individual inability to work. The Pregnancy Discrimination Act requires employers to treat pregnancy the same way they would treat any other disability. Although the act does not provide for pregnancy leave with pay, if an organization has a policy of granting sick leave for any disability, pregnancy should be treated likewise. Similarly, if an organization provides medical benefits for any disabilities or illnesses, it must extend the same benefits for pregnancy and related medical conditions. Extending this logic, in *Newport News Shipbuilding & Dry Dock Co. v. EEOC* (1983), the Supreme Court ruled that if pregnant female employees receive certain medical benefits, spouses of male employees are also entitled to the same benefits.

Benefits regarding abortion represent an exception to this equal medical coverage. An employer is not bound to pay health insurance to cover abortions unless the health of the mother is at risk. If, after an abortion, a medical complication arises, then that must be covered by the organization's health insurance.

In *California Federal Savings and Loan Association v. Guerra* (1987), the Supreme Court upheld a state law providing for benefits (extended paid/unpaid maternity leave) to pregnant women employees which were unavailable to male employees. The Court ruled that the Pregnancy Discrimination Act's requirement of matching pregnancy benefits with other disability benefits was to "construct a floor beneath which pregnancy disability benefits may not drop—not a ceiling beyond which they may not rise."

In a number of cases, justifying discrimination against pregnant women by arguing that nonpregnancy is a bona fide occupational qualification has received attention. Although each situation is unique, courts have accepted a BFOQ as a

Under the Pregnancy Discrimination Act of 1978, it is illegal for an employer to terminate or refuse to promote an employee because she is pregnant. (McCrea Adams)

defense when public safety is at risk (*Levin v. Delta Airlines*, 1984; *Burwell v. Eastern Airlines*, 1980; *Harris v. Pan Am World Airways*, 1980).   —*Kamala Arogyaswamy*

See also Affirmative action; Age discrimination; Civil Rights Act of 1964; Comparable worth; Equal Employment Opportunity Commission (EEOC); Equal Pay Act; Feminism; *Frontiero v. Richardson*; *Griggs v. Duke Power Co.*; *Muller v. Oregon*; National Organization for Women (NOW); Racial and ethnic discrimination; Sexual harassment; *Washington v. Davis*.

BIBLIOGRAPHY

For a detailed legal perspective, especially regarding the evolution of cases, see Arthur Gutman, *EEO Law and Personnel Practices* (Newbury Park, Calif.: Sage Publications, 1993). For coverage at a more applied level, see Nancy J. Sedmak and Michael D. Levin-Epstein, *A Primer on Equal Employment Opportunity* (5th ed. Washington, D.C.: Bureau of National Affairs, 1991). An important reference is *Questions and Answers Concerning the EEOC Guidelines on Discrimination Because of Sex* (Washington, D.C.: Equal Employment Opportunity Commission, 1977). Since the law is evolving, recent court judgments should be sought. Two worthwhile books on sex discrimination are Jerry A. Jacobs, ed., *Gender Inequality at Work* (Thousand Oaks, Calif.: Sage Publications, 1995), and Nijole V. Benokraitis and Joe R. Feagin, *Modern*

Sexism: Blatant, Subtle, and Covert Discrimination (Englewood Cliffs, N.J.: Prentice Hall, 1995). Finally, for those interested in managerial issues of sex discrimination, the following articles might be referred to: Linda Stroh, Jeanne Brett, and Anne Reilly, "All the Right Stuff: A Comparison of Female and Male Managers' Career Progression," *Journal of Applied Psychology* 77, no.3 (1992), and Jerry Jacobs, "Women's Entry into Management: Trends in Earnings, Authority, and Values Among Salaried Managers," *Administrative Science Quarterly* 37 (June, 1992).

Sex offenses. *See* Rape and sex offenses

Sexual harassment

DEFINITION: Unwelcome sexual advances, requests for sexual favors, and other verbal or physical conduct of a sexual nature, when submission to such conduct is made a term of employment or is used as a basis of employment decisions; harassment also exists when such conduct unreasonably interferes with an individual's work performance or creates an intimidating, hostile, or offensive work environment

SIGNIFICANCE: Under Title VII of the Civil Rights Act of 1964, an employer is obligated to remove artificial barriers to employment; the Supreme Court has interpreted this stricture to mean that an employer is obligated to maintain a workplace free of sexual harassment

Numerous statutes deal with sexual harassment. Principal among them at the federal level are Title VII of the Civil Rights Act of 1964 and the Civil Rights Act of 1991. Many states also have their own legislation. Further, specific types of organizations may also be covered by specific statutes. Title IX of the Education Amendments of 1972, for example, covers the relationship between a university and its students and covers all educational institutions receiving federal assistance. In addition, victims may file claims under the common law relating to torts.

Various statutes dealing with sexual harassment differ somewhat in their coverage. Title VII of the Civil Rights Act 1964 applies to private, state, and local "persons" with fifteen or more employees; it also applies to most federal agencies. ("Persons" here includes individuals, groups, partnerships, educational institutions, labor organizations, employment agencies, and overseas subsidiaries of American companies.)

Under Title VII of the Civil Rights Act, harassment on the basis of sex is prohibited. According to the sex discrimination guidelines of the Equal Employment Opportunity Commission (EEOC), unwelcome sexual advances, requests for sexual favors, and other verbal or physical conduct of a sexual nature constitute sexual harassment. The EEOC guidelines define two types of harassment: *quid pro quo* harassment (when a person's submitting to or rejecting such advances is used as a basis of employment decisions) and "hostile environment" harassment (unwelcome sexual conduct that unreasonably interferes with an individual's job performance or creates an intimidating, hostile, or offensive working environment).

Initially, courts denied that sexual harassment was covered under Title VII. For example, in *Barnes v. Train* (1974), the plaintiff was repeatedly asked for sexual favors. Stating that there was no discrimination under Title VII, the Washington, D.C., district court asserted that the plaintiff "was discriminated against not because she was a woman but because she refused to engage in a sexual affair with her supervisor." (This judgment was later overturned in an appeal, *Barnes v. Costle*, 1977.) Similarly, in *Corne v. Bausch & Lomb* (1975), the plaintiff was forced to resign because of unwelcome sexual advances by her boss. The court rejected the case, stating that the "supervisor was satisfying a personal urge" which "had no relationship to employment."

The turning point came with *Williams v. Saxbe* (1976), in which the circuit court held for the first time that sexual harassment was discrimination under Title VII. The court held that "the conduct of the plaintiff's supervisor created an artificial barrier to employment which was placed before one gender and not another."

Quid Pro Quo Harassment. The next stage in the evolution of the concept of sexual harassment was the establishment of *quid pro quo* harassment. (A *quid pro quo* arrangement is one in which something is given in exchange for something else.) In the appeal case *Barnes v. Costle*, the District of Columbia circuit court suggested two criteria for *prima facie* discrimination: disparate treatment of women versus men and a tangible employment consequence. This judgment was important in that it incorporated the liability of the employer, for unless the employer is liable, no change may be possible in the terms of employment (such as reinstatement). The court held that employers are liable if they knew or should have known of the illegal behavior and failed to take corrective action. Other *quid pro quo* cases include *Henson v. City of Dundee* (1982), *Katz v. Dole* (1983), and *Carrero v. New York City Housing Authority* (1989).

Hostile Environment Harassment. An important case incorporating hostile environment harassment is *Bundy v. Jackson* (1981). In this case, Bundy was repeatedly abused by two of her supervisors over a two-year period. She was subject to sexually stereotyped insults and demeaning propositions. There was no tangible employment consequence during that period. Nevertheless, the court ruled for the plaintiff, stating that a hostile environment makes endurance of sexual intimidation a condition of employment.

In the key hostile environment case, *Meritor Savings Bank v. Vinson* (1986), plaintiff Michelle Vinson was terminated from her job at a bank for taking excessive leave. The plaintiff had had sexual intercourse on numerous occasions with Sidney Taylor, the bank vice president who was her supervisor. The plaintiff alleged that early advances were rebuffed but that she accepted later advances for fear of losing her job. Further, the supervisor fondled her in public and forcibly raped her on several occasions. The Supreme Court found hostile environment harassment. The Court ruled that alleged sexual advances need only be "unwelcome"; the fact that the victim participated "voluntarily" cannot be used as a defense in a sexual harassment suit. In this case, the Court elaborated on the nature of a hostile environment that qualifies as sexual harassment. A hostile environment must be more than trivial and harmless behavior, even if the behavior is annoying. To

The issue of sexual harassment suddenly gained national attention in 1991 when law professor Anita Hill charged Supreme Court nominee Clarence Thomas of having harassed her when he was her supervisor at the Equal Employment Opportunity Commission. (AP/Wide World Photos)

qualify as sexual harassment, the behavior must be sufficiently severe as to "alter the conditions of the victim's employment and create an abusive working environment."

A number of cases have delineated other situations that fall under the category of hostile environment. In one case, a dean verbally assaulted, attacked, and fondled a female professor (*King v. Board of Regents of the University of Wisconsin System*, 1990); in another, a female employee was depicted in obscene cartoons in the men's rest room (*Bennet v. Corroon & Black Corp.*, 1988); in another, a supervisor touched a female employee and attempted to kiss her (*Carrero v. New York City Housing Authority*, 1989). An example of a situation that was not considered hostile environment came up in the case *Rabidue v. Texas-American Petrochemicals, Osceola Refining Co. Div.* (1986). Here it was held that an occasional obscene comment by a coworker and the posting of pictures of scantily clad women or nude women did not constitute sexual harassment. The Court held that such behavior may have been annoying but did not seriously affect the psyches of female employees.

In *Harris v. Forklift Co.* (1993), the Supreme Court produced new guidelines on the issue of whether the victim of hostile environment harassment must show some physical or psychological damage in order to recover damages. In this case, Theresa Harris, the plaintiff, was harassed by Charles Hardy, the president of the company. He would ask Harris and other female employees to retrieve coins from his front pants pocket. He also made derogatory comments such as, "You're a woman, what do you know?" and suggested that Harris accompany him to a Holiday Inn to negotiate a raise. The lower courts, denying Harris' claim, found that Hardy's comments were not "so severe as to be expected to seriously affect her psychological well-being." In a 9-0 decision, however, the Supreme Court, ruling for the plaintiff, rejected the "psychological injury" standard. Justice Sandra Day O'Connor, writing for the Court, stated that "federal law comes into play before the harassing conduct leads to a nervous breakdown." If the victim "subjectively perceives the environment to be abusive" and if the environment may be reasonably perceived as detracting from the employee's job performance, that is sufficient proof of hostile environment. The intent of the harasser is not relevant; what is important is the perception of the victim.

In this case the Court used the concept of a "reasonable person" to determine whether a particular behavior constitutes sexual harassment. The Court asked whether a reasonable person would find the behavior unwelcome. If a reasonable person would find the behavior offensive and if the victim found it unwelcome, that behavior is likely to be construed as sexual harassment. Therefore, while merely offensive behavior is not prohibited, an employer would be breaking the law if a reasonable person would find the workplace so filled with sexual improprieties that it had become a hostile and abusive environment, even if there was no physical or psychological damage.

EEOC guidelines and court rulings in cases such as *King v. Palmer* (1985), *Broderick v. Ruder* (1988), and *Spencer v. General Electric Co.* (1990) suggest that third parties whose employment opportunities are adversely affected by an employer's sexual favoritism can also justifiably claim sexual harassment. Favoritism based upon coerced sexual conduct may constitute *quid pro quo* harassment, while widespread favoritism may constitute hostile environment harassment.

Employer Liability. EEOC guidelines state that an employer is liable for acts of its supervisors "regardless of whether the acts complained of were forbidden by the employer, and regardless of whether the employer knew or should have known of their occurrence." Courts have not accepted such categorical statements, however; in the *Meritor Savings Bank v. Vinson* case discussed earlier, for example, the Supreme Court stated that employers are neither automatically liable nor automatically not liable. The fact that a company has a policy against discrimination and has a grievance procedure in place is not necessarily an adequate defense, especially if the grievance procedure requires a victim first to report the matter to her (or his) supervisor—who may very well be the harasser. Courts of appeal have generally held strict employer liability in *quid pro quo* cases, especially in cases where the supervisor has authority over employment decisions (as in *Volk v. Coler*, 1988). In hostile environment cases, the employer is liable if there is actual knowledge of a supervisor's misconduct (*EEOC v. Hacienda Hotel*, 1989). In cases involving coworker sexual harassment, an employer is liable if the employer knew or should have known of the harassment and failed to take "immediate and appropriate corrective action" (*Paroline v. Unisys Corp.*, 1989). Courts have also ruled for employer liability when a third party, such as a customer, sexually harasses an employee and the employer fails to take any action.

Analysis. Research on judicial outcomes of sexual harassment claims has identified a number of conditions as most likely to increase the chances of a court ruling in favor of the claimant. A ruling for the claimant is most likely when the harassment involves physical contact, when propositions are linked to promises or threats to change the conditions of employment, when the claimant has notified management before filing charges, and when the organization has no formal policy toward harassment. (If the organization has such a policy and it is not conveyed to employees, or if such a policy requires a victim to report the matter to her immediate supervisor, findings for the claimant are also more likely.)

Since 1990, more than ten thousand charges of sexual harassment have been filed each year. Ninety-eight percent of the people charged with harassment are men, and more than 90 percent of the adult victims are women. Sixty-five percent of the cases are filed after dismissals, and 16 percent are filed after people quit voluntarily.   —*Kamala Arogyaswamy*

See also Civil Rights Act of 1964; Equal Employment Opportunity Commission (EEOC); Feminism; National Organization for Women (NOW); Sex discrimination.

BIBLIOGRAPHY

A good source from a legal perspective that includes practical applications and a historical analysis is Alba Conte, *Sexual Harassment in the Workplace: Law and Practice* (New York:

Wiley Law Publications, 1990). For a more detailed legal perspective, especially regarding the evolution of cases, see Arthur Gutman, *EEO Law and Personnel Practices* (Newbury Park, Calif.: Sage Publications, 1993). For applied coverage, see Nancy J. Sedmak and Michael D. Levin-Epstein, *A Primer on Equal Employment Opportunity* (5th ed. Washington, D.C.: Bureau of National Affairs, 1991). Another important reference is the EEOC's *Questions and Answers Concerning the EEOC Guidelines on Discrimination Because of Sex* (Washington, D.C.: Equal Employment Opportunity Commission, 1977). Finally, since sexual harassment law is evolving, recent court judgments should always be examined.

Shapiro v. Thompson

COURT: U.S. Supreme Court

DATE: Decided April 21, 1969

SIGNIFICANCE: Ruling that one-year residence requirements for receiving welfare benefits were unconstitutional, the Court defended a broad right to establish residence in the state of one's choice and to enjoy equal rights with other residents

After living in Connecticut for two months, Vivian Thompson applied for public assistance under the Aid to Families with Dependent Children (AFDC) program. Thompson, pregnant and a mother of one child, was denied assistance because she did not meet the state's one-year residency requirement. She then sued the welfare commissioner, Bernard Shapiro, in federal district court. The district court ruled in her favor based on two principles: that the residency requirement had a "chilling effect on the right to travel" and that it denied Thompson's guarantee of equal protection under the Fourteenth Amendment. Connecticut appealed the ruling to the U.S. Supreme Court, which accepted review and consolidated the case with others dealing with the same requirement to receive welfare.

The Supreme Court decided by a 6-3 vote to strike down the durational residency requirements, with Justice William Brennan delivering the opinion of the majority. Brennan observed that the right to migrate from state to state, implied in several places in the Constitution, was well established in the precedents of the Court. Concerning the second issue, the equal protection clause of the Fourteenth Amendment, Brennan wrote that the residency requirement created two classes of needy residents, with the two classes receiving unequal benefits. Since this classification restricted "the fundamental right of interstate movement," it could only be justified by a "compelling state interest." Although a state had a valid interest in restricting its expenditures, it could not promote this interest "by invidious discrimination between classes of its citizens."

The dissenters in the case accepted the constitutional principle of a right to travel, but they believed that the impact of residency requirements were indirect and quite insubstantial. Justice John M. Harlan attacked the expansion of judicial power that occurred when courts arbitrarily decided that fundamental rights required a more rigorous standard of review.

Shapiro was an important step in the Warren Court's development of "strict scrutiny" doctrine, which required states to show a compelling state interest to justify laws limiting fundamental rights or laws based upon "suspect classifications" such as race. Since the right to interstate migration was recognized as fundamental, *Shapiro* made it difficult for states to justify durational residency requirements for most services. Later the Court would invalidate residency requirements for voting, indigent medical care, and other basic services but would allow them for less basic services, upholding requirements for seeking divorce and for exemption from paying out-of-state tuition at public universities. Contrary to some expectations, *Shapiro* did not mark the beginning of a new governmental obligation to provide the economic necessities of life.

See also Aid to Families with Dependent Children (AFDC); Civil liberties; *Dunn v. Blumstein*; Ninth Amendment; *San Antonio Independent School District v. Rodriguez.*

Shaw v. Reno

COURT: U.S. Supreme Court

DATE: Ruling issued June 28, 1993

SIGNIFICANCE: By calling for close scrutiny of a predominantly black congressional district whose shape it considered "bizarre," the Supreme Court struck a blow against the practice of drawing district boundaries to create "majority-minority" electoral districts

After the 1990 census, the state legislature of North Carolina began the task of "reapportionment," or redrawing its electoral districts. Although about 22 percent of the state's population was African American, no blacks had been elected to Congress for almost a century. To remedy this, and ostensibly to meet provisions of the Voting Rights Act, the legislature created two majority-nonwhite districts. In order to avoid disturbing incumbents' districts, the legislature drew one of the two districts largely along an interstate highway, snaking 160 miles through the north-central part of the state. The resulting district was 53 percent black.

Five voters filed suit against the reapportionment plan, objecting that the race-based district violated their right to participate in a nonracial electoral process. The case reached the Supreme Court, whose 5-4 majority instructed the lower courts to reconsider the constitutionality of such a district in light of its "bizarre" shape and its "uncomfortable resemblance to political apartheid." In essence, the majority expressed its concern about the practice of creating districts on the basis of race and of establishing contorted geographical boundaries. The coupling of the two practices presumably could result in districts that patently violated the Constitution's equal protection clause, unless a compelling state interest could be demonstrated.

When the *Shaw* case was subsequently returned to North Carolina, a federal panel upheld the reapportionment plan after finding that the state did indeed have a compelling interest in complying with the VRA. Nevertheless, the Supreme Court's *Shaw* decision has been the basis for other important decisions concerning racially defined districts. In 1994, for example, a majority-black district in Louisiana was rejected by a federal district court invoking *Shaw*. The court expressed particular concern that the district was intentionally created on the basis of the voters' race. More significant, in 1995 the U.S. Supreme Court extended *Shaw*'s admonitions about racial reapportionment to argue that voters' rights are violated whenever "race was the predominant factor motivating the legislature's decision to place a significant number of voters within or without a particular district," irrespective of shape.

Shaw served as a watershed in the contest between advocates of racial representation and those who champion a "color-blind" electoral system. It came at a time when various racial issues that had for years remained largely outside of sharp political debate—affirmative action, welfare reform, and so forth—had been thrust into the center stage of American political discourse. Although *Shaw* by no means resolved these debates, it helped to clarify the battle lines.

See also Equal protection of the law; Racial and ethnic discrimination; Representation: gerrymandering, malapportionment, and reapportionment; Vote, right to; Voting Rights Act of 1965; *Wesberry v. Sanders*.

Shelley v. Kraemer

COURT: U.S. Supreme Court
DATE: Decided May 3, 1948
SIGNIFICANCE: Although the Supreme Court acknowledged the right of private individuals to make racially restrictive covenants, the Court ruled that state action to enforce such covenants was a violation of the Fourteenth Amendment

After J. D. Shelley, an African American, purchased a house in a predominantly white neighborhood of St. Louis, Missouri, one of the neighbors, Louis Kraemer, sought and obtained an injunction preventing Shelley from taking possession of the property. Unknown to Shelley, the neighboring landowners had signed a contractual agreement barring owners from selling their property to members of "the Negro or Mongolian race." Supported by the National Association for the Advancement of Colored People (NAACP), Shelley challenged the constitutionality of the contract in state court, but the Missouri Supreme Court upheld its legality. Appealing to the U.S. Supreme Court, Shelley's case was argued by the NAACP's leading counsel, Charles Houston and Thurgood Marshall. President Harry S Truman put the weight of the executive branch in favor of the NAACP's position.

This was not the first time that the issue of residential segregation had appeared before the Court. In *Buchanan v. Warley* (1917), the Court had struck down state statutes that limited the right of property owners to sell property to a person of another race, but in *Corrigan v. Buckley* (1926) the Court upheld the right of individuals to make "private" contracts to maintain segregation. *Corrigan* was based on the establishment principle that the first section of the Fourteenth Amendment inhibited the actions of state governments, not those of individuals.

The Court refused to declare restrictive contracts unconstitutional, but it held 6-0 that the Fourteenth Amendment's equal protection clause prohibited state courts from enforcing the

contracts, meaning that the contracts were not enforceable. The decision, written by Chief Justice Fred Vinson, emphasized that one of the basic objectives of the Fourteenth Amendment was to prohibit the states from using race to discriminate "in the enjoyment of property rights." The decision did not directly overturn *Corrigan*, but it interpreted the precedent as involving only the validity of private contracts, not their legal enforcement. In a companion case five years later, *Barrows v. Jackson* (1953), Chief Justice Vinson dissented when the majority used the *Shelley* rationale to block enforcement of restrictive covenants through private damage suits against covenant violators.

Eliminating the last direct method for legally barring African Americans from neighborhoods, *Shelley* was an important early victory in the struggle against state-supported segregation. Civil rights proponents hoped that a logical extension of the case would lead to an abolition of the distinction between private and state action in matters of equal protection, but in later decisions such as *Moose Lodge No. 107 v. Irvis* (1972), the majority of judges were not ready to rule against private conduct that was simply tolerated by the state.

See also Civil Rights Act of 1968; Civil Rights movement; *Heart of Atlanta Motel v. United States*; *Moose Lodge No. 107 v. Irvis*; Restrictive covenant; Segregation, *de facto* and *de jure*.

Sheppard v. Maxwell

COURT: U.S. Supreme Court
DATE: Decided June 6, 1966
SIGNIFICANCE: In *Sheppard v. Maxwell*, the Supreme Court for the first time provided guidelines for trial courts on how to balance the interests of the media in reporting information about a criminal trial and the rights of a criminal defendant

Problems related to too much media publicity about a criminal trial extend back to the 1800's, but it was not until the 1960's that the Supreme Court discussed the effects of publicity in criminal trials. Between 1959 and 1966, the Court reversed five convictions on the grounds that the amount of publicity had affected the defendant's right to a fair trial. It was not until 1966, when it decided *Sheppard v. Maxwell*, that it actually provided practical suggestions to the trial courts on how to solve the issues related to prejudicial publicity.

Sheppard involved the murder conviction of Sam Sheppard, a well-known physician in Cleveland accused of murdering his wife. Even before the arrest of the defendant in this case, the media published countless stories about him, accentuating his alleged failure to cooperate with the investigation and strongly arguing for his arrest. After an article demanded to know why there had been no public inquest, a three-day inquest took place where Sheppard's questioning was covered by television and radio. Another article also seemed to influence the decision to arrest Sheppard, since he was arrested hours after the headline "Why Isn't Sam Sheppard in Jail?" was run. Many articles and editorials implied his guilt and discussed allegedly incriminating evidence that was never introduced at trial. During the trial itself, the media filled the courtroom, and the constant movement of reporters made it difficult for some witnesses to be heard. A special table for media representatives was set in the courtroom, and twenty people were assigned to it. The court also reserved four rows of seats behind the bar railing for television and radio reporters and for representatives of out-of-town newspapers and magazines. A radio station was allowed to broadcast from a room adjacent the room where the jury rested and deliberated. Because of his proximity to reporters in the courtroom, it was almost impossible for the defendant to speak privately with his attorney during the proceedings. Despite this situation, the trial judge did not take steps to limit the effects of the publicity or the behavior of the press during the trial. The Supreme Court reversed the murder conviction, holding that the publicity surrounding the trial had deprived the defendant of his right to a fair trial.

In criticizing the trial court for allowing a "carnival atmosphere in the courtroom" and for failing to control the flow of publicity, the Supreme Court ordered lower courts to take an affirmative role in protecting the rights of the defendants from undue interference by the press. The Court enumerated some ways in which courts could make sure the publicity did not affect the defendant's right to a fair trial. For example, courts could regulate the conduct of reporters in the courtroom, change venue, order a continuance of the trial, isolate witnesses, and control the release of information to the media by law enforcement personnel and counsel.

See also Criminal justice system; Criminal procedure; News media; Privacy, right of; Privileged communications.

Sherbert v. Verner

COURT: U.S. Supreme Court

DATE: Decided June 17, 1963

SIGNIFICANCE: The Supreme Court allowed individuals to make First Amendment claims against governmental policies that indirectly burdened their free exercise of religion and required government to show that any such burdens were justified by a compelling state interest

Adell Sherbert, a member of the Seventh-day Adventist church, worked in a textile mill in South Carolina, and in 1959 her employer informed her that henceforth she would be required to work on Saturdays. Since it was against her religious beliefs to work on the Sabbath, she refused the new conditions, and she was fired. Not able to find employment consistent with her beliefs, she filed for state unemployment benefits. South Carolina law did not allow benefits for applicants who refused to accept work without good cause, and the unemployment office rejected her religious scruples as a justification.

Sherbert and her lawyers filed suit against the unemployment office at state court, but the South Carolina Supreme Court ruled in favor of the state agency. The state court relied on the recent precedent of *Braunfeld v. Brown* (1961), in which the U.S. Supreme Court had allowed for Sunday closing laws (blue laws) even if such laws disadvantaged Jewish merchants whose religious convictions prevented them from working on Saturdays. The state court concluded that the burdens on Sher-

bert were essentially the same as the economic hardships accepted in *Braunfeld*.

The U.S. Supreme Court, however, voted 7-2 that South Carolina's policy was in violation of the religious exercise clause of the First Amendment, made applicable to the states by the Fourteenth Amendment. Writing for the majority, Justice William Brennan began with the premise that religious exercise was a fundamental right and that any governmental burden on this right must be justified by a compelling state interest. In addition, Brennan wrote that the state had the obligation to adopt the alternative which was the least restrictive on religious practice, a test that had previously been used in free speech cases. The state was violating the First Amendment when it presented Sherbert with the "cruel choice" of either forfeiting an economic benefit or abandoning one of the precepts of her religion.

The two dissenters, supported by many informed observers, argued that Brennan's opinion contradicted the reasoning in *Braunfeld*, but Brennan maintained that the two cases were quite different. In the earlier case, he wrote, the state had demonstrated a compelling interest to provide a uniform day of rest for all workers, while in *Sherbert* the state had no compelling reason to refuse to modify its requirements for unemployment benefits.

Sherbert required governments to make exceptions in enforcing laws to accommodate religious practices unless the normal application of the law could be defended according to the tests that it served a compelling state interest and was the least restrictive alternative. The result was a maximum of protection for unpopular religious practices. In *Employment Division, Department of Human Resources of Oregon v. Smith* (1990), however, the Court ruled that indirect burdens were acceptable when state policies had a secular basis and were equally applicable to all citizens.

See also Blue laws; Civil liberties; *Employment Division, Department of Human Resources of Oregon v. Smith*; Religion, free exercise of; *Reynolds v. United States*; *Wisconsin v. Yoder*.

Sheriff

DEFINITION: The chief law enforcement official in a county, usually elected by popular vote

SIGNIFICANCE: A sheriff's duties are to aid the criminal and civil courts by delivering writs, summoning juries, and executing judgments, to maintain the county jail, and to perform various other required duties

The office of sheriff originated in England some time before the Norman conquest of 1066. Each shire, or county, was at that time administered by a representative of the king known as a reeve. The appointed reeve was usually a baron who was an ally of the king. These officials had nearly absolute power within their jurisdiction. Eventually the title "shire reeve" became "sheriff." The sheriff collected taxes, commanded the militia, delivered writs, and judged all criminal and civil cases. Following the reign of William the Conqueror, the role of the

In many counties, particularly in rural areas, the sheriff's department is the agency primarily responsible for law enforcement. (James L. Shaffer)

sheriff was dramatically reduced. Under Henry II, the position assumed an essentially law enforcement role. By the reign of Queen Elizabeth I (1558-1603), most of the duties of the sheriff had been transferred to the newly created offices of constable and justice of the peace.

Sheriffs in the Eighteenth and Nineteenth Centuries. English settlers in colonial America preferred to call their first law enforcement officials constables, as they had responsibilities very similar to those of their English namesakes. It was not until after the American Revolution that the sheriff emerged as the law enforcement agent of frontier justice in the American West. The pre-Civil War American sheriff was typically appointed to his position and exercised wide-ranging powers. Among his many duties were collecting taxes, apprehending criminals, conducting elections, and maintaining the local jail. Typically, the sheriff appointed deputy sheriffs to assist him in his duties, especially with the apprehension of fleeing criminals. As Western territories became states, increasingly the sheriff became a locally elected officeholder.

By the early 1900's, many states had begun to create new law enforcement agencies that took work and duties from local sheriffs. The complexities of organized crime and other developments, including the automobile and the expanding high-

way system, necessitated the creation of highly trained and skilled state and federal police agencies capable of meeting the challenges of modern criminal activity. Most sheriffs, generally popularly elected, did not have the training or professional qualifications to deal with the modern criminal who could move rapidly from one jurisdiction to another. Another often-heard complaint was that the sheriff in many communities was nothing more than the servant of the local elite.

Sheriff's Departments Today. Today the more than three thousand sheriff's departments throughout the United States are a vital part of the law enforcement community. In many counties they still provide the following services: local law enforcement, a county jail and juvenile facility, and service to the county as required by the state constitution or statute. As of 1987, almost one in four law enforcement officers (22.4 percent) served in a sheriff's department. In the states that require the position by law, the duties and responsibilities of the office vary widely from state to state. In many rural and unincorporated areas of the United States, the local sheriff is often the primary source of law enforcement protection. Alaska and New Jersey are the only states that do not maintain the office of sheriff. Today, sheriffs are elected in all but two states.

—*Donald C. Simmons, Jr.*

See also Criminal justice system; District attorney; Frontier, the; Marshals Service, U.S.; *Posse comitatus*; Southern Christian Leadership Conference (SCLC); Spoils system and patronage; State police; Subpoena power.

BIBLIOGRAPHY

The best treatment of the early American sheriff is Frank R. Prassel, *The Western Peace Officer: A Legacy of Law and Order* (Norman: University of Oklahoma Press, 1972); for those more interested in the gunfighting sheriff, refer to Joseph G. Rosa, *The Gunfighter: Man or Myth?* (Norman: University of Oklahoma Press, 1969). For information on the role of the modern American sheriff, see Samuel Walker, *The Police in America: An Introduction* (2d ed. New York: McGraw-Hill, 1992); Lane W. Lancaster, *Government in Rural America* (2d ed. New York: D. Van Nostrand, 1952); and Herbert Sydney Duncombe, *Modern County Government* (Washington, D.C.: National Association of Counties, 1977).

Sherman Antitrust Act

DATE: Became law July 20, 1890

DEFINITION: Outlawed contracts and conspiracies in restraint of trade as well as monopolization or attempts to monopolize by firms in interstate or foreign commerce

SIGNIFICANCE: The Sherman Act effectively put a stop to collusive actions by business firms such as price-fixing, and it restricted the power and growth of large firms

As the economy of the United States grew and modernized following the Civil War, large and aggressive firms developed, first in railroading, then in industry. A conspicuous firm was Standard Oil Company, led by John D. Rockefeller. The firm was efficient and progressive in developing petroleum refining, but it was heavily criticized for such actions as receiving preferential rebates from railroads and engaging in discriminatory price cutting to intimidate competitors. In 1882 the firm was reorganized in the form of a trust, facilitating acquisition of competing firms. Although the trust form went out of use, the term "trust" became a common name for aggressive big-business monopolies.

Opposition to big-business abuses became widespread among farmers and in small-firm sectors such as the grocery business. Both political party platforms in the election of 1888 contained vague antimonopoly statements. Senator John Sherman of Ohio introduced antimonopoly bills beginning in 1888. In 1890 his bill was extensively revised, primarily by Senators George F. Edmunds of Vermont and George F. Hoar of Massachusetts. With little debate and only one opposing vote in Congress, the bill was signed into law by President Benjamin Harrison on July 20, 1890.

The Sherman Antitrust Act outlawed "every contract, combination in the form of trust or otherwise, or conspiracy, in restraint of trade or commerce among the several States or with foreign nations." The law also made it illegal for any person to "monopolize or attempt to monopolize any part" of that trade or commerce. The attorney general was empowered to bring criminal or civil proceedings against violators. Further, private individuals could sue offending firms for triple the value of their losses.

Early Applications. In the law's early years, relatively few cases were brought. Several targeted railroads, despite their regulated status. The law also proved potentially damaging to labor unions, giving rise to triple-damage suits against strikes, picketing, and boycotts. A prosecution directed against the sugar trust was dismissed by the Supreme Court in 1895 for lack of jurisdiction, on grounds that manufacturing was not commerce (*United States v. E. C. Knight Co.*). Collusive behavior among a number of separate firms, however, was not granted such a loophole. In 1899, activities by six producers of cast-iron pipe to agree on contract bids were held illegal in *Addyston Pipe and Steel Co. v. United States*. These two cases indicated that activities involving several firms were much more likely to be found illegal than the operations of a single-firm monopolist. Perhaps in response, the decade of the 1890's witnessed an unprecedented boom in formation of giant corporations through mergers and consolidations. The culmination was the formation of United States Steel Corporation in 1901, capitalized at more than $1 billion.

Busting Big Trusts. Public outcry arose over these mergers. Some large firms were successfully attacked. A giant railroad merger was thrown out in 1904 (*Northern Securities Co. v. United States*). In 1911 two of the most notorious "trusts," Standard Oil and American Tobacco, were convicted of antitrust violations. In each case, the offending firm was ordered broken into several separate firms. Entry into petroleum refining became much easier, making possible the appearance of such new firms as Gulf Oil and Texaco. Prosecution of the ultimate corporate giant, U.S. Steel, was dismissed in 1920.

In 1914, Congress amended the Sherman Act to try to identify more specific actions to be prohibited. The Clayton Act outlawed price discrimination, tying and exclusive-dealing contracts, mergers and acquisitions, and interlocking directorships, where these tended to decrease competition or create a monopoly. The Federal Trade Commission was also established in 1914, charged with preventing "unfair methods of competition" and helping enforce the Clayton Act.

After World War II. Until 1950, Sherman Act prosecutions tended to be relatively effective and stringent against collusive actions by separate firms in interstate commerce—such as price-fixing and agreements to share markets, to boycott suppliers or customers, or to assign market territories. On the other hand, individual large firms were left relatively free, even if they held substantial monopoly power. The last condition appeared to change in 1945, when the government successfully prosecuted the Aluminum Company of America (ALCOA) on grounds that its market share was large enough to constitute a monopoly and that the firm had deliberately set out to achieve this monopoly. While few other firms met the market-share criterion, *United States v. Aluminum Co. of America* established a precedent for successful actions against United Shoe Machinery Co. (1954) and against American Telephone and Telegraph (AT&T). In the AT&T case, settled in 1982, the telephone industry was drastically reorganized. The various regional operating companies became independent, and entry into long-distance telephone service was opened up for new competitors. In 1950, Congress strengthened the restrictions on mergers by the Celler-Kefauver Anti-merger Act.

Evaluations. After more than a century, the Sherman Act remains an important constraint on business activity, although much of the litigation has shifted into areas involving the Clayton Act and its amendments. Some economists believe that antitrust legislation interferes with efficiency and technological innovation and may even inhibit competition. Others believe that it is important in maintaining a sense of fairness, preventing collusion, and keeping open the opportunity for new firms to enter established industries. —*Paul B. Trescott*

See also Antitrust law; Attorney general of the United States; Clayton Antitrust Act; Consent decree; Contract, freedom of; Federal Trade Commission (FTC); Justice, U.S. Department of; Price fixing.

BIBLIOGRAPHY

Historical and economic overviews of trusts and antimonopoly activities include Roger D. Blair and David L. Kaserman, *Antitrust Economics* (Homewood, Ill.: R. D. Irwin, 1985); Theodore P. Kovaleff, ed., *The Antitrust Impulse* (2 vols. Armonk, N.Y.: M. E. Sharpe, 1994); Frederic M. Scherer, *Industrial Market Structure and Economic Performance* (2d ed. Boston: Houghton Mifflin, 1980); and Les Seplaki, *Antitrust and the Economics of the Market* (New York: Harcourt Brace Jovanovich, 1982). A number of specific case studies are presented in Simon N. Whitney, *Antitrust Policy: American Experience in Twenty Industries* (2 vols. New York: Twentieth Century Fund, 1958).

Simpson, O. J., trial

DATE: Trial began September 26, 1994; verdict rendered October 3, 1995

SIGNIFICANCE: The Simpson murder trial confronted the American public with fundamental questions of racial and class differences in the administration of criminal justice in the United States and highlighted deep differences in perspective between whites and people of color

On June 17, 1994, Los Angeles police arrested Orenthal James (O. J.) Simpson, a celebrity and former Heisman Trophy-winning football player, for the murder of his former wife and her friend Ronald Goldman. Five days earlier, Nicole Brown Simpson and Goldman had been brutally stabbed to death outside her Brentwood, California, condominium.

The arrest of the national sports hero caught the attention of millions; the ensuing trial was the most widely viewed criminal proceeding in history. Jury selection began on September 26, 1994, and opening arguments began January 24, 1995. On some television stations the events in the courtroom were broadcast gavel to gavel for the thirteen-month duration of the trial. The jurors were ostensibly insulated from the extensive publicity, as they were sequestered and thus (in theory at least) protected from exposure to uncensored media sources.

The Trial. In the nearly eight months between opening and closing arguments, the jury was introduced to a wide range of detailed evidence. Expert witnesses testified that DNA evidence placed Simpson's blood at the scene of the crime and the victims' blood in Simpson's vehicle and home. Los Angeles Police Department detective Mark Fuhrman testified that he found a bloody glove, a blue knit cap, and bloody shoe prints at the crime scene that allegedly belonged to Simpson, along with a second similar bloody glove at Simpson's estate. A limousine driver hired to take Simpson to the airport the night of the crime testified that a white Ford Bronco was not outside the house when he arrived and that Simpson did not answer the door for more than fifteen minutes. The prosecution also showed that, in the past, Simpson had more than once assaulted his former wife.

The defense raised questions about the evidence, arguing that police misconduct and incompetence had created a "cesspool of contamination." Forensic expert witnesses questioned the validity of the DNA evidence, pointing to sloppy procedures that could have tainted the blood samples. When Simpson, at the prosecution's request, attempted to try on the bloody gloves, they seemed too small for his hands. The defense emphasized this occurrence in its closing arguments, telling the jury, "If it doesn't fit, you must acquit." It was discovered that Detective Fuhrman, in previously taped interviews with an aspiring screenwriter, had recounted stories in which he planted evi-

Defendant O. J. Simpson, flanked by two of his attorneys, Johnnie Cochran, Jr. (left), and Robert Shapiro. (AP/Wide World Photos)

dence against African American defendants and—contrary to his earlier sworn testimony—used racial epithets.

The long, closely scrutinized trial and the stress of sequestration took its toll on the jurors. Ten of the original jurors were dismissed, some at their own request and others for cause. By the end of the trial, only two alternate jurors remained.

After hearing the closing arguments, the jury deliberated a mere four hours before returning with a verdict. The next day, at the time scheduled for the reading of the verdict, daily life in the United States came to a near standstill. More Americans watched the reading of the verdict on television than had watched Neil Armstrong walk on the moon. The jury acquitted Simpson on all charges. Because of constitutional protections against double jeopardy, he could not be subject to another criminal prosecution. At the end of 1995, however, he found himself faced with civil suits brought by the families of the victims. In a civil lawsuit, the jury's decision need not be unanimous, and the burden of proof is lower.

Legal Issues and Social Context. The Simpson trial focused attention on several contemporary social problems. In the initial phase of the trial, for example, domestic violence was much discussed. Later, some activists against domestic violence saw the verdict as a dramatic setback in which the jury condoned a case of a violent man abusing and then killing his former wife.

Racial tensions surrounded many aspects of this trial of an African American accused of killing two white victims. The police department investigating the crime had a reputation for racist acts against people of color, a reputation that had been reinforced a few years earlier by the trial of white officers accused of beating Rodney King, a black man—a beating captured on videotape and broadcast internationally. Some commentators claimed that defense attorney Johnnie Cochran played "the race card" in his closing statement when he asked the jury (consisting of nine blacks, two whites, and one Hispanic) to "send a message" to the Los Angeles police about their sloppy and arguably racist behavior. Opinion polls showed the American public deeply divided along racial lines. An ABC news poll showed that 83 percent of African Americans but only 37 percent of whites agreed with the verdict, a finding which underscored the fact that black Americans and white Americans have sharply differing views regarding the nation's judicial system.

Some commentators claimed that the jury's verdict illustrated a case of jury nullification, saying that the jury disregarded the facts in the case and refused to convict a guilty man. Others argued that the defense team had simply done its job and successfully created reasonable doubt in the minds of the jurors by emphasizing flaws in key pieces of evidence and prosecution witnesses. Many pointed to the pivotal role of Simpson's wealth, which enabled him to hire a legal "dream team," saying that if Simpson had been poor, clearly he would have been convicted.   —*Lynda Frost*

See also Criminal procedure; DNA testing; Domestic violence; Jury nullification; Jury system; King, Rodney, trial and aftermath; Reasonable doubt; Standards of proof.

Sinclair, Upton (Sept. 20, 1878, Baltimore, Md.—Nov. 25, 1968, Bound Brook, N.J.)

IDENTIFICATION: Author and reformer

SIGNIFICANCE: Through his "muckraking" journalist in such works as *The Jungle*, Sinclair helped institute industrial and social reforms throughout the opening decades of the twentieth century

Upton Sinclair started writing while a student at the City College of New York, which he began attending at fifteen. His early novels include *Springtime and Harvest* (1901, later retitled *King Midas*), *The Journal of Arthur Stirling* (1903), *Manassas* (1904), and *A Captain of Industry* (1906). He is best known, however, for *The Jungle* (1906), a brutally graphic exposé of the Chicago stockyards which led to the strengthening of food adulteration laws. True to his beliefs, Sinclair invested the profits from this, his most successful book, in the Helicon Home Colony, a socialist community in Englewood, New Jersey. *The Jungle* was followed by *The Metropolis* (1908), *The Moneychangers* (1908), and the semi-autobiographical *Love's Pilgrimage* (1911). In 1915 Sinclair moved to California, where he continued to write such books as *King Coal* (1917), *Oil!* (1927), and *Boston* (1928), which addressed the Sacco and Vanzetti case. During the Depression he began to take an active role in California politics, and in 1934 he formed EPIC (End Poverty in California), an alliance of progressives and the unemployed that took control of the state Democratic Party and nearly won him the governorship. Sinclair made several more unsuccessful attempts at public office before returning to literature in 1940 with the first of a series of eleven novels tracing the career of the fictional Lanny Budd from World War I to the Cold War. The third of these, *Dragon's Teeth* (1942), won him the Pulitzer Prize.

See also Food and Drug Administration (FDA); Progressivism; Pure Food and Drug Act; Sacco and Vanzetti trial and executions; Socialism.

Skinner v. Railway Labor Executives' Association

COURT: U.S. Supreme Court

DATE: Decided March 21, 1989

SIGNIFICANCE: In this case the Supreme Court ruled that drug and alcohol testing in the workplace was not a violation of the Fourth Amendment

The Fourth Amendment to the U.S. Constitution protects not only against unreasonable search and seizure of persons and places but also against the issuance of warrants for search and seizure unless just cause is demonstrated.

The Federal Railroad Administration (FRA), in response to evidence that drug and alcohol abuse was becoming a problem in the nation's railways, established regulations to address the problem. These regulations required blood and urine samples from employees to test for drugs or alcohol after train accidents where deaths, injuries, or property damage occurred. Employees also had to submit to breath or urine tests if there was reasonable suspicion that they were under the influence of drugs or alcohol, even if no accident had occurred.

Industry	Percent of Businesses with Testing Programs	Total Number of Businesses in the Industry
Mining	21.6	31,600
Communications and public utilities	17.6	37,500
Transportation	14.9	153,500
Manufacturing:		
Durable goods	9.9	193,900
Nondurable goods	9.1	141,200
Wholesale trade	5.3	467,900
Finance, insurance, and real estate	3.2	403,900
Construction	2.3	458,100
Services	1.4	1,553,400
Retail trade	.7	1,101,800
All establishments	3.2	4,542,800

TYPES OF BUSINESSES WITH DRUG-TESTING PROGRAMS

Source: U.S. Department of Justice, Bureau of Justice Statistics, *Drugs, Crime, and the Justice System.* Washington, D.C.: U.S. Government Printing Office, 1992. Primary source is Bureau of Labor Statistics, 1989.

Railway labor organizations filed suit in the U.S. District Court for the Northern District of California. The court held the regulations to be constitutional. The railway organizations then appealed in the U.S. Court of Appeals for the Ninth Circuit. The appeals court reversed the lower trial court's decision, holding that such tests were search and seizure without warrant and constituted a violation of an employee's Fourth Amendment rights.

The U.S. Supreme Court, on *certiorari*, reversed the court of appeals ruling and upheld the original decision, finding that Fourth Amendment rights had not been violated. In addition, the Court noted that the FRA regulations were well known to, and understood by, the railway workers subject to them.

The Court found that the tests were not unconstitutional even when a warrant had not been issued. The justices cited the need to ensure the safety of the public using the railways. Because evidence of drug or alcohol use could disappear from a person's body within a brief period of time, timely testing was essential for accurate results. Obtaining a warrant would take too long. Furthermore, they said that the railway did not need to prove that there was particular reason to suspect drug or alcohol use before testing employees who had not been involved in accidents. The justices pointed out the need to discourage all employees from using drugs or alcohol during working hours or shortly before. In general, the Court held that the greater good of protecting the public outweighed the private rights of individuals responsible for ensuring travel safety.

The opinion was written by Justice Anthony Kennedy with Chief Justice William H. Rehnquist and Justices Byron R. White, Harry A. Blackmun, Sandra Day O'Connor, and An-

tonin Scalia concurring. Justice John Paul Stevens concurred in part and concurred in the judgment. Justices Thurgood Marshall and William J. Brennan dissented.

See also Constitutional interpretation; Drug use and sale, illegal; Labor unions; *National Treasury Employees Union v. Von Raab*; Search and seizure; *Terry v. Ohio*.

Skyjacking

DEFINITION: The forcible takeover of an aircraft in flight or on the ground for political or criminal purposes

SIGNIFICANCE: Skyjacking was a frequent tactic of criminals and political terrorists during the 1960's and 1970's as a means of securing ransom monies, releases of political prisoners, and other concessions

During the 1960's and 1970's, skyjacking was frequently used by political groups to achieve political goals. Skyjackers demanded ransom for the release of passengers, crew, and aircraft; releases of political prisoners; the publication or broadcast of political messages; political asylum or safe passage to a friendly nation; and other concessions. In the early 1960's, skyjackers generally were seeking political asylum. For example, there were numerous skyjackings to Cuba by American radicals, until the Cuban government began imprisoning skyjackers.

By the early 1970's, skyjackings had become more violent and more dramatic. The events escalated from simple takeovers with a list of demands to weeklong (and longer) skyjackings involving airports in several countries and ending with spectacular bombings. Criminal skyjackings were rare, but the D. B. Cooper case—involving a skyjacker who parachuted from an airliner and disappeared into the forests of the Pacific Northwest with the ransom money—has almost become legend.

For the United States, Cuba's discouragement of skyjackings during the late 1960's reduced the number of takeovers dramatically. The Palestinian Liberation Organization (PLO) decided to stop hijackings by its members in 1972, and the number of international skyjackings decreased significantly. The adoption of international antiskyjacking conventions also contributed to the decline in takeovers. The Tokyo Convention of 1963 outlawed attacks on civilian aircraft, and the Hague Convention of 1970 and the Montreal Convention of 1971 clarified jurisdiction over skyjackings and other attacks on aviation and ratified the policy of "prosecute or extradite," requiring signatories to apprehend skyjackers and either try them or extradite them to a nation that will. In the United States, the Anti-hijacking Act of 1974 reaffirmed the responsibility of airlines to provide security. Successful rescues of hostages in Entebbe, Uganda, in 1976 and Mogadishu, Somalia, in 1977 encouraged military operations against skyjackers, but rescue attempts were often unsuccessful and hostages and rescuers were killed because the circumstances were quite different from those in Entebbe and Mogadishu.

After a dramatic TWA skyjacking in 1985, security measures were increased at U.S. airports, and security at foreign airports was increasingly monitored. As a result, skyjackings

Chief Justice Salmon P. Chase vigorously dissented from the Court's Slaughterhouse Cases *decision, arguing that it undermined the rights of freedmen.* (Painting by William F. Cogswell, collection of the Supreme Court of the United States)

of flights from major international airports have become uncommon, although there are concerns about security at smaller airports in United States and at many international airports. Skyjackings still occur but are more likely to involve persons seeking political asylum and trying not to harm their hostages.

See also Extradition; Federal Bureau of Investigation (FBI); International law; Terrorism.

Slander. *See* Defamation

Slaughterhouse Cases

COURT: U.S. Supreme Court

DATE: Decided April 14, 1873

SIGNIFICANCE: In these cases, the U.S. Supreme Court for the first time interpreted the three Reconstruction-era amendments to the U.S. Constitution—the Thirteenth, Fourteenth, and Fifteenth Amendments—and upheld a state statute granting monopoly status to a corporation

The state of Louisiana created a corporation in 1869 and gave it monopoly status to operate a meat-slaughtering facility south of the city of New Orleans. It prohibited all other slaughterhouse operations in the three parishes surrounding the city. The goal of the law was to remove slaughterhouse operations from areas that polluted Mississippi River water traveling through the city and consolidate them at one central location downstream from the city. The law also regulated the prices charged for use of the facility by butchers. Butchers not included in the monopoly claimed the law was unconstitutional under the recently adopted Thirteenth and Fourteenth Amendments to the U.S. Constitution. The Louisiana Supreme Court affirmed the law, and the case was appealed to the U.S. Supreme Court.

Justice Samuel F. Miller, writing for the five-member majority of the Court, upheld the law. He used the case to reflect on the purpose of the three Reconstruction-era amendments to the U.S. Constitution, the Thirteenth, Fourteenth, and Fifteenth Amendments which had been ratified between 1865 and 1870. He wrote that the three taken together were intended to end slavery and the effects of slavery on African Americans. This portion of the opinion is important, as it reflects contemporaneous thinking on the rationale for the ratification of the three amendments.

Justice Miller rejected the claim that granting a monopoly to the corporation created an "involuntary servitude" in violation of the Thirteenth Amendment, noting that the amendment intended to apply narrowly to the incidents of slavery. He also refused to find that the state of Louisiana had violated the Fourteenth Amendment protection of the "privileges and immunities of citizens of the United States" by awarding the monopoly. He refused to give the Fourteenth Amendment a broad interpretation or permit the concept of due process to be used to challenge state law through the U.S. Constitution.

The four-member minority opinion authored by Justice Stephen J. Field sharply disagreed with the majority. Justice Field wrote that the Fourteenth Amendment protects a broad array of privileges and immunities from state interference. Justice Joseph P. Bradley wrote a second dissenting opinion asserting that the Fourteenth Amendment due process clause requires that persons be protected from state actions and that the clause should be given a broad interpretation. This minority view later gained support by the Court majority in the use of substantive due process to limit state regulation of economic activities. It also has been used as a source to protect fundamental rights such as the right to privacy and in criminal law.

See also Civil rights; Civil War; Civil War Amendments; Due process of law; *Lochner v. New York*; Reconstruction.

Slavery

DEFINITION: In the United States, the system of labor before 1865 in which African Americans were owned by whites and compelled to work for their owners

SIGNIFICANCE: Slavery defined the legal treatment of African Americans for two-and-one-half centuries, and the crusade against slavery gave rise to modern concepts of citizenship and civil rights

The first African laborers in the English colonies of North America arrived in Virginia in 1619. By the 1770's, slaves made up one-fifth of the population of the English colonies. At this time, slave labor was used in every colony, including those in the North. Only in the South, however, did slavery dominate economic life. Slaves were used primarily to grow staple crops such as tobacco and rice for exportation to Europe and the Caribbean.

During the eighteenth century, slavery was weakened by several forces. The religious movement known as the Great Awakening challenged the excessive materialism of slaveholding and emphasized the spiritual equality of the races. The American Revolution undermined the ideological foundations of slavery by popularizing the ideas of liberty and equality. Between 1776 and 1804, every northern state abolished slavery. Even in the South, private manumissions (freeing of slaves) increased and many southerners argued that slavery was declining. Tobacco cultivation exhausted the soil, and rice cultivation was limited by geography to seacoast areas.

The nineteenth century Industrial Revolution reinvigorated slavery by bringing a new crop, cotton, to importance. As textile factories in Britain began purchasing large quantities of cotton, slave plantations multiplied from the Atlantic Coast to Texas. Southern slaveholders began to defend slavery militantly. Simultaneously, northern concern about the South's disproportionate share of political power promoted the growth of the antislavery movement.

Slavery and the Territories. As Americans moved westward, the issue of whether slavery should expand into the new territories became increasingly important. Americans realized that new western states would determine the balance of political power between North and South. Congress initially divided the new territories between North and South. In the Northwest Ordinance (1787), Congress banned slavery in the lands north of the Ohio River while implicitly accepting slavery south of the Ohio. In regard to the Louisiana Purchase, the Missouri Compromise of 1820 banned slavery north of the line 36° 30′ latitude while allowing slavery to exist south of the line.

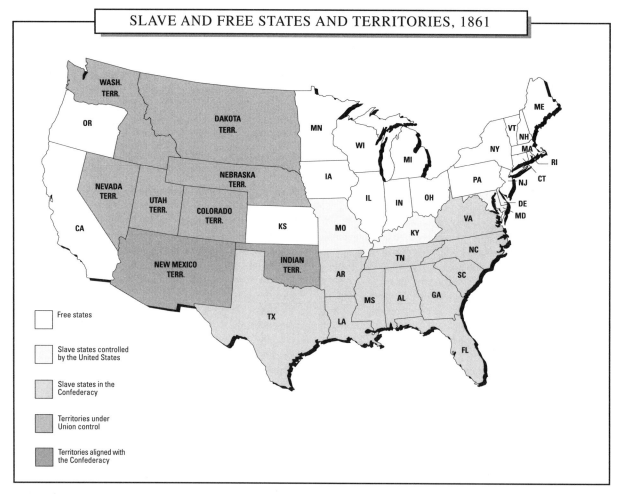

SLAVE AND FREE STATES AND TERRITORIES, 1861

Free states

Slave states controlled
by the United States

Slave states in the
Confederacy

Territories under
Union control

Territories aligned with
the Confederacy

Source: Adapted from Eric Foner and John A Garraty, eds., *The Reader's Companion to American History.* Boston: Houghton Mifflin, 1991.

The Missouri Compromise resolved the issue of slavery in the territories until the Mexican War of 1846-1848 added new western lands to the United States. Subsequently, four positions emerged regarding the issue. Many northerners favored the Wilmot Proviso, a proposal to ban slavery in the territories. Other Americans favored popular sovereignty, which would allow the people of the territories to decide the issue for themselves. Some Americans favored extending the Missouri Compromise line to the Pacific Coast. Many southerners believed the federal government should protect slavery in the territories.

In the 1850's, the popular sovereignty approach gained ascendancy. The Compromise of 1850 applied popular sovereignty to California, New Mexico, and Utah. The Kansas-Nebraska Act (1854) repealed the old Missouri Compromise line and enacted popular sovereignty for the Louisiana Purchase. The Kansas-Nebraska Act created such great controversy that the existing political alignment was shattered. Opponents of the act created a new antislavery political party, the Republican Party, while supporters of the act reconstructed the Democratic Party as a proslavery party.

Disagreements regarding slavery-related issues and sectional competition for political power led ultimately to the outbreak of the Civil War in 1861. During the war, northern military officials increasingly believed that freeing the South's slaves would severely injure the Confederacy. President Abraham Lincoln issued the Emancipation Proclamation in 1863, proclaiming that the Union Army would henceforth liberate the Confederacy's slaves. In 1865, the Thirteenth Amendment to the U.S. Constitution freed all remaining slaves belonging to American citizens.

Slavery and the U.S. Constitution. Slavery significantly influenced the writing of the U.S. Constitution. The Constitutional Convention of 1787 nearly broke up because of disagreements regarding sectional issues. Ultimately the sectional impasse was resolved with the Compromise of 1787. Direct taxes and representation in the House of Representatives were to be apportioned according to the three-fifths rule: All free people and three-fifths of the slaves were to be counted in determining a state's tax burden and congressional representation. Congress could prohibit the importation of slaves into the United States after the lapse of twenty years. States were prohibited from freeing fugitive slaves, and slaveholders were given the right to cross state boundaries to recapture fugitives. Congress was prevented from taxing exports so that slavery would not be injured by excessive taxes on the products of slave labor. Finally, to ensure that the compromise would not be abrogated, the clauses regarding the international slave trade and the three-fifths rule were declared by the Constitution to be unamendable.

As the Civil War approached, Americans debated the significance of these actions. What was the relationship between the U.S. Constitution and slavery? Before 1860, most Americans believed that the Constitution did not establish a federal right to own slaves. Slavery was thought to exist as a result of state laws, and the federal government was thought to have few constitutional powers regarding slavery. Northerners and southerners disagreed regarding the practical application of this idea. Southerners believed the federal government was increasingly intruding into matters related to slavery. They called for an end to federal interference with slavery. North-

erners argued that the federal government had been indirectly providing protection to slavery for years. They called for the withdrawal of this protection.

In the 1840's and 1850's, militants on both sides developed new constitutional theories regarding slavery. Some southerners claimed that there was a federal right to own slaves, established in the fugitive slave clause and the privileges and immunities clause of the U.S. Constitution. The federal government, they said, must protect the right of citizens to own slaves in the territories. Some southern extremists argued that the federal right to own slaves was so comprehensive that even northern states could not outlaw slavery within their own boundaries. Ironically, the branch of the abolitionist movement led by William Lloyd Garrison agreed with this argument, claiming that the Constitution protected slavery and arguing that northern states should abandon this corrupt document by withdrawing from the Union.

Another branch of the abolitionist movement, led by Gerrit Smith and William Goodell, argued to the contrary that the

The Alexandria, Virginia, slave warehouse of Price, Birch & Co. in the 1850's. (National Archives)

Constitution was best read as an antislavery document. They claimed that citizenship was based on residence in the United States and that slaves therefore were citizens. The privileges and immunities clause of the Constitution, they claimed, prevented both the states and the federal government from giving unequal treatment to citizens. The due process clause of the Fifth Amendment prevented citizens from losing their liberty without due process of law. Slavery violated these principles, and judges therefore ought to declare slavery unconstitutional. While this interpretation of the Constitution seemed extreme and utopian at the time, after the Civil War, the abolitionists' constitutional ideas were incorporated into the Fourteenth Amendment.

Fugitive Slave Laws. One of the most significant controversies regarding slavery involved fugitive slave laws. In 1793, Congress adopted legislation to enforce the fugitive slave clause of the U.S. Constitution. The Fugitive Slave Act of 1793 allowed slaveholders to obtain warrants from either state or federal courts for the rendition of fugitive slaves. In the 1820's and 1830's, several states passed personal liberty laws to prevent state officials from assisting in the recapture process. In *Prigg v. Pennsylvania* (1842), the U.S. Supreme Court upheld the constitutionality of personal liberty laws by ruling that the enforcement of fugitive slave laws rested entirely in the hands of the federal government.

Without the assistance of state officials, slaveholders found that it was difficult to recapture their slaves. Southerners clamored for federal assistance. Congress responded by passing a new Fugitive Slave Act as a part of the Compromise of 1850. A new group of federal officials was created for the sole purpose of assisting slaveholders recapture slaves. State officials were forbidden to resist the rendition of fugitives. Even ordinary citizens could be compelled to serve in posses for the purpose of capturing fugitives. To prevent blacks who were seized as fugitives from challenging their seizure, their legal rights, including the right of *habeas corpus*, were abolished.

The Fugitive Slave Act of 1850 was met with strong opposition in the North. Hundreds of fugitives, and even some free blacks, migrated to Canada to avoid seizure under the new law. Many northern communities formed vigilance committees to assist fugitives, and in a few cases northern mobs tried to rescue fugitives from the hands of government officials.

One rescue in 1854 led to a conflict between Wisconsin and the federal government. This case is notable because Wisconsin, a northern state, used states' rights arguments to challenge federal authority, a ploy normally used by southerners to defend slavery. Sherman M. Booth, an abolitionist, was arrested by federal marshals for participating in the rescue of a fugitive slave. The Wisconsin State Supreme Court twice issued writs of *habeas corpus* to free Booth from federal imprisonment and declared the federal Fugitive Slave Act to be unconstitutional. The U.S. Supreme Court in *Ableman v. Booth* (1859) reasserted the primacy of federal over state law and the right of the federal government to enforce its own laws through its own courts. The Wisconsin court accepted this decision, now be-

lieving that it did not help the antislavery cause to promote the idea of states' rights and nullification of federal law.

Legal Treatment of Slaves. African laborers occupied an ambiguous status in the American colonies before 1660 because English law did not recognize the status of slavery. Some Africans were held as slaves; others were held as indentured servants, persons whose term of labor expired after several years. Indentured servants enjoyed certain additional legal protections since, unlike slaves, their physical bodies were not owned by their masters. After 1660, Virginia and Maryland constructed elaborate slave codes to establish the legal status of slavery. For the next two centuries, the vast majority of blacks in America were slaves.

The evolving law of slavery in the English colonies and later the United States was harsher than the law of slavery in Latin America. The colonies of Spain and Portugal inherited a well-developed law of slavery from the mother countries. These inherited law codes had been strongly influenced by the efforts of the Catholic Church to recognize slaves as moral beings. In the Spanish colonies, the marriage of slaves was legally recognized. Husbands and wives could not be separated by sale. Slaves had the right to own property. Slaves were subject to the practice of *coartación*, by which they had the right to buy their freedom by paying a fair price to their masters.

Because there were no English precedents for slavery, American slave codes tended to reflect the practical needs of slave masters in a difficult environment to control their bondsmen through brute force. It should be emphasized that despite the differences in formal law codes, the actual treatment of slaves was probably better in the English colonies than in Latin America, where the labor demands were greater and where masters located far from imperial authority often flouted benevolent imperial law.

In making and enforcing slave codes, Americans recognized slaves as both people and property. As property, slaves generally had few legal rights as independent beings. Slaves could not own property, enter into contracts, sue or be sued, or marry legally. Slaves had no freedom of movement. Masters could sell their slaves without restriction, and there was no legal protection for slave families against forced separation through sale. The status of slave children was inherited from their mothers, a departure from the traditional common-law doctrine that children inherited the status of their fathers.

In some ways, the masters' property rights in slaves were limited by compelling public interest. Most southern states made it difficult for masters to free their slaves on the theory that free blacks were a nuisance to society. Most southern states also tried to prevent slaves from becoming a threat to society. State laws often required slaves to carry passes when traveling away from their masters' homes. Laws in several states prohibited slaves from living alone without the supervision of whites. In all but two states, it was illegal for anyone to teach slaves to read or write. Some states banned the use of alcohol and firearms by slaves; others outlawed trading and

A woodcut from an antislavery publication depicting slaves being flogged. (Library of Congress)

gambling by slaves. While these laws were primarily a burden to the slave population, they also restricted the manner in which masters could manage and use their property.

Southern law codes occasionally recognized slaves as people as well as property. By the mid-nineteenth century, most states provided slaves with a minimal degree of protection against physical assaults by whites, although these laws were generally poorly enforced. All states outlawed the murder and harsh treatment of slaves. While masters were occasionally put on trial for murder of their slaves, evidence suggests that most homicidal masters either received light sentences or were not punished. Laws protecting slaves against other forms of inhumane treatment (such as excessive beatings or starvation diets) were almost never enforced. In practice, masters could beat or starve their slaves with impunity. Battery of slaves by strangers was illegal and was often punished by southern courts. Rape of slaves by whites, however, was not illegal. Masters had the full legal right to rape their own slaves, although masters could charge other whites with criminal trespass for an act of rape without the master's permission.

Under the law, blacks were assumed to be slaves unless they could prove otherwise, meaning that free blacks were forced always to carry legal documents certifying their freedom. Many actions, including the use of alcohol and firearms, were illegal for slaves but not for whites. Penalties for crimes were generally more severe for slaves than for whites. For slaves, capital crimes—those for which death was the penalty—included not only murder but also manslaughter, rape, arson, insurrection,

and robbery. Even attempted murders, insurrections, and rapes were subject to the death penalty.

Despite the harshness of the law, actual executions of slaves were rare because even slave criminals were valuable property. State laws generally required governments to pay compensation to the masters of executed slaves. The fact that the labor of slaves was valuable meant that, in all states except Louisiana, imprisonment was rarely used as punishment for slave criminals. Instead, most penalties involved physical punishments such as whipping, branding, or ear-cropping, punishments which were rarely used against whites after the early nineteenth century. Slaves convicted of rape sometimes saw their death sentences commuted to castration. In all cases of physical punishment, the state inflicted physical pain as punishment to the criminals and then sent them back to work. For incorrigible slave criminals, states sometimes deported them outside the state or the country. Other slaves were sentenced to hard labor on public work projects.

It is difficult to measure accurately the incidence of crime or the fairness of punishment regarding slaves. A characteristic feature of slave societies was that they gave much responsibility for policing the behavior of slaves to masters rather than to the government. While statistics of crime and punishment can be compiled from police and judicial records, these records do not record crimes punished unofficially by masters and slave patrols.

The best evidence regarding the incidence of crime comes from the state of Virginia, which several studies suggest was typical of most southern states. Slaves were most often charged with crimes against property, primarily stealing and arson. About 80 percent of those slaves charged with stealing were accused of taking clothing, food, or livestock, suggesting that slaves stole to acquire basic necessities of life denied to them by their masters. Slaves were less often charged with crimes against persons: assault, rape, and murder. Slaves were accused of killing about equal numbers of whites and blacks but were about twice as likely to be convicted of killing whites as of killing blacks.

While southern courts did not give blacks and whites equal treatment, the courts made some effort to be fair to slaves, probably because of the influence of wealthy slaveholders with an economic interest in the acquittal of their property. The proportion of slaves among those people accused of crime was about equal to the proportion of slaves in the population. Slaves appear to have been convicted at nearly the same rate as whites. Southern law codes also reflected the slaveholders' interests. Many states required that slaves have access to counsel and protected them against self-incrimination and double jeopardy. Slaves, however, could not testify in court against whites, meaning that it was nearly impossible to prosecute crimes against slaves when blacks were the only available witnesses.

—Harold D. Tallant

See also Abolitionist movement; Black codes; Civil War; Civil War Amendments; Emancipation Proclamation; Free Soil Party; Fugitive Slave Laws; Kansas-Nebraska Act; Missouri Compromise of 1820; Reconstruction; *Scott v. Sandford.*

BIBLIOGRAPHY

The most readable and comprehensive survey of slavery and the law is Harold M. Hyman and William M. Wiecek, *Equal Justice Under Law: Constitutional Development, 1835-1875* (New York: Harper & Row, 1982). Alan Watson, *Slave Law in the Americas* (Athens: University of Georgia Press, 1989), offers a succinct comparison of the law of slavery in several Western Hemisphere societies. Mark V. Tushnet, *The American Law of Slavery, 1810-1860: Considerations of Humanity and Interest* (Princeton, N.J.: Princeton University Press, 1981), discusses the tension within American law regarding the slaves' dual role as both property and people. Two works which survey the impact of the antislavery movement on legal and constitutional issues are William M. Wiecek, *The Sources of Antislavery Constitutionalism in America, 1760-1848* (Ithaca, N.Y.: Cornell University Press, 1977), and Robert M. Cover, *Justice Accused: Antislavery and the Judicial Process* (New Haven, Conn.: Yale University Press, 1975). The best survey of the legal treatment of slaves is Philip J. Schwarz, *Twice Condemned: Slaves and the Criminal Laws of Virginia, 1705-1865* (Baton Rouge: Louisiana State University Press, 1988). See also A. Leon Higginbotham, Jr., *In the Matter of Color: Race and the American Legal Process, the Colonial Period* (New York: Oxford University Press, 1978).

Small-claims court

DEFINITION: A special court, often a subdivision of a regular court, that expeditiously, informally, and inexpensively settles small claims—generally claims of less than $1,000

SIGNIFICANCE: The informality of the small-claims system makes it possible for small disputes to be settled without attorneys and formal legal procedures; the expenses involved are quite small

Proceedings in a small-claims court are very informal. The plaintiff and the defendant usually represent themselves without the benefit or expense of an attorney. (In some cases it may be wise to get the advice and suggestions of an attorney before going to small-claims court in order to understand better one's legal situation. Reading the appropriate law books in a local library, however, may be all that is necessary.) Often all the court does is to arrange for the payment of small claims and accounts. The tone is conciliatory, and the judge tries to work out a mutually fair settlement.

Almost all of the fifty states now have small-claims courts. These courts handle such cases as a person seeking restitution from a dry cleaner who has ruined a suit, a couple wanting a car dealer to repair a car he sold them, or one party trying to get another to pay back a debt that is owed. Contract law is involved if an agreement has been signed. If it has not, the law still recognizes spoken and implied contracts.

There are no juries in small-claims court, and the judge must follow the formal standard of proof as in a regular civil trial; proof must be demonstrated by a preponderance of the evidence. The judge must determine the facts in the case and then apply the law the best he or she can.

Small-claims courts are not a separate level of justice, but rather a special procedure that is part of a larger, more formal court. Judges rotate in and out of the court, typically spending only a week there at a time. Part of the purpose of the courts is to expedite the case load, so small-claims hearings customarily last only fifteen to thirty minutes. Sometimes the judge will interrupt an explanation and say that he has heard enough and has a strong enough basis for a judgment. Most small-claims courts have a $1,000 limit on claims they can hear. The plaintiffs usually win, perhaps as much as 80 percent of the time. When the plaintiff does not win, it is usually because the jurisdiction of the court does not extend as far as the plaintiff's description of the situation.

It is sound judicial administration to have small-claims courts, not only because of the speed of the process and the settlement of many disputes but also because of the effect on the parties involved. A large-scale political or judicial system often seems so complicated and slow that many citizens feel alienated from their government. Small-claims courts have an opposite psychological effect and serve a worthwhile purpose in showing that the government can be responsive to their own small problems.

Small-claims courts should not be confused with the Court of Claims, created in 1855 solely to try claims against the United States government. The United States government is not a party in a small-claims court. Small-claims disputes are between two private citizens in a civil matter. *—William H. Burnside*

See also Civil procedure; Contract law; Equity; Evidence, rules of; Judicial review; Judicial system, U.S.; Litigation; Standards of proof.

BIBLIOGRAPHY

Two sources that deal exclusively with small-claims courts are Robert L. Spurrier, *Inexpensive Justice: Self-Representation in the Small Claims Court* (3d ed. Port Washington, N.Y.: Associated Faculty Press, 1983), and Steven Weller and John C. Ruhnka, *Practical Observations on the Small Claims Court* (Williamsburg, Va.: National Center for State Courts, 1979). Any standard law dictionary, such as Henry A. Black, *Black's Law Dictionary* (5th ed. St. Paul, Minn.: West, 1979), gives succinct definitions of relevant terms. Other useful works are Bernard Schwartz, *The Law in America: A History* (New York: McGraw-Hill, 1974), and Alexander H. Pekelis, *Law and Social Action*, edited by Milton R. Konvitz (New York: Da Capo Press, 1970).

Smith Act

DATE: June 28, 1940

DEFINITION: Officially known as the Alien Registration Act, the Smith Act required aliens to register with the U.S. government and made it a crime to advocate overthrowing American governments by force

SIGNIFICANCE: The Smith Act became the U.S. government's primary legal tool for attacking the American Communist Party during the early years of the Cold War

As World War II approached, fears of foreign-inspired subversive activity grew in the United States. Concerned especially that the buildup of American defenses might be threatened by sabotage, Congress reacted by passing the Alien Registration Act, which came to be more generally known as the Smith Act for its major proponent, Congressman Howard W. Smith of Virginia.

The Smith Act had two major thrusts. The first sought greater control over aliens living in the United States. Under the act, aliens had to register with the government, be fingerprinted, carry identity cards, and report yearly. (The registration requirement was dropped in 1982.) Those involved in what were regarded as subversive activities could be deported. The other major provisions of the act were directed at disloyal activities. These made it a crime for anyone to advocate the overthrow of the federal government or other American governments by force or violence, to enter a conspiracy to advocate such a course of action, or to become a knowing member of such a group. Penalties for those convicted under the act included a ten-thousand-dollar fine, up to ten years in prison, or both.

Though a wartime measure, the Smith Act was used relatively little during World War II. As postwar tension between the United States and the Soviet Union developed into Cold War, however, the act came to the fore as concerns about the possibility of Communist subversion in the United States rose. By the late 1940's, there were increasing concerns about the activities of members of the American Communist Party and sympathetic groups, and charges of communist penetration of the government were increasingly made. The administration of President Harry S Truman was charged with being slow to meet the communist challenge at home. Partly in response, the Truman Administration used the Smith Act to attack the party's organization.

In 1948 Eugene Dennis and ten other communist leaders were arrested and charged under the act. They were convicted and sentenced to prison. They appealed, arguing that the Smith Act was an unconstitutional violation of the First Amendment's protection of free expression. Their appeal was denied by the Supreme Court in 1951.

Use of the Smith Act continued during the 1950's. Altogether, more than 140 arrests were made under the act. Later Supreme Court decisions in *Yates v. United States* (1957) and *Brandenburg v. Ohio* (1969) broadened the extent of expression protected by the First Amendment, but the Smith Act itself continued to be held as constitutional.

See also *Brandenburg v. Ohio*; Civil liberties; Clear and present danger test; Communist Party, American; *Dennis v. United States*; *Scales v. United States*; Speech and press, freedom of; *Yates v. United States*.

Smith v. Allwright

COURT: U.S. Supreme Court

DATE: Decided April 3, 1944

SIGNIFICANCE: The Supreme Court's ruling in this case overturned the all-white primary in Texas and inspired further efforts to increase African American access to the ballot

The Jim Crow system of racial segregation that characterized the Southern states in the early twentieth century was made possible by the virtual exclusion of African Americans from politics. One of the most effective tools for limiting black political influence was the all-white primary. Under this arrangement—adopted by eight Southern states—primary elections were held to be "private" affairs, outside the reach of the Fourteenth Amendment's prohibition against discriminatory state action and the Fifteenth Amendment's ban on racial discrimination in voting. The Democratic Party was so dominant in most Southern states that winning its primary was tantamount to election.

Texas witnessed the most significant legal challenges to the white primary. In 1927 the U.S. Supreme Court ruled (in *Nixon v. Herndon*) that blacks could not be barred from primaries by state law. The legislature repealed its laws on primary voting and opened the way for the state Democratic convention to ban blacks from participation in its primaries. The Supreme Court upheld this approach in *Grovey v. Townsend* (1935) as "private" action that was beyond the reach of the Constitution. In 1941, however, the Court enlarged the scope of federal jurisdiction by ruling (in *United States v. Classic*) that Congress could regulate primary elections that selected candidates for federal elections. The National Association for the Advancement of Colored People (NAACP) saw an opportunity. Sponsoring a suit by Lonnie Smith, a Houston dentist who had unsuccessfully tried to vote in the Democratic primary, the NAACP argued that the all-white primary was, in fact, a racially discriminatory and unconstitutional election.

The Supreme Court, by an 8-1 majority, agreed. Reversing its previous decision in the *Grovey* case, the Court held that the primary was part of the state's electoral machinery; Smith had been unconstitutionally denied the vote on racial grounds.

The Court's decision marked the end of the white primary. It not only enlarged the scope of voting rights held to be subject to constitutional protection but also inspired two decades of efforts to end racial discrimination in voting that culminated in the Voting Rights Act of 1965.

See also Civil rights; Civil Rights movement; Civil War Amendments; *Classic, United States v.*; *Grovey v. Townsend*; Jim Crow laws; National Association for the Advancement of Colored People (NAACP); *Nixon v. Herndon*; Vote, right to; Voting Rights Act of 1965.

Social Security system

DEFINITION: A program of pensions, other transfer payments, and medical-expense subsidies for elderly, disabled, and unemployed persons, and for certain low-income groups

SIGNIFICANCE: The Social Security system involves a heavy wage tax on most American workers, provides cash benefits and medical-expense reimbursements for most Americans over sixty years of age, and is the source of unemployment compensation and some welfare payments to low-income families

The disastrous economic depression which began in 1929 led to many political proposals for government subsidies to needy and unemployed persons. Strong support developed for a proposal by F. G. Townsend to pay a pension of two hundred dollars a month to each person sixty years of age or older who would retire and spend the money promptly. In response, in 1935, the New Deal government of President Franklin D. Roosevelt created a vast system to provide pensions for the elderly, unemployment compensation for wage earners, and support for specified categories of public assistance.

Old-Age and Disability Pensions. The Social Security Act of 1935 imposed a payroll tax, initially of 2 percent, half paid by the worker and half by the employer, in "covered" employment. A worker paying the tax could become eligible to receive a pension upon retirement at age sixty-five. Pension benefits came as a "right," earned by contributing to the system; no "means test" (particular requirement for eligibility) was imposed on the pensioners. A parallel separate program for railroad workers was created by the Railroad Retirement Act of 1937.

Because unemployment was severe in 1935, a motive for the pension program was to encourage older workers to retire and make way for younger ones. The initial structure of the system, however, primarily involved tax collections, which began in 1937; benefit payments were not scheduled to begin until 1940. This was highly deflationary and contributed to the economic recession of 1937. As a result, in 1939 the law was revised to speed the payment of pension benefits. The benefit system was extended to provide a pension supplement for a retired pensioner with dependent spouse and/or dependent children under sixteen. Should a covered worker die before

being eligible for benefits, pension benefits could also be paid to the surviving spouse and children.

The tax and benefit levels were designed to make the system financially self-supporting and, in early years, to take in more money than was paid out. The inflowing surplus was to constitute a trust fund "invested" in Treasury securities, and the interest paid on these would be added to the fund. Although the system imitated private insurance in many respects, not all workers paying tax would receive benefits. Most were required to put in ten years of covered employment. Also, benefits were not proportional to contributions. Low-wage workers received pensions that represented a higher proportion of their former wage. Persons continuing to earn wages past age sixty-five would have their pension benefits reduced.

In response to the inflation of the 1940's, benefit levels were repeatedly increased. To finance the increases, there were periodic increases in the payroll tax and in the maximum amount of wages subject to tax. By 1994 the tax was 7.65 percent on the worker and an equal amount on the employer. Initially about 60 percent of gainfully employed persons were covered, but extensions in 1950 increased coverage to about 90 percent. Persons were permitted to retire as early as age sixty-two on a reduced scale of benefits.

As of early 1995, the average Social Security retirement benefit paid to individuals was about $700 per month, and to couples, about $1,200 per month. Retirees aged sixty-five to sixty-nine were permitted to earn about $11,000 from employment without penalty. Beyond that level, each additional $3 of earnings would reduce benefits by $1. This offset applied only to income from employment, not to income from other pensions, investments, and property. Beyond age seventy, there was no limit on earnings. Social Security pensions, long exempt from federal income tax, became taxable to a limited degree beginning in 1983.

In 1956, Congress extended the pension program to cover persons unable to work for reason of disability. Unlike age,

AVERAGE MONTHLY SOCIAL SECURITY BENEFITS, 1990	
Type of Beneficiary	*Amount*
Retired workers	$603
Retired worker and wife	1,027
Disabled workers	587
Wives and husbands	298
Children of retired workers	259
Children of deceased workers	406
Children of disabled workers	164
Widowed mothers	409
Widows and widowers, nondisabled	557
Parents	482
Special benefits	167

Source: U.S. Bureau of the Census, *Statistical Abstract of the United States: 1992*. Washington, D.C.: U.S. Government Printing Office, 1992.

disability is a relatively arbitrary concept, and the program has run into problems determining whether a person is really unable to work or simply would prefer not to. The pension program is known by the acronym OASDI (Old Age, Survivors, and Disability Insurance).

Medicare. In 1965 the retirement program was given a major extension with the creation of the Medicare program to subsidize medical expenses incurred by persons receiving Social Security retirement pensions. Medicare benefits are similar to those under private medical insurance in that each beneficiary is free to go to a physician of choice for treatment. A portion of the resulting bill is paid by Social Security. For part A, covering hospital expenses, the wage tax was increased to cover some of the costs. For part B, covering physicians' fees, an insurance premium was levied on the prospective beneficiaries. Individuals are also required to absorb some costs through deductibles and copayments. One consequence of the program was greatly increased consumption of medical services by the elderly. The government's expenditures increased far more than had been predicted. By the early 1990's, three-fourths of part B expenses came from general Treasury revenues, and only one-fourth were covered by user charges. A parallel program called Medicaid made grants to states to subsidize medical care for eligible low-income families.

Indexation. For many years, politicians were tempted to compete for votes by offering increases in Social Security benefits, a practice which eventually threatened the solvency of the system. To reduce such political pressure and yet protect retired persons against inflation, legislation in 1972 began the policy of indexing benefits. Since 1974, benefits have automatically been increased each year in proportion to the increase in the Consumer Price Index.

Unemployment Compensation. A separate section of the Social Security Act of 1935 created a system of unemployment compensation. The individual states were "encouraged" to create their own individual systems. A federal tax of 3 percent was levied on "covered" payrolls, but of this, 90 percent could be deducted from a state tax levied for unemployment benefits. All states quickly developed programs. Workers who had been employed for some minimum period of time could receive unemployment benefits if they lost their jobs. Benefits were a fraction of former wages and were normally conditional on evidence that the unemployed person was actively seeking employment. Benefits could be received only for a limited time period. Each state created a separate trust fund which received the wage tax revenues and paid benefits. Initially only about half the country's wage earners were covered, but the coverage expanded as time passed. As with OASDI benefits, unemployment compensation was paid as a matter of right and was not subject to any means test.

Public Assistance. A third element of the Social Security Act of 1935 was a program to provide grants-in-aid to state governments to subsidize their programs of public assistance—that is, "welfare" programs paid only to persons eligible on the basis of low incomes and poverty. The 1935 law designated three categories: needy elderly persons, blind persons, and families with dependent children. Over time, the Aid to Families with Dependent Children (AFDC) program became the most controversial part of the "welfare" system. Women were often denied benefits if there was an able-bodied male in the household, and critics charged that the program encouraged marital breakups and child-bearing by unmarried women. By the 1990's the number of children in poverty had risen rapidly, many of them born to young women without the financial, educational, emotional, or physiological resources to care for them. AFDC was a major target of proposals for welfare "reform." In 1994, about 4.6 million adults received AFDC payments, reflecting about 9 million children.

The public-assistance elements of Social Security underwent a major revision in 1972, when a transfer benefit called Supplemental Security Income (SSI) was created. Benefits are conditional on financial need, and the program absorbed persons receiving benefits in the previous elderly and blind categories. Persons with disabilities were also eligible. As of early 1995, an individual was eligible for SSI only if owning assets worth $2,000 or less ($3,000 for a couple), not counting home, automobile, and some other personal property. Maximum possible benefits were $458 for an individual and $687 for a couple.

Evaluations. The Social Security system was created to reduce poverty and economic insecurity, and it made major contributions to both objectives. As of 1994, more than 47 million Americans were receiving benefits under OASDI and SSI, totaling more than $300 billion per year. Elderly persons had represented a disproportionately large percentage of those in poverty in the 1950's. By the 1990's, the proportion of elderly in poverty was lower than for other age groups. The damage from unemployment was also much reduced. Critics claimed, however, that the prospect of benefits encouraged individuals to be less careful of their own financial management. Social Security was blamed for the decline in the proportion of personal income which was saved. Labor-force participation by males over sixty declined substantially. Statistical studies of unemployment benefits indicated that they enabled workers to remain unemployed somewhat longer, suggesting that they were less eager to find work.

An important criticism was that OASDI benefits involved unfair income transfers. Certainly in the early years, beneficiaries received far more from the program than they had paid in. As long as the number of retired persons was small compared with the number of workers, this was not a major problem. By the 1980's, however, the proportion of retirees was growing rapidly. Young working families were under a heavy tax burden to enable the fund to pay its promised benefits. In addition, some observers blamed Medicare and Medicaid for driving up medical costs and diverting medical resources away from working families.

The wage tax itself came in for criticism as bearing very heavily on low-income wage earners. Unlike the personal income tax, Social Security taxes make no allowance for dependent children. The heavy wage tax also decreases business incentives to hire more workers.

In the early 1990's, efforts to reduce the federal government's deficit focused attention on Medicare. Numerous proposals were advanced for health-care reform, with the aim of holding medical costs in check and slowing the rapid rise in federal spending. Other elements in Social Security were also under scrutiny as some projections showed the OASDI system losing its self-supporting character early in the twenty-first century.

One important economic benefit of the system has been the provision of a kind of fiscal "automatic stabilizer" for the economy. During a business recession, revenues from the wage taxes tend to decline, while unemployment benefits and retirement claims increase. Benefit payments raise people's disposable incomes and enable them to spend more, thus reducing the severity of the recession. Economic recovery reverses these tendencies.   —*Paul B. Trescott*

See also Aid to Families with Dependent Children (AFDC); Employee Retirement Income Security Act (ERISA); Food stamps; New Deal; Taxation and justice; Welfare state; Workers' compensation.

BIBLIOGRAPHY

The Social Security Administration publishes a vast array of useful materials, chiefly for potential beneficiaries; these include the *Annual Report* and *Handbook of Social Security* as well as numerous pamphlets. A comprehensive study (of more than 900 pages) is Robert J. Myers, *Social Security* (4th ed. Philadelphia: University of Pennsylvania Press, 1993). It deals extensively with Medicare and public assistance as well as OASDI. Myers also wrote *Indexation of Pension and Other Benefits* (Homewood, Ill.: R. D. Irwin, 1978). A readable older study which helps one understand the ideas shaping the system is Robert M. Ball, *Social Security, Today and Tomorrow* (New York: Columbia University Press, 1978). Economic issues are stressed in Zvi Bodie and Alicia H. Munnell, eds., *Pensions and the Economy: Sources, Uses, and Limitations of Data* (Philadelphia: University of Pennsylvania Press, 1992), and Jack L. VanDerhei, ed., *Search for a National Retirement Income Policy* (Homewood, Ill.: R. D. Irwin, 1987).

Socialism

DEFINITION: A philosophy based on "social" or public ownership of production and capital and on the ideal of the equality and well-being of all people

SIGNIFICANCE: Socialism has been widely discussed, but rarely applied in its pure form, since its inception in the early nineteenth century, when it was cultivated in reaction to rampant capitalism and harsh treatment of the working class

Socialist ideas arose during the Industrial Revolution in nineteenth century England, where terrible working conditions prevailed. Men, women, and children often worked sixteen hours a day, six or seven days a week, in dirty, unsafe factories for very low pay. Chief among the socialist theorists was German-born Karl Marx, who developed his theory in *Das Kapital* (1867). According to Marx, human history is the history of class struggle, and there have always been a ruling and an oppressed class. Capitalism, according to Marx, is the bourgeoisie oppressing the proletariat. Workers, he predicted, would eventually revolt and take over the means of production, leading to a "dictatorship of the proletariat." This would soon be superseded by socialism—the abolition of private ownership and a breaking down of class barriers. This would eventually lead to communism, a higher form of society characterized by the complete equality of all people without classes, politics, or possessions.

While socialism became very popular in Europe, where an unequal distribution of wealth led to such movements as the Paris Commune (1871) and the Russian Revolution (1917), it was never especially popular in the United States, where the combined elements of a vast, undeveloped continent with unlimited access to wealth and freedom, a democratic ideal where all men were already considered equal, and the absence of an entrenched aristocracy all served to alienate socialist theory, in which individuality and opportunity do not exist.

Despite this, there was a successful Socialist Party in the United States during the first part of the twentieth century; it reached its height in 1912 and 1920 with presidential candidate Eugene V. Debs. Around the same time, labor unions began to procure higher wages and better working conditions, although they were not politically active. After World War II, when communism was gaining popularity throughout impoverished Europe and Asia, the United States was enjoying an economic boom, thus insulating it from the lure of communism. The negative example of the repressive Soviet Bloc as "communism gone bad" reinforced capitalist beliefs in the United States.

See also Communist Party, American; Debs, Eugene V.; *Debs, In re*; Labor unions; Marxism; Socialist Party, American.

Socialist Party, American

DATE: Founded July, 1901

SIGNIFICANCE: This party was the most successful purely labor party in the United States

The American Socialist Party was formed in 1901 from several earlier organizations. It derived its ideology from the writings of Karl Marx and Friedrich Engels. The Socialists were closely connected to the labor movement and were successful in winning the support of several unions. Most unions, however, particularly those associated with the American Federation of Labor, did not embrace the party.

The party was successful in electing a number of local candidates, including mayors and state legislators, and several members of Congress. It never elected a governor or senator. Its most successful bid for the presidency was in 1912, when its leader, Eugene V. Debs, received almost a million votes, or 6 percent of the electorate. Although the party continued to participate in presidential elections until 1956, particularly behind perennial candidate Norman Thomas, who ran from

1932 to 1956, it never did as well again. Before 1920 members of the party were harassed and persecuted on various pretexts. Debs was imprisoned in 1917 for speaking out against American entrance into World War I. After the war, the party's left resigned and joined more radical formations, particularly the Communist Party, USA. While these more radical groups suffered police and Federal Bureau of Investigation harassment, the Socialist Party was allowed to operate freely with relatively minor official harassment.

See also American Federation of Labor-Congress of Industrial Organizations (AFL-CIO); Communist Party, American; Debs, Eugene V.; *Debs, In re*; Labor unions; Marxism; Pullman strike; *Schenck v. United States*; Socialism; Socialist Party, American.

Solem v. Helm

COURT: U.S. Supreme Court
DATE: Decided June 28, 1983
SIGNIFICANCE: In this case, the Supreme Court interpreted the Eighth Amendment's prohibition on cruel and unusual punishments to limit the ability of states to impose life sentences for multiple convictions on nonviolent felony charges

In 1979, Jerry Helm was convicted of issuing a "no account" check for one hundred dollars. This was his seventh felony conviction in South Dakota. In 1964, 1966, and 1969, he had been convicted of third-degree burglary. He had been convicted of obtaining money under false pretenses in 1972, and in 1973 he was convicted of grand larceny. Moreover, his third drunk-driving conviction in 1975 counted as a felony offense. All the offenses were nonviolent, none involved personal, physical victimization of another person, and alcohol was a contributing factor in each case. Although the maximum penalty for writing a "no account" check would have been five years in prison and a five-thousand-dollar fine, Helm was sentenced to life imprisonment without possibility of parole because anyone convicted of four felonies under South Dakota law may be given the maximum penalty for a class 1 felony—even if he or she has never committed any class 1 felonies. The purpose of the tough sentencing law was to put habitual offenders away forever so that they could not commit additional offenses.

On appeal, the South Dakota Supreme Court rejected Helm's claim that the sentence of life without parole for a nonviolent offense constituted cruel and unusual punishment in violation of the Eighth Amendment. The U.S. court of appeals disagreed and invalidated Helm's sentence. When the U.S. Supreme Court reviewed the case, a narrow five-member majority agreed with Helm's argument.

In a prior decision (*Rummel v. Estelle*, 1980), the U.S. Supreme Court had permitted Texas to impose a life sentence on a man who, over the course of a decade, was convicted of three separate theft offenses in which he stole less than $250. The Supreme Court regarded the *Helm* case as different because South Dakota, unlike Texas, did not permit people with life sentences to become eligible for parole. Thus the realistic impact of Helm's sentence was much harsher than that of life

sentences imposed in other states where prisoners typically earn an eventual parole release if they exhibit good behavior. The Court decided that Helm's punishment was disproportionate to his crimes because sentences of life without parole are typically reserved for people convicted of first-degree murder, kidnapping, or treason—not for people who commit nonviolent offenses involving modest amounts of money.

The importance of *Solem v. Helm* is that the Supreme Court placed limitations on the ability of the states to impose severe sentences on people convicted of multiple nonviolent felonies. The case also reinforced the Court's view that the Eighth Amendment contains an implicit requirement that sentences cannot be disproportionate to the crimes committed.

See also Bill of Rights, U.S.; Cruel and unusual punishment; *Harmelin v. Michigan*; *Rummel v. Estelle*; Sentencing.

Solicitation to commit a crime

DEFINITION: A command or request to a third person to commit a crime
SIGNIFICANCE: The effort to engage another person in crime, regardless of whether the completed crime is committed, is itself the substantive crime of solicitation

Various state statutes or judicial decisions consider sufficient for solicitation a statement that does any of the following: advises, commands, counsels, encourages, entices, entreats, importunes, incites, induces, instigates, procures, requests, solicits, or urges. The words themselves are sufficient, and the act of asking suffices.

By the early 1800's, English and American courts recognized solicitation as a misdemeanor under the common law. Most state statutes in the twentieth century limited solicitation to felonies; some include serious misdemeanors.

One of the "inchoate" or incomplete crimes, together with criminal attempt and conspiracy, the crime of solicitation is completed even if the person solicited refuses to cooperate or repudiates the proposal, and regardless of whether payment or reward is offered, accepted, or refused. Evidence of an offer of payment or reward, however, can be important in proving solicitation. Furthermore, solicitation occurs even if the request was not understood or if the person solicited was incapable of committing the offense.

See also Accessory, accomplice, and aiding and abetting; Attempt to commit a crime; Conspiracy; Contributing to the delinquency of a minor; Entrapment.

Solicitor general of the United States

DEFINITION: The fourth-ranking member of the Department of Justice and the primary legal spokesperson for the executive branch of the government
SIGNIFICANCE: The solicitor general plays a key role in the appellate process, since he or she determines which cases the government will appeal to the Supreme Court and mediates interdepartmental disputes on matters of legal policy

The office of solicitor general was created by Congress as part of the Department of Justice in 1870. Its purpose was to provide the attorney general and by extension the executive branch with legal advice. The solicitor general is the only official required by statute to be "learned in the law." In the modern Department of Justice the solicitor general is a presidential appointee who ranks fourth in authority behind the attorney general, the deputy attorney general, and the associate attorney general. The solicitor general is primarily responsible for deciding what federal cases the government will appeal to the Supreme Court. These decisions are based on a number of factors, including the "ripeness" of the issue, the Court's crowded docket, policy considerations, and the government's legal resources.

The solicitor general determines the government's position and argues the case before the Supreme Court if the Court accepts the case. The Supreme Court accepts about 75 percent of cases in which the solicitor general is a party or an *amicus curiae* (friend of the court) as compared with fewer than 5 percent of other petitioners. This makes the solicitor general the "gatekeeper" affecting the flow of cases to the Supreme Court. The Court grants the solicitor general special privileges with regard to court procedures in recognition of this role as the government's attorney. At times, the Court will ask the solicitor general for an opinion on complicated cases. By tradition, the Court expects the solicitor general not to be narrowly partisan but to take a longer view of issues and to do so with candor. This special relationship with the Supreme Court has led the solicitor general to be informally called the "tenth justice."

Because of this dual role as representative of the executive branch and counselor to the Court, solicitor generals have taken an independent stance and viewed their primary loyalty to be to the idea of law and justice. This has led to tension with the executive branch. For example, Rex Lee, solicitor general from 1981 to 1985, refused on more than one occasion to put forth arguments advanced by the Reagan Administration if he thought they were weak or inappropriate. This refusal to be, as he put it, "pamphleteer general," finally led to his resignation. His successor, Charles Fried (1985-1989), was less reluctant to ask the Court to reverse matters for political reasons, which caused him to lose credibility and effectiveness before the Court. Independence remains a vital characteristic of the office and makes it a crucial component of the American justice system. Solicitor generals have included William Howard Taft (1890-1892), John Davis (1912-1918), Charles Evans Hughes (1929-1930), Stanley Reed (1935-1938), Archibald Cox (1961-1965), Thurgood Marshall (1965-1967), and Robert Bork (1973-1977).

See also Attorney general of the United States; Hughes, Charles Evans; Justice, U.S. Department of; Marshall, Thurgood; Supreme Court of the United States; Taft, William Howard.

Southern Christian Leadership Conference (SCLC)

DATE: Founded 1957

SIGNIFICANCE: The SCLC was one of the major organizations instrumental in the Civil Rights movement in the American South in the 1950's and 1960's; the organization was based

in Atlanta, Georgia, and led by Martin Luther King, Jr., from its formation until his assassination in 1968

The Southern Christian Leadership Conference originated in a bus boycott organized in 1955 to protest segregation in Montgomery, Alabama. Martin Luther King, Jr., a young minister, led the Montgomery Improvement Association, which spearheaded the boycott. His leadership marked the emergence of African American ministers as organizers in the Civil Rights movement. King and other black ministers became increasingly involved in the Civil Rights movement.

The SCLC was formed in December, 1957, as a result of this church-led protest movement and others that had occurred in Southern communities. The SCLC was distinctly different from the National Association for the Advancement of Colored People (NAACP), long the premiere organization involved in the struggle for the rights of African Americans. In contrast to the NAACP, the SCLC was confined to the South. It did not have individual memberships, in part so that it would not be seen as competing with the NAACP. Instead, it was an umbrella organization bringing together local affiliates in a loose alliance. Each affiliate paid the SCLC a fee of $25, in return receiving a certificate of affiliation signed by King. Each affiliate had the right to send five delegates to the group's annual meeting. Most affiliates were composed of African American ministers and their churches. At least two-thirds of the thirty-three members of the governing board were ministers, primarily Baptist. Northern activists, including Bayard Rustin and Stanley Levison, assisted the SCLC in solving problems of organizational cohesion, financial stability, and political direction. The SCLC, however, is identified primarily with King as its leader.

Methods. The approach used by the SCLC was a combination of grassroots activism and political strategy. Its major campaigns concentrated on the use of nonviolent direct action techniques such as marches, demonstrations, boycotts, and civil disobedience to protest segregation and discrimination. Politically, the SCLC worked within the system to change laws.

The organization's initial project, in 1958, was a voter registration drive in the South. As the 1960's began, other groups began launching protest movements of various types. In 1960, African American students launched sit-in demonstrations at lunch counters to protest segregation, and in 1961, the Congress of Racial Equality initiated Freedom Rides on interstate buses. These protests served as training in the use of nonviolent protest methods. In 1961, the SCLC became involved in mass nonviolent demonstrations against segregation in Albany, Georgia, learning how to mobilize the African American community in the process. Although the Albany campaign failed, the SCLC learned the importance of having a strong local base, a clear chain of command, and a coherent strategy. In 1963, the SCLC was successful in desegregating facilities in Birmingham, Alabama. Publicity from that movement, including televised coverage of police officers beating black demonstrators, was a major impetus to passage of the Civil Rights Act of 1964. In 1965, the SCLC was involved in a

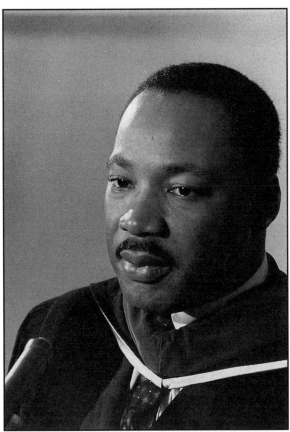

Martin Luther King, Jr., rose to national prominence as leader of the SCLC. (Library of Congress)

voting rights campaign in Selma, Alabama. This led directly to passage of the Voting Rights Act of 1965, one of the major achievements of the Civil Rights movement.

After 1965, the SCLC began to look beyond the South. A 1966 attempt to end housing segregation in Chicago failed, in part because the SCLC lacked a base outside the South. King and the SCLC also began to focus on problems of poverty following urban riots in 1964. This effort culminated in the Poor People's Campaign. King was assassinated on April 4, 1968, when he went to Memphis, Tennessee, to support striking sanitation workers as part of his Poor People's Campaign. The campaign continued, and the planned march to Washington, D.C., took place under the leadership of the Reverend Ralph Abernathy. The SCLC held demonstrations in the nation's capital in May and June of 1968.

Following King's death, Abernathy became president of the SCLC. The SCLC subsequently declined in importance. Abernathy lacked King's leadership abilities, and following the major achievements of the 1960's, support for the Civil Rights movement as a whole diminished. In the 1970's, the SCLC faded as an effective force in achieving social and economic progress for African American and poor people. In 1973, Abernathy announced his resignation as president of the SCLC.

Assessment. In 1986, King's birthday was made a national holiday in recognition of his civil rights work. King is the leader most clearly identified with the Civil Rights movement. Passage of the Voting Rights Act of 1965 was one of the notable achievements of the SCLC. That act resulted in an increase in African American voter registration from 2 million to approximately 3.8 million in ten years. This in turn led to a large increase in the numbers of African American elected officials and other elected officials responsive to the needs of the African American community. Although that community continued to face problems, the efforts of the SCLC aided black Americans in securing equal rights within the American system of justice. The SCLC later concentrated its efforts on issues involving African American families and voter registration in the South. —*William V. Moore*

See also Civil Rights Act of 1964; Civil Rights movement; Congress of Racial Equality (CORE); King, Martin Luther, Jr.; National Association for the Advancement of Colored People (NAACP); Segregation, *de facto* and *de jure*; Student Nonviolent Coordinating Committee (SNCC); Voting Rights Act of 1965.

BIBLIOGRAPHY

Numerous books document the contributions of King and various civil rights groups. Among them are Taylor Branch, *Parting the Waters: America in the King Years, 1954-63* (New York: Simon & Schuster, 1988); Adam Fairclough, *To Redeem the Soul of America: The Southern Christian Leadership Conference and Martin Luther King, Jr.* (Athens: University of Georgia Press, 1987); David J. Garrow, *Bearing the Cross: Martin Luther King, Jr., and the Southern Christian Leadership Conference* (New York: William Morrow, 1986); Stephen B. Oates, *Let the Trumpet Sound: The Life of Martin Luther King, Jr.* (New York: Harper and Row, 1982); and Robert Weisbrot, *Freedom Bound: A History of America's Civil Rights Movement* (New York: W. W. Norton, 1990).

Special weapons and tactics (SWAT) teams

DEFINITION: Teams of police officers specially trained to handle situations beyond the control of normally equipped and trained police officers

SIGNIFICANCE: SWAT teams are most appropriately used in cases involving hostages, protection of public figures, or other extremely volatile and unpredictable situations that call for quick and effective response to minimize impact and potential damage in the community

The mission of a normal special weapons and tactics (SWAT) team is to respond to situations considered beyond the capability of regularly equipped and trained police officers. These situations are rarely predictable, and the response of a SWAT team is critical in bringing them under control as quickly as possible. There are several types of events that call for SWAT teams. These include situations involving hostages, protecting dignitaries or other public officials, searching for escaped criminals known to be extremely dangerous, countering snipers in riot-control situations, and serving warrants on extremely dangerous individuals. Other conditions may also arise in which the senior leadership in a community may desire the presence of a SWAT team even if no specific threat exists at the time.

The size of SWAT teams varies as much as the mission and the departmental leadership style. Normally, individual SWAT team cells range in size from four to eight people, with the capability of building larger teams or adding individuals with specialized skills. Individual applicants must be capable of handling intensely stressful situations, have above-average intelligence, be physically fit and psychologically sound, and be capable of taking a leadership role if necessary. SWAT units require extensive training on a continual basis to maintain a high degree of proficiency in individual and team skills. This requirement can cause some controversy in smaller police departments, whose budgetary restrictions can be quite severe. As a result, many municipalities continually reassess the necessity of maintaining a standing SWAT team. Many municipalities have moved toward accepting a form of umbrella coverage from counties or from larger nearby municipalities should the need arise.

Armament is considerable, ranging from individual sidearms to shotguns and automatic weapons and sometimes even to heavier armor-piercing weaponry. Command, control, and communications are critical in SWAT team operations. Throughout any situation where a SWAT team is utilized, police and political authorities up and down the chain of command must be able to communicate quickly with the team and its individual members. While the capabilities of SWAT teams are significant in terms of potential firepower, their primary function is not to use their power but rather to rely on negotiation or persuasion, using deadly or lethal force only as a last resort.

See also Federal Bureau of Investigation (FBI); Police; Sheriff; State police; Terrorism.

Speech and press, freedom of

DEFINITION: The right to speak, write, publish, or distribute expressive materials without government censorship or unjustifiable regulations

SIGNIFICANCE: Freedom of expression, guaranteed by the First and Fourteenth Amendments, is recognized as a fundamental human right essential to individual autonomy, constitutional democracy, the growth of knowledge, and the possibility of social change

The First Amendment, which became law in 1791, prohibits Congress from "abridging the freedom of speech or of the press." It is clear that this clause was never intended to prohibit all restrictions on oral and written expressions, for some verbal expressions have traditionally been recognized as crimes, such as offers of bribes, perjury, and agreements for conspiracy. Even when the content of expression is protected, moreover, government has a legitimate interest in making reasonable regulations regarding time, manner, and place, such as prohibitions against the delivery of speeches in libraries and hospitals. Accordingly, when courts examine a limitation on expression, they must first decide whether the category of speech or press content has constitutional protection. If the category is

protected, courts must then decide whether other compelling interests justify regulations.

Original Understanding and Early History. In the period when the First Amendment was produced, freedom of speech and press in common law meant the absence of governmental restraint prior to the event, but after the event government had the right to punish an expression of blasphemy, immorality, or seditious libel (verbal attacks on public authority). William Blackstone's writings were especially influential in promoting this perspective. In 1789, James Madison wanted to go beyond the common-law understanding of free expression when he proposed his original version of what became the First Amendment, but Congress modified his wording to make the amendment consistent with the standards of the day. Congress also failed to approve Madison's proposal for an amendment that would have guaranteed freedom of the press in the states.

The first controversy about the meaning of the speech and press clause in the First Amendment occurred when Congress passed the Sedition Act of 1798, imposing criminal penalties for "any false, scandalous writing against the government of the United States." The Federalists who dominated the national government argued that the statute was constitutional because there was no prior restraint, and some Supreme Court justices were involved in prosecutions under the statute. Madison and other Jeffersonian Republicans, in contrast, argued that the First Amendment prohibited the federal government from punishing people for seditious libel, although they recognized that state legislatures might pass such laws. After Thomas Jefferson became president in 1801, he encouraged the states to prosecute Federalist editors who attacked his administration.

Into the nineteenth century, the Blackstonian interpretations of free expression continued to be commonly accepted, as exemplified in Joseph Story's commentary of 1833 and in Thomas Cooley's treatise of 1868. Still, there was a growing sentiment against laws punishing seditious libel, reflecting a more liberal appreciation of the value of unrestrained political debate. Congress refused to support President Andrew Jackson's proposal to prohibit abolitionist materials from the mails, and many Americans were appalled at the extent to which southern states criminalized speeches and writings that attacked the institution of slavery.

The Fourteenth Amendment. After the Civil War, a common theme in the drafting and ratification of the Fourteenth Amendment was that southern laws prohibiting abolitionist discourse had violated American principles of free government. Although it is not clear whether the intent of the amendment was to make all the Bill of Rights applicable to the states, there was a general understanding that speech and press freedom was one of the "privileges or immunities" of American citizens. Clearly this freedom was not intended to extend to pornographic materials, for the same Congress that passed the Fourteenth Amendment also made it illegal to transport such materials in the mails or through customs.

For many decades the Supreme Court interpreted the Fourteenth Amendment so that the Bill of Rights was not binding

SELECT COURT CASES RELATED TO FREEDOM OF EXPRESSION

Date	Medium	Case Name	Result
1868	books	*Regina v. Hicklin*	First legal standard for obscenity: tendency to corrupt minds of those most susceptible.
1919	circulars	*Abrams v. United States*	Conviction for conspiracy to advocate resistance to war affirmed. In dissent Justice Holmes cited "argument from truth": Truth can be found only in the marketplace of ideas.
1931	newspaper	*Near v. Minnesota*	State law allowing "prior restraint" of newspaper unconstitutional.
1934	books	*United States v. One Book Entitled Ulysses*	Ending of Hicklin rule; entire work judged by dominant effect on average people.
1942	speech	*Chaplinsky v. New Hampshire*	Obscenity and insulting or fighting words unprotected by the First Amendment.
1952	film	*Joseph Burstyn, Inc. v. Wilson*	Film could not be banned as sacrilegious; film is expressive communication protected by First Amendment.
1957	books, circulars, ads	*Roth v. United States*	First set of standards to determine obscenity beyond First Amendment protection.
1958	speech	*Speiser v. Randall*	Mandatory loyalty oath a violation of free speech.
1961	film	*Times Film Corp. v. Chicago*	Screening prior to permit not void as prior restraint.
1963	books	*Bantam Books v. Sullivan*	Procedure used to police books for obscenity violates First and Fourteenth Amendments.
1964	film	*Jacobellis v. Ohio*	Film found not obscene under *Roth* standard.
1965	film	*Freedman v. Maryland*	Procedural requirements in case of film censorship unconstitutional; this case terminated film censorship as such in the United States.
1966	book	*Memoirs v. Massachusetts*	Refined the *Roth* standard; *Fanny Hill* found not obscene.
1968	symbolic speech	*United States v. O'Brien*	Burning draft card not protected symbolic speech; interfered with valid government interests.
1971	words on clothing	*Cohen v. California*	Epithet printed on jacket did not constitute obscenity but was protected speech: "One man's vulgarity is another man's lyric."
1971	newspaper	*New York Times Co. v. United States*	Prior restraint unjustified in Pentagon Papers case.
1973	film	*Paris Adult Theatre I. v. Slaton*	Companion case to *Miller*, below; material found to be hard-core pornography not protected under First Amendment.
1973	books, photos, and brochures	*Miller v. California*	Conviction of obscenity upheld; three-pronged test for obscenity established, overruling previous standards.
1974	film	*Jenkins v. Georgia*	Application of *Miller*; film *Carnal Knowledge* not obscene.
1975	film	*Ernoznik v. Jacksonville*	Ordinance prohibiting film with nude scenes at drive-in unconstitutional.
1982	film	*New York v. Ferber*	Statute prohibiting sexual performance of children upheld; child pornography passed *Miller* test.
1982	books	*Board of Education v. Pico*	Removal of books from school libraries on grounds of being anti-Christian, anti-Semitic, and "just plain filthy" violated terms of First Amendment.
1989	symbolic speech	*Texas v. Johnson*	Burning American flag considered protected free speech.
1990	dance	*Miller et al. v. Civil City of South Bend*	Nude dancing not obscene; protected expression under First Amendment.
1991	dance/grants	*Bella Lewitzky Dance Foundation v. Frohnmayer*	Decency oath unconstitutional condition for grant funds.
1991	performance art/grants	*Karen Finley et al. v. NEA and Frohnmayer*	Denial of grant funds based on decency provision in violation of First Amendment.

on the states. This was one of the results of the Court's narrow construction of the privileges or immunities clause in the *Slaughterhouse Cases* (1873), and as late as 1922 the Court reaffirmed that the First Amendment was applicable only to the federal government. In *Gitlow v. New York* (1925), however, the Court used the approach of substantive due process to conclude that the due process clause incorporated First Amendment principles of free speech and press. At the time, this break with the Court's precedents did not appear very significant because of the Court's conservative interpretation of protected expression, but the situation would change dramatically as the Court progressively took a more liberal perspective.

Advocacy of Illegal Acts. Shortly after the United States declared war on Germany in 1917, Congress passed the Espionage Act, which, among other things, provided criminal sanctions for antiwar propaganda intended to cause disloyalty in the armed forces or to obstruct recruiting efforts. The Sedition Act of 1918 added additional restrictions on the right of dissent. About two thousand people were prosecuted under these laws, with most accused of using words that seemed to encourage illegal acts, such as resistance to the draft. By 1925 some two-thirds of the states had laws similar to the federal statutes.

Following the war, the Supreme Court had to decide whether convictions under the various espionage and sedition laws violated the First and Fourteenth Amendments. In a series of decisions, including *Schenck v. United States* (1919) and *Gitlow v. New York* (1925), the Court's majority upheld almost all the laws and convictions, usually basing its decisions on the "bad tendency doctrine," allowing government to prosecute words that logically led to forbidden actions. The two liberal justices of the period, Oliver Wendell Holmes, Jr., and Louis D. Brandeis, dissented in many of the cases. It was in this context that Holmes invented his famous "clear and present danger" test, which allowed punishment only for speech-acts such as falsely shouting "Fire!" in a theater.

The freedom to dissent really began with *Fiske v. Kansas* (1927), when the Supreme Court overturned the conviction of a socialist found guilty for verbally attacking the American government without any clear advocacy of illegal action. During the 1940's, an increasingly liberal Court maintained that First Amendment freedoms enjoyed a "preferred position," meaning that they were at the top of a hierarchy of constitutional values. With World War II and the Cold War, however, fear of fascism and communism created a more restrictive climate. The Smith Act of 1940 made it a crime to advocate or to belong to an organization that advocated the violent overthrow of the government, and the Internal Security Act of 1950 required members of the Communist Party to register with the Department of Justice. In *Dennis v. United States* (1951), the Court emphasized that a real threat of communism justified both statutes according to the clear and present danger test.

Within a few years, however, the Court again began to adopt a more libertarian position. In *Yates v. United States* (1957), it applied a balancing test in which First Amendment rights were weighed against society's right to self-preservation, and it made a distinction between advocacy of abstract beliefs (protected by the First Amendment) and the actual incitement to commit illegal acts (not protected). The *Yates* distinction between abstract doctrine and actions made it very difficult for prosecutors to obtain convictions. In *Brandenburg v. Ohio* (1969), the Court increased the difficulty when it ruled that government may not punish the advocacy of illegal action except where such advocacy is directed at "producing imminent lawless action and is likely to incite or produce such action."

Libel. Threats of punishment for defamation of character by spoken word (slander) or by written word (libel) clearly place a major restraint on the freedom of expression. In the twentieth century, cases of criminal libel have been very rare, although some states retained laws with criminal penalties for libel against groups. In *Beauharnais v. Illinois* (1952), the Court upheld the conviction of an outspoken leader of a white racist organization, based on a statute that outlawed defamatory or derogatory publications about "any race, color, creed, or religion." While *Beauharnais* has never been formally overturned, almost all the Court's subsequent decisions appear inconsistent with such enforcements of criminal libel laws.

Government always has indirect involvement in private libel suits, because laws determine the rules under which suits occur. There is a special challenge to freedom of expression when public officials seek damages for libel against private persons, for it is often impossible to criticize a governmental action without also criticizing a public official. Confronting this issue in *New York Times Co. v. Sullivan* (1964), the Supreme Court ruled that officials may win libel suits only if they can show "actual malice," which means that a defamatory statement is known to be false or is made with a "reckless disregard" for the truth. In subsequent cases, the *New York Times* standard was extended to libel against "public persons" and to persons appearing in stories of "public or general interest." In 1974, the Court announced that a "private individual" must prove only that a writer or publisher was negligent in failing to use normal care while reporting a story.

Doctrine of "No Prior Restraint." The common-law doctrine on prior restraint applied primarily to a system of administrative control exercised by licensers and censors, but the Supreme Court took a broad construction of the doctrine in the case of *Near v. Minnesota* (1931), when it voted 5 to 4 to strike down a statute that allowed injunction relief to stop any "malicious, scandalous and defamatory" publication. The Court's majority was willing to allow injunctions only in an emergency situation, such as the need to prevent the publication of critical wartime information that would help the enemy.

During the Vietnam War, a researcher sneaked classified documents to American newspapers, and President Richard M. Nixon's administration sought a restraining order to prevent publication, alleging a need to protect national security. In *New York Times Co. v. United States* (1971), the Court voted 6 to 3 to deny the government's request, with the rationale that

Evangelist Jerry Falwell sued Hustler *magazine publisher Larry Flynt for libel because of a cartoon depiction of him in the magazine; in 1984 the jury found Flynt not guilty of libel but, in an unusual move, held that Flynt should pay Falwell $200,000 in damages nevertheless.* (AP/Wide World Photos)

the government had failed to show that publication would pose a significant threat to national security. The implication of this and other cases was that a court might prevent a publication in very exceptional circumstances, but that anyone seeking the restraining order would be required to overcome a rigorous burden of proof.

Fair Trials and Free Press. In the 1960's, the Supreme Court was faced with the difficult issue of whether inflammatory pretrial and trial publicity can make it impossible for a defendant to receive a fair trial as guaranteed by the Sixth Amendment. Beginning in 1959, the Court overturned several criminal convictions on the grounds of prejudicial publicity. In the case of *Sheppard v. Maxwell* (1966), the Court instructed trial judges to take remedial measures such as changing the venue, carefully screening out prospective jurors with fixed opinions, and controlling information released to the press by witnesses, the police, and counsel. Some judges then issued restraining orders (called "gag orders") on what the press might report before the trial, and the press objected to the practice as an unconstitutional prior restraint. In *Nebraska Press Association v. Stuart* (1976), the Court struck down such an order as a violation of press freedom, and although the Court did not rule that gag orders were unconstitutional in all circumstances, the decision made them extremely difficult to justify.

Some trial judges then tried to minimize the problem of pretrial publicity by denying press representatives' access to pretrial hearings and even to trials. Confronted with this approach, the Court was badly divided and issued several contradictory decisions, but in *Richmond Newspapers, Inc. v. Virginia* (1980) the Court held that criminal trials must be open to both the press and the public except under exceptional circumstances. The decision marked the first time the Court recognized a First Amendment right of access for the purpose of news reporting. Six years later, the Court extended the right to all pretrial hearings except when there was a "substantial probability" that limiting access was essential to a fair trial—a very difficult hurdle to overcome.

Symbolic Expression and Expressive Conduct. The framers of the First Amendment wanted to protect communication by spoken and written language (often called "pure speech"), but in the twentieth century the Supreme Court extended protection to communication with nonverbal symbols and "speech-plus-conduct." The first such case was *Stromberg v. California* (1931), when the Court struck down a state law that prohibited the displaying of red flags as symbols of protest. In a similar case, *Tinker v. Des Moines Independent Community School District* (1969), the Court upheld the constitutional right of students in the public schools to wear black armbands in symbolic protest against American foreign policy in Vietnam. Yet symbolic expression involves complexities not found in pure speech. In *United States v. O'Brien* (1968), for example, the Court ruled that the burning of draft cards to protest foreign policy was not a protected form of expression. When speech and acts are combined, the Court reasoned, important governmental interests can justify "incidental limitations on First Amendment freedoms."

For many Americans, the most unacceptable form of symbolic expression is disrespectful treatment of the American flag. The Court declined to deal directly with the constitutionality of criminal sanctions against flag desecration until the case of *Texas v. Johnson* (1989), at which time the Court voted 5 to 4 that the burning of a flag communicated a message that was protected by the First Amendment. The following year, the Court overturned a federal statute prohibiting flag burning. In an interesting contrast, in *Barnes v. Glen Theatre, Inc.* (1991) the Court voted 5 to 4 that the erotic message contained in nude dancing was not a protected form of symbolic expression.

Fighting Words. In an often-quoted decision, *Chaplinsky v. New Hampshire* (1942), the Supreme Court determined that several categories of utterances are "no essential part of any exposition of ideas" and were "of such slight social value as a step to truth that any benefit that may be derived from them is clearly outweighed by the social interest in order and morality." Based on this premise, the *Chaplinsky* decision upheld the conviction of an individual for using "fighting words"—face-to-face insults or epithets. While continuing to hold that the category of fighting words was not protected, the Court applied the category so narrowly so as almost to eliminate its use in criminal law. Also, the Court carefully insisted that the category of fighting words is not to be confused with "offensive" or "shocking" speech, which is protected by the First Amendment.

In the 1980's, a number of states, communities, and universities tried to expand on the "fighting words" exception by prohibiting various kinds of "hate speech." Lower courts overturned many such regulations as overly broad and as having a chilling effect on public debate. In *R.A.V. v. City of St. Paul* (1992), the Supreme Court unanimously overturned a city ordinance that made it a crime to use a symbol such as a burning cross or a swastika in a way likely to arouse anger or alarm "on the basis of race, color, creed, religion, or gender." In contrast, the Court in *Wisconsin v. Mitchell* (1993) upheld a hate-crime statute that provided for enhanced penalties for those convicted of physical assault when victims were chosen because of a racial, gender, or ethnic bias. The Court reasoned that the law punished only unprotected conduct and that traditionally many factors might be considered in the determination of a proper sentence. Libertarians disagreed with the decision because the law meant that the defendant's words would be examined to determine the existence of a bias, implying punishment for expression of opinions.

Pornography and Obscenity. There is no evidence that the First Amendment was originally understood to protect materials deemed pornographic or indecent. Although the matter was usually left up to the states, between 1842 and 1956 Congress passed some twenty antipornography statutes applicable to the mails and to customs, with the oppressive Comstock Law of 1873 providing prison terms up to five years for a first offense. Courts often enforced the laws with the common-law test from *Queen v. Hicklin* (1868), a test that considered the effect of isolated passages on the most susceptible person in society.

The Supreme Court has held that obscenity is not protected by the first amendment but has made the definition of obscenity strict. (James L. Shaffer)

The case of *Roth v. United States* (1957) represented the seventh time that the Supreme Court approved of federal prosecutions of pornography. Although the *Roth* decision concluded that "obscenity" was not protected by the First Amendment, it repudiated the Hicklin test and endorsed a less restrictive test that employed contemporary standards to determine whether the dominant theme of the work as a whole appealed to "prurient interests." In a 1966 case dealing with the 1749 novel *Fanny Hill*, the Court took the libertarian position that government might proscribe only materials that are "utterly without redeeming social value." After retreating from this view, the Court in *Miller v. California* (1973) finally appeared to reach a consensus on a three-part test: The dominant theme must be to the prurient interest; state law must precisely define the patently offensive sexual material which is proscribed; and the work as a whole must lack "serious literary, artistic, political, and scientific value." The Miller test allowed government to make so-called "hard-core pornography" illegal, but it protected R-rated films such as *Carnal Knowledge* (1971).

Because "child pornography" appeared to promote the sexual exploitation of children, in *New York v. Ferber* (1982) the Court ruled that materials depicting sexual conduct of children did not have First Amendment protection even if the materials did not satisfy the *Miller* definition of obscenity.

Broadcasting Regulations. Radio, television, and other electronic media using a limited number of transmission frequencies have long been subject to regulations not applicable to the print media. In 1934 Congress created the Federal Communications Commission (FCC) to award broadcasting licenses and to enforce laws and rules about programming. The "fairness doctrine" established by Congress in 1959 required the presentation of both sides of controversial issues and the opportunity for persons to reply to attacks. When a station challenged the doctrine in *Red Lion Broadcasting Co. Inc. v. Federal Communications Commission* (1969), the Court ruled the regulation to be consistent with the First Amendment, justified by the special demands of a scarce public resource. President Ronald Reagan, however, opposed the fairness doctrine, and it was abolished by the FCC in 1987.

Many radio and television stations also disliked the statutory ban on indecent words, especially because the ban did not require the proscribed words to meet the *Miller* test for obscenity. When challenged in *Federal Communications Commission v. Pacifica Foundation* (1978), the regulation was upheld as constitutional, with the rationale emphasizing two points: first, that broadcasting is uniquely accessible to children, and second, that the ban on specific words does not censor the expression of offensive opinions. In contrast, the issue of *Sable Communications v. Federal Communications Commission* (1989) was a federal statute that totally banned both indecent and obscene telephone recordings (or "dial-a-porn"). This time, a unanimous Court overturned that portion of the law proscribing indecent speech, with the explanation that the goal of protecting children did not justify such a broad infringement on the First Amendment rights of adults.

—*Thomas T. Lewis*

See also Alien and Sedition Acts; Bill of Rights, U.S.; Censorship; Comstock Law; Constitutional law; Defamation; Incorporation doctrine; *Near v. Minnesota*; *New York Times Co. v. United States*; News media; *O'Brien, United States v.*

BIBLIOGRAPHY

A good collection of court decisions and commentary is in vol. 2 of David O'Brien, *Constitutional Law and Politics* (2d ed. New York: W. W. Norton, 1995). John D. Stevens provides a readable and concise historical account in *Shaping the First Amendment: The Development of Free Expression* (Beverly Hills, Calif.: Sage, 1982). Lucas A. Powe, Jr., presents a useful treatment in *The Fourth Estate and the Constitution: Freedom of the Press in America* (Berkeley: University of California Press, 1991). Also see Jeffery Smith, *Printers and Press Freedom* (New York: Oxford University Press, 1988). Catharine MacKinnon makes the case for regulation of pornography from a feminist perspective in *Only Words* (Cambridge, Mass.: Harvard University Press, 1993). For the libertarian view, see Edward DeGrazia, *Girls Lean Back Everywhere: The Law of Obscenity and the Assault on Genius* (New York: Random House, 1993). The most scholarly account of early seditious libel is Leonard Levy, *Emergence of a Free Press* (New York: Oxford University Press, 1985). Leonard Levy presents an excellent collection of documents in *Freedom of the Press from Zenger to Jefferson: Early American Libertarian Theories* (Indianapolis, Ind.: Bobbs-Merrill, 1966). For a useful introduction to the work of the FCC, see Lucas A. Powe, Jr., *American Broadcasting and the First Amendment* (Berkeley: University of California Press, 1987). For information about freedom of speech issues in other countries, a useful beginning point is Ilan Peleg, ed., *Patterns of Censorship Around the World* (Boulder, Colo.: Westview Press, 1993).

Speedy trial, right to

DEFINITION: The Sixth Amendment guarantees an accused person the right to a "speedy and public trial"

SIGNIFICANCE: This right is designed to prevent a person from being held in jail indefinitely or for a long period of time without having been found guilty in a trial and sentenced to imprisonment

Speed is a relative concept, so how quickly a case must come to trial to be considered "speedy" has been the subject of interpretation and debate. An accused person should not have to remain in jail for an inordinately long time without having been found guilty of a crime. On the other hand, if the accused really is guilty, then society needs to be protected from the person. Another problem with a delayed trial is the possible effect of too much elapsed time on the memories of the witnesses in the case. They may forget or reconstruct the details, move away, or even die before being able to testify in a trial.

In *Barker v. Wingo* (1972), the Supreme Court established a four-part test to try to determine whether the accused has been denied the right to a speedy trial. How long has the delay been; why was there a delay; has the defendant tried to obtain a speedy trial; and how, and to what extent, has the delay hurt the accused?

A court often allows delays of less than a year between indictment and trial. It also takes into consideration requests for postponement that originate with the defense. (It would make no sense for the defendant to cause the delay and then request dismissal for lack of a speedy trial.) On the other hand, a case may be ordered dismissed and the charges dropped because excessive postponements were requested by the prosecution while the accused was held in jail against his or her protest that a speedy trial was being denied. The U.S. Supreme Court extended the guarantee of a speedy trial to state as well as federal courts in *Klopfer v. North Carolina* (1967).

The Speedy Trial Act of 1974 requires that an arrested person be charged within thirty days of the arrest and arraigned within ten days of being charged; the trial must begin within sixty days of the arraignment. There are a few exceptions to this "counting of days," but in general, if trial does not begin within that specified period of time, the defendant can move for dismissal.

See also *Barker v. Wingo*; Bill of Rights, U.S.; Criminal procedure; *Habeas corpus*; Indictment.

Spoils system and patronage

DEFINITION: "Patronage" is the use of the constitutional power of appointment to give someone a public office as a reward for faithful political party service; when that power is abused or used in a wholesale fashion, it is described as a "spoils system," alluding to the wartime practice whereby a victorious army would loot its foe's possessions, known as the "spoils of war"

SIGNIFICANCE: The debate over the power of appointment and public policy has led to the establishment of a civil service system that is designed to add continuity to public administration without impairing the abilities of a new political leader to carry out his or her policies

For political leaders to carry out their ideas and policies, they must have loyal associates who agree with their objectives and seek to implement their plans. If leaders have subordinates disagreeing with them philosophically and working against them, it is obvious that they cannot achieve their goals or implement their policies. For that reason presidents, governors, and department heads have the power to appoint their subordinates.

There are, however, many government positions that require clerical or administrative skills and do not establish public policy. If people doing those kinds of jobs lose their positions just because they are members of a different political party, it is argued, the power of appointment is being abused. Opposing arguments include the points that public policy is affected by how vigorously it is enforced and that if lesser officials do not agree with policy objectives and "drag their feet," then the implementation of policy is impaired. In addition, the argument is made that people who worked hard to get their political party elected to office deserve to get a reward. Further, fresh faces and new personnel can sometimes add a new dynamic to an organization. (Opponents in turn counter this idea with the argument that constant changes in personnel impair the efficiency and continuity of an organization.)

Which type of person has a greater interest in achieving the goals of public policy, a career bureaucrat or a political appointee? There is not an automatic answer to this question, so for two hundred years the issue of political appointments versus civil service career bureaucracy has been debated in the United States.

Appointive powers. The power of appointment is found in the U.S. Constitution in Article II, section 2, which states that the president

shall nominate, and by and with the advice and consent of the Senate, shall appoint ambassadors, other public ministers and consuls, judges of the Supreme Court, and all other officers of the United States, whose appointments are not herein otherwise provided for, and which shall be established by law; but the Congress may by law vest the appointment of such inferior officers, as they think proper, in the President alone, in the courts of law, or in the heads of departments.

Thus there are four different methods of federal appointment: by the president alone, by the president with the advice and consent of the Senate, by courts, and by department heads. Patronage and the spoils system can be used in any of the four.

History. The election of Thomas Jefferson to the presidency in 1800 marked the first change of political parties. He made many changes when he came to office. President Andrew Jackson also did so some years later, and he was accused of instituting a "spoils system." During President Jackson's first year he removed 919 out of 10,000 government employees, and during the eight years he was in office he changed about 20 percent of government offices.

Jackson was consistent to the ideas he believed in, however; the central idea of Jacksonian democracy was belief in self-government, in the broad sense of individuals and families governing their own affairs without governmental interference. The government, they believed, should be elected by, and respond to, the people. Jacksonians did not look to gov-

President Andrew Jackson is associated with the institution of the spoils system in the early nineteenth century. (Library of Congress)

ernment for help, but they did fear that government could become a tyrant, or dictator. The Jacksonians therefore were against career bureaucrats; they wanted public officials changed with each new administration. They called this procedure "rotation in office." It was their political enemies who used the term "spoils system."

The debate continued throughout the nineteenth century until the establishment of the civil service later in the century. That system was well-known to the Progressive movement of the early twentieth century, but the federal government did not start growing to its present enormous size until the New Deal period of the 1930's. The major complaint soon was directed not toward a spoils system but to the inertia of the huge federal bureaucracy, which sometimes seems to lumber along unresponsively to either public opinion or public elections.

—William H. Burnside

See also Administrative law; Civil service system; Jacksonian democracy; Machine politics; New Deal; Political corruption; Progressivism.

BIBLIOGRAPHY

Patronage and the appointment powers are discussed in most basic texts on American government and the United

States Constitution. The spoils system and civil service reform are discussed in all United States history textbooks, particularly in discussions of the nineteenth century. C. Herman Pritchett, *The American Constitution* (3d ed. New York: McGraw-Hill, 1977), and Bernard Bailyn et al., *The Great Republic* (Lexington, Mass.: D. C. Heath, 1977), are examples. Clarence B. Carson, *The Sections and the Civil War, 1826-1877* (Wadley, Ala.: American Textbook Committee, 1985), has an extensive section on Jacksonian democracy and the spoils system. Civil service reform during the late nineteenth century is dealt with extensively in volume two of Samuel Eliot Morison et al., *The Growth of the American Republic* (New York: Oxford University Press, 1969).

Sports law

DEFINITION: Legal aspects of the world of athletics

SIGNIFICANCE: Although sports law constitutes a relatively minor part of American jurisprudence, widespread interest in athletics and the celebrity of many of those involved makes the field among the legal world's most publicized

Sports and the law intersect on many levels. While most such connections may be properly considered as minor subsets of other legal specialties, the public fascination with athletics causes sports-related legislation, crime, litigation, and the like to draw significant levels of attention—and, often, to involve substantial amounts of money.

For example, suits arising over injuries relating to athletic competition represent a small but lucrative genre of tort law; prosecutions of star athletes for illicit drug use, involvement with gamblers, or a host of other sins rank among the most celebrated of criminal cases; gender-related discrepancies in the distribution of funds by public-school athletic departments are among the most widely discussed violations of civil rights laws; and the never-ending wranglings between professional athletes and their employers rank among the best-known American labor law and antitrust debates. Each subgenre of sports law has its own specialists and has produced its own literature.

Moreover, many of the most famous sports-related legal cases have become thoroughly entwined with the American social fabric, from the arguments over the Olympian Jim Thorpe's amateur status and the baseball "Black Sox" scandal in the early part of the century, through the midcentury college basketball point-shaving scandals and the legal maneuvering surrounding the move of the Brooklyn Dodgers to Los Angeles, to the more recent wave of professional sports strikes and the modern scandals involving Pete Rose and Tonya Harding. Although many lament the intrusion of such prosaic concerns on their recreations, the simple truth is that the world of athletics, though prized as a refuge from mundane troubles, has long reflected the litigious nature of American society.

See also Assault; Civil law; Contract law; Tort.

Standards of proof

DEFINITION: The rule that determines how much and what sort of evidence is enough to win in a court of law

SIGNIFICANCE: Without well-established and uniformly applied standards of proof, no one could be assured of a fair trial

There are three separate standards of proof, two for "civil" (noncriminal) cases and another for criminal cases. In most civil cases, the standard is generally said to require proving a case "by a preponderance of the evidence." This means convincing the court that one side's position is more likely true than the other side's position. In these cases, the same standard applies to both sides.

In some civil cases, such as those involving fraud, the party bringing the lawsuit is required to prove a case by providing "clear and convincing evidence." Under this standard, the court must be persuaded that the accusation or claim is highly probable, not merely more likely true than not true.

These civil standards are basically "judge-made"; that is, they were developed as part of the English common law, and those traditions have been followed by American courts. The distinction between the two types of civil cases has its origin in ancient English law, where there were two court systems, one of law and one of "equity." Cases heard in law courts were decided under the "preponderance" standard, while those heard in courts of equity were decided under the "clear and convincing" standard.

Although most modern American court systems have only courts of law, the ancient distinction still remains. Sometimes the standard to be applied is included in the law the court is asked to enforce; where the statute does not say, however, the courts resort to the common-law tradition and to their understanding of the legislature's purposes in passing the law.

In a criminal case, the party bringing the case is the government, which is usually far more powerful and with much less to lose than the other side. A much higher standard of proof is applied to the government: Before it can win, it must prove its position "beyond a reasonable doubt." That means the accused person cannot be found guilty unless the court is convinced that the government has definitely proved every necessary part of its case. This standard has long been followed in both England and the United States, and it has been expressly required in American criminal cases since 1970, when the United States Supreme Court formally adopted that language in *In re Winship* (1970).

See also Burden of proof; Civil procedure; Criminal procedure; Equity; Evidence, rules of; Presumption of innocence; Reasonable doubt.

Standing

DEFINITION: The personal stake of a litigant in a matter necessary for the litigant to seek judicial resolution of the matter

SIGNIFICANCE: The "standing" doctrine acts as a restraint on the ability of parties to pursue suits in which they have no personal interest or stake even though the claim they assert may be valid

Generally a party may not invoke the jurisdiction of a court unless he or she has some personal interest in the matter being litigated. A plaintiff seeking relief from a court must show that the plaintiff has some legally protected interest that the defendant's actions threaten. This requirement, sometimes referred to as the requirement of "standing to sue," ensures that courts will not be called upon to resolve hypothetical grievances and reserves the judicial function for the resolution of real controversies between adverse parties. The American system of justice is adversarial—that is, it relies upon antagonistic interests to present and clarify the opposing sides of an issue presented for judicial resolution. Accordingly, the standing requirement assures that suits will involve concrete disputes brought by parties with the kind of first-hand interest that will assure that a court will be informed of the issues at stake in a particular matter. It prevents the use of courts by individuals who have no more than a general interest in the resolution of some controversy.

A determination that a party lacks standing does not resolve the underlying merits of a legal dispute but rather prevents a court from reaching substantive issues asserted in a suit. In state courts the requirement of standing is usually self-imposed by the judiciary. In federal courts, however, the requirement of standing is one element of the Constitution's restriction of federal jurisdiction to the decision of "cases or controversies." Federal courts may not, without trespassing upon this constitutional limitation, entertain suits by parties without a real and substantial stake in the matter. A party's lack of such a stake deprives the federal court of jurisdiction—that is, authority to decide the matter.

For example, not everyone opposed on principle to some law has standing to challenge its constitutionality. The Supreme Court has held that the mere desire of a citizen to have his or her government act constitutionally does not confer standing on that citizen to challenge an arguably unconstitutional act. Instead, the citizen must demonstrate some personal injury, traceable to the government action and capable of redress by a court. Similarly, not everyone who objects to the wisdom or legality of some governmental expenditure has standing to challenge the expenditure. Thus, the Supreme Court has determined that a citizen opposed to the federal government providing certain welfare benefits had no standing to pursue the objection through litigation in court. The chief exception to result has been the Court's holding that a citizen taxpayer has standing to challenge expenditures of money that violate the First Amendment's prohibition against any establishment of religion by the government.

See also Civil procedure; Litigation; Suit; Supreme Court of the United States; Tort; Tort reform.

Stanford v. Kentucky

COURT: U.S. Supreme Court

DATE: Decided June 26, 1989

SIGNIFICANCE: In this case, the Supreme Court held that the Eighth Amendment's prohibition against "cruel and unusual punishment" did not prevent the execution of individuals who were juveniles at the time they committed the crimes for which they were executed

The Supreme Court's decision addressed two cases, one involving a seventeen-year-old male convicted of first-degree murder for having robbed a gas station and then raped, sodomized, and shot a station attendant to death, and the other involving a sixteen-year-old sentenced to death for having robbed a convenience store, stabbed the attendant, and left her to die. Both criminal defendants had been tried as adults.

The Supreme Court held that the Eighth Amendment's "cruel and unusual punishment" clause did not bar states from executing individuals who were sixteen and seventeen years of age at the time they committed the applicable crimes. The Court noted that such executions were not the kinds of punishment considered cruel and unusual at the time the Bill of Rights was adopted. Furthermore, the Court concluded that the executions at issue in the case were not contrary to "evolving standards of decency that mark the progress of a maturing society." Justice Sandra Day O'Connor concurred in this holding but wrote separately to emphasize her belief that the Court had a constitutional obligation to assure in each case that a particular defendant's blameworthiness was proportional to the sentence imposed. Justice Antonin Scalia, who wrote the majority opinion and the opinion of four justices on this point, argued that the Court had never invalidated a punishment solely because of an asserted disproportion between the punishment and the defendant's blameworthiness.

Justices William J. Brennan, Thurgood Marshall, Harry A. Blackmun, and John Paul Stevens dissented. These justices stated that the "cruel and unusual punishment" clause of the Eighth Amendment bars the execution of any person for a crime committed while the person was under the age eighteen. Justice Brennan, writing for the dissenters, asserted that such executions violated contemporary standards of decency. He pointed out that the laws of a majority of states would not have permitted the executions at issue in this case and that in the vast majority of cases involving juvenile offenders, juries did not impose the death penalty. The justice concluded by arguing that the imposition of the death penalty for juvenile crimes served the interests of neither retribution nor deterrence. Capital punishment in these cases did not serve the interests of retribution since, according to Justice Brennan, the penalty was disproportionate to the defendants' blameworthiness. The punishment did not advance the interests of deterrence since juveniles were not likely to make the kind of cost-benefit analysis that would dissuade them from committing a crime for fear of receiving the death penalty.

See also Bill of Rights, U.S.; Capital punishment; Constitution, U.S.; Cruel and unusual punishment; Juvenile justice system; Punishment.

Stanton, Elizabeth Cady (Nov. 12, 1815, Johnstown, N.Y.—Oct. 26, 1902, New York, N.Y.)

IDENTIFICATION: Social reformer and feminist

SIGNIFICANCE: Stanton was a pioneer women's rights leader and the foremost critic of women's subordination to men in the nineteenth century

Stanton dedicated her life to changing laws and social practices that prevented women from enjoying their rights as individuals. Observations of her father's practice as an attorney and judge provided Stanton with an early awareness of the discriminatory effects of laws as applied to women and slaves. In 1840 she married abolitionist Henry Stanton and attended the London Anti-Slavery Convention. There she met Lucretia Mott and experienced the exclusion of female delegates from the floor. Stanton and Mott organized the Seneca Falls Convention in 1848, the first women's rights gathering in the United States. Stanton drafted the Declaration of Sentiments that was adopted at the convention.

In 1850, Stanton met Susan B. Anthony, sparking a long-term friendship and collaboration. They founded the Women's State Temperance Society (1852-1853) and *The Revolution* (1868-1870), a women's rights weekly. Stanton, Anthony, and Matilda Joslyn Gage wrote the first three volumes of *The History of Woman Suffrage* (1881-1888).

After the Civil War, Stanton focused more exclusively on women's rights, including issues of child rearing, marriage and divorce, property rights, and suffrage. Stanton was the founder and president of the National Woman Suffrage Association (in 1869) and the National American Woman Suffrage Association (in 1890). Later in life, Stanton focused on gender inequalities in religion. She provided a feminist critique of the Bible in *The Woman's Bible* (1895, 1898).

Stanton wrote extensively and traveled widely to express her views. In 1854 she was the first woman to speak to the New York legislature. In 1894 she spoke in favor of the woman suffrage amendment before a U.S. Senate committee. Applying a natural law perspective, Stanton's philosophy was that a woman was first and foremost an individual, with all the rights of choice and personal development which men were expected to have as individuals.

See also Abolitionist movement; Anthony, Susan B.; Feminism; Natural law and natural rights; Seneca Falls Convention; Woman's suffrage.

Stare decisis

DEFINITION: The decision of a case on the basis of judicial precedent in similar cases

SIGNIFICANCE: This principle gives continuity and predictability to the entire body of common-law decisions

Stare decisis comes from a Latin term meaning "to stand by things that have been settled." Under this principle of law, judicial decisions that have been made in cases similar to the one under consideration are accepted as authoritative. *Stare decisis* involves, in addition to how judges in the past decided similar cases, what the basic judicial principles followed were. (It is accepted that specific circumstance will vary.) Often more than one case will be cited to illustrate the stability and continuity of the principles judged to apply in the current case. The principle applies only to the actual decision and not to the arguments substantiating that decision. Thus, a later case could be decided similarly to an earlier one but for different reasons.

Legal Continuity. Many arguments on questions of the law have already been settled in earlier cases. When the same point is again in controversy in a trial court, the earlier precedent is judged to be binding on the later court decision. This principle provides a degree of certitude as to what the law actually says about similar issues. It gives a consistency to court decisions that might not be possible if earlier decisions were not consulted. Appellate courts similarly follow the principle of *stare decisis*, but they are not under the same obligation as is a trial court. If two principles of the law come into conflict, or if the court seeks to remedy a continued and obvious injustice, appellate courts can deviate from judicial precedent and break new ground.

Precedents Overruled. Precedents can be overruled and, in fact, have been many times. Courts often look at the presumed results of a decision. Occasionally such a prediction will prompt the judge to alter a decision. The judicial philosophy of a particular judge or justice can also influence a court decision. Judicial activists are more likely to overturn a precedent than are judges who believes it is their duty to defer to legislative intent. In the absence of clear legislation, that philosophy tends to follow decisions of earlier courts.

In *Helvering v. Hallock* (1940), Supreme Court Justice Felix Frankfurter called *stare decisis* "a principle of policy and not a mechanical formula," especially when adhering to the principle would involve "collision with a prior doctrine more embracing in its scope, intrinsically sounder, and verified by experience." It is not unusual for the United States Supreme Court to overrule its own decisions. The New Deal era Court, for example, did that several times. The most celebrated Court reversal was *Brown v. Board of Education* in 1954, which overruled the "separate but equal" segregation doctrine of *Plessy v. Ferguson* (1896).

Overruling judicial precedent is a serious responsibility because it not only changes what has been accepted as law but also implies that the judge or judges making the earlier rules were either mistaken or philosophically wrong. A court must show respect for the knowledge and intelligence of previous judges. Even when an earlier decision can be shown to be legally or constitutionally flawed, stability is a consideration. If changing a decision would disrupt society excessively or create political chaos, judges are reluctant to break with the continuity of precedent.

Res Judicata. Closely related to *stare decisis* is the principle of *res judicata* ("a matter settled by judgment"). This means that once a matter is judicially settled by the courts, continued suits on the same matter will not be permitted. Once decided, a decision is laid to rest. —*William H. Burnside*

See also Appellate process; Case law; Common law; Constitutional interpretation; Evidence, rules of; Judicial review; Judicial system, U.S.; Supreme Court of the United States.

BIBLIOGRAPHY

Any standard law dictionary, such as Henry C. Black, *Black's Law Dictionary* (5th ed. St. Paul, Minn.: West, 1979), gives succinct discussions of legal terms. Other useful works are Bernard Schwartz, *The Law in America: A History* (New York: McGraw-Hill, 1974); Oliver Wendell Holmes, Jr., *The Common Law* (Boston: Little, Brown, 1909); Bryan Garner, *A Dictionary of Modern Legal Usage* (New York: Oxford University Press, 1987); and Alexander H. Pekelis, *Law and Social Action* (New York: Da Capo Press, 1970).

State police

DEFINITION: A public law enforcement agency with statewide jurisdiction, most typically a state's highway patrol

SIGNIFICANCE: Modern transportation, communications, and crime control technologies have contributed to the development and expansion of statewide policing agencies

The Texas Rangers, founded in 1835, several years before Texas gained statehood, were a territorial equivalent to a state police. They were a paramilitary force organized to protect settlers against Indians. Later, when Texas became a state, they were used for border patrol duties. They were a lawless lot, notorious for brutal treatment of Indians, Mexicans, and African Americans, until Texas brought them under the Department of Public Safety in the 1930's.

Massachusetts established its state police in 1865, primarily to control vice and bring hard-drinking Irish Catholic immigrants under control. Some became competent detectives and were kept on in rural communities after 1876, when Massachusetts, embarrassed by the bigotry within the force, officially disbanded the state police.

Civil unrest and crime arising from industrial expansion led to the creation of other state police. In particular, steel-mill and coal-mining areas were plagued with labor violence. In 1865, the Pennsylvania State Legislature responded by creating the infamous Iron and Coal Police, who were little more-than thugs used by mill and mine owners to terrorize striking workers.

By the beginning of the twentieth century, with worker unionization and a great tide of immigration, conditions had worsened. Spurred by the violent anthracite coal strike of 1902 and a federal commission's finger-pointing, Pennsylvania organized a state police modeled on the quasi-military constabularies of Ireland and the Philippines. Officers were army veterans with anti-insurrection training. By World War I, with notable impartiality, they had brought peace to the troubled region, but they had also gained some notoriety for their blatant attempts to recast immigrants in an "American" mold.

Between 1908 and 1923, fourteen states created similar forces. Most were less impartial than the Pennsylvania State Police, particularly in the West, where they were violently antiunion and probusiness. Their use soon declined, however, for in the economic boom era of the 1920's, new laws brought the immigration flood to a trickle and labor-organizing efforts to a standstill. State police thus needed another purpose for their continued existence.

Automobiles and Highways. The automobile provided a very good purpose. By 1920, the automobile was rapidly becoming a necessity of middle-class families, not merely the toy of the rich. Cars were rolling off assembly lines onto the country's ever-expanding roads. Once out of town and city jurisdiction, drivers were growing reckless and dangerous. Better roads also gave criminals ready access to and escape from cities and towns, making robberies a growing problem.

A few states responded by creating agencies with authority over both traffic regulation and criminal investigation, but most limited their state police to highway patrols. Between 1920 and 1940, twenty-six states created new state police, but only ten of them had powers extending much beyond regulating traffic.

Dealing with criminals was another matter. Twenty-four states had centralized criminal-identification bureaus by 1934, but the most important advances came with new technologies such as the two-way radio and expanded telephone service, which made the coordinated pursuit of fugitives and roadblocks effective crime-fighting strategies.

The Refurbished Image. During the 1930's, state police were still being used in dubious ways—for example, to block entry into states by Dust Bowl refugees. By the eve of World War II, however, they enjoyed a much improved reputation. They had brought increased safety to the highways through patrolling and public education programs. They had also earned respect as courteous professionals, virtually free of political influence and class biases.

The postwar era at first brought few changes. There was less recruitment from the armed services but little rethinking of the structure and role of state police. In 1959, a new series of state initiatives began by addressing the issue of police training. Syndicated crime also became a major focus because of its dramatic spread. To fight organized crime, including auto theft and drug trafficking, most states formed computer links with the National Crime Information Center, begun in 1967. Interstate cooperation was also instituted. For example, the New England State Police Compact provided for the pooling of crime-fighting resources. The Omnibus Crime Control and Safe Streets Act (1968) also helped, providing extensive federal funds for various state training and research programs and authorizing state control of coordinated anticrime planning.

Highway Safety—a Common Denominator. No two states have identical state-police infrastructures, but most have agencies with similar functions. Highway patrol officers or "troopers" are undoubtedly the most visible state police, but many statewide criminal justice responsibilities fall to agents with special police powers stemming from myriad laws and regulations relating to alcoholic beverages, narcotics, consumer affairs, corrections, gaming and racing, state parks and recreation, hunting and fishing, and fire investigations. In a generic sense, officers who have statewide policing authority are state police, whatever their official designation. Also, they frequently work in cooperation with state highway patrols—for drug interdiction, for example.

Still, in the usual, popular sense, state police are the troopers charged with ensuring public safety on the United States' net-

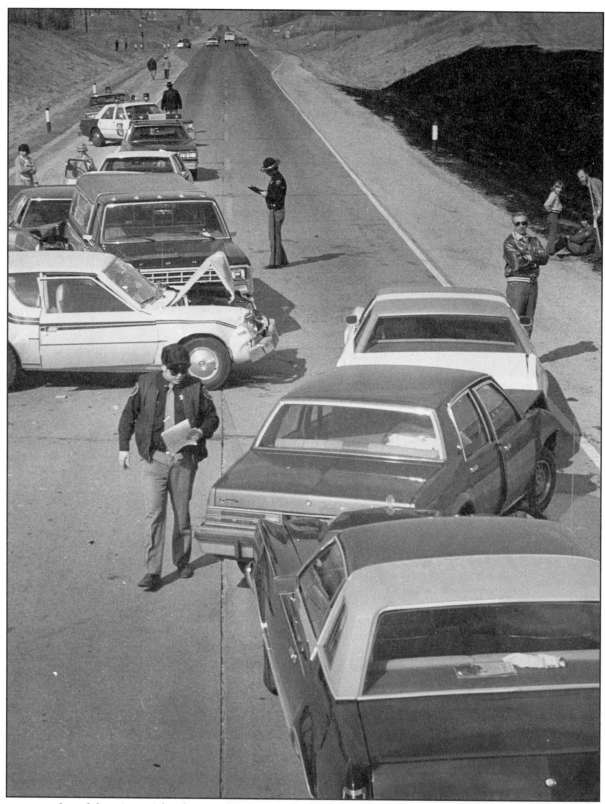

One of the primary jobs of state police forces is the maintenance of highway safety. (James L. Shaffer)

work of federal and state highways. They now hover in helicopters and catch speeders using radar guns, but their basic mission has not changed much since Detroit began manufacturing cars that were within the average person's means.

—John W. Fiero

See also Drug use and sale, illegal; Federal Bureau of Investigation (FBI); National Crime Information Center; Sheriff; Transportation law.

BIBLIOGRAPHY

Concise histories and overviews include David R. Johnson, *American Law Enforcement: A History* (St. Louis, Mo.: Forum Press, 1981); Thomas A. Reppetto, *The Blue Parade* (New York: Free Press, 1978); Bruce Smith, *The State Police: Organization and Administration* (Montclair, N.J.: Patterson Smith, 1969); Thomas F. Adams, *Law Enforcement: An Introduction to the Police Role in the Community* (Englewood Cliffs, N.J.: Prentice-Hall, 1968); and Ron Stern, *Law Enforcement Careers* (Tarzana, Calif.: Lawman Press, 1988). For an inside view, see Marie Bartlett Maher, *Trooper Down: Life and Death on the Highway Patrol* (Chapel Hill, N.C.: Algonquin Books, 1988).

States' rights

DEFINITION: A basic belief, marked by historical variations, that the states retain certain constitutional rights, liberties, and authority that the federal government cannot take from them

SIGNIFICANCE: Historically, states' rights doctrines have generated philosophical debates; fueled social, racial, and political conflicts; and, upon occasion, threatened the Union's existence

The Constitution's Tenth Amendment (1791) delegates to the national government exclusive powers which states cannot exercise, denotes concurrent powers whose delegation to the federal government does not restrict state authority, and denotes federal powers that limit but do not entirely preclude their exercise by the states—that is, powers that are neither exclusive nor entirely concurrent.

Defining this distribution of power and adjusting its balance between a central government and those of the states periodically were subjects of serious philosophical and political conflict until the close of the Civil War in 1865. Subsequently, although no armed challenge to federal authority arose, the doctrine of states' rights reemerged vigorously during the 1940's and 1950's. It represented a conservative southern protest against the growth of federal power and, of equal importance, an attempt to prevent federal authority from altering white southern resistance to the extension of full civil rights to African Americans.

Interposition. There were striking assertions of states' rights prior to the Civil War. Arguing that the Constitution was a compact which left state sovereignty intact, Thomas Jefferson in the Kentucky Resolutions (1798-1799) and, almost simultaneously, James Madison in the Virginia Resolutions declared that when the federal government exercised powers not delegated to it, the states possessed the right not to obey. Moreover, as one means of redress, states could "interpose" themselves between federal authority and their people to check the "evil" that flowed from unconstitutional federal legislation.

Southerners were not alone in holding such views. In 1815, for example, delegates from five New England states assembled secretly as the Hartford Convention protesting federal policies during the War of 1812. Closely following language of the Virginia and Kentucky resolves, convention spokesmen asserted that when there are deliberate and dangerous federal infractions of the Constitution, the states have the right to interpose themselves as they choose. While neither the authors of the Kentucky and Virginia resolves nor outspoken members of the Hartford Convention initiated direct action to implement "interposition," a belief in states' rights persisted as a set of widespread convictions.

Nullification. As the predominantly agricultural South lost its lengthy sectional control over national politics and yielded to the political and industrial ascendancy of New England and the Upper Midwest, southerners fought against northern-inspired federal legislation. In 1828 and 1829, southern spokesmen attacked federal protectionist tariffs and public lands legislation by proclaiming states' rights. Asserting the compact theory of the Constitution, the independence of the states, and the states' right to determine—free of federal judicial interference—when their liberties were infringed upon by the federal government, they deplored the "consolidation" of federal power and reiterated their right of interposition. It was a short step from interposition to the remedy of nullification.

The idea of nullifying uncongenial federal legislation had arisen during the tariff controversies of 1828 and was elaborated upon in 1832 by leading political figures in South Carolina, Georgia, Mississippi, and Virginia, most notably by John C. Calhoun. Only President Andrew Jackson's threat to use federal force avoided the breakup of the Union.

Secession. The compact theory of the Constitution, interposition, and nullification all implied an independent state's right to secede to preserve its liberty and sovereignty. Such interpretations during the 1850's resulted in deepening sectional animosities, the erosion of compromises, and the breakdown of the dominant political parties, primarily over slavery issues. The election of President Abraham Lincoln and ascension to power of the young, sectional Republican Party precipitated secessionist movements during 1860, first in the Deep South, and ultimately by eleven states. Thereafter, the sovereignty of the federal government and the indissolubility of the Union were settled on the battlefields of the Civil War and belatedly confirmed by the U.S. Supreme Court's decision in *Texas v. White* (1869).

Dixiecrats and States' Rights. Since the Civil War both state and federal powers have expanded steadily. Federal power unquestionably has grown more dramatically than that of the states, especially since the 1930's. The range of congressional power has been vastly extended, for example, by broadened Supreme Court interpretations of the commerce clause and of the Fourteenth and Sixteenth Amendments. Into the 1990's, executive powers were magnified by war powers and expanded foreign policy powers even more than were those of the Congress, leading many observers to speak of the emergence of an "imperial presidency" between the 1960's and 1980's.

General acquiescence to federal sovereignty did not quiet outcries in behalf of states' rights. Political protests, like those of the Dixiecrats, or States' Rights Party, erupted in the late 1940's and early 1950's. The resistance of some southern governors to the racial integration of public schools and extensions of civil rights affirmed deeply rooted local and sectional traditions hostile to federal policies regarding racial relations. Many other states' rights advocates reflected popular fear and disenchantment with the sheer power, pervasiveness, and cost of federal government that began with President Franklin Roosevelt's New Deal programs (1933-1938). Characterized as "states' rights constitutionalism," such views embody ap-
prehensions which first plagued drafters of the Constitution and are as old as the Republic. —*Mary E. Virginia*

See also Alien and Sedition Acts; Civil rights; Civil War; Conservatism, modern American; Constitution, U.S.; Federalism; Jeffersonian democracy; Segregation, *de facto* and *de jure*; States' Rights Party.

BIBLIOGRAPHY

Amid an abundance of fine readings are Robert A. Garson, *The Democratic Party and the Politics of Sectionalism, 1941-1948* (Baton Rouge: Louisiana State University Press, 1974); Robert A. Goldwin, ed., *A Nation of States* (Chicago: Rand McNally, 1974); Clinton Rossiter, ed., *The Federalist Papers* (New York: New American Library, 1961); Wendell Holmes Stephenson and E. Merton Coulter, *A History of the South* (Baton Rouge: Louisiana State University Press, 1976); and Gordon S. Wood, *The Creation of the American Republic, 1776-1797* (Chapel Hill: University of North Carolina Press, 1969).

States' rights became a rallying cry for proponents of segregation in the 1950's and 1960's. Here Alabama governor George Wallace (far left) raises a hand in his attempt to block black enrollment at the University of Alabama in 1963. (AP/Wide World Photos)

States' Rights Party

DATE: Established 1948

SIGNIFICANCE: Establishment of the States' Rights Party symbolized conservative southern dissatisfaction with the Democratic Party's recognition of civil rights as an important part of its agenda

Minneapolis Mayor Hubert H. Humphrey persuaded Democratic National Convention delegates to add a strong civil rights plank to the party platform in 1948. That decision enhanced the party's reputation as a champion of civil rights, but it also alienated many southern conservatives. Shortly after the convention, disaffected southerners met at Birmingham, Alabama, created the States' Rights Party (the "Dixiecrats"), and nominated Governor Strom Thurmond of South Carolina and Governor Fielding Wright of Mississippi for president and vice president.

The Dixiecrat campaign focused on dissatisfaction with various civil rights initiatives of the Democratic Party and President Harry S Truman. Thurmond carried Mississippi, Alabama, South Carolina, and Louisiana, and he received thirty-nine electoral votes. The States' Rights Party marked a transitional phase of southern politics during which Democrats learned that they could vote for a presidential candidate other than the Democratic nominee, and the Democratic Party learned that it could espouse social justice causes and win a national election without solid southern support.

See also Civil rights; Civil Rights movement; Democratic Party; Segregation, *de facto* and *de jure*; States' rights.

Status offense

DEFINITION: An act which is defined as illegal only if committed by a person below the age of majority (usually eighteen), such as running away, truancy, and incorrigibility

SIGNIFICANCE: Status offenses represent one of the areas of law that demonstrate the law's differing treatment of adults and minors

Status offenses are acts defined as crimes only if the offender is a juvenile; these acts are considered legal for adults. Status offenses are not the same as juvenile delinquency, which consists of acts that are illegal regardless of age (delinquency specifically refers to crimes committed by juveniles rather than by adults). Status offenses typically consist of such acts as running away, truancy, using tobacco, drinking alcohol, violating curfew, and incorrigibility (disobeying parents). Not all status offenses are clearly defined; examples of such offenses include immorality, promiscuity, and moral depravity. While punishment for these types of crimes is usually not severe, juveniles can be incarcerated in secure facilities for chronic status offending. In some jurisdictions, juveniles are incarcerated in adult facilities for status offenses. The Office of Juvenile Justice and Delinquency Prevention (OJJDP) was created, in part, to focus on removing status offenders from secure facilities.

See also *In loco parentis*; Juvenile delinquency; Juvenile Justice and Delinquency Prevention, Office of; Juvenile Justice and Delinquency Prevention Act; Juvenile justice system; Majority, age of.

Statute of limitations

DEFINITION: The period of time during which an action may be brought to enforce a legal right

SIGNIFICANCE: Statutes of limitations reflect the notion that legal challenges should be made in a timely fashion and defendants should not be required to defend stale claims

Statutes of limitations restrict the period of time during which an action may be brought to enforce legal rights. The requirement of a statute of limitations encourages lawsuits to be brought promptly when evidence is fresh and also grants the defendant the comfort that after a reasonable time he or she will be free from potential claims. Statutes of limitations in the civil context are often called "statutes of repose."

The statute of limitations requires that a party must file a suit in a court of competent jurisdiction before the statute expires (or "runs," in common parlance) if the court is to have jurisdiction over the matter. If a party attempts to file a suit after the expiration of the statute, the defendants will plead as an "affirmative defense" that the statute of limitations has expired. If indeed it has, the case will be dismissed.

A statute of limitations has three parts. First, it defines when the limitations period begins to run. For example, for a tort action, the statute usually begins when the injury occurs. For a contract action, the alleged breach of contract starts the statute of limitations running. Second, the statute of limitations states the period of time during which actions may be brought. Different types of actions have different limitation periods. Disfavored actions, such as defamation of character, have relatively short statutes of one year or so. Negligence actions usually have a two-year to three-year period of limitations, while contract actions and actions based on written instruments have limitation periods of five or six years. Third, a statute defines what "tolls" the limitations period— that is, stops it from running. For example, the commencement of an action by filing suit tolls the statute of limitations, and a statute is often tolled during the legal incapacity of the plaintiff (for example, during the period of time the plaintiff is a minor).

Statutes of limitations also apply in criminal law: The state must indict or otherwise bring official charges against a defendant within the specified period of time. If the statute runs without charges being filed, the defendant is forever protected from prosecution and may even confess without fear of punishment. In the criminal context, a statute of limitations is an act of grace of the state, which surrenders its right to prosecute alleged wrongdoers. Thus, the state is more likely to surrender the right to prosecute for minor crimes than for serious ones. For example, the statute of limitations for a misdemeanor assault is typically one year. By contrast, there is no statute of limitations for murder, and in difficult cases the state can (and often does) bring charges after many years.

See also Civil procedure; Criminal procedure; Litigation; Suit.

Statutory rape

DEFINITION: Consensual sexual intercourse between a person who has reached the age of majority and a person who is a minor

SIGNIFICANCE: Laws regarding statutory rape have historically used sexist language, having been directed against adult males having consensual sex with minor females

Statutory rape is a crime of age. Unlike forcible rape, which is defined as forcible sexual intercourse, statutory rape involves consensual sexual relations between two people. There is an assumption that juveniles (or minors) cannot make appropriate decisions about sexual behavior and that sexual relations between a juvenile and an adult are the result of coercion or pressure on the juvenile. The definition of statutory rape as a crime is an attempt to protect children from being sexually assaulted. Some parents of teenagers, however, have successfully helped to convict their child's adult boyfriend or girlfriend of statutory rape if sexual intercourse has occurred.

Statutory rape has historically been defined in terms of juvenile females having sexual intercourse with adult males. This definition has resulted in some debate, since it makes the assumptions that girls are unable to make appropriate decisions about sex but boys are, and boys cannot be coerced into sex by an adult (man or woman).

See also Child abuse; Child molestation; Contributing to the delinquency of a minor; Rape and sex offenses.

Steffens, Lincoln (Apr. 6, 1866, San Francisco, Calif.— Aug. 9, 1936, Carmel, Calif.)

IDENTIFICATION: American journalist

SIGNIFICANCE: Steffens' *The Shame of the Cities*, an attack on urban political corruption, made Steffens the foremost American political journalist of his time and greatly influenced reformists of the Progressive era

Educated at the University of California at Berkeley and in Europe, Lincoln Steffens, like many contemporaries, originally sought scientific solutions to social problems. From 1901 to 1906, he was a "muckraking" journalist with *McClure's Magazine*; the term described journalists dedicated to sensationalistic exposure of social evil. Steffens focused on the unseen and corrupt alliances that actually ruled cities, despite the illusions of voters. His articles, collected as *The Shame of the Cities* (1904), made him the foremost political journalist of his day. After publication of *The Struggle for Self-Government* (1906) and *Upbuilders* (1909), he turned to the structure of society, rather than individuals within it. His defense of violent radicalism, in the United States and abroad, lost him much popularity, but, in 1931, with publication of *The Autobiography of Lincoln Steffens*, he regained importance as an authority on the lasting problems of urban corruption.

See also Bribery; Commercialized vice; Machine politics; Police corruption and misconduct; Political corruption; Progressivism; Spoils system and patronage.

Sterilization and American law

DEFINITION: Sterilization is a voluntary or involuntary medical procedure rendering the patient sterile or incapable of procreation

SIGNIFICANCE: State statutes permitting compulsory sterilization for eugenic or punitive reasons raise questions with regard to "cruel and unusual punishment," the right of procreational privacy, human experimentation, and the interpretation of "compelling state interest"

Early in the twentieth century, most states enacted laws providing for the compulsory sterilization of persons categorized as mentally ill or deficient, epileptics, sexual perverts, and habitual criminals. The constitutionality of compulsory sterilization measures for eugenic reasons was sustained by *Buck v. Bell* (1927), wherein the Supreme Court upheld a Virginia court's decision to order compulsory sterilization of a "feebleminded" eighteen-year-old woman. This controversial case—in which an analogy was drawn between compulsory eugenic sterilization and compulsory vaccination—became the impetus for the enacting of similar statutes by other states.

Compelling state interest in protecting the public from supporting eugenically defective persons has been largely undisputed, although safeguards have been added to ensure the protection of the incompetent patient. Compulsory sterilization as a punitive measure, on the other hand, has been successfully rejected in a number of cases by invoking the Fourteenth Amendment's "equal protection" clause (*Skinner v. Oklahoma*, 1942) and the Eighth Amendment's "cruel and unusual punishment" clause (*Davis v. Berry*, 1914, and *Mickle v. Henrichs*, 1918), although compulsory sterilization is still sometimes ordered as a condition for probation.

See also Birth control, right to; *Buck v. Bell*; Cruel and unusual punishment; Rape and sex offenses.

Sting operation

DEFINITION: A large-scale undercover operation designed to expose fencing, money laundering, drug trafficking, political corruption, or other major criminal activity

SIGNIFICANCE: Large operations involving major criminal activity are often so powerful and secretive that the only way to expose them is to pose as a part of the operation and penetrate its inner workings

A sting operation generally involves a variety of investigators and undercover police personnel posing as participants in a major criminal activity. For example, detectives in a medium to large city may have a problem with an increase in thefts of personal property. The undercover operatives may decide that the best way to counter the problem is to set up a phony pawn shop front, making it known that they are willing to buy and sell almost anything. Through the use of hidden cameras and other recording devices, they record all transactions and attempt to identify and trace the merchandise they buy. Once enough evidence is obtained and a direct link between the contraband items and the suspects is obtained, the suspects are arrested and prosecuted. Significant effort must be expended to ensure that any action taken by the undercover operatives cannot be considered entrapment.

See also Detectives, police; Entrapment; Evidence, rules of; Federal Bureau of Investigation (FBI); Police; Search and seizure.

Stone, Harlan Fiske (Oct. 11, 1872, Chesterfield, N.H.— Apr. 22, 1946, Washington, D.C.)

IDENTIFICATION: Chief justice of the United States, 1941-1946

SIGNIFICANCE: As a member of the U.S. Supreme Court from 1925 to 1946, Stone generally defended the doctrine of judicial self-restraint, and he often supported libertarian ideals

In his active career, Harlan Stone was a practicing lawyer, professor, and dean at the Columbia Law School, attorney general, associate justice of the Supreme Court, and finally the twelfth chief justice. In 1924 he resigned his deanship to become attorney general, in which position he helped restore confidence to the Justice Department after the fiasco of the Teapot Dome Scandal. From his appointment to the Supreme Court in 1925 until the "judicial revolution of 1937," he was known as one of the "three great dissenters" who voted to allow economic regulations, including most New Deal reforms. His most influential opinion was *United States v. Carolene Products Co.* (1938), with its famous Footnote Four advocating heightened judicial scrutiny when dealing with

Chief Justice Harlan Fiske Stone presided over a Court with bitter philosophical and political divisions. (Painting by Charles J. Fox, collection of the Supreme Court of the United States)

fundamental rights and equality for minorities. Stone is recognized for the objectivity and balanced judgment in his six hundred opinions, but as chief justice from 1941 to 1946, he was less successful in attempts to minimize the bitter conflict among the Court's associate justices.

See also Attorney general of the United States; Brandeis, Louis D.; Cardozo, Benjamin Nathan; New Deal; Supreme Court of the United States; Teapot Dome scandal.

Story, Joseph (Sept. 18, 1779, Marblehead, Mass.— Sept. 10, 1845, Cambridge, Mass.)

IDENTIFICATION: Eminent American jurist and United States Supreme Court justice, 1812-1845

SIGNIFICANCE: Story played a pivotal role in the development of nineteenth century jurisprudence, enlarging federal jurisdiction in his role as a justice, helping to found Harvard Law School, and authoring a series of esteemed legal treatises

When he was appointed to the Supreme Court in 1811, at thirty-two, Joseph Story was the youngest man ever to receive this honor. On the court, Story served as Chief Justice John Marshall's second, working closely with the chief justice to forge the Court into an instrument of legal nationalism. His opinion in *Martin v. Hunter's Lessee* (1816) established the Supreme Court as the tribunal of last resort in appeals from civil cases concerning federal law. When Marshall died in 1835, Story was considered his obvious successor, but he was passed over, largely for political reasons. Thereafter, he customarily found himself dissenting from the Court majority. While serving on the Court, he also was a professor at Harvard Law School, helping to establish the national approach to legal education that became the standard. He also wrote a celebrated series of nine *Commentaries* on the law, first published between 1832 and 1845 and reprinted many times thereafter.

See also Federalism; Jurisprudence; Marshall, John; Supreme Court of the United States.

Stowe, Harriet Beecher (June 14, 1811, Litchfield, Conn.—July 1, 1896, Hartford, Conn.)

IDENTIFICATION: Novelist and reformer

SIGNIFICANCE: As the author of *Uncle Tom's Cabin*, the most widely read and controversial novel of the nineteenth century, Stowe had a tremendous influence on the abolitionist movement in the United States

In 1832 Harriet Beecher's family moved to Cincinnati, where her father, Lyman, became president of Lane Theological Seminary. In 1836 she married Calvin Stowe, a recently widowed professor of biblical literature. Despite six difficult pregnancies and the responsibilities of motherhood, Stowe continued to write and sell short stories and sketches, as she had since 1833. Troubled by the Fugitive Slave Law of 1850 and inspired by a vision she had received in church, Harriet decided to raise the nation's consciousness against slavery. Serialized in *The Nation*, an antislavery journal, *Uncle Tom's Cabin: Or, Life Among the Lowly* (1852) was an immediate best-seller in the United States and England. So profound was this novel's influ-

ence on the growing antislavery movement in the United States that upon meeting Stowe in 1862 Abraham Lincoln is said to have joked, "So this is the little lady who made this big war."

See also Abolitionist movement; Fugitive Slave Laws; Garrison, William Lloyd; Slavery.

Strict liability

DEFINITION: Strict liability imposes liability on a person or entity that causes injury to another even though that person or entity is without fault

SIGNIFICANCE: The doctrine of strict liability allows a person to recover damages for injuries caused by another party without having to prove the fault of the other party

Historically, legal liability was imposed only if a party causing an injury was at fault. The minimum degree of fault for imposing liability was negligence. Strict liability is considered a radical theory by many academics because it imposes legal liability without an individual or entity being at fault. The rationale for imposing liability without fault is that often traditional legal theories fail to redress injuries unless a party is at fault. The purpose of strict liability is to shift the loss from the injured party to the party who was in the best position to prevent the injury.

Strict liability has been applied in extremely hazardous and abnormally dangerous activities such as the use of explosives. Courts have recognized that even though a person may use explosives properly and with the proper degree of care, explosives are somewhat unpredictable and may injure others. In these types of circumstances, strict liability may be imposed.

Strict liability has also been applied in situations involving animals that cause injury to others. For example, strict liability has been imposed where a party keeps a wild animal outside its natural environment and the animal causes property damage or personal injury. Strict liability may also be applied to damage caused by domestic animals that have exhibited dangerous propensities, such as a vicious dog. Strict liability also has been imposed on the owners of livestock when that livestock trespasses on another's property and causes damage.

Products liability is an area where strict liability has become increasingly important. In strict product liability, a manufacturer, distributor, or vendor of a product can be held strictly liable if a product is defective and unreasonably dangerous and causes injury to the user because of the defect.

States have also enacted statutes that extend strict liability to certain situations. Workers' compensation statutes impose strict liability on employers for injuries to employees that occur in the workplace, regardless of fault. Payments are made to an injured employee from a common insurance fund created from employer-paid premiums. Statutes also impose strict liability on certain crimes. Examples of strict liability crimes include adulterating or misbranding drugs, polluting the air and water, and statutory rape.

Still other states have enacted statutes codifying court decisions regarding strict liability. For example, several states have statutes that impose strict liability on dog owners for damages suffered by a person bitten by the dog.

There are defenses to strict liability; they focus on the injured party's contribution of fault to the injury. For example, misuse of a product or assumption of the risk may be valid defenses to certain strict liability actions. Further, privileges may exist to defend against injuries occurring in ultrahazardous activities where there is a desirable social benefit from the activity.

See also Negligence; Products liability; Workers' compensation.

Student Nonviolent Coordinating Committee (SNCC)

DATE: Established April, 1960
SIGNIFICANCE: In the early 1960's, SNCC helped to eliminate discrimination at lunch counters and promote voter registration of African Americans in the South

The insistence of four African American students from the North Carolina Agricultural and Technical College that they be served at a Woolworth's lunch counter in Greensboro, North Carolina, in February of 1960 sparked the student sit-ins of the 1960's. The students' sit-in at the Woolworth's lunch counter precipitated similar protests in more than sixty-five cities. The need to coordinate what began as spontaneous and haphazard events resulted in the establishment of the Student Nonviolent Coordinating Committee (SNCC).

SNCC was founded in April of 1960 by a group of southern African American students, many of whom participated in the sit-ins. They were assisted by long-time civil rights leader Ella Baker, who insisted that the new student organization pursue its own path. SNCC concentrated its efforts in the South, as its leadership determined that the more immediate problems of racial discrimination and the denial of constitutional rights were occurring there. SNCC spent most of its early years, especially in 1964 and 1965, attempting to register African Americans to vote. The voter registration campaign that SNCC and the Congress of Racial Equality (CORE) carried out, along with the passage of the 1965 Voting Rights Act, proved to have a tremendous impact on southern politics, especially within the Democratic Party.

Despite its various successes, SNCC appeared to be an organization that was in constant turmoil. It was continually struggling with which direction it should take as an incipient social justice organization. SNCC's uncertainty was reflected in the group's frequent changes in leadership. James Farmer, a former Chicago teacher and the first executive secretary of SNCC, attempted to mold it into a highly structured and formalized organization. He was replaced by John Lewis, who was committed to nonviolent integrated struggle. In 1966 Lewis was replaced by Stokely Carmichael (Kwame Toure), who advocated total black membership and would later initiate the move toward "black power." SNCC officially adopted "black power" as its slogan at its 1966 convention. Under Carmichael, SNCC decided to stop using integrated teams of field workers. He took the position that if whites really wanted to help, then they should organize whites in their communities. By 1969 Carmichael had been replaced by H. Rap Brown, who was perceived to be even more militant and changed the group's name to the Student National Coordinating Committee.

SNCC's new philosophy alienated whites, but more important, it put SNCC (along with CORE) at odds with the more traditional civil rights organizations, especially the National Association for the Advancement of Colored People (NAACP) and the Southern Christian Leadership Conference (SCLC). While its new philosophy was embraced by many young African Americans, it moved SNCC further from what many perceived to be the paradigm of the civil rights struggle. Consequently, much of the group's financial support dried up, and the young people who were committed to nonviolent integrated struggle slowly deserted its ranks. By 1970, SNCC had ceased to exist.

See also Black Panther Party; Black Power movement; Civil Rights movement; Congress of Racial Equality (CORE); National Association for the Advancement of Colored People (NAACP); Southern Christian Leadership Conference (SCLC).

Students for a Democratic Society (SDS)

DATE: Established 1960
SIGNIFICANCE: SDS was the most prominent "New Left" student organization working for social change in the 1960's

In its 1962 manifesto, the "Port Huron statement," Students for a Democratic Society offered a critique of materialistic, imperialistic, and bureaucratic Cold War America. The group called for the uniting of working-class and poor Americans to institute a truly "participatory democracy," one in which power would shift from impersonal institutions to individuals and community organizations, resulting in expanded social, economic, and educational opportunities. To this end it formed the Economic Research and Action Project in 1964 in nine U.S. cities.

Students for a Democratic Society was also a leading actor in the anti-Vietnam War movement, organizing one of the first major marches against the war in April, 1965; it considered the war to be imperialistic and immoral. It also led the student takeover of Columbia University in 1968 in response to Columbia's proposed expansion into the surrounding poor community.

Ideological tensions within the antiwar movement as well as the difficulty of organizing the working class led to the decline of SDS by 1970. Its most lasting impact was its Port Huron statement, a vision of a humane and just society.

See also Campus Unrest, President's Commission on; Chicago seven trial; COINTELPRO; Conscientious objection; Kent State student killings; Morality and foreign policy; Socialist Party, American; Vietnam War.

Sturges v. Crowninshield

COURT: U.S. Supreme Court
DATE: Decided February 17, 1819
SIGNIFICANCE: In this case, the Supreme Court provided its first evaluation of the constitutionality of state bankruptcy statutes

Sturges and Crowninshield were parties to two contracts involving promissory notes dated March 22, 1811. When the defendant in the case, the maker of the notes, could not repay them, he was sued in federal court. The court relieved him from repaying his debts on the basis of the New York bankruptcy statute, passed April 3, 1811. The plaintiff, who had lent money in good faith and prior to enactment of the New York law, appealed this decision, basing his case on two arguments: first, that individual states did not have the power to pass bankruptcy laws, which were the exclusive province of Congress, and second, that even if states were vested with such power under the Constitution, the New York law was invalid because, in permitting discharge of debts incurred before the statute was passed, it violated the contract clause (Article I, section 10) of the Constitution, which prohibits states from passing laws that impair the obligations of contracts. The judges of the circuit court were divided as to whether the ruling in favor of the defendant should be overturned, thus obliging the Supreme Court to decide the appeal.

The Supreme Court, by a vote of 6 to 0, voided the New York statute. Although Chief Justice John Marshall, writing for the Court, rejected the argument that the federal government had exclusive jurisdiction over insolvency laws, he did find the New York law an unconstitutional state interference with contracts.

Although Article I, section 8 of the Constitution empowers Congress to establish "uniform Laws on the subject of Bankruptcies throughout the United States," in 1819 there was no national bankruptcy law. In the absence of a comprehensive national scheme, Marshall declared, states were free to create their own systems of bankruptcy relief—so long as they did not discharge contracts involving debt. Since this is the very point of bankruptcy laws, *Sturges v. Crowninshield* left states in confusion until the Court again addressed the question in *Ogden v. Saunders* (1827), holding that states could pass insolvency laws so long as they did not permit discharge of debts that predated the laws.

Ogden, however, did not resolve the bankruptcy problem. Although various states, primarily northern ones, did attempt schemes for discharging insolvent debtors, they found they had difficulty meeting the needs of both debtors and creditors. Some states, fearful that bankruptcy laws would discourage lending altogether, did not even enter the field. Finally, in 1898, Congress put the controversy to rest by passing national bankruptcy legislation which preempted state insolvency laws. Flaws in the administration of the system were further addressed with the Bankruptcy Reform Act of 1978, which created a separate system of bankruptcy courts to enforce the new legislation.

See also Bankruptcy; Contract, freedom of; Contract law; Federalism; Marshall, John; *Ogden v. Saunders*; Supremacy clause.

Subpoena power

DEFINITION: The power of the courts to require a person with knowledge of relevant events to testify at a trial

SIGNIFICANCE: The constitutional right of an accused person to be able to demand that people appear and testify at his or her trial is intended to help provide the accused with the most effective defense possible

Among other important rights guaranteed to accused persons by the United States Constitution, the Sixth Amendment of the Bill of Rights guarantees a person the basic right "to have compulsory process for obtaining witnesses in his favor." That process is the right to request that a subpoena be issued to compel people who have direct knowledge of one's case to appear in court to testify on one's behalf. Regardless of whether they are "too busy" or do not want to appear, the law compels them to testify.

If subpoenaed, a person is legally required to appear in court. Failure to appear can result in a fine or imprisonment for contempt of court. Sometimes testimony can be postponed or taken by deposition (sworn testimony put into writing), but a subpoenaed person is not given the option of refusing to testify.

The technical term for an ordinary subpoena ordering someone to testify in court is *subpoena ad testificandum*. There is also a type of subpoena that orders someone to turn over specific documents or papers to the court. That is called a *subpoena duces tecum*.

Occasionally a person not wanting to turn over a paper to a court may plead the right of privacy or attempt to invoke the Fourth Amendment prohibition against warrantless searches and seizures. Courts have seldom paid much attention to such protests. Even the Fifth Amendment provision against self-incrimination has seldom prevented courts from ordering documents turned over. Administrative agencies in the executive branch normally have these same powers of subpoena. The federal government has always taken a broad interpretation of its own powers. The argument for these powers is the right of the accused to build as strong a case as possible in his or her own defense.

See also Bribery; Civil procedure; Commercialized vice; Contempt of court; Criminal procedure; Evidence, rules of; Machine politics; Police corruption and misconduct; Political corruption; Privacy, right of; Search and seizure; Spoils system and patronage; Watergate scandal.

Suicide and euthanasia

DEFINITION: Respectively, the deliberate termination of one's own life and the act of ending the life of someone suffering an incurable illness or condition

SIGNIFICANCE: Developments reflect governmental efforts to come to terms with the right of individuals to control their demise in an age when invasive medical technologies can, sometimes painfully, extend biological existence long beyond the point of productive life

Issues involving life and death altered profoundly during the twentieth century. One hundred years ago, numerous ailments and injuries that can today be treated were invariably fatal, and people usually died in their homes. Death has since become a less private matter. Injuries and diseases often involve hospitals, where invasive procedures can be used to delay the death of both the comatose and the conscious beyond their ability to partake of life. In response to these developments, some citizens have asserted a right to die, lest painful medical technologies prolong their lives while exhausting their resources and sapping their dignity.

Background. The state's interest in preserving life as long as possible remains an established part of government and law. Many states in the United States still make attempted suicide a crime; some treat it as murder if a person persuades another to commit suicide or aids in the act. Killing a person even to end suffering is, technically, a form of premeditated homicide in most states.

Yet the concept of euthanasia (or mercy killing) as an act of putting to death persons suffering from incurable and painful ailments is not new. The term's origin can be traced at least to the seventeenth century, when it meant "quiet and easy death." Older still is the common-law right of individuals to protect their bodies from unjustifiable interference.

In the United States, the euthanasia movement came into being in the mid-twentieth century. By the 1970's public opinion and practice in the United States began to favor euthanasia's legalization. Opinion polls taken during the mid-1970's persistently showed a majority in favor of allowing people to end their lives when suffering from painful and incurable disease. More remarkably, studies of trials involving mercy killings since the 1950's indicate that in a significant majority of cases the accused were found not guilty. Similarly, case studies of the behavior of medical professionals indicate that during the 1970's more than half of the physicians in major city hospitals practiced some form of euthanasia on at least one occasion (typically by withholding extraordinary treatment from a suffering, incurable patient).

Right-to-die court cases also began to surface during the early 1970's. In Florida in 1971, for example, a lower court spoke of an individual's right not to be hurt in upholding a dying hemophiliac's decision to refuse additional transfusions. Still, as late as 1976, no state legislature, higher state court, or federal entity had upheld an individual's right to refuse life-sustaining medical treatment or prescribed a manner by which such a right could be legally asserted.

The Quinlan Case. The pivotal moment for the right-to-die issue in the American justice system was the case involving Karen Anne Quinlan, a young woman who collapsed into a vegetative state after ingesting a combination of tranquilizing drugs and alcohol. Quinlan's parents, advised by the physicians attending their daughter that there was no hope of her recovery, requested that the respirator prolonging her life be disconnected. When the hospital refused, Quinlan's parents went to court. In 1976, the New Jersey Supreme Court granted their motion, ruling that under some circumstances an individual's right to privacy outweighs a state's interest in preserving life and permits the withdrawal of invasive life-supporting procedures.

The court's opinion was limited to the circumstances of the case and included a four-part procedure for withdrawing medical care under even those circumstances. The attending physi-

cian had to conclude that recovery was impossible, a hospital's ethics committee had to agree, the attending physician had to agree to the removal of the life-prolonging equipment, and the patient's parents or guardian had to request the action and waive liability action against the hospital and physicians before such passive euthanasia could be practiced.

The case nevertheless had a broad impact on several fronts. The photographs of the once-lovely young woman, combined with the stories of the hopelessness of her condition and the mechanical devices being used to prolong her life, generated a national debate on such issues as the quality of life versus biological existence and suicide versus the passive withdrawal of extraordinary life-sustaining mechanisms. By 1980, public opinion polls showed the number of people favoring a right to die had grown to more than 70 percent.

The Quinlan case also led to the adoption of a variety of state laws and arrangements to enable competent adults to choose the medical treatment they might receive when no longer able to refuse attention. Generically known as "natural death acts," these statutes are of two broad types: living wills, which enable adults to create written directives instructing

The parents of Karen Anne Quinlan sought the right to let their daughter die once physicians told them she could never recover from her coma. The case attracted national attention in the mid-1970's. (AP/Wide World Photos)

physicians to withhold (or provide) life-sustaining procedures in the event of a terminal accident or illness, and advance directives (ADs), which use "durable power of attorney for health care" documents to empower proxies to make decisions involving this care when patients can no longer make such determinations themselves. ADs provide the greater flexibility because they keep the ultimate decision over whether to continue treatment in the patient's hands or those of a proxy. Living wills leave the interpretation of instructions and the decision to withhold or withdraw life-maintaining processes to physicians. Both arrangements typically require that two physicians certify the terminal nature of a patient's condition before medical care can be withdrawn, and both free physicians from civil or criminal liability in terminating care. The first Natural Death Act was passed by California the same year as the *Quinlan* decision; by 1994 every state except Nebraska had adopted some form of living will law.

Meanwhile, the Quinlan case opened the door to further court activity in states without natural death legislation. In most instances, these cases widened the circumstances under which patients—or their parents, guardians, or even close associates—could end life-prolonging procedures. Some states,

however, moved in the opposite direction. New York and Missouri, for example, demanded a higher standard of proof of intent (evidence indicating that the patient would have wanted the procedures discontinued) than New Jersey had required in the Quinlan case.

The Right to Die and the Federal Government. Missouri's unwillingness to allow the parents of an accident victim to remove the nutrition-providing tubes maintaining the life of their daughter produced the Supreme Court's first right-to-die decision, *Cruzan v. Director, Missouri Department of Health* (1990). Although Cruzan had existed in a vegetative state for seven years, Missouri refused to permit the tubes' withdrawal because the patient had never explicitly told family or friends prior to her accident that she would not want her life prolonged in such a manner.

In recognizing a patient's right to die, the Supreme Court adopted the "clear and convincing" evidence of intent test rather than the more restrictive "unequivocal proof" test that Missouri favored. The Court also recognized a person's right to refuse both artificial-mechanical means of sustaining bodily functions and food and hydration injections. On the other hand, *Cruzan* did not establish a broad, constitutional right to die. The *Cruzan*

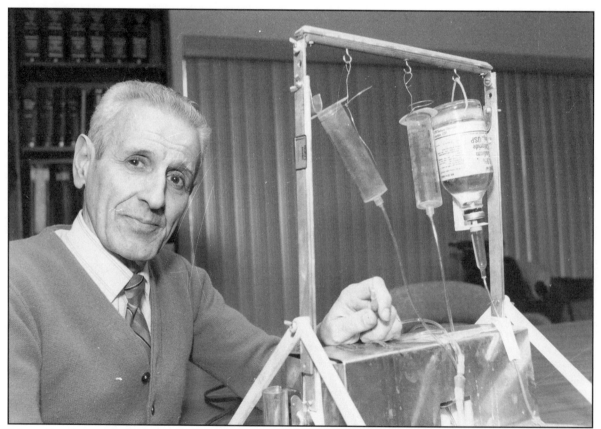

Right-to-die advocate Dr. Jack Kevorkian engendered tremendous controversy in the early 1990's for assisting terminally ill patients in ending their lives with the help of a device that the press nicknamed the "suicide machine." (AP/Wide World Photos)

decision rests not on the constitutional right to privacy but on the due process clause of the Fourteenth Amendment and the long-established right of individuals to be free from physical harm.

Cruzan also left the states as the principal actors affecting the right to die. Hence, because only a half-dozen states recognize as living wills expressions not contained in a formal document, the right to die can extensively depend on where a person resides. Most important, the *Cruzan* ruling applies only to those who have signed or formally expressed a living will desire to avoid heroic, life-sustaining measures (only 15 percent of the American people have living wills). Individuals falling into a coma without leaving clear and convincing evidence of such a desire have no federally recognized right to die under *Cruzan*.

To plug this gap at least somewhat, Congress passed the Patient Self-Determination Act in 1991. Based on recommendations of the 1983 President's Commission for the Study of Ethical Problems in Medicine and Biomedical and Behavioral Research, *Deciding to Forego Life-Sustaining Treatment: A Report on the Ethical, Medical, and Legal Issues in Treatment Decisions*, the act requires that medical facilities receiving Medicare and Medicaid payments inform patients of their right to execute living wills and advance directives.

Passive and Active Euthanasia and the Law. Prior to the 1990's, litigation and statutory law focused on passive (or "negative") euthanasia and the circumstances under which life-sustaining treatment could be withdrawn or withheld from terminal, often comatose patients. The states' adoption of "death with dignity" laws essentially addressed these issues by enabling those with living wills to refuse extraordinary measures during the advanced stages of terminal infirmities. Subsequently, most litigation has revolved around hearings to determine whether those failing to execute living wills before losing consciousness had otherwise evinced a clear desire to avoid extraordinary life-prolonging measures. Legal action of this nature is required in every state. Otherwise, the withdrawal of medical attention would constitute involuntary euthanasia, prosecutable as murder in many jurisdictions.

Meanwhile, for the conscious person suffering a lingering illness, the suicide option has become less controversial. Derek Humphry's *Lawful Exit: The Limits of Freedom for Help in Dying* (1993), something of a suicide manual written by the founder of the Hemlock Society, sold well in a limited but expanding market. Most intriguing, the key political issue has shifted from passive to active euthanasia, also known as physician-assisted suicide, which came to national attention between 1993 and 1995 through the cases brought against physician Jack Kevorkian by the state of Michigan for allegedly aiding incurably ill patients in the taking of their lives. Physician-assisted suicide takes two forms. The less controversial has the physician prescribing a lethal drug which the patient, acting alone, takes. In the more controversial form, the doctor administers a lethal injection. Not only is the latter illegal virtually everywhere in the United States, but during the 1990's it was still viewed as a violation of medical norms. To medical ethicists, passive euthanasia is an acceptable com-

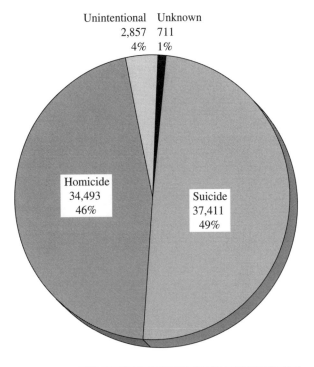

FIREARM-RELATED DEATHS, 1990-1991

Unintentional 2,857 4%

Unknown 711 1%

Homicide 34,493 46%

Suicide 37,411 49%

Source: Data are from U.S. Department of Justice, Bureau of Justice Statistics, *Sourcebook of Criminal Justice Statistics—1993*. Washington, D.C.: U.S. Government Printing Office, 1994.

Note: Data are based on death certificate information. Percentages are rounded.

promise between doctors' obligation to save lives and their obligation to ease suffering. Active euthanasia, they argue, flagrantly violates the physician's oath to preserve life.

Ethical considerations aside, the 1990's witnessed activity to legalize active euthanasia, much as the 1970's produced laws providing a legal framework for passive euthanasia. Voters in Washington State in 1991 and California in 1992 were presented with initiatives that would have allowed assistance in dying for terminally ill patients with less than six months to live. In both instances doctors would have been permitted to administer a lethal injection, and in both instances the propositions were defeated by a 54-46 percent vote. In November, 1994, however, Ballot Measure 16 passed in Oregon, enabling physicians in that state, within the framework of well-defined procedures designed to ensure the patient's actual intent, to prescribe lethal drugs for patients requesting them. In passing this legislation, Oregon became the first American state to permit a form of active, though entirely voluntary, euthanasia.

—*Joseph R. Rudolph, Jr.*

See also *Cruzan v. Director, Missouri Department of Health*; Legal ethics; Medical and health law; Medical malpractice; Wills, trusts, and estate planning.

BIBLIOGRAPHY

Excellent general works include Baruch A. Brody, ed., *Suicide and Euthanasia: Historical and Contemporary Themes* (Boston: Kluwer Academic Publishers, 1989), and Robert N. Wennberg, *Terminal Choices: Euthanasia, Suicide, and the Right to Die* (Grand Rapids, Michigan: Wm. B. Eerdmans, 1989). On the ethical issues involved in the topic, see especially James P. Moreland and Norman L. Geisler, *The Life and Death Debate: Moral Issues of Our Time* (New York: Praeger, 1990), and James Rachels, *The End of Life: Euthanasia and Morality* (New York: Oxford University Press, 1986). Particularly helpful works focusing on the legal issues include Henry R. Glick, *The Right to Die: Policy Innovation and Its Consequences* (New York: Columbia University Press, 1992), and Melvin I. Urofsky, *Letting Go: Death, Dying, and the Law* (New York: Charles Scribner's Sons, 1993).

Suit

DEFINITION: A civil proceeding brought to obtain redress of an injury or enforcement of a right

SIGNIFICANCE: Suits are the fundamental units of the civil adversary system, which seeks to redress grievances through concrete controversies between particular parties

A suit is a legal proceeding of a civil—rather than criminal—nature. In it, one or more plaintiffs initiates a formal action before a court to obtain a legal remedy against one or more defendants for the redress of some injury or the procurement of some right. A civil suit is generally to be distinguished from a criminal proceeding, in which government seeks to punish parties believed to have violated some criminal law. In the American system of justice, suits occur within an adversarial framework. Opposing parties, typically one or more plaintiffs and defendants, contend against each other for results they believe just. A judge acts as an independent arbiter of the conflicting claims rather than as a prosecutor of any particular claim (in contrast to "inquisitorial" systems of justice).

Formerly, the word "suit" was commonly used to describe a proceeding at equity, in contrast with an action at law. A proceeding in equity attempted to serve the broad interests of justice without strict adherence to the formal rules of the common law. Actions at law were heard by common-law courts and, if successful, normally yielded a remedy in the form of money damages. Suits in equity were brought before separate courts of equity, empowered to administer a broader range of "equitable" remedies, including injunctions. Today, most jurisdictions have abolished the distinction between common law and equity courts, and both forms of action may be heard by the same court. Moreover, "suit" may now refer either to an action at law for damages or to a proceeding for equitable relief. All civil actions are therefore "suits."

The conduct of a suit is governed by formal rules of civil procedure. For example, the Federal Rules of Civil Procedure govern civil actions in federal district and appellate courts. A typical suit is commenced by the plaintiff's filing of a complaint of petition for relief against one or more defendants and the summoning of the defendant or defendants to answer the complaint. Having made their respective complaint and answer, the parties to the suit then generally engage in pretrial discovery of information relevant to their dispute. Procedural mechanisms such as a motion to dismiss a suit and a motion for summary judgment sometimes serve to foreshorten suits with no merit or resolve uncontroverted issues without the time and expense of a trial on the merits. Most suits, however, proceed to trial before either a judge or a jury. Thereafter the court before which the suit is brought renders a decision in the form of a judgment, an official determination of the rights and claims of the parties made a subject of the suit.

See also Civil procedure; Civil remedies; Class action; Equity; Judicial system, U.S.; Litigation; Tort; Tort reform.

Supremacy clause

DATE: U.S. Constitution ratified June 21, 1788

DEFINITION: The portion of the U.S. Constitution declaring it the supreme law of the land

SIGNIFICANCE: The supremacy clause means that federal law generally supersedes conflicting state law

Article VI of the U.S. Constitution states that the Constitution and laws of the United States and all treaties made by the United States shall be the supreme law of the land. This statement is known as the supremacy clause. It establishes a hierarchy of law in the United States that requires all other laws to conform to the terms of the Constitution.

The supremacy clause also means that if a state passes a law conflicting with a law of the U.S. Congress, the state law is said to be preempted by the federal law. Many state laws regulating business and employment matters have been preempted because they conflict with federal law. Preemption permitted tremendous growth in federal regulation of business. Uniform federal provisions have been held to apply in all the states and to take precedence over the oftentimes conflicting rules found in the several states. Thus, in many areas of the law, workers and consumers are protected equally across the country.

See also Constitution, U.S.; Constitutional law; *Cooper v. Aaron*; Federalism; States' rights.

Supreme Court of the United States

DEFINITION: The highest court in the federal court system

SIGNIFICANCE: The Supreme Court interprets the Constitution, sets limits to the scope and power of the legislative and executive branches of government, and establishes policies that affect the daily lives of Americans

The United States has a dual court system—one state, one federal. Within this system, the Supreme Court wields enormous power. Sitting at the top of the federal judiciary, it is the court of last resort in the federal court system and for the fifty state courts when a federal question is involved. From this position, the Court acts as the nation's conscience, determines the meaning of the Constitution, declares the acts of both Congress and the president unconstitutional when these acts do not conform with the Court's interpretation of constitutional principles, and protects the rights and liberties of minorities from the tyranny of hostile majorities.

Article III. Because of disagreements over how the federal courts should be organized and how much power they should have, the framers left Article III of the Constitution, which established the judicial branch of government, short and vague. The only court required by the Constitution is the Supreme Court. The establishment of lower federal courts is left to Congress, as is the power to add to or subtract from the number of judges that sit on the Court. In the first century of its existence, the number of Supreme Court justices ranged from five to ten. In 1869, it was changed to nine. Justices are appointed by the president with the approval of the Senate.

The founding fathers clearly intended the courts to be independent of Congress and the executive branch. In order to immunize federal judges from retaliation for unpopular decisions, Article III provides them with lifetime appointments as well as the guarantee that their salaries will not be reduced while they hold office. The only constitutional mechanism for their removal is impeachment, a cumbersome and little-used procedure. As of 1995, no Supreme Court justice had ever been removed from the bench in this manner.

Article III also limits the Court's original jurisdiction, or authority to hear a case first, to cases involving ambassadors, other public ministers and consuls, and certain cases in which a state is a party. Throughout the entire history of the Court, fewer than two hundred cases have arisen out of its original jurisdiction. Most of the cases that come before the Court each year are heard on appeal from U.S. courts of appeal and state courts of last resort. The Court's appellate jurisdiction, or authority to hear cases on appeal from lower courts, is left to Congress. Today, because of a combination of congressional acts and court decisions, the Supreme Court has control of its own agenda. It decides what cases it wants to hear and denies a hearing to those that it does not want to hear.

The Power of the Court. The Supreme Court got off to a slow and shaky start. In the first decade of its existence, it conducted little business and commanded little respect. When it convened for the first time on February 1, 1790, two justices did not even bother to attend, and both resigned before the end of the first term. At a later date, the first chief justice also resigned to become envoy to England because he was not convinced that the Court would ever acquire the dignity and respect that he believed it should be afforded.

From 1790 to 1803, little happened to dispel the concerns of the first chief justice. During this period, Congress did pass the Judiciary Act of 1789, which established the federal court system, but the role of the Supreme Court was still ambiguous, particularly in regard to the all-important power of judicial review—the power to declare the acts of Congress, the president, and the legislatures of the various states unconstitutional if they are judged to be in conflict with the Constitution. On this matter, the Constitution was silent. Without the power of judicial review, the Supreme Court could never realistically be considered a coequal branch of government. When Thomas

Jefferson appointed John Marshall chief justice in 1801, however, the Court's fortune was destined to change.

Marshall devoted his thirty-four years as chief justice to enhancing the prestige and powers of the Court. His most famous decision came in the case of *Marbury v. Madison* (1803), when the Court, speaking through Marshall, declared section 13 of the Judiciary Act of 1789 unconstitutional because it conflicted with the specific limitations the Constitution places on the original jurisdiction of the Supreme Court. Section 13 was a relatively insignificant part of the act, but by striking down this minor provision of a law passed by Congress, the Court established its right to exercise judicial review over the legislative branch of government. Subsequent cases extended the power of judicial review to presidential acts and to the actions of state legislatures.

The impact of Supreme Court decisions often reaches far beyond the particulars of a given case and creates public policy as far-reaching as any produced by Congress or the president of the United States. For example, on May 17, 1954, when the Court ruled in *Brown v. Board of Education* against segregation in public schools, it signaled the end of legally created segregation of the races in the United States. The *Brown* case stands as testimony to the depth and breadth of the Court's policy-making power. Yet vast power is subject to vast abuse. In *Plessy v. Ferguson* (1896), the same Court had upheld a Louisiana statute requiring the segregation of railroad cars and in so doing had reinforced the right of states to segregate the races for the use of drinking fountains, washrooms, restaurants, and other public facilities. Though the *Plessy* decision is now considered both immoral and ill conceived, from 1896 through 1954 the segregation of public facilities in the United States was constitutional. What is constitutional is what the Supreme Court says is constitutional, and what is unconstitutional is what the Supreme Court says is unconstitutional. Such is its awesome power.

The enormous power of the Supreme Court does not, however, go unchecked. In the first place, the justices have no police force or army at their disposal. They are dependent upon the executive branch for the enforcement of their decisions. Occasionally, this enforcement is not forthcoming. A classic example was President Andrew Jackson's refusal to return land that the state of Georgia had seized from the Cherokee Nation between 1827 and 1830. Jackson was able to get away with defying the Court's *Cherokee Nation v. Georgia* (1831) decision because public opinion weighed heavily in his favor and against the Native Americans. The point here is that the Court cannot entirely ignore public opinion. The Court's powers are also restrained by the other branches of government and the states. The fact that justices are appointed by the president with the consent of the Senate ensures the other two branches of government a major role in determining the composition of the Court and, indirectly, the character of the Court's decisions. Finally, Congress and the states can undo a Court decision interpreting the Constitution of the United States by changing that document through the amendment process.

The Justices. Supreme Court justices are not representative of the general population. The typical justice is a white male Protestant from a relatively well-to-do family. As of 1995, only two African Americans (Thurgood Marshall and Clarence Thomas) and two women (Sandra Day O'Connor and Ruth Bader Ginsburg) had served on the Court. Most of its justices have previous judicial experience.

The criteria for selecting justices are highly political. As a general rule, presidents appoint individuals from their own political party. Approximately 90 percent of all nominees to the federal bench since the time of President Franklin D. Roosevelt have been members of the president's party who are believed to share the president's ideological views. Once justices are appointed to the Supreme Court, however, predictions about their future decisions often prove extremely unreliable, as President Eisenhower learned after his selection of Earl Warren as chief justice. Eisenhower's choice of Warren had been based to a large extent upon Warren's solid conservative record as governor of California, yet Chief Justice Warren led the way toward some of the most liberal decisions in the Court's history.

When a justice dies or steps down and a vacancy occurs, the president and his staff put together a list of possible nominees whose names are gathered from a wide variety of sources, including the attorney general, influential members of the legal community, party leaders, and interest groups. The Justice Department then helps the president screen potential nominees and subjects serious contenders to a background check by the Federal Bureau of Investigation. Since 1946, the Standing Committee on the Federal Judiciary of the American Bar Association, the largest organization of lawyers in the United States, ranks prospective nominees on a four-point scale ranging from "exceptionally well qualified" to "not qualified."

Once a nominee has been chosen, the president submits the nomination to the Senate, which must confirm the nomination by a majority vote. It is before the Senate Judiciary Committee that major battles over judicial confirmation, when they occur, usually take place. Nevertheless, the presumption is that presidents should be allowed considerable discretion in judicial appointments. As of 1995, the Senate had refused to confirm

The Supreme Court in November, 1994. From left are (front row) Antonin Scalia, John Paul Stevens, Chief Justice William Rehnquist, Sandra Day O'Connor, and Anthony Kennedy. Behind them, from left, are Ruth Bader Ginsburg, David Souter, Clarence Thomas, and Stephen Breyer. (AP/Wide World Photos)

October Terms	Cases Argued During Term	Cases Disposed of by Full Opinions	Cases Disposed of by Per Curiam Opinions	Cases Set for Reargument	Cases Granted Review This Term	Cases Reviewed and Decided Without Oral Argument	Total to Be Available for Argument at Outset of Following Term
ACTIVITIES OF THE U.S. SUPREME COURT, 1983-1992							
1983	184	174	6	4	149	86	80
1984	175	159	11	5	185	82	87
1985	172	161	10	1	187	103	101
1986	175	164	10	1	167	113	91
1987	167	151	9	7	180	95	105
1988	170	156	12	2	147	110	81
1989	146	143	3	0	122	80	57
1990	125	121	4	0	141	115	70
1991	127	120	3	4	120	77	66
1992	116	111	4	0	97	113	46

Source: U.S. Department of Justice, Bureau of Justice Statistics, *Sourcebook of Criminal Justice Statistics—1993*. Washington, D.C.: U.S. Government Printing Office, 1994.

Note: Figures represent status at the conclusion of the Supreme Court's October term.

29 of the 138 presidential nominees to the Supreme Court, and only 7 of these in the twentieth century.

The formal powers of the chief justice are relatively meager. The chief justice decides which petitions for a hearing are to be considered by the full Court, presides over the Court in oral argument and in conference, and assigns the writing of opinions whenever the chief justice is in the majority, which is most of the time. In those instances in which this is not the case, the senior justice in the majority assigns the opinion. These powers, by themselves, do not guarantee leadership as much as afford the opportunity to lead. Not surprisingly, then, the power of chief justices to provide intellectual leadership and policy direction for the Court has varied considerably with the personality and ability of the incumbents.

The Administration of Justice. Because the Supreme Court makes national policy that has such far-reaching impact on every American citizen, it is important to have an understanding of how justices decide which cases to hear and how they formulate and arrive at their decisions. In the later twentieth century, the caseload of the Supreme Court increased dramatically, from fewer than nine hundred in 1930 to more than six thousand a year in the 1990's. Yet of the thousands of cases that find their way to the Court's calendar each year, fewer than two hundred are selected by the justices for consideration. For the vast majority that are denied review, the decisions of the lower courts are left standing. The method for deciding which cases warrant oral arguments and full consideration by the Court is the informal "rule of four." By tradition, when four or more justices agree that a case should be heard, the Court issues a writ of *certiorari*, or order to the lower court to prepare a record of the case and to send it up to the Supreme Court for review.

Not only are the odds against a case ever receiving full consideration by the Supreme Court, but the costs are also extremely high. Unlike litigants in most European countries, parties in the United States must pay their own way. This is referred to as the "American rule." The Court's filing fee is three hundred dollars; another one hundred dollars is added if a case is granted oral argument. While other fees may be encountered, the direct costs to a litigant are well under a thousand dollars. Nevertheless, before the case reaches the Supreme Court, the costs of bringing a case through the trial and appeal process can cost millions of dollars.

Not all litigants bear these expenses themselves. Interest groups often assume the costs for cases in which they have an interest. For indigent (without funds) defendants in criminal cases, the government provides an attorney without cost. Indigents in noncriminal cases can petition the Court *in forma pauperis* (in the manner of a pauper) for exemption from the usual fees.

Once the Court agrees to review a case, the lawyers for each side submit a brief that summarizes the lower court's opinion, presents their arguments, and discusses past cases on which the Court has ruled that are relevant to the legal issues in question. Sometimes other written briefs, called *amicus curiae* (friend of the court) briefs, may be submitted by individuals, organizations, or government agencies that have an interest in the case. After these briefs are circulated among the justices, a date is set for the attorneys to present their oral arguments. During oral arguments, the justices often interrupt to ask questions or to request additional information. At times, the justices may even try to help attorneys if they are having a difficult time.

After hearing oral arguments, the justices meet in a conference room where no outsiders are allowed. There, in complete secrecy, they debate the cases before them. The chief justice summarizes the facts and legal issues involved in each case and makes suggestions for their disposal. Then each justice, in order of seniority, presents his or her views or conclusions. Cases are decided on the base of majority rule. In the event of a tie, the

CHIEF JUSTICES OF THE UNITED STATES		
Chief Justice	Years Served	Appointed by
John Jay	1789-1795	George Washington
Oliver Ellsworth	1796-1800	George Washington
John Marshall	1801-1835	John Adams
Roger B. Taney	1836-1864	Andrew Jackson
Salmon P. Chase	1864-1873	Abraham Lincoln
Morrison R. Waite	1874-1888	Ulysses S. Grant
Melville W. Fuller	1888-1910	Grover Cleveland
Edward D. White	1910-1921	William Howard Taft
William Howard Taft	1921-1930	Warren G. Harding
Charles Evans Hughes	1930-1941	Herbert Hoover
Harlan Fiske Stone	1941-1946	Franklin D. Roosevelt
Fred M. Vinson	1946-1953	Harry S Truman
Earl Warren	1953-1969	Dwight D. Eisenhower
Warren E. Burger	1969-1986	Richard M. Nixon
William Rehnquist	1986-	Ronald Reagan

ruling of the lower court is left standing. (A tie is possible when one of the nine justices is absent.) Yet the conference vote is not binding. The justices are free to change their votes until the moment when the final opinion is read in open court.

After the conference vote, an opinion must be written. This is the most difficult and time-consuming task of a Supreme Court justice. Writing an opinion for a major case can take months. Once an opinion is drafted, it is circulated among the other justices for review and comment. Because these cases involve complex and difficult issues, it is often the case that the first draft is not acceptable to a majority. Frequently, an opinion has to be redrafted and recirculated several times before a majority can be reached. The goal of the author is always to achieve the largest majority possible. This frequently entails considerable political negotiating and bargaining among the justices. Yet a decisive majority is important because the legal system of the United States is based upon the principle of *stare decisis* (let the decision stand) or precedent, which means that the principles of law established in earlier cases should be accepted as authoritative in similar cases. The greater the majority, the clearer the message. This is particularly true where the Supreme Court is concerned, for this court is expected to provide direction and guidance to the entire judicial system.

When in the majority, the chief justice decides who will write the opinion. On the other hand, when the chief justice is the minority, the senior justice in the majority makes the assignment. There are five kinds of opinions: (1) *per curiam* (brief and unsigned) opinions, (2) unanimous opinions, when all the justices agree, (3) majority opinions, when the Court is divided, (4) concurring opinions, when one or more of the justices agree with the ruling but for different reasons which they wish to state, and (5) dissenting opinions, written by one or more of the justices on the losing side.

Judicial Activism. The Supreme Court has always generated political controversy. Yet the more activist role of the Court in recent times has brought the issue of judicial power to the forefront of the political debate. Supporters of judicial activism argue that the Court corrects injustices that the White House, Congress, state legislatures, and city councils fail to address, such as racial discrimination in public facilities prior to *Brown v. Board of Education*. Such corrections, they argue, are vital for a democratic society. Critics of judicial activism advocate judicial restraint. From their perspective, no matter how desirable Court-declared rights and principles might be, when the justices depart from their proper roles as interpreters of the Constitution to undertake broad and sweeping policy initiatives, they become nonelected sovereigns in black robes usurping the legitimate authority of Congress and state legislatures.

Other Court observers believe that both those who support judicial activism and those who advocate judicial restraint fail to grasp the complexity of the issues that come before the Court. According to this group, the Court should take an activist role whenever legislation restricts the democratic process by which decisions are made or whenever legislation interferes with the rights of minorities. In all other instances, they contend, established political process should be allowed to work without interference from the Court. Given the power of the Court in the American political system, it is little wonder that questions over its proper role fuel one of the perennial debates of American politics. —*Thomas J. Mortillaro*

See also Brandeis, Louis D.; Burger, Warren; Cardozo, Benjamin Nathan; *Certiorari*, writ of; Constitution, U.S.; Constitutional interpretation; Constitutional law; Court-packing plan of Franklin D. Roosevelt; Douglas, William O.; Judicial review; Judicial system, U.S.; Marshall, John; Marshall, Thurgood; Rehnquist, William; Retroactivity of Supreme Court decisions; Taney, Roger Brooke; Warren, Earl.

BIBLIOGRAPHY

Probably the most accessible overview of the Supreme Court for the beginner is David M. O'Brien's *Storm Center: The Supreme Court in American Politics* (3d ed. New York: W. W. Norton, 1993), in which the author discusses how personality, politics, and the law come together and impact the daily lives of Americans. More expository and analytical but still very readable overviews are Lawrence Baum's *The Supreme Court* (5th ed. Washington, D.C.: Congressional Quarterly Press, 1995); Henry J. Abraham's *The Judiciary: The Supreme Court in the Governmental Process* (7th ed. Boston, Mass.: Allyn and Bacon, 1987); and Stephen L. Wasby's *The Supreme Court in the Federal Judicial System* (4th ed. Chicago: Nelson-Hall, 1993). Case studies are a particularly engaging way to learn about the workings of the Supreme Court. John A. Garraty, ed., presents a series of fascinating studies of landmark cases that read like exciting short stories in *Quarrels That Have Shaped the Constitution* (rev. ed. New York: Perennial Library, 1987).

Swann v. Charlotte-Mecklenburg Board of Education

COURT: U.S. Supreme Court

DATE: Decided April 20, 1971

SIGNIFICANCE: In this case, the U.S. Supreme Court determined that lower courts may properly order local school boards to use extensive school busing to desegregate urban schools

By the end of the 1960's, a significant percentage of southern school boards had desegregated their schools. The primary exception to this trend was urban schools. Many urban schools by the end of the 1960's were still segregated because of significant residential segregation. In 1968, in *Green v. County School Board of New Kent County*, the Supreme Court ruled that school boards had an "affirmative duty" to take all necessary actions to integrate schools. The question after the *Green* decision was what type of affirmative action must an urban school board faced with considerable residential segregation take in order to integrate its schools.

In the late 1960's, a group of black parents, with the assistance of the National Association for the Advancement of Colored People Legal Defense and Educational Fund, filed a lawsuit seeking to force the school board in Charlotte, North Carolina, to implement an extensive school busing plan to integrate its schools. Prior to the litigation, children in the Charlotte-Mecklenburg school system were assigned to schools on the basis of their residence. As a result, many schools remained all-white or all-black because of the city's residential segregation.

In February of 1970, federal district court judge James McMillan ordered the Charlotte-Mecklenburg Board of Education to adopt an extensive busing plan that would integrate

The Swann v. Charlotte-Mecklenburg Board of Education *decision ushered in the controversial era of busing to reduce* de facto *segregation in schools. Here thousands of marchers protest busing in Boston in 1975.* (AP/Wide World Photos)

every school in the school system. McMillan's busing plan sparked a firestorm of opposition, with politicians throughout the state and nation, including President Richard Nixon, criticizing his action. In June, 1970, the U.S. Supreme Court decided to review the case to decide whether urban school boards were required to engage in extensive school busing to overcome residential segregation. It was understood throughout the country that the *Swann* case would settle the issue of whether school boards would be obliged to engage in school busing to integrate their schools.

In April, 1971, the U.S. Supreme Court unanimously held that school busing was an appropriate method for eliminating segregated schools and that Judge McMillan had acted properly in ordering the Charlotte-Mecklenburg School Board to engage in extensive busing. The Court did say that not every majority black school had to be eliminated in order to satisfy constitutional demands, but it did strongly affirm the legitimacy of busing as a means of integrating urban schools.

In the wake of the *Swann* decision, lower court judges throughout the South ordered urban school boards to adopt school busing plans. In the meantime, members of Congress sought passage of both legislation and constitutional amendments restricting the application of the *Swann* decision. Efforts to amend the Constitution failed, and the legislation that Congress enacted did not significantly inhibit the ability of courts to require school busing. As a result of the *Swann* decision, most urban school systems eventually adopted pupil-assignment plans involving school busing.

See also *Brown v. Board of Education*; Busing; Civil Rights movement; *Green v. County School Board of New Kent County*; *Milliken v. Bradley*; National Association for the Advancement of Colored People Legal Defense and Educational Fund; Segregation, *de facto* and *de jure*.

Sweatt v. Painter

COURT: U.S. Supreme Court

DATE: Decided June 5, 1950

SIGNIFICANCE: This unanimous Supreme Court declared that the "separate but equal" standard established in *Plessy v. Ferguson* was unattainable in higher education

Plessy v. Ferguson (1896) established the "separate but equal" doctrine that provided the legal justification for segregation.

Civil rights organizations, including the National Association for the Advancement of Colored People (NAACP), although opposed to "separate but equal," decided to use the courts in an attempt to make sure that the "equal" part of the "separate but equal" doctrine was being enforced. In a series of cases running from 1936 to the *Sweatt* decision in 1950, the NAACP attacked the lack of law schools and graduate programs for blacks throughout the South.

If no professional schools existed, clearly the "separate but equal" doctrine was not being met. When African Americans started seeking admission to professional schools throughout the South, many states established "overnight" law schools and professional schools in order to comply with *Plessy*. These schools were certainly separate, but were they equal? Herman Sweatt, a Houston, Texas, postal worker, applied to admission to the University of Texas Law School in 1946. He was denied admission on the grounds that Texas had just created a law school for blacks. To avoid integration, Texas had rented a few rooms in Houston and hired two black lawyers as its faculty.

Sweatt refused to attend the "black law school," saying that it was inferior and he would be deprived of the "equal protection of the law." A unanimous Supreme Court sided with Sweatt, whose case was argued by Thurgood Marshall of the NAACP. Even if the facilities at the two Texas schools were equal, the Court concluded that inequality might exist with respect to other factors "which make for greatness in a law school." Such factors include the reputation of the faculty and administration and the prestige of the alumni. "It is difficult to believe," said Chief Justice Fred M. Vinson, Jr., "that one who had a free choice between these law schools would consider the question close."

The Court ordered that Sweatt be admitted to the University of Texas Law School. The *Sweatt* case marked the first time the Supreme Court found a black professional school to be unequal in quality. Although the Court refused to reexamine *Plessy v. Ferguson*, the decision in *Sweatt* paved the way for the NAACP to launch a direct assault in overturning *Plessy* in *Brown v. Board of Education* only four years later.

See also *Brown v. Board of Education*; Civil Rights movement; Law schools; Marshall, Thurgood; National Association for the Advancement of Colored People (NAACP); *Plessy v. Ferguson*; Vinson, Fred M.

Taft, William Howard (Sept. 15, 1857, Cincinnati, Ohio—Mar. 8, 1930, Washington, D.C.)

IDENTIFICATION: President of the United States, 1909-1913; chief justice of the United States, 1921-1930

SIGNIFICANCE: As president, Taft was a conservative; as chief justice, he brought harmony and greater efficiency to the Supreme Court

William Howard Taft was the only president of the United States also to have been chief justice. Taft succeeded fellow Republican Theodore Roosevelt to the presidency in 1909 but, once there, proved too conservative to retain the support of progressive Republicans. Taft increased enforcement of antitrust legislation and strengthened the Interstate Commerce Commission. Roosevelt split off from the Republicans and ran against Taft in 1912, which allowed Democrat Woodrow Wilson to win the election.

As chief justice, Taft worked to achieve unanimity where possible and to reduce the number of dissenting opinions written by individual justices. He also sought to give an overburdened Supreme Court greater power over which cases it would select to review, thus lightening its workload considerably. Taft firmly believed that the goal of courts was to protect the happiness of the American people through speedy and effective administrative of justice. The primary concerns of the Taft Court were to protect property rights and, for the most part, to uphold existing laws. Taft's written decisions tended to weaken the rights of organized labor and to protect the privileges and rights of business and law enforcement officers.

See also Constitutional law; Contract, freedom of; Immigration laws; President of the United States; Supreme Court of the United States.

Taft-Hartley Act. *See* Labor-Management Relations Act

Takings clause

DEFINITION: The part of the Fifth Amendment to the U.S. Constitution that guarantees that private property shall not "be taken for public use, without just compensation"

SIGNIFICANCE: The taking of property for governmental purpose (for the benefit of the public at large) is allowable as long as the property owner is fairly compensated; the courts have ruled that certain regulations regarding the use of property may also constitute "takings"

As part of the Bill of Rights, the Fifth Amendment provides that whenever the government appropriates the use of privately owned property, it must appropriately compensate the owner. The concept protected in the Constitution is that al-

William Howard Taft served both as U.S. president and as chief justice of the United States. (Deane Keller, collection of the Supreme Court of the United States)

though the legislature has ultimate authority over private property, a check on misuse of this power is to require compensation to the owner. The Constitution separates this takings clause from the due process clause by only a semicolon: "nor shall any person be . . . deprived of life, liberty, or property, without due process of law; nor shall private property be taken for public use, without just compensation."

Under prerevolutionary English practice, the government could take whatever it needed or wanted without having a public purpose and without paying under the principles of sovereignty. Although James Mason, author of the takings clause, apparently thought it applicable only to the physical taking of property, as a legitimate exercise of the power of eminent domain, today it also applies to regulations the government may make while exercising its "police power." Justice Oliver Wendell Holmes stated that "while property may be regulated to a certain extent, if regulation goes too far it will be recognized as a taking." Consequently, even if a regulation, for example, satisfies the due process clause, it may still violate the takings clause. If it does, the government must abandon the regulation or compensate the affected property owner. The takings clause applies to the states as well as other governmental entities through the Fourteenth Amendment.

While the concept of "taking" is a flexible one, applicable to both real and personal property, in most cases the property is physically appropriated, invaded, or used, on either a temporary or permanent basis. Often restrictions on how persons may utilize their property are found to constitute takings, unless there is a "legitimate state interest" relating to harm to the public's health, morals, or safety. The restriction must not interfere with the owner's right to otherwise use and dispose of the property. According to the Supreme Court, there is no taking, however, unless the owner is "denied the economically viable use of his land."

See also Bill of Rights, U.S.; Constitutional law; Due process of law; Eminent domain; *Nollan v. California Coastal Commission*; Nuisance; Property rights; Zoning.

Taney, Roger Brooke (Mar. 17, 1777, Calvert County, Md.—Oct. 12, 1864, Washington, D.C.)

IDENTIFICATION: Chief justice of the United States, 1836-1864

SIGNIFICANCE: The last of the great chief justices the Court would see for many decades, Taney is most remembered as the author of the infamous Dred Scott decision (*Scott v. Sandford*, 1857)

Roger Brooke Taney was one of Maryland's most prominent attorneys when he was elected to the state senate in 1816 as a Federalist. When the party dissolved shortly thereafter, he became a Democrat, eventually joining the administration of President Andrew Jackson in 1831. Taney served first as attorney general, but he came into his own as a partisan politician during Jackson's war with the Bank of the United States. When Jackson decided to destroy the bank by removing its federal fund deposits, he went through two successive secre-

taries of the treasury who refused to carry out his orders before settling on Taney as the hatchet man.

Jackson wanted to reward Taney, but the Senate, which the president had alienated, refused in 1834 to nominate Taney as secretary of the treasury. The next year, however, a vacancy on the Supreme Court offered Jackson another opportunity. Although the Senate indefinitely postponed its decision on Taney's confirmation as associate justice, it finally gave in and confirmed him as chief justice a year later.

Coming to the post directly after the great and much-loved Chief Justice John Marshall, Taney had large shoes to fill, and it did not help that he had a reputation as a political hack. Although it was initially feared that the Democratic loyalist would undo the advances in constitutional nationalism made by the Marshall Court, the Taney Court in fact helped to balance the federal bias developed during Marshall's leadership by emphasizing a more equitable sovereignty shared with the states. Early opinions such as *Charles River Bridge v. Warren Bridge Co.* (1837), written by Taney, introduced tenets of Jacksonian democracy such as the belief that private property rights must be offset by community rights, which are promoted by police powers vested in the states.

Such modifications of prior constitutional readings proceeded gradually and, over time, added to the Court's prestige. Unfortunately, toward the end of his tenure, Taney presided over *Scott v. Sandford* (1857), in which the dogmatism of the states' rights movement got the upper hand. Although each justice wrote a separate opinion in the case, Taney delivered the inflammatory opinion of the Court declaring that slaves are not persons but property.

Taney lived for seven years after *Scott v. Sandford*, during which his reputation and that of the Court steadily diminished as the Civil War raged on. He died a frustrated, angry man whose tainted legacy long survived him. It took many decades for Taney once again to be valued as one of the country's great jurists.

See also *Charles River Bridge v. Warren Bridge Co.*; *Habeas corpus*; Jacksonian democracy; Lincoln, Abraham; *Scott v. Sandford*; States' rights.

Tariff

DEFINITION: Although the term can refer to any scale of charges, it most commonly refers to taxes on products imported from other countries

SIGNIFICANCE: Tariffs have been a major source of government revenue, but now they are primarily important as a focal point for debates about the impact of imported goods on the national economy

An important motivation for forming the United States government in 1787 was to remove tariffs on goods moving from one state to another. Prior to the Civil War, the tariff was the principal source of revenue for the federal government. Only with the coming of the federal income tax since 1913 has tariff revenue lost its significance.

Political pressure for high tariffs comes from industries which feel the pressure of competition from imported prod-

Chief Justice Roger Taney left a mixed legacy that included his Scott v. Sandford *opinion that slaves should be considered property rather than people.* (Mathew Brady, collection of the Supreme Court of the United States)

ucts. Tariffs are termed "protective" when they are used to influence buyers to spend less on imports and more on substitute domestic products. Such tariffs are defended as "saving jobs," but in practice they often support relatively inefficient firms. Funds spent to buy imports will in turn be used overseas to buy American export products, and the exporting industries are likely to be those which make more efficient use of the nation's resources. A relative absence of import barriers benefits consumers by keeping prices down and encouraging competition, as American automobile buyers began to discover in the 1960's. Some industries (such as textiles and shoe manufacturing) and their workers believe that import competition is unjust, since the countries of origin often pay much lower wages.

Historically, low tariffs were favored by farmers producing products for export, such as cotton and grain. Bitter controversies have centered on tariff policy, with the 1994 dispute over the North American Free Trade Agreement (NAFTA) simply one example. Increases in tariff rates by the United States tend to injure the economies of the countries supplying it with imports. This situation has been known to provoke retaliation, which can make all countries worse off. As the world economy slid into deep depression after 1929, many countries raised tariffs and other import barriers to try to stem flows of funds to other countries. The Smoot-Hawley tariff in the United States (1930) was a notorious example. In the mid-1930's, Secretary of State Cordell Hull instituted a new policy of negotiating with other countries for mutual tariff reductions. In the period after World War II, emphasis shifted to multilateral negotiations of trade concessions. These centered on the General Agreement on Tariffs and Trade (GATT), set up in 1947.

Since the 1940's, the general level of U.S. import tariffs has declined. In 1993, about 40 percent of U.S. imports entered duty-free, and customs collections averaged only about 5 percent of dutiable imports. Other types of import restrictions, however, such as quotas, have often been used. Efforts by low-income countries to achieve economic development have been impeded by the unwillingness of the developed countries to accept more imports from the developing areas.

See also Capitalism; Commerce clause; Constitution, U.S.; International law; Taxation and justice.

Tax evasion

DEFINITION: The deliberate failure to pay taxes by either not filing a tax return or filing a fraudulent or illegal tax return

SIGNIFICANCE: Tax evasion is an "unreported" crime that must be discovered by the Internal Revenue Service through various channels; tax evasion is estimated to cost the U.S. government—and therefore, honest taxpayers—well over $100 billion a year

Tax evasion may be considered a type of white-collar crime. Forms of tax evasion include not filing taxes, underreporting income, overstating expenses, fraud, and willfully disregarding tax laws. Tax evaders are subject to both civil and criminal penalties depending on the seriousness of the crime.

The existence of the "underground economy" is the primary factor in tax evasion. The tax loss attributable to the underground economy and the underreporting of income for the year 1994 was estimated to be $150 billion. This "underground" ranges from self-employed people such as plumbers, doctors, accountants, and small business owners to people who work part time performing such services as babysitting and home repairs and do not report income to the Internal Revenue Service. Significant "off the books" income is commonplace today in the United States. Furthermore, a widespread perception of the tax system as unfair and excessive

CRIMINAL TAX FRAUD CASES INITIATED BY THE INTERNAL REVENUE SERVICE CRIMINAL INVESTIGATION DIVISION				
	Cases Initiated by Criminal Investigation Division	*Disposed of by Criminal Investigation Division*		*Disposed of by Office of Chief Counsel*	
		Prosecution Recommended	*Prosecution Not Recommended*	*Prosecution Not Warranted, Including Cases Declined by the U.S. Dept. of Justice*	*Convictions*
1984	6,194	2,990	3,446	267	1,806
1985	6,065	3,234	3,015	253	2,025
1986	5,861	3,524	2,654	249	2,460
1987	5,511	3,526	2,354	186	2,556
1988	4,899	3,044	2,167	277	2,491
1989	5,417	3,242	2,011	199	2,282
1990	5,280	3,228	2,015	192	2,472
1991	5,208	3,677	1,951	142	2,911
1992	6,537	4,252	1,823	97	2,950
1993	6,146	4,266	1,726	142	3,216

Source: U.S. Department of Justice, Bureau of Justice Statistics, *Sourcebook of Criminal Justice Statistics—1993.* Washington, D.C.: U.S. Government Printing Office, 1994.

Note: The Criminal Tax Division of the Office of Chief Counsel handles criminal tax matters for the IRS, including reviewing cases for possible prosecution and working with the Department of Justice.

The trial and 1992 conviction of wealthy hotel owner Leona Helmsley (nicknamed the "queen of mean") for tax evasion generated considerable publicity. (AP/Wide World Photos)

does little to discourage tax evasion. Often, taxpayers view tax evasion as a smart, even necessary way to make ends meet. In addition, many taxpayers justify tax evasion with arguments to the effect of "the government wastes their money anyway."

Internal Revenue Service. The Internal Revenue Service (IRS) is given wide-ranging powers to collect taxes. The IRS is the keeper and collector of taxes and the enforcer of the tax law for the United States government. The IRS has the power to request information from taxpayers concerning their tax matters. It also has the power to place liens on homes, to seize bank accounts and assets, and to garnish wages. In essence, the IRS is allowed to do whatever is necessary to collect taxes as long as it is constitutionally acceptable.

Accountants must provide information about their clients to the IRS upon request. Accountants do not have the same protection of the law regarding privileged communication that ministers, psychiatrists, or lawyers do. In fact, the IRS can bar an accountant from preparing tax returns if the preparer refuses to provide information to it.

Audits. For the most part, the U.S. tax code relies on the voluntary compliance of the taxpayers in filing and paying their taxes. To ensure that taxes are being filed and paid correctly, however, the IRS performs audits on selected tax returns.

The probability of a return being audited depends on a number of factors. One is the type of tax return and deductions involved: If a taxpayer has a cash-based business, income of more than $100,000, excessive deductions, or unusual deductions such as theft losses, the chance of an audit by the IRS increases. Audit chances also increase if a taxpayer has been audited in a previous year and assessed a substantial deficiency. Another factor is a mismatch between informational filings such as W-2's and 1099's and the information on the taxpayer's tax return. Through the Taxpayer Compliance Measurement Program (TCMP), the IRS also audits a number of returns randomly to develop and update the mathematical formulas used in selecting returns for audit. Since taxpayers are asked to verify all items on their tax return, this type of audit is the most tedious. Information provided by outsiders, such as informants, may also lead to an audit. The IRS gives rewards to informants if an underpaid tax liability is assessed.

All taxpayers will receive a notice if obvious mathematical mistakes are found on their tax returns. In these cases, taxpayers are merely asked to agree to the assessment and to send in the amount due.

Audits of a more serious nature are called office or field audits. Office audits are conducted by an agent at the IRS office. Taxpayers are usually asked to bring in information to substantiate certain deductions. Field audits are usually more extensive, requiring the auditor to be on the taxpayer's premises (home or office) so that information is readily available. In most cases, the IRS and the taxpayer will settle the case after the audit. If the taxpayer does not agree to the IRS's assessment at the time, the taxpayer must go through an appeal process and perhaps go to court.

Penalties. The Internal Revenue Code requires the timely filing of returns, the proper reporting of tax liabilities, the timely payment of taxes, and the proper withholding of taxes by employers. To promote taxpayer compliance, the IRS can charge numerous penalties. The following are the most commonly assessed penalties. The failure to file penalty is 5 percent per month of the net tax due up to a maximum of 25 percent. The failure to pay penalty is 5 percent per month to a maximum of 25 percent. The negligence penalty is 20 percent of the tax underpayment attributable to negligence (defined as the "careless, reckless, and intentional" disregard of tax laws). The substantial understate- ment of tax liability penalty is 10 percent of the amount of the understatement of the tax liability. A 75 percent civil fraud penalty can be imposed if the IRS can prove fraud. Criminal penalties—both monetary fines and imprisonment—may also apply.

Famous Cases. One well-publicized case of tax evasion was that of Leona Helmsley. Helmsley was found guilty in 1992 of underreporting income and of channeling personal expenses through her corporation. Helmsley was fined and served a prison sentence. Zoë Baird, President Bill Clinton's first nominee for U.S. attorney general in 1993, was involved in a different type of tax evasion. She had not paid employment taxes for a child-care worker, and as a result she was forced to withdraw as a nominee.

The most famous criminal tax evasion case was probably that involving mobster Al Capone. Capone was imprisoned for tax evasion for failure to file tax returns for the years 1922-1925. He thereupon filed delinquent returns in the amount of $4,082. He refused to pay the amount, however, claiming poverty. Instead, Capone made a compromise offer of $1,000. Because bank records of deposits showed that more than $2 million had been deposited in his bank accounts over a five-year period, it was not difficult for the IRS to prove tax evasion, and Capone was imprisoned.   —*Marsha M. Huber*

See also Capone, Alphonse (Al); Fraud; Internal Revenue Service (IRS); Money laundering; Taxation and justice; Treasury, U.S. Department of the.

BIBLIOGRAPHY

For further information on tax evasion, see Teresa Tritch, "The $150 Billion Tax Cheats," *Money*, April 1, 1995; Frank A. Cowell, *Cheating the Government: The Economics of Evasion* (Cambridge, Mass.: MIT Press, 1990); and Walter Ingo, *The Secret Money Market: Inside the Dark World of Tax Evasion, Financial Fraud, Insider Trading, Money Laundering, and Capital Flight* (New York: Harper & Row, 1990). For tax fraud, see Darrell McGowen, Daniel G. O'Day, and Kenneth E. North, *Criminal Tax Fraud* (2d ed. Charlottesville, Va.: Michie, 1994), and Elliot Silverman, "Turning the Other Cheek: Tax Fraud, Tax Protest, and the Willfulness Requirement," *Taxes*, May 1, 1991. For the underground economy, see Dan Bawley, *The Subterranean Economy* (New York: McGraw-Hill, 1982). For famous cases, see Richard Hammer, *The Helmsleys: The Rise and Fall of Harry and Leona* (New York: New American Library, 1990), and A. Lodge, "What Al Capone Started," *Journal of Accountancy* 160 (November, 1985).

Tax Reform Act of 1986

DATE: Became law October 22, 1986

DEFINITION: The most sweeping reform of the federal income tax law since World War II

SIGNIFICANCE: The Tax Reform Act of 1986 reduced top marginal income tax rates substantially and it also eliminated or reduced several popular deductions

The purposes of the act were to reduce the tax rates and to broaden the tax base. The basic rate of corporate tax was reduced from 46 percent to 34 percent, and the marginal rate of individual income tax at higher levels of income fell from 50 percent to 28 percent. The Tax Reform Act also eliminated investment tax credits, slowed depreciation schedules, and scrapped several other deductions for corporations. On the individual side, it eliminated sales tax deduction, scrapped preferential treatment of capital gains, and imposed limits on passive losses and deductibility of individual retirement account (IRA) contributions. The Tax Reform Act enjoyed broad bipartisan congressional support. Critics argued that it would reduce nonresident investment, the gross national product (GNP), and the competitiveness of U.S. business. Supporters argued that it would remove distortions from the economy and improve fairness. Nonresident investment proved to be stable, and savings increased marginally in the 1987-1989 period. Fairness in the tax system, however, did not improve. The Congress repealed parts of the act in 1990; the top tax rate increased to 31 percent, payroll taxes increased, and itemized deductions were limited.

See also Internal Revenue Service (IRS); Reagan, Ronald; Taxation and justice.

Tax revolt movement

DATE: The modern tax revolt movement began in the late 1970's

SIGNIFICANCE: The tax revolt movement, said to have been initiated by California voters' passage of Proposition 13, resulted in many states' reducing a variety of types of taxes

In June of 1978, rapidly rising property tax rates in California led to a grassroots movement to limit property taxes. Led by conservative activists Howard Jarvis and Paul Gann, the movement coalesced around Proposition 13, which cut property taxes by 57 percent, rolling back the rates to 1 percent of a property's market value, with a maximum raise thereafter of no more than 2 percent a year. That tax revolt marked a revival of tax protest in United States, and within a year more than a dozen states had instituted taxation or spending limits, with thirty-seven states overall reducing property taxes. By 1979, sales tax cuts alone totalled $4 billion.

Although the modern tax reform movement has been criticized as being "class" driven (that is, by property owners—among those pushing hardest for Proposition 13, for example, were well-to-do people with substantial real estate holdings), the tax protest movement has involved many common citizens who thought that government was taking too much of their money. The debate involved a central, democratic issue, namely whether free people could retain more of the fruits of their labor rather than less. It also necessarily involved discussions of what government services should be cut back or eliminated if there was no longer money to pay for them.

The historical heritage of tax protests dates to the American Revolution, which erupted largely over a system of taxes on tea and other goods (among the taxes that had angered the colonists were the Tea Act and the Stamp Act of 1765). After the war, the new United States Congress retained the authority to levy taxes but refrained from passing any taxes other than import duties, which themselves generated considerable opposition. Tax revolts were infrequent in the early republic because tax rates were low, there was no federal income tax, and any taxes raised were enacted at the state level, where the votes had influence to shape the type and degree of taxation. The most famous tax revolt of the early national period came in the 1790's with the Whiskey Rebellion, an angry response to a specific tax against farmers.

Most twentieth century tax protests have involved property taxes, with a revival of tax strikes occurring in the 1930's. City and state taxes had risen in the 1920's, with many city levies increasing by 30 percent in the decade. Hundreds of taxpayer leagues formed in the early 1930's, and they started to coordinate their activities. An early key test came in Milwaukee in 1933, where the mayor had made a campaign issue of the "tax delinquents." The taxpayers won, restricting future taxation and limiting the city's annual spending. Chicago witnessed one of the most massive, organized tax resistance campaigns in history. The Association of Real Estate Taxpayers—with about thirty thousand members—mounted a string of lawsuits to revise tax assessments. The group experienced remarkable success for almost three years until internal dissension reduced the group's power.

More recently, Jarvis and Gann's Proposition 13 initiated a restructuring of taxation programs across the United States. The California protest movement also provided an alternative approach to reform when traditional means (such as gaining control of state legislatures and local districts) were closed: the popular initiative or referendum processes. As an increasing number of states adopted the initiative/referendum concept, taxpayers found that they could force tax increases into the public view and debate them on their merits, as opposed to receiving tax increases after the fact. In the 1980's and 1990's, many initiatives resulted in states' limiting property or income taxes, repealing or limiting sales taxes, and repealing or limiting the effects of special assessments for school bonds or specific funds.

See also Fries Rebellion; Internal Revenue Service (IRS); Tax Reform Act of 1986; Taxation and justice.

Taxation and justice

DEFINITION: The issue of how taxes are to be imposed upon and collected from taxpayers fairly

SIGNIFICANCE: Every citizen feels, directly or indirectly, the impact of the allocation and collection of taxes, and the problem of imposing taxes very often drives political debate on nontax issues

In its earliest days, the U.S. government relied upon tariffs to fund its activities. In the late 1800's, however, it became clear that the revenues generated from tariffs were insufficient. Congress enacted a personal income tax in 1894, but this tax was held unconstitutional in *Pollock v. Farmers' Loan & Trust Co.* (1895). Political compromise allowed enactment of a corporate tax in 1909 as a strategy to stave off a personal income tax. This tax raised relatively few funds, and the need for additional money was overwhelming. Thus, the Sixteenth Amendment to the U.S. Constitution was ratified in 1913. This amendment empowered Congress "to lay and collect taxes on incomes, from whatever source derived, without apportionment among the several States, and without regard to any census or enumeration." The federal government now relies on other taxes as well, such as excise taxes, the corporate income tax, and the federal estate tax, but the personal income tax raises the vast majority of funds for general expenditures. Thus, it is the allocation of the federal personal income tax burden that raises the most issues of justice in taxation. In general, there are three major policy issues in the imposition of taxes: fairness, administrative practicality, and rational economic effects.

Allocating the Tax Burden Fairly. In order for taxpayers to accept the imposition of taxes, they must perceive the tax burden as being allocated fairly. Theories abound for different methods of allocating the income tax burden among taxpayers, but the one most widely accepted is that the income tax should be allocated among taxpayers according to their relative abilities to pay tax. In accordance with principles of horizontal equity, taxpayers with similar abilities to pay tax should pay similar amounts of tax. Likewise, a taxpayer with a greater ability to pay tax should pay more in taxes than another taxpayer with a lesser ability to pay. (This is known as vertical equity.) This principle is easy to state but much harder to implement, because it is impossible to measure directly any particular taxpayer's ability to pay with any degree of accuracy. One might interview every single taxpayer, finding out all about each taxpayer's work, family, medical history, and so forth, but this approach would consume enormous administrative resources and would perhaps still not generate reliable information about relative ability to pay.

Because it is impossible to devise a perfect system for measuring taxpayers' relative abilities to pay tax, the federal tax system (and those of most states) uses an indirect measure of ability to pay: "taxable income." If ability to pay rises and falls with taxable income, the tax system will be fair in the sense of allocating tax based on ability to pay. Thus, the proper determination of taxable income is crucial in developing a fair tax system.

Taxable income is computed by first including all of a taxpayer's income in his or her gross income, and then allowing certain deductions. For example, a wage earner includes in his or her gross income all of his or her wages, certain fringe benefits, and bonuses. Then the taxpayer is entitled to subtract certain deductions from gross income—for example, certain medical expenses and home mortgage interest. The resulting figure is taxable income, upon which the income tax is imposed.

Much debate surrounds the proper computation of taxable income. While most common types of income (wages, salary, dividends, interest, and royalties) are included in gross income, some types of income are excluded. For example, certain housing provided by an employer and certain types of fringe benefits may be excluded from gross income by statute. Even more debate plagues the allowance of deductions. A deduction represents Congress' decision that an expense has caused the taxpayer to be "less able to pay" taxes. Certainly the rationale for the allowance of business deductions against business income is obvious: The income tax seeks to measure the net business income of the taxpayer. Certain personal deductions also recognize expenditures that leave the taxpayer worse off in an economic sense, and thus less able to contribute to the tax burden. The deductions for casualty (fire, earthquake, flood, and so on) losses and extraordinary medical expenses are examples of such personal deductions. Yet the rationale for other deductions is less clear and can best be explained by taxpayers' (and politicians') historic attachment to them. For example, it is difficult to explain the deduction for home mortgage interest and property taxes on the basis of a taxpayer's ability to pay, but any attempt to remove such deductions provokes enormous controversy.

The difficulty in accurately measuring ability to pay has led to a variety of responses. One proposal is the "flat tax." This proposal imposes a relatively low tax on all gross incomes, at the same rate for all taxpayers. While the flat tax is attractive for its simplicity, this advantage must be weighed against its possible violation of notions of horizontal equity. It probably works best for wage or salary earners because their gross incomes more or less equals their net incomes. For others, however, whose gross incomes are very different from their net incomes (such as small business owners) the flat tax can result in a tax on economic losses. Another proposal is the "value added tax," which most other industrialized countries already incorporate into their taxing systems. This tax, similar to a sales tax, imposes a small charge on the addition of value at each stage of production of goods or services.

Effective Tax Administration. In addition to being fair, the tax system must not be overly burdensome to administer. The taxpayer must be protected from undue governmental intrusion into his or her life, yet the system must also be designed so that it collects the tax at a reasonable cost. The federal system and most state tax systems in the United States are "self-assessment" systems, which means that each income taxpayer prepares his or her return (or has it prepared by a professional), under penalty of perjury. Thus, the viability of the system depends on taxpayers being honest on their tax returns. The increasing use of information reporting and computerized comparisons of tax returns with information reports increases the likelihood that the Internal Revenue Service (IRS) will be able to monitor compliance.

An important aspect of tax administration is the ability of taxpayers to respond to proposed changes to their tax returns. After an audit by the IRS in which it proposes changes to a taxpayer's return, the taxpayer has a right to an administrative hearing at the appeals division of the IRS. If the case is not settled there, the IRS issues a statutory notice of deficiency (also known as a "90-day letter") which sets forth the proposed changes. If the taxpayer does not agree with these changes, he or she may file a petition with the U.S. Tax Court, without first paying the tax. The IRS may not collect the tax until a decision is entered by the Tax Court. Alternatively, the taxpayer may pay the tax and file a claim for a refund with the IRS. If the IRS denies or ignores the claim, the taxpayer may file suit in a U.S. district court for a refund of the taxes paid. Appeal of tax cases from both the U.S. Tax Court and the district courts is to the circuit court for the jurisdiction in which the taxpayer resides.

Rational Economic Effects. The third goal of the income tax system is to create rational economic effects. Every change in the income tax laws produces changes in taxpayer behavior, both expected and unexpected. For example, the enactment of tax credits for investment in equipment is likely to encourage this type of investment, but it may have unintended results as well—such as investment solely to gain tax benefits. While it is impossible to predict all of the economic effects of any particular tax provisions, it is important for legislators to consider the probable effects of every proposed change. In this way, the less desirable economic effects of tax provisions can perhaps be avoided.

Tax Rates: Progressivity and the Capital Gains Debate. The flat tax, mentioned above, raises another important question regarding taxation: Should tax rates be different for taxpayers with differing amounts or types of income? Proponents of the flat tax suggest that tax rates should be identical for all taxpayers on the grounds that each taxpayer should bear a proportionate share of the tax burden. Other theorists argue that income tax rates should rise as income rises—in other words, should be progressive—for several reasons. First, progressive tax rates serve an important redistributional function in society; those with the highest incomes pay proportionately more of their incomes as taxes than those with the lowest incomes. Second, as income rises, the marginal detriment to the taxpayer of additional tax falls, so that the high-income taxpayer with a 70 percent tax rate "suffers" the same as a low-income taxpayer at a 20 percent rate. Both of these justifications are highly controversial. The first argument depends on political values about which there can be no certainty, and the second on virtually unmeasurable information about the marginal detriment of additional taxes.

Another area of intense political debate is the proper taxation of capital gains, income from the sale of investment assets such as stock, bonds, or land. For many years prior to the Tax Reform Act of 1986, the federal tax rate on capital gain income was lower than the rate on other types of income. Justifications for a lower tax rate on capital gains come in four varieties.

First, these assets appreciate in value over a period of years, yet this appreciation is not taxed during those years. When the sale occurs, the "bunching" of income in one year arguably overstates the taxpayer's income for that year, and thus a lower tax rate is appropriate. Second, some of the taxpayer's capital gain is not true gain; it is the result of inflation during the years of investment. Third, offering a lower tax rate on capital gains offsets the "lock-in" effect, the tendency of holders of investment assets to continue to hold them solely to avoid tax. Finally, the opportunity of a lower tax rate for these assets encourages investment in them, which arguably is a desirable economic effect. All these theories are controversial, and debate is complicated by the fact that there are little reliable data on the real impact of the lock-in effect or the additional incentive effects of a lower tax rate. While the Tax Reform Act of 1986 temporarily removed the preference for capital gains, it did not eliminate the debate.

State Taxation. Another significant tax burden is state and local taxation. State and local governments typically rely on income taxes (usually following the federal model of the income tax), property taxes, and sales taxes for their operating revenues. In particular, the sales tax deserves some attention. Arguably, the sales tax is a regressive tax—it falls more heavily on those with lower incomes than those with higher incomes. People with lower incomes spend a proportionately larger amount of their incomes than do high-income taxpayers. Problems of regressivity lead most states to exempt from the sales tax certain essential goods and services, such as groceries and medical care.   —*Gwendolyn Griffith*

See also Internal Revenue Service (IRS); Poll tax; Tax evasion; Tax Reform Act of 1986; Tax revolt movement.

BIBLIOGRAPHY

A very complete treatise on the income taxation of individuals, with excellent examples, is Boris Bittker and Martin McMahon, Jr., *Federal Income Taxation of Individuals* (Boston: Warren, Gorham & Lamont, 1990), and for corporations, James T. O'Hara, Michael C. Durst, Gwendolyn Griffith, and Nancy E. Shurtz, *Corporate Taxation* (Colorado Springs, Colo.: Shephard's/McGraw-Hill, 1992). For a discussion of the theory and policy of the federal income tax rules and regulations, see Joseph M. Dodge, *The Logic of Tax: Federal Income Tax Theory and Policy* (St. Paul, Minn.: West, 1989), and Marvin A. Chirelstein, *Federal Income Taxation: A Guide to the Leading Cases and Concepts* (7th ed. Westbury, N.Y.: Foundation Press, 1994). For a discussion of tax reform efforts leading to the 1986 act, see Department of the Treasury, *Tax Reform for Fairness, Simplicity, and Economic Growth* (Washington, D.C.: U.S. Government Printing Office, 1984).

Teapot Dome scandal

DATE: 1921-1923

PLACE: Teapot Dome, Wyoming; Elk Hills, California; Washington, D.C.

SIGNIFICANCE: Arguably the worst scandal that had tainted a presidential administration until that time, Teapot Dome resulted in the first criminal prosecution and imprisonment of a cabinet official

Although President Warren G. Harding filled several key positions in his probusiness administration with able conservative politicians, he also made numerous lesser appointments of political cronies of questionable talent and integrity. His administration was consequently racked with scandal.

At Secretary of the Interior Albert B. Fall's urging, Harding, in 1921, transferred control of naval oil reserves at Teapot Dome, Wyoming, and Elk Hills, California, to the Department of the Interior. Fall, without competitive bidding, leased the oil deposits to the private interests of Harry F. Sinclair and Edward L. Doheny, both of whom loaned Fall money (about $100,000 and $300,000, respectively). Following a Senate investigation, Fall was convicted of accepting bribes, sentenced to a year in prison, and fined $100,000. In 1931, he was also convicted of conspiracy to defraud the government.

The Teapot Dome scandal became synonymous with governmental corruption. It led to the passage of the Federal Corrupt Practices Act (1925), which attempted to regulate political financing.

See also Bribery; Conspiracy; Political corruption; Spoils system and patronage.

President Warren G. Harding's administration was rocked by the Teapot Dome scandal in the early 1920's (Library of Congress)

Telecommunications law

DEFINITION: The body of laws and regulations that govern electronic communications

SIGNIFICANCE: Telecommunications law has always lagged behind technology and has inevitably created controversies over whether, and how, various forms of electronic communication should be regulated

A number of areas of law have been notable for the fact that the law has been at least one step behind rapid technological developments. Among these areas are banking law, commercial law, and telecommunications law. Telecommunications began in the nineteenth century with the invention of the telegraph and telephone and then expanded dramatically in the twentieth century with the addition of radio, television, cable television, satellite, and computer communications. Telecommunications is therefore a broad field as far as the technologies and types of communication it covers. Moreover, in the largest sense, telecommunications law covers aspects of these technologies ranging from assigning frequencies and issuing licenses to broadcasters to regulating the content of various media—from television to the Internet.

Communications Act of 1934. The first commercial radio station in the United States, Pittsburgh's KDKA, began broadcasting in 1920. Others rapidly followed, and the first permanent radio network, the National Broadcasting Company (NBC), was established in 1926. It soon became apparent that a coherent national policy was required in order to regulate broadcasting. The regulation of telecommunications began in earnest with passage of the Communications Act of 1934, which established both the Federal Communications Commission (FCC) and a philosophy for governing use of the airwaves. Telecommunications law long consisted primarily of this legislation and its amendments. The broadcast media, the act stated, are different from the print media: The airwaves are a public trust, and frequencies should be licensed to private users who will act according to "public interest, convenience, and necessity." No one can own a broadcast frequency.

This approach was largely a result of a belief that usable broadcasting frequencies were "scarce." It was the FCC's job to allocate them for various private, governmental, and commercial uses. Although frequencies ultimately turned out to be less scarce than had been thought, the broadcasting industry has had to operate within a context of regulation unknown to the print medium. Whereas the print media have virtually unlimited freedom of speech (as guaranteed by the First Amendment), the FCC has the power to regulate broadcast content, and it can fine broadcasters or revoke or simply not renew—the license of a station broadcasting objectionable programming. (Measures as harsh as revocation or nonrenewal, however, are rarely taken.)

The FCC also promulgated the "fairness doctrine," requiring stations to provide equal time for the presentation of opposing views regarding any controversial opinions presented. The fairness doctrine was part of the FCC's broader mission to require radio and television stations to be "socially responsible"; another example is the requirement that television stations provide children's programming.

Expanding Technologies. In 1949, during a freeze on the issuing of new television licenses (while the FCC was sifting through a host of technical issues), a few small companies began to transmit television programming via cable; first called community antenna television (CATV), the business soon became known as cable television. The FCC at first decided that it would not regulate cable operations, but it changed its mind in 1965—it first regulated microwave-fed cable systems, then all cable television. It placed numerous restrictions and requirements on cable television operators, one of which was that they carry local stations and limit the number of distant stations they carried. Major cable legislation has included the 1984 Cable Communications Policy Act, which substantially deregulated the industry.

Another new communications technology began when the first communications satellites began operating in 1962. The Communications Satellite Act of 1962 amended the Communications Act and created the Communications Satellite Corporation (COMSAT), a private corporation, to help provide effective international satellite communication. In 1968, the FCC, worried about the effect the availability of satellite facilities and transmissions would have on the cable television industry, halted the growth of the cable industry for four years.

Through the decades, the FCC adopted new policies and regulations piecemeal as technology advanced, telecommunication practices changed, and the Communications Act was amended. By 1976, the face of telecommunications had changed so much that Congress considered significant changes in legislation; Representative Lionel Van Deerlin announced plans for a major revision of the 1934 act. Such changes were not to be, however; three years later, Van Deerlin gave up the attempt in the face of opposition from many quarters. Nevertheless, "deregulation" was the word of the 1980's, and the head of the FCC publicly questioned underlying assumptions of the 1934 act, including the scarcity doctrine.

Calls for Change in the 1990's. By the late 1980's, the telecommunications field was again undergoing revolutionary changes. The proliferation of computers, computer networks, and individual users equipped with modems was transforming the landscape. By the mid-1990's, millions of individuals, as well as businesses and institutions, were communicating via electronic mail and newsgroups through services giving them access to the Internet. There were other changes as well. Major long-distance carriers were operating in competition with American Telephone and Telegraph (AT&T), and they wanted to be allowed to expand into new areas that technology would now support, such as carrying television signals and competing with the cable companies. In turn, cable companies, which had grown tremendously in fifteen years, wanted to be freed of what they viewed as outdated restrictions. Somewhat contradictory currents were also at work in Washington, where there were simultaneous calls for continuing economic deregulation

and for increasing regulation of the content of radio, television, and the Internet.

In 1995, both houses of Congress passed new telecommunication bills that contained sweeping changes. The final form of the bill was enacted into law in 1996, and its essence was significant deregulation. Among the major changes were allowing long-distance telephone carriers, local telephone companies, and cable television operators to enter one another's markets, loosening restrictions on the number of stations a broadcaster can own, and deregulating charges for premium cable services.

Included in the act was a provision requiring the installation of an electronic chip (the "V-chip") in new television sets to allow parents to restrict electronically the programs their children are allowed to view. Also part of the act was a prohibition on the broadcasting of "indecent" material over computer networks unless steps are taken to restrict children's access to the material. This last provision, the subject of considerable controversy, pitted advocates of unregulated free speech on the Internet against those fearful of, among other things, exposing children to obscenity.

The possible effects of the 1996 act were heatedly debated before it was passed. Consumer advocates were certain that higher cable television rates would result from deregulation; supporters of deregulation countered that increased competition should ultimately lower rates for all telecommunications services affected. It was acknowledged that concentration of ownership of broadcasting facilities would increase significantly, but there was uncertainty regarding how important that was, as increasing satellite and telephone-line transmission of television signals made such concentration seem less ominous. Regarding criminalizing objectionable content on the Internet, both advocates and opponents realized that the near impossibility of effective enforcement was a major problem.

—*Matthew Fisher*

See also Bill of Rights, U.S.; Electronic surveillance; News media; Speech and press, freedom of.

BIBLIOGRAPHY

Publications on telecommunications law are destined to be outdated nearly as soon as they are published, and this was never more true than in the mid-1990's. Nevertheless, bearing this in mind, useful sources include Michael K. Kellogg, John Thorne, and Peter W. Huber, *Federal Telecommunications Law* (Boston: Little, Brown, 1992); Charles H. Kennedy, An *Introduction to U.S. Communications Law* (Boston: Artech House, 1994); Daniel L. Brenner, *Law and Regulation of Common Carriers in the Communications Industry* (Boulder, Colo.: Westview Press, 1992); and Robert L. Hilliard, *The Federal Communications Commission: A Primer* (Boston: Focal Press, 1991).

Temperance movement

DEFINITION: The temperance movement called for a restriction on the production and consumption of alcoholic beverages

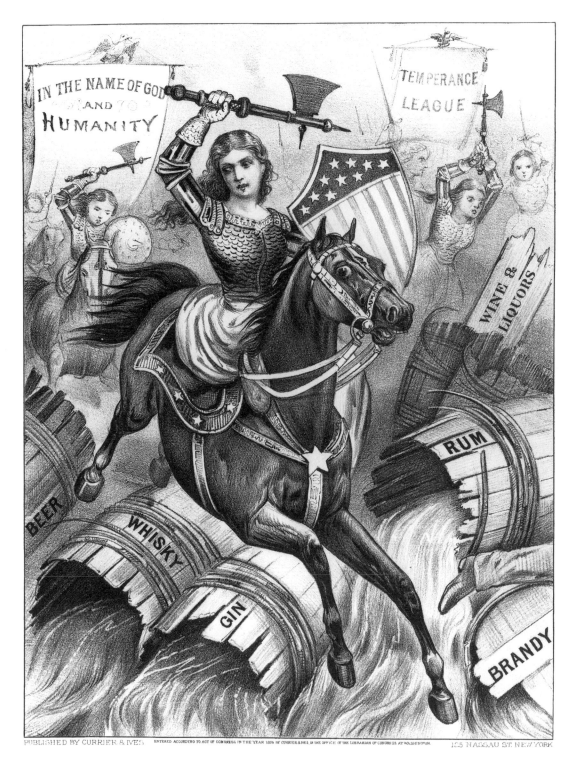

WOMANS HOLY WAR.

Grand Charge on the Enemy's Works.

An 1874 depiction of the temperance movement as a "holy war." (Library of Congress)

SIGNIFICANCE: The temperance movement led to the 1919 ratification of the Eighteenth Amendment to the U.S. Constitution

Considered broadly, temperance can mean either total abstinence from alcohol or simply its moderate use. Alcohol consumption in the United States rose at a steady rate throughout the eighteenth and early nineteenth centuries. In 1826, evangelical Protestants formed the first national temperance organization, The American Temperance Society. Led by ministers such as Lyman Beecher, this organization called for total abstinence from alcohol.

Alcohol abuse became an increasingly important issue throughout the nineteenth century. Champions of alcohol reform argued that liquor control would solve a host of societal ills ranging from poor race relations to domestic violence. The drive to curb alcohol abuse spawned more organizations that incorporated a wide segment of the American populace. In 1879 Frances Willard became the first president of the newly formed Women's Christian Temperance Union (WCTU), the nation's first mass organization of women. National prohibition was adopted in December, 1917, as a wartime measure aimed at conserving grain stores. The Eighteenth Amendment to the Constitution was ratified in 1919, enacted on January 1, 1920, and repealed in 1933.

See also Abolitionist movement; Prohibition; Wickersham Commission.

Ten most wanted criminals

DEFINITION: A list of ten particularly notorious criminals sought by the Federal Bureau of Investigation (FBI)

SIGNIFICANCE: The use of mass media to publicize descriptions of most-wanted fugitives has enhanced the image of the Federal Bureau of Investigation, involved citizens in law enforcement, and resulted in the arrest of many criminals

Advertising the descriptions of wanted criminals dates back to 1772, when London magistrate John Fielding published the first issue of *The Quarterly Pursuit of Criminals*. This quarterly was supplemented by *The Weekly Pursuit* and *The Extraordinary Pursuit*. By 1786, a weekly crime bulletin, *Public Hue and Cry*, had appeared; this became *The Police Gazette* by 1828. An official publication, its offices were moved to Scotland Yard in 1883, and a daily *Police Gazette* has been published since 1914. In the United States, a *Police Gazette*, first published in 1846, was originally designed to publicize descriptions of criminals and deserters from the Mexican war, but it became a general magazine of popular theater, sports, and scandal. Official publications were supplemented by wanted posters that appeared throughout much of the nineteenth century, especially in the American West.

The FBI first became involved in a "Ten Most Wanted Fugitives" program in 1947, when newspaper wire services began distributing feature stories on criminals sought by the FBI. In 1950, the FBI officially began its "Ten Most Wanted Fugitives" list, publicizing descriptions through newspapers, magazines, radio, and television. By 1956, ninety-eight descriptions had been publicized, and eighty-eight criminals had been captured.

The list was part of an ongoing effort to strengthen the public image of the FBI; FBI director J. Edgar Hoover believed that a strong image was the bureau's best weapon. Hoover's efforts led to the film *G-Men* (1935), starring James Cagney, and a radio show, also called "G-Men," which began July 10, 1935. "War on Crime," an official FBI comic strip, began May 18, 1936. Other efforts included a pulp detective magazine and books such as Courtney Ryley Cooper's *Ten Thousand Public Enemies* (1935) and Don Whitehead's *FBI Story* (1956), filmed under that title, with James Stewart, in 1957.

Hoover's most successful efforts, however, involved the public in the law enforcement process. Early television stations often ran photographs of most-wanted criminals before signing off at night, while, in 1965, a Hoover-coordinated television series, *The FBI*, began. It lasted nine years and featured a monthly photograph of a top-ten fugitive and an appeal for information. At the time of Hoover's death in 1972, the show was viewed by forty million Americans and syndicated in fifty other countries.

Two American television shows continued the tradition into the 1990's. *America's Most Wanted* first aired in February, 1988. By September, twenty-two fugitives had been captured; by 1992, the number had risen to almost two hundred, and host John Walsh received the FBI's highest civilian commendation. *Unsolved Mysteries* began at the same time. A monthly British Broadcasting Company (BBC) show, *Crime Watch UK*, brings similar information to British viewers.

See also Crime; Federal Bureau of Investigation (FBI); Hoover, J. Edgar; News media.

Tennessee v. Garner

COURT: U.S. Supreme Court

DATE: Decided March 27, 1985

SIGNIFICANCE: This case significantly limited the power of police officers to use deadly force in effecting an arrest

Most arrests do not entail problems, but occasionally the accused will resist arrest or flee. There are also occasions when law enforcement officers must make an instantaneous decision on the severity of any threat posed to the officers. The common law developed the rule that law enforcement officers could use all necessary and reasonable force, including deadly force, to arrest a suspected felon, regardless of whether the suspect committed an act of violence or posed a threat to the arresting officers.

The common-law rule became increasingly controversial during the 1960's and 1970's, but courts adhered to it. There were numerous objections of a constitutional, legal, and humanistic nature. The main objection was that, in essence, the rule allowed police officers to become judge, jury, and even executioner. Indeed, many jurisdictions which did not use capital punishment allowed officers to use deadly force through "fleeing felon" statutes modeled after the common law.

In *Tennessee v. Garner*, a fifteen-year-old boy, Edward Garner, broke a window and entered an unoccupied residence in suburban Memphis on the night of October 3, 1974. A neighbor called the police. Two police officers responded and intercepted the minor as he ran from the back of the house to a six-foot cyclone fence in the backyard. By shining a flashlight on the suspect, the officers could tell that the suspect was a youth and apparently unarmed. There was therefore no indication that the boy had committed a felony involving violence, nor did he pose an apparent threat to the officers' safety. The suspect ignored the officers' directive to stop. Instead, he tried to escape. One officer took aim and fatally shot the suspect in the back as he climbed over the fence. The officer had acted in accordance with his training, the Tennessee fleeing felon statute, and police department policy. The deceased had ten dollars worth of money and jewelry in his possession stolen from the house.

The decedent's father brought suit against the officers, their superiors, and the city under the federal civil rights statute to recover damages for wrongful death caused by violation of the decedent's constitutional rights. The lawsuit was filed in federal court in a successful attempt to circumvent the common law. The Supreme Court overturned the common-law rule in a 6-3 decision. Justice Byron White delivered the majority opinion, which held that deadly force may be used to effectuate an arrest only in cases where it is necessary to prevent the escape of the suspect and the officer has probable cause to believe that the suspect poses a significant threat of death or serious physical injury to the officer or others. The Court noted that most major police departments have forbidden the use of deadly force against nonviolent suspects. The practical effect of *Tennessee v. Garner* was that lawsuits involving wrongful death causes of action against state law enforcement officers will be brought in federal courts and will invoke federal constitutional law.

See also Arrest; Deadly force, police use of; Discretion; Reasonable force.

Terrorism

DEFINITION: Violence or the threat of violence, usually against innocent civilians, in pursuit of a political objective

SIGNIFICANCE: Recent decades have witnessed an upsurge in terrorism, especially international terrorism; American citizens have been the leading targets of international terrorism, but, until relatively recently, U.S. territory has been largely spared

Terrorism is often called a weapon of the weak. It is used by those who have political objectives but do not have the power to influence governments or the wherewithal to engage in conventional warfare. In many cases, terrorist violence is used to attract world attention to a political cause or to protest the policies of governments. This explains why terrorist acts are often designed to attract maximum media coverage. Terrorism may also represent an attempt specifically to incite a government to react violently, thereby alienating citizens and creating

sympathy for the group resorting to the terrorist acts. Victims of terrorism may include people working for the governments or organizations that the terrorists oppose, such as policemen and soldiers. They may be citizens of countries against which the terrorists are protesting—for example, Israelis killed by Palestinian terrorists. Finally, they may be citizens of countries that are viewed as assisting those whom the terrorists are fighting: Leon Klinghoffer, for example, an American passenger aboard the Italian cruise ship *Achille Lauro*, was murdered by Palestinian terrorists after that vessel was hijacked in 1986.

Defining Terrorism. Defining terrorism or terrorist groups is complicated because of the propensity of authorities to define violent groups of whom they approve as "freedom fighters" or "partisans" and those of whom they disapprove as "terrorists." International terrorism involves the movement of persons across national frontiers or the provision of assistance to terrorists by foreign governments. Everyone has become more vulnerable to terrorist acts because of revolutions in transportation and communications that make it easier for terrorists to strike anywhere and because of the growing sophistication of armaments, which gives individuals or small groups the capacity to inflict greater violence than ever before.

Terrorists often commit many of the same acts committed by common (that is, nonpolitical) criminals. Either may threaten or use violence and may commit criminal acts such as theft, kidnapping, or murder. Before the Russian Revolution of 1917, Bolsheviks routinely robbed banks to finance their revolutionary activities, and during the 1960's and 1970's, groups such as the Weather Underground and Symbionese Liberation Army committed robberies as part of their efforts to overthrow what they believed to be the United States' oppressive and racist political system. Sometimes alliances are formed between groups of common criminals and terrorist groups, such as that between growers and refiners of cocaine in Latin America and the Peruvian terrorist group Shining Path, which provides the drug rings with protection in return for a share of the profits. Foreign businessmen, including American executives, have been kidnapped and held for ransom in Latin America, and the perpetrators often claim that they are trying to overthrow the political system in their country. The difference between common crime and terrorism lies largely in the motives of perpetrators. Terrorism is crime which has a political objective, while common crime is undertaken for private motives such as profit or revenge. Common criminals have been known to allege that they have political motives in an attempt to elicit sympathy from a jury.

Another difficult distinction is that between domestic and international terrorism. During the Vietnam War, terrorist acts such as bombing the offices of university faculty members, making bomb threats, and destroying government property were undertaken by Americans, especially of draft age. They were sometimes accused of having been inspired by the Vietnamese communists. Sometimes domestic terrorists appear to emulate the tactics of foreign terrorists whom they read about or see on television. The necessity of combating both varieties of terrorism creates some bureaucratic confusion, because the Federal Bureau of Investigation (FBI) is in charge of gathering information about and capturing terrorists in the United States, while the Central Intelligence Agency (CIA) investigates overseas sources of terrorism.

The Motives of Terrorists. Terrorists have a variety of political motives. Some of the most infamous groups are those seeking independence or autonomy for a national or ethnic group. In Europe, the Provisional wing of the Irish Republican Army has waged a campaign of bombings, assassinations, and brutal beatings in Ulster and in England to force the British out of Northern Ireland. A number of groups in the Middle East, including Hamas, Hizballah, and the Popular Front for the Liberation of Palestine (PFLP), seek a Palestinian national home and refuse to accept steps toward compromise and peace in the region. They continue to carry out suicide bombings and attacks both against Israelis and against Arabs whom they accuse of collaborating with the enemy.

Some terrorists are inspired by vague revolutionary ideologies. The two most famous examples in Western Europe were the Red Army Faction (RAF) in West Germany and the Italian Red Brigades. The West German group gained notoriety by assassinating German businessmen and attacking U.S. mili-

tary bases. Among their acts of terrorism, the Red Brigades murdered a former Italian prime minister and kidnapped an American general. Some groups favor Marxist ideology, while others are fascistic.

State Sponsorship of Terrorism. Some states believe that it is in their interest to assist terrorist groups. In some cases, terrorist groups are actually created by governments to carry out violent acts on their behalf. From time to time, the regime of Libya's Muammar Qadhafi has employed agents to murder Libyan dissidents residing overseas, and the regime of Iraq's Saddam Hussein was accused of trying to assassinate former U.S. president George Bush on the occasion of his trip to Kuwait in 1993.

It is more common, however, for states to provide arms, safe haven, and other facilities to terrorists whom they hope to use for their own purposes. In some instances, diplomats take advantage of their legal immunity from search and arrest to carry weapons or store weapons for terrorists whom they sponsor. Such incidents as the 1983 suicide bombing of the U.S. Marine barracks in Beirut, the 1986 bombing of a West German discotheque frequented by U.S. soldiers, and the 1988 bombing of a Pan American airliner over Scotland were almost certainly sponsored by governments that wanted to harm

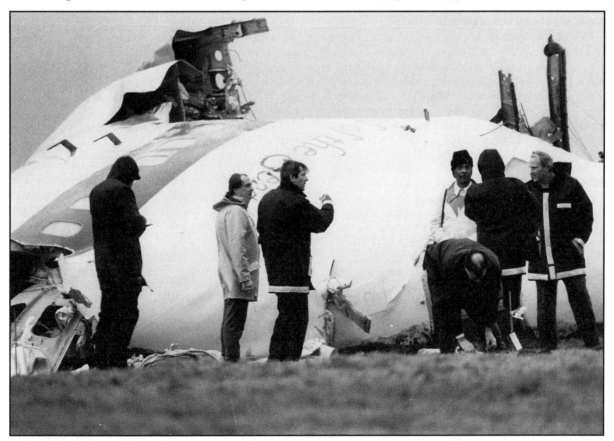

Investigators inspecting the nose section of the Pan American jetliner destroyed over Lockerbie, Scotland, by terrorists in 1988. (AP/Wide World Photos)

American interests without showing their hand. By law, the U.S. government must identify annually regimes that it believes sponsor terrorism. Among the countries that have been so identified are Iran, Iraq, Syria, the former South Yemen, and North Korea.

The Tactics of Terrorists. Terrorists use a variety of tactics to intimidate or harm their adversaries. In the 1970's, skyjackings, involving demands in return for the release of hostages, were common and provided perpetrators and their causes with widespread publicity. Skyjacking declined, however, as airport and airplane security improved. The bombing of planes continues, however, especially by groups that seek to avenge themselves against foes.

Some groups, such as the Italian Red Brigades and Hizballah, make extensive use of kidnapping to publicize their causes or to obtain funds. Some, notably small groups of Islamic fundamentalists, resort to suicide bombing—a tactic that is difficult to deter—while others plant bombs in public buildings. Some groups create terror by resorting to indiscriminate grenade or machine gun attacks. Another tactic is the assassination of public figures who serve as symbols of an enemy. For example, the Irish Republican Army assassinated Lord Mountbatten, a member of the British royal family and the last viceroy of India, in 1979 and in 1984 sought to assassinate British prime minister Margaret Thatcher.

Weapons of Mass Destruction. Perhaps the greatest threat of terrorism in the future involves the possibility that terrorists may acquire weapons of mass destruction, such as nuclear or chemical weapons. Concern has long existed that a terrorist group might steal a nuclear device from a U.S. base, perhaps in Italy or Turkey, or seek to sabotage a nuclear power plant. In recent years, the prospect of nuclear terrorism has increased dramatically because of the break-up of the Soviet Union, the growing power of organized crime in Russia, and the economic difficulties confronting Russia, Ukraine, and other Soviet successor states. During 1994 a number of incidents involving efforts to sell weapons-grade plutonium, probably stolen from Russian nuclear installations, were reported by the German police. It was also reported in 1994 that the United States had secretly transported a large quantity of weapons-grade uranium out of Kazakhstan because of fears that it might be sold or stolen. The availability of technical information and the miniaturization of weaponry mean that the unavailability of fissionable material is the major obstacle preventing terrorists from building nuclear devices. Fissionable materials could also be used to poison a population by means of radioactivity released in the atmosphere or the water supply. As of the mid-1990's there had been no confirmed possession of nuclear materials by terrorists, but there had been a number of (baseless) threats made.

Even more worrisome is the possibility that chemical or biological weapons, which are more widely distributed than nuclear weapons, might fall into the hands of terrorists. The fact that some countries—Iraq and probably Libya—have obtained such weapons and are known to have abetted terrorists is frightening indeed. In 1978 and 1979, the German police found in a house a large amount of the chemicals necessary to produce toxic nerve gas. In 1980, French police raided a safe house of the Red Army Faction and found the toxin that causes botulism; ten years later, the French turned up the same type of toxin in another RAF safe house. Such materials are easy to transport and hide, and modern urban areas, including their water supplies, are vulnerable to chemical and biological contamination.

Patterns of World Terrorism. Terrorism is not a new phenomenon. It was a terrorist incident, the assassination of the heir to the throne of Austria-Hungary, that triggered World War I. Two especially shocking and bloody acts in the early 1970's, however—the massacres of Israeli athletes at the Munich Olympics by members of the Palestinian terrorist group Black September and of twenty-six travelers by the Japanese United Red Army at Israel's Lod Airport—brought the threat of terrorist violence home to millions in the West.

The total number of international terrorist incidents soared in the late 1960's and early 1970's and remained relatively constant until the early 1990's, when it began to decline. Terrorist incidents have been especially prevalent in the Middle East, Western Europe, and Latin America, but U.S. citizens and property have been the most frequent targets of such attacks. There are a number of reasons why U.S. interests are selected for attack by terrorists. First, Americans and American property are relatively vulnerable because they are to be found in every corner of the world. In addition, the United States is viewed as the world's leading capitalist society and as an ally of governments (such as Israel and Egypt) that terrorists have targeted. Finally, attacks on the interests of the United States, the world's only remaining superpower, are certain to receive considerable publicity.

CASUALTIES RESULTING FROM INTERNATIONAL TERRORISM INVOLVING U.S. CITIZENS, 1981-1993			
	Total	*Dead*	*Wounded*
Total	**2,197**	**586**	**1,611**
1981	47	7	40
1982	19	8	11
1983	386	271	115
1984	42	11	31
1985	195	38	157
1986	112	12	100
1987	54	7	47
1988	232	192	40
1989	34	15	19
1990	44	10	34
1991	21	7	14
1992	3	2	1
1993	1,008	6	1,002

Source: U.S. Department of Justice, Bureau of Justice Statistics, *Sourcebook of Criminal Justice Statistics—1993*. Washington, D.C.: U.S. Government Printing Office, 1994.

The seizure of the U.S. embassy in Teheran, Iran, along with sixty-six hostages, by Revolutionary Guards in 1979 and the subsequent kidnapping of Western hostages, including a number of Americans, by Iranian sympathizers in Lebanon galvanized U.S. anti-terrorist efforts. American revulsion at terrorism increased greatly with the highly publicized seizure of Trans World Airlines (TWA) flight 847 en route to Athens in June, 1985 (thirty-nine U.S. citizens were held as hostages for more than two weeks), and the destruction of Pan American Flight 103 over Lockerbie, Scotland, in December, 1988, with the death of 259 passengers and eleven local residents. These events made it clear that Americans everywhere were vulnerable to terrorist acts.

Responses to Terrorism. To the public, the most evident response to terrorism is the screening of passengers at airline terminals and other facilities to prevent the smuggling of bombs, guns, or other weapons. Growing concern in recent years about suicide bombings of the sort that took the lives of several hundred American marines in Beirut, Lebanon, in 1983 has led to the proliferation of concrete barricades around public buildings in the United States. In addition, the establishment of the Special Operations and Research Unit and the Terrorist Research and Analytical Center within the FBI has increased the capacity of that agency to cope with domestic terrorist threats. There are, however, inherent limits to improving security in a democracy such as the United States, where measures such as preventive detention and random search and seizure are unconstitutional.

Beyond passive actions such as those noted above, it has proved difficult for U.S. officials to institute effective measures against terrorism. When the Reagan Administration came to office in 1981, Secretary of State Alexander Haig made it clear that combating terrorism was a high government priority, declaring that international terrorism was the "ultimate abuse of human rights." In 1986, using bases in Great Britain, the United States bombed Libya in retaliation for what Washington said was Libyan involvement in a bombing in Europe that took the lives of American servicemen. U.S. officials have publicly refused to negotiate with terrorists, but they have done so privately. The U.S. army has trained special antiterrorist units, and many U.S. cities have created special police teams to deal with terrorist acts; such approaches have had some success.

The United States has been significantly less successful in dealing with terrorism against its citizens who travel or reside overseas. Advances in weapons technology such as the use of plastic bombs (plastic explosives) complicate the task of security personnel. Easy access to weapons and the ability to move quickly across international boundaries make it difficult for any society to insulate itself. In Western Europe, for example, there are virtually no impediments any longer to the free movement of persons across borders. Thus, a terrorist who gains access to one member of the European Union enjoys easy access to all others.

In some cases of lax security—for example, the airport at Lagos, Nigeria—the U.S. government may alert Americans to avoid such facilities. Another problem is that some foreign governments refuse to cooperate with the United States, as did Libya when U.S. authorities demanded the extradition of individuals accused of having carried out the bombing of Pan American flight 103. In still other instances, governments seek to avoid retaliation and refuse to extradite or prosecute accused terrorists whom they have in custody. Thus, the Italian and Yugoslav governments allowed a terrorist responsible for planning the 1986 seizure of the cruise ship *Achille Lauro* to escape, and, following the kidnapping of some Germans in Lebanon, the German government in 1987 refused to extradite a Palestinian who was accused of involvement in the skyjacking of a TWA flight. In other episodes, the Greek and French governments refused to cooperate in turning over to American authorities those accused of terrorist acts against U.S. citizens. For this reason, U.S. law permits the seizure of alleged terrorists overseas by American authorities, with or without the permission of the host country, and in 1985 U.S. authorities exercised this right against an accused skyjacker.

No single country, no matter how powerful, can cope alone with international terrorism, and any effective strategy against terrorism must involve cooperation among many states. In the 1990's, cooperation began to increase. For example, after Libya refused to surrender those accused of having plotted the destruction of Pan American flight 103, the United Nations, at American and French insistence, imposed economic sanctions on the Libyans. The intelligence services of the major Western democracies routinely exchange intelligence information with one another and with Interpol regarding the movement and activities of suspected terrorists. Perhaps the most important successes in the fight against terrorism in recent years followed the end of the Cold War and the collapse of communism in Eastern Europe and the former Soviet Union. As a consequence, terrorists were deprived of safe havens they had formerly enjoyed in East Berlin, Prague, and elsewhere, and considerable useful intelligence information was made available to Western antiterrorist experts. Ultimately, all countries have an interest in cooperating with those who are the victims of terrorism lest they also become victims.

Domestic Terrorism. The United States' relative freedom from terrorist attacks came to an abrupt end with the 1993 World Trade Center bombing. Secretary of State Warren Christopher spoke of how terrorist attacks "have brought home the ruthless persistence of evil, cowardice and intolerance in the world—and the frightening ease with which terrorists can obtain destructive technology." The discovery that Islamic militants were planning to set off car bombs in the highway tunnels under New York's Hudson River indicated the vulnerability of urban America to terrorist attacks. For its part, the FBI was authorized to track down the alleged mastermind of the Trade Center bombing, Ramzi Yousef, whom they captured in Pakistan and returned to face trial in the United States.

The United States' sense of vulnerability to terrorism increased dramatically with the car bombing of the Alfred P. Murrah Federal Building in Oklahoma City on April 19, 1995, with the loss of hundreds of lives, including numerous children in a day-care center. Suspicion initially fell upon foreign extremists, but the investigation instead led to the arrest of two young Americans, Timothy James McVeigh and Terry Lynn Nichols. Moreover, the explosive used was not a sophisticated bomb but a common and easily acquired fertilizer, ammonium nitrate, soaked in fuel oil.

McVeigh was a decorated army veteran of the Persian Gulf War and a former member of the National Rifle Association (NRA), and both he and Nichols, also a veteran, had links to a fringe right-wing militia in Michigan. Like members of that group and similar paramilitary groups around the United States such as Aryan Nation and Posse Comitatus, McVeigh and Nichols harbored an almost paranoic fear that the United States government was hatching a gigantic plot to curb individual freedoms. They believed that gun control, United Na-

tions peacekeeping, and incidents such as the April 19, 1993, shoot-out between federal agents and the Branch Davidian religious cult in Waco, Texas (resulting in the death of eighty Branch Davidians, including their leader David Koresh), and the FBI siege at the home of white separatist Randy Weaver in Ruby Ridge, Idaho, in August, 1992 (in which Weaver's wife and son were killed), were part of this plot. Indeed, McVeigh once claimed that the army had implanted a microchip in his buttocks to help the government spy on him. For the most part, extremist militias such as the one in Michigan are well armed and spout a confused ideology frequently consisting of racist, anticommunist, anti-Semitic, and antigovernment rhetoric.

Other events in 1995 highlighted the vulnerability of modern society to the acts of determined terrorists. In mid-1995 a threat to plant a bomb aboard an airplane by someone claiming to be the mysterious Unabomber spread fear among passen-

The federal building in Oklahoma City, bombed by domestic terrorists in 1995; the blast killed hundreds of people, including a number of children. Here rescue workers are attending a memorial service for the victims. (AP/Wide World Photos)

TERRORIST INCIDENTS IN THE UNITED STATES, 1982-1992	
Type and Target	Number
Total	**165**
Type of incident	
Bombing attacks	130
Malicious destruction of property	4
Acts of sabotage	2
Hostile takeover	4
Arson	8
Kidnapping; assaults; alleged assassinations; assassinations	11
Robbery; attempted robbery	5
Hijacking	1
Type of target	
Private residence/vehicle	18
Military personnel/establishments	33
Educational establishments	6
Commercial establishments	60
State and United States government buildings/property	31
Diplomatic establishments	17

Source: U.S. Department of Justice, Bureau of Justice Statistics, *Sourcebook of Criminal Justice Statistics—1993*. Washington, D.C.: U.S. Government Printing Office, 1994.

gers and prompted an increase in airport security efforts. Since 1978, the so-called Unabomber has used the mail to send packaged bombs in sixteen attacks on scientists or others somehow involved with technology. Even more frightening was a poison-gas attack on the Tokyo subway in late March, 1995, by followers of Shoko Asahara's doomsday religious cult, Aum Shinrikyo (Aum Supreme Truth), killing five and disabling thousands. Then, in July, seven passengers were killed in a terrorist bombing of the Paris Metro. Such incidents showed that despite efforts to increase security—such as closing off Washington's Pennsylvania Avenue to vehicular traffic in front of the White House—modern society cannot prevent determined terrorists from striking. *—Richard W. Mansbach*

See also Branch Davidians, federal raid on; Extradition; Federal Bureau of Investigation (FBI); International law; Interpol; Skyjacking; Special weapons and tactics (SWAT) teams; Weather Underground.

BIBLIOGRAPHY

Albert Parry's *Terrorism from Robespierre to Arafat* (New York: Vanguard Press, 1976) provides a historical perspective of terrorism. A useful introduction to the subject is Donna M. Schlagheck, *International Terrorism* (Lexington, Mass.: Lexington Books, 1988). A highly accessible set of readings is Charles W. Kegley, Jr., ed., *International Terrorism: Characteristics, Causes, Controls* (New York: St. Martin's Press, 1990). The sources of terrorism and the strategies available to deal with the threat are analyzed in Brian Jenkins, *International Terrorism: A New Mode of Conflict* (Los Angeles, Crescent Publications, 1975). An excellent source of data about

terrorist acts is Edward F. Mickolus, Todd Sandler, and Jean M. Murdock, *International Terrorism in the 1980's* (Ames: Iowa State University Press, 1989). Peter C. Sederberg's *Terrorist Myths: Illusion, Rhetoric, and Reality* (Englewood Cliffs, N.J.: Prentice Hall, 1989) provides background and analysis of the sources of terrorism and some of the alternatives to coping with it. The best analysis of the challenge posed by terrorism to liberal societies is Paul Wilkinson, *Terrorism and the Liberal State* (2d ed. New York: New York University Press, 1986).

Terry v. Ohio

COURT: U.S. Supreme Court

DATE: Ruling issued June 10, 1968

SIGNIFICANCE: In this case, the Supreme Court ruled that, if an officer had reasonable suspicion that he was dealing with an armed individual, he could subject that person to a limited search of the outer clothing, a procedure sometimes known as "stop and frisk"

In October, 1963, veteran detective Martin McFadden observed suspicious activity by two men in a Cleveland business district. Suspecting a daylight robbery, McFadden approached John Terry and Richard Chilton and identified himself as a police officer. When his attempts to question the men on their activities were ignored, McFadden seized the two and patted down their outer clothing. Feeling a weapon on each, McFadden removed the guns and arrested the men for carrying concealed weapons. In a pretrial motion, Terry and Chilton contended that the guns were seized during an illegal search. The Court of Common Pleas overruled the motion and sentenced the men to three years. Chilton died before the case was appealed.

In June, 1968, the Supreme Court ruled 8 to 1 to uphold Terry's conviction. Writing for the majority, Chief Justice Earl Warren concluded that the issue at hand was "whether it is always unreasonable for a policeman to seize a person and subject him to a limited search for weapons unless there is probable cause for an arrest." In deciding this issue, the Court divided the case into the "seizure" and the "search." The decision defined a seizure as occurring any time a police officer restrains an individual's freedom to walk away.

Determining the constitutionality of the search required a balance between the Fourth Amendment's protection from unreasonable searches and seizures with the safety to the individuals involved. Warren concluded that a limited search was allowable if based on "specific reasonable inferences" drawn upon "the facts in the light of [the officer's] experience." In addition, the Court stipulated that "the issue is whether a reasonably prudent man in the circumstances would be warranted in the belief that his safety or that of others was in danger." Dissenting with the decision, Justice William O. Douglas looked to the legal differences between "probable cause" and "reasonable suspicion." Relying on the protection found in the Fourth Amendment, Douglas saw the search in question as an "infringement on personal liberty" because McFadden had no probable cause for arrest prior to the search.

Terry v. Ohio allowed a significant change in police procedures. It provided a police officer, once identified as such, with a legal right to perform a limited search of suspicious individuals by means of a protective pat-down. This provision helped to lower the number of injuries and deaths during initial confrontations between individuals and police officers. In addition, the police were authorized to seize any nonthreatening contraband, such as drugs or drug paraphernalia, found during a *Terry* search. Recognizing the potential for abuse in allowing "stop and frisk" actions by police, however, the Court was careful to outline the Fourth Amendment limitations that apply to stop and frisk searches. In *Sibron v. New York*, a companion case to *Terry*, the Court held that if the reason for the search is to find evidence rather than to check for weapons, then any evidence found is inadmissible.

See also Evidence, rules of; *Katz v. United States*; *Mapp v. Ohio*; Search and seizure; *Weeks v. United States*.

Texas v. Johnson

COURT: U.S. Supreme Court

DATE: Decided June 21, 1989

SIGNIFICANCE: The First Amendment protects symbolic forms of expression, including the right of a protester to burn an American flag as part of a political demonstration

While the Republican National Convention was taking place in Dallas in 1984, Gregory Lee Johnson participated in a political demonstration to protest the policies of the Reagan Administration and of certain Dallas-based corporations. In front of city hall, Johnson doused an American flag with kerosene and set it on fire. While the flag burned, protesters chanted, "America, the red, white, and blue, we spit on you." Several witnesses testified that they had been seriously offended, but no one was injured or threatened with physical injury. Following the demonstration, a witness collected the flag's remains and buried them in his backyard. Johnson was

In Texas v. Johnson, *the Supreme Court ruled that burning the U.S. flag is constitutionally protected symbolic speech.* (AP/Wide World Photos)

charged with the desecration of a venerated object in violation of the Texas Penal Code. He was convicted, sentenced to one year in prison, and fined two thousand dollars. The Court of Appeals for the Fifth District of Texas at Dallas affirmed the conviction. The Court of Criminal Appeals of Texas, however, reversed the lower courts. By a 5-4 vote, the U.S. Supreme Court affirmed the appeals court's decision.

Justice William J. Brennan, joined by Justices Thurgood Marshall, Harry Blackmun, Antonin Scalia, and Anthony Kennedy, wrote the majority opinion. Brennan noted that the First Amendment protects "expressive conduct" as well as written and spoken words. While a state can prevent "imminent lawless action," in this case Johnson's symbolic expression of displeasure with government policies did not lead to a disturbance of the peace and did not oppose the state's interest in maintaining order. Instead, Johnson's expression was restricted because of the content of his message. "If there is a bedrock principle underlying the First Amendment," Brennan observed, "it is that the Government may not prohibit the expression of an idea simply because society finds the idea itself offensive or disagreeable." Toleration of Johnson's criticism reaffirms the freedom that the flag represents. Brennan continued, "[t]he way to preserve the flag's special role is not to punish those who feel differently about such matters. It is to persuade them that they are wrong. . . . We can imagine no more appropriate response to burning a flag than waving one's own, no better way to counter a flag burner's message than by saluting the flag that burns."

Chief Justice William Rehnquist, in a dissenting opinion joined by Justices Byron White and Sandra Day O'Connor, emphasized the unique role of the flag and the "profoundly offensive" nature of Johnson's conduct. In a separate dissent, Justice John Paul Stevens argued that Johnson had been prosecuted not for his criticism of government policies but for the method he chose to express his views.

This case is important for establishing that flag burning as a symbolic form of expression is protected by the First Amendment.

See also Bill of Rights, U.S.; Civil disobedience; *Eichman, United States v.*; *O'Brien, United States v.*; Speech and press, freedom of; *Tinker v. Des Moines Independent Community School District*.

Theft

DEFINITION: A crime involving the taking and carrying away of the property of another without consent and with intent to deprive the owner of its possession permanently

SIGNIFICANCE: Larceny is the oldest crime against property and the most frequently underreported offense, often because of the small value of items stolen

According to 1990 U.S. Department of Justice statistics, more than 70 percent of felony arrests are for property offenses, drug violations, and robbery. Reports to police in 1992 revealed 7,915,200 larcenies nationwide, with the total value of property stolen placed at $3.8 billion. The most common form

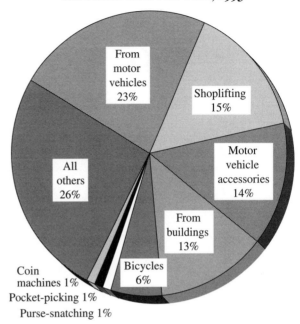

REPORTED THEFT BY TYPE, 1993

From motor vehicles 23%

Shoplifting 15%

Motor vehicle accessories 14%

All others 26%

From buildings 13%

Bicycles 6%

Coin machines 1%

Pocket-picking 1%

Purse-snatching 1%

Source: U.S. Department of Justice, Federal Bureau of Investigation, *Crime in the United States* (Uniform Crime Reports). Washington, D.C.: U.S. Government Printing Office, 1994.
Note: Motor vehicle theft not included.

of larceny in the late twentieth century was theft of motor vehicle parts, accessories, and contents. Yet larceny, the most common crime against property, is the most frequently underreported, often because small thefts rarely come to the attention of the police. In 1992, the average value of items reported stolen was about $480.

Motor vehicle theft is the most commonly reported crime, as insurance companies require police reports before they will reimburse car owners for their losses. In 1992, more than 1.6 million motor vehicles were reported stolen, with the average value per vehicle placed at $4,713, for a total of $7.6 billion. Arrest reports for motor vehicle theft in 1990 revealed that 62 percent of all arrestees were under twenty-one years of age and 90 percent were male. Motor vehicle theft often becomes violent in cases of "carjacking." The Federal Bureau of Investigation (FBI) estimates that carjacking constitutes slightly more than 1 percent of all motor vehicle thefts. "Joyriding," a temporary rather than permanent deprivation, is also included within the theft/larceny offenses.

Components of Larceny. Larceny involves the taking and carrying away of the personal property of another without consent and with intent to steal or to deprive the owner of its possession permanently. The first element of larceny involves a "taking." This may be in the form of purse snatching, pickpocketing, shoplifting, or the like. The taking must be deliber-

Shoplifting is one of the most widespread forms of theft. (James L. Shaffer)

ate and conducted with the intent to deprive the owner of possession of the property permanently. Many states have expanded these requirements to include use, transfer, concealing, or retaining possession. Personal property has also been broadened to include movable property or anything of value. Personal property can be tangible or intangible, including utilities (water, gas, electricity, and oil). The Model Penal Code expands on intangibles as theft of services, including labor, professional services, telephone or other public services, accommodations, admission to exhibits, and use of vehicles or other movable property.

Unauthorized computer use has presented dilemmas in larceny/theft cases. Some courts have held that unauthorized use of computer time is not larceny, despite ruling that electrical services can be the object of theft. Other courts have

reached the opposite conclusion. The Counterfeit Access Device and Computer Fraud and Abuse Act of the Comprehensive Crime Control Act of 1984 makes it illegal to access a computer knowingly without authorization, to use a computer for nonauthorized attempts to gain government secrets or financial records of private institutions or persons, or to use a computer to modify a program or block authorized access.

Under common law there were no degrees of larceny; all such crimes were felonies. Modern statutes divide larceny into two degrees: grand larceny and petit larceny. The distinction depends on the value of the articles stolen. The line of demarcation between the two degrees is generally a trivial amount, such as fifty, one hundred, or two hundred dollars. Value is governed by fair market value, if that can be determined. If it is unavailable, cost value is used. Consolidation of the various larceny offenses under "theft" is considered a more realistic approach, because the necessity of determining the manner in which the property has been misappropriated is largely eliminated.

Other Offenses. Embezzlement is a crime against ownership of property. One who is in rightful possession of property and later decides to convert (retain possession of) it is said to have embezzled. Examples of potential embezzlers include those to whom property is given for repair or safekeeping and public officials such as stockbrokers, bank tellers, and others in positions of trust.

False pretenses depends on the misrepresentation of a past or present fact. Relying on the misrepresentation, the owner is deceived into giving up possession of the property. Con games fall into this category, as do the phony telemarketing schemes which cause Americans to lose nearly one billion dollars annually. The elderly are especially vulnerable to telephone swindlers.

Larceny by trick is similar to false pretenses, but in the former, title is intentionally passed, whereas in the latter only possession is surrendered because of some trick, deception, or fraud. If the victim expects return of the property, the crime is larceny by trick; if not, it is false pretenses.

Robbery and Burglary. Robbery involves the stealing of property plus the element of force or fear; it is usually classified as a crime against the person rather than a crime against property. Absent force or fear of the use of force, there is no crime of robbery. A majority of courts now hold that when force or threat of force is not used in stealing property, but only in escaping from the scene or keeping the property, the crime of robbery has still been committed.

Burglary involves unlawful entry into a building or occupied structure with intent to commit a felony or theft. Use of force to gain entry is not required. Certain state statutes specify "intent to commit a felony or petit larceny"; others have eliminated larceny as one of the crimes that can be the object of burglary; still others state "intent to commit a felony or larceny." The problem involves proving intent to commit a felony, especially when there is no evidence of commission of another crime.

—Marcia J. Weiss

See also Burglary; Carjacking; Computer crime; Crime; Embezzlement; Motor vehicle theft; Robbery.

BIBLIOGRAPHY

The issues surrounding burglary and theft are addressed in John M. MacDonald, C. Donald Brannan, and Robert E. Nicoletti, *Burglary and Theft* (Springfield, Ill.: Charles C Thomas, 1980). More general works include Neil C. Chamelin and Kenneth R. Evans, *Criminal Law for Police Officers* (4th ed. Englewood Cliffs, N.J.: Prentice-Hall, 1987); Joel Samaha, *Criminal Law* (4th ed. St. Paul, Minn.: West, 1993); Thomas J. Gardner and Terry M. Anderson, *Criminal Law: Principles and Cases* (5th ed. St. Paul, Minn.: West, 1992); Arnold H. Loewy, *Criminal Law in a Nutshell* (2d ed. St. Paul, Minn.: West, 1987).

Thirteenth Amendment. *See* Civil War Amendments

Thornburgh v. American College of Obstetricians and Gynecologists

COURT: U.S. Supreme Court

DATE: Decided issued June 11, 1986

SIGNIFICANCE: The Court upheld a woman's right to abortion, striking down a number of provisions that would have limited that right and placed restrictions on physicians

In June, 1982, Pennsylvania enacted the Abortion Control Act, which placed severe restrictions on access to abortion. Before signing an abortion consent form, a woman had to read, or hear read, material about abortion alternatives, stages of fetal development, and psychological and physical harm that abortion might cause. Physicians were required to file extensive information about the women on whom they performed abortions and provide criteria by which fetal viability was determined in each case. A second physician was required to attest fetal viability. Additionally, physicians were required to use the abortion method that best protected the viability of the fetus. Failure to comply was a third-degree felony.

Following passage, a case was filed with the U.S. Court of Appeals, Third Circuit, by the American College of Obstetricians and Gynecologists against the state of Pennsylvania, represented by Governor Richard Thornburgh. This court ruled against all the major restrictions, citing earlier Supreme Court decisions. Pennsylvania then filed an appeal with the Supreme Court. Opponents of abortion were hopeful that an increasingly conservative Court would use this case to overturn the major provisions of *Roe v. Wade* (1973).

The Supreme Court, by a 5-4 majority, upheld the findings of the appeals court. The consent requirements were deemed an attempt to persuade women to change their minds, not to provide necessary information for informed consent. The restrictions placed on physicians were ruled as impinging on the doctor-patient relationship and limiting physicians' professional judgment. Restricting the method of abortion was viewed as giving fetal rights priority over the health and well-being of the mother. The Court did reaffirm the states' right to intervene on behalf of the fetus, but only during the last trimester of pregnancy. It also invoked the concept of *stare decisis* (let past decisions stand) in affirming a woman's right to abortion. It argued that constant reinterpretation of the law undermines societal stability.

The dissenting minority questioned the fundamental right to abortion, arguing that no such right is found in the Constitution. It declared its belief that *Roe v. Wade* had gone too far in affirming a woman's right to privacy, arguing that fetal rights should be strengthened. These issues have continued to be part of the public debate surrounding abortion and have reappeared in other state laws and cases brought before the Supreme Court. The narrow majority decision in this case continues to generate hope among abortion opponents that continued challenges will eventually result in strict and severe limitations being placed on abortion.

See also Abortion; *Akron v. Akron Center for Reproductive Health*; *Doe v. Bolton*; *Harris v. McRae*; *Maher v. Roe*;

Planned Parenthood of Central Missouri v. Danforth; *Planned Parenthood v. Casey*; *Roe v. Wade*.

Tilton v. Richardson

Court: U.S. Supreme Court

Date: Decided October 12, 1971

Significance: The Court held that it is constitutional for the federal government to provide grants to private sectarian colleges for the construction of academic buildings used solely for secular purposes

The Higher Education Facilities Act of 1963 provided private colleges, both religious and secular, with federal grants and loans to construct academic buildings. The subsidized buildings were not to be used for religious instruction or worship for at least twenty years, but one section of the act allowed buildings to be used for any purpose after that period. The act was administered by the commissioner of education, and the commissioner required institutions receiving grants to provide assurances that the religious restrictions would be observed.

Eleanor Tilton and other taxpayers filed suit in a federal district court against the federal officials who administered the act, charging that grants to four church-related colleges in Connecticut were a violation of the establishment clause of the First Amendment. After the district court dismissed the complaint, the taxpayers appealed their suit to the U.S. Supreme Court.

The Court ruled 5 to 4 to uphold the provisions of the 1963 law that allowed religious colleges and universities to obtain federal funding for buildings used only for secular instruction, but the Court found that the part of the law ending the ban on religious practices after twenty years to be an unconstitutional contribution to a religious body. In defending the major portion of the law, Chief Justice Warren Burger wrote that the crucial question was not whether the law provided some benefit to a religious institution but whether the primary effect of the law was to advance religion. In making a distinction between the 1963 law and cases in which the Court had ruled against state subsidies to primary and secondary schools, Burger argued that church-related colleges were not dealing with impressionable children, that the colleges under consideration did not have religious indoctrination as one of their substantial purposes, that buildings were themselves religiously neutral with little need for government surveillance, and that onetime grants required only minimal inspection. Cumulatively, Burger concluded that these factors lessened the potential for the grants to cause divisive religious fragmentation. He did acknowledge, however, that it might be unconstitutional for government to provide grants to a college which had religious indoctrination as one of its primary missions.

Since first dealing with the issue in *Everson v. Board of Education* (1947), the Court has had a difficult time interpreting the establishment clause in its relationship to governmental assistance to students attending religious schools. Sometimes the Court has supported the strict separationist view, which is suspicious of even indirect aid to religious education, while in other cases the Court has tended to promote accommodation and emphasize neutrality. The *Tilton* decision indicated that the Court was willing to allow an extreme accommodationist position when the case involved religious colleges and universities.

See also Establishment of religion; *Lemon v. Kurtzman*; *Mueller v. Allen*.

Tinker v. Des Moines Independent Community School District

Court: U.S. Supreme Court

Date: Decided February 24, 1969

Significance: In this case, the Supreme Court decided that students attending public junior high and high school have a constitutional right to express their opinions on important public policy issues as long as they do not materially disrupt the school's educational program while doing so

In December, 1965, several students met at one of their homes and agreed to wear black armbands to their respective schools to demonstrate their opposition to the war in Vietnam. School authorities, upon learning of the students' plans, adopted a policy requiring the suspension of any student who wore an armband to school and refused to remove it. Five students wore black armbands to school and were suspended from class and sent home when they refused to obey the school's policy. Three of these students and their parents filed suit in federal district court on the grounds that the suspension of the students violated their First Amendment rights to freedom of speech. The district court dismissed their complaint, and the Court of Appeals for the Eighth Circuit affirmed that decision.

The Supreme Court by a vote of 7 to 2 reversed the decision of the lower court. In ringing terms, the Court declared that students and teachers do not "shed their constitutional rights to freedom of speech or expression at the schoolhouse gate." The Court was particularly concerned that the school authorities permitted students to wear other political symbols to class without sanction but had determined to discipline only those students who wore armbands to protest the Vietnam War. This kind of regulatory discrimination against a specific viewpoint of speech directly challenged the most basic of free speech principles: Government cannot prohibit the expression of one opinion while allowing other points of view to be openly debated.

Despite its endorsement of the free speech rights of students in *Tinker*, the Court was careful not to undermine the legitimate authority of school officials. The majority opinion of Justice Abe Fortas made it clear that while students had a constitutionally protected right to express their beliefs at school, their freedom of speech was not unlimited in its scope. Student expressive activities could be appropriately regulated to prevent any disturbance of the school's educational programs. The First Amendment did not protect disruptive speech or expression that impinged on the rights of other students. In the case before it, however, there was no evidence that the passive wearing of armbands caused disruption or interfered with school activities. The Court rejected the argument that the speculative concerns of school officials, who feared that a protest against the Vietnam War might prove disorderly, constituted a sufficient basis for forbidding the students' speech. "In our system," Justice Fortas wrote, "undifferentiated fear or apprehension of disturbance is not enough to overcome the right to freedom of expression."

The primary holding in *Tinker* is that bedrock principles of freedom of speech apply to public school students. No case prior to *Tinker* had stated this rule as forcefully or as clearly. The Court's decision in *Tinker* did not purport to resolve all the conflicts that might arise between student speakers and school authorities. Subsequent decisions have demonstrated, for example, that when student speech is part of the school's educational program and bears the imprimatur of the school, officials have the discretion to regulate nondisruptive expression on the grounds that it does not further the school's educational goals.

See also Bill of Rights, U.S.; *O'Brien, United States v.*; School law; Speech and press, freedom of; Vietnam War.

Tison v. Arizona

COURT: U.S. Supreme Court
DATE: Decided April 21, 1987
SIGNIFICANCE: In this case, the Supreme Court created a flexible standard for applying the death penalty to felony-murder accomplices who demonstrate reckless disregard for human life even though they do not directly participate in killing a victim

On July 30, 1978, brothers Donny, age twenty-one, Ricky, age twenty, and Raymond Tison, age nineteen, smuggled guns into the Arizona State Prison and helped in the escape of their father Gary, a convicted murderer, and another convicted murderer. The group changed cars and made their escape on a desert highway. When they had a flat tire, they flagged down a passing car containing young parents, a baby, and a teenage cousin and held the family at gunpoint. Gary Tison ordered his sons to load their possessions into the young family's car. As the brothers loaded the car and pushed their own disabled car into the desert, their father and the other prison escapee brutally murdered the entire family, including the baby, with shotgun blasts at close range. The escaping group traveled for several more days before encountering a police roadblock. During the ensuing shootout, Donny was killed, Gary escaped into the desert but soon died from exposure, and Ricky, Raymond, and the other convict were captured.

As accomplices to the killing of the young family, Ricky and Raymond Tison were charged with felony murder. When they were sentenced to death, they appealed their sentences based on a Supreme Court decision (*Enmund v. Florida*, 1982) which had declared that felony-murder accomplices cannot be sentenced to death if they do not directly participate in the actual killing. After the Arizona Supreme Court upheld the sentences, the Tisons took their case to the U.S. Supreme Court.

In a 5-4 decision, the U.S. Supreme Court created a flexible standard for imposing the death penalty. The Court declared that felony-murder accomplices could receive the death penalty if they demonstrated "reckless disregard for human life," even if they did not directly participate in the killing. The justices used this new standard to uphold the capital sentences imposed on the Tisons because they viewed the brothers' active involvement in supplying weapons to convicted murderers and kidnapping the young family as a demonstration of "reckless disregard."

In *Tison v. Arizona* the Supreme Court gave state prosecutors greater flexibility to seek the death penalty against accomplices who participate in crimes that result in homicides. This new flexibility came at the price of greater inconsistency in the application of capital punishment. Under the prior rule, it was relatively clear which offenders were eligible for the death penalty, based on their direct participation in a killing. By contrast, under the *Tison* rule, jurors and judges applying the vague "reckless indifference" standard have broad opportunities to impose capital punishment based on their negative feelings toward the accomplice or their revulsion at the crime without precise consideration of the defendant's actual participation.

See also Accessory, accomplice, and aiding and abetting; Capital punishment; Cruel and unusual punishment; Felony; Murder and homicide.

Tort

DEFINITION: Any "wrongful act" that is actionable in civil court for which damages can be recovered; torts are wrongs that are not covered by contract law
SIGNIFICANCE: Tort actions cover a wide variety of behaviors and represent a significant portion of the cases in civil court

There was no general principle of tort liability in English common law, but the king's court allowed the recovery of damages for various types of trespass that resulted in injury. The law of torts evolved from a common-law tradition making it possible to recover damages in civil court for a wrongful act. The connection of torts with wrongful acts has the potential to be confusing; there is no implication of criminality or moral delinquency in the use of the term "wrongful." The concepts of tort and crime differ in many ways. Nevertheless, many common-law criminal acts are actionable as torts. Assault, for example, is both a common-law crime and actionable as a tort.

In a tort case, the defendant incurs liability when his or her action or failure to act causes a breach of a legal duty and results in a foreseeable injury or harm to a legally recognized right of a plaintiff. Not every injury or harm is considered a tort (thereby being actionable). There is no liability for the inevitable accident or an event considered an act of God.

A tradition in Anglo-American law is that the government cannot be sued without giving its permission. In a 1907 decision upholding sovereign immunity, Justice Oliver Wendell Holmes, Jr., held that "there can be no legal right as against the authority that makes the law on which the right depends." The

U.S. Congress passed the Tort Claims Act in 1946, authorizing the U.S. district courts to adjudicate liability for all tort claims of injury or harm resulting from the acts or failure to act of the federal government's employees, officers, and agencies. It directed the courts, furthermore, to hold the federal government as responsible as a private individual, in the same circumstances and to the same degree.

In tort law, the standard by which actions are judged is the action's (or failure to act's) reasonableness in the circumstances. The remedy for a tort claim is generally a monetary award for damages. In a case of wrongful death, the monetary damages may be the present value of all future income that the individual would have earned had the person lived a normal life expectancy. The determination of such a value usually requires the services of a professional economist as an expert witness. In the case of a nuisance, an injunction may be the proper remedy.

The law of torts permits any and all parties to be held liable. The liability is held to be vicarious liability, and even the plaintiff may be wholly or partially responsible for the injury. In cases in which the plaintiff is held partially responsible, a proportional reduction in any damage award may be made to the degree that the plaintiff is held responsible.

See also Civil law; Civil procedure; Contract law; Litigation; Suit; Tort reform.

Tort reform

Definition: Changes in the expansion or reduction of a tort defendant's liability, especially in the areas of products liability and medical malpractice

Significance: Until the 1980's, tort reforms generally expanded the rights of injured parties; since the 1980's, tort reforms have tended to shrink the liability exposure of defendants in business and the professions

For people injured by malpractice, dangerous products, or accidents, the tort system provides medical and rehabilitative costs, replaces lost income, compensates victims for pain and suffering, and sometimes punishes the defendant beyond the victim's damage by imposing punitive damages. When this system of compensation becomes costly, inconsistent, inefficient, or unpopular for other reasons, the result has usually been a call for reform.

Nineteenth Century Judicial Reforms. Before the middle of the nineteenth century, common law imposed a strict standard upon defendants whose acts caused another's injury. Unless an injury-causing accident was inevitable, the defendant was absolutely liable. Defendant liability began to shrink, however, with decisions such as *Brown v. Kendall* in 1850. After that decision, defendants were liable only if their negligence caused the injury, thus shifting the burden from defendant to plaintiff, with a corresponding shift from absolute liability to liability based on negligence. Under a negligence theory, plaintiffs had to demonstrate that they were owed a duty of due care, that the duty was breached, and that the breach was the proximate cause of the injury (that is, that it was legally held to be the cause).

Industrial Interests Influence Reform. The early nineteenth century industrial economy influenced how and to what extent parties injured by the negligence of others would be compensated. Nineteenth century tort law assumed that with industrial progress, some injuries would go uncompensated. Railroads and other new machines of industry led to accidents whose costs, it was believed, should not burden or discourage commercial enterprise. Therefore, it was not uncommon in the nineteenth century for a railroad company to escape liability when a railroad employee's negligence injured a fellow worker (*Farwell v. Boston and Worcester Railroad*, 1842). Accidents on the job were considered an ordinary risk of employment. Furthermore, with a system of compensation based on negligence, the excuses of "assumption of risk" and "contributory negligence" became available for industrial and business defendants to avoid full liability and responsibility. The costs of workplace accidents were borne by the workers themselves.

Later Judicial Reforms. With increasing consumer awareness, judicial tort reform eroded defenses and immunities. Greater exposure for liability was placed on business enterprises to the extent that fault gave way to strict liability in areas such as products liability. For example, the *McPherson v. Buick Motor Co.* (1916) decision exposed manufacturers to greater tort liability by no longer requiring that, in order to seek damages, an injured party be in a contractual arrangement with the party that caused the injury or damage.

Emergence of Strict Liability. Judicial reforms imposed strict liability in products liability cases with the *Escola v. Coca-Cola Bottling Co. of Fresno* decision in 1944. A strict liability approach no longer required that the injured party prove negligence to impose liability upon the manufacturer of a defective product. By the 1960's, particularly with the decision in *Greenman v. Yuba Power Products Inc.* (1963), the term "defect" was steadily enlarged to include product design and warnings about a product's use. As the relationship between consumer and manufacturer changed over time, the tort system attempted to keep pace with the changes in that relationship.

Other reforms led to the recognition of injuries such as wrongful death, under which a decedent's family could claim damage, and to emotional distress, whereby a plaintiff who may not have suffered physical injury could still sue for the emotional stress caused, for example, by witnessing the death of a family member. By the 1970's, defendant liability had broadened sufficiently to include failure to warn potential victims of a mental patient's intent to harm them (*Tarasoff v. Regents of University of California*, 1976).

No-Fault Reforms. Two no-fault compensation systems appeared in the twentieth century to provide compensation for people injured under specified conditions. Between 1910 and 1920, forty-two states enacted workers' compensation schemes for those injured on the job. With the enactment of workers' compensation legislation, injured workers no longer had to litigate to recover medical costs and wages lost after workplace accidents. Although under this scheme injured workers surrendered the right to compensation for pain and suffering, they were spared the expense, delays, and uncertainty of litigation. This system effectively moved injured workers' claims from the tort system to the administrative office.

In the 1970's a system of no-fault automobile insurance emerged amid considerable public debate. During the 1970's, automobile insurance premiums were rising quickly. Insurance companies argued that large damage awards and the high administrative costs of litigation increased the costs of insuring automobiles. Academic studies and consumer advocate Ralph Nader supported enactment of no-fault insurance systems. As under workers' compensation schemes, under no-fault insurance the liability equation no longer included fault, so claims could be settled quickly and efficiently and insurers could keep insurance premiums affordable. Twenty-four states adopted some form of no-fault automobile insurance scheme during the 1970's.

The Insurance Crisis. In the 1980's, liability insurance premiums suddenly escalated. Because of premium increases, many consumers, businesses, and service providers were forced to spend more on liability insurance coverage or to withdraw from the marketplace. In some states children's day care centers closed, helpful but potentially risky products such as medicines became too expensive to market, and some obstetricians and anesthesiologists practiced without insurance. Debate flourished about the reasons for the crisis. Chief among the suggested causes was that the insurance industry had miscalculated its underwriting cycle, resulting in reduced insurance funds. A second suggestion was that insurance companies were simply gouging consumers; however, with the unavailability of some liability insurance policies at any cost, this seems unlikely. A third suggestion was that increased tort liability litigation was taking its financial toll.

Tort Reform from 1970 to the 1990's. The tort reforms of the 1970's responded to the medical crisis that some states faced. Both California and Indiana, for example, passed legislation in 1975 to limit medical malpractice awards. In 1979 the Model Uniform Products Liability Act appeared as a reform proposal for states to follow in drafting their own products liability legislation, and the 1980's saw reforms focused on products liability. Since 1986 nearly every state has made legislative changes to its tort law. States have modified or abolished joint and several liability, restricted products liability suits, capped or prohibited punitive damages (or required "clear and convincing" evidence for the award), capped noneconomic damages, and reduced damages where other compensation may be available.

The impetus for reform came from the perception that unchecked litigation and enormous damage awards had increased the price of goods and services, increased taxes, reduced government services, increased liability insurance premiums, and forced some firms from the marketplace. Furthermore, proponents of reform argued that businesses, industry, and the professions were increasingly targets of tort litiga-

tion because of the "deep pockets" of the enterprise or its insurer. Increased business costs, it was argued, weakened American businesses on the world market. Reform advocates also criticized the tort system for its seemingly haphazard treatment of injured parties—some plaintiffs received windfall damages and others received nothing. Proponents of reforms included the American Tort Reform Association, the United States Chamber of Commerce, and the American Medical Association.

Opponents of reform argued that commercial and industrial interests created the perception that the tort system was failing. Proposed reforms were characterized not only as attacks on the protections the system afforded injured victims but also as attacks on access to a legal system designed to compensate injured parties. Critics also emphasized the fact that women have most often been the consumers of products that have resulted in massive litigation in recent years. The Dalkon Shield contraceptive device, silicone breast implants, and the anti-diethylstilbestrol (DES) miscarriage drug were products that injured women and resulted in thousands of plaintiffs and large damage awards. Organizations opposing reforms included groups such as the Association of Trial Lawyers of America, the American Bar Association, and the Consumer Federation of America.

Statistical Debate. Although proponents view tort reforms as a partial solution to increases in litigation and increases in associated costs, it is unclear whether American society actually became increasingly litigious during this period, since there are no statistics that show how many injured and deserving parties chose not to file a lawsuit. For example, while civil litigation in federal district courts between 1980 and 1990 increased from 168,789 to 207,742 cases, tort-related cases accounted for only 18 percent of cases filed in 1980 and increased by only 2 percent to 20 percent of all civil cases filed in 1990. In some years in that decade the percentage of tort cases even decreased. These statistics suggest that the tort system might be the wrong target if civil litigation is to be reduced.

Although the number of tort claims during the 1980's and 1990's remained relatively constant, the few cases involving large damage awards captured the attention of the public and the politicians. According to the Rand Corporation's Institute for Civil Justice, people on both sides of the debate selected their statistics carefully. While tort litigation had not increased greatly in the 1980's and 1990's, parts of the tort litigation system saw tremendous growth. For example, mass latent-injury cases stemming from the use of products such as asbestos showed expanded litigation. Lobbyists quoting those statistics would find alarming trends of increased numbers of plaintiffs suing and very high damage awards for successful plaintiffs. On the other hand, lobbyists would find little change over time in the costs and amount of litigation associated with automobile accidents.

Tort law is designed to provide medical treatment for victims, to replace lost income, to compensate for pain and suffering, and to punish egregious defendants by means of punitive damages. Tort reform is a product of public opinion and political action. Business and industry have a strong interest in persuading Congress to enact reform favorable to potential defendants. Furthermore, tort reform involves insurance reform, which traditionally has been defeated rather easily by the insurance industry. The industry is relatively free from federal control, since it is largely exempt from the regulations of federal antitrust laws. Proposed reforms that would be favorable to potential defendants who produce products such as asbestos and tobacco, which have received highly unfavorable press reports, are subject to strict scrutiny by consumer rights groups as well as politicians, whose futures depend on public opinion. Finally, given the large number of congressional committees involved in producing the legislation, both time constraints and political compromises limit the amount of reform that occurs. —*Paul Albert Bateman*

See also Civil law; Civil procedure; Compensatory damages; Consumer rights movement; Litigation; Negligence; Products liability; Punitive damages; Strict liability; Tort.

BIBLIOGRAPHY

The American Law Institute's *Enterprise Responsibility for Personal Injury: Unedited Transcript of Discussion of Reporters' Study at 1991 Annual Meeting* (Philadelphia: American Law Institute, 1991) addresses the complexities of liability problems and tort reform. Several law reviews have devoted symposia to the topic, including *San Diego Law Review* 30 (1993), which comments on the "Reporters' Study," *Ohio State Law Journal* 48 (no. 2, 1987), and *Denver University Law Review* 64 (no. 4, 1988). For a discussion of the relationship between proposed reforms and national health care, see *Cornell Law Review* 79 (no. 6, 1994). For a practitioner's view on the need for tort reform, see Robert V. Wills, *Lawyers Are Killing America: A Trial Lawyer's Appeal for Genuine Tort Reform* (Santa Barbara, Calif.: Capra Press, 1990). For a historical review of the issue, see Kermit L. Hall, ed., *Tort Law in American History: Major Historical Interpretations* (New York: Garland, 1987).

Transportation law

DEFINITION: Laws regarding the transportation of persons and goods, covering such issues as public health and safety, commercial relationships, and access to public airways, waterways, and land

SIGNIFICANCE: Transportation is a broad group of industries subject to government regulations defining legal relationships, assuring safety, and protecting the environment

Transportation law usually focuses on specific modes of transportation, such as automobiles or aircraft, and takes the form of regulations governing such functions as driver or pilot qualifications and training, vehicle maintenance, operating procedures, safety precautions, access to publicly owned rights-of-way or property, and effects on the environment. Transportation law also is a very broad legal category that may include related issues, such as bailments, the legal responsibility of transporters or shippers for the storage and shipment of goods owned by someone else.

Automobile Registration. The variety of regulations governing automobile transportation includes everything from automobile registration requirements (that establish legal title and assure payment of state taxes and licensing fees) to safety requirements in designing and constructing automobiles and restrictions on the emission of air pollutants. In terms of the latter restrictions, the Clean Air Act of 1970 and 1977 amendments place limits on the amount of automobile emissions that are permissible in communities with high levels of air pollution. Auto emission standards have been set by the Environmental Protection Agency (EPA) and are monitored periodically by state and federal officials. Increasing gasoline mileage requirements for automobiles has been one part of the regulatory effort. Reducing automobile traffic in areas with poor air quality has been another. In 1980, the EPA withheld federal funds for highway construction from the state of Colorado for failing to regulate emissions.

The National Highway Traffic Safety Administration (NHTSA) in the U.S. Department of Transportation is responsible for highway safety, and it issues recalls of automobiles for defective and potentially dangerous parts. Recalls often require repairs of thousands of vehicles and can cost automobile makers millions of dollars. An NHTSA rule requiring that automobile bumpers be strong enough to withstand a 5 miles per hour crash was very controversial and caused political conflict between members of Congress from steel-producing and aluminum-producing states, the latter favoring the 5 miles per hour requirement (which encouraged the use of lighter aluminum bumpers), and the former favoring a 2.5 miles per hour requirement that would encourage the continued use of steel bumpers.

During the 1980's, President Ronald Reagan's appointees to executive positions in the NHTSA and EPA attempted to abolish or delay implementation of safety and environmental regulations for new automobiles and trucks. Requirements to include airbags to protect drivers and passengers involved in crashes were delayed for years. One of the most hotly contested issues has been federally mandated speed limits as a condition for qualifying for federal highway funds, and laws were changed in 1995 to permit states to increase the limits.

Aircraft and Airline Regulation. The Federal Aviation Administration (FAA) is responsible for regulating air traffic, investigating aircraft crashes, monitoring aircraft maintenance, setting standards for pilot training, and overseeing a broad spectrum of operational requirements. The FAA also has legal authority to "ground" aircraft and airlines that are judged unsafe or cannot document proper training of their crews and proper maintenance of their aircraft. Deregulation proposals during the 1980's included letting the airlines themselves decide how they would meet training and maintenance standards. Apart from safety standards, deregulation of the airline industry resulted in a very volatile industry with the collapse of several major airlines and an expansion of local, or commuter, airlines. The effects of deregulation on aviation safety are uncertain, although crashes of commuter aircraft in the 1990's suggest that pilot training and maintenance may have become substandard. Stricter regulations were subsequently issued by the FAA.

Railroad Regulation. A series of legislative acts around the beginning of the twentieth century set standards for automatic couplers, brakes, and signals. The Locomotive Inspection Act of 1911 required railroads to implement and maintain self-inspection programs, with the Interstate Commerce Commission (ICC) being responsible for setting standards and monitoring procedures. ICC inspectors focused primarily on train and track maintenance records. The 1960's and 1970's saw the

expansion of regulatory efforts aimed at increasing safety, and the railroad responsibilities of the ICC were transferred to the newly created Federal Railroad Administration. Major issues in railroad regulation in the 1980's and 1990's, following a series of rail accidents, were drug testing of train engineers and improving track and bridge maintenance.

Transportation law includes the regulation of many other modes of transport, including pipelines, maritime transport, and commercial trucking. Laws regarding pipelines largely relate to environmental issues, setting load standards for pipes, and dissipation of the heat generated by liquids moving through pipes. Maritime regulation—of vessels, crew training, port facilities, sea lanes and inland waterways, and the water-

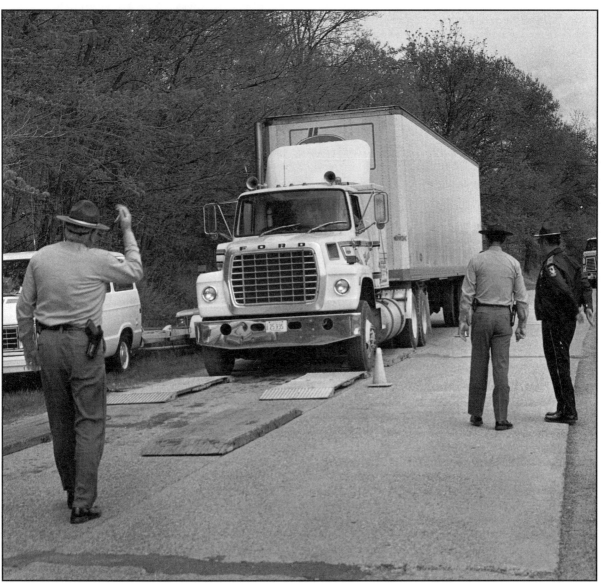

The trucking industry is regulated with regard to driver licensing, truck maintenance, maximum loads allowable, and the types of materials that can be transported. (James L. Shaffer)

borne transportation of goods and passengers—is a mixture of domestic and international law. Legal authority on the "high seas," as well as in the "high skies," is based in international law. While the United States has had vessel inspection programs dating from 1838, an academy to train maritime service officers, and other standards to protect the safety of goods and passengers in transit, the regulation of international shipping and passenger liners has been slow to develop. Disasters aboard cruise ships have drawn attention to the lack of effective regulation and encouraged U.S. monitoring of vessels using U.S. ports. Maritime law, like other forms of transportation law, tends to develop in response to demands by the public or business firms to address specific problems.

Regulations or laws regarding the trucking industry focus on the qualifications and licensing of drivers, driver training, truck maintenance, maximum loads, and the kinds of materials that may be transported. Operational restrictions include limits on the number of hours drivers are permitted to operate vehicles without rest. The state of California has a preventive maintenance requirement that involves state inspectors monitoring the records of trucking firms. There are growing concerns about poor maintenance of large transport trucks and violations of driver-safety standards. As a result, a number of states are increasing their inspection of vehicles to assure that lights, brakes, and other equipment work and that drivers are not exceeding the time limits on driving without rest.

—*William L. Waugh, Jr.*

See also Commerce clause; Environmental law; Federal Trade Commission (FTC); Interstate Commerce Commission (ICC); Regulatory crime; *Skinner v. Railway Labor Executives' Association*; State police.

BIBLIOGRAPHY

Transportation law is specialized, and it is easiest to study by focusing on a particular mode of transportation, such as rail or aircraft, or on a transportation function, such as the transportation of passengers or freight. The American Bar Association has a section that regularly publishes a newsletter on transportation law which can be found in law libraries; academic analyses can be found in the University of Denver College of Law's *Transportation Law Journal*. Because the literature largely focuses on government regulation of transportation, books on regulation offer the broadest perspective on transportation law. Detailed information on the process of government regulation can be found in Cornelius M. Kerwin, *Rulemaking: How Government Agencies Write Law and Make Policy* (Washington, D.C.: Congressional Quarterly Press, 1994). An excellent analysis of the effectiveness of regulatory law in transportation and other areas can be found in Eugene Bardach and Robert A. Kagan, *Going by the Book: The Problem of Regulatory Unreasonableness* (Philadelphia: Temple University Press, 1982). One of the most well-known critiques of the Reagan Administration's attempts to abolish or weaken government regulations is Susan J. Tolchin and Martin Tolchin's *Dismantling America: The Rush to Deregulate* (Boston: Houghton Mifflin, 1983). Histories of the Interstate Commerce

Commission, Federal Trade Commission, Federal Aviation Administration, Bureau of Marine Inspection and Navigation, and other regulatory agencies are also available in libraries.

Treason

DEFINITION: Betraying a nation or a sovereign ruler through activities which jeopardize their interests or security

SIGNIFICANCE: Treason has traditionally been regarded as the highest crime known to society because it is a breach of loyalty on the part of individuals who aim at destroying the existing political and social order, thereby affecting many others

At one point in history, persons who even criticized the policies or actions of their rulers might have found themselves convicted of treason. With the establishment of modern democratic nations, however, the meaning of treason changed. The framers of the Constitution of the United States had learned that men in power sometimes falsely or loosely accuse their enemies of treason as a tool to eliminate them. Therefore, they defined treason restrictively in order to protect the rights of citizens to oppose the actions of their government in all reasonable ways.

Constitutional Definitions. Article III, section 3 of the U.S. Constitution defines treason as "levying War against them [the United States] or in adhering to their Enemies, giving them Aid and Comfort." Generally, levying war consists of being part of a group of armed persons actually moving against the government. The charge of giving aid and comfort to the enemies of the United States requires evidence of deliberate promotion of the cause of a recognized enemy. This approach may be contrasted, for example, with Japanese treason laws, which place special emphasis on acts designed to promote war, so that a Japanese citizen may be punished for advocating that Japan go to war against another nation.

The U.S. Constitution also states that no persons can be convicted of treason on the basis of circumstantial evidence alone. The accused must make an open confession in open court, or there must exist two witnesses to an overt act of treason. Their testimony, either by itself or along with other evidence, must be able to convince a jury of the defendant's guilt. Thus, obtaining a conviction in a court of law is often difficult because treasonous acts are usually committed covertly (through espionage), and people are not prone to incriminating themselves.

Another special problem in obtaining convictions in cases involving treason is the practice of foreign nations granting political asylum to people accused of treason in their native countries. Curiously, though treason may be regarded by the offended country as the worst of all crimes, it is not subject to extradition, since it is ultimately regarded as political in nature. A murderer who kills one person can be extradited, while one guilty of treason, who may have sent many to their deaths—or even threatened the lives of millions, during the nuclear age—is protected.

Punishment for Treason. In the United States, Congress alone holds the constitutional power to determine and declare

Treason, a breach of loyalty, is considered one of the most serious crimes against society; the U.S. Constitution defines treason in Article III. (James L. Shaffer)

what penalties shall be meted out for treason. Death or life in prison is the usual penalty. Such a severe sentence is in keeping with the view, derived from English legal theory, that treason is a most heinous crime. The Constitution also puts limits on the mode of execution, however, disallowing extreme forms of punishment. Historically, in England, offenders were put to death in a cruel manner: Their bowels were taken out while they were alive and were burned in their presence. Their heads were cut off and their bodies divided into quarters. Such cruelties were eschewed by the Constitutional Convention.

A person convicted of treason is branded a traitor. (The words treason, traitor, and treachery all derive from the Latin word *tradere*, which means to give up or to betray.) In sixteenth and seventeenth century England, it was impossible for the relatives of a traitor to inherit anything from the convict. Such a practice of automatic estate forfeiture was expressly forbidden in the Constitution by its framers. As James Madison explained, the Constitutional Convention restrained Congress from extending the consequences of guilt beyond the guilty party.

Impact of Treason Cases. Famous cases of treason may be found in almost all historical periods. Perhaps the most notorious early traitor in American history was Benedict Arnold, whose very name has become synonymous with disloyalty. Arnold, a revered patriot hero who held a high position in the Continental Army, offered to hand over the West Point fortifications to the British for money—a frequent motive behind treason. The plot was discovered. Arnold and his wife barely escaped to England, where he was pensioned as a British officer until his death.

Far more important for legal history and precedent than Benedict Arnold, however, was the case of Aaron Burr, the third vice president of the newly established United States. He was charged with treason for conspiring to take over western territories of the United States during the administration of President Thomas Jefferson. Public opinion was against Burr. The trial judge, however, was John Marshall, a strong Federalist who insisted upon the narrow constitutional definition of treason. He refused to allow testimony regarding Burr's supposed intentions. He demanded two witnesses to each overt act of treason. Ultimately, the jurors declared that Burr had not been proved guilty according to constitutional requirements. The significance of this trial for the American justice system was tremendous. Marshall helped protect the civil rights of all Americans. Had he admitted circumstantial evidence in the case, it would have become easier for subsequent governmental leaders to use trumped-up conspiracy charges to silence legitimate political opposition.

Among the most sensational treason cases in American history was that of Julius and Ethel Rosenberg. They were charged with conspiracy to transmit secret atomic data to the Soviet Union. In 1951, a jury convicted the couple of treason, and Judge Irving Kaufman sentenced them to die for what he termed a loathsome offense. Despite prolonged appeals, they were electrocuted in 1953—the only people in American history ever executed in peacetime for espionage. Their dramatic trial, combined with a fear of atomic weapons in the hands of the dreaded communists, inspired a new wave of congressional treason hunting, which had an impact on American life for several years thereafter. —*Andrew C. Skinner*

See also Bill of attainder; Citizenship; Conspiracy; Constitution, U.S.; Espionage; McCarthyism; Rosenberg trial and executions.

BIBLIOGRAPHY

Bradley Chapin, *The American Law of Treason: Revolutionary and Early National Origins* (Seattle: University of Washington Press, 1964), is a good historical source; Allen Dulles, *The Craft of Intelligence* (New York: Harper & Row, 1963), gives much information about the organizations and practice of espionage in the world. Chapman Pincher, *Traitors* (New York: St. Martin's Press, 1987), is a thorough discussion about why people engage in treason, and Pincher describes some of the most famous traitors in history. Also see Theodore R. Sarbin, Ralph M. Carney, and Carson Eoyang, eds., *Citizen Espionage: Studies in Trust and Betrayal* (Westport, Conn.: Praeger, 1994); Rebecca West, *The New Meaning of Treason* (New York: Viking Press, 1964); and John Wexley, *The Judgement of Julius and Ethel Rosenberg* (New York: Cameron and Kahn, 1955).

Treasury, U.S. Department of the

DATE: Established September 2, 1789

SIGNIFICANCE: The Department of the Treasury advises Congress and the president on tax policy, acts as financial agent for the federal government, manufactures currency, and enforces tax laws

Two government agencies carry the primary responsibility of advising the U.S. government on economic policy and enacting that policy. The Federal Reserve System and its board of governors help set monetary policy (the government's actions in controlling such economic factors as the supply of money, interest rates, and inflation). The Department of the Treasury advises on and, in part, administers fiscal policy, which encompasses all matters of taxation and government expenditures. The secretary of the treasury heads the department and is appointed by the president.

The Treasury Department has the power, delegated to it by Congress, to make fundamental policy decisions concerning the management of government accounts and of the public debt. Although officials of the Treasury Department advise the president and Congress on policy matters, the department is expected to conduct its operations in accordance with established policies and in cooperation with the Federal Reserve System, an agency independent of political control. The Federal Reserve System and its board of governors were granted independence from the political process to avoid the risk that the nation's monetary system would be manipulated for political advantage. The Federal Reserve System is entrusted with the power of being the government's bank—in which the Treasury Department keeps the government's accounts—and with implementing monetary policy. The Treasury Department is limited in its role regarding monetary policy; it reacts to the actions of the Federal Reserve System and prints money as required.

Perhaps the major role of the Department of the Treasury lies in its criminal justice responsibilities. The Treasury Department regulates wire transfers, investigates tax abuses, and prevents money laundering and the circulation of counterfeit currency. For most U.S. citizens, the most familiar part of the Treasury Department is the Internal Revenue Service (IRS). The Treasury Department also includes the Bureau of Alcohol, Tobacco, and Firearms (ATF), the United States Customs Service, and the United States Secret Service, among other agencies.

The Internal Revenue Service. The Internal Revenue Service (IRS) is responsible for administering and enforcing internal revenue laws and related statutes, except those related to alcohol, tobacco, firearms, and explosives, which are regulated by the Bureau of Alcohol, Tobacco, and Firearms. The IRS is charged with collecting the proper amount of income tax revenue at the least cost to the public and in a manner that warrants public confidence in the agency's integrity, efficiency, and fairness.

The IRS encourages voluntary compliance with tax laws, and it determines the extent and causes of noncompliance. It does this in part through selective auditing of tax returns. In a tax audit, a tax examiner checks the information on a tax return against records provided by the tax filer. Tax evasion is recognized as a significant problem of tax collection. Most often, filers fail to report income or provide false information regarding their rights to deductions. Improved data collection methods have made the job of the IRS easier; employers and financial institutions now are required to provide information directly to the IRS to be checked against tax returns.

Money Laundering. For a long time, fund transfers between banks were made primarily over international and domestic telegraph and telex networks. These forms of communication required a large staff of handlers and were vulnerable to fraud. Rapid technological advances have increased the speed and efficiency of wire transfers so that errors have been greatly reduced.

The efficiency of the system has not gone unnoticed by those who illicitly accumulate and distribute large amounts of cash. Up to 75 percent of all drug trafficking proceeds are "laundered" through wire transfers. Money laundering is the process of disguising the source of funds so that they appear to have been acquired through legal means. Although money laundering is generally associated with drug trafficking, it is also employed to disguise money earned from illegal gambling, extortion, bribery, prostitution, and loansharking.

The Treasury Department regulates bank operations through the comptroller of the currency, who supervises and periodically examines national banks. Individual states are responsible for banks operating under state charters. Money laundering can occur through banks by layering funds within accounts and transferring those funds electronically. When laundered funds are returned to the legitimate economy, they appear to have been derived from legal sources such as real estate deals, loans from front companies, and import and export invoicing. To identify a money laundering operation, the Treasury Department must associate funds with some illegal activity. The Internal Revenue Service often becomes involved in the uncovering of money laundering schemes because such schemes can be used to evade income taxes.

The Bank Secrecy Act. The core statutes governing currency transaction reporting and recordkeeping are found within the provisions of the Bank Secrecy Act, administered by the Department of the Treasury. These provisions are designed to assist in the detection and prosecution of illegal fund transfers. Agencies involved in this effort include the U.S. Customs Service, Internal Revenue Service, Office of Financial Enforcement, and Office of Financial Crime Enforcement Network (FINCEN). The FINCEN was established by order of the secretary of the treasury in order to provide a government-wide, multisource intelligence and analytical network in support of the detection, investigation, and prosecution of domestic and international illegal fund transfers and other financial crimes. The FINCEN branch of the Treasury Department has no authority to conduct independent investigations but is designed to assist the Justice Department with tactical and strategic information sources and with criminal investigations.

The Bank Secrecy Act's reporting requirements include the Currency Transaction Report (CTR) and the Report of International Transportation of Currency or Monetary Instruments (CMIR). Generally, the CTR and CMIR are required when customers of financial institutions make transactions at or exceeding ten thousand dollars in currency or, in the case of CMIR, of currency or financial instruments of any kind that are transported into or out of the United States. The act also requires the Report of Foreign Bank and Financial Accounts, which must be filed by persons with signature authority or a financial interest in foreign bank security or deposit accounts at or exceeding ten thousand dollars.

Financial institutions must file these currency transaction reports with the Internal Revenue Service within fifteen days of a reportable transaction. CMIR reports are filed with the commissioner of customs. If currency is transported, the filing must occur at the time of entry into the United States. The recipient is required to file within fifteen days of receipt. Financial institutions must also provide the identity and the occupation of the individual who conducted the transaction with the financial institution, the identity of the individual on whose behalf the transaction was conducted, and the account number involved in the transaction.

The Bank Secrecy Act's recordkeeping and reporting requirements apply only to domestic financial institutions and foreign banking entities doing business in the United States. The act does not extend to financial institutions offshore, even those that are branches of the U.S. institutions doing business outside U.S. borders.

The Bank Secrecy Act was enacted in 1970, but enforcement was virtually nonexistent until the 1980's. The act was designed to help deter white-collar crimes such as income tax evasion by furnishing law enforcement officials with greater evidence of illegal financial transactions. Bank Secrecy Act regulations authorize the secretary of the treasury to target transactions with certain foreign institutions and transactions of domestic financial institutions that take place in certain geographic regions of the United States. These regulations provide the secretary with broad discretion in channeling resources to particular institutions and regions that might be prone to abuses and illicit manipulation.

The Coast Guard and Customs Service. The Coast Guard and the U.S. Customs Service aid in the discovery and prosecution of money laundering schemes and investigate a variety of other types of crime. Although the legitimate world payments systems have fostered the evolution of a relatively cashless society, cash has assumed an even greater importance as the medium of exchange within the criminal world. Specifically, almost 90 percent of the total $180 billion of coin and currency in circulation outside banks is estimated by the Federal Reserve Bank to be held in unreported hoards.

The most pervasive method of illegal fund transfer is physically smuggling currency or financial instruments across borders. Cash provides criminal enterprises with a ready medium of exchange. The large volume of currency and monetary instruments that legitimately traverse borders makes identifying illegal funds problematic, because these funds are often mixed with, and may be indistinguishable from, legitimate currency, cashier's checks, and bearer bond transactions. The Customs Service and Coast Guard acknowledge that bulk currency is physically disposed of through various means, including the commingling of funds with legitimate business proceeds, smuggling, and converting cash into deposits or assets at banks. The requirement of reporting currency transactions of ten thousand dollars or more means that laundering involves making deposits in smaller increments. In a process called "smurfing," couriers make multiple purchases of money orders, cashier's checks, or other financial instruments in order to reduce the risk of detection at the inspection point.

The Coast Guard and Customs Service also monitor other types of transfers across borders. The Customs Service assesses and collects customs duties, excise taxes, and fees due on imported merchandise. It is also charged with seizing contraband material, including narcotics and illegal drugs. In this effort it is aided by the Coast Guard, because shipment by boat is one of the primary means of smuggling illegal drugs into the United States. Goods that are legal may also draw the attention of the Customs Service, because those who bring them into the United States may attempt to avoid paying customs duties or taxes. —*Sam R. Hakim*

See also Alcohol, Tobacco, and Firearms (ATF), Bureau of; Coast Guard, U.S.; Counterfeiting and forgery; Drug Enforcement Administration (DEA); Internal Revenue Service (IRS); Money laundering; Secret Service; Tax evasion.

BIBLIOGRAPHY

For overviews, see Thomas E. Luebke, ed., *Department of the Treasury* (U.S. Government Printing Office, 1986), and the useful, though dated, David C. Cooke, *Your Treasury Department* (New York: W. W. Norton, 1964). An excellent survey of the Treasury Department's monitoring and regulation of fund transfers is U.S. General Accounting Office, *Electronic Funds Transfer: Information on Three Critical Banking Systems* (Washington, D.C.: U.S. General Accounting Office, February, 1989). For details on the investigation of financial crimes, see U.S. General Accounting Office, *Money Laundering: Treasury's Financial Crimes Enforcement Network* (Washington, D.C.: U.S. General Accounting Office, March, 1991). See also the Department of the Treasury notice *Organization, Functions, Authority Delegations: Financial Crimes Enforcement Network* (Federal Register 18433-03, 1990). For information on the use and volume of cash transactions in illicit activities, see the report by the President's Commission on Organized Crime entitled *The Cash Connection* (Washington, D.C.: U.S. Government Printing Office, 1984).

Triangle Shirtwaist Factory fire

DATE: March 25, 1911

PLACE: New York City

SIGNIFICANCE: This tragedy, which left 146 dead, helped spur union organization and worker safety laws

On March 25, 1911, a fifteen-minute fire in the Triangle Shirtwaist Factory left 146 workers dead and caused a national

The main work room of the Triangle Shirtwaist Factory after it was destroyed by fire in 1911. (AP/Wide World Photos)

outrage that led to the enactment of worker safety laws and gave impetus to unionization in the clothing industry. The making of women's blouses (shirtwaists) was a boom business in American cities after 1900 because of the popularity of the fashion and its utility for the new generation of working women. A 1909 strike led to the organization of the International Ladies Garment Workers Union (ILGWU). Triangle, however, even though its workers were among the principal organizers of the strike, remained a nonunion "sweatshop" occupying the eighth, ninth, and tenth floors of the Asch building, next to the New York University.

Its ability to provide steady employment even during slack periods made it attractive to immigrant seamstresses. Management kept the doors of the factory locked to prevent workers from leaving without permission. This situation made escape from the fire impossible for the victims. Triangle's owners, Max Blanck and Isaac Harris, were tried for manslaughter, but the antilabor judge directed the jury to acquit them. The 1911 tragedy raised the consciousness of the public regarding workers' safety. Stringent codes were enacted, but lax enforcement led to continued danger in American workplaces.

See also Labor law; Labor unions; Occupational Safety and Health Administration (OSHA).

Truman, Harry S (May 8, 1884, Lamar, Mo.—Dec. 26, 1972, Kansas City, Mo.)

IDENTIFICATION: President of the United States, 1945-1953

SIGNIFICANCE: Truman was president when the United States made the transition from World War II to peacetime and during the beginning of the Cold War

As president, Harry S Truman was given the task of returning the nation to a peacetime economy. As millions of veterans returned to civilian pursuits, the society had to be substantially revamped to accommodate them. He established a committee on civil rights to strengthen existing civil rights laws and laws protecting the right to vote. At his insistence, with full appreciation of the political risks, civil rights proposals were contained in the Democratic Party's platform in the 1948 elections. He also oversaw the integration of the nation's armed forces.

Truman's Point Four program made benefits of scientific and technical progress available to the world's hungry and needy. His Fair Deal program was an ambitious attempt to continue the social and economic reforms dispensed by Franklin D. Roosevelt's New Deal. Its twenty-four programs covered many aspects of Truman's view of social justice, including medical insurance, immigration policy, farm supports, public housing, civil rights, conservation, free collective bargaining, and public power. He also advocated a higher minimum wage, increased Social Security benefits, and housing aid for all Americans. Truman's candor and close identification with the needs and aspirations of common people provided him with the necessary support to pursue domestic initiatives concerning social justice.

President Harry S Truman oversaw the return to a peacetime economy after World War II; his Fair Deal program continued the thrust of Franklin D. Roosevelt's New Deal. (Library of Congress)

See also Democratic Party; Eisenhower, Dwight D.; House Committee on Un-American Activities (HUAC); Roosevelt, Franklin D.; Welfare state.

Truth in Lending Act

DATE: Became law May 29, 1968

DEFINITION: The Truth in Lending Act requires that lenders provide customers with standardized credit information regarding finance charges and annual percentage rates

SIGNIFICANCE: Enacted as Title I of the Consumer Credit Protection Act, the Truth in Lending Act permitted more informed borrower decisions by establishing standard disclosures for creditors

In the late 1960's, Congress became concerned that consumers were confused by the many ways credit costs were charged. Rather than legislate the method for imposing credit charges, Congress proposed that credit terms be disclosed in a uniform manner. Ideally, uniform disclosure would provide consumers with the information needed to compare credit terms and make informed decisions on the use of credit. The Truth in Lending Act (TIL Act) was introduced in 1960 by Senator Paul H. Douglas. Eight years of discussion and disagreement ensued concerning the need for such disclosure information. The credit industry voiced much concern over the difficulty in computing an annual rate. The average sales clerk, they agreed, would be unable to compute it without substantially increasing the cost of extending credit. They further stated that consumers did not really care about annual rates and would be confused by the information. In fact, they might be shocked and reduce drastically the volume of credit purchases made. These concerns were dispelled in 1966 when the state of Massachusetts passed a TIL law and none of these problems materialized; however, debate concerning the method of computing and when these computations would be required continued. Finally, in 1968, the TIL Act was passed, establishing standard disclosures for consumer credit nationwide. Federal Reserve Regulation Z implements the disclosure laws laid out in this act and requires lenders to (1) provide borrowers with meaningful, written information on essential credit terms, (2) respond to consumer complaints of billing errors, (3) identify credit transactions on statements of accounts, (4) provide certain credit card rights, (5) provide estimates of disclosure information before consummation of mortgage transactions, (6) provide disclosure of credit terms in adjustable rate mortgages and home equity lines of credit, and (7) comply with special advertising rules. Under these rules, the dollar cost of credit must be disclosed as the "finance charge," and the cost must be calculated as a percentage of the amount being loaned, according to a uniform method for computing the "annual percentage rate."

The TIL Act is primarily a disclosure law. Some people mistakenly believe it is the law responsible for governing such things as usury rates, late payment charges, and methods of rebating unearned finance charges. While this act requires disclosure regarding these practices, it does not regulate the practices themselves.

Because of the complexity of the TIL Act, ten years after its enactment more than 80 percent of banks were not in full compliance. This situation led to the passage in 1980 of the Truth in Lending Simplification and Reform Act. This act was designed to make compliance easier, provide simpler disclosures to consumers, and significantly reduce the number of lawsuits that were being filed for technical violation of the law.

See also Banking law; Commercial law; Consumer fraud.

Uniform Crime Reports (UCR)

DEFINITION: An annual publication that provides information on crimes and arrests as reported by local law enforcement agencies to the Federal Bureau of Investigation (FBI)

SIGNIFICANCE: The UCR is regarded as the nation's official record of crime; despite its flaws, it represents the single best source on annual crime statistics for cities, states, and other geographical areas

The Uniform Crime Reports has been published annually as *Crime in the United States* by the Federal Bureau of Investigation since 1930. Its data are based on monthly reports voluntarily submitted by more than sixteen thousand local law enforcement agencies about crime within their jurisdictions. Part I of the UCR summarizes the number of serious offenses known to the police for four violent crimes (forcible rape, homicide, robbery, and aggravated assault) and four property crimes (auto theft, burglary, larceny, and arson). Part I also reports the number of cases "cleared," usually through arrest. Part II provides information on the number of arrests for all other crimes, excluding traffic violations. The crime rate (reported as crimes per 100,000 people), trends over time, and the characteristics of persons arrested for different types of crimes are also supplied.

The accuracy of the UCR in measuring crime has been challenged on a number of grounds. A major criticism is that many crimes are not reported, as victims may fear reprisal or wish to remain anonymous. The UCR is also affected by record-keeping practices and the types of rules used in counting multiple offenses. Another problem is that, although the percentage of participating departments has increased over time, a small number still do not comply. Departments also differ in how they classify crimes and in their interpretation of the UCR reporting guidelines. Despite these problems, the UCR is the most systematic and comprehensive annual compilation of statistics on crime in the United States.

It should be noted that there is also a survey that questions households to determine how many people report having been victims of crime. It is *Criminal Victimization in the United States*, also called the National Crime Victimization Survey (NCVS), and has been published annually by the Bureau of Justice Statistics since 1975.

See also Crime; Crime Index; Federal Bureau of Investigation (FBI); Justice Statistics, Bureau of; National Crime Victimization Survey.

United Farm Workers (UFW)

DATE: Founded 1962

SIGNIFICANCE: Using a social justice platform, the United Farm Workers union won collective bargaining rights for previously unorganized agricultural workers and helped create the Latino civil rights movement

César Chávez, Dolores Huerta, and others formed the National Farm Workers Association, the precursor to the United Farm Workers (UFW) union in 1962. The founders emerged from the Community Service Organization (CSO), a Mexican American self-help association based in Los Angeles.

Like the Civil Rights movement, the UFW received much support from students and church members who saw agricultural workers' call for better wages, higher standards in working and sanitary conditions, and union recognition as moral and social justice issues. In the 1960's a majority of United States farm workers were Mexican or Mexican American. Unlike other occupations, agricultural work was not covered under the auspices of the National Labor Relations Act (Wagner Act) and thus was not protected under the aegis of the National Labor Relations Board. Major unions were not interested in organizing migratory Hispanic workers. The UFW was developed in response to this lack of legal protection or union advocacy. Its approach was based on a platform of philosophical tactics developed by Chávez, who was a student of the nonviolent teachings of Mahatma (Mohandas) Gandhi and Martin Luther

César Chávez (seated) and California vineyard owners at 1970 ceremony after a new contract that included a pay raise ended a five-year grape boycott. (AP/Wide World Photos)

King, Jr. In addition to strikes and picketing, the UFW used fasting, mass consumer boycotts, and peaceful demonstration to publicize their cause and exert pressure on growers.

In 1965 the UFW joined the Delano grape strike and organized the first of a series of national boycotts of grapes and wine. A three-hundred-mile march from Delano, California, to the state capital of Sacramento took place Easter Sunday, 1966; the march was patterned after the Freedom March from Selma, Alabama, two years before. The march combined the penitence and pilgrimage traditions of Mexican and Filipino culture and Catholic religion with the political purposes of the union. The boycott received wide public support from coast to coast, and union victory in the grape fields came in 1970 with contracts signed with major table grape growers. Organizing then shifted to lettuce fields, with a major boycott campaign focused on iceberg lettuce.

The early 1970's were characterized by backlashes against the UFW, but by 1974 there was a resurgence of strength, and new contracts were signed with growers. Renewed pressure resulted in the passage of the Agricultural Labor Relations Act (1975), the first law that recognized the collective bargaining rights of farmworkers. The UFW's effectiveness declined in the 1980's as antiunion and anti-immigrant sentiment increased under federal and state Republican administrations, undercutting the UFW's organizing power, and the Agricultural Labor Relations Board worked in the interests of growers.

Although overall membership has declined in the 1990's and Chávez's charismatic leadership was lost with his death in 1993, the UFW continues to represent workers, lead boycotts, and lobby legislatures and Congress. The Citizenship Participation Day Department, the political wing of the UFW, provides testimony and carries on public education programs about immigration laws, environmental issues surrounding the use of pesticides, and the health concerns of migrant workers.

See also Chávez, César; Labor unions; National Labor Relations Act (NLRA); Nonviolent resistance; Selma-to-Montgomery civil rights march.

United States Code

DEFINITION: The official collection of federal statutes in force, which are edited to eliminate duplication and arranged under appropriate headings

SIGNIFICANCE: The U.S. Code provides easy access to federal legislation which has been "codified"—that is, assembled and presented in a uniform format

Prior to 1926, when Congress authorized preparation of the U.S. Code, federal laws were added as they appeared to the Revised Statutes of 1875. This agglomeration of legislation was difficult to use, because laws were often redundant and their relevance often unclear. The first U.S. Code rearranged the laws in force in 1926 under fifty titles and published them in four volumes; subsequently these were updated annually with a cumulative supplement. Every six years, the federal government publishes a new edition of the code following the same format, and the number of volumes continues to grow.

Another official collection of federal legislation, the United States Code Annotated (the USCA), is similarly structured. It contains, in addition to the texts of federal laws, notes on state and federal judicial decisions applying individual laws, together with cross-references to other sections of the code, historical annotations, and library references.

The laws enacted by Congress are also collected in a chronological arrangement; issued annually, this arrangement is known as the United States Statutes at Large. The U.S. Statutes at Large are indexed but are not arranged by subject matter. Congress numbers the volumes of the Statutes at Large, which also contain amendments to the Constitution and presidential proclamations.

See also Civil law; Common law; Constitution, U.S.; Criminal law.

United States Parole Commission

DATE: Established 1976

SIGNIFICANCE: From 1910 to October 31, 1987, the primary method of release from prison for federal prisoners was parole, the discretionary early release from a prison sentence followed by a period of supervision in the community

In 1976 the Parole Commission and Reorganization Act changed the name of the United States Board of Parole to the United States Parole Commission (USPC) and increased the membership from seven to nine members, with six-year staggered terms. The new act classified the commission as an independent decision-making agency within the U.S. Department of Justice for administrative purposes. It also organized the commission into five regions, formalized due process parole rights of prisoners, established a National Appeals Board, approved the use of parole guidelines which recognized offense severity and actuarial factors for decision-making purposes, and formalized the use of hearing examiners for in-person hearings. The commission's rules and procedures are published in the *Code of Federal Regulations*.

The USPC has always been a small organization (it had fewer than 350 employees in 1989), because the U.S. Bureau of Prisons provides institutional services and U.S. probation officers act as parole agents. The USPC lost parole jurisdiction over all federal offenders sentenced on or after November 1, 1987, as a result of the Comprehensive Crime Control Act of 1984, which created the United States Sentencing Commission and abolished federal parole. The commission is scheduled to exist until 1997 in order to process cases sentenced prior to November 1, 1987.

See also *Everson v. Board of Education*; Parole; Prison and jail systems; Prisons, Bureau of; Probation; United States Sentencing Commission.

United States Sentencing Commission

DATE: Created 1984; formally organized 1985

SIGNIFICANCE: Since November 1, 1987, sentencing guidelines prepared by the United States Sentencing Commission have controlled all sentences for violations of federal law

A major provision of the Comprehensive Crime Control Act of 1984 was the creation of the United States Sentencing Commission as an independent agency within the judicial branch of government. The commission consists of seven voting commissioners. The attorney general and chair of the U.S. Parole Commission serve as nonvoting commissioners. The membership must be bipartisan, and three commissioners must be federal judges. All commissioners are appointed by the president and confirmed by the Senate.

The stated mandates for the commission include the design and implementation of sentencing guidelines and ongoing criminal justice research. The sentencing guidelines are to consider traditional purposes of punishment such as retribution, deterrence, incapacitation, and rehabilitation. Also, they should replace disparity in sentencing with elements of certainty and fairness. The responsibility for ongoing research related to criminal justice and the punishment of offenders requires that data be collected on a regular basis, and that regular reports be written.

The commission was formally organized in October, 1985. A workable set of sentencing guidelines prepared by the U.S. Sentencing Commission was submitted to Congress during April, 1987, for approval. The guidelines became the criteria for all federal sentences on November 1, 1987. Since that time the commission has refined and expanded the scope of the guidelines.

Initially, several federal judges resisted implementation of the guidelines, arguing that they violated the separation of powers section of the Constitution and that they consisted of legislation that could not be delegated to the judicial branch of government by Congress. Ultimately, in the decision *Mistretta v. United States* (1989), the Supreme Court found the activities of the U.S. Sentencing Commission constitutional.

The sentencing guidelines are similar in structure to the federal parole guidelines that had preceded them, with the exception that they are more detailed. The guidelines use a matrix composed of two axes, one for forty-three offense levels ordered in rows, the other of columns for six criminal history categories. The guidelines for a specific case are calculated by U.S. probation officers who first analyze the offense behavior to determine which of the forty-three offense severity levels apply. As offense scores increase, associated penalties also increase. Next, points are assigned to the criminal history category score based on an analysis of the offender's background. This score is an actuarial instrument (it indicates the statistical likelihood of future antisocial behavior) and acts to penalize repeat offenders with a high probability of recidivism. The convergence of the two scores on the matrix represents the sentence that should customarily be imposed by a federal judge as a range of months. For example an offender with an offense level of 7 and a criminal history category of IV would have an eight-to-fourteen-month guideline. With respective scores of 39 and VI, the offender's guideline would be 360 months to life.

The ultimate sentence imposed by a federal judge must be within the guidelines unless extenuating reasons for overriding them are articulated in writing by the sentencing judge. If a defendant receives a sentence that is either above or below the guidelines, both the prosecution and defense have the legal right to appeal to a circuit court.

See also Comprehensive Crime Control Act of 1984; Model Penal Code; Punishment; Sentencing; Sentencing guidelines, U.S.; United States Parole Commission.

United States v. . . . *See name of other party*

United Steelworkers of America v. Weber

COURT: U.S. Supreme Court

DATE: Decided June 27, 1979

SIGNIFICANCE: The Court ruled that an employer could establish voluntary programs of racial preference, including quotas, in order to eliminate manifest racial imbalance, even without evidence that the employer was guilty of discrimination

Title VII of the Civil Rights Act of 1964 made it illegal "to discriminate against any individual because of his race, color, religion, sex, or national origin." Within a few years, federal agencies began to use "racial imbalance" as *prima facie* evidence of invidious discrimination, and they encouraged employers to use numerical goals, timetables, and sometimes quotas to promote minority participation in areas of employment where they had been traditionally underrepresented. The Kaiser Corporation's plant in Gramercy, Louisiana, found that while African Americans made up 39 percent of the local workforce, they occupied fewer than 2 percent of the craft positions in the plant. Fearing that this imbalance might jeopardize government contracts, the corporation and the labor union agreed to a "voluntary" affirmative action plan that included a special training program for craft positions. Admission to the training program was based on seniority, except

SENTENCES IMPOSED FOR VIOLENT CRIMES UNDER U.S. SENTENCING COMMISSION GUIDELINES, 1993			
	Sentences to Imprisonment		
Primary Offense	Total Cases	Average Length (in Months)	Median Length (in Months)
Murder	80	288.6	240.0
Manslaughter	36	38.6	30.0
Kidnapping, hostage-taking	46	99.1	63.0
Sexual abuse	136	84.4	34.5
Assault	279	39.7	24.0
Robbery	1,602	113.7	84.0
Arson	76	61.3	36.5

Source: U.S. Department of Justice, Bureau of Justice Statistics, *Sourcebook of Criminal Justice Statistics—1993.* Washington, D.C.: U.S. Government Printing Office, 1994.

that half the positions were reserved for African Americans even if they had less seniority.

Brian Weber, a white employee with five years of experience, was disappointed when he was not admitted into the program while two black employees with less seniority did gain admission. He sued both the company and the union with the argument that he was a victim of discrimination in violation of the 1964 Civil Rights Act. After Weber prevailed in both the district court and the court of appeals, the union petitioned the U.S. Supreme Court to review the judgments.

The Court voted 5 to 2 to reverse the lower courts' decision and to uphold the affirmative action program at the Gramercy plant. Writing for the majority, Justice William J. Brennan looked to the spirit rather than the literal wording of Title VII. Since the purpose of the law was to advance employment opportunities for members of racial minorities, he reasoned that the law did not prohibit preferences as a means of integrating minorities into the mainstream of American society. the program, moreover, did not "unnecessarily trammel" the interests of Weber; it was only a "temporary measure" to stop when a target was reached. Further, it had the limited goal of ending "a manifest racial imbalance." Finally, Brennan noted that if the Court had "misperceived" the intent of Congress, the decision could be corrected easily by legislative action.

In a strongly worded dissent, Justice William H. Rehnquist proclaimed that "no racial discrimination in employment is permissible under Title VII." Noting the explicit wording of the law, he also quoted extensively from the congressional debates to show that the framers of Title VII envisioned a law allowing no preference based on race or gender.

The *Weber* decision was one of the Court's most controversial cases to deal with the question of "reverse discrimination." Supporters of race-conscious remedies for past societal discrimination were delighted that the Court did not apply the strict scrutiny test to an affirmative action program that involved racial preference and quotas. In later cases the justices would continue to be divided over the issue of *Weber*; they would tend to alternate between approving and disapproving affirmative action programs.

See also Affirmative action; Civil Rights Act of 1964; *Fullilove v. Klutznick*; Racial and ethnic discrimination; *Regents of the University of California v. Bakke*; *Richmond v. J. A. Croson Co.*

Vagrancy laws

DEFINITION: Vagrancy, or the condition of being without "visible means of support," is not a crime per se, but ordinances and statutes have often made it a punishable public offense

SIGNIFICANCE: Dealing with the homeless vagrant has become a major urban problem that cannot be solved through the strict enforcement of outmoded vagrancy laws that are no longer practical or constitutionally appropriate

Under English common law, a "vagrant" was construed as any able-bodied and destitute individual who refused work and attempted to live by begging. Before the Industrial Revolution most rural workers were agrarian laborers, and vagrants who roamed the land in search of better wages violated statutes against internal migration.

Economic factors forced changes in such laws. The enclosure movement ended much tenant farming, thereby ending the need to tie workers to the land. Next, the Industrial Revolution encouraged unemployed workers to seek factory jobs in mushrooming urban centers. The older vagrant and poor laws had restricted those who were unable to work to their home parishes and sent itinerant "loafers" and "idlers" to workhouses or forced them to return to their home communities. Under the new conditions, with worker migration inevitable, vagrancy laws shifted their focus to community worries about potential criminal behavior and the financial burden of caring for indigent drifters.

Eventually vagrancy came to be viewed as a form of disorderly conduct, and that association is reflected even in the earliest vagrancy laws in the United States. Under the Articles of Confederation, "paupers" and "vagabonds" were denied the right of free movement from one state to another, and both colonial and ensuing state vagrancy statutes had similar restrictions on the movement of indigent individuals. Under most vagrancy laws, indolent drifters could be jailed or required to move outside the legal jurisdiction of the enforcing agency.

In bad economic times, vagrancy laws could be stringently enforced. For example, during the Great Depression, some states used such laws to justify burning "Hoovervilles" (makeshift settlements of homeless people) and erecting blockades to prevent migrants from entering to look for work. Police have at times put the laws to other questionable uses—for example, in the service of controlling labor unrest or upholding community standards based on racial or class discrimination.

Beginning in the 1960's, in part as a result of the Civil Rights movement, vagrancy laws increasingly came under judicial review. In 1972, the U.S. Supreme Court, in *Papachristou v. City of Jacksonville*, struck down a Florida vagrancy law because of its vagueness and condemnation of innocent behavior. Because the Florida law was very similar in scope and wording to laws in other states, the Court's finding forced the revision of many state laws. Most were refashioned to comply with the Model Penal Code, which makes no mention of idleness, the original basis of vagrancy statutes in common law. Civil rights advocates have argued that the code itself contains constitutionally suspect provisions against loitering and prowling. Given the growing concerns over the nation's high crime rate, however, it remains to be seen whether the civil rights of "potential criminals" will gain much additional protection.

See also Breach of the peace; Civil liberties; Civil rights; Disorderly conduct; Homelessness; Model Penal Code; Public order offenses.

Vandalism

DEFINITION: The willful or malicious destruction or defacement of any public or private property without the consent of the owner or persons having custody or control

SIGNIFICANCE: Vandalism accounts for approximately 3 percent of all arrests and is one of the most frequent crimes committed by offenders under eighteen years of age; it is generally classified as a misdemeanor

Vandalism is committed by relatively young offenders. In 1992, 44.9 percent of vandalism arrests were of juveniles (individuals under eighteen years of age). By comparison, 16.4 percent of arrests for all crimes were of juveniles. Older offenders are more likely to commit violent crime and less likely to be involved in property crime, including vandalism. Approximately 76.1 percent of 1992 vandalism arrests were of white offenders, whereas 67.6 percent of all arrests were of non-Hispanic white offenders.

Vandalism arrests have increased at a much higher rate than have arrests for other crimes. Between 1983 and 1992, vandalism arrests increased by 49.2 percent, while arrests for all crime increased by 20.3 percent. Major factors in this increase include the increase in "tagging" (the illegal spray painting of gang symbols and other logos) and other organized gang activities.

Arrests for illegal gang activity, including tagging, have shown dramatic increases since 1980. This growth is largely attributable to the fact that major cities have recognized the extensive nature of gang activity and policed it more effectively. Most major American police departments now have a gang-suppression unit that is similar to the Boston Anti-Gang Violence Division. These units, often led by a command-level officer, spend much of their resources combating vandalism and drug-related crime.

Community-oriented policing, a relatively recent crime suppression strategy, is designed to combat youth crime, including vandalism. In community-oriented policing, police agen-

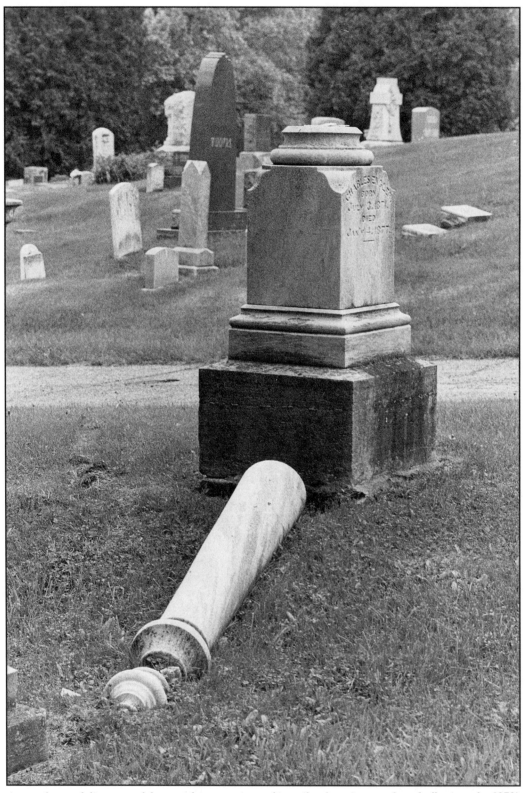

Arrests for vandalism, one of the most frequent crimes of juveniles, have increased markedly since the 1970's.
(James L. Shaffer)

cies reach out to the communities they serve by increasing official police involvement in community organizations, schools, and businesses. Patrol officers are moved from service units to foot patrol, giving the community a view of police officers as real people rather than distant figures in squad cars.

See also Gangs, youth; Hate crimes; Juvenile delinquency; Juvenile justice system.

Veterans' rights

DEFINITION: Rights and benefits given to veterans of military service, including programs in housing, employment, education, health care, and insurance

SIGNIFICANCE: The U.S. federal government and state and local governments have given veterans preferential treatment in employment and have provided a broad range of benefits ranging from home loans and medical care to educational benefits

Following most of America's wars, federal, state, and local governments have passed legislation establishing special preferences and benefits for military veterans. The promises of benefits are generally viewed as "rights," and, as a consequence, veterans' rights usually have a very broad interpretation.

The extension of benefits to veterans has followed a clear pattern. In the decades following the American Revolution, "fitness of character" was the principal criterion upon which government hiring decisions were based, and former military officers enjoyed considerable preference in hiring. The preference was based on the veterans' proven loyalty to the government and the likelihood that they were from the upper classes.

Following the Civil War, veterans were given land in the West to encourage development, as well as to reward service and to reduce unemployment. Some medical benefits were extended to disabled veterans following the Civil War and the Spanish American War. For example, an 1865 federal act gave disabled veterans preference for appointments to public jobs. A number of states passed similar legislation during the late 1800's, and World War I veterans were added in 1919. During the 1930's, the U.S. Civil Service Commission gave special examinations to disabled veterans and, if they passed, moved them to the top of hiring lists. Veterans' preference in public employment, however, did not expand significantly until passage of the Veterans Preference Act of 1944.

Preference in Employment. Veterans' preference in employment is perhaps the most familiar benefit. While preference legislation has primarily focused on protecting the reemployment rights of veterans returning to civilian life after active duty, veterans' preference means much more. The federal government and many state and local governments typically add five points to the civil service examination scores of veterans and ten points to the scores of disabled veterans. Some state and local governments automatically move qualified veterans to the top of the register. This is termed an "absolute preference." Some governments extend the benefits to the families of disabled veterans. The extra points often elevate veterans to the top of hiring lists or registers and increase their prospects of being hired.

Once hired, veterans have also enjoyed greater protection from dismissal. The Veterans' Preference Act of 1944 gave the Civil Service Commission authority to reinstate veterans removed from their positions, while the commission could only review and make recommendations concerning removals of nonveterans. When the federal civil service was reformed in 1978, President Jimmy Carter proposed changes in veterans' preference, because it was seen as a violation of the principle that hiring should be on merit or job qualifications, but Congress intervened to protect and expand the provisions.

Veterans are also offered some protection in reductions-inforce or layoffs. When veterans' positions are eliminated, they can find other positions at an equal or lower rank and "bump" nonveteran occupants out of their jobs. In some state and local governments, veterans are also given preference in promotions and other personnel actions.

Challenges to Preference. On the whole, veterans' preference reduces flexibility in hiring, rewarding, disciplining, and laying off public workers and violates the merit principle. Indeed, veterans' preference has had a significant impact on the composition of the federal civil service, particularly at the senior level, in terms of reducing opportunities for women. Also, because the preference is not merit-based, it may have had a negative impact on the overall quality of the senior civil service. While there has been growing criticism of veterans' preference because it violates merit principles, there has been less criticism of programs to employ disabled veterans. The Vietnam Era Veterans' Readjustment Assistance Act of 1974 was passed to facilitate the employment of veterans and disabled veterans who can reasonably be expected to benefit from vocational rehabilitation services.

The challenges to veterans' preference in employment have not been successful. In *Washington v. Davis* (1976), the Supreme Court reaffirmed that personnel practices are acceptable if there is no intent to discriminate. In *Personnel Administrator of Massachusetts v. Feeney* (1979), the "absolute preference" for veterans in Massachusetts was upheld because there was no intent to discriminate against women, and women veterans were provided the same benefit. In fact, the Equal Employment Opportunity Act of 1972 prohibits discrimination in employment, with the specific exception of veterans' preferences. Notwithstanding the unsuccessful challenges to veterans' preference, some limits are increasingly being placed on "double dipping," or using military service credit to qualify for additional civilian pension benefits.

Other Benefits. Other veterans' benefits have included educational and medical assistance. The "GI Bill" educational benefits, which were originally extended to veterans returning home after World War II and the Korean War and to Vietnam-era veterans without requiring them to contribute directly, became a voluntary contribution program (with the federal government matching the veterans' contributions) in the 1970's. The Department of Veterans' Affairs Home Loan Guaranty Program was created to stimulate home buying after World War II by permitting veterans to purchase homes without a down payment and by underwriting the loans. The Veterans Administration, now Veterans' Affairs, hospital system still provides health care for disabled, aged, and indigent veterans, although budget cuts during the 1970's and 1980's forced cutbacks in care. Veterans are also provided with burial benefits, although space in veterans' cemeteries is becoming scarce.

Public support for veterans' rights and programs is diminishing because of the smaller percentage of the population who have served in the military, including the declining number of members of Congress who are veterans. Support from the American Legion, the Veterans of Foreign Wars (VFW), and other veterans' groups remains strong; however, fewer younger veterans are joining the American Legion and VFW because of a lack of identification with World War II and Korean War vets and political differences with the national organizations. The strength of the veterans' lobby, however, is evident in the elevation of the Veterans Administration to the cabinet-level Department of Veterans' Affairs in the 1980's.

—William L. Waugh, Jr.

See also Civil service system; Equal Employment Opportunity Act; GI Bill of Rights; Sex discrimination; Vietnam War; *Washington v. Davis.*

BIBLIOGRAPHY

Overviews of veterans' employment rights can be found in Lloyd G. Nigro, *The New Public Personnel Administration* (4th ed. Itasca, Ill.: F. E. Peacock, 1994); and N. Joseph Cayer, "Merit System Reform in the States," in *Public Personnel Administration: Problems and Prospects*, edited by Steven W. Hays and Richard C. Kearney (3d ed. Englewood Cliffs, N.J.: Prentice Hall, 1995). Brochures on the full range of veterans' rights and benefits are available through the U.S. Department of Veterans' Affairs.

Victim assistance programs

DEFINITION: Advocacy and support services, often funded or administered by government, which guide victims of crime through the legal system and help them cope with emotional distress

SIGNIFICANCE: Victim assistance programs address a common criticism of the criminal justice system: that by focusing on justice for defendants and society at large, it overlooks the emotional, legal, and physical needs of crime victims

The first victim assistance programs in the United States were created in the early 1970's. They were located in large urban areas and focused primarily on sexual assault of women. These programs offered limited support services to women for whom the criminal justice system might seem intimidating and insensitive. Since that time, victim assistance programs have expanded in number and scope. By the mid-1990's programs were in place throughout the country, addressing victims not only of sexual assault but also of child abuse, spousal battery, and other violent crimes.

Victim assistance programs typically offer services in three general areas: counseling and support, legal assistance, and public awareness and legislative reform. Counseling and support is perhaps the most common function, helping victims to cope with post-traumatic stress disorder, rape trauma syndrome, and other conditions caused by an assault. Individual and group counseling, crisis intervention, medical referrals, and relocation services are some of the resources typically available. Programs also offer legal assistance for crime victims who are testifying, seeking restraining orders, or otherwise facing the criminal justice system. Services include orientation to the justice system and courtroom assistance. Finally, victim assistance services act as advocates for crime victims generally, raising public awareness of certain crimes and how to prevent them, and advocating legislative reforms.

The federal government has promoted victim assistance programs through legislation and funding. The federal Law Enforcement Assistance Administration funded the creation of model victim assistance programs in 1974. The federal Victim and Witness Protection Act of 1982 established "fair treatment standards" for victims and witnesses of crimes. Two years later, the Victims of Crime Act (VOCA) established a fund which provides grants to states to compensate crime victims, and for state and local programs that provide direct assistance to crime victims and their families. In 1994 the Violent Crime Control and Law Enforcement Act augmented the VOCA fund and authorized funding of more than $1 billion for fighting violence against women.

National nongovernment organizations also have been established for promoting victims' rights and victim assistance. Two advocacy groups, the National Organization for Victim Assistance (NOVA) and the Victims' Assistance Legal Organization (VALOR), were created in 1975 and 1981, respectively. In 1985, the National Victim Center was established to help promote the rights and needs of crime victims by working with thousands of local criminal justice and victim service organizations around the country.

See also Criminal justice system; Mothers Against Drunk Driving (MADD); National Organization for Victim Assistance (NOVA); Rape and sex offenses; Victims of Crime Act; Violent Crime Control and Law Enforcement Act of 1994.

Victimless crimes

DEFINITION: Legally prohibited activities or exchanges among willing parties that do not harm anyone except, possibly, the parties willingly involved; typical examples include gambling, prostitution, and drug use

SIGNIFICANCE: The concept of victimless crimes (also called consensual crimes or public order offenses) is frequently applied to debates about decriminalization and the advisability of attempting to "legislate morality"

Although the concept of victimless crime was suggested in the work of criminologists in the 1950's, it first found explicit statement in a 1965 study by Edwin Schur that was published under the title *Crimes Without Victims*. Schur identified and discussed three types of behavior as examples of victimless crimes: abortion, drug addiction, and homosexuality. As he stated, "In each case the offending behavior involves a willing and private exchange of strongly demanded yet officially proscribed goods and services: this element of consent precludes the existence of a victim—in the usual sense." Other scholars have made use of the idea, including criminologist Jerome Skolnick, who applied it to offenses such as gambling, marijuana use, and prostitution, and jurist Herbert Packer, who cited fornication and narcotic use as crimes without victims. A number of other offenses, including drinking in public, vagrancy, and selling or viewing pornography, have also been called victimless crimes.

At issue is the debate over whether the law should forbid activities for which it is difficult or impossible to determine precisely who is being harmed and how. It has been argued that the law should not forbid activities as long as they harm no one except, perhaps, the people willingly involved in them. Some legal scholars argue that the United States has become an "over-criminalized" society. On the other hand, others point out that some supposedly "victimless" crimes indeed generate harm (as drug addiction leads to theft and robbery as addicts try to support their habit). There is also a widespread belief that certain activities should be prohibited because they are harmful to society at large—this is essentially a moral and philosophical position and is therefore difficult to evaluate empirically.

The concept of victimless crime has been used in efforts to reform criminal law by reducing the kinds of conduct subject to criminal penalties. Some argue that criminal offenses which lack victims in the traditional sense are good candidates for decriminalization. Decriminalization frequently entails reducing punishments from possible jail time to a fine; public drunkenness and the possession of small amounts of marijuana are offenses that have been decriminalized in some states.

Schur points out that victimless crimes often involve conduct about which there is a lack of public consensus that the conduct is seriously wrong. Moreover, the fact that many such offenses cause no measurable harm (except for possible harm to the participating individuals) gives rise to serious difficulties with enforceability. If there is no clear harm to another, there is no complainant (a crime victim who requests that an alleged criminal be prosecuted). Law enforcement officials therefore have difficulty detecting such crimes and gathering evidence to establish the guilty parties. Thus, efforts to control more serious crimes may suffer because of the time-consuming distractions of investigating victimless crimes. Two further undesirable effects are often cited. One is that criminalizing such conduct often gives rise to illicit traffic in the goods and services legally proscribed. The conduct is not actually discouraged, and law enforcement faces the additional problem of dealing with a thriving black market. The second unwelcome consequence is that otherwise law-abiding persons are stigmatized as criminals and are thus degraded.

Despite its initial attractiveness and apparent utility, the appeal of the notion of victimless crimes has declined; by the early 1990's, criminologists were more likely to talk of consensual crimes or public order offenses. An early manifestation of difficulty with the concept of victimless crime was that different authors provided different lists of such crimes, sug-

gesting that the concept lacked clarity and focus. An underlying difficulty is the fact that defining "victim" or "victimization" is a complex and controversial undertaking. Being physically injured or being deprived of a valued possession are clear-cut cases of victimization. It is also arguable, however, that damaging another person's reputation or esteem or causing mental distress or anguish through one's actions or insults should be considered as victimizing that person. Feminist critiques of pornography and prostitution, for example, condemn such practices as degrading and demeaning to the women involved and, in effect, to all women. Even if meaningful consent were present, they contend, there would still be real victims of these practices.

See also Breach of the peace; Commercialized vice; Drug legalization debate; Gambling law; Public order offenses.

Victims of Crime Act

DATE: Signed into law October 12, 1984
DEFINITION: Legislation that established a Crime Victims Fund to help finance state compensation programs as well as assist victims of federal crimes
SIGNIFICANCE: Demonstrating the federal commitment to assist crime victims, the Victims of Crime Act quickly became

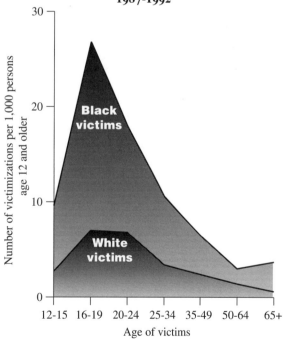

ESTIMATED RATES PER 1,000 PERSONS OF VIOLENT VICTIMIZATION WITH A HANDGUN, 1987-1992

Source: U.S. Department of Justice, Bureau of Justice Statistics, *Sourcebook of Criminal Justice Statistics—1993*. Washington, D.C.: U.S. Government Printing Office, 1994.

a key component in the funding of programs throughout the nation

In the early 1980's, many groups worked for the right of crime victims to receive fair treatment. In 1981, President Ronald Reagan, a supporter of the movement, proclaimed an annual National Victims of Crime Week. In April, 1982, Reagan established the President's Task Force on Victims of Crime, which made sixty-eight recommendations to help victims. On October 18, 1982, he signed the Victim and Witness Protection Act, which increased penalties on those who tried to intimidate victims or witnesses, mandated restitution to victims from offenders, and required the consideration of victim impact statements at sentencing in federal criminal trials.

The Victims of Crime Act of 1984 (VOCA) established the Crime Victims Fund, which at first had a cap of $100 million a year. Each state was to receive at least $100,000, and 5 percent of the fund would go to victims of federal crimes. Rather than coming from the taxpayer, revenues for the fund are obtained from fines, penalty fees, forfeitures of bail bonds, and literary profits from convicted offenders. By 1988, the fund was supporting fifteen hundred programs a year, and its maximum was increased to $150 million. VOCA was well received by the public, and it encouraged states to do more to assist victims.

See also Crime; Criminal justice system; National Organization for Victim Assistance (NOVA); Victim assistance programs; Violent Crime Control and Law Enforcement Act of 1994.

Vietnam War

DEFINITION: U.S. aid and "advisers," 1950's-1964; U.S. troop involvement, 1965-1973; fall of Saigon, April, 1975

SIGNIFICANCE: The war in Vietnam raised significant political and social justice issues, including the constitutional powers of the presidency, free speech, the composition of the armed forces, and the reintegration of veterans into society

American involvement in the war in Vietnam was the result of Cold War politics. After World War II the United States supported its ally France in French attempts to regain former colonial possessions in Indochina. In 1954, when the French left Indochina after the siege at Dien Bien Phu, the Eisenhower Administration gave full backing to a pro-American South Vietnamese dictatorship. Subsequent administrations increased American commitment in Vietnam.

The Powers of the Presidency. On August 7, 1964, Congress approved the so-called Gulf of Tonkin Resolution, the U.S. government's response to an alleged attack by North Vietnamese patrol boats on U.S. naval vessels in the Gulf of Tonkin, off the coast of North Vietnam. The resolution authorized President Lyndon B. Johnson to take "all necessary measures to repel any armed attacks against the forces of the United States and to prevent further aggression" and to "promote the maintenance of international peace and security in Southeast Asia."

Johnson used the resolution as a blank check to expand American involvement in the conflict. By essentially forfeiting its constitutional right to declare war, Congress had made it possible for Johnson and, later, Richard Nixon to expand the U.S. commitment of equipment and troops. In the spring of 1970, the Nixon Administration went so far as to bomb two neutral countries, Cambodia and Laos, because the Viet Cong were transporting arms through both countries into South Vietnam and maintained supply bases within their borders. At that point, the Senate repealed the 1964 resolution. On January 27, 1973, the United States and North Vietnam signed a cease-fire agreement, mandating the withdrawal of all remaining U.S. troops within sixty days.

Reacting to the Vietnam experience, Congress passed the War Powers Act on November 7, 1973, which limited deployment of troops without notification of Congress to sixty days. The act was intended to define and circumscribe the powers of the president when acting as the commander in chief of the armed forces.

Opposition to the War. Demonstrations against the war began in earnest in 1965, along with the first burning of a draft card in protest of the war. Many of the early demonstrations against the war were organized by Students for a Democratic Society (SDS), and opponents of the war were generally viewed scornfully as leftists and college radicals. As American involvement in Southeast Asia increased, however, opposition to the war drew wider and wider circles, until it involved people of all ages and walks of life. The war began to polarize American society. Riots occurred in Chicago in 1968 during the Democratic presidential convention; the rioting was later determined to have been provoked by the local police in a "police riot." Nevertheless, the U.S. Department of Justice leveled conspiracy charges against Rennie Davis, Dave Dellinger, Tom Hayden, Abbie Hoffman, Jerry Rubin, John Froines, Lee Weiner, and Bobby Seale, dubbed the "Chicago eight." (The Chicago seven trial did not include Bobby Seale, who was tried separately.)

Particular events in the war, as they were reported in the press, fueled antiwar protests and increased the ranks of protesters. One such event was the March, 1968, massacre of civilians at the village of My Lai, which became public knowledge in the fall of 1969 when Lieutenant William Calley was charged with murdering more than a hundred Vietnamese civilians; photographs of the atrocity were printed in *Life* magazine. Another was the American bombing of Cambodia and Laos in 1970. In May, 1970, protests against the bombing were disrupting classes at Kent State University in Ohio, and Governor James Rhodes ordered the state's national guard to patrol the Kent State campus. On May 4, National Guardsmen opened fire, killing four students. In response to the Kent State deaths, five hundred college campuses and four million students across the nation went on strike.

The Draft. Conscription (the draft) and the Selective Service system were among the main targets of the war's opponents. The most attention-getting way to show objection to the war and the draft was the burning of draft cards. Prosecution of draft card burners was inconsistent. While during the height of resistance hundreds of men burned their cards publicly, the

Justice Department brought action against fewer than fifty draft card burners, and only forty were actually convicted. Many observers expected the courts to overturn those convictions. In the 1968 case *United States v. O'Brien*, however, the Supreme Court upheld the law against draft card burning even though the decision seemed to run counter to decisions in other freedom of speech cases.

Among opponents of the draft, conscientious objectors (COs) created the most sustained legal problems. The Selective Service system tended to treat conscientious objectors—individuals who are excused from combatant military service, traditionally for religious reasons—inconsistently, often failing to follow due process of law. Many COs were Jehovah's Witnesses, Quakers, Mennonites, and others whose religious beliefs included strict pacifism. As the war progressed and the death toll rose, interest in becoming a CO rose drastically. In the mid-1960's, the military approved fewer than 30 percent of the several hundred applications for CO status it received. By the late 1960's, CO applicants attempted to take advantage of existing case law pertaining to civilian COs. The military, however, continued to reject CO applications, overlooking precedents in the case law. In 1970, the Supreme Court ruled in *Welsh v. United States* and two other cases that its 1965 decision in *United States v. Seeger* applied to members of the military as well as civilians. The Supreme Court had ruled in *Seeger* that sincere pacifists were entitled to CO status even if their motivation had no foundation in religious beliefs. The courts further ruled that the military could not reject the CO application of a person who was already a member of the service unless the military could point to factual evidence in his or her military record to support the conclusion that the applicant did not have sincere motives. Soon the number of successful CO applications rose, and the military faced a growing number of lawsuits. In 1971 and 1972, two-thirds of CO applications were successful.

Whether draft evaders (as well as soldiers who went AWOL, or "absent without leave") should be prosecuted or given clemency became a growing debate as American in-

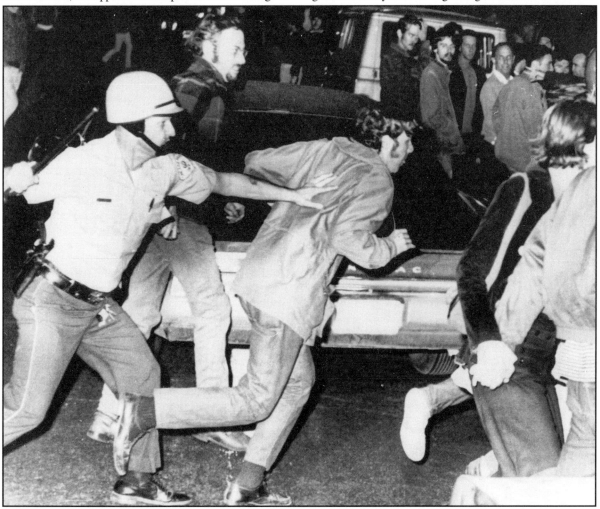

Police chasing antiwar demonstrators near Chicago's Lincoln Park in August, 1968. (AP/Wide World Photos)

volvement in the war came to an end. After 1973, when the United States signed a cease-fire agreement with North Vietnam, the call for clemency no longer fell on deaf ears. In 1974, President Gerald R. Ford created a President's Clemency Board. Considering the generally lenient treatment of draft offenders by then, the Ford program actually offered little improvement; only 2,600 people applied. Another 265,650 received pardons from President Jimmy Carter in 1977.

Military Service and Social Justice. The administration of the draft itself raised issues of social justice. Of 26,800,000 men of draft age, 15,980,000 never served. Of these, 15,410,000 were deferred, exempted, or disqualified. Of 570,000 draft offenders, 209,517 were accused; 197,750 cases were dropped, 3,250 people were imprisoned, and 5,500 received probation or a suspended sentence. Among those who escaped the draft were recipients of deferments (mostly student deferments), draft evaders, nonregistrants, and conscientious objectors. The fact that potential draftees could receive student deferments while attending college struck many observers as unfair, given that the young people likely to be in college were disproportionately white and middle- or upper-class.

For those who served, issues of social and racial justice played a significant role. Among the American forces stationed in Vietnam, fewer than 1 percent were ever needed for combat missions, but that 1 percent was most likely to consist

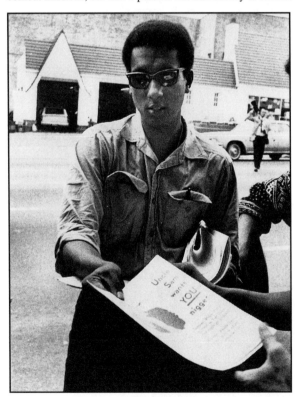

A man distributes flyers expressing outrage at the overrepresentation of minorities among the ground troops fighting the Vietnam War. (AP/Wide World Photos)

of minorities from disadvantaged backgrounds. Front-line combat personnel were, on average, a cross section of American minorities. In addition, soldiers of low-income background were about twice as likely to serve in Vietnam and about twice as likely to end up in combat service than soldiers from high-income backgrounds.

Agent Orange. Many of the soldiers who went to Vietnam came home with new problems, such as drug dependencies and post-traumatic stress disorder (PTSD). Those afflicted with post-traumatic stress disorder had extraordinary difficulties reintegrating into civilian life. In addition, severe health problems were experienced by those soldiers who had been exposed to an herbicide called Agent Orange, which contained the highly toxic chemical dioxin. During the war, American planes sprayed nearly thirteen million gallons of Agent Orange. The herbicide created health problems for those with significant exposure to it, and it caused birth defects in their children.

The government, Dow Chemical (the principal supplier of Agent Orange), and other companies involved were aware of the possibly fatal consequences of exposure to dioxin but ignored or publicly denied them. The Veterans Administration downplayed the effects of Agent Orange and dismissed veterans' complaints for many years. Veterans had little legal recourse against the Veterans Administration, since federal law barred them from taking Veterans Administration benefit decisions to court.

In 1983, veterans and their families brought a class action suit. Long Island U.S. circuit court judge Jack Weinstein decided against Dow and a number of other makers of Agent Orange, forcing the companies to release crucial documents proving that Dow and others acted in full knowledge of the possible health consequences of the substance. In May, 1984, the involved parties reached a settlement which created a $184 million fund. Dow and the other companies involved appealed the case. In 1989, the U.S. Agent Orange Settlement Fund finally began distributing funds. On average, single lump-sum benefits ranged between $340 and $3,400. By 1993, about sixty-five thousand claims had been filed. By December 29, $22 million was left in the fund, and the claim deadline was extended from December 31, 1994, to January 17, 1995.

In February, 1994, events took another turn when the Supreme Court in *Ivy v. Diamond Shamrock* and *Hartman v. Diamond Shamrock* denied review of cases requesting reopening litigation by two groups of Vietnam veterans and their families. In both cases, the veterans had received benefits but in amounts considered insufficient. On the other hand, the Court has agreed to hear arguments by Hercules and William T. Thompson, two companies that made the herbicide, who were seeking $30 million in costs in relation to the 1984 class action suit. The companies claim that it was not their fault that the government used the defoliant in Vietnam, thereby exposing humans to the toxic chemical dioxin.   —*Thomas Winter*

See also Chicago seven trial; Conscientious objection; Conscription; Johnson, Lyndon B.; Kent State student killings; My

Lai massacre; *New York Times Co. v. United States*; Nixon, Richard M.; Students for a Democratic Society (SDS); *Tinker v. Des Moines Independent Community School District*; Weather Underground.

BIBLIOGRAPHY

The body of literature on the Vietnam War is vast. One excellent comprehensive study of the war and its broad historical and regional context is Stanley Karnow, *Vietnam: A History* (rev. ed. New York: Viking Press, 1983). A good short study is George C. Herring, *America's Longest War: The United States and Vietnam, 1950-1975* (2d ed. New York: McGraw-Hill, 1986). For a more recent perspective, see Marilyn B. Young, *The Vietnam Wars, 1945-1990* (New York: HarperCollins, 1991). On the draft, see Lawrence M. Baskir and William A. Strauss, *Chance and Circumstance: The Draft, the War, and the Vietnam Generation* (New York: Alfred A. Knopf, 1978). On Agent Orange and its legal implications, see Peter H. Schuck, *Agent Orange on Trial: Mass Toxic Disasters in the Courts* (Cambridge, Mass.: The Belknap Press of Harvard University Press, 1986). The lasting problems that the war caused for many Americans are well covered by Myra MacPherson, *Long Time Passing: Vietnam and the Haunted Generation* (Garden City, N.Y.: Doubleday, 1984).

Vigilantism

DEFINITION: The illegal, private pursuit of justice that occurs when a group of people "take the law into their own hands"

SIGNIFICANCE: Vigilantism occurs when people view formal procedures for administering justice as inadequate for their protection; vigilantism often involves the dispensing of summary justice and therefore carries with it the likelihood of abuse and injustice

Through most of human existence, people who were viewed as wrongdoers or as disruptive elements in society were often dealt with informally by other members of society. In a sense, then, people have always taken it on themselves to enforce society's rules when necessary. As complex societies codified laws and organized judicial systems and police forces, however, the enforcement of law and the punishment of lawbreakers became the domain of officially sanctioned government entities. By definition, vigilantism can exist only when there is a formal justice system in place that the vigilantes are circumventing by their actions. Some experts also view group activity as a defining characteristic of vigilantism; according to this view, the lone self-appointed upholder of justice would not be seen as a true vigilante. Vigilante groups believe that the government is not protecting the lives, well-being, or property of its citizens and feel that they must act—even though they are acting outside the law—to ensure that justice is being done.

Vigilantism in American History. Vigilantism occupies a fabled place in American, and especially western, legal history. Much has been written about it, and undoubtedly much embellishment of events has occurred. The dispensing of "frontier justice" is a staple of fictional portrayals of the West

in books, films, and television programs. Although acts of vigilantism certainly occurred from colonial times (and in England and Europe before), the peak years of vigilante activity in the United States were roughly between 1850 and 1900.

American vigilantism has been viewed as arising on the frontier when early settlers had to band together for their mutual protection from criminals preying on them. Early vigilante groups, which were given names such as "regulators" and "committees of public safety," sometimes carried out periodic round-ups and punishment of suspected criminals because of the absence of reliable local law enforcement officials. Regrettably, innocent suspects were often punished for crimes that they did not commit. Vigilante groups notoriously spent too little time examining and weighing evidence, and they were inclined to inflict excessive punishment on those they apprehended. Especially well-known groups are the San Francisco vigilantes of the 1850's, vigilantes in the Montana Territory, and the violent vigilante groups of the Southwest in the latter half of the nineteenth century. After the Reconstruction era, the American South also saw considerable activity that could be considered vigilantism, in the form of lynchings and harassment of blacks deemed guilty of wrongdoing, although in truth these vicious activities represented a combination of vigilantism and terrorism designed to keep African Americans subservient to whites. The activities and organization of the Ku Klux Klan exemplified this combination.

In San Francisco of the 1850's—a wild boom town in the wake of the 1848 California Gold Rush—there were two different "vigilance committees." The merchants of the time considered the town to be crime-ridden and out of control. The first committee was formed in June of 1851 and was active for only about a month, but in that time it hanged one man and drove twenty-eight others out of town. The committee's main targets were Australian men—Australians tended to be stereotyped as criminals at the time. (Most of Australia's first residents were criminals expelled from England.) The second San Francisco committee was formed in 1856 and was a much bigger organization than the first; it had more than six thousand members. It hanged at least four people and forced at least thirty "rowdies" out of San Francisco. This committee also took on the city's political machine; some have argued that, from the beginning, its real purpose was to wrest political power from the (largely Irish Catholic) Democrats through violence and intimidation. In other cases, apparently sincere efforts at law enforcement by vigilante groups have been accompanied by vigilantes who have sought to control rival ethnic and racial groups, to impose personal moral codes, and to terrorize newcomers or any other outsiders who are seen as undesirable.

Punishments meted out by vigilante groups included whipping, tar and feathering, torture, mutilation, and murder. The term "lynching" first arose to describe whippings carried out by eighteenth century American vigilantes led by a Virginian named Charles Lynch. As the extent of vigilante violence grew in the nineteenth century, lynching became identified with the summary execution of "undesirables" by any vigilante group, but particularly of blacks by whites in the South.

Vigilante Organization. Some vigilantes formed well-organized voluntary vigilance committees aimed at combating perceived threats to the group or community—threats which may have been real, exaggerated, or totally imaginary. In many instances the leadership of a vigilante group was drawn from the elite members of the community. This was true of the 1856 San Francisco group, for example. Although vigilante activities have always been illegal, members of vigilante groups saw themselves as upholding and enforcing the law, not as violating it. The Vigilance Committee of Payette, Idaho, had its own constitution and by-laws. It guaranteed accused persons a jury trial (only a majority vote in a seven-member jury was required for conviction, however, and the verdict was final). Three punishments were allowable: banishment, public whipping, and death. It should be noted that, although many vigilante groups conducted some sort of trial, convictions overwhelmingly outnumbered acquittals.

Modern Definitions. A distinction should be drawn between vigilante groups and other types of groups with whom they are sometimes considered. The essential element of a vigilante group is that it wishes to administer justice (although, admittedly, justice as the group itself defines it) and punish wrongdoers whom the law is unwilling or unable to punish. A number of other types of modern groups that are sometimes grouped with vigilantes—hate groups, terrorist groups, survivalists—do not have this goal. Those people on the extreme fringes of movements such as the right to life movement, the animal rights movement, and the radical ecology movement have sometimes been called modern vigilantes (as well as criminals and terrorists), and in a sense they might be considered moral vigilantes, on a crusade to enforce a moral code that the legal system does not uphold.

Fear of crime in city streets and in mass transit systems has spawned groups that are sometimes, though generally inaccurately, deemed vigilante groups. These organizations range from the local neighborhood watch groups who seek to keep down crime in neighborhoods to transit and subway patrols such as New York's Guardian Angels. None of these "defensive" groups is truly definable as a vigilante movement, because few of their members have any wish to take the law into their own hands. They most often act as watchdogs, as deterrents to crime, and as eyes and ears for law enforcement agencies, although undoubtedly some members of these groups have occasionally pushed the limits of acceptable behavior when carrying out citizen's arrests.

At the individual level, vigilantism is a relatively rare occurrence. Events such as the widely publicized case of "subway vigilante" Bernhard Goetz, a white man who shot four black youths he said had threatened him on the New York subway in 1984, are quite uncommon. Also, as noted previously, by some definitions Goetz would not be considered a vigilante at all, since vigilantism, according to some scholars, requires a group acting in concert. —*Sanford S. Singer*

See also Citizen's arrest; Frontier, the; Hate crimes; Ku Klux Klan (KKK); Lynching; Neighborhood watch programs; *Posse comitatus*; Self-defense.

BIBLIOGRAPHY

Robert P. Ingalls, *Urban Vigilantes in the New South: Tampa, 1882-1936* (Gainesville: University Press of Florida, 1993), presents an interesting record of various types of vigilantism in the South. William E. Burrows, *Vigilante* (New York: Harcourt Brace Jovanovich, 1976), and Arnold Madison, *Vigilantism in America* (New York: Seabury Press, 1973), give overviews of American vigilantism. In H. Jon Rosenbaum and Peter C. Sederberg, eds., *Vigilante Politics* (Philadelphia: University of Pennsylvania Press, 1976), various aspects of individual involvement in vigilante-type activities, including overforceful citizen's arrests, are discussed. Finally, see Christian G. Fritz, "Popular Sovereignty, Vigilantism, and the Constitutional Right of Revolution," *Pacific Historical Review* 63 (February, 1994).

Village of Skokie v. National Socialist Party of America

COURT: Illinois Supreme Court

DATE: Ruling issued January 27, 1978

SIGNIFICANCE: The *Skokie* decision upheld a broad interpretation of free speech, declaring that the promotion of even as odious an ideology as Nazism is protected by the First Amendment

Frank Collin, a neo-Nazi leader of the National Socialist Party of America (NSPA), sought permission to hold an NSPA demonstration in Marquette Park, a white neighborhood of Chicago. The city, fearing a repeat of riots and racial assaults which had occurred during the previous three summers, used various legal devices to deny the Nazi Party a parade permit. Collin met or circumvented those requirements, until ultimately the city required a $250,000 bond to pay for any damages which might arise from the parade. The American Civil Liberties Union (ACLU) helped Collin challenge the city's requirement in federal court.

While the Marquette case was being litigated, Collin decided to move his demonstration to the village of Skokie, a largely Jewish suburb whose citizens include several thousand survivors of the Holocaust. Like Marquette Park, Skokie tried to stop Collin's group from demonstrating, securing from the Cook County Circuit Court an injunction against the NSPA. Skokie also quickly passed several ordinances which restricted the granting of parade permits through strict insurance bond requirements, a prohibition on the display of certain military uniforms, and a prohibition on the dissemination of material promoting or inciting racial or religious hatred. Thus there were two issues to be contested: the ordinances and the injunction.

In *Village of Skokie v. National Socialist Party of America*, the Illinois Supreme Court invalidated the injunction on First Amendment grounds, finding that there were not adequate grounds for the prior restraint of the NSPA's symbolic speech. Invoking *Cohen v. California* (1971), the Court rejected

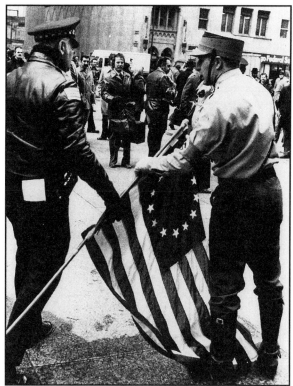

At a 1977 rally in Chicago, the National Socialist Party of America announced its plans to march in Skokie; here, at that rally, a police officer takes an American flag from a party member who is standing on it. (AP/Wide World Photos)

Skokie's claim that the symbols of the NSPA, including the swastika, amounted to "fighting words" which were not protected speech. The issue of the ordinances was decided by the U.S. district court in *Collin v. Smith*, which also held in favor of the NSPA. That ruling was upheld upon appeal to the U.S. appeals court.

Despite Collin's legal successes, various Jewish and other groups from around the country threatened to block the planned Nazi march on Skokie. As Collin considered his options, the federal district court in Chicago, obviously heeding the Skokie decision, ruled in *Collin v. O'Malley* (1978) that Collin be granted the original parade permit for Marquette Park without the bond requirement. Collin moved the demonstration back to Marquette Park.

The *Skokie* decision (along with *Collin v. Smith* and *Collin v. O'Malley*) reflected a firm commitment to a broad interpretation of free speech. Although the U.S. Supreme Court in earlier years had noted that free speech is not a limitless right (as in the case of "fighting words" against specific individuals), in these cases the federal and state courts refused to find hateful speech directed against a general group (in this case, Jews) to be unprotected.

See also American Civil Liberties Union (ACLU); Bill of Rights, U.S.; Censorship; Speech and press, freedom of.

Vinson, Fred M. (Jan. 22, 1890, Louisa, Ky.—Sept. 8, 1953, Washington, D.C.)

IDENTIFICATION: Chief justice of the United States, 1946-1953

SIGNIFICANCE: Vinson was appointed by Harry Truman to heal deep divisions within the Supreme Court, but he has been criticized as being one of the weakest leaders in the Court's history

Having served in all three branches of the federal government when he was appointed chief justice, Fred Vinson seemed like a good candidate for the job. Unfortunately, his brethren did not partake of this view, regarding him as deficient in education and experience. It was rumored that he was lazy and let his clerk do much of his writing for him. To be fair, however, he was appointed chief justice at a time when the Court had deep and rancorous divisions, and Vinson was a pragmatist rather than a philosopher. Vinson believed that overwork had contributed to some justices' early deaths, and he succeeded in reducing the Court's increasingly heavy workload.

One measure of his shortcomings as a leader and unifier of the Supreme Court is the large number of dissents he filed. He remained true to principles of judicial restraint, however, and after 1949, owing more to personnel changes than to his persuasiveness, his attitudes gained ascendancy. Even then, how-

Fred M. Vinson, chief justice of the United States from 1946 to 1953, was a pragmatist rather than a philosophical leader. (James Whitmore, collection of the Supreme Court of the United States)

ever, the role of intellectual leader passed from the activist Hugo Black to the conservative Felix Frankfurter. Yet before he died in 1953, Vinson's advocacy of civil liberties helped set the stage for the revolution that would take place under his successor, Earl Warren.

See also Black, Hugo L.; *Dennis v. United States*; Frankfurter, Felix; Supreme Court of the United States; Truman, Harry S; Warren, Earl.

Violent Crime Control and Law Enforcement Act of 1994

Date: Enacted September 13, 1994

Definition: Legislation that provided significant funds for hiring and training community police officers and set more severe punishments for a number of crimes

Significance: The 1994 crime bill was the largest bill ever passed to combat crime in the United States

The Violent Crime Control and Law Enforcement Act of 1994 was created to control the amount of violent crime in the United States. The focus of the act is on federal crimes, and it increases punishment for many existing criminal acts. One of

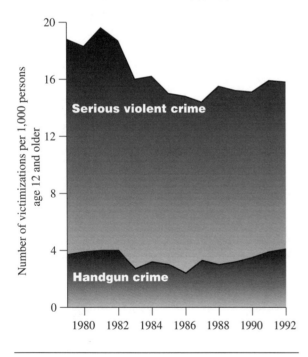

Estimated Rate of Violent Victimizations per 1,000 Persons, 1979-1992

Source: U.S. Department of Justice, Bureau of Justice Statistics, *Sourcebook of Criminal Justice Statistics—1993*. Washington, D.C.: U.S. Government Printing Office, 1994.

Note: Data are from National Crime Victimization Survey and represent victims' reports of violent crime. "Serious violent crime" includes rape, robbery, and aggravated assault.

the more controversial provisions of the act had to do with firearms ownership. The act bans the manufacture of certain types of "assault weapons" and limits the number of rounds weapons can hold. Because of this, the National Rifle Association opposed the bill, arguing that such restrictions impinge on the rights specified in the United States Constitution. Such opposition meant that the bill had to go through several revisions before being accepted by Congress and President Bill Clinton. The final bill also placed restrictions on the purchase of weapons, and it contained a provision that individuals who have been convicted of crimes of domestic violence are prohibited from purchasing weapons.

Besides addressing weapon ownership, the Violent Crime Control and Law Enforcement Act increased the penalties for a large number of crimes, specifically gang-related crimes, terrorism, illegal immigration, and fraud at the federal level. Terrorism and illegal immigration are both crimes that are under federal jurisdiction. While fraud and gang-related crimes are not necessarily under federal jurisdiction, the definition of these crimes was expanded under the act. For example, using telephone lines to commit fraud is a federal crime and therefore can be punished under the 1994 act's provisions. The act also dictates that individuals who have been incarcerated for sex crimes must notify the community to which they are moving following the term of incarceration.

Finally, the act allocated a large amount of funding for research in criminal justice topics, especially domestic violence and community policing. Over eight billion dollars was set aside to hire and train more than 100,000 new police officers. These officers would be trained to work with community members to help reduce crime in their neighborhoods.

See also Arms, right to keep and bear; Community-oriented policing; Comprehensive Crime Control Act of 1984; Domestic violence; Fraud; Gangs, youth; Illegal aliens; National Rifle Association (NRA); Omnibus Crime Control and Safe Streets Act of 1968.

Voir dire

Definition: The preliminary examination of prospective jurors to determine their qualifications and suitability

Significance: *Voir dire* is conducted both by judges and the attorneys participating in a case; it is a basic part of the justice system designed to achieve fair trials

Designed to enhance an American citizen's constitutional rights in criminal cases and general right to a fair trial in all litigation judged by juries, *voir dire* ("to see and say [the truth]") is part of the pretrial process of jury selection. Both presiding judges and the attorneys representing the parties to an action may examine the background of prospective jurors and question them to ascertain their suitability and qualifications. Those found unqualified for such reasons as bias or unfamiliarity with English may be excused "for cause." Also as a result of the *voir dire* process, jurors may be excused by attorneys exercising peremptory challenges: An attorney has the right to excuse, without citing a reason, a certain number of prospective jurors (the specific number is normally set by the presiding judge).

The use of *voir dire* by attorneys to "shape" juries through their use of the challenges system has frequently been criticized. The U.S. Constitution guarantees criminally accused persons the right to a fair trial by an impartial jury of his or her peers. Critics of the *voir dire* process argue that its results go beyond protecting this guarantee, however, as defense attorneys naturally attempt, especially through their use of peremptory challenges, to empanel jury members they believe to be least likely to convict their client.

See also Civil procedure; Criminal procedure; Jury system.

Vote, right to

DEFINITION: The ability to influence the choice of public officials and policy by participation in free elections

SIGNIFICANCE: The right to vote allows citizens to participate in the making of law through the choice of lawmakers and provides a means of holding government accountable to the people

The right to vote is one of the most fundamental rights of American citizenship, and its widespread distribution is one of the essential features of American democracy. The expansion of voting rights has been an important theme in the evolution of American democracy, as has been the increasing role of the federal government in defining such rights.

Early Voting Rights. In colonial America, voting rights were limited to adult white males who could meet a property qualification. It was generally felt that ownership of property was necessary to prove a stake in society. During and after the American Revolution, property qualifications were reduced or replaced with a requirement that a voter be a taxpayer. Voting continued to be seen as a privilege rather than a basic right of citizenship.

The Constitution of 1787 said little about voting rights. The definition of who could vote was left to the states, with the proviso that the requirements for voting for members of the House of Representatives be the same as those for voting for members of the largest house of the state legislature. The franchise remained almost exclusively limited to white males.

Expansion of Voting Rights. By the 1830's, there was a noticeable trend in the direction of manhood suffrage—that is, toward allowing adult white male citizens to vote whether they owned property or not. Though all women and most black men continued to be excluded from voting, manhood suffrage was an important step in establishing a connection between citizenship and voting rights.

The Civil War set the stage for a significant broadening of voting rights as well as for a growing federal role in their definition. During Reconstruction, Congress required that the former Confederate states allow adult male African Americans to vote. The Fourteenth Amendment (1868) reinforced this by including a provision (never actually used) that allowed reduction of a state's representation in Congress if it denied the vote to its adult male citizens. The Fifteenth Amendment (1870)

MAJOR EXPANSIONS OF VOTING RIGHTS		
Date	*Action*	*Significance or Intent*
1870	Fifteenth Amendment	Guaranteed the vote to African Americans.
1920	Nineteenth Amendment	Guaranteed the vote to women.
1961	Twenty-third Amendment	Gave District of Columbia residents right to vote in presidential elections.
1964	Twenty-fourth Amendment	Prohibited use of poll taxes or other taxes to restrict voting rights.
1965	Voting Rights Act	Banned voting tests in the South and some other areas.
1970	Voting Rights Act	Suspended literacy tests for voting.
1971	Twenty-sixth Amendment	Extended vote to eighteen-year-olds.
1972	*Dunn v. Blumstein*	Supreme Court held that long residency requirements for voting were unconstitutional.
1975	Voting Rights Act	Required that voting information be bilingual in parts of twenty-four states.
1982	Voting Rights Act	Extended 1965 act for twenty-five years.

went even further, saying that the right to vote could not be denied on the basis of race, color, or previous condition of servitude. Since blacks were already voting in the South under congressionally mandated changes in state constitutions, the most immediate effect of the Fifteenth Amendment was to enfranchise blacks in the North, where most states still limited suffrage to whites.

The Fifteenth Amendment illustrates the point that the right to vote and its actual use are two different things. By the 1890's, southern states were finding ways to limit black voting without formally restricting the right to vote on a racial basis. Techniques such as unevenly applied literacy tests, poll taxes, and the all-white primary (sometimes backed up by the threat of violence) effectively reduced African American voting to insignificance.

During the same period, the woman suffrage movement exerted increasing pressure in an effort to gain access to the ballot. Beginning with Wyoming in 1890, a number of states recognized the right of women to vote; however, women could not vote on a nationwide basis until ratification of the Nineteenth Amendment in 1920.

The Civil Rights Movement. Reviving the Fifteenth Amendment and ending restrictions on black voting rights

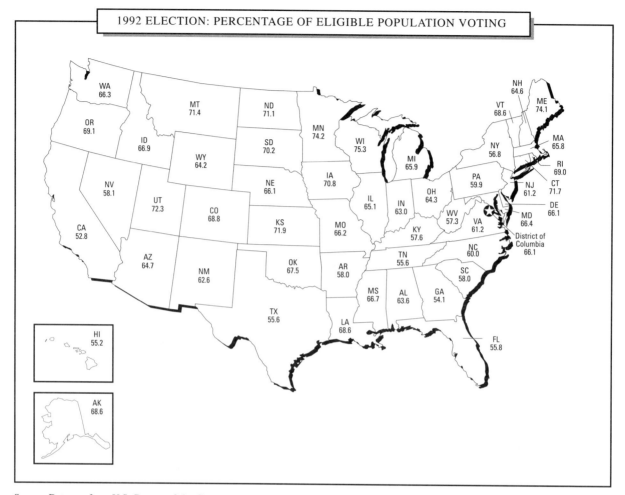

1992 ELECTION: PERCENTAGE OF ELIGIBLE POPULATION VOTING

Source: Data are from U.S. Bureau of the Census, *Voting and Registration in the Election of November 1992.*

in the southern and border states became a major goal of the Civil Rights movement that developed after World War II. Early civil rights laws made limited attempts to protect voting rights, and in 1964, the Twenty-fourth Amendment banned the poll tax in federal elections. It was not, however, until the Selma-to-Montgomery civil rights march dramatized the issue that Congress acted effectively. The result was the Voting Rights Act of 1965. The act provided for federal supervision of elections in southern counties where African Americans did not vote in numbers consistent with their presence in the population. Originally limited to five years, the act was subsequently renewed and extended to cover Native Americans and Hispanics.

The trend toward greater federal definition of voting rights continued in other ways. The Twenty-sixth Amendment (1971) enfranchised millions of new voters by lowering the voting age to eighteen. The federal courts also struck down many state laws limiting the vote to longtime residents. By the 1970's, residency requirements of longer than thirty days were no longer permitted.

Late Twentieth Century Controversies. Despite the extension of voting rights to virtually all adult citizens, the right to vote continued to excite controversy. The Supreme Court expanded its definition of the right to vote beyond access to the ballot itself. Beginning with *Baker v. Carr* (1962), the Court adopted a "one person, one vote" rule that forced changes in the apportionment of state legislatures and local governments. During the 1970's, claims by racial and ethnic groups that apportionment should take into account not only population but also the presence and interests of previously underrepresented groups received a sympathetic hearing. By the 1990's, this approach had created a complicated and controversial area of the law. Less controversial, but troubling, was the irony that as the right to vote expanded, the proportion of Americans actually voting declined. —*William C. Lowe*

See also *Baker v. Carr;* Citizenship; Civil Rights Act of 1957; Civil Rights movement; Civil War Amendments; Poll tax; *Reynolds v. Sims;* Selma-to-Montgomery civil rights march; *Smith v. Allwright;* Voting Rights Act of 1965; *Wesberry v. Sanders.*

BIBLIOGRAPHY

Five works that offer informative historical perspectives on voting in the United States are Lorn S. Foster, ed., *The Voting Rights Act: Consequences and Implications* (New York: Praeger, 1985); Steven Lawson, *Black Ballots: Voting Rights in the South, 1944-1969* (New York: Columbia University Press, 1976); Frances Fox Piven and Richard A. Cloward, *Why Americans Don't Vote* (New York: Pantheon Books, 1988); Donald W. Rogers, ed., *Voting and the Spirit of American Democracy* (Urbana: University of Illinois Press, 1992); Chilton Williamson, *American Suffrage: From Property to Democracy, 1760-1860* (Princeton, N.J.: Princeton University Press, 1960).

Voting Rights Act of 1965

DATE: August 6, 1965

DEFINITION: Legislation designed to surmount obstacles still remaining in the way of minority voters

SIGNIFICANCE: The passage of this act, ensuring a federal role in cases of disfranchisement, greatly increased the political participation of African Americans, particularly in the South, and other minority citizens

This legislation essentially abolished a number of practices that had been used at various times to disqualify African American voters, primarily in the South, including literacy, education, and character tests. It authorized the U.S. attorney general to send federal examiners into areas where voter discrimination was suspected; in effect, it allowed federal voting registrars to supersede state ones. Affected jurisdictions could be free from federal scrutiny once they showed that they had not employed discriminatory practices for five years from the time of initial federal intervention. Yet perhaps the most sweeping part of the act was its "preclearance requirements," which applied to areas with low voter registration or participation: They required that any reapportionment plans or proposed changes in electoral requirements would have to be approved by the Justice Department before they could take effect. The act also included a finding that poll taxes were preventing blacks from voting in state elections, spurring the Supreme Court to hold that poll taxes were illegal in 1966 (poll taxes in federal elections had been abolished in 1964).

The act was amended in 1970, 1975, and 1982. The 1970 amendment prohibited literacy tests throughout the country until 1975. The 1975 amendment maintained the provisions of the 1970 amendment, suspending literacy tests indefinitely, after failing to enlist enough supporters to apply the Voting Rights Act to language minorities as well as racial minorities. The 1982 amendment, effective for twenty-five years, directed

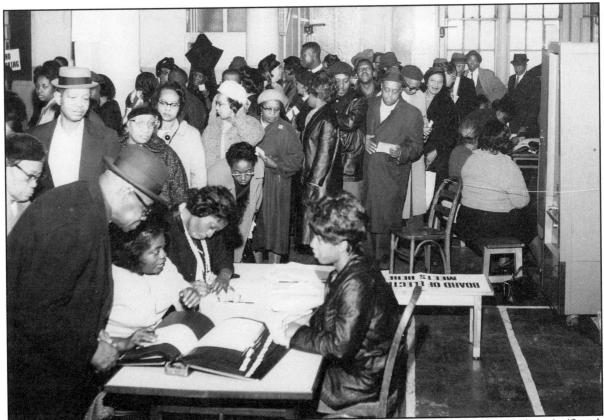

The Voting Rights Act of 1965 abolished a number of practices used to keep African Americans from voting, significantly increasing their political participation. (AP/Wide World Photos)

the federal courts to examine the effect, in addition to the intent, of practices that discriminated against black voting opportunities. This amendment was passed as a result of a 1980 Supreme Court decision (*City of Mobile v. Bolden*) stating that civil rights litigants had to prove that municipalities intended to discriminate against blacks by adopting particular voting procedures.

Generally, the federal courts have granted the widest possible latitude to the interpretation of discrimination under the Voting Rights Act. A 1992 Supreme Court decision against local black elected officials in Alabama, however, represented a retreat from this traditional stance and a possible narrowing of electoral rights protected by the act.

Background to Enactment. With the relative success of the Civil Rights movement in integrating public accommodations by 1960, the movement shifted its attention to procuring for African Americans the right to vote. The Fifteenth Amendment to the Constitution, passed immediately after the Civil War, guaranteed blacks the right to vote; however, this legislation was evaded in most southern states by various legal means, such as poll taxes and literacy tests. The fear of white reprisals against those blacks who were bold enough to register, coupled with extralegal roadblocks to voting, prevented all but a tiny percentage of blacks in the South from voting.

The voter registration effort represented a combined effort of the Student Nonviolent Coordinating Committee (SNCC), a civil rights organization composed primarily of young people, and the Southern Christian Leadership Conference (SCLC), led by Martin Luther King, Jr., a proponent of the use of passive nonviolence as an effective social protest tactic. To attract national attention to the campaign for voting rights and to spur the passage of voting rights legislation through Congress, the SCLC and SNCC concentrated their energy in Selma, Alabama, a town in which blacks represented a majority of the population but only a handful of its voters. The so-called Selma campaign was successful in that the violence perpetrated against civil rights protesters—mass arrests and incarceration, the indiscriminate use of tear gas and billy clubs, and the killing of a white cleric—resulted in demands for an immediate legislative response to the injustice.

Congressional Legislation. Spurred by the events in Selma, President Lyndon B. Johnson submitted an administration voting rights bill to Congress in mid-March, 1965. Federal intervention would be triggered wherever less than half the adult population had voted in the 1964 presidential elec-

tion and where other mechanisms had been used to prevent African Americans from voting. This "triggering" formula was controversial and sparked lively debate in Congress, but President Johnson used his legendary skills of persuasion, developed over many years as a former Senate majority leader, to see the legislation through to passage. He was aided by then Senate minority leader Everett Dirksen. Along the way, Johnson was able to muster enough bipartisan support for the legislation to prevent Senator James Eastland, chairman of the Judiciary Committee, from allowing the bill to die in committee. In late May, 1965, by a vote of 70-30, the Johnson Administration was able to override a Senate filibuster (a tactic that often had been employed successfully by southern senators to derail civil rights legislation). The fact that public opinion polls revealed that more than 75 percent of the American public supported the Voting Rights Act was also instrumental to the act's final passage.

Impact of the Act. Passage of the act resulted in a dramatic increase in African American voter registration. By the end of the 1960's, more than 60 percent of blacks in the Deep South were registered. This increase in black voter registration also meant that significant numbers of African Americans were elected to office, although primarily at the local, county, and state levels. The act has proved to be a landmark piece of legislation in ensuring that all American citizens can exercise their constitutionally guaranteed right to vote, a fundamental precept of American citizenship and justice.

—Craig M. Eckert

See also Citizenship; Civil rights; Civil Rights Act of 1964; Civil Rights movement; Johnson, Lyndon B.; King, Martin Luther, Jr.; Poll tax; Selma-to-Montgomery civil rights march; Southern Christian Leadership Conference (SCLC); Student Nonviolent Coordinating Committee (SNCC); Vote, right to.

BIBLIOGRAPHY

Books pertinent to this issue include Steven F. Lawson, *Running for Freedom: Civil Rights and Black Politics in America Since 1941* (New York: McGraw-Hill, 1991); Robert Weisbrot, *Freedom Bound: A History of America's Civil Rights Movement* (New York: Plume, 1991); Juan Williams, *Eyes on the Prize: America's Civil Rights Years, 1954-1965* (New York: Viking, 1987); David Garrow, *Protest at Selma: Martin Luther King, Jr., and the Voting Rights Act of 1965* (New Haven, Conn.: Yale University Press, 1978); Lyndon B. Johnson, *The Vantage Point: Perspectives of the Presidency, 1963-1969* (New York: Holt, Rinehart and Winston, 1971).

Waite, Morrison Remick (Nov. 29, 1816, Lyme, Conn.— Mar. 23, 1888, Washington, D.C.)

IDENTIFICATION: Chief justice of the United States, 1874-1888

SIGNIFICANCE: Assuming leadership of the Court in the wake of the *Scott v. Sandford* debacle of 1857 and the political maneuverings of his predecessor, Waite restored a measure of authority to the judicial branch of government

Morrison R. Waite was a prosperous lawyer from Ohio who lacked a national reputation when he became President Ulysses S. Grant's fourth choice to succeed Salmon P. Chase as chief justice. The nomination came as a complete surprise to Waite, as well as to others, but given Grant's troubles in filling the post, Waite's relative obscurity seemed his primary recommendation. Waite, who had never argued a case before the Supreme Court or served as a judge, was initially treated with condescension by his brethren. He quickly took command, however, becoming an able if not inspiring administrator. Un-

Morrison R. Waite, chief justice of the United States from 1874 to 1888, had never even served as a judge before President Grant nominated him for the post. (Collection of the Supreme Court of the United States)

like Chase, he spurned any suggestion that he run for president; he also managed to sidestep involvement in another misguided Court foray into politics, the 1876 electoral commission that was convened to decide the standoff between presidential candidates Samuel J. Tilden and Rutherford B. Hayes. Instead, he presided over a Court that delivered a series of decisions concerning civil rights and economic regulation which have long affected American life.

See also *Civil Rights Cases*; Supreme Court of the United States.

Wallace v. Jaffree

COURT: U.S. Supreme Court

DATE: Decided June 4, 1985

SIGNIFICANCE: The Court ruled against a state law permitting a moment of silence for "meditation or voluntary prayer" in the public schools, based on the law's sectarian intent

In 1978, the Alabama legislature authorized a one-minute period of silence to begin each school day in the public schools, and about half of the states in the 1970's passed similar laws. Many citizens, especially in the South, wanted public schools also to conduct oral prayer activities. In 1981, the Alabama legislature specified that the period of silence could be used "for meditation or voluntary prayer," and the next year the legislature ignored Supreme Court precedents and authorized teachers to lead willing students in a vocal prayer.

Ishmael Jaffree, an outspoken humanist of Mobile County, became angry when teachers of his minor children conducted prayer activities, with peer ridicule for those not participating. After local officials refused to stop the practice, Jaffree filed a complaint in federal court against various officials, including Governor George Wallace. The complaint challenged the constitutionality of the 1981 and 1982 laws. Although the district court ruled against Jaffree, based on the argument that the Supreme Court had been mistaken in 1947 when it made the establishment clause applicable to the states, the court of appeals reversed the judgment and found that the two laws were unconstitutional because they advanced and encouraged religious activities.

The U.S. Supreme Court unanimously affirmed the unconstitutionality of the 1982 law allowing vocal prayers, and the Court voted 6 to 3 to strike down the 1981 law allowing a moment of silence for meditation or prayer. Writing the majority opinion, Justice John Paul Stevens focused all of his attention on the 1981 law. Failing to find any secular motive behind the law, Stevens argued that the expression "meditation or voluntary prayer" indicated the legislature's desire to "endorse prayer as a favored practice," and he quoted the sponsor as introducing the bill as "an effort to return voluntary prayer to our public schools." Stevens found no problem with the simple moment of silence as enacted in the law of 1978.

In a long and vigorous dissent, Justice William H. Rehnquist reviewed the history of the establishment clause and rejected the idea that the clause required a "wall of separation between church and state." He concluded that the Framers intended only to prevent a national establishment of religion and to prohibit federal preference for one religion over another. Chief Justice Warren Burger's dissent emphasized that only two years earlier, in *Marsh v. Chambers* (1983), the Court had relied on history to allow oral prayers in legislative sessions. He wrote that to treat prayer as a step toward an established religion "borders on, if it does not trespass, the ridiculous." The dissenters did not reject the idea that the establishment clause applied to the states through the Fourteenth Amendment.

In the *Jaffree* decision, the Court went rather far in insisting on neutrality between religion and secularism in the public schools. The majority of the Court made it clear that a moment of silence was acceptable so long as schools did not encourage students to use the time for religious activity. In 1992 the Court would again deal with the issue of state-encouraged prayer in *Weisman v. Lee*, ruling that invocations and benedictions at public school graduation ceremonies violated the First Amendment.

See also *Abington School District v. Schempp*; *Engel v. Vitale*; Establishment of religion; *Everson v. Board of Education*; *Lemon v. Kurtzman*; *Lynch v. Donnelly*; School prayer.

Walnut Street Jail

DEFINITION: A Philadelphia prison facility that began operations in 1789 and is considered the first modern penitentiary

SIGNIFICANCE: The Walnut Street Jail served as a model for U.S. prisons in the nineteenth century

Philadelphia's Walnut Street Jail was established as a state prison in 1789; it had previously been used as a short-term confinement facility. The prison was inspired by reformers, Benjamin Franklin among them, with the goal of introducing humane treatment of prisoners. It was the first modern penitentiary and was designed to hold prisoners for specific periods of incarceration, providing rehabilitation as well as punishment. The goal of rehabilitation was influenced by Quaker beliefs.

A new, more secure wing with separate cells was erected for the most incorrigible prisoners, but most prisoners lived and worked together (they were segregated by sex). The prison introduced the first prison school, designed to educate prisoners and lead them to more productive lives. The prison was a model for others in the United States. Although some of its ideas had previously been used in Europe, the Walnut Street Jail set a new course in penology for the United States and the world. By 1820 overcrowding in the prison and public objections to its methods that emphasized rehabilitation led to its demise, but many of its innovations continued.

See also Auburn system; Incapacitation; Prison and jail systems; Punishment; Rehabilitation.

War crimes

DEFINITION: Violations of customary and treaty law limiting the behavior of armed forces during time of war

SIGNIFICANCE: The tendency for war to become a contest of unlimited brutality and destruction is offset by traditional, recognized rules of war that protect the lives of innocent civilians, wounded and disarmed soldiers, prisoners of war, and noncombatants

The idea of war crimes, though rooted in a long tradition of efforts to ensure humane treatment for innocent parties, traces its modern development to the American Civil War and subsequent efforts to codify the laws and customs of war. Closely related to the evolution of war crimes is the development of the laws of war.

Historical Development. Building on principles regarding the treatment of hostages and repatriation of prisoners at the time of the Roman Empire, Christianity forwarded the notion that even during time of war, humane treatment should be accorded civilians, prisoners of war, and unarmed or disarmed enemy soldiers. Augustine developed the notion of a just war, which could be fought only under lawful authority. The purpose of just war was to seek peace and punish evil, not to despoil and pillage. The intention or motive for war, then, had to be just, but the war also had to be fought mercifully and humanely. These notions encouraged the ideas of chivalry and fairness concerning the practice of war during the Middle Ages. After the Thirty Years' War, which ended in 1648, the nations of Europe developed even broader customary principles to regulate hostilities, avoid unnecessary suffering, and protect useless destruction of property. Wars, where practicable, were to be fought on battlefields, away from civilian populations; during sieges, however, civilians were directly affected. Still, while humane action by military commanders and soldiers might have been encouraged, no principle existed whereby those who violated the customs and usages of war could be tried or punished as war criminals.

The movement in the latter direction took shape during and after the American Civil War, which saw the first effort to codify the laws of war and saw one of the first "war crimes trials," in which southern captain Henri Wirz was convicted of inhumane treatment of Union prisoners of war in Andersonville Prison. The trial was controversial, and many questioned whether Wirz was not a scapegoat at a time when many other violators of the laws of war in both the North and South were not prosecuted. Still, the egregious conditions at Andersonville stimulated considerable popular resentment, and this fact, combined with much testimony regarding barbarities committed personally by Wirz, led to his conviction and execution. Wirz alone was tried and punished among many who were culpable.

A more important and influential development arising from the Civil War concerned the codification of the laws of war. In 1863, Francis Lieber, of Columbia University, at the request of President Abraham Lincoln, produced a manual which codified the existing principles and customs of land warfare. Lieber's *Instructions for the Government of the Armies of the United States in the Field* was adopted by the Union army in the same year. By the beginning of the twentieth century, several other nations had modeled their national military manuals after it, even as momentum built to codify the international laws of war. This effort culminated in the Hague Conferences of 1899 and 1907 and in the promulgation of the 1907 Hague Convention Respecting the Laws and Customs of War on Land. Many of the rules codified in the 1907 convention had already been accepted by nations as binding customary laws; the convention merely clarified them and identified other areas of growing consensus.

Still, the notion of trying war crimes by international tribunals did not emerge until after World War I. Until then it was assumed that governments bore responsibility for compensating victims of war crimes committed by its armed forces and that war criminals would be dealt with by their own governments—or, if captured, by the injured belligerent government. After World War I, this began to change, as the Versailles Treaty called for the investigation and punishment of war crimes committed by the forces of the Axis powers. Few were brought to trial, however, and those found guilty of various offenses received light sentences.

The traditional laws of war concerning punishment for war crimes rested on the notion that individuals are not direct subjects of international law. Trials for war crimes, then, took place under the jurisdiction of a country's military or civil jurisdiction. In the United States, the Uniform Code of Military Justice specifies crimes which are subject to court-martial, and among these are war crimes. The assignment of blame for war crimes, however, rested on determining who in the military chain of command was responsible for the crime. Usually soldiers were obliged to follow orders. If ordered to commit a war crime, soldiers could defend their action by citing the *respondeat superior* principle, the defense of superior orders. In such cases the superior who gave the order was held responsible for the war crime. Soldiers who exceeded their orders could be held accountable when committing war crimes on

At the Nuremberg war crimes trials following World War II, Nazi leaders were brought to trial. Among those in the box are Hermann Goering (taking notes) and, to his left, Rudolf Hess. (AP/Wide World Photos)

their own authority. This traditional attitude changed rather dramatically in the wake of the Nuremberg trials after World War II.

Nuremberg Legacy. The wholesale violations of the laws of war that took place during World War II shocked the conscience of humanity. For the first time in history, the international community responded by bringing to justice several thousand persons who were found guilty of war crimes. The Nuremberg trials set a new precedent in regard to the *respondeat superior* question. No longer could a soldier simply follow illegal orders with impunity. To obey an order knowing that it called for the commission of a war crime was to participate in the crime. Yet the Nuremberg tribunal acknowledged that several factors could be taken into account in mitigating punishment for those following orders in commission of war crimes. These included recognition of the fact that situations in time of war may be ambiguous, that some "war crimes" are controversial, that actions which might constitute war crimes in themselves may be acts of retaliation for prior war crimes perpetrated by an enemy force, and that refusal to obey orders may endanger a soldier's life.

These principles came into sharp focus in the 1970-1971 court-martial of Lieutenant William Calley, who was found guilty of the premeditated murder of twenty-two Vietnamese civilians at My Lai. The Vietnam War, like all guerrilla wars, blurred the distinction between armed combatants and civilians. This fact made observation of the laws of war in Vietnam particularly difficult. Calley appealed to this as an element of his defense. Nevertheless, the court-martial held that Calley had exceeded orders given to him by his superior officer. Relatedly, enemy forces had evacuated My Lai, so it no longer held military significance. Even if one could say the massacre represented a reprisal, the laws of war specifically prohibit reprisals against innocent civilians. Under the Nuremberg principles, Calley was justifiably convicted. Of the twenty-five officers and enlisted men charged with participating in the My Lai massacre, nineteen were not tried for lack of evidence and the rest, save Calley, were acquitted. On appeal, Calley's life sentence was reduced, and he eventually became a federal parolee, illustrating that military and civil courts are reluctant to mete out harsh punishments even for those convicted of war crimes.

The Geneva Conventions. In 1949, the International Committee for the Red Cross convinced governments that it was time to revise and update the laws of war as a result of their widespread violation during World War II. The Fourth Geneva Convention Relative to the Protection of Civilian Persons in Time of War was the most central effort to strengthen the traditional distinction between combatants and noncombatants. In 1977 two additional protocols dealing with treatment of civilians in times of international and domestic civil wars were promulgated, although they have had less widespread application than the 1949 conventions. The Geneva Conventions also articulated principles for the humane treatment of prisoners of war.

Taking the 1907 Hague Convention, the Nuremberg tribunal, and the Geneva Conventions and protocols into account, a more comprehensive list of war crimes now exists than ever before. Among the war crimes prohibited are firing on undefended localities that lack military significance, the poisoning of streams and wells, pillaging, killing or wounding captives, killing or attacking harmless civilians, aerial bombardment for the mere purpose of terrorizing a population, and attacking hospitals. Practices smacking of deceit, especially those practices which attempt to hide military operations under the guise of civilian activity, also constitute war crimes because they blur the distinction between combatants and civilians. Such practices include using hospitals as military posts, the wearing of civilian garb or enemy uniforms by soldiers on military missions, abusing flags of truce or surrender, misuse of Red Cross emblems, and treachery in asking for quarter by feigning wounds or sickness. Also forbidden are the taking and killing of hostages, torture and inhuman treatment (including biological experiments on prisoners or civilians), forcing civilians to perform prohibited labor, and the wanton destruction of cultural and religious sites and buildings.

Although the laws of war have been greatly augmented since World War II, acts of cruelty and barbarity, especially in the context of civil wars, are still quite prevalent. Individuals, for the first time in history, can be held directly accountable for violations of the laws of war and thus, in this sense, may be viewed as direct subjects of international law. If war crimes are to be deterred, however, governments must be willing, either collectively or through their national legal systems, to prosecute war crimes and punish the offenders. To this day, governments have been reluctant, for political reasons, to prosecute war crimes aggressively. Still, by aggressively training elements of their armed forces, providing instruction in the laws of war, and instilling principles of military justice and discipline, governments provide a foundation from which the brutalities and inhumanity of war, which is always an unfortunate and necessarily deadly exercise, can be mitigated.

—*Robert F. Gorman*

See also Civil War; Espionage; International law; My Lai massacre; Natural law and natural rights; Nuclear weapons; Vietnam War.

BIBLIOGRAPHY

For a comprehensive treatment of both the laws of war and war crimes more specifically, see Gerhard von Glahn's *Law Among Nations: An Introduction to Public International Law* (6th ed. New York: Macmillan, 1992). Those interested in learning more about Andersonville Prison and the trial of Henri Wirz should see John McElroy, *This Was Andersonville* (New York: Bonanza Books, 1957). Among other things, this book contains a partial transcript of Wirz's trial as a war criminal. For a detailed analysis and copy of the U.S. Uniform Code of Military Justice, see William B. Aycock and Seymour W. Wurfel, *Military Law Under the Uniform Code of Military Justice* (Westport, Conn.: Greenwood Press, 1972). For treatments of the My Lai massacre and the trial of Lt. William

Calley, see Peter A. French, ed., *Individual and Collective Responsibility: Massacre at My Lai* (Cambridge, Mass.: Schenkman, 1972), and Joseph Goldstein, Burke Marshall, and Jack Schwartz, *The My Lai Massacre and Its Cover-up: Beyond the Reach of Law?* (New York: The Free Press, 1976). The latter contains useful excerpts of treaties and cases related to the My Lai massacre. On the general question of military ethics, see Richard A. Gabriel, *To Serve with Honor: A Treatise on Military Ethics and the Way of the Soldier* (Westport, Conn.: Greenwood Press, 1982), and Nicholas Fotion and Gerard Elfstrom, *Military Ethics: Guidelines for Peace and War* (London: Routledge and Kegan Paul, 1986).

War on Poverty

DATE: Launched in 1964, phased out in 1970's and 1980's

DEFINITION: An effort by the federal government in the 1960's to eliminate poverty by creating a variety of social programs

SIGNIFICANCE: The War on Poverty expanded the welfare state; it represents an ambitious attempt by the federal government to aid the poor

In his first State of the Union address (January 8, 1964), President Lyndon B. Johnson declared "unconditional war on poverty in America." This was part of Johnson's plan to create a "Great Society" free of poverty and racism. Congress responded by enacting the Economic Opportunity Act, which established several antipoverty programs. The Office of Economic Opportunity (OEO) acted as the coordinating agency.

Promising to give "a hand, not a handout," the government provided job training for the unemployed, work-study assistance for low-income college students, and adult basic education for the functionally illiterate. Welfare payments were increased to assist the poor while they remained jobless. The War on Poverty was controversial from the beginning. Radicals criticized the government for failing to redistribute more income to the poor, while conservatives complained that increased benefits discouraged the poor from leaving the welfare rolls.

The long-term effects of the War on Poverty are still debated. Congress terminated the OEO in 1973, but some of its functions are carried on by other federal agencies. Welfare payments still provide assistance to those in need, but the "war" has not been won; in fact, the poverty rate has declined very little.

See also Great Society; Johnson, Lyndon B.; Liberalism, modern American; New Deal; Vietnam War; Welfare state.

The Head Start program for disadvantaged children was one part of the War on Poverty that survived beyond the 1970's. (Diane C. Lyell)

Wards Cove Packing Co. v. Atonio

Court: U.S. Supreme Court

Date: Ruling issued June 5, 1989

Significance: This decision threatened to narrow the scope of the law against employment discrimination sharply

Five salmon canneries, owned by Wards Cove Packing Company and Castle & Cooke, recruited seasonal labor for the peak of the fishing season at remote areas in Alaska. Unskilled cannery workers were recruited from Alaska Natives in the region and through the Seattle local of the International Longshoreman's and Warehouseman's Union; two-thirds of these employees were either Alaska Natives or Filipino Americans, including Frank Atonio and twenty-one other plaintiffs. Higher-paid on-site noncannery support staff, including accountants, boat captains, chefs, electricians, engineers, managers, and physicians, were recruited from company offices in Oregon and Washington, largely by word of mouth; some 85 percent of these employees were white. For all employees, the companies provided race-segregated eating and sleeping facilities.

Plaintiff cannery workers, who believed that they were qualified to hold support staff positions but were never selected for these higher-paying jobs, filed suit in 1974 against the companies under Title VII of the Civil Rights Act of 1964. Their argument was based on statistics that showed ethnic differences in the two classes of workers, cannery versus noncannery. In addition to evidence of segregated company housing, they asserted disparate treatment and adverse impact arguments regarding criteria and procedures used to screen them out. Among these criteria, they claimed that there were preferences for relatives of existing employees (nepotism), rehire preferences, English language requirements, failure to promote from within, and a general lack of objective screening and selection criteria. The procedures to which they objected were separate hiring channels and word-of-mouth recruitment rather than open postings of job opportunities.

Justice Byron White delivered the opinion of a divided Court (the vote was 5-4). According to the majority, the comparison between ethnic groups in the two types of jobs was irrelevant because they were drawn from different labor market pools. The Court then went beyond the case to assert that a statistical difference between ethnic groups does not give *prima facie* evidence of discrimination under Title VII unless intent to discriminate is proved. To provide that proof, plaintiffs must show that specific criteria, even vague and subjective criteria, statistically account for the difference. Moreover, an employer may defend criteria that have been proved to account for the difference if they are "reasoned."

The decision had a deleterious impact on efforts to redress employment discrimination, as it reversed the broad language of *Griggs v. Duke Power Co.* (1971) by requiring proof of intent, by allowing the use of separate hiring channels, and by no longer insisting that employers must prove that biased hiring criteria are absolutely essential for job performance. Congress responded by passing the Civil Rights Act of 1991, which codified the original *Griggs* ruling into law.

See also Civil Rights Act of 1964; Civil Rights Act of 1991; Equality of opportunity; *Griggs v. Duke Power Co.*; Racial and ethnic discrimination; *Washington v. Davis*.

Warren, Earl (Mar. 19, 1891, Los Angeles, Calif.—July 9, 1974, Washington, D.C.)

Identification: Chief justice of the United States, 1953-1969

Significance: Chief Justice Earl Warren led the Supreme Court during the most active era of judicial protection of civil rights and civil liberties in the Court's history

Earl Warren grew up in Bakersfield, California. He attended the University of California at Berkeley, where he received his law degree. Among the several state offices he held was that of attorney general of California in 1941, when the Japanese bombed Pearl Harbor, and he supported the relocation of Japanese Americans from the West Coast. For many years thereafter, he believed that the action had been necessary but later in his life came to regret it. Warren, a Republican, was three times elected governor of California. In the 1952 presidential election, he campaigned for the Republican nominee, Dwight D. Eisenhower. President Eisenhower appointed Warren to the first vacancy on the Supreme Court, which was the position of Chief Justice. He held the position from 1953 to 1969, when he retired. During those years, he held one notable extrajudicial position: chairman of the bipartisan commission appointed by President Lyndon B. Johnson to investigate the assassination of President John F. Kennedy. The commission came to be known as the Warren Commission.

Earl Warren was not a legal scholar; he did not decide cases by applying sophisticated legal theories. His approach was to ask whether what had happened was fair or right. Because of its detrimental effect on the motivation of African American children, Warren did not believe that racial segregation in the public schools was right; in *Brown v. Board of Education* (1954), for a unanimous Supreme Court, he wrote that it denied the equal protection of the laws guaranteed by the Fourteenth Amendment. Because the District of Columbia is not a state, the Fourteenth Amendment does not apply to it; however, Warren believed that segregated schools were just as wrong there as in states, and in *Bolling v. Sharpe* (1954) he wrote that such segregation constituted a denial of the due process of law guaranteed by the Fifth Amendment.

Even though he had once prosecuted criminals and his father had been a murder victim, Warren was equally concerned about fairness in the criminal process. In *Miranda v. Arizona* (1966), he wrote that the police must inform people prior to in-custody interrogation of their right to remain silent. The police were also required to inform them of their right to have an attorney present, if they elected to answer questions, and to tell them that an attorney would be appointed if they could not afford to retain one.

Warren did not believe that it was fair or right that a minority of the population could dominate a legislative body. He believed that the apportionment decisions, based on the principle of one person, one vote, were the most important decisions

The liberal era of the Supreme Court under Earl Warren left a lasting imprint on American law; Warren wrote the majority opinions in both Brown v. Board of Education *(1954) and* Miranda v. Arizona *(1966). (Supreme Court Historical Society)*

rendered during his years on the Court because they made the political system more democratic. He wrote the majority opinion in *Reynolds v. Sims* (1964) requiring that both houses of state legislatures be apportioned on the basis of population.

See also *Bolling v. Sharpe*; *Brown v. Board of Education*; Japanese American internment; Liberalism, modern American; *Miranda v. Arizona*; *Reynolds v. Sims*; Supreme Court of the United States; Warren Commission.

Warren Commission

DATE: Created November 29, 1963; issued final report September 24, 1964

SIGNIFICANCE: The Warren Commission, charged with investigating the circumstances of John F. Kennedy's assassination, did a slipshod and unconvincing job, thereby leaving the door open for numerous theories as to who might have been involved in the assassination and why

President John F. Kennedy was assassinated in Dallas, Texas, on November 22, 1963, while riding in a motorcade. Lee Harvey Oswald was charged with the assassination, but before he could be brought to trial he was in turn assassinated by Jack

Ruby. A week after Kennedy's assassination, President Lyndon Johnson established a fact-finding commission to investigate the tragedy. He appointed Chief Justice Earl Warren to head the commission. Other members included Allen Dulles, Gerald Ford, and Arlen Specter. The commission was to determine whether Oswald had been a lone assassin or whether there were others involved.

The Warren Commission released its twenty-six-volume report in September, 1964. The commission concluded that Kennedy had been killed by a single assassin: Oswald had acted alone, and no domestic or foreign conspiracy was involved. Doubts about this conclusion surfaced immediately, and they have increased as the years have gone by. Substantial problems and oversights in the commission's investigation show that the commission was at best inept and at worst trying to bend the evidence to prove that there was only one man involved. Based on the testimony of 552 people and on physical and photographic evidence, the Warren Report held that there was "no credible evidence" of a conspiracy. Oswald, it said, had shot Kennedy from the Texas Book Depository with a rifle he owned; Oswald's rifle ballistically matched a bullet

Bearers lift the casket of President John F. Kennedy at Arlington Cemetery on November 25, 1963. The Warren Commission's investigation of the assassination was handled so poorly that conspiracy theories have abounded. (AP/Wide World Photos)

found on a stretcher. Among the problems with this theory, however, are unanswered questions about the seemingly improbable angles and pattern of bullet wounds and the fact that a number of witnesses reported hearing a gunshot from a grassy knoll to the front and right of Kennedy.

The primary legacy of the Warren Commission has been to encourage distrust of "truth" as it is presented by government; subsequent events, including the Vietnam War and the Watergate hearings, added to this distrust. Shortly after the Warren Report, New Orleans district attorney Jim Garrison embarked on a personal crusade to uncover a conspiracy, but although he generated interest and publicity, he did not marshal convincing evidence of a plot. A congressional committee created in 1976 concluded that Kennedy was "probably" assassinated as the result of a conspiracy. In the early 1990's, after the 1991 film *JFK* brought the issue to national prominence again, President Bill Clinton appointed a panel to release numerous documents relating to the assassination that Johnson had classified as secret. A number of facts came to light, but again, no concrete evidence of conspiracy emerged. Thousands of articles and books have tried to unravel the mystery. A number of theories have peen proposed as to who might have been involved. One idea is that the CIA and/or Cuban leader Fidel Castro con-

spired with the Soviet Union to kill Kennedy; another is that organized crime planned the assassination.

See also Johnson, Lyndon B.; Kennedy, John F.; Warren, Earl.

Washington, Booker T. (Apr. 5, 1856, Hale's Ford, Va.—Nov. 14, 1915, Tuskegee, Ala.)

IDENTIFICATION: Black educator and leader

SIGNIFICANCE: Washington is a famous example of the rise of blacks through education in the decades after Emancipation; until 1912 his philosophy that black people could advance only by self-improvement and education dominated civil rights thinking

Booker Taliaferro Washington was born to a slave mother and an anonymous white father. After Emancipation and a rudimentary education, he was graduated from Hampton Normal and Agricultural Institute in Virginia, and in 1879 he joined its faculty. In 1881 Washington founded the Tuskegee Normal and Industrial Institute. It was run entirely by blacks. Under his presidency it became, and remains, a foremost center for black education.

While Washington's nationwide fund-raising lectures were winning support for Tuskegee from northern capitalists (Andrew Carnegie contributed $600,000), blacks in the South were entering a dreadful period. Despite passage of the Fourteenth Amendment in 1866, hooded Klansmen terrorized blacks to keep them from voting. Within a generation after the war, southern Jim Crow laws had deprived blacks of the vote and firmly established segregation.

In this climate, Washington's 1895 speech at the Atlanta Cotton States and International Exposition, announcing his views on race, gave him national visibility: If whites would hire blacks, he said, "[Y]ou and your family will be surrounded by the most patient, faithful, law-abiding, and unresentful people." He promised that blacks would postpone their demand for equal rights in return for jobs and schools. This "Atlanta Compromise" essentially defined race relations in the United States until 1912. In the press Washington became Frederick Douglass' successor as spokesman for blacks.

Washington's writings include *The Future of the American Negro* (1899); his autobiography, *Up from Slavery* (1901); *Character Building* (1902); *Working with the Hands* (1904); *Life of Frederick Douglass* (1907); and *The Negro in Business* (1907). All expounded his Social Darwinist optimism about the future of blacks in America: Through thrift, hard work, education, and self-help, they could join the ranks of the fittest and win acceptance by whites. He urged blacks to stay in the South despite the terrorism and to accept segregation. Washington's National Negro Business League (founded in 1900) had the same focus.

Washington became the nation's foremost black politician. Presidents Theodore Roosevelt and William Howard Taft appointed blacks and southern whites only with his recommendation. The "Tuskegee machine," as W. E. B. Du Bois termed Washington and his northern financiers, decided what schools received funding. Washington subsidized black newspapers to assure their promotion of his ideas and public image.

White Americans admired him (he received honorary degrees from Harvard University in 1896 and from Dartmouth College in 1901) as an embodiment of the American dream and as sharing their own views on the race question.

After 1900 Du Bois and the National Association for the Advancement of Colored People, founded in 1909, increasingly criticized Washington's soft civil rights stance, arguing that emphasizing vocational training was in effect accepting black inferiority. Blacks were not moving ahead. Most still sharecropped under slavery conditions or were janitors and porters. Prodded by these considerations and personal debasements, Washington personally funded lawsuits supporting black causes. He understood, but never fully embraced, militancy. The defeat of Taft in 1912 ended his political influence.

Washington's personal accomplishment—rising from slavery to fame and influence—was immense. After his death, Du Bois called him "the greatest Negro leader since Frederick Douglass."

See also Civil rights; Douglass, Frederick; Du Bois, W. E. B.; Emancipation Proclamation; Jim Crow laws; Ku Klux Klan (KKK); National Association for the Advancement of Colored People (NAACP); Racial and ethnic discrimination.

Washington v. Davis

COURT: U.S. Supreme Court

DATE: Decided June 7, 1976

SIGNIFICANCE: The Supreme Court held that evidence of the disparate impact of challenged employment practices is insufficient to prove discrimination

African American members of the Washington, D.C., Metropolitan Police Department, as well as unsuccessful applicants to the department, sued the department, claiming that its hiring and promotion policies were racially discriminatory. In particular, they cited a written test that a disproportionately high number of blacks failed. The district court found for the police department, but the appellate court, relying on the Supreme Court precedent of *Griggs v. Duke Power Co.* (1971), reversed that decision, finding the disparate impact of the test to be evidence of employment discrimination. When *Washington v. Davis* came before the Supreme Court, however, Justice Byron White's opinion for the Court stated unequivocally that evidence of discriminatory purpose must be present for such tests to be found unconstitutional. The lower appellate court was reversed.

Griggs had been a landmark employment discrimination case which made disparate impact the test for employment discrimination under Title VII of the 1964 Civil Rights Act. In *Washington*, however, the plaintiffs were claiming that the police department's employment practices violated their right to equal protection under the due process clause of the Fifth Amendment. The standards for determining discrimination proscribed under Title VII were not, said the Court, the same as those applied to a claim of unconstitutional racial discrimination, which requires some evidence of intent to discriminate. Here, the Court found, the personnel test at issue was neutral on its face; in addition, it was rationally related to a legitimate purpose: improving employees' communications skills.

The Court indicated that intent to discriminate could be inferred from a totality of circumstances, including disparate impact, but it declined to spell out a more precise test for unconstitutional employment discrimination. In fact, the majority opinion confused the issue. As Justice John Paul Stevens indicates in his concurring opinion, disparate impact and discriminatory purpose are often indistinguishable. When disparate impact becomes proof of discriminatory purpose, the two standards are conflated. Furthermore, by augmenting the consequences of past discrimination, employment policies not intended to be discriminatory can produce results identical to those resulting from conspicuously discriminatory ones.

The test for what constitutes evidence of discriminatory intent was left indeterminate until the Supreme Court strengthened it in *Personnel Administrator of Massachusetts v. Feeney* (1979) to the advantage of employers. In *Feeney*, the Court held that even if discriminatory results of a prospective statute are foreseeable at the time it is passed by the legislature, it is only unconstitutional if these results constitute the reason for passage. The consequences for subsequent civil rights litigants pressing discrimination suits against state employers were profound.

See also Civil Rights Act of 1964; Due process of law; Equal protection of the law; *Griggs v. Duke Power Co.*; Racial and ethnic discrimination; *Wards Cove Packing Co. v. Atonio.*

Watergate scandal

DATE: June 17, 1972—August 9, 1974

PLACE: Washington, D.C.

SIGNIFICANCE: "Watergate" was a major constitutional crisis caused by the obstruction of justice committed by President Richard M. Nixon and several of his most influential assistants; although Nixon denied personal involvement in the Watergate cover-up for more than two years, proof of his guilt was eventually revealed, and he was forced to resign the presidency on August 9, 1974

During the spring of 1972, opinion polls indicated that President Richard Nixon would easily win reelection against the expected Democratic nominee, Senator George McGovern from South Dakota. Several members of the Committee to Reelect the President, however, did not want to take any chances. Wanting to learn of the strategy the Democrats planned to use in their campaign against Nixon, they decided to break into the national headquarters of the Democratic Party in Washington's Watergate Hotel. A custodian in the Watergate Hotel noticed a door ajar in the Democratic Party offices and notified the District of Columbia police, who arrested the would-be burglars. They were charged with breaking and entering.

Although three of the criminals, E. Howard Hunt, James McCord, and G. Gordon Liddy, worked for the Committee to Reelect the President, no one could prove at that time that any member of the Nixon Administration had been involved in planning the break-in or in paying money to the seven defendants to remain quiet. More than two years later it was proved that on June 23, 1972, President Nixon himself had ordered the Central Intelligence Agency to interfere with the Federal Bureau of Investigation's probe of the break-in. Moreover, Nixon's main assistants, John Erlichman and Bob Haldeman, approved the secret payment of large sums of money to the seven defendants. Nixon clearly hoped that the defendants would not reveal the participation of their superiors in the break-in. Throughout the remaining months before the November, 1972, election, the cover-up was successful. President Nixon and his staff stated repeatedly that no one other than the seven defendants had been involved in the crime. Nixon won a landslide victory against Senator McGovern.

Judge Sirica's Role. During their trial in January, 1973, the defendants affirmed that they had acted alone, thereby committing perjury. The cover-up began to unravel in March, 1973, however, when the time came for federal district court judge John Sirica to sentence the five defendants who had pleaded guilty and the two whom the jurors had found guilty. Judge Sirica suspected that he had been lied to during the trial, and he was determined to do something to discover the truth. He offered the seven felons a choice: If they chose to cooperate with prosecutors and the recently formed Senate Select Committee on Presidential Campaign Activities, chaired by Senator Sam Ervin, Jr., from North Carolina, they would not serve much time in jail, but if they continued to be uncooperative, he would sentence each of them to forty-five years in federal prison, the maximum sentence permitted for their crime.

Judge Sirica's tactic astounded President Nixon's assistants in the White House, but it also produced the desired effect by persuading James McCord, one of the convicted felons, that it was in his self-interest to cooperate with Sirica. McCord wrote a letter to Sirica explaining that he and his partners had been paid to perjure themselves during the trial. McCord admitted that others had been involved in the cover-up. Nixon decided to continue to deny his personal involvement in the cover-up and to blame others in his administration for the scandal, which was threatening to endanger his presidency. He revealed a complete lack of loyalty to those who had served him faithfully for several years; he also abused his authority by the false claim of executive privilege to conceal his own participation in the Watergate scandal. His contempt for the rule of law and his abuse of the great power of the White House caused some Americans to lose respect for the office of the presidency. Although Nixon strove mightily to remain in power, eventually even most members of his own party abandoned him. He was forced to resign in disgrace in August, 1974. Many unexpected events had occurred between Judge Sirica's decision in March, 1973, and Nixon's resignation in August, 1974.

The Special Prosecutor and the Senate Hearings. On April 30, 1973, Nixon accepted the resignations of Erlichman, Haldeman, his personal counsel John Dean, and Attorney General Richard Kleindienst, all of whom had participated in the cover-up. He appointed a well-respected Republican, Elliot Richardson, as his new attorney general and granted Richardson the authority to appoint an independent special prosecutor. Nixon badly misjudged the character of both Richardson and Archibald Cox, the new special prosecutor. He thought that he could somehow control them. Richardson was a Republican, and Cox was a Democrat (Cox was teaching law at Harvard University). Despite their political differences, neither Richardson nor Cox would compromise their ethical beliefs. Neither had political ambitions, and both were very honest lawyers. Soon after his appointment as special prosecutor, Cox made it clear that he would seek the truth, no matter where the search led him. Richardson strove to reestablish the integrity of the Department of Justice, which had been used for political purposes by Richard Kleindienst and his predecessor, John Mitchell.

After Senator Ervin's Select Committee began its hearings in May, 1973, it became clear that many morally questionable decisions had been made by influential people in the Nixon White House and that specific laws had most probably been violated by many members of his administration. It remained unclear whether President Nixon himself had been involved in the cover-up. Senator Howard Baker of Tennessee, the ranking Republican member of the committee, asked many witnesses what the president knew and when the president had learned of certain facts. These hearings, which were televised live, persuaded the American public that the four Democratic and three

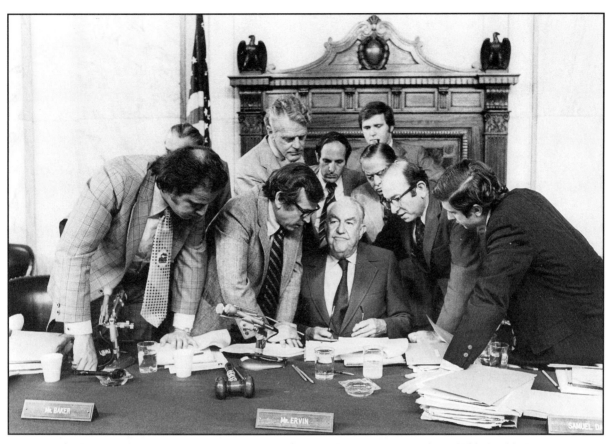

The Senate committee investigating Watergate; chairman Sam Ervin is seated. (AP/Wide World Photos)

Republican senators on the select committee were objectively seeking truth. Although many people believed that President Nixon must have known of the Watergate cover-up, there was no proof that he had committed the high crimes and misdemeanors which would justify removing him from office.

The White House Tapes. An unexpected revelation, one which would eventually produce the necessary proof of President Nixon's personal involvement in the criminal obstruction of justice, was made before the Ervin Committee on July 16, 1973, when Alexander Butterfield, who had previously served as an assistant in the White House, stated under oath that from 1971 until his departure from the White House on March 14, 1973, all conversations in the Oval Office had been secretly recorded and that these tapes had been kept by order of the president. Senators Ervin and Baker and Special Prosecutor Cox immediately understood that these tapes could provide incontrovertible proof of the president's innocence or guilt. In response to subpoenas from the Senate Committee and Archibald Cox, President Nixon invoked "executive privilege" and refused to turn over the relevant tapes.

The American public understood that President Nixon's actions had provoked a constitutional crisis. Would the United States remain a country governed by law, or would the president be free to disregard laws which displeased him? After

Nixon's refusal to comply with the subpoena from Archibald Cox, the special prosecutor asked Judge Sirica to enforce this subpoena. Sirica did so, and the Federal Appeals Court of the District of Columbia upheld the validity of the subpoena in October, 1973. Unless the U.S. Supreme Court voted to overrule the decision of the appeals court, Nixon would have to turn over the relevant tapes or be held in contempt of court, which would most certainly cause his impeachment by the House of Representatives and removal from office by the Senate.

In a desperate attempt to put an end to the work of the special prosecutor, Nixon ordered Attorney General Richardson on Saturday, October 20, 1973, to fire Cox and to abolish the office of the special prosecutor. Both Attorney General Richardson and Assistant Attorney General William Ruckelshaus refused to implement this unethical order, and they were both fired by President Nixon. Robert Bork, then the U.S. solicitor general and third in command in the Department of Justice, complied with Nixon's wishes and fired Cox. This abuse of presidential power came to be known as the "Saturday night massacre." On November 1, 1973, President Nixon had to appoint yet another attorney general, Senator William Saxbe of Ohio. Leon Jaworski was appointed as the new special prosecutor. President Nixon's attempt to destroy the independence of the American judicial system had failed, and

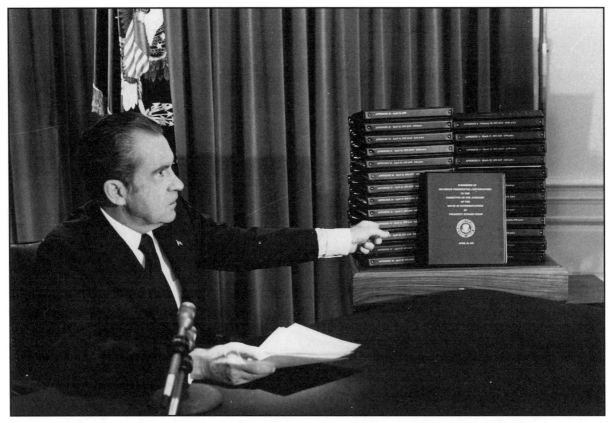

President Richard Nixon appeared on television in an unsuccessful attempt to avoid relinquishing the White House tapes: He offered to provide the special prosecutor with edited transcripts of the tapes. (AP/Wide World Photos)

he was even forced to agree that he would not attempt to fire special prosecutor Jaworski without the approval of Republican and Democratic leaders from the House and the Senate.

Nixon's Resignation. Although Richard Nixon would not resign for several months, it was clear that the end was near. President Nixon's special counsel, James St. Clair, asked the U.S. Supreme Court to reverse the decision of the Federal Appeals Court of the District of Columbia, but in a unanimous decision written by Chief Justice Warren Burger (*United States v. Nixon*), the U.S. Supreme Court affirmed on July 24, 1974, the decision of the lower court and ordered President Nixon to turn over the subpoenaed tapes to the special prosecutor. Nixon's guilt soon became obvious to almost everyone: In a conversation recorded on June 23, 1972, he had ordered the CIA to interfere with the FBI's investigation of the break-in. This action clearly constituted criminal obstruction of justice. By a vote of twenty-seven to eleven, the House Judiciary Committee under the chairmanship of Congressman Peter Rodino from New Jersey voted on July 27, 1974, to impeach President Nixon. All twenty-one Democrats on the committee as well as six of the seventeen Republicans voted for impeachment. When it was explained to President Nixon by such Republican leaders as Senators Hugh Scott of Pennsylvania and Barry Goldwater of Arizona that almost no Republicans

would support him in either the House of Representatives or the Senate, Nixon finally decided to resign in order to avoid the public humiliation of being impeached by the House of Representatives and then removed from office by the Senate.

Vice President Gerald Ford was sworn in as president on August 9, 1974. On September 8, 1974, President Ford granted Richard Nixon a full pardon for all crimes which he had committed during his presidency. Many of Nixon's top assistants, including Erlichman, Haldeman, and Mitchell, were later convicted of their crimes and sentenced to prison. The Watergate scandal cast a long shadow over the presidency and to some extent—especially combined with the deep divisions caused by the Vietnam War—the government as a whole for many years. In particular, both politicians and the public were suspicious of presidential power, and special prosecutors were appointed on a number of occasions to investigate possible wrongdoing. Among the activities investigated by special prosecutors were the Iran-Contra scandal that tainted the Reagan and Bush administrations and the Whitewater allegations against Bill Clinton and members of his administration. —*Edmund J. Campion*

See also Burger, Warren; Constitutional law; Ford, Gerald R.; Lying to Congress; Nixon, Richard M.; Pardoning power; Political campaign law; Political corruption; Subpoena power; Supreme Court of the United States.

BIBLIOGRAPHY

A very clear history of the Watergate scandal can be found in Theodore H. White, *Breach of Faith: The Fall of Richard Nixon* (New York: Atheneum Press, 1975). Senator Sam Ervin, Jr., expressed his views in *The Whole Truth: The Watergate Conspiracy* (New York: Random House, 1980). Nixon's unsuccessful attempts to manipulate public opinion are analyzed very well in Frank Mankiewicz, *U.S. v. Richard M. Nixon: The Final Crisis* (New York: New York Times Book Co., 1975). The work of the special prosecutors both before and after Nixon's resignation has been described very clearly in James Doyle, *Not Above the Law: The Battles of Watergate Prosecutors Cox and Jaworski* (New York: William Morrow, 1977), and Richard Ben-Veniste and George Frampton, Jr., *Stonewall: The Real Story of the Watergate Prosecution* (New York: Simon & Schuster, 1977).

Weather Underground

DATE: Established 1968
SIGNIFICANCE: The Weather Underground's actions contributed to the dominant view that student revolution was essentially violent, dangerous, and anarchistic

The Weather Underground, a relatively small group which began as a faction of Students for a Democratic Society (SDS), attracted widespread attention for its political platform. It judged American capitalist society to be incapable of providing true justice through either mainstream politics or more radical approaches. Instead, the Weather Underground advocated the formation of small, tightly knit collectives dedicated to armed revolution, the rejection of conventional norms, and the eventual overthrow of the U.S. government.

The Weather Underground was a prime organizer of the "Days of Rage," dedicated to disrupting the Democratic Party's 1968 presidential convention in Chicago. It also carried out bombings, resulting in property damage but no fatalities, throughout the United States. It generated national attention when three of its members accidentally killed themselves while manufacturing bombs in New York City's Greenwich Village in March, 1970.

The Weather Underground was the subject of intense and effective law enforcement surveillance and repression. Even other leftist organizations were often unsympathetic to its advocacy of random violence and its general ineffectiveness, thereby rendering its impact minimal, except perhaps in causing mainstream Americans to be less sympathetic to radical groups in general.

See also Campus Unrest, President's Commission on; Chicago seven trial; COINTELPRO; Socialism; Students for a Democratic Society (SDS); Terrorism; Vietnam War.

Webster v. Reproductive Health Services

COURT: U.S. Supreme Court
DATE: Ruling issued July 3, 1989
SIGNIFICANCE: In this case, the Supreme Court confirmed the basic principles of *Roe v. Wade* with regard to a woman's right to abortion but significantly expanded the ability of the states to regulate abortion, at least partially eroding the intent of *Roe v. Wade*

In June of 1986, the state of Missouri passed into law a statute which amended existing state laws regarding abortion. The following month, several health care professionals brought a class action suit challenging the constitutionality of five provisions of the new law. These were (1) the pronouncement by the state legislature that life begins at conception, (2) the connected pronouncement that unborn children have a legally protectable right to life, (3) mandatory viability tests prior to abortions after twenty or more weeks of pregnancy, (4) prohibition against public facilities and personnel performing abortions except to save the life of the mother, and (5) prohibition against public funds or personnel being used to counsel women to have an abortion except in life-threatening situations. *Amicus curiae* briefs were submitted by the federal government not only supporting the Missouri law but also arguing that *Roe v. Wade* (1973), which had established constitutionally protected abortion rights, should be overturned altogether.

The Court responded in a divided and complex way. Provisions (1) and (2) were taken to be abstract theoretical constructs without legal consequence, and thus to be beyond the interests of the court. By a narrow 5-4 vote, the Court upheld the Missouri law (reversing district and appeals court decisions). Four of the majority justices believed that this decision effectively overturned or at least fundamentally altered the impact of *Roe v. Wade*. The fifth, Sandra Day O'Connor, supported the right of Missouri to regulate abortion in the ways listed above but opined that such a decision did not fundamentally disturb *Roe v. Wade*. Thus *Roe v. Wade* was upheld, also by a 5-4 vote, with O'Connor providing the fifth vote for each majority.

The Court's decision preserved a basic right to abortion for the first two trimesters of pregnancy but also gave the states considerable leeway in regulating abortions. This had two cross-cutting effects. Other states passed laws similar to Missouri's and included new provisions such as parental notification for minors, which the Court approved as long as they included a process for permitting exceptions where appropriate. On the other hand, abortion rights advocates now found it easier to organize "pro-choice" voters against "pro-life" candidates and, more specifically, against George Bush in the 1992 presidential election. Despite an attempt to moderate his views, Bush was beaten in 1992 partly by voters who feared that the next Bush Supreme Court appointee would further erode or overturn *Roe v. Wade*. New president Bill Clinton appointed two pro-choice justices within his first two years in office.

See also Abortion; *Akron v. Akron Center for Reproductive Health*; Bush, George; *Maher v. Roe*; *Planned Parenthood of Central Missouri v. Danforth*; *Planned Parenthood v. Casey*; *Roe v. Wade*; *Thornburgh v. American College of Obstetricians and Gynecologists*.

Weeks v. United States

COURT: U.S. Supreme Court

DATE: Decided February 24, 1914

SIGNIFICANCE: In order to enforce the privacy values of the Fourth Amendment, the Court ordered that illegally obtained evidence must be excluded from criminal trials in federal courts; this order is commonly called the "exclusionary rule"

After Fremont Weeks was arrested for illegally sending lottery tickets through the U.S. mail service, a federal marshal accompanied by a police officer, without a search warrant, broke into Weeks's private home and seized incriminating evidence. Although the defendant argued that the search and seizure contradicted the requirements of the Fourth Amendment, the resulting evidence was used to convict him in a federal district court. Weeks appealed his case to the Supreme Court.

Until the *Weeks* decision, American courts had followed the common-law practice of allowing federal prosecutors to use evidence unlawfully seized by law enforcement officers. Many constitutional scholars had argued that the traditional practice encouraged governmental violations of liberties guaranteed in the Constitution, and they insisted that it was inconsistent with the Fourth Amendment's purpose of treating people's houses as their castles. Based on this point of view, the Supreme Court in *Boyd v. United States* (1886) criticized and implicitly rejected the common-law practice, but the Court stopped short of explicitly ruling the inadmissibility of evidence obtained illegally. The *Boyd* pronouncements on privacy values, without any means of enforcement, appeared to have no impact on the behavior of those who enforced the laws.

In *Weeks* an impatient Court unanimously required federal courts thereafter to apply the exclusionary rule in all criminal prosecutions. In the official opinion, Justice William Day declared that without the exclusionary rule, the Fourth Amendment was of "no value" and "might as well be stricken from the Constitution." The noble goal of punishing the guilty must not be used as an excuse to sacrifice the "fundamental rights" established by the Constitution. Day's opinion did not clearly articulate whether the application of the exclusionary rule was an individual right guaranteed by the Constitution or whether it was simply a judicial device developed to prevent unreasonable searches and seizures. Although these two views would continue to be debated by the Court, most justices have accepted Day's conclusion that the exclusionary rule is the only practical means of requiring government to conform to constitutional rules.

The immediate impact of the *Weeks* decision was limited, because it did not apply to state courts where most criminal prosecutions took place. When the Court ruled that the Fourth Amendment was binding on the states in *Wolf v. Colorado* (1949), the Court did not require states to follow the exclusionary rule, and until *Elkins v. United States* (1960), the so-called silver platter doctrine permitted federal prosecutors to make use of evidence illegally seized by agents of the states.

Finally, in *Mapp v. Ohio* (1961), the Supreme Court required the application of the exclusionary rule in state courts. The exclusionary rule has always been controversial, for it sometimes makes it more difficult to prosecute criminals. Critics argue that there are alternative means of protecting the rights of the Fourth Amendment, but defenders reply that the alternatives do not provide effective protection.

See also Evidence, rules of; *Katz v. United States*; *Mapp v. Ohio*; Search and seizure; *Wolf v. Colorado*.

Welfare state

DEFINITION: The welfare state is characterized by government assurances to the citizenry of a national minimum of protection against disability, ill health, unemployment, inadequate housing, and the physical and economic insecurities of old age

SIGNIFICANCE: The activities of most modern states reflect the assumption that for the good of the whole community, governments are charged with planning and spending to provide whatever may be regarded as the basic conditions of social justice

Governmental efforts to ensure social justice in the United States are best understood in the context of the politics of a complex federal system. This is a system involving fifty states, thousands of municipalities, and more than 100,000 other governmental units. Each of these has distinctive powers and important capacities to determine what revenues, if any, are redistributed to ensure or project measures of social justice. The views of the many communities that these governments represent are often disparate and subject to differing interpretations, a fact which has made the development of federally sponsored, nationwide programs of social justice uniquely difficult and highly politicized in the United States.

Nevertheless, the notion that because of these difficulties the United States lagged behind other modern governments such as those of Great Britain, Germany, and the Scandinavian countries in creating basic elements of a "welfare state," and that it did not begin to do so until the New Deal policies of President Franklin D. Roosevelt in the 1930's, must be modified. Long before the New Deal, millions of Americans were beneficiaries of federal and state policies and expenditures directed toward the improvement of their social welfare.

European Background. The origins of the modern welfare state usually are attributed to the highly centralized, authoritarian German regime of Chancellor Otto von Bismarck (1815-1898), who on behalf of Kaiser Wilhelm I dominated German government from 1862 to 1890. Seeking to undercut the rising power of German socialists and to undermine working-class dissent, Bismarck initiated a series of comprehensive social reforms between 1883 and 1887. These reforms established maximum hours of work, limited woman and child labor, and legislated universal accident, sickness, and old-age insurance.

It was primarily the British experience, however, that attracted and informed the social welfare ideas of early twentieth century American intellectuals and social reformers. By 1914,

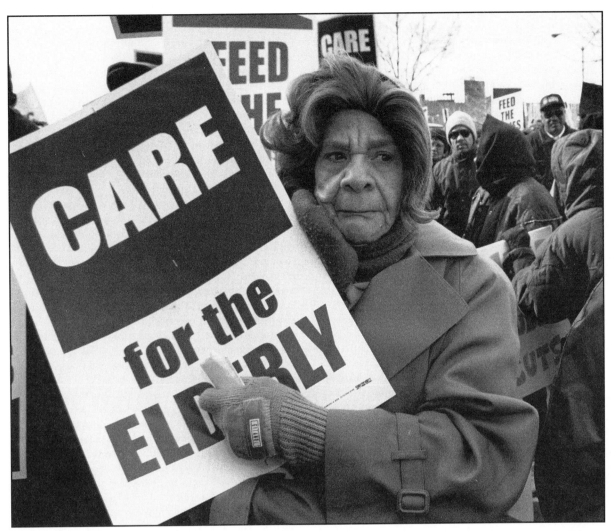

The provision of retirement benefits and health care for the elderly is one of the central aspects of the welfare state. (Jim West)

the British government, under political pressure from well-organized trade unionists and stimulated by moderate socialists, civil servants, settlement house leaders, and reform-minded intellectuals, had provided workers' compensation (1906), old-age pensions (1908), and unemployment and health insurance (1911). After World War I and throughout the Depression and mass unemployment of the 1920's and 1930's, Britain expanded social insurance programs paid for by public revenues and payroll taxes. Following World War II, with plans ready for postwar reconstruction, the British revised and extended programs of social justice. Much of this effort was guided by William Beveridge's reform recommendations (in the Beveridge Report, *Social Insurance and Allied Services*, 1942), from which, in the English-speaking world, came the term "welfare state": a state pledged to provide basic social services covering every individual from "cradle to grave." Beyond revisions of unemployment insurance, disability in-

surance, workers' compensation, and old-age insurance, the British added free universal health care, nationalized hospitals, and (by 1947, through the Town and Country Act) a national housing program. Similar national programs almost simultaneously were underway in Scandinavian countries as well as in socialist or communist nations such as the Soviet Union.

Early American Experience. The American experience with extensions of social justice, beginning in the nineteenth century, was strikingly different from policies initiated in Great Britain and elsewhere. There were a number of reasons for this. Until the mid-1920's, the United States remained predominantly an agricultural nation. Its trade union movements were small and weak; capitalists, corporations, and the business communities, including farmers, generally exercised dominant influences over government policymaking. Its civil service and bureaucracies were modest in size and in political influence; suspicions of governmental power traditionally were strong. At least rhetorically, many Americans prided themselves on their individualism and their general capacity to care for themselves without government "interference." All these factors militated against national planning and the implementation of universalized social welfare programs.

Large, politically influential groups of Americans, nonetheless, received the benefits of social legislation enacted by federal and state governments during the nineteenth and early twentieth centuries—well prior to the New Deal. Since free or cheap land represented a capital subsidy, for example, millions of farmers (as well as speculators and other business interests, notably transcontinental railroads) profited from the distribution of the public domain—in other words, from federal land subsidies. Between 1862 and 1904, under such federal legislation as the Homestead Act (1862), more than 147 million acres were distributed free, while more than 610 million acres were sold cheaply, ostensibly to farmers. After the 1840's millions of American children likewise received free public educations—in the most comprehensive educational programs in the industrializing world—from state and local governments.

In addition, under the Arrears Pension Act (1879), the Dependent Pension Act (1890), and related federal legislation on behalf of Civil War veterans, their widows, and dependents, nearly a million pensioners by the mid-1890's received handsome service pensions (including land), as well as disability and old-age pensions. State governments invariably augmented these benefits. By the 1890's, the federal government alone was spending 41 percent of its income on the relatively lavish veterans' benefits that were collected by more than one-third of northern men and by a substantial number of widowed women.

Civil War veterans were not alone in benefiting from federal and state social welfare legislation. Historical studies have revealed that middle-class and working-class women's groups were primarily responsible in nearly every state for winning legislation limiting women's hours of labor and, in fifteen states by 1913, for winning minimum wage laws. In nearly every state women's groups secured pensions for widows with children and for aged women. U.S. Supreme Court decisions such as *Muller v. Oregon* (1908) threw an additional protective mantle over some of this "maternalist protective labor legislation" years before male wage earners were covered by such laws. Thus, although the American political structure long precluded universalized social welfare legislation, millions of its citizens benefitted from federal and state aid designed to help them meet many basic needs.

The New Deal. The unprecedented social and economic disasters that attended the Great Depression during the decade after 1929 created the political pressures from which flowed the New Deal legislation of President Franklin D. Roosevelt. Between 1933 and 1938, New Deal policies, many experimental in character, took two major directions. Each necessitated unprecedented peacetime federal spending. The earliest programs were designed to alleviate the shocks of massive unemployment as well as to subsidize the rehabilitation of major banking and business failures and encourage job retention. To relieve unemployment, for example, federal agencies were established to create "public works" under the auspices of the Works Progress Administration, the Public Works Administration, the National Youth Administration, and the Civilian Conservation Corps. Further legislation helped refinance homeowners' and farm mortgages, extended crop loans, set a floor under wages and a ceiling on hours for millions of workers, prevented mortgage foreclosures, initiated a national housing program for low-income families, instituted retirement pensions for railroad employees, mandated minimum wages and maximum hours for employees working under government contracts, and paid adjusted pensions to World War I veterans. Intended as "relief" measures, little of this type of New Deal legislation contributed to a universalized effort to extend social welfare or social justice to all American citizens.

The enactment of one federal "entitlement" program, however, emerged as the nearest approximation to a genuinely national social welfare program: the Social Security Act of 1935, the centerpiece of New Deal welfare statism. Paid for by wage earners' contributions and by a payroll tax on their employers, Social Security assured wage earners retirement income based on their highest level of earnings, along with additional benefits for them and their dependents. Social Security established a framework for the United States' major programs of unemployment insurance, public assistance, and old-age retirement insurance at both federal and state levels. Modest additions to social welfare legislation have included the GI Bill of 1944, which rewarded 13 million World War II veterans with educational benefits—a temporary measure—and the Medicare, Medicaid, food stamp, and Aid to Families with Dependent Children (AFDC) programs launched during the Great Society campaign of President Lyndon B. Johnson (in office 1963-1969).

SOCIAL WELFARE SPENDING, 1989, IN MILLIONS OF DOLLARS		
Program Categories	Federal	State and Local
Total	563,191	392,676
Social insurance	387,290	80,765
Public aid	79,852	47,623
Health and medical programs	24,215	32,651
Veterans programs	29,638	466
Education	18,520	220,111
Housing	15,184	2,943
Other social welfare	8,492	8,117

Source: U.S. Department of Commerce, Bureau of the Census, *Statistical Abstract of the United States, 1992.* Washington, D.C.: U.S. Government Printing Office, 1992.

Note: "Social insurance" includes Social Security, Medicare, public employee retirement, and workers' compensation; "Public aid" includes Medicaid, Supplemental Security Income (SSI), and food stamps.

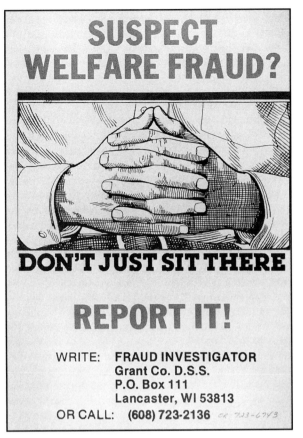

SUSPECT
WELFARE FRAUD?

DON'T JUST SIT THERE

REPORT IT!

WRITE: **FRAUD INVESTIGATOR**
Grant Co. D.S.S.
P.O. Box 111
Lancaster, WI 53813
OR CALL: **(608) 723-2136**

Fraud in the various components of the welfare system is certainly considerable, but its extent is impossible to determine with any precision. (James L. Shaffer)

Reevaluations and Uncertainty. Beginning in the 1970's, as "big government" fell into popular—hence political—disfavor, and as congressional struggles to achieve a balanced budget and cut the deficit curtailed spending, national social welfare entitlement programs, including Social Security, came under attack by the media, legislators, and Presidents Richard Nixon, Jimmy Carter, Ronald Reagan, and George Bush. Social Security, despite its inequities, appeared immune, largely because of its broad middle-class political base and support from well-organized interest groups such as the American Association of Retired Persons. However, those programs which popularly were stigmatized by the term "welfare"—implying government "handouts" for people who did not work—were more vulnerable. Although facts were difficult to marshal and varied from state to state, there was widespread agreement among experts and legislators that "welfare" programs were not only inordinately expensive but also desperately in need of reform. Again without precise information, there were suspicions and estimations of widespread welfare fraud. Generally, such programs centered on aid to persons of low income, many of whom had been living for years in poverty and on public assistance, constituting what some soci-

ologists called a "culture of poverty." Many were black, Hispanic, or immigrant residents of inner cities, poorly educated and often unemployable. Their vulnerability to the loss of public assistance was enhanced by their lack of political clout.

During the 1990's, debate over the future of social welfare and entitlement programs intensified. Running for president in 1992, Bill Clinton vowed to push for a national health care program that would cover all Americans, some 25 million of whom still had neither public nor private health insurance. Public opinion polls indicated that a majority of Americans supported the idea. The plan his administration produced, however, was widely criticized and was defeated by a Congress that was trying to reduce the budget deficit. In the congressional elections of 1994, Republicans won a majority of the seats in both houses and began to examine all government social spending more critically than ever. Significant cuts to such long-standing programs as Medicare and Medicaid were heatedly debated, and even Social Security was subjected to reevaluation of such elements as its formula for computing cost-of-living increases. By the mid-1990's, while it appeared unlikely that such broad middle-class programs such as Social Security would be destroyed, it appeared equally unlikely that social welfare programs would soon be expanded.

—*Clifton K. Yearley*

See also Aid to Families with Dependent Children (AFDC); Conservatism, modern American; Food stamps; GI Bill of Rights; Great Society; Johnson, Lyndon B.; Liberalism, modern American; New Deal; Roosevelt, Franklin D.; Social Security system; War on Poverty.

BIBLIOGRAPHY

Since welfare states operate by redistributing a nation's income to fulfill social objectives, they invariably have been controversial not only among general publics but also among policy experts; these controversies have produced abundant readings. Two award-winning books by Theda Skocpol are important to this literature: *Social Policy in the United States* (Princeton, N.J.: Princeton University Press, 1995) focuses on the political distinctiveness of the United States' development of social welfare in comparison with British welfarism, and *Protecting Soldiers and Mothers* (Cambridge, Mass.: Harvard University Press, 1992) emphasizes new historical evidence on nineteenth century welfare in the United States. Paul Pierson's *Dismantling the Welfare State?* (Cambridge, England: Cambridge University Press, 1994) compares attempts by two conservatives, British prime minister Margaret Thatcher and American president Ronald Reagan, to curtail their nations' welfare programs. Peter G. Peterson and Neil Howe's *On Borrowed Time* (San Francisco, Calif.: ICS Press, 1988) takes an apocalyptic view of how the growth of American welfare spending threatens the nation's future. Theodore R. Marmor, Jerry L. Mashaw, and Philip L. Harvey examine the consequences of persistent public myths about American welfare in contrast to the realities in *America's Misunderstood Welfare State* (New York: Basic Books, 1990). Margaret Weir, Ann S. Orloff, and Theda Skocpol, eds., present an enlightening and, in viewpoint, generally prowelfare collection of essays in *The Politics of Social Policy in the United States* (Princeton, N.J.: Princeton University Press, 1988). An instructive survey is Edward Berkowitz and Kim McQuaid's *Creating the Welfare State* (New York: Praeger, 1980).

Wesberry v. Sanders

COURT: U.S. Supreme Court
DATE: Ruling issued February 17, 1964
SIGNIFICANCE: This decision required that congressional districts within a state be approximately equal in size

The topic of representation in Congress and state legislatures—with the related issues of apportionment and districting—was long avoided by the federal courts. When in the 1946 case of *Colegrove v. Green* the Supreme Court was asked to consider the imbalance in size of congressional districts in Illinois (which had not been redistricted since 1901), it declined to enter "the political thicket" and said that such matters were the proper concern of legislative bodies. In 1929, Congress had stopped mandating that states redraw district lines after each census. The result was that by the 1960's there were substantial inequalities in the sizes of congressional (and state legislative) districts in many states, a situation that usually meant the decided overrepresentation of rural populations.

An important indication that change might be on the way came in the case of *Baker v. Carr* (1962). In this case the U.S. Supreme Court ruled that questions of apportionment and districting were within the jurisdiction of federal courts, effectively reversing the doctrine it had followed in the *Colegrove* case. The court took up the question directly when it agreed to hear *Wesberry v. Sanders*. This case had its origins in a class action suit by voters in Fulton County, Georgia, who claimed that they were cheated of fair representation. They pointed out that their urban and suburban fifth district was approximately three times larger than the rural ninth district, though each was represented by one congressman. The Court upheld their challenge by a 7-2 majority. It based its decision on Article I, section 2 of the Constitution, which says that representatives should be chosen "by the People of the several States." The court interpreted this to mean that one person's vote should be equal to another's.

Wesberry was followed by other "reapportionment decisions." In *Reynolds v. Sims* (also 1964) the Court reached a similar conclusion with regard to state legislative districts (though grounding its decision here in the Fourteenth Amendment's equal protection clause).

By mandating equality in population among congressional districts, the Court brought a considerable shift in congressional representation and political power from rural areas to urban and—especially—suburban ones that would continue for the rest of the century. Other decisions had a similar effect at the state level, though the Court did tolerate greater differences in size among state legislative districts than among congressional districts. Once established, the doctrine of "one person, one vote" raised other questions, such as the extent to which racial and ethnic considerations should be factored into apportionment and districting.

See also *Baker v. Carr*; *Colegrove v. Green*; Representation: gerrymandering, malapportionment, and reapportionment; *Reynolds v. Sims*; Vote, right to.

West Coast Hotel Co. v. Parrish

COURT: U.S. Supreme Court
DATE: Decided March 29, 1937
SIGNIFICANCE: In this case, the U.S. Supreme Court upheld a state minimum wage law and signaled the end of an era declaring many similar state laws unconstitutional on the basis of substantive due process

The state of Washington enacted a minimum wage law for women in 1913. Elsie Parrish, a hotel chambermaid, sued her employer, the West Coast Hotel Company, for her minimum wage under the terms of the Washington law. She was seeking $14.50 for forty-eight hours of work. The Washington Supreme Court upheld the law, and the employer appealed to the U.S. Supreme Court. Chief Justice Charles Evans Hughes, writing for the narrow five-member majority, upheld the law under the U.S. Constitution's Fourteenth Amendment. The majority held that the protection of women workers was a legitimate end for the states to regulate. Further, a minimum wage for women provides for their subsistence and is a permissible means for the state to achieve the desired end. This decision reversed several earlier cases which had declared similar state statutes unconstitutional under the Lochner doctrine. This doctrine was generally based on the Court's 1905 decision in *Lochner v. New York*, which struck down a New York maximum hours law as unconstitutional. The Lochner doctrine applied the Fourteenth Amendment due process clause to invalidate state legislation under the grounds of substantive due process. The Court had held state regulation of business activities to be an invasion of the fundamental freedom of individuals to enter into contracts of their own free choice. Such an argument was used many times to strike down state laws as unconstitutional that protected workers such as maximum hours laws.

The West Coast Hotel Company case is significant in that it was decided during the era of the "Court-packing plan" of President Franklin D. Roosevelt, during which the Court majority changed and reversed some of its earlier decisions. The *West Coast Hotel* decision vote by Justice Owen J. Roberts is cited as the "switch in time that saved nine" when he apparently changed his vote from his position in an earlier case. The Court then started to uphold many pieces of the Roosevelt Administration's New Deal legislation and signaled the beginning of the modern era of judicial scrutiny of state and federal legislation.

Subsequently, the rationale of the Court has been criticized for relying too much on an argument that it is necessary to provide special protection to women in the workplace. In many early cases, during the period 1906-1937, courts had been willing to uphold legislation that characterized women as weaker and in need of more state protection. These laws have since generally given way to less sexually stereotypical laws that apply to all employees, not simply women.

See also Court-packing plan of Franklin D. Roosevelt; *Darby Lumber Co., United States v.*; Due process of law; Hughes, Charles Evans; *Lochner v. New York*; New Deal.

West Virginia State Board of Education v. Barnette

COURT: U.S. Supreme Court

DATE: Decided June 14, 1943

SIGNIFICANCE: In an important recognition of freedom of conscience, the Supreme Court held in favor of Jehovah's Witnesses children who had refused to salute the flag and recite the Pledge of Allegiance at their public school

On June 3, 1940, the Supreme Court decided *Minersville School District v. Gobitis* and upheld a state law requiring public school children to salute the flag and recite the Pledge of Allegiance. The Justices voted 8-1 to reject the argument by Jehovah's Witnesses children and their parents that they should be excused from the ceremony because of their religious beliefs.

Reaction to the ruling was highly critical among scholars and in the legal profession. Newspaper editorials disapproved of the outcome. Local school officials reacted enthusiastically, however, enacting similar provisions all across the country. The heightened sense of loyalty and patriotism during World War II contributed to public outrages against Jehovah's Witnesses, including physical attacks and torchings of their meeting halls.

The Board of Education of West Virginia resolved that the flag salute and the Pledge of Allegiance be a regular part of the school day and that refusal to participate be regarded as an act of insubordination. Jehovah's Witnesses children were expelled in large numbers and threatened with being sent to reformatories; their parents were threatened with criminal prosecution for causing delinquency. In response, the parents brought suit in federal court. They explained that according to their religious belief the flag ceremony violated the Book of Exodus prohibition against bowing down before graven images.

The Supreme Court had changed by the time this case reached it. Justice James Byrnes had replaced Justice James McReynolds. Chief Justice Charles Evans Hughes had retired, and Justice Harlan Stone, who had dissented in *Gobitis*, was elevated to chief justice. Justice Robert H. Jackson was appointed to Stone's seat. Other justices simply changed their mind, perhaps affected by the almost universal condemnation of the decision and its aftermath of violence. Justices Hugo Black, William O. Douglas, and Frank Murphy took the unusual step of announcing in an intervening case that they now believed that *Gobitis* had been wrongly decided.

On Flag Day, Justice Jackson announced the 6-3 decision overruling *Gobitis*. His words are a stirring defense of the values of free speech and freedom of religion: "If there is any fixed star in our constitutional constellation, it is that no official, high or petty, can prescribe what shall be orthodox in politics, nationalism, religion, or other matters of opinion or force citizens to confess by word or act their faith therein." Justice Felix Frankfurter, who authored the *Gobitis* decision, wrote an eloquent dissent defending the principle of judicial self-restraint and urging deference to local elected leaders.

This landmark decision signaled the justices' new institutional willingness to intervene actively against majorities and state laws on behalf of minorities and civil liberties. It remains an important part of the First Amendment doctrine that protects free speech and free exercise of religion.

See also Civil disobedience; Civil liberties; Religion, free exercise of; School prayer.

Whig Party

DATE: Organized 1834

SIGNIFICANCE: The Whig Party, begun as an anti-Jackson party and including John C. Calhoun and Henry Clay, was influential in its advocacy of a national bank system to be partly owned by the federal government

The Whig Party first appeared as a national party in 1834. It represented an amalgamation of the southern nullifiers led by John C. Calhoun of South Carolina and members of the former National Republican Party loyal to Henry Clay of Kentucky. Later, a third group, represented by Daniel Webster of Massachusetts, temporarily joined the Whigs. The name "whigs" appeared in 1832 as a term of opposition to the administration of Andrew Jackson, whose followers were labeled "tories."

Whigs in general came from the ranks of planters and merchants in the South, merchants and businessmen in the North, and westerners anxious for federal aid toward the expansion of internal roadways and harbors. Pinning down the Whigs on specific policies, however, depended entirely on the individual in question. Calhoun, for example, strongly favored "states' rights" and developed a thorough constitutional defense of the concept. The other prominent Whig, Henry Clay, was a nationalist who sought to weave together the various sections of the country by providing all sections certain benefits at the hands of the federal government. Whigs won relatively few elections—Whig presidential candidates won only two, and both Whigs died in office before the end of their first term—leaving the Whigs little in the way of a judicial legacy. Daniel Webster, who argued *Charles River Bridge v. Warren Bridge Co.* for the Charles River Bridge Company, fought for a strict interpretation of contract clauses in the Constitution, but his views could hardly be considered typical of a "Whig concept of justice."

The Whigs had their most important influence in the numerous arguments, bills, and battles related to the Second Bank of the United States and the sub-treasury system; they unsuccessfully struggled to maintain a national bank that would be owned in part by the federal government. More often, the Whigs were the anti-Jackson party that provided an outlet for those who saw the Democrats as excessively aggrandizing power in the hands of the executive branch.

See also Calhoun, John C.; *Charles River Bridge v. Warren Bridge Co.*; Clay, Henry; Jacksonian democracy; States' rights.

White, Edward Douglass (Nov. 3, 1845, near Thibodaux, La.—May 19, 1921, Washington, D.C.)

IDENTIFICATION: Ninth chief justice of the United States

SIGNIFICANCE: White provided moderately conservative leadership to the Supreme Court during the Progressive era

White was elected to the Louisiana senate in 1875. In 1879, he became an associate justice of the Louisiana Supreme Court, but he left the bench in 1880. He reentered politics in 1891 with election to the United States Senate, where he served until President Grover Cleveland appointed him an associate justice of the U.S. Supreme Court in 1894. President William Howard Taft elevated him to chief justice in 1910. He was the first associate justice to be appointed chief justice. During his twenty-seven years on the Court, White generally wrote or concurred in conservative opinions but occasionally assumed a liberal position. His decisions in *Pollock v. Farmer's Loan & Trust Company* (1895), *Lochner v. New York* (1905), the Insular Cases (1901-1904), and various antitrust cases reveal his progressivism. He also helped to preserve the concept of dual federalism in the relationship between state and national gov-

Edward Douglass White was the first Supreme Court associate justice to be named chief justice of the United States. (Painting by Albert Rosenthal, collection of the Supreme Court of the United States)

ernment authority. He died May 19, 1921, from complications of bladder surgery.

See also Federalism; *Lochner v. New York*; Supreme Court of the United States.

White-collar crime

DEFINITION: Offenses against criminal or regulatory laws committed by individuals, organizations, or government agencies using the power afforded by their otherwise legitimate occupation, business, or public office

SIGNIFICANCE: White-collar crime accounts for more economic, physical, and social harm to the United States than do all serious conventional crimes, while being the least controlled type of crime

Ever since Edwin Sutherland first introduced the concept in 1939, "white-collar crime" has been controversial. Questions about whether it is "real" crime, whether its offenders should be treated as criminals, and what types of offenses should be included remain unresolved. Such problems, together with the complexity of white-collar offenses, their relative invisibility, the wide dispersal of their victims, the difficulty of enforcement, and their historical neglect by academic criminology, have brought numerous attempts at redefinition.

Three features of white-collar crime are particularly important in defining it. First, the offender must occupy a legitimate structural position in society, such as legal occupation or political office, and his or her primary activity must be involved with that position. This excludes primarily criminal enterprises, such as organized crime. Second, the offense must involve an illegal use of the power afforded by legitimate positions for the purpose of increasing the economic, political, or social standing of the perpetrator. Third, both offenders and victims of white-collar crime may consist of individuals or large groups of individuals.

Corporate and Occupational Crime. Emphasis on one or more of these features has given rise to several distinctions and typologies. One of the most enduring distinctions is between "corporate crime"—offenses committed by corporate officials, primarily on behalf of and by the corporation as a whole—and "occupational crime," offenses committed by individuals, primarily for themselves, in the course of their occupation.

Corporate crime, also called business crime, organizational crime, elite deviance, and corporate deviance, is referred to by some as "crimes of the powerful" or "suite crime." Hence power refers to the offenders' structural position in society rather than to their use of power in offending. Thus, crimes by wage-earning employees would be considered crimes of the powerless. Examples of corporate crime include price-fixing (as was once practiced by Standard Oil), environmental pollution (such as that caused by the *Exxon Valdez* oil spill), health and safety violations, unsafe production, food and drug violations, antitrust cases, deceptive advertising, manufacture of faulty products, bribery and corruption, consumer fraud and unnecessary services, corporate tax evasion and illegal stock manipulations, off-the-books employment, and industrial es-

pionage. "Elite deviance" also refers to crimes by governments, or "state crime." Examples include police entrapment, systemic police corruption, invasion of privacy, government medical experiments, human rights violations against U.S. citizens, and political repression against other nations.

Occupational crime, on the other hand, describes individual offenses by officials, professionals, or employees. Any classification which detracts from an emphasis on crimes of the powerful should be excluded, however; for this reason "crimes of the occupationally powerful," although a somewhat awkward phrase, is a preferred concept. It includes crimes by persons in powerful positions, offices, or professions. It also retains Sutherland's concept of offenders as persons of "respectability and high social status." Examples include insider trading, bribery of police officers, corruption of politicians, computer fraud, Medicaid and Medicare fraud by doctors, and tax evasion by the self-employed. While many white-collar crimes involve gaining money, materials, or services by deceptive means, some are intended to obtain political or social advantage. In either case, victims may suffer physical harm, including death, as well as violations of their human rights and trust.

Cost, Extent, and Seriousness. Given the diversity and complexity of white-collar crime and its varied and dispersed victims, estimates of the economic cost of white-collar crime vary enormously. Some experts put white-collar crime costs between five and twenty-five times the total cost of conventional crime, with consumer fraud alone accounting for more than half this cost. The 1980's savings and loan crisis has been conservatively estimated to cost about $500 billion, and evidence suggests that white-collar crime was the major factor in 70 to 80 percent of thrift failures. One study found that two-thirds of Fortune 500 companies had convictions ranging from price-fixing to hazardous waste dumping between 1975 and 1985.

According to government-funded research over a two-year period, civil and criminal actions filed with twenty-five federal agencies against 477 of the country's largest manufacturing corporations and 105 of the largest wholesale and retail services revealed that 60 percent of the corporations had at least one legal action against them, with an average of 4.2 violations. Multiple violators, averaging 23.5 violations per corporation, accounted for 13 percent of those charged (8 percent of all corporations studied), and 38 companies committed 52 percent of all violations.

Contrary to popular belief, public opinion research suggests that the majority of Americans rank specific white-collar crimes more seriously than some conventional crimes and favor harsh punishments, including imprisonment. In one poll, the manufacturer of unsafe automobiles was seen as worse than a mugger, and a corporate price-fixer worse than a burglar.

Causes. The central explanatory issue is whether white-collar crime is an individual or systemic problem. Individual explanations rely on psychological theories, according to which either behavioral traits or social learning may lead to amoral, antisocial personalities. Social-structural or systemic explanations argue that capital accumulation and the pursuit of the profit in an uncertain environment pressure corporations to reduce financial risk through cheating. Capitalist organizations are hierarchically differentiated into replaceable role positions whose incumbents are socialized to conform to company expectations. Each position, and each subunit, conducts a specialized part of the process of achieving the overall goals, none of which need be harmful in isolation. The combined process may be harmful, even lethal, but no individual can easily be held accountable. Organizational recruitment into powerful positions includes a selection process whereby precisely the psychological and moral qualities that lead to legitimate success (such as high ambition, shrewdness, and moral flexibility) also facilitate rule breaking. This situation is more likely to be the case where loyalty to the corporation has been cultivated through involvement, inducement, and social reward and where disloyalty is met with the threat of replacement by the more compliant.

Laws and Enforcement Problems. Several problems exist in attempting to control white-collar crime. First, state crime and government agency crime are especially difficult to control because government entities rely on self-regulation by the very agencies responsible for control. In addition, participants are reluctant to "blow the whistle" on their colleagues. Several major obstacles to controlling crime relate to powerful corporate influence on the legislative process, which reduces the effectiveness of laws controlling harmful corporate practices. Historically the United States has tried to deal with collective actors with laws intended to be applied to individuals. In the 1970's this changed as various protected categories were established and formal penalties were increased. Laws were still regulatory rather than criminal, however, and they contained numerous loopholes built in by corporate lobbying at the legislative stage. Moreover, enforcement agencies are understaffed; notably, there are not enough inspectors. Typically laws are symbolic rather than real and are too general to be effective. In addition, corporations practice a "politics of resistance," including preemptive public relations campaigns, the use of the media to spin the original story, employment of extensive legal advice, and use of the *nolo contendere* (no contest) plea to avoid civil liability (the plea is entered in 73 percent of all antitrust convictions).

Arrests, Prosecutions, and Convictions. In the year 1992 there were 424,200 arrests for fraud, an increase of 24.7 percent over 1983. In 1992, 57.9 percent of fraud arrestees were men, 64.6 percent were white, and 95.7 percent were over eighteen years old. There were 8,184 suspects in criminal matters concluded by U.S. attorneys for a variety of regulatory offenses in 1991, up 39.0 percent from 1982. Defendants handled by U.S. attorneys in 1993 for a variety of white-collar crimes, such as various frauds (including health care frauds and tax frauds), antitrust violations, and bank embezzlements, amounted to 5,721; 81.8 percent were convicted.

Suspects convicted in U.S. district courts in 1992 for regulatory offenses numbered 2,179, up 20.2 percent from 1982. Of 2,054 people convicted for regulatory offenses in 1990, 9.9 percent were fined, 59.0 percent received probation, and 38.9 percent received prison sentences (either with or without other punishments) for an average sentence of 26.7 months (only 12.9 months for antitrust violations), with the average time served being 18.2 months.

Evidence exists that, beginning in the 1980's, local prosecutors increasingly prosecuted economic crime, occupational safety and health violations, and illegal toxic dumping. More than 25 percent of respondents to a survey of 632 district attorneys said that corporate prosecutions had increased during their tenure and that they expected this to continue. Most commonly prosecuted (in 1988) was consumer fraud, followed by environmental offenses, false claims, insurance fraud, and securities fraud. Major limitations to prosecution are a lack of resources, the complex and technical nature of the offenses, the difficulty of establishing intent, and the reluctance of victims to cooperate. By the mid-1990's, changes in the U.S. government had reversed the trend toward more enforcement and had weakened legislation by placing limits on penalties (penalties that were already widely viewed as too inadequate to be effective).

Department of Justice data show that between 1982 and 1992 convictions in U.S. district courts for several regulatory offenses increased by about 20 percent. Antitrust convictions went down from 163 in 1982 to 69 in 1992, the lowest figure in ten years. Convictions for various types of fraud increased by 17 percent in the same period, but that increase occurred between 1982 and 1985; since then, the conviction rate for frauds has been stable at around 10,000 cases per year.

Even at its best, enforcement has been lax and has had little follow-through. As of 1982, for example, 60 percent of convicted corporations had not paid their fines, which left $38 billion uncollected. In addition, fines are relatively insignificant: Calculated as a proportion of income and standardized to a person earning $30,000, the average fine works out to the equivalent of $3.60. The typical Occupational Safety and Health Administration (OSHA) penalty for offending decreased from $2,093 in 1972 to $511 in 1990, and in twenty years only one person had received a jail sentence. The number of OSHA inspectors decreased by 15 percent in the 1980's, and the average firm can expect an inspection once every twenty-two years. Only one-third of the publicized fines are collected.

Some evidence suggests that public support of whistleblowing and such practices as encouraging employees to take video recorders into corporate board rooms could help control white-collar crime. Some experts suggest the use of negative publicity and public shaming. Others advocate changing American corporate structures—including the implementation of corporate chartering, licensing, and strict liability rules for executives—and making boards of directors directly accountable for a corporation's actions. Others recommend increasing enforcement through a greater number of inspectors, interagency cooperation, independent research, and random inspections. Sentencing suggestions include corporate divestiture, community and public service, and funding for research on prevention of white-collar crime. Some experts have argued that until political influence is controlled—by controlling lobbyists, political action committees, and campaign financing—little progress will be made. —*Stuart Henry*

See also Bribery; Computer crime; Consumer fraud; Embezzlement; Fraud; Insider trading; Political corruption; Securities and Exchange Commission (SEC); Tax evasion; Theft.

BIBLIOGRAPHY

Three excellent anthologies, M. David Ermann and Richard J. Lundman, eds., *Corporate and Governmental Deviance* (4th ed. New York: Oxford University Press, 1992); Kip Schlegel and David Weisburd, eds., *White-Collar Crime Reconsidered* (Boston: Northeastern University Press, 1992); and Gilbert Geis and Paul Jesilow, eds., *White-Collar Crime* (Newbury Park, Calif.: Sage Periodicals Press, 1993), give theoretical overviews and specific case illustrations of a variety of white-collar crime, including problems of enforcement, sentencing, sanctions, and deterrence. For a critical overview and synthesis, see Tony G. Poveda, *Rethinking White-Collar Crime* (Westport, Conn.: Praeger, 1994). Marshall Clinard and Peter Yeager, *Corporate Crime* (New York: Free Press, 1980), is one of the best studies of crimes by the top five hundred manufacturing companies. On fraud-facilitated leveraged buyouts and junk bonds, see Mary Zey, *Banking on Fraud* (New York: Aldine de Gruyter, 1993), and for the savings and loan crisis see Stephen Pizzo et al., *Inside Job* (New York: McGraw Hill, 1989). For a study of law creation and the effectiveness of safe production see Nancy Frank, *Crimes Against Health and Safety* (New York: Harrow and Heston, 1985). Finally, on crimes of government policy, an excellent source is Gregg Barak, *Crimes by the Capitalist State* (Albany, N.Y.: State University of New York Press, 1991).

Wickard v. Filburn

COURT: U.S. Supreme Court
DATE: Decided November 9, 1942
SIGNIFICANCE: This case effectively eliminated the use of the interstate commerce clause of the Constitution as a restraint on federal authority

Beginning in 1933, the federal government attempted to raise farm prices by measures intended to restrict output. After the Agricultural Adjustment Act of 1933 had been declared unconstitutional in 1936, Congress adopted the Agricultural Adjustment Act of 1938. The law authorized the secretary of agriculture to establish a national acreage allotment for wheat that would be translated into a permissible quota for each farmer. Farmers were given an opportunity to reject the national quota level in an annual referendum vote. Production in excess of the quota would incur a financial penalty.

Roscoe Filburn, an Ohio farmer, produced 239 bushels of wheat in excess of his allotment and was assessed a penalty of $117. He obtained an injunction from a federal district court against Secretary of Agriculture Claude Wickard. Filburn used much of his wheat output on his own farm, chiefly for feed and seed. He claimed that the government policy went beyond the boundaries of interstate commerce. He further argued that a

speech by Wickard had misled farmers into supporting the quota in the referendum, and that the increase in penalties by a statutory amendment in May, 1941, was improper when applied to production already undertaken.

The Supreme Court rejected Filburn's claim and upheld federal authority. The contentions concerning Wickard's speech and the penalty increase, both of which had been accepted by the district court, were dismissed. As for the commerce clause, the Court noted its previous broad construction in *United States v. Darby Lumber Co.* (1941), upholding the federal minimum-wage law. They acknowledged that the 1938 law extended regulatory authority to production not entering commerce but being consumed on the farm. Such an extension was not improper: "[E]ven if appellee's activity be local and though it may not be regarded as commerce, it may still . . . be reached by Congress if it exerts a substantial economic effect on interstate commerce." Home-consumed production of wheat in the aggregate was a potentially important influence on the price of wheat. The propriety of such regulation was a political question, said the Court, rather than an issue of constitutionality.

Taking this decision and the *Darby* case in combination, the Supreme Court clearly served notice that it was not inclined to limit the scope of federal authority by reference to the commerce clause. Thus the doctrine of *United States v. E. C. Knight Co.* (1895), that "commerce succeeds to [that is, follows] manufacture, and is not a part of it," was put aside. It is probably not mere coincidence that the *Filburn* case came during World War II, which involved such extreme extensions of federal authority as the military draft and direct controls over wages and prices. The decisions in *Filburn* and *Darby* also removed obstacles to later extensions of federal authority into employment discrimination, health and safety, and environmental protection.

See also *Carter v. Carter Coal Co.*; Commerce clause; *Darby Lumber Co., United States v.*; Federalism; New Deal.

Wickersham Commission

DATE: May, 1929, to January 19, 1931
SIGNIFICANCE: The Wickersham Commission's final report confirmed that after a decade of Prohibition the Eighteenth Amendment was still proving difficult to enforce

After ten years of national Prohibition mandated by the Eighteenth Amendment (1919), President Herbert Hoover appointed former attorney general George Wickersham to head the new Law Observance and Enforcement Commission. The commission's function was to study the effectiveness of the Eighteenth Amendment as a basis for future policy recommendations. It was common public knowledge that Prohibition had been marked by a national crime wave (witness the criminal career of Al Capone), by widespread bootlegging and smuggling, as well as by the corruption of police and public officials.

In 1931, the commission (generally called the Wickersham Commission) reported that law enforcement was being rendered ineffectual by the high profits of the illegal liquor trade and that the general public was disaffected with the Eighteenth

Amendment. The commission called for revisions in the approach to Prohibition, chiefly in recommending placing enforcement entirely in federal hands, but it did not call for the amendment's repeal. President Hoover continued to oppose repeal.

See also Capone, Alphonse (Al); Commercialized vice; Federal Bureau of Investigation (FBI); Prohibition; Temperance movement.

Wills, trusts, and estate planning

Definition: The set of rules governing the transfer of wealth at death

Significance: By determining who gets the property of someone who dies, these rules affect the distribution of wealth in society; they also affect the extent to which the dead can influence the lives of their survivors

State law dominates the nontax aspects of this topic, and states' approaches vary widely. Some states have adopted some or all of the Uniform Probate Code (UPC), a statute designed as a model to both modernize and unify the law. Congress has established a federal tax law governing gifts, estates, and "generation-skipping transfers." One important distinction is between "probate" and "nonprobate" property. In general, probate property is property someone owns alone. Nonprobate property usually is shared. Joint bank accounts or stocks, life insurance, living trusts, and real property owned in joint tenancy all avoid the probate system. Avoiding probate, however, does not mean avoiding federal tax; they are two different systems.

Intestacy. Each state has an "intestate" statute that tells how to distribute probate property not covered by a will. The statute applies to people who never made wills, people whose wills are invalid, and people whose wills do not cover all their property. The details vary among states, but common patterns emerge. Principal problems include how much to presume about what distributions most people would prefer, and whether other public policies, such as fair treatment of surviving relatives, should override those presumed intentions.

Spouses and descendants have the first claims. Many states share the estate between the surviving spouse and the descendants. Others give everything to the surviving spouse and rely on the spouse to serve as a conduit to the children. If the surviving spouse is not the parent of the children, as commonly happens in second-marriage situations, the children may get a larger intestate share. That approach protects the children against the possibility that they will get nothing at the step-parent's death. If no spouse or descendants exist, the property usually goes to various descendants of the decedent's grandparents or to the next-closest surviving relative.

Wills. To change the result of an intestacy scheme, an individual makes a will, a formal document telling how to distribute property. A will may also name an executor to handle the estate or appoint a guardian for minors or incapacitated relatives. State laws vary on the elements involved in creating a valid will. In almost all situations, it must be in writing and

signed by the person making it, but many states add other formal requirements.

One controversy is the extent to which the law should require a long list of formalities. Wills that fail on formal grounds may still reflect the maker's intention. To make will execution easier, some states have adopted the UPC's approach of shortening the list of formalities. Others allow wills executed in "substantial compliance" with the statute. A third approach is to recognize noncomplying wills if there is clear evidence that the testator intended the document to be a will.

Trusts. Trusts are extremely flexible devices for holding property in a way to benefit families. One can create a trust by giving property to someone else (the trustee) with instructions to manage the property for the benefit of others. Testamentary trusts are created by will. Living trusts are created during the creator's lifetime, so the creators have the choice of giving the property to a trustee or naming themselves as trustees. Trusts can provide solutions to a wide variety of planning problems: providing for college, supporting children with disabilities, caring for aging parents. Living trusts have become particularly popular as probate-evidence devices.

Two justice issues surrounding trusts are the related questions of the extent to which trust income or assets should be available to creditors of trust beneficiaries and how long a trust ought to continue. "Spendthrift" trusts prohibit creditors from attaching trust property to enforce their claims. Although commentators have long argued that such trusts favor the rich, virtually all states allow them. Most states, however, effectively limit the time period a noncharitable trust can continue to about a hundred years. Under this approach, property eventually returns to the control of people living at the time rather than being subject to the directions of people who died long ago.

Another question is whether people can use trusts to defeat the claims of their surviving spouses. In states not following the community property system, a spouse disappointed with a will's terms can "elect against" it and instead take a share of the probate estate. Spouses in community property states typically have no such right because they are already guaranteed their share of the community property.

An elective share extending only to probate property ignores the vast amounts of property not subject to the probate system. For example, one spouse might defeat the other's claim by putting everything in trust and leaving the survivor with nothing in the probate estate to elect against. Some states prevent this result by allowing surviving spouses to claim a share of trust property as well.

Estate Planning. Estate planning is the process by which lawyers and other advisers use a wide variety of devices and doctrines to develop ideas meeting clients' family and business needs.

Tax. Most states impose one of two types of death taxes. The first, estate taxes, are based on the wealth of the decedent. The second, inheritance taxes, are based on how much each recipient gets. The federal government also imposes a comprehensive system of gift, estate, and generation-skipping transfers. The last of those is assessed primarily against long-term trusts of very wealthy people. —*Roger W. Andersen*

See also Fiduciary trust; Property rights; Taxation and justice.

BIBLIOGRAPHY

A popular source for general audiences is Norman F. Dacey's *How to Avoid Probate* (5th ed. New York: HarperPerennial, 1993). An accessible student text is Roger W. Andersen, *Understanding Trusts and Estates* (New York: Matthew Bender, 1994). Comprehensive treatments include William H. Page, *Page on the Law of Wills* (Rev. by Jeffrey A. Schoenblum. Cincinnati: Anderson, 1991); and Austin W. Scott and William F. Fratcher, *The Law of Trusts* (4th ed. Boston: Little, Brown, 1987-1994).

Wilson, James (Sept. 14, 1742, Carskerdo, Fifeshire, Scotland—Aug. 21, 1798, Edenton, N.C.)

IDENTIFICATION: Supreme Court justice, 1789-1798

SIGNIFICANCE: One of only six Americans to have signed both the Declaration of Independence and the Constitution, this founding father and eminent jurist ended his days a fugitive

As a strong Federalist, an advocate of popular sovereignty, and one of the principal theoreticians of the Constitution, James Wilson had every reason to hope for public office, but his highly visible investment activities—sometimes tainted by conflicts of interest and frequently throwing him into debt—probably made him unelectable. Instead, he offered himself to President George Washington as a candidate for chief justice, but he was passed over in 1789 and again in 1796. Wilson served almost nine years on the Supreme Court as an associate justice, and during most of that time he continued to speculate in land. His record as a justice was spotty, and after his investments began to fail in the 1790's, he was hounded by creditors and even jailed once for debt. In 1798, amid rumors of impeachment, he sought refuge with fellow justice James Iredell in Edenton, North Carolina, where, in an inn near the courthouse, he died at the age of fifty-five.

See also Constitution, U.S.; Federalist Party; Supreme Court of the United States.

Wilson, Woodrow (Dec. 28, 1856, Staunton, Va.—Feb. 3, 1924, Washington, D.C.)

IDENTIFICATION: President of the United States, 1913-1921

SIGNIFICANCE: Responsible for significant reform legislation, Wilson is most famous as a promoter of the League of Nations

Woodrow Wilson was graduated from Princeton University in 1879, obtained an LL.B from the University of Virginia in 1881, and took a Ph.D. in history from The Johns Hopkins University in 1886. After short appointments at Bryn Mawr College (1885-1888) and Wesleyan University (1888), he joined Princeton University in 1890. In 1902, he became university president and began an intensive reorganization. After being stymied in regard to a system of resident colleges and a new graduate college organization, Wilson ran for governor of New Jersey. As governor (1910-1912) he secured passage of extensive regulatory and reform legislation.

In 1912, Wilson was elected president of the United States, advocating reform and business regulation. His administration passed the Underwood Simmons Law (1913), cutting tariffs and instituting an income tax, the Glass-Owens Act (1913), providing for the Federal Reserve System and curbing concentration of monetary wealth, the Clayton Antitrust Act, the Sherman Antitrust Act, and the Adamson Act, mandating an eight-hour day in the railroad industry. It also established the Federal Trade Commission. In foreign affairs Wilson established a policy of nonrecognition of governments founded on revolution or established by constitutional violation.

During World War I Wilson set up broad controls over the economy, restricted civil rights, and established a draft. Following the war, Wilson tried to make moral peace embodying his Fourteen Points. He established the League of Nations, but the United States Senate refused to ratify the Treaty of Versailles. Wilson wrote a dozen books, including *Congressional Government* (1885) and *Constitutional Government in the United States* (1908).

See also Clayton Antitrust Act; Conscription; Espionage Act; Federal Trade Commission (FTC); International law; Sherman Antitrust Act.

President Woodrow Wilson's administration pressed Congress to pass reform legislation; he also established the League of Nations after World War I. (Library of Congress)

Wiretapping. *See* **Electronic surveillance**

Wisconsin v. Mitchell

COURT: U.S. Supreme Court
DATE: Decided June 11, 1993
SIGNIFICANCE: This hate crime case was the first of its type to be heard by the U.S. Supreme Court; this landmark decision has opened the way for more extensive hate crime legislation, and it signals that such legislation will be upheld as constitutional by the court in most cases

Following a showing of the 1988 film *Mississippi Burning*, several African American men and boys congregated at an apartment complex to talk about the film. After a discussion of a scene in the film in which a young African American boy is beaten by a white man, the accused, Todd Mitchell, asked those who joined him outside if they were ready to go after a white man.

Walking on the opposite side of the street and saying nothing, fourteen-year-old Gregory Riddick approached the complex. Mitchell selected three individuals from the group to go after Riddick. The victim was beaten, and his tennis shoes were stolen.

In a Kenosha, Wisconsin, trial court, Mitchell was convicted as a party to the crime of aggravated battery. By Wisconsin law, this crime carries a maximum prison sentence of two years. Mitchell's sentence was extended to four years, however, under a state statute commonly known as the "hate crimes" statute. This statute provides for sentence extensions if it can be determined that the victim was selected because of his or her race, religion, color, disability, sexual orientation, national origin, or ancestry.

Mitchell appealed his conviction and the extended sentence. His conviction was upheld by the court of appeals, but the Supreme Court of Wisconsin reversed the decision of the appellate court. Wisconsin's Supreme Court held that the "hate crimes" statute violated the defendant's First Amendment protection for freedom of speech because it was unconstitutionally overbroad and punished only what the state legislature found to be offensive. Moreover, the state Supreme Court believed that this statute would have a "chilling effect" on a citizen's freedom of speech; that is, a citizen would fear reprisal for actions which might follow the utterance of prejudiced or biased speech.

The United States Supreme Court reversed the state court's decision. Chief Justice William Rehnquist wrote the opinion in this unanimous decision. The Court held that Mitchell's First Amendment rights to free speech had not been violated. The Court pointed out that the statute was not aimed at speech but at conduct, which is not protected by the First Amendment. The Court also addressed the "chilling effect" of the statute, finding that such would not be the case and that the state Supreme Court's hypothesis was far too speculative to be entertained. This decision indicates that the Supreme Court appears ready to uphold legislation designed to enhance punishment for criminal acts based on bigotry and bias without making bigoted or biased speech itself a crime.

See also Assault; Hate crimes; Racial and ethnic discrimination; *R.A.V. v. City of St. Paul*; Speech and press, freedom of.

Wisconsin v. Yoder

COURT: U.S. Supreme Court
DATE: Decided May 15, 1972
SIGNIFICANCE: Balancing the state's interest in education against the freedom to exercise one's religion, the Supreme Court insisted that any governmental burden on this freedom must be justified by a compelling state interest

Jonas Yoder and two other members of Amish churches were convicted and fined five dollars each for violating Wisconsin's compulsory school-attendance law, which required children to attend school until the age of sixteen. Following their religious traditions, these Amish parents refused to send their children, ages fourteen and fifteen, to school beyond the eighth grade. The parents argued that the Wisconsin law violated their free exercise of religion, as protected by the First and Fourteenth Amendments. After the Wisconsin Supreme Court ruled in favor of the parents, the state of Wisconsin appealed to the U.S. Supreme Court.

The Court voted 6 to 1 (although Justice William Douglas' dissent was only in part) to uphold the position of the parents. Writing for the majority, Chief Justice Warren Burger began with the premise that the free exercise of religion was a fundamental right that could be overbalanced only by state interests of the "highest order." The Amish objected to formal education beyond the eighth grade because they believed that secondary education exposed children to "worldly" influences that tended to distance Amish youth from their religious community. According to traditions of almost three centuries, Burger stated, it was impossible to separate the Amish faith from a simple, nonsecular mode of life, and government institutions were prohibited from evaluating the desirability of particular religious beliefs.

Burger acknowledged that normally the state might enforce compulsory education laws because of the state's interest that children learn to become "self-sufficient participants in society." The Amish community, however, had a long-established system of informal vocational training that prepared children for life in an agrarian community. Burger indicated that nonreligious motivations would not justify exemption from school-attendance laws.

In a partial dissent, Justice Douglas argued that the issue was the religious freedom of the children rather than that of the parents. He insisted that exemption should not be granted until the children were asked if they wished a high-school education. The majority refused to consider this point, however, since only the parents were parties to litigation, and because of traditional rights of parents to control the religious education of their children.

Yoder was important as the Court's most advanced reaffirmation of the principles of *Sherbert v. Verner* (1963), requiring that states accommodate religious practices according to the dual criteria of the compelling state interest test and the least restrictive alternative test. In *Employment Division, Department of Human Resources of Oregon v. Smith* (1990), however, the Court adopted a more restrictive view of the right for legal exemption based on religious exercise.

See also Civil liberties; *Employment Division, Department of Human Resources of Oregon v. Smith*; *Pierce v. Society of Sisters*; Religion, free exercise of; *Reynolds v. United States*; *Sherbert v. Verner*.

Witherspoon v. Illinois

COURT: U.S. Supreme Court
DATE: Decided June 3, 1968
SIGNIFICANCE: In this groundbreaking decision, the Supreme Court decided that prospective jurors with reservations about the death penalty could not be excluded from service in a criminal proceeding

The Sixth Amendment to the U.S. Constitution guarantees accused citizens the right to trial by an impartial jury of peers. This deceptively simple guarantee has come under fire in cases too numerous to mention. During the 1960's, many noteworthy cases advanced to the Supreme Court regarding the composition and unanimity of the jury in criminal cases. In 1968, the *Witherspoon* case compounded the jury-selection question with the issue of capital punishment.

Using an Illinois statute, the prosecution at William Witherspoon's murder trial in Cook County, Illinois, eliminated almost half of the potential jurors by challenging those who had reservations about their ability to impose a death sentence. This exclusion occurred without any determination of the level of reservation; that is, the potential jurors were excluded for any degree of uncertainty about imposition of a death sentence. The defendant, Witherspoon, appealed his case on the grounds that such a broad exclusion of jurors prevented him from being tried by an impartial jury as guaranteed in the Sixth Amendment. Witherspoon claimed that a jury absent of those opposed or at least uncertain about capital punishment would under no circumstances be impartial or representative of the community.

The Supreme Court agreed in a majority opinion written by Justice Potter Stewart. Witherspoon's death sentence was voided by the Court; however, his conviction was not overturned. The Court agreed with the defendant that a jury devoid of objectors to capital punishment was sure to be "woefully short" of the impartiality guaranteed by the Sixth Amendment and extended to the states under the Fourteenth Amendment. In the majority opinion, the Court stated that those prospective jurors who expressed a total disinclination toward ever imposing the death penalty could be excluded; however, persons who merely had reservations in the matter could not be excluded for their reservations alone.

The Court went on to state that juries must attempt to mirror the feelings of the community. In any given community there will be a certain number of people who are unsure of their feelings about capital punishment. This point of view should not be avoided in jury selection, the Court ruled, as inclusion of such undecided jurors will insure neutrality on the sentencing issue and will allow the jury more adequately to reflect the conscience of the community.

While ruling that a jury totally committed to the imposition of the death penalty cannot be selected deliberately, as this would deprive a defendant of life without due process, the Court did not issue a constitutional rule that would have required the reversal of every jury selected under the Illinois statute. The Court did not state that a jury composed of persons in favor of capital punishment would be predisposed to convict, only that such a jury would be predisposed in the sentencing element of a trial.

The *Witherspoon* decision was an early test of the Supreme Court's position on capital punishment as well as on jury composition and selection. The Court indicated its willingness to uphold criminal convictions while examining the sentencing procedures being used in the states. At no point in its opinion did the Court express disfavor for the death penalty; rather, the opinion targeted only the constitutional implications of the jury-selection process. In other words, the *Witherspoon* decision indicated that within constitutional bounds, communities would be left to choose whether or not to impose the death penalty.

See also Capital punishment; Criminal procedure; Jury system; *Voir dire*.

Wolf v. Colorado

COURT U.S. Supreme Court
DATE: Decided June 27, 1949
SIGNIFICANCE: The decision of the U.S. Supreme Court in this search and seizure case emphasized the importance of the individual protections guaranteed by the Fourth Amendment against illegal searches and seizures but failed to mandate use of the exclusionary rule in state courts

The United States Supreme Court has heard a number of cases related to the protection against unlawful searches and seizures guaranteed by the Fourth Amendment of the U.S. Constitution. Until early in the twentieth century, rules of common law allowed the admission of illegally obtained evidence in criminal trials throughout the country. A case decided by the U.S. Supreme Court in 1914, *Weeks v. United States*, changed the rules of evidence in federal criminal proceedings by instituting an "exclusionary rule" that required the barring of illegally obtained evidence in those trials.

The exclusionary rule in criminal trials prohibits the use of evidence which has been gained from an unconstitutional search and seizure. This rule was designed to give teeth to the Fourth Amendment in order to protect the integrity of trial courts from tainted evidence and to decrease police misconduct in the collection of evidence.

Wolf v. Colorado was the first case to argue that this exclusionary rule should also be mandatory for state criminal proceedings. Wolf was accused and convicted of performing illegal abortions. The evidence introduced at trial included his appointment book, which had been taken by a deputy sheriff without a warrant. After acquiring the appointment book, the deputy sheriff questioned patients whose names he saw in the book. By doing so, he obtained enough evidence to charge the doctor with performing illegal abortions. Wolf appealed his conviction on the basis that the evidence used to convict him was a product of an illegal search and seizure in violation of his Fourth Amendment liberties.

Writing for the majority, Justice Felix Frankfurter stated with undeniable enthusiasm that the Fourth Amendment protections are a vital and basic part of the concept of "ordered liberty." That is to say, the protections against illegal searches and seizures are fundamental to the American notion of freedom. The Court sustained Wolf's conviction, however, and stopped short of requiring use of the exclusionary rule in state courts. Rather, state courts were given the option of using or not using evidence which was obtained illegally. Justice Hugo Black wrote a concurring opinion, and Justice William Douglas wrote the dissenting opinion, which was joined by Justices Frank Murphy and Wiley Rutledge. It is important to note that the dissenting justices only disagreed with the Court's finding inasmuch as the Court failed to exclude the evidence.

This decision stood throughout the 1950's; however, by the turn of the decade, the Court was beginning to fine tune this position. Several loopholes in the earlier *Weeks* decision were closed, and by 1961, the Court was ready to hold the states accountable for Fourth Amendment protections through the application of the Fourteenth Amendment. *Mapp v. Ohio* (1961) extended the application of the exclusionary rule to state criminal proceedings, effectively overturning the decision rendered in *Wolf*.

This controversial rule of evidence has been revisited on numerous occasions in both judicial and political arenas. Indeed, throughout the 1970's and 1980's, the Court itself continued to redefine the criteria for determining that evidence had been obtained illegally. Critics of the exclusionary rule tout the numbers of criminals released and unpunished, the apathy among police forces across the nation, and so on. Advocates of the exclusionary rule seek to remind policy makers and the public of dangers of unrestrained governmental interference and police powers. Both sides continue to argue their cases in the light of the ever-changing political landscape.

See also Evidence, rules of; *Mapp v. Ohio*; Search and seizure; *Weeks v. United States*.

Woman suffrage

DEFINITION: The legal right of women to vote as the political equals of men

SIGNIFICANCE: Essential to full citizenship and a prerequisite for political redress, women's right to vote altered a common-law prejudice that women are men's legal inferiors and gradually contributed to feminist activism and the democratization of the American family

Ratification of the U.S. Constitution's Nineteenth Amendment in 1920 belatedly extended the franchise to American women in state and federal elections. As the ratification process began in 1918, women were without the vote in twenty-four of the then forty-eight states. With the exception of New Mexico, all these nonsuffrage states formed a tier that stretched, solidly in 1917, down the eastern seaboard from Maine to Louisiana. Twelve states permitted women to vote only in presidential elections, two others only in primaries. Only fifteen (mostly western) states extended full voting privileges to women.

Background. By 1920, agitation for granting woman suffrage was more than a century old. True, the general estate of white females in the United States during the eighteenth and early nineteenth centuries was more fortunate than conditions most women endured elsewhere. Nevertheless, their denial of the vote for 120 years after the Constitution went into effect was perceived by a vocal minority of women and sympathetic men as a glaring anomaly in an ostensibly free and increasingly democratic society.

A few white women participated in voting during the colonial era, and some enjoyed voting rights, again locally, through the nineteenth century, but these were insignificant exceptions to the prevailing practices of a male-dominated society. Furthermore, general preclusion of woman suffrage contrasted sharply with extensions of male suffrage. Universal white manhood suffrage, for example, was a reality by the mid-1840's, a distinctively American achievement. Moreover, in 1870, as a part of post-Civil War Reconstruction, ratification of the Fifteenth Amendment prohibited denial of the vote because of race, color, or previous conditions of servitude, thus granting the franchise to black males recently emancipated by the Thirteenth Amendment in 1865. Opinions held by a majority of eighteenth and nineteenth century women about the value of the franchise are unknown, but thousands of educated and articulate women certainly regarded denial of the vote as a glaring discontinuity in the overall advance of American democracy.

Early Pioneers. American women whose enthusiasm for equality remained latent at the end of the revolutionary era and the opening of the nineteenth century were receptive to the message of England's Mary Wollstonecraft. Although Wollstonecraft died in her thirties while giving birth, *A Vindication of the Rights of Women* (1792), her pathbreaking feminist document, enjoyed wide currency in North America. Wollstonecraft espoused women's full participation with men in a joint exercise of equal civil and political rights, along with women's liberation from their traditional status through access to education. Probably because many American women had already entertained ideas expressed in *A Vindication of the Rights of Women*, a few seized upon it as a source of inspiration—as did Theodosia Burr (and her husband, Aaron)—despite popular satires against it.

Among female reformers and their allies, woman suffrage had lower priority before the 1840's than did legal reforms in married women's property rights and alterations in laws of divorce. Their successes in these efforts opened wider vistas for them. In New York State, for example, victories in securing such changes encouraged a few women to participate in the utopian and reformist movements that flourished through the 1830's. In this context, women made impressive contributions

Upon gaining the vote in 1920, women had a legitimized political voice; here the League of Women Voters presents its proposed planks for the Democratic platform for the 1920 election. (Library of Congress)

to the abolitionist movement. Their eagerness to participate was signaled by the attendance of two American Quaker schoolteachers, Lucretia Mott and Elizabeth Cady Stanton, at the World Anti-Slavery Convention gathered in London in 1840. Though they were refused seats at the London convention, Mott and Stanton returned home with strengthened convictions. Within a few years, both women and male abolitionists were joined in American antislavery organizations by such reformers as Angelina and Sarah Grimké, Lucy Stone, Frances (Fanny) Wright, and Abby Kelley Foster. Often a divisive element within abolitionist ranks and usually discriminated against, women nevertheless found abolitionism a training ground that equipped them to move on to suffrage and other feminist reforms.

Seneca Falls. A gathering of about three hundred women in the Wesleyan chapel at Seneca Falls, New York, in July, 1848, has been widely viewed as the beginning of the woman suffrage movement in the United States. Its leaders were Elizabeth Cady Stanton and Lucretia Mott, both of whom may have

been converted to giving primacy to the suffrage issue by Massachusetts-born Oberlin College graduate Lucy Stone. Modeling their own Declaration of Sentiments on the Declaration of Independence, the women at Seneca Falls proclaimed the equality of the sexes and proceeded to pass a dozen resolutions enumerating specific women's rights. Curiously, the sole proposal not passed unanimously was the right to vote.

The extension of women's rights had been so long delayed that discussions of them inevitably produced differing priorities among their advocates and consequently caused divisions among them. In addition, many women were still committed overwhelmingly to domestic pursuits, and their energies were dispersed through other emancipating activities such as educational reform, temperance, and abolition. Nevertheless, the Seneca Falls declaration solicited wide public attention, and two years later Lucy Stone was able to found the Woman's Rights Convention in Worcester, Massachusetts, an organization of both female and male reformers dedicated primarily to woman suffrage. Unfortunately, the rancorous sectional

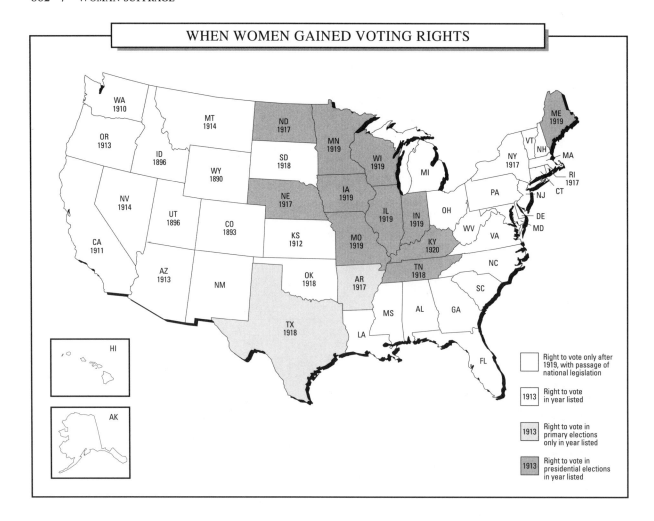

WHEN WOMEN GAINED VOTING RIGHTS

WA 1910
OR 1913
ID 1896
MT 1914
ND 1917
MN 1919
WI 1919
MI
ME 1919
VT
NH
NY 1917
MA
RI 1917
CT
NV 1914
UT 1896
WY 1890
SD 1918
NE 1917
IA 1919
IL 1919
IN 1919
OH
PA
NJ
DE
MD
CA 1911
CO 1893
KS 1912
MO 1919
KY 1920
WV
VA
AZ 1913
NM
OK 1918
AR 1917
TN 1918
NC
SC
TX 1918
MS
AL
GA
LA
FL

HI

AK

Right to vote only after 1919, with passage of national legislation

1913 Right to vote in year listed

1913 Right to vote in primary elections only in year listed

1913 Right to vote in presidential elections in year listed

controversies of the 1850's that soon led to Civil War preempted public interest in woman suffrage—indeed in all reforms except the antislavery movement.

Post-Civil War Campaigns. Suffragists had always believed that their close identification with the efforts of northern abolitionists to free the slaves would advance the suffrage cause and their own emancipation. Convinced by male anti-slavery leaders of the overwhelming importance of abolition, Mott, Stanton, Kelley, Wright and other female suffragists acquiesced to taking back seats during the turbulent 1850's until blacks were freed and the former abolitionists could reciprocate by aiding the fight for the vote. Female suffragists had similar hopes of winning public support as a consequence of the often remarkable services they had rendered the Union during the Civil War.

Understandable as they were, these expectations were dashed during the early phase of Reconstruction (1867-1870). While suffragists were gratified by the Wyoming Territory's extension of the vote to women in 1869, they found themselves abandoned by postwar politicians and former abolitionists. The Reconstruction Act of 1867 enfranchised black

males, not women, throughout the South. The Fourteenth Amendment imposed penalties for denying the black male vote. The Fifteenth Amendment, which proclaimed that the vote could not be denied because of race, color, or previous condition of servitude, despite female suffragists' voluble protests and lobbying, notably lacked inclusion of the word "sex." Indeed, the amendment had been designed primarily to ensure that northern states, most of which long had excluded blacks from the franchise, mandated its extension to black men.

These Reconstruction battles disabused suffragists of the idea that they were automatically connected with former abolitionists, with black leaders, and with Republican politicians. They also split woman suffrage advocates into two organizations, each established in 1869: Lucy Stone's American Woman Suffrage Association (AWSA) and Susan B. Anthony's and Elizabeth Stanton's National Woman Suffrage Association (NWSA). Thereafter, the two organizations concentrated upon securing constitutional amendments which would give the vote to women. Lucy Stone's AWSA sought amendments to state constitutions, while the NWSA fought for an amendment to the U.S. Constitution. After years of such

WORKERS' COMPENSATION / 863

tactical (and to some extent, personal) divisions, the two organizations combined as NAWSA in 1890.

In the interim, the national suffrage crusade had drawn into its ranks such women as Julia Ward Howe, Anne Howard Shaw, Carrie Chapman Catt, Matilda Joslyn Gage, Martha C. Wright, Pauline Wright-Davis, Belva Ann Bennett Lockwood, Ann Preston, Eliza Farnham, Lydia Fowles, Lydia Child, Marianna W. Johnson, and Ida Husted Harper. Moreover, between 1881 and 1922, Anthony and Stanton, with assistance from Gage and Harper, produced a massive six-volume compilation of documents and essays entitled *The History of Woman Suffrage*, which became a mine of information—and inspiration—for future generations of feminists.

The tenacity, intrepidity, public protests—some occasioning violence—and spirited lobbying of these women won them the vote in four Rocky Mountain states between 1869 and 1896 as well as in seventeen additional states between 1910 and 1918. Then, in 1913, using the leverage of female voters in states that had enfranchised them and drawing on the reform impetus of the Progressive era, Lucy Burns and Alice Paul formed the National Woman's Party to press Washington for an amendment to the federal Constitution. These efforts were given a final fillip by America's entrance into World War I. Women's immense contributions to the nation's industrial mobilization when they replaced millions of men in service were generally recognized and, as a consequence, enough traditional attitudes were changed to secure passage of the Nineteenth Amendment in 1920.

Evaluation. Suffragists who envisioned the vote as the opening of a revolution in women's rights were, as Carrie Chapman Catt reminded them in 1920, destined to be disappointed. The Nineteenth Amendment failed to usher them into the traditional seats of power. Nor were enfranchised women able to mobilize into reformist political blocs or into a viable third party. Moreover, for some feminists of a later generation, such as Betty Friedan, many of the potential gains of the Nineteenth Amendment were smothered, along with other women's rights, by a societal emphasis on "super-domesticity" during the so-called second Victorian era that developed during the two decades after World War II. Friedan's views were echoed with variations by other feminists who downplayed the importance of suffrage, insisting that effecting attitudinal changes and securing legislation allowing women full access to economic, educational, and professional opportunities were more vital than the vote. Not least, some male political scientists concluded that the Nineteenth Amendment simply doubled the vote without altering its quality: Women, they noted, generally tended to vote the same way that their husbands and male relatives did.

Other commentators reached different conclusions. Between the 1970's and 1990's, they cited the more open character of the American family as one result of women gaining full citizenship. Despite continuing prejudices and discriminations, they argued, women were more politically aware, confident, and active in both public and voluntary associations than

they had been prior to 1920. By the 1990's, they were inside the public arena as mayors, governors, congresswomen, cabinet officers, and bureau chiefs in growing numbers (although numbers well short of a share of offices commensurate with their majority in the general population). Moreover, they were gradually translating democratic values into the lives and values of their families, a contrast even with the situation in most other developed nations. If nothing else, the vote offered something women had not possessed before the Nineteenth Amendment: a means of political redress against a battery of discriminations.   —*Mary E. Virginia*

See also Anthony, Susan B.; Citizenship; Feminism; Seneca Falls Convention; Stanton, Elizabeth Cady; Vote, right to.

BIBLIOGRAPHY

The following are engaging, well-written scholarly works. Lois W. Banner, *Elizabeth Cady Stanton* (Boston: Little, Brown, 1980), contrasts the effects of Stanton's conservative background and radical activities on shaping her personality; Kathleen Barry, *Susan B. Anthony* (New York: New York University Press, 1988), concentrates on Anthony's character development rather than on her activities; Mari Jo Buhle and Paul Buhle, eds., *A Concise History of Woman Suffrage: Selections from the Classic Work of Stanton, Anthony, Gage, and Harper* (Urbana: University of Illinois Press, 1978), is an invaluable historical collection on the evolution of the suffrage movement; and Ellen C. DuBois, *Feminism and Suffrage* (Ithaca, N.Y.: Cornell University Press, 1978), covers the subject from Seneca Falls to 1869. Eleanor Flexner, *Century of Struggle* (New York: Atheneum, 1973), places suffrage in the broader setting of women's rights; Linda Kerber, *Women of the Republic* (New York: W. W. Norton, 1986), makes useful mention of Wollstonecraft's influence and of suffrage in the early republic; Aileen Kraditor, *The Ideas of the Woman Suffrage Movement, 1890-1920* (New York: Columbia University Press, 1965), examines suffragism in relation to antisuffragism, domesticity, religion, and sectional politics; and David Morgan, *Suffragists and Democrats: The Politics of Woman Suffrage in America* (East Lansing: Michigan State University Press, 1972), emphasizes suffragism's early twentieth century role in the broad sweep of American politics.

Workers' compensation

DEFINITION: A legally mandated system under which employers are required to pay specific amounts to employees who suffer an injury during the course of employment, generally without regard to the cause of the injury, in exchange for which employees are required to give up their common-law right to sue their employers for that injury

SIGNIFICANCE: Instead of focussing on the traditional legal issues of cause and fault, workers' compensation aims to determine quickly and efficiently whether an employee was injured while working and, if so, to provide prompt compensation

The first broad workers' compensation statute was enacted in New York in 1910, but it was soon afterward held unconstitutional by the New York Court of Appeals. In 1917 the U.S. Supreme Court expressly held such statutes constitutional, and the concept spread quickly. By 1949 every state had adopted some form of workers' compensation. Each state devises and administers its own workers' compensation system. However, most systems have a number of elements in common.

Workers' compensation is a relatively informal system. Because the basic question in workers' compensation is whether an employee was injured in the course of employment, and because the basic purpose is to compensate or rehabilitate that employee quickly, workers' compensation systems are more informal and less technical than traditional legal systems. Rules of evidence and procedure are relaxed, and claims are required to be resolved in a period of months, rather than years. Most states handle initial claims administratively, though some have special courts for that purpose. Most claims are settled short of litigation, although nearly every state requires that any settlement be approved by the administrative board or court.

Participation is nearly universal. Most categories of employers and employees are required to participate in the program, either by express requirement or by legal presumption. The exceptions are usually such categories as domestic and agricultural workers and small firms. Although the employers bear the initial cost of the compensation, usually through insurance purchased for that purpose, those costs are ultimately passed on to the general public.

WORKERS' COMPENSATION BENEFITS PAID, 1989

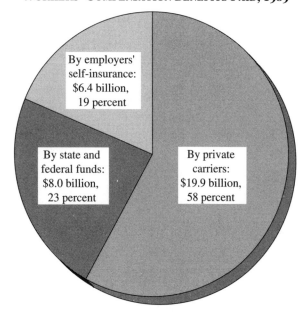

By employers' self-insurance: $6.4 billion, 19 percent

By state and federal funds: $8.0 billion, 23 percent

By private carriers: $19.9 billion, 58 percent

Source: Data are from U.S. Department of Commerce, Bureau of the Census, *Statistical Abstract of the United States, 1992.* Washington, D.C.: U.S. Government Printing Office, 1992.

In order to compensate injured employees promptly, nearly all states provide a "schedule" that sets out the compensation rate for injury to a particular body part. The compensation is usually paid in terms of a weekly benefit rate, with each scheduled loss entitled to a certain number of weekly payments. The benefits are calculated without reference to the actual wages earned by the employee before the injury.

Each claim also requires determining whether the injury is temporary or permanent, and whether it is total or partial. When an employee has suffered an injury not on the schedule, it is necessary to determine how much disability that employee has suffered, up to a legislatively mandated maximum level.

Rehabilitation is a part of the system. If an employee is permanently unable to return to the work he or she had once performed, many states provide that the employee may be eligible for an award of vocational rehabilitation, though the amounts and types of that rehabilitation vary by state.

See also Insurance law; Labor law; Negligence; Occupational Safety and Health Administration (OSHA); Social Security system.

World Court

DATE: Established June 26, 1945
PLACE: The Hague, The Netherlands
SIGNIFICANCE: The World Court provides the opportunity for states within the international system to settle their disputes by the rule of law rather than the use of force

The World Court, also known as the International Court of Justice (ICJ), is the judicial organ of the United Nations (U.N.). The mission and structure of the World Court are set forth in Articles 92 to 96 of the U.N. Charter and in the Statute of the International Court of Justice. All member states of the United Nations, including the United States, are automatically parties to the Statute of the ICJ.

The World Court is the successor to the Permanent Court of International Justice (PCIJ). The PCIJ was created by the League of Nations in 1920 and ceased to exist in 1946. The Statute of the PCIJ served as the model for the Statute of the ICJ. The Security Council and the General Assembly of the United Nations elect the fifteen judges that compose the World Court. Five of the fifteen judges are elected every three years; they serve nine-year terms. Each judge is eligible for reelection. No two judges may be of the same nationality.

The World Court can issue two types of rulings. One is an advisory opinion; the other is a binding decision. Advisory opinions are issued in response to requests made of the court to resolve a question of international law. The actor making the request is not bound by the opinion issued. The parties in a contentious case brought before the court, however, are bound by the court's decision. A contentious case is one in which the two parties to a dispute agree to allow the court to resolve the dispute by determining which party's position is justified by international law.

States that are parties to a contentious case before the World Court must recognize the court's jurisdiction to rule on the case. If a state has not granted the court jurisdiction to resolve a particular type of dispute, then the court cannot settle that dispute. Only states can be parties in contentious cases heard by the World Court. The court does not have the authority to adjudicate disputes involving individuals or nonstate actors, such as transnational corporations or international organizations.

The World Court decides contentious cases on the basis of a majority vote, with at least nine of the fifteen judges participating. (It is possible for a smaller panel of judges to hear a case if both parties to a dispute agree to it.) The decisions and awards made by the World Court cannot be appealed. The court can rehear a case, however, if new information comes to light. The World Court does not have the ability to force a state to comply with its rulings in contentious cases. If a state ignores one of its decisions, the court can only request that the U.N. Security Council take action to enforce the decision.

See also International law; Positive law; War crimes.

Yates v. United States

COURT: U.S. Supreme Court

DATE: Decided June 17, 1957

SIGNIFICANCE: The U.S. Supreme Court's decision in this case advanced protections for both freedom of speech and freedom of assembly or political association; this case rendered ineffective the government's attempt to prosecute members of the Communist Party of America under the Smith Act

Following the rise of communism around the globe, leaders in the United States moved to stamp out any signs of communist activity in the country. Fourteen middle-level Communist Party leaders were accused under the Smith Act (1940) of organizing and participating in a conspiracy to advocate the forceful overthrow of the United States government. In a stunning 6-1 decision, with two justices not participating, the Supreme Court reversed their convictions, acquitting five and remanding the remaining nine for new trials.

The Court maintained that the government had waited much too long to charge the defendants with organizing the Communist Party in the United States. Indeed, the Court stated that the three-year statute of limitations had expired. The Court also found that the trial judge had been mistaken in his directions to the jury in regard to what they must find in order to convince the defendants on the advocacy charges. Finally, the Court declared the evidence in several cases to be entirely insufficient. After this decision was rendered, the government dropped all nine of the remanded cases.

The question before the court was simple enough. When placed in balance, which is of greater consequence: the value of preserving free speech or the value of preserving a government's interest which might be adversely affected by such speech? This basic question continues to raise controversy and foster strong emotions even though the issue of communism itself has been removed.

In an earlier case, *Dennis v. United States* (1951), the Court upheld the Smith Act as constitutional, allowing for numerous conspiracy convictions from 1951 through 1957. The Yates decision did not directly overrule Dennis, but it clarified the distinction between advocating illegal acts and holding abstract doctrinal beliefs which, the Court said, had been ignored by trial courts. After *Yates*, the government was required to show very specific illegal acts by the accused in order to gain a conviction. Membership in a political organization was insignificant in and of itself. Strict standards of proof had to be met.

This decision marked a dramatic and important change in the Court's attitude toward the Smith Act and a move away from the *Dennis* decision. Only four years later, however, the Court upheld a section of the Smith Act which made it a crime to be a member of a group advocating the overthrow by force of the government. This case, *Scales v. United States* (1961), was neither a retreat from *Yates* nor a return to *Dennis*, because the Court insisted that evidentiary requirements similar to those found in *Yates* be met. That is, a person's "membership" has to meet certain criteria. It must be both knowing and active. Additionally, the person must show "specific intent" to bring about the forceful overthrow of the government. This case, in combination with *Yates*, made conviction under the Smith Act virtually impossible.

See also Communist Party, American; *Dennis v. United States*; *Scales v. United States*; Smith Act.

Zoning

DEFINITION: The placing of restrictions on land in terms of construction, improvement, and use

SIGNIFICANCE: Zoning affords local governments the power to address a range of justice issues, including the affordability of housing, the integration of neighborhoods, and the preservation of quality of life; however, zoning also raises legal questions about just compensation for the "taking" of a property's use

Almost all land in the incorporated cities and towns of the United States, and much land in the surrounding counties, is subject to land-use controls established by local ordinances. Zoning is the designating of the various parcels of land for specific purposes, such as residential, commercial, industrial, and open space. In addition to specifying permissible use, zoning ordinances typically regulate the acceptable types of construction and other improvements on the property. The benefits of zoning are obvious in terms of community plan-

ning, as they facilitate the logical and orderly development of neighborhoods, commercial districts, park lands, and sanitation districts. Zoning permits long-range planning and allows purchasers of property to know the nature of the surrounding areas once it is built out—possibly some decades in the future.

Beyond its practical benefits, zoning involves several justice issues. Particularly in terms of residential zoning, housing affordability and discrimination are relevant. By specifying maximum density (units per acre) of residential construction, zoning affects the affordability of housing through land costs. Low-density housing requirements can make housing prohibitively expensive for lower-income households. Off-street parking requirements, floor area ratios, and other zoning standards may further add to housing costs. Highly restrictive zoning may effectively turn neighborhoods and even entire towns into elite enclaves. Some have gone so far as to charge that such situations amount to *de facto* racial discrimination. Conversely, a broad range of residential zoning standards in a single area

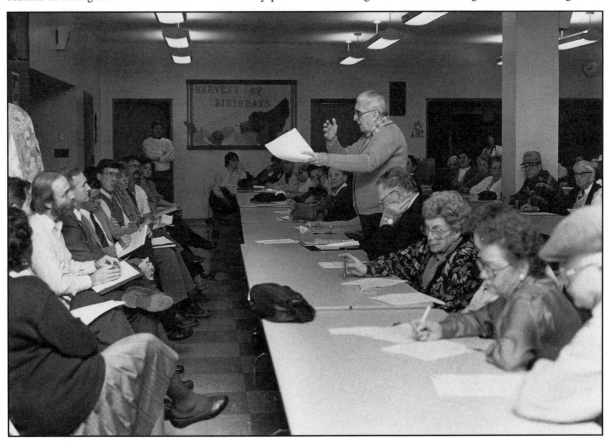

At zoning hearings, local residents are given the opportunity to express their opinions. (James L. Shaffer)

(for example, including apartments, condominiums, mobile homes, and single-family homes) can encourage the creation of financially and racially integrated neighborhoods. Federal and various state fair housing laws prohibit intentional discrimination through zoning, but it is difficult to distinguish between regulations which stem from legitimate purposes, such as public health and safety, and those which unfairly place excessive "quality of life" standards above the need for affordable housing within a region.

Zoning also raises justice issues for the owners of land. By definition, land use controls such as zoning place some limits on the rights of ownership. This fact raises questions about just compensation: Do governmental restrictions upon one's land constitute a "taking" of all or part of the land's value, thus requiring compensation? Moreover, how should compensation, if necessary, be calculated? Over time, the courts have broadened the tolerable level of abridgment of property rights in the public interest. Nevertheless, standards vary from court to court and from place to place, leaving much room for controversy.

See also Environmental law; Property rights; Real estate law; Restrictive covenant; Takings clause.

THE DECLARATION OF INDEPENDENCE

In Congress, July 4, 1776
The unanimous declaration of the thirteen United States of America

When in the Course of human Events, it becomes necessary for one People to dissolve the Political Bands which have connected them with another, and to assume among the Powers of the Earth, the separate and equal Station to which the Laws of Nature and of Nature's God entitle them, a decent Respect to the Opinions of Mankind requires that they should declare the causes which impel them to the Separation.

We hold these Truths to be self-evident, that all Men are created equal, that they are endowed by their Creator with certain unalienable Rights, that among these are Life, Liberty, and the Pursuit of Happiness—That to secure these Rights, Governments are instituted among Men, deriving their just Powers from the Consent of the Governed, that whenever any Form of Government becomes destructive of these Ends, it is the Right of the People to alter or to abolish it, and to institute new Government, laying its Foundation on such Principles, and organizing its Powers in such Form, as to them shall seem most likely to effect their Safety and Happiness. Prudence, indeed, will dictate that Governments long established should not be changed for light and transient Causes; and accordingly all Experience hath shewn, that Mankind are more disposed to suffer, while Evils are sufferable, than to right themselves by abolishing the Forms to which they are accustomed. But when a long Train of Abuses and Usurpations, pursuing invariably the same Object, evinces a Design to reduce them under absolute Despotism, it is their Right, it is their Duty, to throw off such Government, and to provide new Guards for their future Security. Such has been the patient Sufferance of these Colonies; and such is now the Necessity which constrains them to alter their former Systems of Government. The History of the present King of Great-Britain is a History of repeated Injuries and Usurpations, all having in direct Object the Establishment of an absolute Tyranny over these States. To prove this, let Facts be submitted to a candid World.

He has refused his Assent to Laws, the most wholesome and necessary for the public Good.

He has forbidden his Governors to pass Laws of immediate and pressing Importance, unless suspended in their Operation till his Assent should be obtained; and when so suspended, he has utterly neglected to attend to them.

He has refused to pass other Laws for the Accommodation of large Districts of People, unless those People would relinquish the Right of Representation in the Legislature, a Right inestimable to them, and formidable to Tyrants only.

He has called together Legislative Bodies at Places unusual, uncomfortable, and distant from the Depository of their public Records, for the sole Purpose of fatiguing them into Compliance with his Measures.

He has dissolved Representative Houses repeatedly, for opposing with manly Firmness his Invasions on the Rights of the People.

He has refused for a long Time, after such Dissolutions, to cause others to be elected; whereby the Legislative Powers, incapable of Annihilation, have returned to the People at large for their exercise; the State remaining in the mean time exposed to all the Dangers of Invasion from without, and Convulsions within.

He has endeavoured to prevent the Population of these States; for that Purpose obstructing the Laws for Naturalization of Foreigners; refusing to pass others to encourage their Migrations hither, and raising the Conditions of new Appropriations of Lands.

He has obstructed the Administration of Justice, by refusing his Assent to Laws for establishing Judiciary Powers.

He has made Judges dependent on his Will alone, for the Tenure of their Offices, and the Amount and Payment of their Salaries.

He has erected a Multitude of new Offices, and sent hither Swarms of Officers to harass our People, and eat out their Substance.

He has kept among us, in Times of Peace, Standing Armies, without the consent of our Legislatures.

He has affected to render the Military independent of and superior to the Civil Power.

He has combined with others to subject us to a Jurisdiction foreign to our Constitution, and unacknowledged by our Laws; giving his Assent to their Acts of pretended Legislation:

For quartering large Bodies of Armed Troops among us:

For protecting them, by a mock Trial, from Punishment for any Murders which they should commit on the Inhabitants of these States:

For cutting off our Trade with all Parts of the World:

For imposing Taxes on us without our Consent:

For depriving us, in many Cases, of the Benefits of Trial by Jury:

For transporting us beyond Seas to be tried for pretended Offences:

For abolishing the free System of English Laws in a neighbouring Province, establishing therein an arbitrary Government, and enlarging its Boundaries, so as to render it at once an Example and fit Instrument for introducing the same absolute Rule into these Colonies:

For taking away our Charters, abolishing our most valuable Laws, and altering fundamentally the Forms of our Governments:

For suspending our own Legislatures, and declaring themselves invested with Power to legislate for us in all Cases whatsoever.

He has abdicated Government here, by declaring us out of his Protection and waging War against us.

He has plundered our Seas, ravaged our Coasts, burnt our Towns, and destroyed the Lives of our People.

He is, at this Time, transporting large Armies of foreign Mercenaries to compleat the Works of Death, Desolation, and Tyranny, already begun with circumstances of Cruelty and Perfidy, scarcely paralleled in the most barbarous Ages, and totally unworthy the Head of a civilized Nation.

He has constrained our fellow Citizens taken Captive on the high Seas to bear Arms against their Country, to become the Executioners of their Friends and Brethren, or to fall themselves by their Hands.

He has excited domestic Insurrections amongst us, and has endeavoured to bring on the Inhabitants of our Frontiers, the merciless Indian Savages, whose known Rule of Warfare, is an undistinguished Destruction, of all Ages, Sexes and Conditions.

In every stage of these Oppressions we have Petitioned for Redress in the most humble Terms: Our repeated Petitions have been answered only by repeated Injury. A Prince, whose Character is thus marked by every act which may define a Tyrant, is unfit to be the Ruler of a free People.

Nor have we been wanting in Attentions to our British Brethren. We have warned them from Time to Time of Attempts by their Legislature to extend an unwarrantable Jurisdiction over us. We have reminded them of the Circumstances of our Emigration and Settlement here. We have appealed to their native Justice and Magnanimity, and we have conjured them by the Ties of our common Kindred to disavow these Usurpations, which, would inevitably interrupt our Connections and Correspondence. They too have been deaf to the Voice of Justice and of Consanguinity. We must, therefore, acquiesce in the Necessity, which denounces our Separation, and hold them, as we hold the rest of Mankind, Enemies in War, in Peace, Friends.

We, therefore, the Representatives of the UNITED STATES OF AMERICA, in General Congress, Assembled, appealing to the Supreme Judge of the World for the Rectitude of our Intentions, do, in the Name, and by Authority of the good People of these Colonies, solemnly Publish and Declare, That these United Colonies are, and of Right ought to be, FREE AND INDEPENDENT STATES; that they are absolved from all Allegiance to the British Crown, and that all political Connection between them and the State of Great-Britain, is and ought to be totally dissolved; and that as FREE AND INDEPENDENT STATES, they have full Power to levy War, conclude Peace, contract Alliances, establish Commerce, and to do all other Acts and Things which INDEPENDENT STATES may of right do. And for the support of this Declaration, with a firm Reliance on the Protection of divine Providence, we mutually pledge to each other our Lives, our Fortunes, and our sacred Honor.

Signed by Order and in Behalf of the Congress,

JOHN HANCOCK, PRESIDENT.

THE CONSTITUTION OF THE UNITED STATES OF AMERICA

We the People of the United States, in Order to form a more perfect Union, establish Justice, insure domestic Tranquility, provide for the common defence, promote the general Welfare, and secure the Blessings of Liberty to ourselves and our Posterity, do ordain and establish this Constitution for the United States of America.

ARTICLE I.

SECTION 1. All legislative Powers herein granted shall be vested in a Congress of the United States, which shall consist of a Senate and House of Representatives.

SECTION 2. The House of Representatives shall be composed of Members chosen every second Year by the People of the several States, and the Electors in each State shall have the Qualifications requisite for Electors of the most numerous Branch of the State Legislature.

No Person shall be a Representative who shall not have attained to the Age of twenty five Years, and been seven Years a Citizen of the United States, and who shall not, when elected, be an Inhabitant of that State in which he shall be chosen.

Representatives and direct Taxes shall be apportioned among the several States which may be included within this Union, according to their respective Numbers, which shall be determined by adding to the whole Number of free Persons, including those bound to Service for a Term of Years, and excluding Indians not taxed, three fifths of all other Persons. The actual Enumeration shall be made within three Years after the first Meeting of the Congress of the United States, and within every subsequent Term of ten Years, in such Manner as they shall by Law direct. The number of Representatives shall not exceed one for every thirty Thousand, but each State shall have at Least one Representative; and until such enumeration shall be made, the State of New Hampshire shall be entitled to chuse three, Massachusetts eight, Rhode-Island and Providence Plantations one, Connecticut five, New-York six, New Jersey four, Pennsylvania eight, Delaware one, Maryland six, Virginia ten, North Carolina five, South Carolina five, and Georgia three.

When vacancies happen in the Representation from any State, the Executive Authority thereof shall issue Writs of Election to fill such Vacancies.

The House of Representatives shall chuse their Speaker and other Officers; and shall have the sole Power of Impeachment.

SECTION 3. The Senate of the United States shall be composed of two Senators from each State, chosen by the Legislature thereof, for six Years; and each Senator shall have one Vote.

Immediately after they shall be assembled in Consequence of the first Election, they shall be divided as equally as may be into three Classes. The Seats of the Senators of the first Class shall be vacated at the Expiration of the second Year, of the second Class at the Expiration of the fourth Year, and of the third Class at the Expiration of the sixth Year, so that one third may be chosen every second Year; and if Vacancies happen by Resignation, or otherwise, during the Recess of the Legislature of any State, the Executive thereof may make temporary Appointments until the next Meeting of the Legislature, which shall then fill such Vacancies.

No Person shall be a Senator who shall not have attained to the Age of thirty Years, and been nine Years a Citizen of the United States, and who shall not, when elected, be an Inhabitant of that State for which he shall be chosen.

The Vice President of the United States shall be President of the Senate, but shall have no Vote, unless they be equally divided.

The Senate shall chuse their other Officers, and also a President pro tempore, in the Absence of the Vice President, or when he shall exercise the Office of President of the United States.

The Senate shall have the sole Power to try all Impeachments. When sitting for that Purpose, they shall be on Oath or Affirmation. When the President of the United States is tried, the Chief Justice shall preside: And no Person shall be convicted without the Concurrence of two thirds of the Members present.

Judgment in Cases of Impeachment shall not extend further than to removal from Office, and disqualification to hold and enjoy any Office of honor, Trust or Profit under the United States: but the Party convicted shall nevertheless be liable and subject to Indictment, Trial, Judgment and Punishment, according to Law.

SECTION 4. The Times, Places and Manner of holding Elections for Senators and Representatives, shall be prescribed in each State by the Legislature thereof; but the Congress may at any time by Law make or alter such Regulations, except as to the Places of chusing Senators.

The Congress shall assemble at least once in every Year, and such Meeting shall be on the first Monday in December, unless they shall by Law appoint a different Day.

SECTION 5. Each House shall be the Judge of the Elections, Returns and Qualifications of its own Members, and a Majority of each shall constitute a Quorum to do Business; but a smaller Number may adjourn from day to day, and may be authorized to compel the Attendance of absent Members, in such Manner, and under such Penalties as each House may provide.

Each House may determine the Rules of its Proceedings, punish its Members for disorderly Behaviour, and, with the Concurrence of two thirds, expel a Member.

Each House shall keep a Journal of its Proceedings, and from time to time publish the same, excepting such Parts as may in their Judgment require Secrecy; and the Yeas and Nays of the Members of either House on any question shall, at the Desire of one fifth of those Present, be entered on the Journal.

Neither House, during the Session of Congress, shall, without the Consent of the other, adjourn for more than three days, nor to any other Place than that in which the two Houses shall be sitting.

SECTION 6. The Senators and Representatives shall receive a Compensation for their Services, to be ascertained by Law, and paid out of the Treasury of the United States. They shall in all Cases, except Treason, Felony and Breach of the Peace, be privileged from Arrest during their Attendance at the Session of their respective Houses, and in going to and returning from the same; and for any Speech or Debate in either House, they shall not be questioned in any other Place.

No Senator or Representative shall, during the Time for which he was elected, be appointed to any civil Office under the Authority of the United States, which shall have been created, or the Emoluments whereof shall have been encreased during such time; and no Person holding any Office under the United States, shall be a Member of either House during his Continuance in Office.

SECTION 7. All Bills for raising Revenue shall originate in the House of Representatives; but the Senate may propose or concur with Amendments as on other Bills.

Every Bill which shall have passed the House of Representatives and the Senate, shall, before it becomes a Law, be presented to the President of the United States; If he approve he shall sign it, but if not he shall return it, with his Objections to that House in which it shall have originated, who shall enter the Objections at large on their Journal, and proceed to reconsider it. If after such Reconsideration two thirds of that House shall agree to pass the Bill, it shall be sent, together with the Objections, to the other House, by which it shall likewise be reconsidered, and if approved by two thirds of that House, it shall become a Law. But in all such Cases the Votes of both Houses shall be determined by yeas and Nays, and the Names of the Persons voting for and against the Bill shall be entered on the Journal of each House respectively. If any Bill shall not be returned by the President within ten Days (Sundays excepted) after it shall have been presented to him, the Same shall be a Law, in like Manner as if he had signed it, unless the Congress by their Adjournment prevent its Return, in which Case it shall not be a Law.

Every Order, Resolution, or Vote to which the Concurrence of the Senate and House of Representatives may be necessary (except on a question of Adjournment) shall be presented to the President of the United States; and before the Same shall take Effect, shall be approved by him, or being disapproved by him, shall be repassed by two thirds of the Senate and House of Representatives, according to the Rules and Limitations prescribed in the Case of a Bill.

SECTION 8. The Congress shall have Power To lay and collect Taxes, Duties, Imposts and Excises, to pay the Debts and provide for the common Defence and general Welfare of the United States; but all Duties, Imposts and Excises shall be uniform throughout the United States;

To borrow Money on the credit of the United States;

To regulate Commerce with foreign Nations, and among the several States, and with the Indian Tribes;

To establish an uniform Rule of Naturalization, and uniform Laws on the subject of Bankruptcies throughout the United States;

To coin Money, regulate the Value thereof, and of foreign Coin, and fix the Standard of Weights and Measures;

To provide for the Punishment of counterfeiting the Securities and current Coin of the United States;

To establish Post Offices and post Roads;

To promote the Progress of Science and useful Arts, by securing for limited Times to Authors and Inventors the exclusive Right to their respective Writings and Discoveries;

To constitute Tribunals inferior to the supreme Court;

To define and punish Piracies and Felonies committed on the high Seas, and Offenses against the Law of Nations;

To declare War, grant Letters of Marque and Reprisal, and make Rules concerning Captures on Land and Water;

To raise and support Armies, but no Appropriation of Money to that Use shall be for a longer Term than two Years;

To provide and maintain a Navy;

To make Rules for the Government and Regulation of the land and naval Forces;

To provide for calling forth the Militia to execute the Laws of the Union, suppress Insurrections and repel Invasions;

To provide for organizing, arming, and disciplining, the Militia, and for governing such Part of them as may be employed in the Service of the United States, reserving to the States respectively, the Appointment of the Officers, and the Authority of training the Militia according to the discipline prescribed by Congress;

To exercise exclusive Legislation in all Cases whatsoever, over such District (not exceeding ten Miles square) as may, by Cession of particular States, and the Acceptance of Congress, become the Seat of the Government of the United States, and to exercise like Authority over all Places purchased by the Consent of the Legislature of the State in which the Same shall be, for the Erection of Forts, Magazines, Arsenals, dock-Yards and other needful Buildings;—And

To make all Laws which shall be necessary and proper for carrying into Execution the foregoing Powers, and all other Powers vested by this Constitution in the Government of the United States, or in any Department or Officer thereof.

SECTION 9. The Migration or Importation of such Persons as any of the States now existing shall think proper to admit, shall not be prohibited by the Congress prior to the Year one thousand eight hundred and eight, but a Tax or duty may be imposed on such Importation, not exceeding ten dollars for each Person.

The Privilege of the Writ of Habeas Corpus shall not be suspended, unless when in Cases of Rebellion or Invasion the public Safety may require it.

No Bill of Attainder or ex post facto Law shall be passed.

No Capitation, or other direct, Tax shall be laid, unless in Proportion to the Census or Enumeration herein before directed to be taken.

No Tax or Duty shall be laid on Articles exported from any State.

No Preference shall be given by any Regulation of Commerce or Revenue to the Ports of one State over those of another: nor shall Vessels bound to, or from, one State, be obliged to enter, clear, or pay Duties in another.

No Money shall be drawn from the Treasury, but in Consequence of Appropriations made by Law; and a regular Statement and Account of the Receipts and Expenditures of all public Money shall be published from time to time.

No Title of Nobility shall be granted by the United States: And no Person holding any Office of Profit or Trust under them, shall, without the Consent of the Congress, accept of any present, Emolument, Office, or Title, of any kind whatever, from any King, Prince, or foreign State.

SECTION 10. No State shall enter into any Treaty, Alliance, or Confederation; grant Letters of Marque and Reprisal; coin Money; emit Bills of Credit; make any Thing but gold and silver Coin a Tender in Payment of Debts; pass any Bill of Attainder, ex post facto Law, or Law impairing the Obligation of Contracts, or grant any Title of Nobility.

No State shall, without the Consent of the Congress, lay any Imposts or Duties on Imports or Exports, except what may be absolutely necessary for executing it's inspection Laws: and the net Produce of all Duties and Imposts, laid by any State on Imports or Exports, shall be for the Use of the Treasury of the United States; and all such Laws shall be subject to the Revision and Control of the Congress.

No State shall, without the Consent of Congress, lay any Duty of Tonnage, keep Troops, or Ships of War in time of Peace, enter into any Agreement or Compact with another State, or with a foreign Power, or engage in War, unless actually invaded, or in such imminent Danger as will not admit of delay.

ARTICLE II.

SECTION 1. The executive Power shall be vested in a President of the United States of America. He shall hold his Office during the Term of four Years, and, together with the Vice President, chosen for the same Term, be elected, as follows

Each State shall appoint, in such Manner as the Legislature thereof may direct, a Number of Electors, equal to the whole Number of Senators and Representatives to which the State may be entitled in the Congress: but no Senator or Representative, or Person holding an Office of Trust or Profit under the United States, shall be appointed an Elector.

The Electors shall meet in their respective States, and vote by Ballot for two Persons, of whom one at least shall not be an Inhabitant of the same State with themselves. And they shall make a List of all the Persons voted for, and of the Number of Votes for each; which List they shall sign and certify, and transmit sealed to the Seat of the Government of the United States, directed to the President of the Senate. The President of the Senate shall, in the Presence of the Senate and House of Representatives, open all the Certificates, and the Votes shall then be counted. The Person having the greatest Number of Votes shall be the President, if such Number be a Majority of the whole Number of Electors appointed; and if there be more than one who have such Majority, and have an equal Number of Votes, then the House of Representatives shall immediately chuse by Ballot one of them for President; and if no Person have a Majority, then from the five highest on the List the said

House shall in like manner chuse the President. But in chusing the President, the Votes shall be taken by States, the Representation from each State having one Vote; A quorum for this Purpose shall consist of a Member or Members from two thirds of the States, and a Majority of all the States shall be necessary to a Choice. In every Case, after the Choice of the President, the Person having the greatest Number of Votes of the Electors shall be the Vice President. But if there should remain two or more who have equal Votes, the Senate shall chuse from them by Ballot the Vice President.

The Congress may determine the Time of chusing the Electors, and the Day on which they shall give their Votes; which Day shall be the same throughout the United States.

No Person except a natural born Citizen, or a Citizen of the United States, at the time of the Adoption of this Constitution, shall be eligible to the Office of the President; neither shall any person be eligible to that Office who shall not have attained to the Age of thirty five Years, and been fourteen Years a Resident within the United States.

In Case of the Removal of the President from Office, or of his Death, Resignation, or Inability to discharge the Powers and Duties of the said Office, the Same shall devolve on the Vice President, and the Congress may by Law provide for the Case of Removal, Death, Resignation or Inability, both of the President and Vice President, declaring what Officer shall then act as President, and such Officer shall act accordingly, until the Disability be removed, or a President shall be elected.

The President shall, at stated Times, receive for his Services, a Compensation, which shall neither be increased nor diminished during the Period for which he shall have been elected, and he shall not receive within that Period any other Emolument from the United States, or any of them.

Before he enter the Execution of his Office, he shall take the following Oath or Affirmation:—"I do solemnly swear (or affirm) that I will faithfully execute the Office of President of the United States, and will to the best of my Ability, preserve, protect and defend the Constitution of the United States."

SECTION 2. The President shall be Commander in Chief of the Army and Navy of the United States, and of the Militia of the several States, when called into the actual Service of the United States; he may require the Opinion, in writing, of the principal Officer in each of the executive Departments, upon any Subject relating to the Duties of their respective Offices, and he shall have Power to grant Reprieves and Pardons for Offenses against the United States, except in Cases of Impeachment.

He shall have Power, by and with the Advice and Consent of the Senate, to make Treaties, provided two thirds of the Senators present concur; and he shall nominate, and by and with the Advice and Consent of the Senate, shall appoint Ambassadors, other public Ministers and Consuls, Judges of the supreme Court, and all other Officers of the United States, whose Appointments are not herein otherwise provided for, and which shall be established by Law: but the Congress may by Law vest the Appointment of such inferior Officers, as they think proper, in the President alone, in the Courts of Law, or in the Heads of Departments.

The President shall have Power to fill up all Vacancies that may happen during the Recess of the Senate, by granting Commissions which shall expire at the End of their next Session.

SECTION 3. He shall from time to time give to the Congress Information of the State of the Union, and recommend to their Consideration such Measures as he shall judge necessary and expedient; he may, on extraordinary Occasions, convene both Houses, or either of them, and in Case of Disagreement between them, with Respect to the Time of Adjournment, he may adjourn them to such Time as he shall think proper; he shall receive Ambassadors and other public Ministers; he shall take Care that the Laws be faithfully executed, and shall Commission all the Officers of the United States.

SECTION 4. The President, Vice President and all civil Officers of the United States, shall be removed from Office on Impeachment for, and Conviction of, Treason, Bribery, or other high Crimes and Misdemeanors.

ARTICLE III.

SECTION 1. The judicial Power of the United States, shall be vested in one supreme Court, and in such inferior Courts as the Congress may from time to time ordain and establish. The Judges, both of the supreme and inferior Courts, shall hold their Offices during good Behaviour, and shall, at stated Times, receive for their Services, a Compensation, which shall not be diminished during their Continuance in Office.

SECTION 2. The judicial Power shall extend to all Cases, in Law and Equity, arising under this Constitution, the Laws of the United States, and Treaties made, or which shall be made, under their Authority;—to all Cases affecting Ambassadors, other public Ministers and Consuls;—to all Cases of admiralty and maritime Jurisdiction;—to Controversies to which the United States shall be a Party;—to Controversies between two or more States; between a State and Citizens of another State; between Citizens of different States,—between Citizens of the same State claiming Lands under Grants of different States, and between a State, or the Citizens thereof, and foreign States, Citizens or Subjects.

In all Cases affecting Ambassadors, other public Ministers and Consuls, and those in which a State shall be Party, the supreme Court shall have original Jurisdiction. In all the other Cases before mentioned, the supreme Court shall have appellate Jurisdiction, both as to Law and Fact, with such Exceptions, and under such Regulations as the Congress shall make.

The Trial of all Crimes, except in Cases of Impeachment, shall be by Jury; and such Trial shall be held in the State where the said Crimes shall have been committed; but when not committed within any State, the Trial shall be at such Place or Places as the Congress may by Law have directed.

SECTION 3. Treason against the United States, shall consist only in levying War against them, or in adhering to their Enemies, giving them Aid and Comfort. No Person shall be convicted of Treason unless on the Testimony of two Witnesses to the same overt Act, or on Confession in open Court.

The Congress shall have Power to declare the Punishment of Treason, but no Attainder of Treason shall work Corruption of Blood, or Forfeiture except during the Life of the Person attainted.

ARTICLE IV.

SECTION 1. Full Faith and Credit shall be given in each State to the public Acts, Records, and judicial Proceedings of every other State; And the Congress may by general Laws prescribe the Manner in which such Acts, Records and Proceedings shall be proved, and the Effect thereof.

SECTION 2. The Citizens of each State shall be entitled to all Privileges and Immunities of Citizens in the several States.

A Person charged in any State with Treason, Felony, or other Crime, who shall flee from Justice, and be found in another State, shall on Demand of the executive Authority of the State from which he fled, be delivered up, to be removed to the State having Jurisdiction of the Crime.

No person held to Service or Labour in one State, under the Laws thereof, escaping into another, shall, in Consequence of any Law or Regulation therein, be discharged from such Service or Labour, but shall be delivered up on Claim of the Party to whom such Service or Labour may be due.

SECTION 3. New States may be admitted by the Congress into this Union; but no new State shall be formed or erected within the Jurisdiction of any other State; nor any State be formed by the Junction of two or more States, or Parts of States, without the Consent of the Legislatures of the States concerned as well as of the Congress.

The Congress shall have Power to dispose of and make all needful Rules and Regulations respecting the Territory or other Property belonging to the United States; and nothing in this Constitution shall be so construed as to Prejudice any Claims of the United States, or of any particular State.

SECTION 4. The United States shall guarantee to every State in this Union a Republican Form of Government, and shall protect each of them against Invasion; and on Application of the Legislature, or of the Executive (when the Legislature cannot be convened) against domestic Violence.

ARTICLE V.

The Congress, whenever two thirds of both Houses shall deem it necessary, shall propose Amendments to this Constitution, or, on the Application of the Legislatures of two thirds of the several States, shall call a Convention for proposing Amendments, which, in either Case, shall be valid to all Intents and Purposes, as Part of this Constitution, when ratified by the Legislatures of three fourths of the several States, or by Conventions in three fourths thereof, as the one or the other Mode of Ratification may be proposed by the Congress; Provided that no Amendment which may be made prior to the Year One thousand eight hundred and eight shall in any Manner affect the first and fourth Clauses in the Ninth Section of the first Article; and that no State, without its Consent, shall be deprived of it's equal Suffrage in the Senate.

ARTICLE VI.

All Debts contracted and Engagements entered into, before the Adoption of this Constitution, shall be as valid against the United States under this Constitution, as under the Confederation.

This Constitution, and the Laws of the United States which shall be made in Pursuance thereof; and all Treaties made, or which shall be made, under the Authority of the United States, shall be the supreme Law of the Land; and the Judges in every State shall be bound thereby, any Thing in the Constitution or Laws of any State to the Contrary notwithstanding.

The Senators and Representatives before mentioned, and the Members of the several State Legislatures, and all executive and judicial Officers, both of the United States and of the several States, shall be bound by Oath or Affirmation, to support this Constitution; but no religious Test shall ever be required as a Qualification to any Office or public Trust under the United States.

ARTICLE VII.

The Ratification of the Conventions of nine States, shall be sufficient for the Establishment of this Constitution between the States so ratifying the Same.

Done in Convention by the Unanimous Consent of the States present the Seventeenth Day of September in the Year of our Lord one thousand seven hundred and Eighty seven and of the Independence of the United States of America the Twelfth. In Witness whereof We have hereunto subscribed our Names,

Gº: Washington—Presidᵗ and deputy from Virginia

New Hampshire	John Langdon Nicholas Gilman
Massachusetts	Nathaniel Gorham Rufus King
Connecticut	Wᵐ Samˡ Johnson Roger Sherman
New York	Alexander Hamilton
New Jersey	Wil: Livingston David Brearley Wᵐ Paterson Jona: Dayton
Pennsylvania	B Franklin Thomas Mifflin Robᵗ Morris Geo. Clymer Thoˢ. FitzSimons Jared Ingersoll James Wilson Gouv Morris

Delaware	Geo: Read Gunning Bedord jun John Dickinson Richard Bassett Jaco: Broom
Maryland	James McHenry Dan of Sᵗ Thoˢ. Jenifer Danˡ Carroll
Virginia	John Blair— James Madison Jr.
North Carolina	Wᵐ. Blount Richᵈ Dobbs Spaight. Hu Williamson
South Carolina	J. Rutledge Charles Cotesworth Pinckney Charles Pickney Pierce Butler
Georgia	William Few Abr Baldwin

Attest William Jackson Secretary

AMENDMENTS TO THE U.S. CONSTITUTION

AMENDMENT I.

Congress shall make no law respecting an establishment of religion, or prohibiting the free exercise thereof; or abridging the freedom of speech, or of the press, or the right of the people peaceably to assemble, and to petition the Government for a redress of grievances.   [ratified December, 1791]

AMENDMENT II.

A well regulated Militia, being necessary to the security of a free State, the right of the people to keep and bear Arms, shall not be infringed.   [ratified December, 1791]

AMENDMENT III.

No Soldier shall, in time of peace be quartered in any house, without the consent of the Owner, nor in time of war, but in a manner to be prescribed by law.   [ratified December, 1791]

AMENDMENT IV.

The right of the people to be secure in their persons, houses, papers, and effects, against unreasonable searches and seizures, shall not be violated, and no Warrants shall issue, but upon probable cause, supported by Oath or affirmation, and particularly describing the place to be searched, and the persons or things to be seized.   [ratified December, 1791]

AMENDMENT V.

No person shall be held to answer for a capital, or otherwise infamous crime, unless on a presentment or indictment of a Grand Jury, except in cases arising in the land or naval forces, or in the Militia, when in actual service in time of War or public danger; nor shall any person be subject for the same offence to be twice put in jeopardy of life or limb, nor shall be compelled in any criminal case to be a witness against himself, nor be deprived of life, liberty, or property, without due process of law; nor shall private property be taken for public use without just compensation.   [ratified December, 1791]

AMENDMENT VI.

In all criminal prosecutions, the accused shall enjoy the right to a speedy and public trial, by an impartial jury of the State and district wherein the crime shall have been committed; which district shall have been previously ascertained by law, and to be informed of the nature and cause of the accusation; to be confronted with the witnesses against him; to have compulsory process for obtaining witnesses in his favor, and to have the assistance of counsel for his defence.   [ratified December, 1791]

AMENDMENT VII.

In Suits at common law, where the value in controversy shall exceed twenty dollars, the right of trial by jury shall be preserved, and no fact tried by a jury shall be otherwise reexamined in any Court of the United States, than according to the rules of the common law.   [ratified December, 1791]

AMENDMENT VIII.

Excessive bail shall not be required, nor excessive fines imposed, nor cruel and unusual punishments inflicted.   [ratified December, 1791]

AMENDMENT IX.

The enumeration in the Constitution, of certain rights, shall not be construed to deny or disparage others retained by the people.   [ratified December, 1791]

AMENDMENT X.

The powers not delegated to the United States by the Constitution, nor prohibited by it to the States, are reserved to the States respectively, or to the people.   [ratified December, 1791]

AMENDMENT XI.

The Judicial power of the United States shall not be construed to extend to any suit in law or equity, commenced or prosecuted against one of the United States by Citizens of another State, or by Citizens or Subjects of any Foreign State.   [ratified February, 1795]

AMENDMENT XII.

The Electors shall meet in their respective states, and vote by ballot for President and Vice President, one of whom, at least, shall not be an inhabitant of the same state with themselves; they shall name in their ballots the person voted for as President, and in distinct ballots the person voted for as Vice-President, and they shall make distinct lists of all persons voted for as President, and of all persons voted for as Vice-President, and of the number of votes for each, which lists they shall sign and certify, and transmit sealed to the seat of the government of the United States, directed to the President of the Senate;—The President of the Senate shall, in the presence of the Senate and House of Representatives, open all the certificates and the votes shall then be counted;—The person having the greatest number of votes for President, shall be the President, if such number be a majority of the whole number of Electors appointed; and if no person have such majority, then from the persons having the highest numbers not exceeding three on the list of those voted for as President, the House of Representatives shall choose immediately, by ballot, the President. But in choosing the President, the votes shall be taken by states, the representation from each state having one vote; a quorum for this purpose shall consist of a member or members from two-thirds of the states, and a majority of all the states shall be necessary to a choice. And if the House of Representatives shall not choose a President whenever the right of choice shall devolve upon them, before the fourth day of March next following, then the Vice-President shall act as President, as in the case of the death or other constitutional disability of the President.—The person having the greatest number of votes as Vice-President, shall be the Vice-President, if such number be a majority of the whole number of Electors appointed, and if no person have a majority, then from the two highest numbers on the list, the Senate shall choose the Vice-President; a quorum for the purpose shall consist of two-thirds of the whole number of Senators, and a majority of the whole number shall be necessary to a choice. But no person constitutionally ineligible to the office of President shall be eligible to that of Vice-President of the United States. [ratified June, 1804]

AMENDMENT XIII.

SECTION 1. Neither slavery nor involuntary servitude, except as a punishment for crime whereof the party shall have been duly convicted, shall exist within the United States, or any place subject to their jurisdiction.

SECTION 2. Congress shall have power to enforce this article by appropriate legislation. [ratified December, 1865]

AMENDMENT XIV.

SECTION 1. All persons born or naturalized in the United States and subject to the jurisdiction thereof, are citizens of the United States and of the State wherein they reside. No State shall make or enforce any law which shall abridge the privileges or immunities of citizens of the United States; nor shall any State deprive any person of life, liberty, or property, without due process of law; nor deny to any person within its jurisdiction the equal protection of the laws.

SECTION 2. Representatives shall be apportioned among the several States according to their respective numbers, counting the whole number of persons in each State, excluding Indians not taxed. But when the right to vote at any election for the choice of electors for President and Vice President of the United States, Representatives in Congress, the Executive and Judicial officers of a State, or the members of the Legislature thereof, is denied to any of the male inhabitants of such State, being twenty-one years of age, and citizens of the United States, or in any way abridged, except for participation in rebellion, or other crime, the basis of representation therein shall be reduced in the proportion which the number of such male citizens shall bear to the whole number of male citizens twenty-one years of age in such State.

SECTION 3. No person shall be a Senator or Representative in Congress, or elector of President and Vice President, or hold any office, civil or military, under the United States, or under any State, who, having previously taken an oath, as a member of Congress, or as an officer of the United States, or as a member of any State legislature, or as an executive or judicial officer of any State, to support the Constitution of the United States, shall have engaged in insurrection or rebellion against the same, or given aid or comfort to the enemies thereof. But Congress may by a vote of two-thirds of each House, remove such disability.

SECTION 4. The validity of the public debt of the United States, authorized by law, including debts incurred for payment of pensions and bounties for services in suppressing insurrection or rebellion, shall not be questioned. But neither the United States nor any State shall assume or pay any debt or obligation incurred in aid of insurrection or rebellion against the United States, or any claim for the loss or emancipation of any slave; but all such debts, obligations and claims shall be held illegal and void.

SECTION 5. The Congress shall have power to enforce, by appropriate legislation, the provisions of this article.
[ratified July, 1868]

AMENDMENT XV.

SECTION 1. The right of citizens of the United States to vote shall not be denied or abridged by the United States or by any State on account of race, color, or previous condition of servitude.

SECTION 2. The Congress shall have power to enforce this article by appropriate legislation. [ratified February, 1870]

AMENDMENT XVI.

The Congress shall have power to lay and collect taxes on incomes, from whatever source derived, without apportionment among the several States, and without regard to any census or enumeration. [ratified February, 1913]

AMENDMENT XVII.

The Senate of the United States shall be composed of two Senators from each State, elected by the people thereof, for six years; and each Senator shall have one vote. The electors in each State shall have the qualifications requisite for electors of the most numerous branch of the State legislatures.

When vacancies happen in the representation of any State in the Senate, the executive authority of such State shall issue writs of election to fill such vacancies: *Provided*, That the legislature of any State may empower the executive thereof to make temporary appointments until the people fill the vacancies by election as the legislature may direct.

This amendment shall not be so construed as to affect the election or term of any Senator chosen before it becomes valid as part of the Constitution. [ratified April, 1913]

AMENDMENT XVIII.

SECTION 1. After one year from the ratification of this article the manufacture, sale, or transportation of intoxicating liquors within, the importation thereof into, or the exportation thereof from the United States and all territory subject to the jurisdiction thereof for beverage purposes is hereby prohibited.

SECTION 2. The Congress and the several States shall have concurrent power to enforce this article by appropriate legislation.

SECTION 3. This article shall be inoperative unless it shall have been ratified as an amendment to the Constitution by the legislatures of the several States, as provided in the Constitution, within seven years from the date of the submission hereof to the States by the Congress.

[ratified January, 1919, repealed December, 1933]

AMENDMENT XIX.

The right of citizens of the United States to vote shall not be denied or abridged by the United States or by any State on account of sex.

Congress shall have power to enforce this article by appropriate legislation.   [ratified August, 1920]

AMENDMENT XX.

SECTION 1. The terms of the President and Vice President shall end at noon on the 20th day of January, and the terms of Senators and Representatives at noon on the 3d day of January, of the years in which such terms would have ended if this article had not been ratified; and the terms of their successors shall then begin.

SECTION 2. The Congress shall assemble at least once in every year, and such meeting shall begin at noon on the 3d day of January, unless they shall by law appoint a different day.

SECTION 3. If, at the time fixed for the beginning of the term of the President, the President elect shall have died, the Vice President elect shall become President. If a President shall not have been chosen before the time fixed for the beginning of his term, or if the President elect shall have failed to qualify, then the Vice President elect shall act as President until a President shall have qualified; and the Congress may by law provide for the case wherein neither a President elect nor a Vice President elect shall have qualified, declaring who shall then act as President, or the manner in which one who is to act shall be selected, and such person shall act accordingly until a President or Vice President shall have qualified.

SECTION 4. The Congress may by law provide for the case of the death of any of the persons from whom the House of Representatives may choose a President whenever the right of choice shall have devolved upon them, and for the case of the death of any of the persons from whom the Senate may choose a Vice President whenever the right of choice shall have devolved upon them.

SECTION 5. Sections 1 and 2 shall take effect on the 15th day of October following the ratification of this article.

SECTION 6. This article shall be inoperative unless it shall have been ratified as an amendment to the Constitution by the legislatures of three-fourths of the several States within seven years from the date of its submission. [ratified January, 1933]

AMENDMENT XXI.

SECTION 1. The eighteenth article of amendment to the Constitution of the United States is hereby repealed.

SECTION 2. The transportation or importation into any State, Territory, or possession of the United States for delivery or use therein of intoxicating liquors, in violation of the laws thereof, is hereby prohibited.

SECTION 3. This article shall be inoperative unless it shall have been ratified as an amendment to the Constitution by conventions in the several States, as provided in the Constitution, within seven years from the date of the submission hereof to the States by the Congress.   [ratified December, 1933]

AMENDMENT XXII.

SECTION 1. No person shall be elected to the office of the President more than twice, and no person who has held the office of President, or acted as President, for more than two years of a term to which some other person was elected President shall be elected to the office of the President more than once. But this Article shall not apply to any person holding the office of President when this Article was proposed by the Congress, and shall not prevent any person who may be holding the office of President, or acting as President, during the term within which this Article becomes operative from holding the office of President or acting as President during the remainder of such term.

SECTION 2. This article shall be inoperative unless it shall have been ratified as an amendment to the Constitution by the legislatures of three-fourths of the several States within seven years from the date of its submission to the States by the Congress.   [ratified February, 1951]

AMENDMENT XXIII.

SECTION 1. The District constituting the seat of Government of the United States shall appoint in such manner as the Congress may direct:

A number of electors of President and Vice President equal to the whole number of Senators and Representatives in Congress to which the District would be entitled if it were a State, but in no event more than the least populous State; they shall be in addition to those appointed by the States, but they shall be considered, for the purposes of the election of President and Vice President, to be electors appointed by a State; and they shall meet in the District and perform such duties as provided by the twelfth article of amendment.

SECTION 2. The Congress shall have power to enforce this article by appropriate legislation.   [ratified March, 1961]

AMENDMENT XXIV.

SECTION 1. The right of citizens of the United States to vote in any primary or other election for President or Vice President, for electors for President or Vice President, or for Senator or Representative in Congress, shall not be denied or abridged by the United States or any State by reason of failure to pay any poll tax or other tax.

SECTION 2. The Congress shall have power to enforce this article by appropriate legislation.   [ratified January, 1964]

AMENDMENT XXV.

SECTION 1. In case of the removal of the President from office or of his death or resignation, the Vice President shall become President.

SECTION 2. Whenever there is a vacancy in the office of the Vice President, the President shall nominate a Vice President who shall take office upon confirmation by a majority vote of both Houses of Congress.

SECTION 3. Whenever the President transmits to the President pro tempore of the Senate and the Speaker of the House of Representatives his written declaration that he is unable to discharge the powers and duties of his office, and until he transmits to them a written declaration to the contrary, such powers and duties shall be discharged by the Vice President as Acting President.

SECTION 4. Whenever the Vice President and a majority of either the principal officers of the executive departments or of such other body as Congress may by law provide, transmit to the President pro tempore of the Senate and the Speaker of the House of Representatives their written declaration that the President is unable to discharge the powers and duties of his office, the Vice President shall immediately assume the powers and duties of the office as Acting President.

Thereafter, when the President transmits to the President pro tempore of the Senate and the Speaker of the House of Representatives his written declaration that no inability exists, he shall resume the powers and duties of his office unless the Vice President and a majority of either the principal officers of the executive department or of such other body as Congress may by law provide, transmit within four days to the President pro tempore of the Senate and the Speaker of the House of Representatives their written declaration that the President is unable to discharge the powers and duties of his office. Thereupon Congress shall decide the issue, assembling within forty-eight hours for that purpose if not in session. If the Congress, within twenty-one days after receipt of the latter written declaration, or, if Congress is not in session, within twenty-one days after Congress is required to assemble, determines by two-thirds vote of both Houses that the President is unable to discharge the powers and duties of his office, the Vice President shall continue to discharge the same as Acting President; otherwise, the President shall resume the powers and duties of his office. [ratified February, 1967]

AMENDMENT XXVI.

SECTION 1. The right of citizens of the United States, who are eighteen years of age or older, to vote shall not be denied or abridged by the United States or by any State on account of age.

SECTION 2. The Congress shall have power to enforce this article by appropriate legislation. [ratified July, 1971]

AMENDMENT XXVII.

No law, varying the compensation for the services of the Senators and Representatives, shall take effect, until an election of Representatives shall have intervened.

[ratified May 7, 1992]

ARREST TRENDS, 1984-1993

Offense Charged	Number of Persons Arrested								
	Total All Ages			Under 18 Years of Age			18 Years of Age and Over		
	1984	1993	Percent Change	1984	1993	Percent Change	1984	1993	Percent Change
TOTAL	8,828,447	10,448,491	+18.4	1,466,212	1,791,083	+22.2	7,362,235	8,657,408	+17.6
Index crimes									
Murder and nonnegligent manslaughter	15,126	18,856	+24.7	1,154	3,092	+167.9	13,972	15,764	+12.8
Forcible rape	28,565	29,432	+3.0	4,357	4,750	+9.0	24,208	24,682	+2.0
Robbery	115,522	143,877	+24.5	29,018	40,499	+39.6	86,504	103,378	+19.5
Aggravated assault	241,664	408,148	+68.9	31,315	62,039	+98.1	210,349	346,109	+64.5
Burglary	338,737	308,849	−8.8	125,718	104,901	−16.6	213,019	203,948	−4.3
Larceny-theft	981,812	1,131,768	+15.3	320,960	352,866	+9.9	660,852	778,902	+17.9
Motor vehicle theft	96,975	156,711	+61.6	33,771	69,465	+105.7	63,204	87,246	+38.0
Arson	14,288	14,504	+1.5	5,978	7,183	+20.2	8,310	7,321	−11.9
Index crimes totals									
Violent crime[1]	400,877	600,313	+49.7	65,844	110,380	+67.6	335,033	489,933	+46.2
Property crime[2]	1,431,812	1,611,832	+12.6	486,427	534,415	+9.9	945,385	1,077,417	+14.0
Crime Index total	1,832,689	2,212,145	+20.7	552,271	644,795	+16.8	1,280,418	1,567,350	+22.4
Other crimes									
Other assaults	423,258	870,146	+105.6	65,444	138,713	+112.0	357,814	731,433	+104.4
Forgery and counterfeiting	65,486	80,989	+23.7	6,300	5,858	−7.0	59,186	75,131	+26.9
Fraud	230,346	296,737	+28.8	17,356	13,301	−23.4	212,990	283,436	+33.1
Embezzlement	7,315	10,092	+38.0	477	586	+22.9	6,838	9,506	+39.0
Stolen property; buying, receiving, possessing	96,632	122,256	+26.5	22,783	32,485	+42.6	73,849	89,771	+21.6
Vandalism	182,347	235,170	+29.0	80,885	105,866	+30.9	101,462	129,304	+27.4
Weapons; carrying, possessing, etc.	139,928	204,433	+46.1	21,000	47,369	+125.6	118,928	157,064	+32.1
Prostitution and commercialized vice	96,262	83,346	−13.4	2,524	923	−63.4	93,738	82,423	−12.1
Sex offenses (except forcible rape and prostitution)	77,653	80,332	+3.4	13,104	15,038	+14.8	64,549	65,294	+1.2
Drug abuse violations	568,032	884,771	+55.8	66,425	84,902	+27.8	501,607	799,869	+59.5
Gambling	29,532	14,121	−52.2	744	1,020	+37.1	28,788	13,101	−54.5
Offenses against family and children	37,842	71,119	+87.9	1,439	3,034	+110.8	36,403	68,085	+87.0
Driving under the influence	1,362,499	1,059,517	−22.2	18,635	9,289	−50.2	1,343,864	1,050,228	−21.9
Liquor laws	354,861	357,116	+.6	90,650	77,866	−14.1	264,211	279,250	+5.7
Drunkenness	839,256	558,833	−33.4	22,050	12,588	−42.9	817,206	546,245	−33.2
Disorderly conduct	480,469	542,837	−13.0	67,814	106,779	+57.5	412,655	436,058	+5.7
Vagrancy	28,519	23,000	−19.4	1,914	2,969	+55.1	26,605	20,031	−24.7
All other offenses (except traffic)	1,806,754	2,531,244	+40.1	245,630	277,415	+12.9	1,561,124	2,253,829	+44.4
Suspicion (not included in totals)	15,230	7,412	−51.3	2,448	1,093	−55.4	12,782	6,319	−50.6
Curfew and loitering law violations	62,487	73,502	+17.6	62,487	73,502	+17.6	—	—	—

Source: U.S. Department of Justice, Federal Bureau of Investigation, *Crime in the United States* (Uniform Crime Reports). Washington, D.C.: U.S. Government Printing Office, 1994.

Note: Data reflect agencies (7,978 in 1993) reporting to the FBI's Uniform Crime Reporting Program. "Index crimes" is a designation used by the program for tracking eight serious types of crime.

[1] Murder, forcible rape, robbery, and aggravated assault.

[2] Burglary, larceny-theft, motor vehicle theft, and arson.

CRIMINAL VICTIMIZATION REPORTS, 1992

Type of Victimization	Estimated Number of Victimizations	Reported to Police Yes[1]	No	Not Known and Not Available	Type of Victimization	Estimated Number of Victimizations	Reported to Police Yes[1]	No	Not Known and Not Available
All crimes	**33,649,340**	**38.7%**	**60.0%**	**1.3%**	Personal larceny with contact	484,810	30.9	69.1	0.0[2]
					Purse snatching	152,300	46.7	53.3	0.0[2]
Personal crimes	18,831,980	36.7	61.8	1.5	Completed	109,570	57.9	42.1	0.0[2]
					Attempted	42,730	18.0[2]	82.0[2]	0.0[2]
Crimes of violence	6,621,140	49.8	49.1	1.2	Pocket picking	332,500	23.7	76.3	0.0[2]
Completed	2,409,520	60.0	38.6	1.4[2]	Personal larceny				
Attempted	4,211,610	43.9	55.0	1.1	without contact	11,726,020	29.5	68.7	1.8
					Completed	11,006,280	30.3	67.9	1.8
Rape	140,930	52.5	47.5	0.0[2]	Less than $50	4,390,870	15.3	83.7	1.0
Completed	40,730	83.0[2]	17.0[2]	0.0[2]	$50 or more	5,942,460	41.5	56.4	2.1
Attempted	100,200	40.0	60.0	0.0[2]	Amount not available	672,930	28.6	66.1	5.3[2]
					Attempted	719,740	17.7	81.0	1.3[2]
Robbery	1,225,510	51.1	48.9	0.0[2]					
Completed	806,460	60.7	39.3	0.0[2]	**Household crimes**	14,817,360	41.3%	57.8%	1.0%
With injury	334,040	69.8	30.2	0.0[2]					
From serious assault	173,480	81.4	18.6[2]	0.0[2]	Completed	12,586,350	42.1	57.0	0.9
From minor assault	160,550	57.3	42.7	0.0[2]	Attempted	2,231,010	36.4	62.1	1.5[2]
Without injury	472,420	54.2	45.8	0.0[2]					
Attempted	419,040	32.7	67.3	0.0[2]	Burglary	4,757,420	53.5	44.8	1.7
With injury	103,320	43.2	56.8	0.0[2]	Completed	3,785,070	58.3	40.1	1.6
From serious assault	55,750	45.9[2]	54.1[2]	0.0[2]	Forcible entry	1,602,130	76.0	22.8	1.2[2]
From minor assault	47,560	40.0[2]	60.0[2]	0.0[2]	Unlawful entry				
Without injury	315,720	29.3	70.7	0.0[2]	without force	2,182,930	45.3	52.8	1.8[2]
					Attempted forcible entry	972,340	34.8	63.1	2.1[2]
Assault	5,254,690	49.4	49.1	1.5					
Aggravated	1,848,530	61.6	37.3	1.2[2]	Household larceny	8,101,150	26.0	73.5	0.5
Completed with injury	657,550	69.0	30.1	0.9[2]	Completed	7,581,760	26.0	73.4	0.6
Attempted with weapon	1,190,970	57.5	41.2	1.3[2]	Less than $50	2,800,570	12.5	87.3	0.1[2]
Simple	3,406,160	42.8	55.6	1.7	$50 or more	4,200,090	35.8	63.5	0.7[2]
Completed with injury	904,770	51.9	45.1	3.0[2]	Amount not available	581,090	19.6	78.5	1.9[2]
Attempted with weapon	2,501,390	39.4	59.4	1.2[2]	Attempted	519,380	26.3	73.7	0.0[2]
Crimes of theft	12,210,830	29.5	68.7	1.7	Motor vehicle theft	1,958,780	74.7	24.3	1.0[2]
					Completed	1,219,510	92.2	7.3	0.5[2]
Completed	11,448,350	30.3	67.9	1.8	Attempted	739,270	45.7	52.5	1.8[2]
Attempted	762,480	17.7	81.0	1.2[2]					

Source: U.S. Department of Justice, Bureau of Justice Statistics, *Criminal Victimization in the United States, 1992* (National Crime Victimization Survey). Washington, D.C.: U.S. Department of Justice, 1994.

Note: National Crime Victimization Survey data, collected by the U.S. Census Bureau, represent a continuous survey of a sample of housing units in the United States; approximately 61,000 housing units participated. Subcategories may not sum to total because of rounding.

[1] Represents the rates at which victimizations were reported to the police, or "police reporting rates."

[2] Estimate is based on about 10 or fewer sample cases.

FAMOUS AMERICAN TRIALS

Date	Trial	Issue or Charge	Result or Significance
1634	Roger Williams	Religious dissent	Williams was found guilty of blasphemy and exiled from Massachusetts Bay Colony; he subsequently founded Rhode Island.
1636	Anne Marbury Hutchinson	Religious dissent	Anne Hutchinson was convicted of sedition and contempt and exiled; she founded Portsmith, Rhode Island.
1690	Rebecca Nurse and others	Witchcraft	In the Salem Witch trials, Rebecca Nurse and five others (all old men and women) were convicted of witchcraft and hanged.
1735	John Peter Zenger	Seditious libel	Zenger published a newspaper opposed to the New York colonial government. He was arrested and imprisoned. Defended by Alexander Hamilton, Zenger proved that his statements were true and was acquitted. This trial set the pattern for freedom of the press in America.
1770	William McCauley and others	Manslaughter	McCauley and six other British soldiers were tried for killing five men in a riot on Boston Commons in March, 1870 (the "Boston massacre"). John Adams defended them. Four were acquitted and two were convicted. The latter were branded and released.
1802	Aaron Burr	Treason	Burr planned to create a personal empire in the Mississippi Valley. President Thomas Jefferson charged him with treason. The judge, Chief Justice John Marshall, narrowly defined the charge, and Burr was quickly acquitted. Popular sentiment was so much against Burr, however, that he was forced into European exile for a number of years.
1804	Samuel Chase	Impeachment	Chase was impeached by Jeffersonian Democrats for his opposition during sedition trials, but the Senate refused to convict him.
1859	John Brown	Treason, murder	Brown's trial on charges stemming from his antislavery raid at Harpers Ferry lasted four days. Supporters' plans to free him failed. The jury convicted him in forty-five minutes, and he was hanged two months later.
1862	Rda-in-yan-ka, Big Eagle, and others	Murder	After a Sioux uprising in 1862 in Minnesota in which more than four hundred whites were killed, a mass trial was held. Three hundred and six were sentenced to death and eighteen to prison. President Lincoln commuted all but thirty-nine of the death sentences. Rda-in-yan-ka was hanged and Big Eagle was imprisoned.
1865	Mary Surratt	Conspiracy to murder, treason	Linked to the assassination of President Lincoln because the conspirators stayed at her boarding house, Surratt was found guilty and hanged although there was no direct evidence against her.
1866	Samuel A. Mudd	Conspiracy to murder	Mudd treated John Wilkes Booth after he killed Lincoln. Although he claimed he did not know of the assassination, he was sentenced to life imprisonment.
1868	Andrew Johnson	Impeachment for high crimes and misdemeanors	Johnson, a southern pro-Union Democrat, became president after Lincoln's assassination. The Republican Congress passed a law limiting his ability to control his cabinet. When he refused to abide, an impeachment trial in the Senate began. Johnson was acquitted when seven Republicans refused to join the others in a guilty verdict: The charge failed by one vote to reach the required two-thirds majority.

Date	Trial	Issue or Charge	Result or Significance
1875	John Doyle Lee	Murder	A Mormon and Indian agent, Lee was involved in a dispute with a band of California-bound settlers. He encouraged a group of Paiute Indians to kill them and participated in the massacre at Mountain Meadows, Utah. After two trials he was executed.
1881	Charles J. Guiteau	Murder	The assassin of President John Garfield, Guiteau was convicted and executed.
1886	August Spies and others	Accessory to murder	Spies and seven others were tried for abetting the murder of policemen killed by a bomb during a labor demonstration in Chicago (the Haymarket Riot). Although their connection to the crime could not be proved, they were charged because they were labor leaders and outspoken anarchists. They were convicted—seven sentenced to hang and one, Oscar Neebe, to life imprisonment. One committed suicide. Two death sentences were commuted. Four of the men were hanged, including Spies. The remaining three were pardoned by Illinois governor John Peter Altgel in 1893.
1901	Leon Czolgosz	Murder	Czolgosz was the anarchist assassin of President William McKinley. He was rapidly tried and convicted in Buffalo, New York, where the assassination took place. He was executed by electrocution.
1906	William Dudley ("Big Bill") Haywood	Murder	Haywood was accused with others of murdering Frank Steunenberg, governor of Idaho. They were defended by Clarence Darrow and acquitted.
1907	Harry Thaw	Murder	Thaw, a wealthy socialite married to the dancer Evelyn Nesbit, shot and killed her lover, prominent architect Stanford White. He was acquitted on grounds of insanity.
1911	J. J. and J. B. McNamara	Murder	The McNamara brothers bombed the *Los Angeles Times* building during a labor dispute. Twenty-one decision persons were killed. Their attorney, Clarence Darrow, pleaded guilty to save their lives. They were sentenced to long prison terms.
1914	Joe Hill (Joe Emmanuel Hagglund)	Murder	Hill, a Swedish-born labor organizer and composer, was falsely charged with murder. He was convicted on doubtful evidence and executed despite widespread appeals for reconsideration including one from President Wilson.
1917	Margaret Sanger	Creating a public nuisance	Sanger, a nurse and advocate of artificial birth control, then illegal in most states, was arrested and convicted of creating a public nuisance. She was sentenced to thirty days.
1917	Emma Goldman	Hindering conscription	Goldman, an anarchist and pacifist, opposed American entry into World War I. She was tried for impeding conscription, denaturalized, and returned to her native Russia in 1919.
1918	Eugene V. Debs	Sedition	Debs, a labor leader and pioneer American socialist, was tried and convicted of violating the Espionage Act. Sentenced to ten years, he was pardoned by President Harding in 1921.

Date	Trial	Issue or Charge	Result or Significance
1924	Nicola Sacco and Bartolomeo Vanzetti	Murder, robbery	Sacco and Vanzetti were Italian-born anarchists who were tried and convicted of armed robbery and murder in 1921. Although the evidence was flimsy and there was indication of other guilty persons, the authorities refused appeals and new trials. They were convicted largely because of their political beliefs. The case provoked worldwide condemnation and mass demonstrations. Sacco and Vanzetti were executed in 1927. Fifty years later Massachusetts governor Michael Dukakis exonerated them.
1921-1922	Roscoe "Fatty" Arbuckle	Manslaughter	Arbuckle, a famous film star, was arrested after the death of a young actress at a Hollywood party. After three trials he was acquitted, but his film career was ruined because of the scandal.
1924	Nathan Leopold and Richard Loeb	Murder	Celebrated case involving the brutal homosexual rape and murder of young Bobby Franks by two wealthy young men, Leopold and Loeb. Clarence Darrow successfully argued against their execution in a bench trial. They were given life imprisonment. Loeb was killed in prison; Leopold was paroled in 1968.
1925	John T. Scopes	Teaching evolution	In what was dubbed the "monkey trial," Scopes, a high school teacher, deliberately broke Tennessee's law against teaching Darwinian evolution. The trial gained national publicity because it pitted William Jennings Bryan as prosecutor against Clarence Darrow for the defense. Scopes was convicted and given a nominal fine. The U.S. Supreme Court overturned the conviction, but the statute remained.
1926	Albert Fall	Accepting bribes	Secretary of the interior under President Harding, Fall was at the center of the Teapot Dome scandal (he gave out generous leases on public land). He was convicted and served one year in prison.
1927	Harry Daugherty	Conspiracy to defraud the government	Daugherty, President Harding's attorney general, was involved in the Teapot Dome scandal. His two trials ended in hung juries.
1931	Haywood Patterson and others	Rape	Patterson and eight other African Americans were falsely charged with rape in Scottsboro, Alabama. All-white juries quickly convicted them in three trials, and all nine were sentenced to execution. The "Scottsboro" case drew national attention and involved complex political and racial issues. The U.S. Supreme Court overturned the convictions because the defendants were denied due process and the right to counsel.
1931	Al Capone	Income tax evasion	Capone, a notorious gangster involved in the illegal manufacture and sale of alcohol and other rackets, had long evaded arrest. Federal authorities finally charged him with violating the tax laws. He was convicted and sentenced to eleven years and fined $80,000.
1936	Bruno Richard Hauptmann	Kidnapping, murder	Hauptmann was charged in the sensational "baby Lindbergh" case. He was accused of kidnapping and murdering the son of famous aviator Charles Lindbergh. Although the evidence was circumstantial, he was convicted and executed. The media reporting of the event was extremely controversial.

Date	Trial	Issue or Charge	Result or Significance
1941	Louis (Lepke) Buchalter	Murder	Buchalter, the leader of Murder Incorporated, organized crime's assassination ring in 1930's New York, was convicted in one of a series of trials against racketeers that brought district attorney Thomas E. Dewey to prominence. Buchalter was executed.
1948	Caryl Chessman	Kidnapping	Chessman forced his victim from one car to another and raped her. In a trial in which he defended himself, he was convicted on the technical charge of kidnapping rather than rape and sentenced to death. His execution was postponed for twelve years, during which time he wrote a number of successful books. The controversial nature of the charge, the length of the delay, and his personal publicity made his case a cause célèbre.
1949	Julius and Ethel Rosenberg	Espionage	The Rosenbergs were convicted of passing atomic secrets to the Soviet Union in a controversial trial. Despite many appeals for their sentences to be commuted to life imprisonment, they were executed.
1950	Alger Hiss	Perjury	Hiss was tried and convicted in a second trial after a first one ended in a hung jury. He was charged with lying about his communist connections. The trials were public sensations, contributing to the hysteria of the McCarthy period.
1951	Elizabeth Gurley Flynn	Smith Act (membership in the Communist Party)	Flynn, a prominent radical labor leader and Communist Party member, was convicted under the Smith Act.
1954	Sam Sheppard	Murder	Sheppard was convicted of murdering his wife and sentenced to life imprisonment. The U.S. Supreme Court in 1965 overturned the conviction because the publicity associated with the case had denied him a fair trial.
1964	Jack Ruby	Murder	The killer of Lee Harvey Oswald, President Kennedy's assassin, was defended by attorney Melvin Belli. He was convicted and sentenced to death, but the conviction was reversed in 1966 on appeal.
1967	Jimmy Hoffa	Jury tampering and mishandling union funds	Hoffa was an object of the Department of Justice's war on union corruption. He was convicted in 1967 after several trials and then pardoned in 1971.
1968	James Earl Ray	Murder	Ray was convicted of murdering the civil rights leader Martin Luther King, Jr., and sentenced to life imprisonment.
1969-1970	Rennie Davis and others	Conspiracy, intent to incite riot	The "Chicago eight" (later seven), were arrested for disrupting the 1968 Democratic convention. Conspiracy charges were dismissed, but five were convicted of intent to incite riot; they were sentenced to five years and fined. Prominent attorney William Kunstler defended them. The convictions were reversed in 1972.
1969	Angela Davis	Accessory to murder	Charged because her guns were used in a prison escape attempt, Davis was acquitted in a case which brought international publicity. Her membership in the Communist Party was thought to be part of the reason behind the charge.

Date	Trial	Issue or Charge	Result or Significance
1971	Charles Manson and others	Murder	Manson, the leader of a counterculture commune (the "Manson family"), was charged with the murder of actress Sharon Tate and more than six others. Although the murders were carried out by his followers, and he was not present, he was seen as primarily responsible. Manson was sentenced to death, but later the sentence was commuted when California overturned its death penalty. The trial attracted international attention.
1971	William J. Calley	Murder	Calley, an army lieutenant, commanded a platoon which massacred women and children in the South Vietnamese village of My Lai during the war. The publicity about the event forced a court-martial of Calley. He was convicted and sentenced to twenty years, but he served little time before being pardoned.
1971	Daniel Ellsberg	Theft, espionage, and conspiracy	Ellsberg leaked the "Pentagon Papers," secret documents that contained information on U.S. violations of international law in the Vietnam War. He was indicted, but the charges were dismissed because of improper government actions in preparing their case.
1973	Spiro Agnew	Accepting bribes	Vice President Agnew pleaded no contest and was sentenced to three years' probation and a $10,000 fine. He resigned as vice president.
1973	John Dean	Perjury	A key figure in the Watergate scandal, Dean pleaded guilty of perjury in the cover-up and was sentenced to prison.
1974	G. Gordon Liddy	Burglary, conspiracy, and wiretapping	One of the principal "plumbers" in the Watergate affair, Liddy was convicted of burglarizing and bugging the Democratic headquarters and was sentenced to seven to twenty years.
1974-1975	John Mitchell, H. R. Haldeman, John Erlichman, and others	Conspiracy	Seven members of the Nixon Administration, White House staff, and Republican National Committee were indicted for illegal conspiracy relating to the 1972 election. Five, including Mitchell, Haldeman, and Erlichman, were convicted and given sentences ranging from two and a half to eight years.
1974	E. Howard Hunt and others	Burglary, conspiracy, and wiretapping	Along with G. Gordon Liddy, Hunt directed the Watergate burglary. He and his four codefendants actually carried out the burglary. Hunt pleaded guilty and was sentenced to thirty months to eight years.
1975	Patricia Hearst	Armed robbery	Kidnapped by the radical terrorist Symbionese Liberation Army, Hearst, the daughter of a newspaper magnate, joined the group and participated in its bank robberies. Her criminal career, capture, and trial were a media sensation. She claimed to have been "brainwashed" but was convicted and sentenced to seven years, commuted by President Jimmy Carter after two and a half years.
1976	Gary Gilmore	Murder	Gilmore was convicted of murder and sentenced to death. His case became controversial when he requested (and received) execution rather than following up the appeals process.

Date	Trial	Issue or Charge	Result or Significance
1982	Claus Von Bulow	Attempted murder	Von Bulow, a financial consultant married to a New England socialite, was convicted of trying to kill her by administering an insulin overdose. He was sentenced to thirty years. The conviction was overturned in 1985 when Von Bulow was represented by attorney Alan Dershowitz.
1984	Raymond James Donovan	Falsifying documents business records	Donovan, President Reagan's secretary of labor, was hounded through his tenure of office by charges of corruption linked to organize crime. He was indicted, tried, and acquitted.
1984, 1986	John DeLorean	Drug trafficking, racketeering, and fraud	In two trials, automobile entrepreneur DeLorean was acquitted on all counts.
1986	Jim Bakker	Conspiracy, fraud	Bakker, a television evangelist, lost his ministry in a sex scandal, and then was convicted of diverting donations for personal use. He was sentenced to forty-five years. The conviction was upheld in appeal, although the sentence was reduced eighteen years.
1989	Oliver North	Conspiracy to defraud, obstruction of Congress	North, a staff member on the National Security Council, was a key figure in the Iran-Contra Affair. He was convicted of covering up the affair and sentenced to a three-year suspended sentence, probation, a fine, and community service.
1990	John Poindexter	Conspiracy, perjury, and obstruction of Congress	Poindexter, as secretary of the Navy, lied during the congressional investigation of the Iran-Contra scandal (the Reagan Administration's illegal trading of arms for hostages). He was convicted on all counts and sentenced to six months. The conviction was reversed on appeal.
1990	Marion Barry	Drug possession	Barry, the mayor of Washington, D.C., was convicted of cocaine possession and sentenced to six months. After serving his term he was again elected mayor.
1992	Jeffrey Dahmer	Murder	Dahmer enticed his victims to his apartment, murdered them, and saved parts of their bodies. He also engaged in cannibalism. The gory nature of his crime made it a sensation. He was ruled sane, convicted of murder, and sentenced to sixteen life terms. He was killed in prison in 1994.
1992	Mike Tyson	Rape	The heavy-weight boxing champion was accused and convicted of raping a participant in a beauty contest in which he was judge.
1992	William Kennedy Smith	Rape	Smith, a member of the prominent Kennedy family, was accused of rape by a woman he invited to the family's compound in Florida. He was acquitted after a televised trial. Comparisons were made with the Tyson trial.
1992, 1993	Stacey Koon, Laurence Powell, and others	Police misconduct, violation of civil rights	Four Los Angeles police officers were charged with using excessive force in arresting African American motorist Rodney King for a traffic violation. The beating of King was videotaped by a witness. The police officers were acquitted by a suburban jury, causing five days of rioting in Los Angeles. In a second trial in federal court, Koon and Powell were convicted of civil rights violations and sentenced to two-and-a-half years.

Date	Trial	Issue or Charge	Result or Significance
1993-1994	Erik and Lyle Menendez	Murder	In a much-publicized case, the brothers murdered their parents and pleaded innocence on the basis that they had been abused as children. Their first trial was declared a mistrial. A second one began in 1995.
1993	Lorena Bobbit	Malicious wounding	Bobbit cut off her husband's penis in retaliation for spousal abuse. (Doctors were able to restore the organ surgically.) She was acquitted.
1994	Byron De La Beckwith	Murder	Beckwith assassinated prominent civil rights activist Medgar Evers in 1963. Although he was known to have committed the crime, racial prejudice in Mississippi, where the murder occurred resulted in two hung juries. A new trial took place in 1994. He was convicted and sentenced to life imprisonment.
1995	Susan Smith	Murder	After murdering her two young sons, Smith claimed that they were kidnapped. She was convicted and sentenced to life imprisonment.
1995	O. J. Simpson	Murder	In a sensational, nationally televised trial lasting almost a year, celebrity and former football star Simpson was charged with murdering his wife and a visitor. A jury took less than a day to acquit him in a decision that had racial overtones and divided the nation.

SELECT SUPREME COURT CASES

Date	Case Name	Citation	Decision
1803	Marbury v. Madison	1 Cranch (5 U.S.) 137	Supreme Court had power to determine constitutionality of federal statutes.
1810	Fletcher v. Peck	6 Cranch (10 U.S.) 87	Supreme Court had power to determine constitutionality of state statutes.
1819	Dartmouth College v. Woodward	4 Wheat. (17 U.S.) 518	State law revising charter of college violated contract clause because college was private corporation.
1819	Sturges v. Crowninshield	4 Wheat. (17 U.S.) 122	State insolvency law discharging previously existing debts violated contract clause.
1827	Ogden v. Saunders	12 Wheat. (25 U.S.) 213	State insolvency law did not violate contract clause when applied to contracts entered into after law's passage.
1831	Cherokee Nation v. Georgia	5 Pet. (30 U.S.) 1	Supreme Court lacked jurisdiction to hear case brought by Cherokees because they were not a sovereign nation.
1833	Barron v. Baltimore	7 Pet. (32 U.S.) 243	Provisions of Bill of Rights limited federal rather than state action.
1837	Charles River Bridge v. Warren Bridge Co.	11 Pet. (36 U.S.) 420	Contract clause did not prevent state from granting proprietors the right to build and collect tolls from bridge and then granting similar right to other individuals to build new bridge.
1857	Scott v. Sandford [sic]	19 How. (60 U.S.) 393	Slaves were not citizens of the United States, and the Missouri Compromise was unconstitutional.
1866	Ex parte Milligan	71 U.S. 2	Trial of civilians before a military tribunal was unconstitutional.
1873	Slaughterhouse Cases	16 Wall. (83 U.S.) 36	State law granting monopoly to one slaughterhouse did not violate Fourteenth Amendment.
1879	Reynolds v. United States	98 U.S. 145	Federal antibigamy law did not violate free exercise of religion rights of Mormons.
1883	Civil Rights Cases	109 U.S. 3	Federal law prohibiting racial discrimination in inns and public conveyances unconstitutionally exceeded Congress' powers under the Thirteenth and Fourteenth Amendments.
1884	Hurtado v. California	110 U.S. 516	Due process clause did not require grand jury indictment in state murder prosecution.
1890	In re Neagle	135 U.S. 1	*Habeas corpus* relief available to remedy violations of acts done under the authority of the United States as well as violations of federal statutes.
1895	In re Debs	158 U.S. 564	Injunction issued against strikers was constitutional since the United States had authority to remove obstructions to commerce.
1896	Plessy v. Ferguson	163 U.S. 537	State requirement of separate railway facilities for black and white passengers did not deny equal protection of law.

Date	Case Name	Citation	Decision
1905	Lochner v. New York	198 U.S. 45	State law limiting hours bakers could work violated due process clause by infringing freedom to contract.
1908	Muller v. Oregon	208 U.S. 412	Law setting maximum work hours for women was not unconstitutional.
1914	Weeks v. United States	232 U.S. 383	Evidence obtained in illegal search must be excluded in a subsequent criminal prosecution.
1915	Guinn v. United States	238 U.S. 347	State voter literacy requirement intended to prevent blacks from voting violated Fifteenth Amendment.
1918	Hammer v. Dagenhart	247 U.S. 251	Federal law prohibiting interstate shipment of goods produced with child labor was in excess of Congress' power under commerce clause.
1919	Abrams v. United States	250 U.S. 616	Federal law punishing criticisms of President Wilson for sending troops to fight in Soviet Russia did not violate First Amendment.
1919	Schenck v. United States	249 U.S. 47	Prosecution of antidraft pamphleteer did not violate First Amendment.
1921	Newberry v. United States	256 U.S. 232	Congress lacked power to limit campaign expenditures in primary elections.
1925	Gitlow v. New York	268 U.S. 652	First Amendment did not prevent state from punishing advocacy of the violent overthrow of government even if such advocacy did not immediately incite criminal action.
1925	Pierce v. Society of Sisters	268 U.S. 510	State law requiring children in grades one through eight to be educated in public schools violated due process clause.
1927	Buck v. Bell	274 U.S. 200	Due process clause not violated when state involuntarily sterilized mentally impaired female.
1927	Nixon v. Herndon	273 U.S. 536	State law excluding blacks from voting in Democratic primaries was unconstitutional.
1928	Olmstead v. United States	277 U.S. 438	Wiretap not involving entry of private premises was not unreasonable search and seizure.
1931	Near v. Minnesota	283 U.S. 697	State law barring publication of newspaper that had printed malicious and defamatory articles violated freedom of press.
1932	Powell v. Alabama	287 U.S. 45	Due process clause required that criminal defendants in rape case have attorney provided.
1934	Home Building and Loan Association v. Blaisdell	290 U.S. 398	State moratorium on repayment of mortgages did not violate contract clause.
1935	Grovey v. Townsend	295 U.S. 45	Equal protection clause not violated by limitation of state Democratic party membership to whites.

Date	Case Name	Citation	Decision
1936	Brown v. Mississippi	297 U.S. 278	Use of coerced confessions in state prosecution violated due process clause.
1936	Carter v. Carter Coal Co.	298 U.S. 238	Congress exceeded its power under the commerce clause by enacting legislation regulating labor in the coal mining industry.
1937	Herndon v. Lowry	301 U.S. 242	First Amendment did not bar statute prohibiting attempts to incite insurrection.
1937	Palko v. Connecticut	302 U.S. 319	Fourteenth Amendment's due process clause did not impose on states the double jeopardy limitation of the Fifth Amendment.
1937	West Coast Hotel Co. v. Parrish	300 U.S. 379	Commerce clause allowed state to regulate minimum wages for women and children.
1940	Chambers v. Florida	309 U.S. 227	Use of improperly obtained confessions violated due process of law.
1941	United States v. Classic	313 U.S. 299	Congress could regulate primary elections since primary was important part of election process for federal office.
1941	United States v. Darby	312 U.S. 100	Commerce clause allowed Congress to regulate wages and hours of workers who manufactured products shipped interstate.
1942	Wickard v. Filburn	317 U.S. 111	Commerce clause allowed Congress to regulate farmers' consumption of wheat for personal use.
1943	Hirabayashi v. United States	320 U.S. 81	Curfew law applied to Japanese Americans did not violate constitutional ban on racial discrimination.
1943	West Virginia State Board of Education v. Barnette	319 U.S. 624	Free exercise of religion clause prohibited schools from compelling Jehovah's Witness children to participate in flag salute ceremony.
1944	Korematsu v. U.S.	323 U.S. 214	Relocation of Japanese Americans to interment camps did not violate constitutional prohibition against racial discrimination.
1944	Smith v. Allwright	321 U.S. 649	Exclusion of blacks from party primaries that selected candidates for state and national offices was "state action" and violated Fourteenth and Fifteenth Amendments.
1946	Colegrove v. Green	328 U.S. 549	Case involving action to compel congressional redistricting was a nonjusticiable political question.
1947	Adamson v. California	332 U.S. 46	Due process clause did not prevent prosecutor in a state criminal proceeding from calling jury's attention to defendant's failure to testify.
1947	Everson v. Board of Education	330 U.S. 1	State reimbursement of parents for costs of transportation to parochial schools did not violate establishment of religion clause.
1948	Shelley v. Kraemer	334 U.S. 1	Fourteenth Amendment prevented state courts from enforcing racially restrictive real estate covenants.

Date	Case Name	Citation	Decision
1949	Wolf v. Colorado	338 U.S. 25	States were not required to exclude evidence obtained through illegal search.
1950	Sweatt v. Painter	339 U.S. 629	State violated equal protection clause by denying black applicant admission to state law school.
1951	Dennis v. United States	341 U.S. 494	First Amendment not violated by conviction for advocating communism.
1954	Brown v. Board of Education	347 U.S. 483	Segregation of public schools violated equal protection clause.
1954	Bolling v. Sharpe	347 U.S. 497	Segregation of schools in the District of Columbia violated equal protection clause.
1957	Roth v. United States	354 U.S. 476	First Amendment did not protect obscene materials.
1957	Yates v. United States	354 U.S. 298	First Amendment prohibited government from prosecuting advocacy of forcible overthrow of government without proof of advocacy of acts to that end.
1958	Cooper v. Aaron	358 U.S. 1	Delaying desegregation of public schools to avoid racial unrest violated equal protection clause.
1959	Barenblatt v. United States	360 U.S. 109	Freedom of speech not violated by contempt conviction of witness before congressional committee for refusal to testify concerning his beliefs and membership in communist club.
1961	Mapp v. Ohio	367 U.S. 643	Fourth Amendment prohibited use of evidence obtained as a result of illegal search.
1961	Scales v. United States	367 U.S. 203	Conviction for "active" membership in the Communist Party did not violate freedom of speech.
1962	Baker v. Carr	369 U.S. 186	Equal protection challenge to state apportionment of legislative districts could be heard by federal courts.
1962	Engel v. Vitale	370 U.S. 421	Recitation of state-composed nondenominational prayer in public schools violated the establishment of religion clause.
1962	Robinson v. California	370 U.S. 660	Classification of drug addition as criminal offense constituted cruel and unusual punishment.
1963	Gideon v. Wainright	372 U.S. 335	Due process clause required state to provide attorneys to defendants charged with serious offenses.
1963	Abington School District v. Schempp	374 U.S. 203	Recitations of Lord's Prayer and Bible readings in public school violated establishment of religion clause.
1963	Sherbert v. Verner	374 U.S. 398	Free exercise of religion clause required state to grant unemployment benefits to Seventh-Day Adventist fired for refusing to work on Saturday, her Sabbath.

Date	Case Name	Citation	Decision
1964	Escobedo v. Illinois	378 U.S. 478	Government prohibited from using confession without informing defendant of right to counsel.
1964	Heart of Atlanta Motel v. United States	379 U.S. 241	Commerce clause permitted Congress to prohibit racial discrimination in privately owned places of public accommodation.
1964	Malloy v. Hogan	378 U.S. 1	Privilege against self-incrimination was applicable to state criminal proceedings.
1964	New York Times Co. v. Sullivan	376 U.S. 254	First Amendment protected press from actions for defamation against public officials unless press acted with actual malice.
1964	Reynolds v. Sims	377 U.S. 533	Equal protection clause required legislative apportionment to accord "one person, one vote."
1964	Wesberry v. Sanders	376 U.S. 1	Substantial disparity in population of congressional districts was unconstitutional.
1965	Griswold v. Connecticut	381 U.S. 479	State law prohibiting married couples from using contraceptives violated right of privacy.
1966	Harper v. Virginia Board of Elections	383 U.S. 663	State poll tax violated equal protection clause.
1966	Miranda v. Arizona	384 U.S. 436	Due process clause required states to inform suspects in police custody of right to remain silent and to have counsel appointed.
1966	Sheppard v. Maxwell	384 U.S. 333	Excessive pretrial publicity violated criminal defendant's right to a fair trial.
1967	In re Gault	387 U.S. 1	Due process clause requires that juveniles be accorded the privilege against self-incrimination and the right to counsel.
1967	Katz v. United States	389 U.S. 347	Wiretap could constitute an illegal search and seizure.
1967	Reitman v. Mulkey	387 U.S. 369	State constitution barring state from interfering with racial discrimination by private individuals in sale or lease of property violated equal protection clause.
1968	Chimel v. California	395 U.S. 752	Warrantless search incident to an arrest may include arrestee's person and area within his immediate control.
1968	Duncan v. Louisiana	391 U.S. 145	Due process clause required states to provide trial by jury to persons charged with serious crimes.
1968	Green v. County School Board	391 U.S. 430	Freedom of choice plan did not satisfy school district's obligation to eliminate racial segregation.
1968	Terry v. Ohio	392 U.S. 1	"Stop and frisk" searches were not unreasonable searches and seizures.
1968	Harris v. United States	390 U.S. 234	Police officers conducting a legal but warrantless search were entitled to seize objects in plain sight.

Date	Case Name	Citation	Decision
1968	Jones v. Alfred H. Mayer Co.	392 U.S. 409	Congress could prohibit private acts of discrimination in housing sales.
1968	United States v. O'Brien	391 U.S. 367	Law prohibiting destruction or mutilation of draft cards did not violate freedom of speech.
1968	Witherspoon v. Illinois	391 U.S. 510	Prosecutors could not exclude potential jurors who expressed general objections to or religious scruples concerning death penalty.
1969	Alexander v. Holmes County Board of Education	396 U.S. 19	Desegregation of public schools required without further delay.
1969	Brandenburg v. Ohio	395 U.S. 444	State could punish advocacy of illegal action only if advocacy incited imminent lawless action and was likely to produce such action.
1969	Shapiro v. Thompson	394 U.S. 618	Durational residency requirement for welfare benefits violated right to travel.
1969	Tinker v. Des Moines School District	393 U.S. 503	First Amendment protected students' rights to wear black armbands to protest Vietnam War.
1970	Brady v. United States	397 U.S. 742	Defendant's guilty plea was not involuntary simply because defendant feared receiving the death penalty at trial.
1970	Dandridge v. Williams	397 U.S. 471	Welfare provision that imposed maximum award per family without regard to family size did not violate equal protection clause.
1971	Bivens v. Six Unknown Named Agents	403 U.S. 388	Victims of illegal search could bring action against federal officers.
1971	Graham v. Richardson	403 U.S. 365	Discrimination against aliens regarding eligibility for welfare benefits violated equal protection clause.
1971	Griffin v. Breckenridge	403 U.S. 88	Congress could punish racially motivated assaults on public highway.
1971	Griggs v. Duke Power Co.	401 U.S. 424	Congress could prohibit employment discrimination based on race and require that job tests be related to job skills.
1971	Lemon v. Kurtzman	403 U.S. 602	Establishment of religion clause prohibited aid to parochial schools which fostered excessive entanglement between government and religion.
1971	New York Times Co. v. United States	403 U.S. 713	First Amendment prohibited injunction to prevent newspapers from publishing the "Pentagon papers."
1971	Reed v. Reed	404 U.S. 71	State law automatically preferring father over mother as executor of child's estate violated equal protection clause.

Date	Case Name	Citation	Decision
1971	Santobello v. New York	404 U.S. 257	Defendant who pled guilty based on prosecutor's commitment regarding sentence recommendation entitled to remand when prosecutor violated commitment.
1971	Swann v. Charlotte-Mecklenburg Board of Education	402 U.S. 1	Flexible use of racial quotas, busing, and gerrymandered school districts was appropriate to remedy segregation in public schools.
1971	Tilton v. Richardson	403 U.S. 672	State grant of construction funds to religious colleges for buildings to be used for secular purposes did not violate establishment of religion clause.
1972	Argersinger v. Hamlin	407 U.S. 25	Right to counsel applies to federal and state trials for offenses involving possible incarceration.
1972	Barker v. Wingo	407 U.S. 514	Right to speedy trial was not violated by delay of five years between arrest and trial when defendant did not desire speedy trial.
1972	Dunn v. Blumstein	405 U.S. 330	Durational residency requirement for voting violated equal protection clause.
1972	Eisenstadt v. Baird	405 U.S. 438	Law allowing only married couples to purchase contraceptives violated equal protection clause.
1972	Furman v. Georgia	408 U.S. 238	Death penalty was unconstitutional when jury had complete discretion in its application.
1972	Lindsey v. Normet	405 U.S. 56	Summary eviction proceedings for tenants did not violate due process clause.
1972	Moose Lodge No. 107 v. Irvis	407 U.S. 163	Granting liquor license to racially discriminatory private club did not violate equal protection clause.
1972	Wisconsin v. Yoder	406 U.S. 205	Free exercise of religion clause required that Amish be exempted from state requirement that children attend high school.
1973	Doe v. Bolton	410 U.S. 179	Requirements that abortions be performed in hospitals, reviewed by other physicians, and limited to state residents violated right to abortion.
1973	Frontiero v. Richardson	411 U.S. 677	Federal law that automatically awarded military dependant benefits differently for males and females violated equal protection clause.
1973	Keyes v. School District No. 1	413 U.S. 189	Districtwide remedies permitted when one part of district engaged in segregation.
1973	Miller v. California	413 U.S. 15	States allowed to regulate obscene material.
1973	Roe v. Wade	410 U.S. 113	Laws restricting abortions except after viability or as necessary to safeguard a woman's health after the first trimester of pregnancy violate right to abortion.

Date	Case Name	Citation	Decision
1973	San Antonio Independent School District v. Rodriguez	411 U.S. 1	State's reliance on local property taxes to fund public education did not violate equal protection clause.
1974	Milliken v. Bradley	418 U.S. 717	Multidistrict remedies for segregated schools were not permissible unless each district involved had engaged in purposeful segregation.
1976	Buckley v. Valeo	424 U.S. 1	Federal limit on amounts candidates for office could spend violated First Amendment.
1976	Elrod v. Burns	427 U.S. 347	Public official of one party who discharges employees who are nonparty members violated First Amendment.
1976	Gregg v. Georgia	428 U.S. 153	Sentencing judge or jury required to consider individual character of defendant and circumstance of crime before imposing death penalty.
1976	Massachusetts Board of Retirement v. Murgia	427 U.S. 307	Mandatory retirement for state police officers did not violate equal protection clause.
1976	Pasadena City Board of Education v. Spangler	427 U.S. 424	District court lacked authority to order yearly adjustments to maintain racial balances in public schools after official segregation had been remedied.
1976	Planned Parenthood v. Danforth	428 U.S. 52	Spousal and parental notification requirements and requirement that physician attempt to preserve fetus' life violated right to abortion.
1976	Runyon v. McCrary	427 U.S. 160	Federal law prevented racially segregated private school from refusing to admit black students.
1976	Washington v. Davis	426 U.S. 229	Requiring police officer candidates to take aptitude test even though more black than white candidates failed did not violate equal protection clause.
1977	Coker v. Georgia	433 U.S. 584	Death sentence for rape constituted cruel and unusual punishment.
1977	Maher v. Roe	432 U.S. 464	State had no obligation to pay for indigent woman's nontherapeutic abortion.
1978	Regents of the University of California v. Bakke	438 U.S. 265	State could not use fixed racial quotas in medical school admissions process but could consider race as one factor in determining admissions.
1979	United Steelworkers of America v. Weber	443 U.S. 193	Employers who voluntarily adopted affirmative action programs did not violate federal antidiscrimination law.
1979	Vance v. Bradley	440 U.S. 93	Mandatory retirement provision for foreign service officials did not violate equal protection clause.
1980	Fullilove v. Klutznick	448 U.S. 448	Congressional affirmative action program involving federal public works projects did not violate equal protection clause.
1980	Harris v. McRae	448 U.S. 297	Congress could restrict federal funding of medically necessary abortions.

Date	Case Name	Citation	Decision
1980	Rummel v. Estelle	445 U.S. 263	Imposition of life sentence after three relatively minor offenses was not unconstitutional.
1981	Rhodes v. Chapman	452 U.S. 337	Housing of two inmates in cell designed for one was not unconstitutional.
1981	Rostker v. Goldberg	453 U.S. 57	Exclusion of women from the draft did not violate equal protection clause.
1982	Hutto v. Davis	454 U.S. 370	Excessiveness of sentence in relation to crime was not unconstitutional.
1982	New York v. Ferber	458 U.S. 747	Freedom of speech was not violated by law making it a crime to promote sexual performances by children (child pornography).
1982	Plyler v. Doe	457 U.S. 202	State could not deny public education to children of illegal aliens.
1983	Akron v. Akron Center for Reproductive Health	462 U.S. 416	Requirement that abortions after first trimester be performed in hospital, that consent of parents be obtained for abortion performed on minor, that physicians inform women of various information, and that twenty-four hour waiting period be imposed all violated right to abortion.
1983	Mueller v. Allen	463 U.S. 388	State income tax deduction for certain educational expenses did not violate the establishment of religion clause when used by parents of parochial school children.
1983	Solem v. Helm	463 U.S. 277	State's imposition of life sentence for the last of a series of nonviolent crimes constituted cruel and unusual punishment.
1984	Lynch v. Donnelly	465 U.S. 668	Inclusion of nativity scene among other items in a holiday display did not violate establishment of religion clause.
1984	Massachusetts v. Sheppard	468 U.S. 981	Exclusionary rule did not apply to results of search conducted by police officers who reasonably relied on warrant later found defective.
1984	Schall v. Martin	467 U.S. 253	Due process clause allowed state to detain suspect who poses serious risk of committing a serious crime before trial.
1984	United States v. Leon	468 U.S. 897	Illegally obtained evidence could be used at trial if police had a search warrant and believed they were acting legally.
1985	New Jersey v. T.L.O.	469 U.S. 325	Fourth Amendment's ban on unreasonable searches and seizures applies to searches of public school students.
1985	Tennessee v. Garner	471 U.S. 1	Police could not use deadly force to stop fleeing felon except to prevent death or serious injury to bystander.
1985	Wallace v. Jaffree	472 U.S. 38	Moment of silence statute intended to restore prayer to public schools violated establishment of religion clause.
1986	Batson v. Kentucky	476 U.S. 79	Prosecutors barred from using peremptory challenges to exclude blacks from jury because of their race.

Date	Case Name	Citation	Decision
1986	Bowers v. Hardwick	478 U.S. 186	Constitutional right of privacy did not protect homosexual conduct.
1986	City of Renton v. Playtime Theaters	475 U.S. 41	Ordinance prohibiting adult theaters from locating within 1,000 feet of residential areas, churches, parks, or schools did not violate freedom of speech.
1986	Ford v. Wainwright	477 U.S. 399	Constitution barred state from executing insane prisoner.
1986	Thornburgh v. American College of Obstetricians and Gynecologists	476 U.S. 747	Right to an abortion violated by state informed consent and reporting requirements as well as by obligation imposed on physician to preserve life of fetus.
1987	Booth v. Maryland	482 U.S. 496	Use of victim impact statement during sentencing phase of capital murder trial was unconstitutional.
1987	Edwards v. Aguillard	482 U.S. 578	State law requiring teaching of "creation science" if evolution was taught violated establishment of religion clause.
1987	Illinois v. Krull	480 U.S. 340	Exclusionary rule did not apply to searches made in objectively reasonable reliance upon law providing for warrantless administrative searches of vehicles.
1987	McCleskey v. Kemp	481 U.S. 279	Statistics showing racial disparities in imposition of death penalty did not prove a violation of equal protection clause.
1987	Nollan v. California Coastal Commission	483 U.S. 825	State violated just compensation clause ("takings clause") by conditioning building permit on owner conveying an easement to the state across owner's property.
1987	Tison v. Arizona	481 U.S. 137	State allowed to execute murder accomplices if they participated in a major way in the crime and displayed reckless indifference to human life.
1989	Texas v. Johnson	491 U.S. 397	Antiflag desecration statute violated the First Amendment.
1989	National Treasury Employees Union v. Raab	489 U.S. 656	Suspicionless drug testing of employees applying for drug interdiction positions was not unconstitutional.
1989	Richmond v. J. A. Croson Co.	488 U.S. 469	Affirmative action program adopted by city in construction contracts violated equal protection clause.
1989	Skinner v. Railway Labor Executives' Association	489 U.S. 602	Required drug testing for railroad workers after major accidents was not unconstitutional.
1989	Stanford v. Kentucky	492 U.S. 361	Death sentence imposed for crime committed while defendant was a minor did not necessarily constitute cruel and unusual punishment.
1989	United States v. Monsanto	491 U.S. 600	Federal drug forfeiture statute allows district court to enter pretrial order freezing assets in defendant's possession even when defendant seeks to use assets to pay attorney.

Date	Case Name	Citation	Decision
1989	Wards Cove Packing Co. v. Atonio	490 U.S. 642	Employer allowed to rebut showing that minorities were underrepresented in workplace by demonstrating a reasonable business justification.
1989	Webster v. Reproductive Health Services	492 U.S. 490	Ban on abortions performed by state employees or in public facilities and requirement that physicians perform a test to determine the viability of a fetus did not violate right to abortion.
1990	Employment Division, Department of Human Resources of Oregon v. Smith	494 U.S. 872	Free exercise of religion clause did not require state to grant an exemption from its drug laws to Native Americans who wished to use peyote in religious ceremonies.
1990	Maryland v. Craig	497 U.S. 836	Right to confront witnesses not necessarily violated when child witness in sexual abuse case testifies via closed circuit television.
1990	Minnick v. Mississippi	498 U.S. 146	Confession was inadmissible when defendant was forced to resume interrogation after consulting with attorney.
1990	Osborne v. Ohio	495 U.S. 103	Law punishing possession or viewing of child pornography did not violate the First Amendment.
1990	United States v. Eichman	496 U.S. 310	Federal law criminalizing mutilation of flag violated freedom of speech.
1991	Arizona v. Fulminante	499 U.S. 279	Admission of involuntary confession was subject to the harmless error rule.
1991	Barnes v. Glen Theatre, Inc.	501 U.S. 560	First Amendment did not prevent state from adopting public indecency law which prohibited nude dancing.
1991	Harmelin v. Michigan	501 U.S. 957	Imposition of mandatory life sentence without parole was not cruel and unusual punishment.
1991	Payne v. Tennessee	501 U.S. 808	Use of victim impact evidence in death penalty sentencing did not automatically constitute cruel and unusual punishment.
1991	Rust v. Sullivan	500 U.S. 173	Federal regulations prohibiting abortion counseling or referrals in federally funded clinics did not violate freedom of speech or right to abortion.
1992	Georgia v. McCollum	112 S.Ct. 2348	Equal protection clause prevented criminal defendant from exercising peremptory challenges on the basis of race.
1992	Lucas v. South Carolina Coastal Council	112 S.Ct. 2886	Zoning ordinance which prevents any economic use of property could violate takings clause.
1992	Planned Parenthood v. Casey	112 S.Ct. 2791	Right to abortion violated by spousal notification requirement but not by twenty-four-hour waiting, informed consent, and reporting requirements.
1992	R.A.V. v. St. Paul	112 S.Ct. 2538	"Hate speech" ordinance violated freedom of speech.

Date	Case Name	Citation	Decision
1992	United States v. Alvarez-Machain	504 U.S. 655	Federal court had jurisdiction to try Mexican national forcibly kidnapped and brought to the United States.
1993	Church of the Lukumi Babalu Aye v. Hialeah	113 S.Ct. 2217	Local ordinances designed to prevent animal sacrifices violated the free exercise of religion clause.
1993	Shaw v. Reno	113 S.Ct. 2816	Redistricting plan crafted solely to maximize minority voting strength may violate equal protection clause.
1993	Wisconsin v. Mitchell	113 S.Ct. 2194	Law enhancing punishment of crimes motivated by racial hatred did not abridge freedom of speech.

Supreme Court Justices

Alphabetical listing of Supreme Court justices. Birth and death dates are given in parentheses below name. Name in boldface indicates service as chief justice of the United States. Asterisk (*) after date in *Tenure* column indicates justice died while in office.

Name	Tenure	Appointed by	Highlights
Henry Baldwin (1780-1844)	1830-1844*	Jackson	First justice consistently to write separate opinions expressing his views. Significant opinion: *Holmes v. Jennison*, 39 U.S. 540 (1840). Other publication: *A General View of the Origin and Nature of the Constitution and Government of the United States* (1937).
Philip Pendleton Barbour (1783-1841)	1836-1841*	Jackson	Significant opinion: *New York v. Miln*, 36 U.S. 102 (1837).
Hugo Lafayette Black (1886-1971)	1937-1971	Franklin D. Roosevelt	Author of incorporation doctrine, which held that the major provisions of the Bill of Rights were imposed on the states through the due process clause of the Fourteenth Amendment. Significant opinions: *Adamson v. California*, 332 U.S. 46 (1947) (dissenting opinion); *Barenblatt v. United States*, 360 U.S. 109 (1959) (dissenting opinion); *Gideon v. Wainwright*, 372 U.S. 335 (1963); *Pointer v. Texas*, 380 U.S. 400 (1965); *Illinois v. Allen*, 397 U.S. 337 (1970); *New York Times Co. v. United States*, 403 U.S. 713 (1971) (concurring opinion).
Harry Andrew Blackmun (1908-)	1970-1994	Nixon	Defender of a general constitutional right of privacy. Significant opinions: *Roe v. Wade*, 410 U.S. 113 (1973); *Andresen v. Maryland*, 427 U.S. 463 (1976); *New York v. Burger*, 482 U.S. 691 (1987); *California v. Acevedo*, 500 U.S. 565 (1991).
John Blair, Jr. (1732-1800)	1790-1796	Washington	Significant opinion: *Chisholm v. Georgia*, 2 U.S. 419 (1793).
Samuel Blatchford (1820-1893)	1882-1893*	Arthur	Wrote one of the earliest opinions interpreting the scope of the privilege against self-incrimination. Energetic supporter of substantive due process doctrine. Significant opinions: *Chicago, Milwaukee, and St. Paul Railway. Co. v. Minnesota*, 134 U.S. 418 (1890); *O'Neil v. Vermont*, 144 U.S. 323 (1892); *Councilman v. Hitchcock*, 142 U.S. 547 (1892).
Joseph P. Bradley (1813-1892)	1870-1892*	Grant	Author of *Boyd v. United States*, 116 U.S. 616 (1886), the first case offering a significant interpretation of the Fourth and Fifth Amendments. Significant opinions: *Legal Tender Cases*, 79 U.S. 603 (1871) (concurring opinion); *Civil Rights Cases*, 109 U.S. 3 (1885); *Munn v. Illinois*, 118 U.S. 557 (1886).
Louis Dembitz Brandeis (1856-1941)	1916-1939	Wilson	As a lawyer was a social reformer known as the "people's attorney." As a justice, argued states should be free to experiment with social and economic regulation and was a consistent defender of individual rights. Significant opinions: *Olmstead v. United States, 277 U.S. 438 (1928) (dissenting opinion); Whitney v. California*, 274 U.S. 357 (1927) (concurring opinion); *New State Ice Co. v. Liebmann*, 285 U.S. 262 (1932) (dissenting opinion).

Name	Tenure	Appointed by	Highlights
William Joseph Brennan, Jr. (1906-1997)	1956-1990	Eisenhower	Author of many important Warren Court-era opinions on individual rights; opposed death penalty. Significant opinions: *Baker v. Carr*, 369 U.S. 186 (1962); *Wong Sun v. United States*, 371 U.S. 471 (1963); *New York Times Co. v. Sullivan*, 376 U.S. 254 (1964); *United States v. Wade*, 388 U.S. 218 (1967); *Warden v. Hayden*, 387 U.S. 294 (1967); *Coleman v. Alabama*, 399 U.S. 1 (1970); *Gregg v. Georgia*, 428 U.S. 153 (1976) (dissenting opinion); *Craig v. Boren*, 429 U.S. 190 (1976); *Dunaway v. New York*, 442 U.S. 200 (1979); *Pennsylvania v. Muniz*, 496 U.S. 582 (1990).
David Josiah Brewer (1837-1910)	1890-1910*	Harrison	Believed many forms of governmental economic and social regulation were unconstitutional under substantive due process doctrine. Significant opinions: *Reagan v. Farmers' Loan & Trust Co.*, 154 U.S. 362 (1894); *In re Debs*, 158 U.S. 564 (1895); *Muller v. Oregon*, 208 U.S. 412 (1908).
Steven Gerald Breyer (1938-)	1994-	Clinton	
Henry Billings Brown (1836-1913)	1891-1906	Harrison	Author of "separate but equal" doctrine concerning racial classifications. Significant opinions: *Pollock v. Farmers' Loan & Trust Co.*, 158 U.S. 601 (1895) (dissenting opinion); *Plessy v. Ferguson*, 163 U.S. 537 (1896); *Holden v. Hardy*, 169 U.S. 366 (1898).
Warren Earl Burger (1907-1995)	1969-1986	Nixon	Critical of Warren-era expansion of constitutional rights available to criminal defendants, but unsuccessful in reversing those decisions. Revived separation of powers as an important constitutional doctrine. Significant opinions: *Harris v. New York*, 401 U.S. 222 (1971); *South Dakota v. Opperman*, 428 U.S. 364 (1976); *United States v. Chadwick*, 433 U.S. 1 (1977); *Richmond Newspapers, Inc. v. Virginia*, 448 U.S. 555 (1980) (plurality opinion); *INS v. Chadha*, 462 U.S. 919 (1983); *Nix v. Williams*, 467 U.S. 431 (1984); *United States v. Sharpe*, 470 U.S. 675 (1985).
Harold Hitz Burton (1888-1964)	1945-1958	Truman	Generally, opposed expansion of rights for criminal defendants in state courts. Significant opinions: *Haley v. Ohio*, 332 U.S. 596 (1948) (dissenting opinion); *Henderson v. United States*, 339 U.S. 816 (1950); *Louisiana v. Resweber*, 329 U.S. 459 (1947) (dissenting opinion).
Pierce Butler (1866-1939)	1923-1939*	Harding	Opposed most New Deal regulatory measures. Significant opinions: *Olmstead v. United States*, 277 U.S. 438 (1928) (dissenting opinion); *United States v. Schwimmer*, 279 U.S. 644 (1929).
James Francis Byrnes (1879-1972)	1941-1942	Franklin D. Roosevelt	Last justice who became a lawyer without attending law school. Resigned from the Court to assist the president in the war effort. Served as secretary of state in the Truman administration.
John Archibald Campbell (1811-1889)	1853-1861	Pierce	Resigned soon after Alabama's secession from the Union and became assistant secretary of war for the Confederacy. Significant opinion: *Scott v. Sandford*, 60 U.S. 393 (1857) (concurring opinion).
John Catron (1786-1865)	1837-1865*	Jackson	Significant opinions: *License Cases*, 46 U.S. 504 (1847); *Scott v. Sandford*, 60 U.S. 393 (1857) (concurring opinion).

Name	Tenure	Appointed by	Highlights
Benjamin Nathan Cardozo (1870-1938)	1932-1938*	Hoover	Distinguished career on the New York Court of Appeals and the United States Supreme Court. One of the great jurists in American history. Significant opinions: *Palko v. Connecticut*, 302 U.S. 319 (1937); *Baldwin v. Seelig*, 294 U.S. 511 (1935); *Stewart Machine Co. v. Davis*, 301 U.S. 548 (1937). Other writings: *The Nature of the Judicial Process* (1921); *The Growth of the Law* (1924); *The Paradoxes of Legal Science* (1928).
Salmon Portland Chase (1808-1873)	1864-1873*	Lincoln	Ardent abolitionist. Presided over impeachment trial of President Andrew Johnson. Significant opinions: *Ex parte Milligan*, 71 U.S. 2 (1866) (concurring opinion); *Ex parte McCardle*, 74 U.S. 506 (1869); *United States v. Klein*, 80 U.S. 128 (1871).
Samuel Chase (1741-1811)	1796-1811*	Washington	Signer of the Declaration of Independence, ardent Federalist, and only justice ever impeached, although not convicted by the Senate. Significant opinions: *Ware v. Hylton*, 3 U.S. 199 (1796); *Calder v. Bull* 3 U.S. 386 (1798).
Tom Campbell Clark (1890-1977)	1949-1967	Truman	Author of *Mapp v. Ohio* opinion, which imposed the exclusionary rule on states. Retired from the Court when his son, Ramsey Clark, became attorney general. Significant opinions: *Jenks v. United States*, 353 U.S. 657 (1957) (dissenting opinion); *Mapp v. Ohio*, 367 U.S. 643 (1961); *School District of Abington v. Schempp*, 374 U.S. 203 (1963); *Sheppard v. Maxwell*, 384 U.S. 333 (1966).
John Hessin Clarke (1857-1945)	1916-1922	Wilson	Resigned from the Court to advocate United States entry into the League of Nations. Significant opinions: *Abrams v. United States*, 250 U.S. 616 (1919); *Hammer v. Dagenhart*, 247 U.S. 251 (1918) (dissenting opinion).
Nathan Clifford (1803-1881)	1858-1881*	Buchanan	
Benjamin Robbins Curtis (1809-1874)	1851-1857	Fillmore	Defense counsel for President Johnson during his impeachment trial. Significant opinions: *Cooley v. Board of Wardens of the Port of Philadelphia*, 53 U.S. 299 (1851); *Scott v. Sandford*, 60 U.S. 393 (1857) (dissenting opinion).
William Cushing (1732-1810)	1790-1810*	Washington	In more than twenty years of service, wrote only nineteen opinions. Significant opinion: *Ware v. Hylton*, 2 U.S. 282 (1796).
William Cushing (1732-1810)	1796	Washington	Chief justice for one week before he decided to decline the office and remain as an associate justice.
Peter Vivian Daniel (1784-1860)	1842-1860*	Van Buren	Consistent advocate of states' rights. Significant opinions: *Cooley v. Board of Wardens of the Port of Philadelphia*, 53 U.S. 299 (1851) (concurring opinion); *Scott v. Sandford*, 60 U.S. 393 (1857) (concurring opinion).
David Davis (1815-1886)	1862-1877	Lincoln	Resigned from the Court to take a seat in the United States Senate. Significant opinion: *Ex parte Milligan*, 71 U.S. 2 (1866).
William Rufus Day (1849-1923)	1903-1922	Theodore Roosevelt	Author of the exclusionary rule remedy for Fourth Amendment violations in federal courts. Significant opinions: *Weeks v. United States*, 232 U.S. 383 (1914); *Hammer v. Dagenhart*, 247 U.S. 251 (1918).

Name	Tenure	Appointed by	Highlights
William Orville Douglas (1898-1980)	1939-1975	Franklin D. Roosevelt	An iconoclast and one of the most outspoken justices. Defender of a broad scope for First Amendment and other individual rights. Significant opinions: *Terminiello v. Chicago*, 337 U.S. 1 (1949); *Griswold v. Connecticut*, 381 U.S. 479 (1965); *Argersinger v. Hamlin*, 407 U.S. 25 (1972). Other writings: *Go East, Young Man* (1974); *The Court Years, 1939-1975* (1980); and more than thirty other books.
Gabriel Duvall (1752-1844)	1811-1835	Madison	One of the first members of the Court to hold strong antislavery views.
Oliver Ellsworth (1745-1807)	1796-1800	Washington	As a senator, the main author of the Judiciary Act of 1789, which established the federal court system.
Stephen Johnson Field (1816-1899)	1863-1897	Lincoln	A zealous advocate of substantive due process doctrine as a means of protecting business from governmental regulation. Survived an assassination attempt by a political rival. Significant opinions: *Slaughterhouse Cases*, 83 U.S. 36 (1873) (dissenting opinion); *Munn v. Illinois*, 94 U.S. 113 (1877) (dissenting opinion). Other writing: *Personal Reminiscences of Early Days in California* (1893).
Abe Fortas (1910-1982)	1965-1969	Lyndon B. Johnson	As a lawyer, successfully argued in *Gideon v. Wainwright*, 372 U.S. 335 (1963), that the right to counsel be applied to the states. Longtime adviser and confidant of President Johnson. Nominated for chief justice in 1968, but withdrew. Resigned after disclosure of alleged financial impropriety involving a former client. Significant opinions: *In re Gault*, 381 U.S. 1 (1967); *Tinker v. Des Moines Independent Community School District*, 393 U.S. 503 (1969).
Felix Frankfurter (1882-1965)	1939-1962	Franklin D. Roosevelt	Opposed imposition of many provisions of the Bill of Rights on the states through the due process clause of the Fourteenth Amendment. Fought with Justice Black over this issue for more than twenty years. Significant opinions: *Adamson v. California*, 332 U.S. 46 (1947) (concurring opinion); *Wolf v. Colorado*, 338 U.S. 25 (1949); *Rochin v. California*, 342 U.S. 165 (1952).
Melville Weston Fuller (1833-1910)	1888-1910*	Cleveland	Opposed an expansive reading of the Congress' power under the commerce clause. Significant opinions: *United States v. E. C. Knight Co.*, 156 U.S. 1 (1895); *Pollock v. Farmers' Loan & Trust Co.*, 158 U.S. 601 (1895); *Champion v. Ames*, 188 U.S. 321 (1903) (dissenting opinion).
Ruth Bader Ginsburg (1933-)	1993-	Clinton	Argued cases before the Court which established intermediate scrutiny under the equal protection clause of the Fourteenth Amendment for gender-based regulations.
Arthur Joseph Goldberg (1908-1990)	1962-1965	Kennedy	Resigned to become ambassador to the United Nations with expectation that he would be permitted to settle the Vietnam War. Significant opinions: *Escobedo v. Illinois*, 378 U.S. 478 (1964); *Aguilar v. Texas*, 378 U.S. 108 (1964); *Griswold v. Connecticut*, 381 U.S. 479 (1965) (concurring opinion).
Horace Gray (1828-1902)	1882-1902*	Arthur	Significant opinions: *Sparf v. Hansen*, 156 U.S. 51 (1895); *United States v. Wong Kim Ark*, 169 U.S. 649 (1898).

Name	Tenure	Appointed by	Highlights
Robert Cooper Grier (1794-1870)	1846-1870	Polk	Significant opinions: *Moore v. Illinois* 55 U.S. 13 (1852); The *Prize Cases*, 67 U.S. 635 (1863).
John Marshall Harlan (1833-1911)	1877-1911*	Hayes	No other justice has written as many dissenting opinons which later became the law of the land. Significant opinions: *Plessy v. Ferguson*, 163 U.S. 537 (1896) (dissenting opinion); *Pollock v. Farmers' Loan & Trust Co.*, 158 U.S. 601 (1895) (dissenting opinion); *Lochner v. New York*, 198 U.S. 45 (1905) (dissenting opinion); *Berea College v. Kentucky*, 211 U.S. 45 (1908) (dissenting opinion).
John Marshall Harlan II (1899-1971)	1955-1971	Eisenhower	Author of the modern approach to the scope of the Fourth Amendment. Significant opinions: *Katz v. United States*, 389 U.S. 347 (1967) (concurring opinion); *Simmons v. United States*, 390 U.S. 377 (1968); *Spinelli v. United States*, 393 U.S. 410 (1969).
Oliver Wendell Holmes, Jr. (1841-1935)	1902-1932	Theodore Roosevelt	Most influential justice in the twentieth century; wrote with an elegant style unmatched in the history of the Court. Significant opinions: *Lochner v. New York*, 198 U.S. 45 (1905) (dissenting opinion); *Schneck v. United States*, 249 U.S. 47 (1919); *Abrams v. United States*, 250 U.S. 616 (1919) (dissenting opinion); *Pennsylvania Coal Co. v. Mohan*, 260 U.S. 393 (1922). Other writings: *Kent's Commentaries on American Law* (12th edition); *The Common Law* (1881).
Charles Evans Hughes (1862-1948)	1910-1916	Taft	Resigned to run (unsuccessfully) as the Republican nominee for president in 1916; later served as secretary of state in the Harding Administration.
Charles Evans Hughes (1862-1948)	1930-1941	Hoover	Successfully defended the Court against President Roosevelt's Court-packing plan. Significant opinions: *Brown v. Mississippi*, 297 U.S. 278 (1936); *Home Building & Loan Association v. Blaisdell*, 290 U.S. 398 (1934); *NLRB v. Jones and Laughlin Steel Corp.*, 301 U.S. 1 (1937).
Ward Hunt (1810-1886)	1873-1882	Grant	
James Iredell (1751-1799)	1790-1799*	Washington	Significant opinion: *Chisholm v. Georgia*, 2 U.S. 419 (1793) (dissenting opinion).
Howell Edmunds Jackson (1832-1895)	1893-1895*	Harrison	
Robert Houghwout Jackson (1892-1954)	1941-1954*	Franklin D. Roosevelt	Took a leave from the Court to serve as chief prosecutor in the Nuremberg war crimes trial of Nazi leaders. Publicly feuded with Justice Black over this and other matters. Significant opinion: *West Virginia State Board of Education v. Barnette*, 319 U.S. 624 (1943). Other writings: *The Struggle for Judicial Supremacy* (1941); *The Supreme Court in the American System of Government* (1955).

Name	Tenure	Appointed by	Highlights
John Jay (1745-1829)	1789-1795	Washington	In 1795, resigned to become governor of New York, and in 1800 declined nomination as chief justice. Only author of *The Federalist Papers* to serve on the Supreme Court. Significant opinion: *Chisholm v. Georgia*, 2 U.S. 419 (1793).
Thomas Johnson (1732-1819)	1791-1793	Washington	Wrote only one opinion.
William Johnson (1771-1834)	1804-1834*	Jefferson	Only member of the Court during this period who directly challenged Chief Justice Marshall's views on the Constitution. Significant opinions: *Gibbons v. Ogden*, 22 U.S. 1 (1824) (concurring opinion); *United States v. Hudson and Goodwin*, 11 U.S. 32 (1832).
Anthony McLeod Kennedy (1936-)	1988-	Reagan	Expanded administrative search exception to warrant requirement to individuals. Significant opinions: *Skinner v. Railway Labor Executives' Association*, 489 U.S. 602 (1989); *Illinois v. Perkins*, 496 U.S. 292 (1990).
Joseph Rucker Lamar (1857-1916)	1911-1916*	Taft	Significant opinion: *Gompers v. Bucks Stove and Range Company*, 221 U.S. 418 (1911).
Lucius Quintus Cincinnatus Lamar (1825-1893)	1888-1893*	Cleveland	Significant opinions: *In re Neagle*, 135 U.S. 1 (1890) (dissenting opinion); *Field v. Clark*, 143 U.S. 649 (1892) (dissenting opinion).
Henry Brockholst Livingston (1757-1823)	1807-1823*	Jefferson	
Horace Harmon Lurton (1844-1914)	1910-1914*	Taft	
John Marshall (1755-1835)	1801-1835*	John Adams	The "great chief justice" who established preeminent role of the Supreme Court in interpreting the Constitution. No other justice has ever so dominated the Supreme Court. His last constitutional law decision held the Bill of Rights did not apply to the states. Significant opinions: *Marbury v. Madison*, 5 U.S. 137 (1803); *McCulloch v. Maryland*, 17 U.S. 316 (1819); *Gibbons v. Ogden*, 22 U.S. 1 (1824); *Barron v. Baltimore*, 32 U.S. 243 (1833).
Thurgood Marshall (1908-1993)	1967-1991	Lyndon B. Johnson	Lead lawyer for the NAACP, successfully argued *Brown v. Board of Education* and other cases before the Supreme Court. Viewed the Constitution as providing significant protection for the individual against unjust actions by the government. Adamantly opposed to the death penalty. Significant opinions: *United States v. Wilson*, 420 U.S. 332 (1975); *Gregg v. Georgia*, 428 U.S. 153 (1976) (dissenting opinion); *Donovan v. Dewey*, 452 U.S. 594 (1981); *Oliver v. United States*, 466 U.S. 170 (1984) (dissenting opinion); *Skinner v. Railway Labor Executives' Association*, 489 U.S. 602 (1989) (dissenting opinion); *Florida v. Bostick*, 501 U.S. 429 (1991) (dissenting opinion).

Name	Tenure	Appointed by	Highlights
Stanley Thomas Matthews (1824-1889)	1881-1889*	Garfield	Closest Senate confirmation vote (24-23). Significant opinions: *Hurtado v. California*, 110 U.S. 516 (1884); *Yick Wo v. Hopkins*, 118 U.S. 356 (1886).
Joseph McKenna (1843-1926)	1898-1925	McKinley	In 1924, after old age rendered him incompetent but he remained on the Court, the other justices agreed to decide no case where his vote was the deciding one. Significant opinions: *Hoke v. United States*, 227 U.S. 308 (1913); *Hammer v. Dagenhart*, 247 U.S. 251 (1918) (dissenting opinion); *Gilbert v. Minnesota*, 254 U.S. 325 (1920).
John McKinley (1780-1852)	1838-1852*	Van Buren	
John McLean (1785-1861)	1830-1861*	Jackson	Adamant antislavery justice. Significant opinions: *Prigg v. Pennsylvania*, 41 U.S. 539 (1842) (dissenting opinion); *Ex parte Dorr*, 44 U.S. 103 (1844); *Scott v. Sandford*, 60 U.S. 393 (1857) (dissenting opinion).
James Clark McReynolds (1862-1946)	1914-1941	Wilson	Arguably, the most reactionary and bigoted, and certainly the least congenial justice ever to serve on the Supreme Court. Opposed use of individual rights in criminal cases and New Deal regulatory measures. Significant opinions: *Berger v. United States*, 255 U.S. 22 (1921) (dissenting opinion); *Carroll v. United States*, 267 U.S. 132 (1925) (dissenting opinion); *Pierce v. Society of Sisters*, 268 U.S. 510 (1925); *Stromberg v. California*, 283 U.S. 359 (1931) (dissenting opinion); *Powell v. Alabama*, 287 U.S. 45 (1932) (dissenting opinion).
Samuel Freeman Miller (1816-1890)	1862-1890*	Lincoln	Opposed using the Fourteenth Amendment to block state regulations of business activity and favored the use of individual rights to check the power of the federal government. Significant opinions: *Slaughterhouse Cases*, 83 U.S. 36 (1873); *Kilbourn v. Thompson*, 103 U.S. 168 (1881); *United States v. Lee*, 106 U.S. 196 (1882).
Sherman Minton (1890-1965)	1949-1956	Truman	Consistently held for the government in criminal cases. Significant opinions: *United States v. Rabinowitz*, 339 U.S. 56 (1950); *United States ex rel. Knauff v. Shaughnessy*, 338 U.S. 537 (1950).
William Henry Moody (1853-1917)	1906-1910	Theodore Roosevelt	Believed states were free to confer or withhold individual rights from criminal defendants. Significant opinion: *Twining v. New Jersey*, 211 U.S. 78 (1908); *Londoner v. Denver*, 210 U.S. 373 (1908).
Alfred Moore (1755-1810)	1800-1804	John Adams	Wrote only one opinion.
Frank Murphy (1890-1949)	1940-1949*	Franklin D. Roosevelt	Argued vigorously for the availability of individual rights as checks on governmental power and opposed the expansion of the scope of warrantless searches and seizures. Significant opinions: *Thornhill v. Alabama*, 310 U.S. 88 (1940); *In re Yamashita*, 327 U.S. 1 (1946) (dissenting opinion); *Harris v. United States*, 331 U.S. 145 (1947) (dissenting opinion); *Wolf v. Colorado*, 338 U.S. 25 (1949) (dissenting opinion).

Name	Tenure	Appointed by	Highlights
Samuel Nelson (1792-1873)	1845-1872	Tyler	Significant opinions: *Scott v. Sandford*, 60 U.S. 393 (1857) (concurring opinion); *Prize Cases*, 67 U.S. 635 (1863) (dissenting opinion); *Ex parte Milligan*, 71 U.S. 2 (1866) (dissenting opinion).
Sandra Day O'Connor (1930-)	1981-	Reagan	First woman to serve on the Supreme Court. Significant opinions: *Strictland v. Washington*, 466 U.S. 668 (1984); *Oregon v. Elstad*, 470 U.S. 298 (1985); *Florida v. Bostick*, 501 U.S. 429 (1991).
William Paterson (1745-1806)	1793-1806*	Washington	Significant opinions: *Hylton v. United States*, 3 U.S. 171 (1796); *Stuart v. Laird*, 5 U.S. 299 (1803).
Rufus Wheeler Peckham (1838-1909)	1896-1909*	Cleveland	Author of best-known substantive due process case, *Lochner v. New York*, 198 U.S. 45 (1905). Believed states were not required to offer defendants all of the rights found in the Bill of Rights. Significant opinions: *Crain v. United States*, 162 U.S. 625 (1896); *White v. United States*, 164 U.S. 100 (1896); *Allegeyer v. Louisiana*, 165 U.S. 578 (1897); *Maxwell v. Dow*, 176 U.S. 581 (1900).
Mahlon Pitney (1858-1924)	1912-1922	Taft	Rejected attempts to apply the Bill of Rights to state criminal justice systems and read the scope of those rights narrowly in federal criminal cases. Significant opinions: *Frank v. Mangum*, 237 U.S. 309 (1915); *Pierce v. United States*, 252 U.S. 239 (1920); *Berger v. United States*, 255 U.S. 22 (1921) (dissenting opinion).
Lewis Franklin Powell, Jr. (1907-)	1972-1987	Nixon	Author of modern "open fields" exception to the Fourth Amendment and of opinion cutting back access to federal *habeas corpus* for state prisoners. Significant opinions: *Barker v. Wingo*, 407 U.S. 514 (1972); *Doyle v. Ohio*, 426 U.S. 610 (1976); *Stone v. Powell*, 428 U.S. 465 (1976); *Solem v. Helm*, 463 U.S. 277 (1983); *Oliver v. United States*, 466 U.S. 170 (1984); *Batson v. Kentucky*, 476 U.S. 79 (1986).
Stanley Forman Reed (1884-1980)	1938-1957	Franklin D. Roosevelt	Significant opinions: *McNabb v. United States*, 318 U.S. 347 (1943) (dissenting opinion); *Adamson v. California*, 332 U.S. 46 (1947); *Winters v. New York*, 333 U.S. 507 (1948); *Gallegos v. Nebraska*, 342 U.S. 55 (1951); *Carlson v. Landon*, 342 U.S. 524 (1952); *Brown v. Allen*, 344 U.S. 443 (1953).
William Hubbs Rehnquist (1924-)	1972-1986	Nixon	Opposed to the Warren-era expansion of constitutional rights of defendants. Author of many opinions limiting the scope of these decisions and adamant critic of the exclusionary rule. Significant opinions: *Rakas v. Illinois*, 439 U.S. 128 (1978); *Illinois v. Gates*, 462 U.S. 213 (1983).
William Hubbs Rehnquist (1924-)	1986-	Reagan	Led the Court in the creation of more exceptions to the warrant requirement of the Fourth Amendment and of limitations on the use of the exclusionary rule. Significant opinions *Colorado v. Connelly*, 479 U.S. 157 (1986); *United States v. Salerno*, 481 U.S. 739 (1987); *Arizona v. Youngblood*, 488 U.S. 51 (1988); *Michigan Department of State Police v. Sitz*, 496 U.S. 444 (1990).

Name	Tenure	Appointed by	Highlights
Owen Josephus Roberts (1875-1955)	1930-1945	Hoover	Changed his vote and saved the Supreme Court from President Franklin D. Roosevelt's Court-packing plan, commonly known as a "switch in time that saved the nine." Consistent defender of individual rights in criminal cases. Significant opinions: *Grau v. United States*, 287 U.S. 124 (1932); *Herndon v. Lowry*, 301 U.S. 242 (1937); *Hague v. Committee for Industrial Organization*, 307 U.S. 496 (1939); *Cantwell v. Connecticut*, 310 U.S. 296 (1940); *Betts v. Brady*, 316 U.S. 455 (1942).
John Rutledge (1739-1800)	1790-1791	Washington	Wrote no opinions and attended no sessions of the Supreme Court. Resigned to become chief justice of the South Carolina Court of Common Pleas.
John Rutledge (1739-1800)	1795	Washington	Took oath and presided over one session where two cases were heard before he was not confirmed by the Senate.
Wiley Blount Rutledge, Jr. (1894-1949)	1943-1949*	Franklin D. Roosevelt	Significant opinions: *Thomas v. Collins*, 323 U.S. 518 (1944); *In re Yamashita*, 327 U.S. 1 (1946) (dissenting opinion).
Edward Terry Sanford (1865-1930)	1923-1930*	Harding	Held that the First Amendment applied to the states through the due process clause of the Fourteenth Amendment. Significant opinions: *Gitlow v. New York*, 268 U.S. 652 (1925); *Fiske v. Kansas*, 274 U.S. 380 (1927).
Antonin Scalia (1936-)	1986-	Reagan	Significant opinions: *Illinois v. Rodriguez*, 497 U.S. 177 (1990); *California v. Hodari D.*, 449 U.S. 621 (1991); *United States v. Williams*, 504 U.S. 36 (1992).
George Shiras (1832-1924)	1892-1903	Harrison	Dissenting opinions offered modern view of the protections offered by the Fifth Amendment. Significant opinions: *Mattox v. United States*, 156 U.S. 237 (1895) (dissenting opinion); *Wong Wing v. United States*, 163 U.S. 228 (1896); *Brown v. Walker*, 161 U.S. 591 (1896) (dissenting opinion).
David Hackett Souter (1939-)	1990-	Bush	
Edwin M. Stanton (1814-1869)	1869*	Grant	Died four days after he was confirmed by the Senate.
John Paul Stevens (1920-)	1975-	Ford	Significant opinions: *Payton v. New York*, 445 U.S. 573 (1980); *United States v. Jacobsen*, 466 U.S. 109 (1984); *Maryland v. Garrison*, 480 U.S. 79 (1987).
Potter Stewart (1915-1985)	1958-1981	Eisenhower	Leader in development of Supreme Court's approach to interpreting the scope of the Fourth Amendment in modern times. Famous for his quip concerning attempts to define obscenity: "[P]erhaps I could never succeed in intelligibly [defining obscenity]. But I know it when I see it; and the motion picture involved in this case is not that." *Jacobellis v. Ohio*, 378 U.S. 184, 197 (1964) (concurring opinion). Significant opinions: *Massiah v. United States*, 377 U.S. 201 (1964); *Stoner v. California*, 376 U.S. 483 (1964); *Katz v. United States*, 389 U.S. 347 (1967); *Chimel v. California*, 395 U.S. 752 (1969); *Gregg v. Georgia*, 428 U.S. 153 (1976) (plurality opinion); *Brewer v. Williams*, 430 U.S. 387 (1977); *Rhode Island v. Innis*, 446 U.S. 291 (1980).

Name	Tenure	Appointed by	Highlights
Harlan Fiske Stone (1872-1946)	1925-1941	Coolidge	Author of footnote four in *United States v. Carolene Products Co.*, 304 U.S. 144 (1938), a key doctrinal innovation leading to modern equal protection analysis under the Fourteenth Amendment.
Harlan Fiske Stone (1872-1946)	1941-1946*	Franklin D. Roosevelt	Led the Supreme Court during the difficult years of World War II.
Joseph Story (1779-1845)	1812-1845*	Madison	Intellectual leader of the Supreme Court who also wrote many of the most significant early commentaries on American law. Significant opinions: *Martin v. Hunter's Lessee*, 14 U.S. 304 (1816); *Charles River Bridge v. Warren Bridge Co.*, 36 U.S. 420 (1837) (dissenting opinion); *United States v. Schooner Amistad*, 40 U.S. 518 (1841); *Swift v. Tyson*, 41 U.S. 1 (1842). Other writings: *Commentaries on the Constitution of the United States* (1833) (3 volumes); *Commentaries on Equity Jurisprudence* (1834); and numerous other books and articles.
William Strong (1808-1895)	1870-1880	Grant	Author of opinions opening jury service to African Americans. Significant opinions: *Strauder v. West Virginia*, 100 U.S. 303 (1880); *Ex parte Virginia*, 100 U.S. 339 (1880); *Virginia v. Rives*, 100 U.S. 313 (1880).
George Sutherland (1862-1942)	1922-1938	Harding	Intellectual leader of the Supreme Court's opposition to New Deal regulatory measures; supported selective application of the Bill of Rights to state criminal justice systems. Significant opinions: *Powell v. Alabama*, 287 U.S. 45 (1932); *Berger v. United States*, 295 U.S. 78 (1935); *Carter v. Carter Coal Co.*, 298 U.S. 238 (1936).
Noah Haynes Swayne (1804-1884)	1862-1881	Lincoln	Most consistent supporter of President Lincoln's orders concerning prosecution of the Civil War. Significant opinion: *Slaughterhouse Cases*, 83 U.S. 36 (1873) (dissenting opinion).
William Howard Taft (1857-1930)	1921-1930	Harding	Only president ever to serve on the Court. As chief justice he actively sought to influence appointments to the Supreme Court. Author of property-based view of the scope of the Fourth Amendment. Significant opinions: *Myers v. United States*, 272 U.S. 52 (1926); *Olmstead v. United States*, 277 U.S. 438 (1928).
Roger Brooke Taney (1777-1864)	1836-1864*	Jackson	Pro-slavery and states' rights chief justice; author of the infamous *Scott v. Sandford* opinion. Resisted many of President Lincoln's orders concerning the prosecution of the Civil War. Significant opinions: *Charles River Bridge v. Warren Bridge Co.*, 36 U.S. 420 (1837); *License Cases*, 46 U.S. 504 (1847); *Scott v. Sandford*, 60 U.S. 393 (1857).
Clarence Thomas (1948-)	1991-	Bush	Most controversial modern Supreme Court appointment; accused of sexual harrassment during confirmation process.
Smith Thompson (1768-1843)	1824-1843*	Monroe	Significant opinion: *Cherokee Nation v. Georgia*, 30 U.S. 1 (1831) (dissenting opinion).
Thomas Todd (1765-1826)	1807-1826*	Jefferson	Never disagreed with Chief Justice Marshall on any constitutional issue.

Name	Tenure	Appointed by	Highlights
Robert Trimble (1777-1828)	1826-1828*	John Q. Adams	Significant opinions: *The Antelope Case*, 25 U.S. 546 (1827); *Ogden v. Saunders*, 25 U.S. 213 (1827).
Willis Van Devanter (1859-1941)	1911-1937	Taft	Significant opinion: *McGrain v. Daugherty*, 273 U.S. 135 (1927).
Frederick Moore Vinson (1890-1953)	1946-1953*	Truman	Significant opinions: *Harris v. United States*, 331 U.S. 145 (1947); *Shelley v. Kraemer*, 334 U.S. 1 (1948); *Stack v. Boyle*, 342 U.S. 1 (1951); *Dennis v. United States*, 341 U.S. 494 (1951).
Morrison Remick Waite (1816-1888)	1874-1888*	Grant	Significant opinions: *United States v. Cruikshank*, 92 U.S. 542 (1876); *Munn v. Illinois*, 94 U.S. 113 (1876).
Earl Warren (1891-1974)	1953-1969	Eisenhower	Second only to Chief Justice Marshall in impact on the Supreme Court's role. Led expansion of constitutional rights for defendants in state courts and the transformation of the meaning of the equal protection clause of the Fourteenth Amendment. Significant opinions: *Brown v. Board of Education*, 347 U.S. 483 (1954); *Watkins v. United States*, 354 U.S. 178 (1957); *Spano v. New York*, 360 U.S. 315 (1959); *Reynolds v. Sims*, 377 U.S. 533 (1964); *Miranda v. Arizona*, 384 U.S. 436 (1966); *Terry v. Ohio*, 392 U.S. 1 (1968).
Bushrod Washington (1762-1829)	1789-1829*	John Adams	Almost always agreed with Chief Justice Marshall's views. Significant opinion: *Ogden v. Saunders*, 25 U.S. 213 (1827).
James Moore Wayne (1790-1867)	1835-1867*	Jackson	Significant opinion: *Louisville, Cincinnati and Charleston Railroad Co. v. Letson*, 43 U.S. 497 (1844).
Byron Raymond White (1917-)	1962-1993	Kennedy	Critical of the exclusionary rule and expansive view of the scope of protection offered by the Fourth Amendment. Significant opinions: *Miranda v. Arizona*, 384 U.S. 436 (1966) (dissenting opinion); *Camara v. Municipal Court of the City and County of San Francisco*, 387 U.S. 523 (1967); *Duncan v. Louisiana*, 391 U.S. 145 (1968); *Chambers v. Maroney*, 399 U.S. 42 (1970); *United States v. Matlock*, 415 U.S. 164 (1974); *Stone v. Powell*, 428 U.S. 465 (1976) (dissenting opinion); *United States v. Leon*, 468 U.S. 897 (1984); *New Jersey v. T.L.O.*, 469 U.S. 325 (1985); *California v. Greenwood*, 486 U.S. 35 (1988).
Edward Douglas White (1845-1921)	1894-1910	Cleveland	Significant opinion: *Rasmussen v. United States*, 197 U.S. 506 (1905).
Edward Douglas White (1845-1921)	1910-1921*	Taft	Significant opinion: *Standard Oil Co. v. United States*, 221 U.S. 1 (1911).
Charles Evans Whittaker (1901-1973)	1957-1962	Eisenhower	Supplied the critical vote in a series of 5-4 decisions in which the Supreme Court rejected individual rights claims in state criminal cases. Significant opinions: *Draper v. United States*, 358 U.S. 307 (1959).

Name	Tenure	Appointed by	Highlights
James Wilson (1742-1798)	1789-1798*	Washington	While on the Court, was imprisoned for failure to pay his debts. Significant opinions: *Chisholm v. Georgia*, 2 U.S. 419 (1793).
Levi Woodbury (1789-1851)	1845-1851*	Polk	Rejected abolitionists' arguments for limiting the impact of the fugitive slave clause of the Constitution. Significant opinion: *Jones v. Van Zandt*, 46 U.S. 215 (1847).
William Burnham Woods (1824-1887)	1881-1887*	Hayes	Significant opinions: *United States v. Lee*, 106 U.S. 196 (1882) (dissenting opinion); *United States v. Harris*, 106 U.S. 629 (1883); *Presser v. Illinois*, 116 U.S. 252 (1886).

Time Line

Significant events and personages related to justice in the United States.

1215   The Magna Carta's thirty-seven clauses address abuses by the British Crown during the reign of King John; they later provide one of the bases for the United States Constitution.

1622   Virginia bars sexual relations between whites and nonwhites.

1624   First "blue law" passed in Virginia mandates church attendance.

1692   Salem witchcraft trials result in the execution of fourteen women and six men.

1765-1769   William Blackstone publishes his *Commentaries*, which form the basis for much British and American law.

1775   American Revolution begins.

1775-1865   The abolitionist movement begins with the establishment of the first antislave society in Philadelphia in 1775. It gains momentum during the presidency of Andrew Jackson (1767-1845) and continues through the end of the Civil War.

1776   Thomas Jefferson (1743-1826) writes the Declaration of Independence, declaring the American colonies independent from Great Britain.

1783   American Revolution officially ends.

1787-1789   United States Constitution is written in Philadelphia in 1787, is ratified in 1788, and becomes effective in 1789. It remains the oldest constitution of any nation in the world.

1789-1791   Congress proposes (1789) and the states ratify (1791) the ten amendments to the Constitution that come to be known as the Bill of Rights.

1789   George Washington (1732-1799) becomes first president of the United States.

1789   Judiciary Act institutes court system in the United States as specified by the Constitution. It also turns matters of admiralty law over to U.S. district courts.

1789   Bureau of Internal Revenue begins collecting excise taxes.

1790   U.S. Supreme Court holds its first session.

1790   First federal copyright statute enacted.

1790   First federal patent bill signed by George Washington.

1790   U.S. Coast Guard begins as Revenue Marine.

1792   Congress passes Militia Act, making state militias available as reserves during wartime.

1793   Passage of Fugitive Slave Act provides for returning fugitive slaves to their owners, reinforcing view of slaves as property.

1798   The Alien and Sedition Acts, aimed at suppressing criticism of and conspiracies against the federal government, are enacted.

1800   Congress passes first Federal Bankruptcy Act.

1803   *Marbury v. Madison* decision establishes Supreme Court's right of judicial review over all federal legislation.

1804   The House of Representatives impeaches Supreme Court Justice Samuel Chase; he is acquitted by the Senate.

1808   First temperance society founded in the United States.

1810   *Fletcher v. Peck* is the first decision of the Supreme Court to affirm the unconstitutionality of a state statute.

1816   Associate Supreme Court justice Joseph Story writes the decision in *Martin v. Hunter's Lessee*, which establishes the Supreme Court's appellate jurisdiction over state courts.

1819 *Dartmouth College v. Woodward* decision establishes sanctity of contracts.

1820 Missouri Compromise admits Maine as a free state and Missouri as a slave state; it bars slavery in the remainder of Louisiana Purchase lands.

1824 Auburn (New York) Prison institutes a system of cell blocks, group labor, and silence for inmates.

1828 First abortion law passes in New York.

1829-1837 "Jacksonian democracy" extends voting rights to give the common citizen a greater voice in government.

1829-1833 Andrew Jackson's method of giving government jobs to his friends and allies becomes known as the spoils system.

1830 First U.S. race riots occur against abolitionists and blacks.

1831 *Cherokee Nation v. Georgia* Supreme Court decision results in forced removal of Cherokees from Georgia to Indian Territory (Oklahoma).

1832 Democratic Party begins first political party conventions.

1833 In *Barron v. Baltimore*, the Supreme Court finds the amendments in the Bill of Rights binding on federal but not state governments.

1834 Whig Party develops in opposition to Andrew Jackson's policies; party disbands by 1860.

1837 *Charles River Bridge v. Warren Bridge Co.* Supreme Court decision establishes responsibilities of private corporations to the public.

1843 B'nai B'rith, parent organization of the Anti-Defamation League, is founded.

1845 Frederick Douglass (1817-1895) publishes his influential account of his years as a slave.

1848 Seneca Falls Convention launches woman suffrage movement in the United States; those in attendance include Elizabeth Cady Stanton (1815-1902) and Frederick Douglass.

1848 Free Soil Party opposes extension of slavery.

1850 John C. Calhoun (1782-1850) reads Senate his denunciation of the North's opposition to extending slavery into the territories.

1850 Henry Clay (1777-1852) sponsors Compromise of 1850 on slavery issue; it includes the Fugitive Slave Law, strengthening the 1793 Fugitive Slave Act and ironically strengthening abolitionist movement.

1852 Harriet Beecher Stowe (1811-1896) publishes *Uncle Tom's Cabin*, which fuels strong antislavery sentiment.

1854 Kansas-Nebraska Act permits settlers in the Kansas and Nebraska territories to decide for themselves whether they want slavery.

1854 Republican Party is formed by Whigs, Democrats, and Free Soil Party members opposed to the spread of slavery.

1857 *Scott v. Sandford* decision (the Dredd Scott decision) denies a slave the right to sue for freedom in federal court.

1858 Abraham Lincoln (1809-1865) and Stephen A. Douglas (1813-1861), both candidates for the U.S. Senate, engage in a series of debates, the main substance of which focuses on extending slavery into the territories.

1859 Abolitionist John Brown (1800-1859) hanged at Harpers Ferry, Virginia, for leading a raid on the armory there and attempting to instigate an insurrection.

1860's Most major cities in the United States have police departments; professional training and standards of conduct, however, will not be in place for many decades.

1861 Abraham Lincoln becomes sixteenth president of the United States.

1861 Civil War begins on April 12.

1861 Chief Justice Roger B. Taney (1777-1864) rules in *Ex parte Merryman* that the right of *habeas corpus* cannot be suspended by the president (only by Congress) during national crises.

1862 Two new laws ban polygamy; they are directed against Mormons in the Utah Territory.

1862-1863 President Lincoln issues the Emancipation Proclamation, freeing slaves under control of the Confederacy.

1862-1872 Bureau of Internal Revenue collects first income taxes.

1865 John Wilkes Booth shoots Abraham Lincoln on April 14; Lincoln dies on April 15. Andrew Johnson (1808-1875) succeeds him as president.

1865 Civil War ends.

1865-1866 Former Confederate states enact "black codes" to control their former slaves.

1865-1870 States ratify Civil War Amendments: the Thirteenth Amendment abolishes slavery, the Fourteenth gives equal protection to all citizens, and the Fifteenth denies states the right to abridge any citizen's voting rights.

1866 Congress passes, over President Johnson's veto, Civil Rights Act that gives former slaves U.S. citizenship.

1866 In *Ex parte Milligan*, the Supreme Court denies the president and the Congress the right to order trials by military tribunals in situations where civil courts are functioning.

1866 Ku Klux Klan is founded.

1867-1868 Congress passes Reconstruction Acts over President Johnson's veto.

1868 Thomas M. Cooley (1824-1898) publishes *The Constitutional Limitations Which Rest upon the Legislative Power of the State of the American Union*, influential for its definition of the government's powers.

1869 Elizabeth Cady Stanton founds National Woman Suffrage Association.

1870-c. 1960 Jim Crow laws enforced to maintain racial segregation.

1871 Congress criminalizes attempts to deny equal protection under the law.

1871 Congress enacts Ku Klux Klan Act, which restrains the organization.

1873 Supreme Court, in its *Slaughterhouse Cases* decision, upholds limited interpretation of Fourteenth Amendment and allows New Orleans slaughterhouse monopoly.

1874 Social Democratic Workingmen's Party founded; name changed to Socialist Labor Party in 1877.

1874 Woman's Christian Temperance Union founded.

1875 Civil Rights Act of 1875 outlaws discrimination regarding public accommodations.

1877 Federal troops withdraw from the South as a result of the Compromise of 1877.

1877 Morrison R. Waite (1816-1888), chief justice from 1874 to 1888, writes *Munn v. Illinois* decision upholding state regulation of business affecting public interests.

1879 Supreme Court decision in *Reynolds v. United States* effectively bans polygamy in the United States.

1878 American Bar Association, the largest organization of attorneys in the United States, is established.

1881 Founding of Federation of Organized Trades and Labor Unions, parent organization of the American Federation of Labor (AFL).

1882 Congress enacts Chinese Exclusion Act, suspending immigration of Chinese laborers until 1892.

1883 In the *Civil Rights Cases*, the Supreme Court declares Civil Rights Act of 1875 unconstitutional, denying blacks equal access to public accommodations.

1883 Pendleton Act establishes the federal Civil Service Commission, instituting a competitive merit system for government service; it puts an end to the spoils system.

1884 In *Hurtado v. California*, the Supreme Court holds that indictments need not be obtained in murder cases in state courts.

1886 Federation of Organized Trades and Labor Union changes name to American Federation of Labor (AFL); Samuel Gompers is its first president.

1887 Congress creates the Interstate Commerce Commission (ICC), primarily to regulate railroad rates.

1889 Jane Addams (1860-1935) founds Hull House in Chicago.

1890 Congress passes Sherman Antitrust Act.

1892 Congress extends Chinese Exclusion Act of 1882.

1893 Anti-Saloon League, a temperance organization, is established.

1894 Pullman Palace Car Company strike begins on May 11 and involves 2,500 employees; strike is broken on July 10 after President Grover Cleveland (1837-1908) deploys a federal antistrike force.

1895 Eugene V. Debs (1855-1926), president of the American Railway Union, imprisoned for six months following the Pullman strike.

1896 In *Plessy v. Ferguson*, Supreme Court upholds the concept that providing "separate but equal" accommodations and facilities for blacks and whites is not an unconstitutional violation of civil rights.

1897 Eugene V. Debs founds the Social Democratic Party of America.

1898 Congress passes Bankruptcy Act, which becomes the basis for modern bankruptcy laws.

1900-1920 Progressivism marks tendency toward reform movements in both major political parties.

1902 Maryland becomes first state to pass workers' compensation legislation to compensate workers injured on the job.

1903 Dick Act sets framework for modern National Guard.

1904 Lincoln Steffens' *The Shame of the Cities* exposes urban political corruption.

1905 W. E. B. Du Bois (1868-1963) helps to organize the Niagara Movement, from which grows the National Association for the Advancement of Colored People (NAACP).

1905 In *Lochner v. New York*. the Supreme Court invalidates a state regulation limiting bakers' working hours to ten hours a day or sixty hours a week.

1906 Publication of Upton Sinclair's exposé of the meat-packing industry, *The Jungle*, leads to enactment of the Pure Food and Drug Act.

1908 In *Muller v. Oregon*, the Supreme Court upholds state statute that sets maximum work hours for women.

1908 Bureau of Investigation established as an investigative wing of the Department of Justice.

1910 Members of the Niagara Movement establish National Association for the Advancement of Colored People (NAACP).

1910 Congress passes the Mann Act, prohibiting the interstate transportation of women for "immoral purposes."

1910-1920 Extensive black migration to the North, coupled with limited job opportunities, leads to twenty-three major riots in large northern cities.

1911 National Urban League established as an interracial organization to protect the rights of blacks from the South who have moved to northern cities.

1914 Clayton Antitrust Act extends and strengthens the Sherman Antitrust Act of 1890.

1914 The *Weeks v. United States* Supreme Court decision holds a warrantless search to be unconstitutional.

1914 Congress establishes the Federal Trade Commission (FTC) to thwart the development of trusts.

1915 Ku Klux Klan is revived and reaches the peak of its influence in the 1920's.

1916 President Woodrow Wilson (1856-1924) appoints Louis Brandeis (1856-1941) associate justice of the Supreme Court.

1916 New York State passes first comprehensive zoning law, exercising government power over the use of land.

1917 United States enters World War I; Espionage Act passed to discourage wartime dissent.

1917 Conscientious objection to military service based on religious grounds recognized as valid.

1918 World War I ends on November 11.

1918 Sedition Act passed by Congress.

1919 In *Abrams v. United States*, the Supreme Court upholds the 1918 Sedition Act.

1919 Prohibition—the banning of the sale or consumption of alcoholic beverages—becomes national law with ratification of the Eighteenth Amendment.

1919 American Communist Party is organized.

1919 Boston police officers strike in protest of work and pay conditions.

1920 American Civil Liberties Union (ACLU) is founded.

1919-1920 Congress passes (1919) and states ratify (1920) Nineteenth Amendment, giving women the right to vote.

1920-1960 John L. Lewis (1880-1969) serves as president of the United Mine Workers' union; serves as first president of the CIO, 1938-1940.

1921 Congress passes Standard State Zoning Enabling Act.

1923 Supreme Court upholds constitutionality of zoning.

1923-1924 Secretary of the Interior Albert Fall (1861-1944) leases federal oil reserves to private corporations, bringing about the Teapot Dome scandal; Supreme Court declares these leases illegal in 1927; Fall is convicted of bribery in 1929.

1924 J. Edgar Hoover (1895-1972) is appointed director of the Bureau of Investigation, a powerful position he will hold for nearly fifty years.

1925 Scopes "monkey" trial finds teacher guilty of breaking a law forbidding the teaching of evolution in public school.

1927 Food and Drug Administration established.

1929 Saint Valentine's Day massacre occurs in Chicago, bringing national attention to the problem of organized crime.

1929 President Herbert Hoover (1874-1964) appoints Wickersham Commission to review U.S. law enforcement.

1930 Wallace Fard founds the Black Muslims (Nation of Islam), a black separatist group.

1931 Social reformer Jane Addams awarded Nobel Peace Prize.

1931 Mobster Al Capone (1899-1947) is arrested and convicted of tax evasion; he serves eight years in prison.

1932 In *Powell v. Alabama*, popularly known as one of the Scottsboro cases, the Supreme Court overturns the death sentences of seven black defendants convicted of raping a white woman, holding that they had not received a fair trial because they had not been appointed counsel

1933 Franklin Delano Roosevelt (1882-1945) becomes thirty-second president of the United States; Roosevelt was the only president to be elected for four consecutive terms.

1933 Congress repeals Eighteenth Amendment and ends Prohibition.

1933 Congress passes National Guard Status Act, establishing basis for the contemporary National Guard.

1933-1940 President Roosevelt institutes the New Deal, a collection of domestic programs designed to combat the Depression.

1934 Securities and Exchange Commission established to enforce the Truth in Securities Act of 1933.

1934 Congress enacts strict new crime laws, including the "Lindbergh law," which makes kidnapping a federal offense if state lines are crossed.

1934 Congress passes Corporation Bankruptcy Act.

1935 President Roosevelt contrives plan to expand the Supreme Court and to "pack" the Court with his appointees.

1935 Social Security Act provides retirement income based on withholding from workers' pay.

1935 Congress passes National Labor Relations Act, which sets up board to settle labor-management conflicts and allows labor the right to engage in collective bargaining.

1935 Congress enacts the Guffey-Snyder Bituminous Coal Stabilization Act to regulate the bituminous coal industry.

1935 Bureau of Investigation renamed Federal Bureau of Investigation (FBI).

1936 Supreme Court's *Carter v. Carter Coal Co.* decision invalidates the Guffey-Snyder Bituminous Coal Stabilization Act of 1935.

1938 Congress passes Chandler Act, revising bankruptcy laws.

1938 Congress establishes House Committee on Un-American Activities (HUAC), chaired by Martin Dies (1901-1972).

1938 Congress of Industrial Organizations (CIO) founded.

1939 Congress passes Hatch Act to discourage political corruption.

1940 Congress passes the anticommunist Smith Act to control subversion.

1941 Japanese forces bomb Pearl Harbor; United States enters World War II.

1942 President Franklin Roosevelt orders the internment of Japanese Americans during World War II.

1944 GI Bill of Rights provides educational and economic benefits for World War II veterans.

1944 Congress passes Violent Crime Control and Law Enforcement Act.

1945 President Roosevelt dies on April 12; Harry S Truman (1884-1972) succeeds him as president.

1945 World War II ends: Germany surrenders to the Allied forces on May 7; United States uses nuclear weapons against Japan in August, forcing Japan's surrender on September 2.

1945 United Nations establishes World Court as its judicial branch.

1947 Taft-Hartley Act amends National Labor Relations Act to limit power of trade unions.

1948 States' Rights (or "Dixiecrat") Party, founded by southern Democrats opposed to integration, runs Strom Thurmond (b. 1902) as its presidential candidate.

1950 McCarthyism begins when Senator Joseph McCarthy (1909-1957) accuses the State Department of employing 205 "card-carrying Communists."

1954 Supreme Court's *Brown v. Board of Education* decision reverses "separate but equal" doctrine in effect since 1896 and mandates desegregation of public schools.

1954 Espionage and Sabotage Act makes espionage and sabotage in peacetime a capital offense.

1955 National Guard is called up in Little Rock, Arkansas, when integration of public schools leads to violence.

1955 American Federation of Labor and Congress of Industrial Organizations merge, forming the AFL-CIO.

1955-1956   Martin Luther King, Jr., leads Montgomery bus boycott, beginning Civil Rights movement of 1950's and 1960's.

1957   Congress passes Civil Rights Act to strengthen federal government's power to enforce voting rights for blacks; establishes a six-member, bipartisan Commission on Civil Rights.

1958   Robert Welch establishes John Birch Society.

1959   Congress passes Landrum-Griffin Act to make labor union elections more democratic.

1959   In *Barenblatt v. United States*, Supreme Court upholds contempt of Congress conviction of a university teacher who refused to answer questions about alleged Communist Party affiliations.

1960   Congress passes Civil Rights Act that increases the government's power to enforce voting rights.

1960   Student Non-Violent Coordinating Committee (SNCC) coordinates students' civil rights sit-ins.

1961   Under the auspices of the Congress of Racial Equality (CORE), a biracial group travels from Washington by interstate bus to force integration of bus terminals in the South.

1962   *Baker v. Carr* results in reapportionment of Tennessee legislative districts and leads to one person, one vote legislation.

1963   *Abington School District v. Schempp* Supreme Court decision bans school prayer.

1963   Southern Christian Leadership Conference (SCLC) is instrumental in leading demonstrations in Birmingham, Alabama, to protest racial discrimination.

1963   President John F. Kennedy (1917-1963) assassinated on November 22. Lyndon B. Johnson (1908-1973) becomes the thirty-sixth president of the United States.

1963-1964   Warren Commission, chaired by Chief Justice Earl Warren (1891-1974), investigates the assassination of President Kennedy.

1964   Martin Luther King, Jr., receives Nobel Peace Prize.

1964   The Senate censures Senator Joseph McCarthy for leveling unproved charges of treason against government officials.

1964   Congress enacts most sweeping Civil Rights Act since Reconstruction.

1964   *Escobedo v. Illinois* Supreme Court decision reiterates a person's right to avoid self-incrimination.

1964-1968   Race riots are recorded in sixty-seven major cities.

1964-1968   President Lyndon Johnson strives to establish the "Great Society."

1964-1973   United States troops are involved in Vietnam War.

1965   Congress enacts Voting Rights Act, which abolishes all racial discrimination in voting.

1965   Malcolm X (Malcolm Little, 1925-1965), black nationalist leader, publishes *The Autobiography of Malcolm X*; he is assassinated on February 21.

1965   Ralph Nader (b. 1934) gains public recognition and begins consumer rights movement with the publication of his exposé of the automobile industry, *Unsafe at Any Speed*.

1966   Establishment of revolutionary black militant group, the Black Panther Party.

1966   Truth in Packaging Law is enacted.

1966   César Chávez (1927-1993) organizes the United Farm Workers' union (UFW).

1966   U.S. Supreme Court expands Fifth Amendment right of defendants to counsel to include having counsel present during interrogation by police in its *Miranda v. Arizona* decision.

1966 Feminist author Betty Friedan (b. 1921) and others found the National Organization for Women (NOW); Friedan serves as its first president.

1967 President Johnson names Thurgood Marshall (1908-1992) to the Supreme Court; Marshall is the Court's first black member.

1967 Age Discrimination Act prohibits discrimination in hiring and other areas based on age.

1967 Congress passes the Freedom of Information Act.

1967 Fifteen states pass laws providing for abortions if continued pregnancy would threaten a woman's physical or mental health.

1967 Supreme Court rules miscegenation laws unconstitutional.

1968 Congress passes Omnibus Crime Control and Safe Streets Act.

1968 Congress enacts Uniform Juvenile Court Act.

1968 Congress enacts Civil Rights Act that prohibits racial discrimination in hiring and in public accommodations.

1968 Congress enacts Truth in Lending Act.

1968 Martin Luther King, Jr., assassinated on April 4.

1968 Lieutenant William Calley perpetrates My Lai massacre during Vietnam War. Massacre revealed in 1970; Calley found guilty in 1971 court-martial.

1968 Robert F. Kennedy (1925-1968) assassinated in Los Angeles. Shot on June 5, he dies the next day.

1968-1969 National Commission on the Causes and Prevention of Violence is formed.

1970 National Guardsmen kill four students at Kent State University in Ohio during an anti-Vietnam War demonstration.

1970 President Richard Nixon appoints President's Commission on Campus Unrest.

1970 Congress passes the Comprehensive Drug Abuse Prevention and Control Act.

1971 Riot at Attica (New York) Correctional Facility.

1971 Supreme Court case *Lemon v. Kurtzman* establishes test (the "Lemon" test) for separation of church and state doctrine.

1972 In *Barker v. Wingo*, the Supreme Court assures the guarantee of a speedy trial.

1972 Supreme Court's *Argersinger v. Hamlin* decision reaffirms a defendant's right to counsel.

1972 In *Lindsey v. Normet* the Supreme Court confirms the right to housing without discrimination.

1972 Congress passes Equal Rights Amendment (ERA); ultimately, the states fail to ratify it.

1972 Congress passes Equal Employment Opportunity Act, which expands Civil Rights Act of 1964; establishes Equal Employment Opportunity Commission (EEOC).

1972 U.S. Supreme Court invalidates capital punishment statutes of federal government and thirty-nine states in *Furman v. Georgia* but stops short of holding the death penalty unconstitutional.

1972 Five men hired by the Committee to Reelect the President break into Democratic Party headquarters at the Watergate office building on June 17; White House admits existence of "plumbers" group on December 11.

1973 Watergate burglars convicted or plead guilty during January; many Nixon officials implicated in a cover-up.

1973 Supreme Court case *Frontiero v. Richardson* invalidates a law authorizing different housing allowances to men and women as sex discrimination.

1973 In its *Roe v. Wade* decision, U.S. Supreme Court rules that the states cannot forbid voluntary abortions.

1974 House Judiciary Committee votes bill of impeachment against Richard Nixon in July; Nixon resigns presidency on August 9; new president Gerald R. Ford (b. 1913) pardons Nixon on September 8.

1974 Congress passes the Employee Retirement Income Security Act.

1974 *Milliken v. Bradley* Supreme Court decision limits busing for integration across district lines.

1976 *Buckley v. Valeo* Supreme Court decision upholds use of public funds in financing political campaigns and strikes down limits on what candidates may spend.

1976 *Gregg v. Georgia* reaffirms that death penalty is not cruel and unusual punishment.

1976 In the *Massachusetts Board of Retirement v. Murgia* decision, the Supreme Court refuses to overturn a mandatory retirement age for police officers.

1977 Supreme Court holds that states do not need to use Medicaid funds to pay for abortions not medically necessary in *Maher v. Roe*.

1977 Congress passes Public Works Employment Act.

1978 In *Regents of the University of California v. Bakke*, the Supreme Court holds that college admissions affirmative action programs cannot use race as their sole criterion.

1978 The *Village of Skokie v. National Socialist Party* Supreme Court decision affirms the First Amendment rights of neo-Nazis.

1981 President Ronald Reagan (b. 1911) appoints Sandra Day O'Connor (b. 1930) to the Supreme Court; she is the first woman to serve on the Court.

1982 In *Hutto v. Davis* the Supreme Court upholds that a lengthy prison sentence for possession of a small amount of marijuana is not cruel and unusual punishment.

1982 The Supreme Court in *Plyler v. Doe* holds that states cannot refuse public schooling to illegal aliens.

1983 In *Akron v. Akron Center for Reproductive Health* the Supreme Court strikes down a range of restrictions on abortion.

1984 In *United States v. Leon* the Supreme Court rules that evidence obtained without a warrant could be admissible if police were acting in "good faith."

1984 Congress passes the Comprehensive Crime Control Act.

1984 Congress enacts the Victim and Witness Protection Act to protect victims and witnesses in criminal proceedings.

1984 Congress passes the Victims of Crime Act.

1984 Mothers Against Drunk Driving (MADD) formed.

1985 In *New Jersey v. T.L.O.* the Supreme Court holds that warrantless searches of students' pockets and purses by school officials are unconstitutional

1986 Congress enacts the Tax Reform Act, proposed by the Ronald Reagan Administration.

1986 In *Bowers v. Hardwick* the Supreme Court holds that the privacy doctrine based on the due process clause does not protect the right of homosexuals to engage in consensual acts of sodomy.

1986 In *City of Renton v. Playtime Theaters*, the Supreme Court upholds zoning regulations as a means of controlling locations of "adult" theaters.

1987 Supreme Court's *Nollan v. California Coastal Commission* decision expands protection of property rights from government limitations.

1989 In *Texas v. Johnson* the Supreme Court holds that burning the American flag is constitutionally protected "symbolic speech."

1989 Supreme Court's *Webster v. Reproductive Health Services* decision upholds some state restrictions on abortion but does not overturn *Roe v. Wade*.

1989 In *National Treasury Employees Union v. Von Raab*, a union sues to prohibit mandatory drug testing of employees, but Supreme Court upholds testing.

1989 In *Richmond v. J. A. Croson Co.*, Supreme Court places limitations on affirmative action programs.

1989 In *Wards Cove Packing Company v. Atonio*, the Court makes it more difficult for plaintiffs to prove employer discrimination.

1990 *Osborne v. Ohio* tests First Amendment rights regarding child pornography; Supreme Court holds child pornography to be unprotected by First Amendment.

1990 In *Maryland v. Craig*, the Supreme Court holds that children may testify via closed-circuit television, thereby not having to face the accused.

1991 *Harmelin v. Michigan* upholds a state law mandating a life-sentence term for drug possession, deeming it not cruel and unusual punishment.

1991 In *Payne v. Tennessee* the Supreme Court overrules previous decisions, holds that victim impact evidence may be permitted in capital cases.

1992 On April 29, a jury in suburban Simi Valley, California, acquits four Los Angeles police officers of beating black motorist Rodney King; widespread rioting and arson break out in Los Angeles.

1992 In *Lucas v. South Carolina Coastal Council* the Supreme Court decides that government land-use regulations may be found to violate prohibition against "taking" land without just compensation.

1993 In Supreme Court case *Church of the Lukumi Babalu Aye v. Hialeah* the Court strikes down ban on animal sacrifices in religious ceremonies.

1993 Congress passes Family Medical Leave Act.

1993 *Shaw v. Reno* Supreme Court case calls for "strict scrutiny" in the drawing of congressional districts, striking a blow against shaping districts specifically so that minorities will be the majority.

1993 In *Wisconsin v. Mitchell* the Supreme Court upholds state hate crimes statute, finding that it is directed at conduct and does not impinge on free speech.

1995 In *Adarand Constructors v. Peña* the Supreme Court holds that a broad Department of Transportation affirmative action program is unconstitutional.

GLOSSARY

Allocution, right of: A criminal defendant's right to have a formal inquiry by the court as to whether the defendant has any legal cause to prevent the court from pronouncing judgment upon him or her in the form of a conviction.

Alternative dispute resolution (ADR): Means other than a formal trial for resolving a legal conflict, including negotiation, mediation, arbitration, and mini-trials.

Answer: A legal pleading responding to the contents of a petition, motion, or brief.

Antitrust law: The body of federal law dealing with the unreasonable restraint of trade in commercial activity.

Appeal: Application to a higher court to review the holding in a case.

Arbitration: A process in which a neutral third party chosen by the disputants resolves the parties' dispute according to their agreement to submit disputes to the third party.

Arraignment: The hearing at which a criminal defendant is formally charged with a crime.

Arrest: The process of detaining an alleged criminal, pursuant to an arrest warrant or because police officers have probable cause to believe that a crime has been committed.

Assault: At common law, the placing of another person in fear of imminent peril. States define assault statutorily and generally divide it into subcategories based on type and severity of assault.

Attempt: In criminal law, an effort to accomplish a crime, moving beyond mere preparation.

Bail: Money or other tangible security posted by a criminal defendant to secure release from custody.

Bankruptcy: The process by which a debtor's debts are discharged (known as a Chapter 7 bankruptcy) or reorganized (known as a Chapter 11 bankruptcy). Federal bankruptcy law is designed to give the debtor a "fresh start" while providing fairness among classes of creditors in access to the debtor's assets.

Battery: At common law, an unlawful beating or other wrongful touching of another inflicted on a person without his or her consent. States define battery statutorily and subdivide it into various categories, such as sexual battery.

Brief: A written submission to a court on issues of law, as applied to the facts, for a particular dispute. A brief follows the specific format prescribed by the court to which it is submitted.

Burglary: At common law, breaking and entering the house of another at nighttime with intent to commit a felony while inside. Statues define burglary statutorily in ways that depart from the common law, often omitting the "nighttime" requirement.

Calendar: The court's schedule of cases to be heard. "Calendar call" is the daily roll call of cases and counsel for cases to be heard that day.

Causation: A concept in tort law requiring that the action taken by the defendant actually cause (directly or indirectly) the damage suffered by the plaintiff.

Caveat emptor: Literally "Let the buyer beware!" A concept (now largely outdated) in contract and tort law that the goods carry no warranty from the seller as to quality or suitability.

Certiorari (writ of): The appellate proceeding for the U.S. Supreme Court to review a decision of one of the appellate courts of the United States system.

Civil procedure: The set of rules governing the process of pretrial, trial, and post-trial litigation in civil cases. The Federal Rules of Civil Procedure govern litigation in federal courts, and each state has its own set of rules for state proceedings.

Codicil: An addition to a signed will, changing or adding to the provisions of the will.

Common law: The body of case law which, as an evolving whole, sets forth the governing law. Common law has been supplanted by statutory law in many instances, but it continues to be of importance in American law in a number of areas, such as tort law. The American common-law tradition is descended from English common law.

Contract: Binding mutual promises between parties to take specified actions. In order for there to be a valid contract, there must be a promise and "consideration" (something given in exchange for that promise).

Corporation: A legal "person" created and recognized under state law that is owned by its shareholders; it carries on business in perpetuity. The shareholders of a corporation are not liable for the debts incurred by the entity unless they specifically undertake a guarantee of those debts.

Criminal procedure: The set of rules governing the process of pretrial, trial, and appeal of litigation in criminal cases.

Cross-examination: The art of asking pointed, direct, and leading questions of a witness to elicit answers that will undermine testimony previously given by the same or other witnesses.

Damages: The economic measure of the harm suffered by a defendant in a contract or tort action. "Compensatory" damages are measured by the actual expenses of the defendant, for both economic loss and pain and suffering, while "punitive" damages are imposed to punish the defendant and deter future conduct.

Defendant: The responding party in a civil matter, or the person charged with the crime in a criminal matter.

Deposition: The process for obtaining testimony from a witness in a civil trial prior to trial, in which the witness is placed under oath, a record is kept, and opposing counsel poses a series of questions to the party and receives his or her answers. The rules of evidence are relaxed in depositions.

Dictum: Language in a court's decision that is not necessary to the holding but which sheds light on some aspect of the legal principle enunciated in the case.

Discovery: The process by which opposing counsel in a dispute create requests for production and written interrogatories, take depositions, and use other methods to unearth the facts of the controversy.

Discrimination: The treatment of one class of persons differently from another, based on some characteristic of the classes such as race, gender, or national origin.

Domestic violence: The infliction of harm by one adult intimate partner (or former intimate partner) on another. The crimes of domestic violence can be assault, battery, or other crimes, and the status of the crime as domestic violence often carries particular consequences such as the availability of a restraining order or mandatory arrest.

Double jeopardy: At common law and in U.S. constitutional law, the prohibition against trying a defendant twice for the same crime. The prohibition prevents an unsuccessful prosecutor from subjecting the defendant to successive retrials by marginally changing the charging crime.

Due process of law: The constitutional requirement, under federal and state law, that a citizen is entitled to the protection of the law and that it will be applied in its usual course without deviation based on the characteristics of the person or the circumstances of the situation.

Equal protection: In U.S. constitutional law, the requirement that the laws be applied without discrimination based on immutable characteristics such as race or national origin.

Evidence: The body of information presented at a trial to the "fact finder" (the judge or jury) upon which the fact finder makes the determinations required.

Ex parte: In court case names (such as *Ex parte Milligan*), refers to an action taken on behalf of the person named. Also refers to a communication by a lawyer to a judge without the presence of, or notice to, opposing counsel; such communications are not favored and are sometimes even considered violations of ethical rules.

Exception: An exception places the trial court on notice of a lawyer's opposition to a particular ruling after the ruling has been made, preserving the matter for appeal.

Exclusionary rule: The rule of evidence stating that prosecution evidence in a criminal proceeding that is obtained by illegal means cannot be admitted at trial.

Expert witness: A person who, because of his or her specialized area of knowledge, is capable of examining evidence and providing an explanation of that evidence and its meaning to the trier of fact (the judge or jury).

Federal Rules of Evidence: A body of federal statutory law which sets forth the parameters for what is considered valid evidence at trial and how such evidence can be presented at trial.

Felony: A more serious crime than a misdemeanor, punishable by imprisonment in a state penitentiary or by death. Rape, burglary, robbery, murder, and some types of assault are felonies.

Felony-murder rule: The common-law rule that, if anyone is killed during the perpetration of a felony, all the co-felons are liable for murder regardless of whether the homicide was intentional or accidental and regardless of which felon actually committed the homicide.

Findings of fact: The determination, by a judge or a jury, of the existence (or nonexistence) of certain facts based on the evidence given at trial.

Fraud: An intentional misrepresentation designed to induce another person to take some detrimental action, such as pay money or purchase an item.

Grand jury: A group of people who hear evidence presented by the prosecution to determine whether there is sufficient likelihood that a crime has been committed to charge a defendant with a crime.

Habeas corpus: A writ ordering a person holding or detaining another person to produce the latter and to submit himself or herself to the judgment of the court as to the propriety of detention. It is used in criminal proceedings on behalf of detained defendants and, though less often, in child custody matters.

Hearing: A court proceeding at which a legal issue is determined by a judge.

Hearsay: Evidence (testimonial or documentary) of a statement made outside the courtroom, when counsel eliciting the testimony is offering it as proof of the truth of the assertions made in the testimony. Hearsay evidence is usually inadmissible because of questions about its reliability: The trier of fact (judge or jury) does not have the opportunity to see the person making the statement and thus cannot evaluate his or her veracity or see how he or she would respond to cross-examination.

Holographic will: A will that does not conform to the standard requirements for a will, usually because it is handwritten and signed by the testator without the required witnesses, which nevertheless will be admitted to probate under certain circumstances.

Homicide: The killing of a human being. Homicide itself is not a crime, but it is a necessary part of the crimes of murder and manslaughter, which require additional proof of the defendant's state of mind.

Hostile witness: A person whose association with an opposing party creates the inference that he or she will not freely offer testimony against that party, allowing the lawyer greater leeway in questioning the witness.

In personam action: A legal action against a person, as opposed to a thing.

In re action: A legal action regarding the status of a matter, such as the marriage of the parties or the probate of an estate.

In rem action: A civil action against a thing, as opposed to a person. For example, a tax proceeding may be brought against the property subject to tax if the owner cannot be located.

Indictment: The grand jury's written charge that a person named in an indictment has done some illegal and punishable act.

Information: A charging instrument signed by a representative of the prosecutor with the power to charge misdemeanors or to bind felonies over to be heard by a grand jury or at a preliminary hearing.

Injunction: A court's order instructing a person to refrain from taking some action.

Judgment: A final ruling on the issues in a case, supported by findings of fact and conclusions of law.

Judgment N.O.V.: A "judgment notwithstanding the verdict." The judge will enter such a judgment, essentially overriding a jury's verdict, when there is not evidence in the record that could possibly support the jury's verdict.

Jurisdiction: The set of controversies over which a court may lawfully render judgment. Proper jurisdiction is a prerequisite to a valid judgment. The petitioner to a court must plead valid jurisdiction, and the parties cannot waive defects in jurisdiction.

Jury: The persons (usually six or twelve in number) charged by the court with the task of fact finding in a trial, including the determination of guilt in a criminal trial.

Jury instructions: A series of directives given by the judge to a jury, educating the jury about the meaning of legal terms and the standards under which they are to make their determination.

Leading question: A question which by its language suggests the answer to a witness.

Legal ethics (professional responsibility): The system of rules governing the conduct of lawyers in their dealings with clients and the legal system.

Lesser included offense: Any offense necessarily included in the definition of the offense which is charged. The defendant cannot be convicted or sentenced for the lesser included offense when charged with the more serious crime.

Lien: A claim or liability against a person's property to secure payment of a debt. In order to be enforceable, a lien must meet certain requirements, generally relating to its filing of record, and multiple liens generally follow the "first in time, first in right" rule.

Limited liability company (LLC): The legal entity created and recognized by state law which consists of an agreement of membership among the members and is recognized as able to do business independently of the members. The members of an LLC are not liable for the debts of the LLC unless they specifically undertake a guarantee of those debts.

Living will: The statutorily prescribed method for a person to instruct doctors and relatives regarding medical treatment in the case of a serious accident or illness that leaves the person unable to communicate his or her wishes.

Mandatory arrest laws: State laws requiring the arrest of alleged criminals when the police find that certain conditions exist. Such laws are enacted in response to a perception that police are improperly exercising their discretion not to arrest, such as in domestic violence situations.

Mandatory sentencing laws: Laws requiring specific sentences for particular crimes. Mandatory sentences generally depend on the type of crime, its context, and characteristics of the defendant such as the number of previous crimes committed.

Manslaughter: At common law, the unlawful killing of a human being without malice, as in a violent quarrel or in the heat of passion.

Mediation: A process of alternative dispute resolution in which a neutral third party assists the disputants in reaching a settlement of their case.

Memorandum of law: A written communication setting forth the facts, the issues, a discussion of the applicable law, and conclusions drawn from applying the law to the facts.

Miranda rights: The requirement of U.S. constitutional law that, upon arrest, a person be informed of his or her rights in custody: generally, the rights to contact a lawyer and not to speak to the police (and a notice that any communications to the police can be used in court). Named from the 1966 Supreme Court case *Miranda v. Arizona.*

Misdemeanor: A crime of a less serious nature than a felony, generally punishable by a fine or imprisonment in a county jail.

Motion: Formal application to a court for a particular order, such as a motion to compel discovery.

Murder: At common law, the killing of a human being with malice aforethought.

Negligence: In tort law, the element of a tort which charges that the defendant failed in his or her duty of care (generally, exercising "reasonable care") to another person. A defendant found to have acted negligently may be liable for damages.

Nolo contendere ("no contest"): A plea by a criminal defendant literally meaning "no contest" (and called that in some jurisdictions). This plea claims neither innocence or guilt, but it has the effect of waiving trial and allowing the court to impose judgment.

Objection: Places the court and opposing counsel on notice that the lawyer is in opposition to something that occurs at trial, such as a question put to a witness. An objection can be sustained (if the judge agrees with the objector) or overruled (if the judge does not agree).

Order: A directive by a court to a person, usually a party to a dispute, governing future conduct.

Overruled: A court's ruling that an objection is not proper and that what the lawyer has objected to can continue.

Parens patriae: The concept that, when a minor is before the court in a custody, neglect, or juvenile matter, the state acts in the stead of the minor's parents to determine the best interests of the child.

Partnership: A legal entity created and recognized by state law consisting of the partnership agreement among the partners, which is able to carry on business independently of its partners. The general partners of a partnership are personally liable for the debts of the partnership, but limited partners of a limited partnership are only liable to the extent of the amount of money they have agreed to contribute to the partnership.

Party: A person who has a direct interest in the subject matter of a lawsuit.

Peremptory challenge: The right of each party's counsel unilaterally to exclude from the jury a potential juror during *voir dire* without stating the reason. Each side usually has a limited number of peremptory challenges, and additional exclusions must be "for cause."

Plaintiff (petitioner): The party instigating the lawsuit or court action in civil matters.

Plea: A criminal defendant's answer to being charged with a crime: guilty, not guilty, or *Nolo contendere* (no contest).

Plea bargain: In criminal law, the negotiated settlement between the defendant, defense attorney, prosecutor, and victim allowing the defendant to plead guilty to a certain offense or offenses. The defendant does not go to trial but instead serves a sentence negotiated by the parties.

Pleading: A legal document conforming to certain standards that is filed with the court, setting forth facts and positions of a party.

Preliminary hearing: Presentation by the prosecution to a judge of the evidence in a criminal matter to determine whether sufficient evidence exists to bind a case over to trial.

Privilege: The concept that certain evidence cannot be compelled by a court because the relationship in which the evidence arose is one granted particular confidentiality, such as attorney-client, doctor-patient, or clergy-penitent

Probable cause: In criminal law, reasonable grounds to believe a crime may have been committed, justifying the issuance of a warrant or the detention of an individual.

Probate: The process by which the will of a decedent is registered with the court, the personal representative (or executor) is formally appointed, and the assets of the estate are distributed.

Prosecutor: The representative of the state in a criminal matter whose responsibilities include appearing before the grand jury to seek indictments, determining what charges to bring against a defendant, and representing the state at trial.

Rape: At common law, the unlawful carnal knowledge of a woman against her will. State statutes now define rape, which is sometimes included within the broader heading "sexual assault," and they sometimes depart from the common-law definition. "Statutory rape" is sexual conduct with a woman under a certain age (often fourteen); consent is not an issue, as she cannot by law give her consent.

Reasonable person standard: In tort law, the standard against which the defendant's conduct is judged with regard to whether the defendant exercised reasonable care under the circumstances. The "reasonable person" is deemed to act reasonably under all circumstances and sets of conditions, and thus the defendant's actions are to be evaluated as to whether they met, exceeded, or fell below this standard.

Recision: The relief granted by a court in a contract action that "undoes" the contract entirely.

Recuse: A request by either side of a dispute (or on the judge's own motion) that a judge rule that he or she not preside over a certain case.

Relevance: An objection to solicited testimony arguing that the evidence will not be relevant to the matter at hand; that is, that it will not shed additional light on the facts at issue.

Remand: An order of an appellate court ordering that a case be sent back to the lower court for a new proceeding, either to determine new facts or to try the case in accordance with the standards of law enunciated by the appellate court.

Reply: A response to an answer filed with the court, giving the party's response to the allegations in the answer.

Restraining order: The order by a court to the respondent to refrain from doing a particular action.

Robbery: At common law, the forceful taking of another person's property in his or her presence and against his or her will. States often define robbery statutorily, altering the common-law definition.

Securities laws: Federal and state laws dealing with the registration of securities (stocks, bonds, and similar investments) and the duty owed by the issuer of securities to the buyers of such investments.

Self-defense: The right of a person to protect his or her person or property from harm by another, which justifies the use of reasonable force.

Settlement: The process by which a dispute is resolved by the parties themselves, without the need for trial, usually through negotiation or mediation. Ninety-five percent of all civil matters are settled prior to trial.

Specific performance: Relief ordered by a court which instructs a party to do a particular action. For example, in an action under a real estate contract, a court may order a party to sell the house to the buyer.

Standing: A prerequisite for a party to seek relief from a court in a particular dispute. The party must have a present and direct interest in the subject matter of a dispute.

Statute of frauds: The requirement that certain types of contracts, typically real property contracts and those whose duration may be for more than a year, be in writing in order to be enforceable.

Statute of limitations: The period of time during which an action may be brought for a particular dispute.

Subpoena: The document (and process) used to require a witness to appear and give testimony.

Subpoena duces tecum: A document demanding the appearance of a person to testify at trial and to bring with him or her original documents and subject them to inspection of the court or parties.

Summons: A document instructing an adverse party to appear in court.

Sustained: A judge's ruling on counsel's objection, indicating agreement with the objection.

Testimony: Oral evidence presented at trial regarding the issues in the case.

Tolling (of the statute of limitations): An event which suspends the running of the statute of limitations.

Tort: The body of law dealing with the "duties of care" that persons have to one another in everyday life. A claim in tort asserts that the defendant failed to exercise the proper amount of care in an activity and that this failure damaged the plaintiff (one example is medical malpractice).

Trial: The process of judicial examination of a criminal or civil dispute in which the parties or their counsel bring the facts and law before the court for final determination.

Trust: An arrangement whereby legal title to property is held by one person (the trustee) for the benefit of another (the beneficiary).

Venue: The county in which a case is to be tried, usually in the place where the alleged injury occurred but occasionally elsewhere under particular circumstances. For example, a criminal defendant may argue for a change of venue if the charged conduct is so notorious in a particular venue that he or she believes a fair trial cannot be had in that jurisdiction.

Verdict: The formal decision by a jury as to the matters submitted to it in a case.

Voir dire: The process of choosing jurors, in which counsel for each party asks questions of potential jurors to determine their suitability for the case.

Warrant: An order issued by a court to a law enforcement officer requiring him or her to perform a particular act, such as an arrest warrant requiring the arrest of a particular person.

Will (last will and testament): The written instrument signed by the testator setting forth instructions regarding disposition of his or her assets after death, which is entered into probate after death. A will generally must be signed by the testator and be witnessed by others.

Witness: A person whose first-hand knowledge is relevant to the issues in a trial.

Writ (writ of assistance): A directive issued by a court to a public official to conform the recipient's conduct to the court's interpretation of the law or to direct a public official to take action on behalf of a citizen.

BIBLIOGRAPHY

The following select bibliography is divided into eight sections: Civil Actions and Obligations, Civil Liberties, Criminal Law and Procedure, History and Biography, The Judicial Process, The Legal Profession and Legal Education, Legal Theory, and Miscellaneous Works.

Civil Actions and Obligations

Coleman, Jules L. *Risks and Wrongs*. New York: Cambridge University Press, 1992.

Fineman, Martha Albertson. *The Illusion of Equality: The Rhetoric and Realty of Divorce Reform*. Chicago: University of Chicago Press, 1991.

Fried, Charles. *Contract as Promise: A Theory of Contractual Obligation*. Cambridge, Mass.: Harvard University Press, 1981.

Glendon, Mary Ann. *The Transformation of Family Law: State, Law and Family in the United States and Western Europe*. Chicago: University of Chicago Press, 1989.

Jackson, Thomas H. *The Logic and Limits of Bankruptcy Law*. Cambridge, Mass.: Harvard University Press, 1986.

Landes, William M., and Richard A. Posner. *The Economic Structure of Tort Law*. Cambridge, Mass.: Harvard University Press, 1987.

Laycock, Douglas. *The Death of the Irreparable Injury Rule*. New York: Oxford University Press, 1991.

Mintz, Morton. *At Any Cost: Corporate Greed, Women, and the Dalkon Shield*. New York: Pantheon Books, 1985.

Olson, Walter K. *The Litigation Explosion: What Happened When America Unleashed the Lawsuit*. New York: Truman Talley, 1991.

Schuck, Peter H. *Agent Orange on Trial: Mass Toxic Disasters in the Courts*. Cambridge, Mass.: Belknap Press of Harvard University Press, 1986.

Shavell, Steven. *Economic Analysis of Accident Law*. Cambridge, Mass.: Harvard University Press, 1987.

Sugarman, Stephen D. *Doing Away with Personal Injury Law: New Compensation Mechanisms for Victims, Consumers and Business*. New York: Quorum Books, 1989.

Weitzman, Lenore J. *The Marriage Contract*. New York: Free Press, 1981.

Civil Liberties

Adams, Arlin M., and Charles J. Emmerich. *A Nation Dedicated to Religious Liberty: The Constitutional Heritage of the Religion Clauses*. Philadelphia: University of Pennsylvania Press, 1990.

Alley, Robert S. *School Prayer: The Court, the Congress, and the First Amendment*. Buffalo, N.Y.: Prometheus Books, 1994.

Arons, Stephen. *Compelling Belief: The Culture of American Schooling*. New York: McGraw-Hill, 1983.

Ashmore, Harry S. *Hearts and Minds: The Anatomy of Racism from Roosevelt to Reagan*. New York: McGraw-Hill , 1982.

Bell, Derrick A. *And We Are Not Saved: The Elusive Quest for Racial Justice*. New York: Basic Books, 1987.

_____. *Faces at the Bottom of the Well: The Permanence of Racism*. New York: Basic Books, 1992.

Bollinger, Lee C. *Images of a Free Press*. Chicago: University of Chicago Press, 1991.

_____. *The Tolerant Society: Free Speech and Extremist Speech in America*. New York: Oxford University Press, 1986.

Carter, Stephen L. *Reflections of an Affirmative Action Baby*. New York: Basic Books, 1991.

De Grazia, Edward. *Girls Lean Back Everywhere: The Law of Obscenity and the Assault on Genius*. New York: Random House, 1992.

Dorsen, Norman, ed. *Our Endangered Rights: The ACLU Report on Civil Liberties Today*. New York: Pantheon Books, 1984.

Dworkin, Ronald M. *Life's Dominion: An Argument About Abortion, Euthanasia, and Individual Freedom*. New York: Alfred A. Knopf, 1993.

_____. *Taking Rights Seriously*. Cambridge, Mass.: Harvard University Press, 1977.

Eastland, Terry, and William J. Bennett. *Counting by Race: Equality from the Founding Fathers to Bakke and Weber*. New York: Basic Books, 1979.

Epstein, Richard. *Forbidden Grounds: The Case Against Employment Discrimination Laws*. Cambridge, Mass.: Harvard University Press, 1992.

Faux, Marian. *Roe v. Wade: The Untold Story of the Landmark Supreme Court Decision That Made Abortion Legal*. New York: Macmillan, 1988.

Foerstel, Herbert N. *Banned in the U.S.A.: A Reference Guide to Book Censorship in Schools and Public*. Westport, Conn.: Greenwood Press, 1994.

Friendly, Fred W. *The Good Guys, the Bad Guys, and the First Amendment: Free Speech vs. Fairness in Broadcasting*. New York: Random House, 1976.

Garrow, David J. *Liberty and Sexuality: The Right to Privacy and the Making of Roe v. Wade*. New York: Macmillan, 1994.

Hentoff, Nat. *Free Speech for Me—but Not for Thee: How the American Left and Right Relentlessly Censor Each Other*. New York: HarperCollins, 1992.

Hopkins, W. Wat. *Actual Malice: Twenty-five Years after Times v. Sullivan*. New York: Praeger, 1989.

Kalven, Harry, Jr. *A Worthy Tradition: Freedom of Speech in America*. Edited by Jamie Kalven. New York: Harper & Row, 1988.

Levy, Leonard W. *Emergence of a Free Press*. New York: Oxford University Press, 1985.

Lewis, Anthony. *Make No Law: The Sullivan Case and the First Amendment*. New York: Random House, 1991.

McClosky, Herbert, and Alida Brill. *Dimensions of Tolerance: What Americans Believe About Civil Liberties.* New York: Russell Sage Foundation, 1983.

MacKinnon, Catharine A. *Only Words.* Cambridge, Mass.: Harvard University Press, 1993.

Nathanson, Bernard. *Aborting America.* Garden City, N.Y.: Doubleday, 1979.

O'Brien, David M. *The Public's Right to Know: The Supreme Court and the First Amendment.* New York: Praeger Publishers, 1981.

Pfeffer, Leo. *Religion, State and the Burger Court.* Buffalo, N.Y.: Prometheus Books, 1984.

Powe, Lucas A., Jr. *American Broadcasting and the First Amendment.* Berkeley: University of California Press, 1987.

Reagan, Ronald. *Abortion and the Conscience of the Nation.* Nashville: Thomas Nelson, 1984.

Richards, David A. J. *Toleration and the Constitution.* New York: Oxford University Press, 1986.

Rosenberg, Norman L. *Protecting the Best Men: An Interpretive History of the Law of Libel.* Chapel Hill: University of North Carolina Press, 1986.

Rosenfeld, Michel. *Affirmative Action and Justice: A Philosophical and Constitutional Inquiry.* New Haven: Yale University Press, 1991.

Ryan, William. *Equality.* New York: Random House, 1981.

Schwartz, Bernard. *Behind Bakke: Affirmative Action and the Supreme Court.* New York: New York University Press, 1988.

Smolla, Rodney A. *Suing the Press: Libel, the Media, and Power.* New York: Oxford University Press, 1986.

Sowell, Thomas. *Civil Rights: Rhetoric or Reality?* New York: William Morrow, 1984.

Spitzer, Matthew L. *Seven Dirty Words and Six Other Stories: Controlling the Content of Print and Broadcast.* New Haven: Yale University Press, 1986.

Strossen, Nadine. *Defending Pornography: Free Speech, Sex, and the Fight for Women's Rights.* New York: Scribner's, 1995.

Tribe, Laurence H. *Abortion: The Clash of Absolutes.* New York: W. W. Norton, 1990.

Urofsky, Melvin I. *A Conflict of Rights: The Supreme Court and Affirmative Action.* New York: Scribner's, 1991.

Waldron, Jeremy. *The Right to Private Property.* New York: Oxford University Press, 1988.

Williams, Patricia L. *The Alchemy of Race and Rights: The Diary of a Law Professor.* Cambridge, Mass.: Harvard University Press, 1991.

Yudof, Mark G. *When Government Speaks: Politics, Law, and Government Expression in America.* Berkeley: University of California Press, 1982.

Criminal Law and Procedure

Baker, Liva. *Miranda: The Crime, the Law, the Politics.* New York: Atheneum, 1983.

Bazelon, David L. *Questioning Authority: Justice and Criminal Law.* New York: Alfred A. Knopf, 1988.

Bedau, Hugo Adam. *The Death Penalty in America.* 3d ed. New York: Oxford University Press, 1982.

Berger, Raoul. *Death Penalties: The Supreme Court's Obstacle Course.* Cambridge, Mass.: Harvard University Press, 1982.

Dershowitz, Alan M. *The Best Defense.* New York: Random House, 1982.

Ewing, Charles. *Battered Women Who Kill: Psychological Self-Defense as Justification.* Lexington, Mass.: Lexington Books, 1987.

Feinberg, Joel. *Harmless Wrongdoing: The Moral Limits of the Criminal Law.* New York: Oxford University Press, 1988.

Fletcher, George P. *A Crime of Self-Defense: Bernhard Goetz and the Law on Trial.* New York: Free Press, 1988.

Katz, Leo. *Bad Acts and Guilty Minds: Conundrums of the Criminal Law.* Chicago: University of Chicago Press. 1987.

Kramer, Rita. *At a Tender Age: Violent Youth and Juvenile Justice.* New York: Henry Holt, 1988.

Lewis, Anthony. *Gideon's Trumpet.* New York: Random House, 1964.

Weinreb, Lloyd L. *Denial of Justice: Criminal Process in the United States.* New York: Free Press, 1977.

White, Welsh S. *The Death Penalty in the Nineties: An Examination of the Modern System of Capital Punishment.* Ann Arbor: University of Michigan Press, 1991.

Winslade, William J., and Judith Wilson Ross. *The Insanity Plea: The Uses and Abuses of the Insanity Defense.* New York: Scribner's, 1983.

History and Biography

Baker, Liva. *Justice from Beacon Hill: The Life and Times of Oliver Wendell Holmes.* New York: HarperCollins, 1991.

Burstein, Paul. *The Struggle for Equal Employment Opportunity in the United States Since the New Deal.* Chicago: University of Chicago Press, 1985.

Burt, Robert. *Two Jewish Justices: Outcasts in the Promised Land.* Berkeley: University of California Press, 1988.

Cover, Robert M. *Justice Accused: Antislavery and the Judicial Process.* New Haven: Yale University Press, 1975.

Currie, David P. *The Constitution in the Supreme Court: The First Hundred Years, 1789-1888.* Chicago: University of Chicago Press, 1985.

————. *The Constitution in the Supreme Court: The Second Century, 1888-1986.* Chicago: University of Chicago Press, 1990.

Eldridge, Larry D. *A Distant Heritage: The Growth of Free Speech in Early America.* New York: New York University Press, 1994.

Friedman, Lawrence M. *A History of American Law.* New York, Simon & Schuster, 1973.

Greenberg, Jack. *Crusaders in the Courts: How a Dedicated Band of Lawyers Fought for the Civil Rights Revolution.* New York: Basic Books, 1994.

Hall, Kermit. *The Magic Mirror: Law in American History.* New York: Oxford University Press, 1989.

Horwitz, Morton J. *The Transformation of American Law, 1780-1860*. Cambridge, Mass.: Harvard University Press, 1977.

————. *The Transformation of American Law, 1870-1960: The Crisis of Legal Orthodoxy*. New York: Oxford University Press, 1992.

Kluger, Richard. *Simple Justice: The History of Brown v. Board of Education and Black America's Struggle for Equality*. New York: Alfred A. Knopf, 1975.

Kurland, Philip B. *Watergate and the Constitution*. Chicago: University of Chicago Press, 1978.

Murphy, Bruce Allen. *The Brandeis/Frankfurter Connection: The Secret Political Activities of Two Supreme Court Justices*. New York: Oxford University Press, 1982.

Novick, Sheldon M. *Honorable Justice: The Life of Oliver Wendell Holmes*. Boston: Little, Brown, 1989.

Paper, Lewis J. *Brandeis*. Englewood Cliffs, New Jersey: Prentice Hall, 1983.

Posner, Richard A. *Cardozo: A Study in Reputation*. Chicago: University of Chicago Press, 1990.

Purcell, Edward A., Jr. *Litigation and Inequality: Federal Diversity Jurisdiction in Industrial America, 1870-1958*. New York: Oxford University Press, 1992.

Strum, Philippa. *Louis D. Brandeis: Justice for the People*. Cambridge, Mass.: Harvard University Press, 1984.

Tushnet, Mark. *Making Civil Rights Law: Thurgood Marshall and the Supreme Court, 1936-1961*. New York: Oxford University Press, 1994.

————. *The NAACP's Legal Strategy Against Segregated Education, 1925-1950*. Chapel Hill: University of North Carolina Press, 1987.

Urofsky, Melvin I. *Louis D. Brandeis and the Progressive Tradition*. Boston: Little, Brown, 1981.

Walker, Samuel. *In Defense of American Liberties: A History of the ACLU*. New York: Oxford University Press, 1990.

White, G. Edward. *Earl Warren: A Public Life*. New York: Oxford University Press, 1982.

————. *Reimagining the Marshall Court: The Marshall Court and Cultural Change, 1815-1835*. New York: Macmillan, 1988.

Woodward, Bob, and Scott Armstrong. *The Brethren*. New York : Simon & Schuster, 1979.

Yarbrough, Tinsley E. *John Marshall Harlan: Great Dissenter of the Warren Court*. New York: Oxford University Press, 1992.

The Judicial Process

Caplan, Lincoln. *The Tenth Justice: The Solicitor General and the Rule of Law*. New York: Alfred A. Knopf, 1987.

Ellickson, Robert C. *Order Without Law: How Neighbors Settle Disputes*. Cambridge, Mass.: Harvard University Press, 1991.

Epstein, Lee, et al. *The Supreme Court Compendium: Data, Decisions, and Developments*. Washington, D.C.: Congressional Quarterly, 1994.

Feeley, Malcolm M. *Court Reform on Trial: Why Simple Solutions Fail*. New York: Basic Books, 1983.

Fletcher, George P. *With Justice for Some: Victims' Rights in Criminal Trials*. Reading, Mass.: Addison-Wesley, 1995.

Forer, Louis G. *Who Owns the Courts?* New York: W. W. Norton, 1984.

Gould, Milton S. *The Witness Who Spoke with God and Other Tales from the Courthouse*. New York: Viking, 1979.

Hans, Valerie P., and Neil Vidmar. *Judging the Jury*. New York: Plenum Press, 1986.

Hastie, Reid, and Steven D. Penrod, and Nancy Pennington. *Inside the Jury*. Cambridge, Mass.: Harvard University Press, 1983.

Hazard, Geoffrey C., Jr., and Michele Taruffo. *American Civil Procedure: An Introduction*. New Haven: Yale University Press, 1993.

Huber, Peter W. *Galileo's Revenge: Junk Science in the Courtroom*. New York: Basic Books, 1991.

Neely, Richard. *The Politics of State Courts*. New York: Free Press, 1988.

O'Brien, David M. *What Process Is Due? Courts and Science-Policy Disputes*. New York: Russell Sage Foundation, 1987.

Posner, Richard A. *The Federal Courts: Crisis and Reform*. Cambridge, Mass.: Harvard University Press, 1985.

Rehnquist, William H. *The Supreme Court: How It Was, How It Is*. New York: Quill, 1987.

Rosenberg, Gerald N. *The Hollow Hope: Can Courts Bring About Social Change?* Chicago: University of Chicago Press, 1991.

Spence, Gerry. *With Justice for None*. New York: Time Books, 1989.

Strick, Anne. *Injustice for All*. New York: Putnam, 1977.

Tribe, Laurence H. *God Save This Honorable Court: How the Choice of Supreme Court Justices Shapes Our History*. New York: Random House, 1985.

The Legal Profession and Legal Education

Abramson, Jill, and Barbara Franklin. *Where They Are Now: The Story of the Women of Harvard Law 1974*. New York: Doubleday, 1986.

Bartlett, Joseph W. *The Law Business: A Tired Monopoly*. Littleton, Colo.: Fred B. Rothman, 1982.

Couric, Emily. *The Trial Lawyers: The Nation's Top Litigators Tell How They Win*. New York: St. Martin's Press, 1988.

Galanter, Marc, and Thomas Palay. *Tournament of Lawyers: The Transformation of the Big Law Firm*. Chicago: University of Chicago Press, 1991.

Granfield, Robert. *Making Elite Lawyers: Visions of Law at Harvard and Beyond*. New York: Routledge, Chapman and Hall, 1992.

Grutman, Roy. *Lawyers and Thieves*. New York: Simon & Schuster, 1990.

Irons, Peter H. *The New Deal Lawyers*. Princeton: Princeton University Press, 1982.

Lopez, Gerald P. *Rebellious Lawyering: One Chicano's Vision of Progressive Law Practice*. Boulder: Westview Press, 1992.

Luban, David. *Lawyers and Justice: An Ethical Study*. Princeton: Princeton University Press, 1988.

McIntyre, Lisa J. *The Public Defender*. Chicago: University of Chicago Press, 1987.

Mann, Kenneth. *Defending White-Collar Crime: A Portrait of Attorneys at Work*. New Haven: Yale University Press, 1985.

Ragano, Frank. *Mob Lawyer*. New York: Scribner's, 1994.

Turow, Scott. *One L*. New York: Putnam, 1977.

Legal Theory

Ackerman, Bruce A. *Private Property and the Constitution*. New Haven: Yale University Press, 1977.

_____. *Social Justice in the Liberal State*. New Haven: Yale University Press, 1980.

_____. *We the People: Foundations*. Cambridge, Mass.: Belknap Press of Harvard University Press, 1991.

Adler, Mortimer Jerome. *We Hold These Truths: Understanding the Ideas and Ideals of the Constitution*. New York: Macmillan, 1987.

Ball, Milner S. *The Word and the Law*. Chicago: University of Chicago Press, 1993.

Berger, Raoul. *Government by Judiciary: The Transformation of the Fourteenth Amendment*. Cambridge, Mass.: Harvard University Press, 1977.

Berns, Walter F. *Taking the Constitution Seriously*. New York: Simon & Schuster, 1987.

Bernstein, Richard B. *Amending America: If We Love the Constitution So Much, Why Do We Keep Trying to Change It?* New York: Times Books, 1993.

Bobbitt, Philip. *Constitutional Interpretation*. Cambridge, Mass.: Basil Blackwell, 1991.

Bork, Robert H. *The Tempting of America: The Political Seduction of the Law*. New York: Free Press, 1990.

Burt, Robert A. *The Constitution in Conflict*. Cambridge, Mass.: Belknap Press of Harvard University Press, 1992.

Calabresi, Guido. *A Common Law for the Age of Statutes*. Cambridge, Mass.: Harvard University Press, 1982.

Carter, Lief H. *Contemporary Constitutional Lawmaking: The Supreme Court and the Art of Politics*. New York: Pergamon Press, 1985.

Cox, Archibald. *The Court and the Constitution*. Boston: Houghton Mifflin, 1987.

Dworkin, Ronald. *Law's Empire*. Cambridge, Mass.: Harvard University Press, 1986.

_____. *A Matter of Principle*. Cambridge, Mass.: Harvard University Press, 1985.

Ely, John Hart. *Democracy and Distrust: A Theory of Judicial Review*. Cambridge, Mass.: Harvard University Press, 1980.

Glendon, Mary Ann. *Rights Talk: The Impoverishment of Political Discourse*. New York: Free Press, 1991.

Goldstein, Joseph. *The Intelligible Constitution*. New York: Oxford University Press, 1992.

Greenawalt, Kent. *Conflicts of Law and Morality*. New York: Oxford University Press, 1987.

_____. *Religious Convictions and Political Choice*. New York: Oxford University Press, 1988

Holmes, Stephen. *The Anatomy of Antiliberalism*. Cambridge, Mass.: Harvard University Press, 1993.

Irons, Peter H. *Brennan vs. Rehnquist: The Battle for the Constitution*. New York: Alfred A. Knopf, 1994.

Kelman, Mark. *A Guide to Critical Legal Studies*. Cambridge, Mass.: Harvard University Press, 1987.

Levinson, Sanford. *Constitutional Faith*. Princeton: Princeton University Press, 1988.

Levy, Leonard W. *Original Intent and the Framers' Constitution*. New York: Macmillan, 1988.

MacKinnon, Catharine A. *Feminism Unmodified: Discourses on Life and Law*. Cambridge, Mass.: Harvard University Press, 1987.

_____. *Toward a Feminist Theory of the State*. Cambridge, Mass.: Harvard University Press, 1989.

Mensch, Elizabeth, and Alan Freeman. *The Politics of Virtue: Is Abortion Debatable?* Durham: Duke University Press, 1993.

Minow, Martha. *Making All the Difference*. Ithaca: Cornell University Press, 1990.

Nagel, Robert. *Constitutional Cultures: The Mentality and Consequences of Judicial Review*. Berkeley: University of California Press, 1989.

Noonan, John Thomas. *Persons and Masks of the Law: Cardozo, Holmes, Jefferson, and Wythe as Makers of the Masks*. New York: Farrar, Straus & Giroux, 1976.

Nozick, Robert. *Anarchy, State, and Utopia*. New York: Basic Books, 1974.

Okin, Susan Moller. *Justice, Gender and the Family*. New York: Basic Books, 1989.

Perry, Michael J. *The Constitution, the Courts, and Human Rights*. New Haven: Yale University Press, 1982.

_____. *Love and Power: The Role of Religion and Morality in American Politics*. New York: Oxford University Press, 1991.

Posner, Richard A. *The Problems of Jurisprudence*. Cambridge, Mass.: Harvard University Press, 1990.

Rawls, John. *Political Liberalism*. New York: Columbia University Press, 1993.

_____. *A Theory of Justice*. Cambridge, Mass.: Belknap Press of Harvard University Press, 1971.

Sunstein, Cass R. *The Partial Constitution*. Cambridge, Mass.: Harvard University Press, 1993.

Tribe, Laurence H. *Constitutional Choices*. Cambridge, Mass.: Harvard University Press, 1985.

Tribe, Laurence H., and Michael C. Dorf. *On Reading the Constitution*. Cambridge, Mass.: Harvard University Press, 1991.

Tushnet, Mark. *Red, White, and Blue: A Critical Analysis of Constitutional Law*. Cambridge, Mass.: Harvard University Press, 1988.

Walzer, Michael. *Spheres of Justice: A Defense of Pluralism and Equality*. New York: Basic Books, 1983.

Miscellaneous Works

Aron, Nan. *Liberty and Justice for All: Public Interest Law in the 1980s and Beyond.* Boulder, Colo.: Westview Press, 1989.

Auerbach, Jerold S. *Justice Without Law?* New York: Oxford University Press, 1983.

Bates, Stephen. *Battleground: One Mother's Crusade, the Religious Right, and the Struggle for Control of Our Classrooms.* New York: Poseidon, 1993.

Birnbaum, Jeffrey H., and Alan S. Murray. *Showdown at Gucci Gulch: Lawmakers, Lobbyists, and the Unlikely Triumph of Tax Reform.* New York: Random House, 1987.

Bork, Robert H. *The Antitrust Paradox: A Policy at War with Itself.* New York: Basic Books, 1978.

Carter, Stephen L. *The Culture of Disbelief: How American Law and Politics Trivialize Religious Devotion.* New York: Basic Books, 1993.

DeBoer, Robby. *Losing Jessica.* New York: Doubleday, 1994.

Edelman, Marian Wright. *Families in Peril.* Cambridge, Mass.: Harvard University Press, 1987.

Ely, John Hart. *War and Responsibility: Constitutional Lessons of Vietnam and Its Aftermath.* Princeton: Princeton University Press, 1993.

Estrich, Susan. *Real Rape.* Cambridge, Mass.: Harvard University Press, 1987.

Fried, Charles. *Order and Law: Arguing the Reagan Revolution, a Firsthand Account.* New York: Simon & Schuster, 1991.

Friedman, Lawrence M. *Total Justice.* New York: Russell Sage Foundation, 1985.

Gilmore, Grant. *The Ages of American Law.* New Haven: Yale University Press, 1977.

Glendon, Mary Ann. *Abortion and Divorce in Western Law.* Cambridge, Mass.: Harvard University Press, 1987.

————. *The New Family and the New Property.* Toronto: Butterworths, 1981.

Goldstein, Joseph, Anna Freud, Albert J. Solnit, and Sonja Goldstein. *In the Best Interests of the Child.* New York: Free Press, 1986.

Guinier, Lani. *The Tyranny of the Majority: Fundamental Fairness in Representative Democracy.* New York: Free Press, 1994.

Howard, Philip K. *The Death of Common Sense: How Law Is Suffocating America.* New York: Random House, 1994.

Karmel, Roberta S. *Regulation by Prosecution: The Securities & Exchange Commission Versus Corporate America.* New York: Simon & Schuster, 1982.

Levy, Leonard, Kenneth Karst, and Dennis Mahoney. *Encyclopedia of the American Constitution.* New York: Macmillan, 1986.

Lieberman, Jethro K. *The Evolving Constitution: How the Supreme Court Has Ruled on Issues from Abortion to Zoning.* New York: Random House, 1992.

Moll, Richard W. *The Lure of the Law.* New York: Viking, 1990.

Moore, Michael S. *Law and Psychiatry: Rethinking the Relationship.* New York: Cambridge University Press, 1984.

Noonan, John T., Jr. *The Believer and the Powers That Are.* New York: Macmillan, 1987.

Posner, Richard A. *Law and Literature: A Misunderstood Relation.* Cambridge, Mass.: Harvard University Press, 1988.

————. *Sex and Reason.* Cambridge, Mass.: Harvard University Press, 1992.

Rabkin, Jeremy A. *Judicial Compulsions: How Public Law Distorts Public Policy.* New York: Basic Books, 1989.

Rembar, Charles. *The Law of the Land: The Evolution of Our Legal System.* New York: Simon & Schuster, 1980.

Schwartz, Herman. *Packing the Courts: The Conservative Campaign to Rewrite the Constitution.* New York: Scribner's, 1988.

Sevilla, Charles M. *Disorder in the Court: Great Fractured Moments in Courtroom History.* New York: W. W. Norton, 1992.

Tribe, Laurence H. *American Constitutional Law.* 2d ed. Mineola, New York: Foundation Press, 1988.

Weiler, Paul C. *Governing the Workplace: The Future of Labor and Employment Law.* Cambridge, Mass.: Harvard University Press, 1990.

Zimring, Franklin E. *The Changing Legal World of Adolescence.* New York: Free Press, 1982.

AMERICAN JUSTICE

LIST OF ENTRIES BY CATEGORY

AREAS OF LAW

Administrative law
Admiralty law
Antitrust law
Banking law
Civil law
Commercial law
Constitutional law
Contract law
Copyrights, patents, and
    trademarks
Criminal law
Environmental law
Family law
Gambling law
Immigration laws
Insurance law
International law
Labor law
Medical and health law
Real estate law
School law
Sports law
Telecommunications law
Transportation law

CIVIL AND CRIMINAL JUSTICE

Adultery
Appellate process
Arraignment
Arrest
Attorney
Bail system
Bailiff
Bankruptcy
Bar examinations and
    licensing of lawyers
Bar, the
Battered child and battered
    wife syndromes
Burden of proof
Capital punishment
Case law
Chief of police
Civil disobedience
Civil procedure
Civilian review boards
Commercialized vice
Common law
Community-oriented policing
Conscientious objection
Coroner
Corporal punishment
Counsel, right to
Crime
Crime Index
Criminal
Criminal intent
Criminal justice system
Criminal procedure
Criminology
Deadly force, police use of
Defamation
Detectives, police
Deterrence
Discretion
District attorney
Domestic violence
Drug legalization debate
Drug use and sale, illegal
Equitable remedies
Equity
Espionage
Evidence, rules of
Felony
Fiduciary trust
Forensic science and medicine
Gangs, youth
Hate crimes
Illegal aliens
Immigration, legal and illegal
Immunity of public officials
Incapacitation
Indictment
Judicial system, U.S.
Jurisprudence
Jury system
Justice
Juvenile delinquency
Juvenile justice system
Labor unions
Law
Law schools
Legal ethics
Legal realism
Lynching
Machine politics
Malfeasance, misfeasance,
    and nonfeasance
Malice
Mandatory sentencing laws
Medical examiner
Medical malpractice
Military justice
Miscarriage of justice
Miscegenation laws
Misdemeanor
Mistrial
Moral relativism
National debt
Negligence
News media
News sources, protection of
Nonviolent resistance
Nuisance
Organized crime
Pardoning power
Pedophilia
Plea bargaining
Police
Police and guards, private
Police brutality
Police corruption and
    misconduct
Political corruption
Positive law
Presumption of innocence
Prison and jail systems
Privileged communications
Products liability
Property rights
Prosecutor, public
Psychopath and sociopath
Public defender
Punishment
Reasonable doubt
Reasonable force
Rehabilitation
Reparations
Restrictive covenant
School prayer
Seditious libel
Self-defense
Sentencing
Sexual harassment
Sheriff
Special weapons and tactics
    (SWAT) teams
Spoils system and patronage
State police
Sterilization and American
    law
Suicide and euthanasia
Ten most wanted criminals
Terrorism
Tort
Tort reform
Vigilantism
Wills, trusts, and estate
    planning
Zoning

CONSTITUTIONAL LAW AND ISSUES

Abortion
Affirmative action
Arms, right to keep and bear
Assembly and association,
    freedom of
Bill of Rights, U.S.
Birth control, right to
Busing
Censorship
Civil liberties
Civil rights
Civil War Amendments
Clear and present danger test
Commerce clause
Constitution, U.S.
Constitutional interpretation
Contract, freedom of
Counsel, right to
Cruel and unusual
    punishment
Double jeopardy
Due process of law
Equal protection of the law
Establishment of religion
Federalism
Incorporation doctrine
Judicial review
Ninth Amendment
Privacy, right of
Religion, free exercise of
Retroactivity of Supreme
    Court decisions
Search and seizure
Self-incrimination, privilege
    against
Speech and press, freedom of
Speedy trial, right to
States' rights
Supremacy clause
Supreme Court of the United
    States
Takings clause

COURT CASES

ORGANIZATIONS

American Bar Association (ABA)

American Civil Liberties Union (ACLU)

American Federation of Labor-Congress of Industrial Organizations (AFL-CIO)

American Indian Movement (AIM)

Anti-Defamation League (ADL)

Black Panther Party

Communist Party, American

Congress of Racial Equality (CORE)

Democratic Party

Federalist Party

Free Soil Party

House Committee on Un-American Activities (HUAC)

International Association of Chiefs of Police

International Brotherhood of Police Officers

Interpol

Jeffersonian Republican Party

John Birch Society

Ku Klux Klan (KKK)

Mexican American Legal Defense and Education Fund (MALDEF)

Mothers Against Drunk Driving (MADD)

Nation of Islam

National Association for the Advancement of Colored People (NAACP)

National Association for the Advancement of Colored People Legal Defense and Educational Fund

National District Attorneys Association

National Organization for Victim Assistance (NOVA)

National Organization for Women (NOW)

National Rifle Association (NRA)

National Urban League

Republican Party

Socialist Party, American

Southern Christian Leadership Conference (SCLC)

States' Rights Party

Student Nonviolent Coordinating Committee (SNCC)

Students for a Democratic Society (SDS)

United Farm Workers (UFW)

Weather Underground

Whig Party

World Court

PERSONS

Addams, Jane

Anthony, Susan B.

Bentham, Jeremy

Black, Hugo L.

Blackstone, William

Brandeis, Louis D.

Brown, John

Bryan, William Jennings

Burger, Warren

Bush, George

Calhoun, John C.

Capone, Alphonse (Al)

Cardozo, Benjamin Nathan

Carter, Jimmy

Chase, Samuel

Chávez, César

Clay, Henry

Cooley, Thomas

Daugherty, Harry M.

Debs, Eugene V.

Dix, Dorothea Lynde

Douglas, Stephen A.

Douglas, William O.

Douglass, Frederick

Du Bois, W. E. B.

Eisenhower, Dwight D.

Ellsworth, Oliver

Field, Stephen J.

Ford, Gerald R.

Frankfurter, Felix

Fuller, Melvin Weston

Gandhi, Mahatma

Garrison, William Lloyd

Garvey, Marcus

Gompers, Samuel

Greeley, Horace

Hand, Learned

Holmes, Oliver Wendell, Jr.

Hoover, J. Edgar

Hughes, Charles Evans

Jackson, Jesse

Jay, John

Johnson, Lyndon B.

Kennedy, John F.

Kennedy, Robert F.

Kent, James

King, Martin Luther, Jr.

Lewis, John L.

Lincoln, Abraham

Livingston, Edward

Long, Huey

Mack, Julian William

Malcolm X

Marshall, John

Marshall, Thurgood

Muhammad, Elijah

Nader, Ralph

Nixon, Richard M.

Pinkerton, Allan

Pound, Roscoe

Randolph, A. Philip

Reagan, Ronald

Rehnquist, William

Roosevelt, Eleanor

Roosevelt, Franklin D.

Rush, Benjamin

Sanger, Margaret

Sinclair, Upton

Stanton, Elizabeth Cady

Steffens, Lincoln

Stone, Harlan Fiske

Story, Joseph

Stowe, Harriet Beecher

Taft, William Howard

Taney, Roger Brooke

Truman, Harry S

Vinson, Fred M.

Waite, Morrison Remick

Warren, Earl

Washington, Booker T.

White, Edward Douglass

Wilson, James

Wilson, Woodrow

SOCIAL JUSTICE AND POLITICAL RIGHTS

Acquired immune deficiency syndrome (AIDS)

Age discrimination

American Indians

Capitalism

Citizenship

Civil rights

Civil Rights movement

Comparable worth

Conservatism, modern American

Declaration of Independence

Democracy

Equality of opportunity

Feminism

Gay rights

Homelessness

Japanese American internment

Liberalism, modern American

McCarthyism

Marxism

Morality and foreign policy

Natural law and natural rights

Nuclear weapons

Poll tax

Racial and ethnic discrimination

Religious sects and cults

Representation: gerrymandering, malapportionment, and reapportionment

Segregation, *de facto* and *de jure*

Sex discrimination

Socialism

Taxation and justice

Veterans' rights

Vietnam War

Vote, right to

War on Poverty

Welfare state

Woman suffrage

CASE INDEX

A page number or range in boldface type indicates a full article devoted to that topic.

INDEX

A page number or range in boldface type indicates a full article devoted to that topic. Page numbers in italic type indicate photographs, drawings, maps, tables, charts, and graphs.

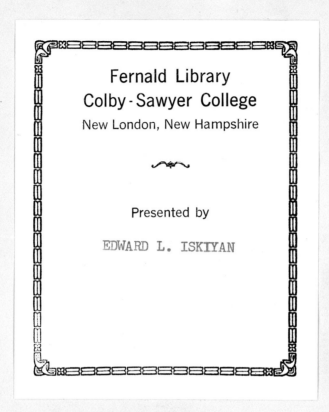

Friendship and Peer Relations

The Origins of Behavior

Michael Lewis and
Leonard A. Rosenblum, Editors

Volume 1
The Effect of the Infant on Its Caregiver

Michael Lewis and
Leonard A. Rosenblum, Editors

Volume 2
The Origins of Fear

Michael Lewis and
Leonard A. Rosenblum, Editors

Volume 3
Structure and Transformation:
Developmental Aspects

Klaus F. Riegel and
George C. Rosenwald, Editors

Volume 4
Friendship and Peer Relations

Michael Lewis and
Leonard A. Rosenblum, Editors

Friendship and Peer Relations

Edited by

Michael Lewis
Educational Testing Service

and

Leonard A. Rosenblum
State University of New York
Downstate Medical Center

A Wiley-Interscience Publication

JOHN WILEY & SONS
New York • London • Sydney • Toronto

Library of Congress Cataloging in Publication Data:

Main entry under title:
Friendship and peer relations.

   (The Origins of Behavior; v. 4)
   "A Wiley-Interscience publication."
   Papers presented . . . at a conference on peer
relations and friendship and held under the auspices . . .
of the Educational Testing Service in Princeton,
New Jersey."
   Includes bibliographies and indexes.
   1. Infant psychology—Congresses. 2. Social
interaction—Congresses. 3. Friendship—Congresses.
I. Lewis, Michael, Jan. 10, 1937– II. Rosenblum,
Leonard A. III. Educational Testing Service.
IV. Series. [DNLM: 1. Interpersonal relations—In
infancy and childhood—Congresses. 2. Peer group—
Congresses. 3. Social behavior—In infancy and
childhood—Congresses. 4. Child development—
Congresses. W1 OR687 v. 4 / WS105 F906]

BF723.I6F74   155.4'22   75-20181
ISBN 0-471-53345-9

Printed in the United States of America

10 9 8 7 6 5 4 3 2 1

Contributors

Elizabeth Bates*
Department of Psychology
University of Colorado
Boulder, Colorado

Lyn J. Bromley
Primate Behavior Laboratory
Downstate Medical Center
Brooklyn, New York

Wanda C. Bronson*
Institute of Human Development
University of California
Berkeley, California

Jeanne Brooks*
Infant Laboratory
Educational Testing Service
Princeton, New Jersey

Christopher L. Coe*
Primate Behavior Laboratory
Downstate Medical Center
Brooklyn, New York

Carol O. Eckerman
Department of Psychology
Duke University
Durham, North Carolina

Harry F. Harlow
Department of Psychology
University of Arizona
Tucson, Arizona

* Conference participants.

Willard W. Hartup*
Institute of Child Development
University of Minnesota
Minneapolis, Minnesota

Jerome Kagan*
Department of Psychology and
Social Relations
Harvard University
Cambridge, Massachusetts

Richard B. Kearsley
Department of Pediatrics
Tufts New England Medical Center
Boston, Massachusetts

Melvin Konner*
Department of Psychology and
Social Relations
Harvard University
Cambridge, Massachusetts

Lee C. Lee*
Department of Human Development
Cornell University
Ithaca, New York

Michael Lewis*
Infant Laboratory
Educational Testing Service
Princeton, New Jersey

Thomas Lucas
Department of Psychology
Clark University
Worcester, Massachusetts

Linda Michalson*
Infant Laboratory
Educational Testing Service
Princeton, New Jersey

Edward Mueller*
Department of Psychology
Boston University
Boston, Massachusetts

Harriet Rheingold*
Department of Psychology
University of North Carolina
Chapel Hill, North Carolina

Leonard A. Rosenblum*
Primate Behavior Laboratory
Downstate Medical Center
Brooklyn, New York

Stephen J. Suomi*
Department of Psychology,
Primate Laboratory
University of Wisconsin
Madison, Wisconsin

Marian Radke Yarrow*
Laboratory of Developmental
Psychology
National Institute of Mental Health
Bethesda, Maryland

Gerald Young*
Infant Laboratory
Educational Testing Service
Princeton, New Jersey

Philip R. Zelazo
Department of Pediatrics
Tufts New England Medical Center
Boston, Massachusetts

Series Preface

"The childhood shows the man,
as morning shows the day."

Milton, Paradise Regained

None can doubt that the study of man begins in the study of childhood. Few would contend that the newborn lacks the challenge of his evolutionary heritage. This series addresses itself to the task of bringing together, on a continuing basis, that confluence of theory and data on ontogeny and phylogeny which will serve to illustrate *The Origins of Behavior.*

Whether our social, human, and professional concerns lie in the psychological disorders of childhood or adulthood or merely in the presumptively normal range of expression in development in different cultures, varied environments, or diverse family constellations, we can never hope to discern order and regularity from the mass of uncertain observation and groundless speculation if we fail to nurture the scientific study of development. Fortunately, the last two decades have seen an enormous burgeoning of effort toward this end, both at the human and nonhuman level. However, despite this growth of effort and interest, no single means of pooling our growing knowledge on development in children and animals and communicating that fusion of material to the broad scientific community now exists. This series seeks to fill the gap. It is our intention to have each volume deal with a specific theme that is either of social or of theoretical relevance to developmental issues. In keeping with the integrated perspective that we consider to be vital, and to provide a meaningful context within which these issues may be considered, each volume in the series will contain a broad range of material and will seek to encompass theoretical and sound empirical studies of the behavior of human infants as well as pertinent aspects of animal behavior with a particular emphasis on the primates. It is our view, furthermore, that not only is it necessary to focus our interest on both human infants and animals, but that the levels of analysis which will explicate the processes of development that are our concern must ultimately involve the study of behavior at all levels of discourse. Thus studies of developmental significance may be found in genetic, physiological, morphological, dyadic, and societal levels and an increased interdigitation of these separate disciplines is among the major goals of this series.

In light of the diversity of topics to be considered, the breadth of material to be covered, and the variety of orientations that will be included in these discourses on the origins of human behavior, we expect this series to serve the needs of the broad social science community, not merely of those interested in behavioral development alone. Just as the series itself will draw upon the knowledge and research of psychologists, ethologists, sociologists, psychiatrists, pediatricians, obstetricians, and devoted scientists and clinicians in a number of related disciplines, it is our hope that the material in this series will provide both stimulation and guidance to all among us who are concerned with man, his past, his present, and his future.

Michael Lewis
Leonard A. Rosenblum
Editors

June 1973

Preface

This volume, the fourth in the series *The Origins of Behavior,* focuses on the infant's social behavior that does not directly involve the relationship with its caregiver. Peer relations and the establishment of friendships represent an appropriate arena within which to consider the infant's social relationships in a broader perspective than that traditionally provided by studies of infant-adult interaction. By broadening the study of the young child's and infant's social relations, we can provide the basis for the development of a theory that considers the child's total social world.

The chapters in this volume derive from papers presented and discussed at a conference on peer relations and friendship held under the auspices and with the support of the Educational Testing Service in Princeton, New Jersey. Chapters reflect the integration of the original papers and the critical comments and thematic discussions of the conference participants. In addition, two conference discussants have contributed written essays on the theme. These, together with the introductory chapter, provide an overview and assessment of the current status of our knowledge regarding early social relations.

The participants in the conference were Dr. Elizabeth Bates, Dr. Wanda C. Bronson, Dr. Jeanne Brooks, Mr. Christopher L. Coe, Dr. Willard W. Hartup, Dr. Jerome Kagan, Dr. Melvin Konner, Dr. Lee C. Lee, Dr. Michael Lewis, Dr. David McNeill, Ms. Linda Michalson, Dr. Edward Mueller, Dr. Harriet L. Rheingold, Dr. Leonard A. Rosenblum, Dr. Stephen J. Suomi, Dr. Marian Yarrow, and Dr. Gerald Young.

Michael Lewis
Leonard A. Rosenblum

Princeton, New Jersey
Brooklyn, New York

August 1975

Contents

Introduction

MICHAEL LEWIS
Infant Laboratory
Educational Testing Service
LEONARD A. ROSENBLUM
Primate Behavior Laboratory
Downstate Medical Center

Bibliographies pertaining to the study of peer relationships and friendship in the life of the infant and young child reveal a rather strange pattern. During the late 1920s and 1930s there were relatively large numbers of studies exploring this problem (e.g., Bridges, 1933; Buhler, 1927; Maudry & Nekula, 1939). From this period until very recently, however, there are hardly any references—with the notable exception of Piaget's work on *Play, Dreams, and Imitation in Childhood* (1951). In the last two or three years there has been a sudden explosion of studies of the early social activities of children with peers.

It is not irrelevant to begin this essay by asking why a 40-year hiatus should have taken place. The explanation for this rather startling phenomenon may have important implications for a series of issues relating not only to scientific concern but also to matters of direct public concern—child care, for example. A review of the two dominant theoretical formulations underlying much of the current work in human development provides some insight into the basis of this prolonged lacuna in peer research. Both psychoanalytic and Piagetian theory have led to a suppression of active study of children's early social behavior other than that directed toward the parents—more specifically, the mother.

One of the single most important underlying tenets of psychoanalytic theory is that the early experiences of the organism are the context and instrument for later development. Without question the issue of primacy underlies much of our belief in the mechanisms of development. Moreover, since it was assumed that the child's social relations are between the infant and its parents, the second important implication of the theory has been the belief that the child's relationship with all other social objects is rooted in the child's interaction with its mother and father. For some reason these tenets and their implications have led to the additional view that the child's social behavior is sequential: first the child-parent relationship, next the child-other. The emphasis on primacy, furthermore, means that the earlier relationship determines the latter ones. Whatever the merits of such a position, it has had the effect of discouraging research exploring the child's early "other" social relationships.

1

Bowlby's (1969) now classical work, based on an ethological-psychoanalytical perspective, was first and foremost an attempt to claim for social relationships a biological imperative. The author argued rather effectively that the mother-infant bond was as biologically important to the survival and well-being of the infant as was the satisfaction of any of the other primary drives. In so arguing, Bowlby's work served to create a still stronger climate in which the child's social world was considered to exist almost exclusively between the infant and its mother. To the extent that this infant-mother dyad was a biological imperative, the child's other social relationships were viewed as derivatives and were neglected or not considered at all.

In *Play, Dreams, and Imitation*, Piaget undertook, within the context of his system of genetic epistemology, an analysis of the young child's social behavior. In this work as elsewhere, the cognitive-structural capacities of the infant and young child, as determined by Piaget, were seen as restricting the child's social behavior. Thus for complex social behavior to occur, at least one member of a social unit must be an adult, that is, an organism capable of the major control and manipulation of the dynamics of the relationship. Without more organized and complex cognitive structures, the egocentric nature of the child's cognitive capacities (as seen, e.g., in its play behavior) should not facilitate the social activity of the infant. Such an analysis, focusing on the relative lack of cognitive facility necessary for social commerce, resulted in the restriction of the study of early child-peer relations.

Interestingly, both theories, or at least parts of them, are being vigorously questioned. The attachment literature, a natural continuation of the psychoanalytic and ethological views, has come under increasing attack. In its place, theories aimed at examining the child's entire social network have begun to appear (e.g., Weinraub, Brooks, & Lewis, 1975). These theories are much less committed to the view that the mother-infant bond is the only important and determining relationship in the child's world. In its place, a larger social network has begun to be examined, one in which fathers, grandparents, adult friends, siblings, and peers all serve an important function in the child's life.

Moreover, the notion of egocentricity has begun to be challenged from a variety of standpoints. The recent work on language use as a function of the age of the listener is a good example (see Shatz & Gelman, 1973). There is little question that children at relatively early ages are capable of using language in a differential and correct fashion in respect to the age of the other social object. So much for any general view of the early egocentric social behavior! Given the influence of psychoanalysis and Piagetian theory, it is little wonder that such slight attention has been accorded to the study of early peer relationships as an example of the child's early "other" social relationships.

In the following sections we attempt to broaden the perspective of the infant's social world. By focusing primarily on the child's peer relationships as an example of the complexity of the network of social interaction—a network in which the child both acts and is acted on—we can argue for a broader view of the young child's social world.

THE SOCIAL NETWORK

If we are to derive a useful framework within which to consider the course of the development of peer relations and friendships in infancy, we need first some conceptual structure for the total set of potential interactive social objects. Only then can we assess the order and interrelations among the diverse set of stimuli within the infant's social domain. In the broadest sense we suggest that the infant's stimulus world can be represented by a structural consideration of all the objects available for interaction. One major differentiation distinguishes the animate and inanimate elements that surround the child. The animate figures with whom interactions occur may be considered to contain both conspecifics (i.e., humans) and other organisms. Furthermore, this set of humans is comprised of several distinguishable subsets: these include the major division of adults and other children. The latter groups are further differentiated in terms at least of their relative familiarity to the infant, hence contain most prominently parents and siblings, respectively. Thus when the child has achieved the primary level of differentiating (through interaction with) the elements in its social sphere, its world may be said to be composed of a network like that in Figure 1, which presents schematically the array of potential social elements. Notice immediately that we have chosen to include within this potential social array the inanimate and animal categories—elements not normally considered to be social. It seems apparent that the very young child's responses to inanimate objects and animals often has a form similar to that exhibited toward people. Thus significant attention, play, and affective response can be directed toward familiar objects such as toys and dolls, and these early inanimate foci must be assumed to be an important part of the child's initially structured environment.

Notice further that within the large array it has been just the parental component, and mostly the mother, that has been the primary focus of attention. However, there is a second dimension for each of the elements in the described space. This familiar-unfamiliar dimension can be used to modulate each element. For example, it is not unreasonable to talk about the amount of interaction a given child has with each of its parents or siblings. Moreover, the dimension of familiarity may vary in its influence as a function of the age or sex of the developing infant (see Rosenblum, et al., chapter 3).

Having enumerated these elemental dimensions of the young child's environment, one task is to delineate the special features of these elements as they interact with and influence the child's social development. *It is vital to note at*

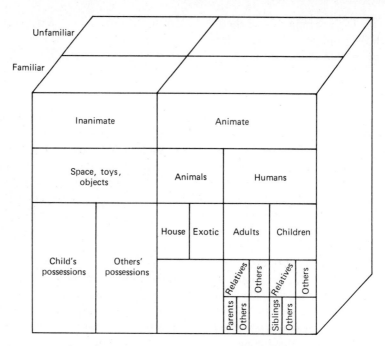

FIGURE 1.   Schematic array of potential social elements.

the outset that no single element is either excluded from social development or provides the singular basis on which it ensues. Moreover, the pattern of *interaction* between these elements is crucial. Sustained and more transient patterns of interactions of varying intensities with each of the elements of the network coalesce in shaping the course of the infant's development. Varying degrees of communality exist between the elements with regard to the infant's commerce with each and the influence each has on subsequent behavior.

THE MEANING OF PEERS

We have seen that substantial, indeed almost exclusive attention has been directed toward an understanding of the special role of parents, primarily the mother, in shaping infant development. Our concern here, however, is to underline the complementary impact of the individuals in the child's environment who share with it parallel levels of maturation and function (i.e., peers, of which siblings represent a significant subset).

For purposes of this discussion, a member of the social network can be considered to be a peer if the member shares with the infant a series of capacities and common physical features. The boundaries of the shared features and capacities vary as a function of development. Thus, for example, a pet can assume the function of a peer because it can share both common features and capacities (a dog makes eye contact and fetches a ball thrown by the child). Similarly, adults by emulating the child and the latter's level of functioning can assume the role of peer. Since the definition of a peer rests at least on shared capacities, we recognize that peer quality is transient. That is, it is directly tied to activity or interaction. For example, in a group of children of varying ages (call it set A), the children who can climb the tree (subset A_1) are, during tree-climbing, peers. During singing activity, however, a second subset of peers (subset A_2) emerges whose members only partially overlap with the first subset. Thus by means of regulated adjustments in behavior, older infants, siblings, and even parents and other adults may within certain contexts function as peers for a period of time. Similarly, the infant itself may modulate its behavior to allow the essential elements of peer relations to be established with younger children or siblings. Hence the essential components of a peer relationship may be considered to be the overt functioning and interaction of individuals at comparable levels of complexity.

SEQUENCES OF DEVELOPMENT

The set of elements capable of eliciting social behavior is considerably larger than it appears at first glance; for that matter, it is a good deal larger than the current research literature suggests. Two central questions need to be asked of such a network. First, is there a hierarchical sequence to the child's differentiation of the elements comprising this set? Second, what are the stimulus dimensions *and* their interaction qualities which lead to this differentiation? Unfortunately, answers to these questions are not readily available.

Consider the hierarchical nature of differentiation. Is it reasonable to consider that the child must be able to differentiate one class of objects from another before it is capable of differentiating a subset from a class? From the point of view of the evolution of the infant's cognitive capacities, what might be considered the sequence of interaction? Inanimate interactions extended to animate ones? The reverse? Or no fixed sequence but rather a movement from one to another object as a function of the nature and intent of the interaction? It has been argued that since inanimate objects are less complicated—that is, are less variable and more predictable—the infant might first develop around these schema and cognitive structures that later can be generalized to deal with animate objects. The difficulty with such a view is that interactions with inanimate objects are capable of being highly variable, whereas at the same time interactions with animate objects can be quite simple. Moreover, if predictability—that is, consistency—is to be considered, one might argue that animate objects are more consistent than inanimate ones. There is little substantiation for theories which attempt to capitalize on either the simplicity or complexity of animate versus inanimate objects and argue on that basis for a sequential course of development. In fact, if we consider the Object Permanence literature, the existing data support the development of person permanence prior to that of object permanence. Thus the interesting question of the sequence of object differentiation in the infant's world does not seem to be easily solved. Indeed, even on the issue of what stimulus or interaction dimensions underlie the differentiation of the elements of the described network, little information can be found. Given the paucity of data and theoretical approaches, we suggest that there is parallel development of response to the various elements within the network previously described. Clearly then, we are now obliged to consider and explore the stimulus or interactional features that affect the development of this social network.

FUNCTIONS OF PEER RELATIONS

The significance for survival of the developing infant's relationship to its caregiver is beyond question. The functions of peer relations are less clear, however. In fact, most statements of function in this regard must be considered merely assumptions now, with little if any systematic data available for support. Even the animal literature, at least that on higher primates, is unclear on the relative significance of early peer relations, either in terms of the particular features of the peer group or even the significance of its total absence early in life. Studies of isolate-rearing, for example, have classically confounded general environmental deprivation and often maternal deprivation with the subject's lack of peer contact. Thus we are forced toward inductive judgments regarding the importance of early peer relations rather than being able to derive our hypotheses from definitive data.

In most instances, for humans as well as most primates, reproduction and adult existence occur within structured social groups that involve interdependent relations in regard to defense, food gathering, and related activities pertinent to survival. In its developing relations with peers, the infant has the opportunity for paced, slowly elaborating enlargement of communicative, aggressive, defensive, and cooperative skills. Whereas immediate interaction with larger, more dexterous and potentially aggressive adults can inhibit or retard the growth of differentiating expression of initially inappropriate or inadequate social responses, interaction with similarly capable age mates or others acting in the role of peers, allows for experimentation and learning without the potential or dire consequences of error. Thus wrestling or play fighting may only have salutory effects on subsequent aggressive or defense potential when engaged with a partner of approximately equal capability, not with one who overwhelms or suppresses the overt expression of such behavior.

Similarly in the course of such early peer interactions, we have the development of specific relationships that serve to facilitate individual recognition and the formation of functional alliances for the future. Since the integration of group activity and specific roles for given individuals are critical tasks of all societies, such early social learning may be strongly selected for during individual and species development.

Indeed, although it is impossible to state precisely the consequences of peer-deficient experience during childhood, given adequate care, we have some strong indications that adequate opportunities for diverse peer relations early in life may represent a setting that is quite conducive to substantially normal social development. Sustained opportunities for active interaction in nursery groups, or in experimental peer groups, can mediate normal development so effectively that one must question the tenability of the frequent assumption that such peer relations substitute for "appropriate" interactions with a caregiver. The possibility exists, and merits our experimental and theoretical attention, that the social interactions with adults supplement or may be substituted for more primary relationships with peers, even very early in life. The ideas that the mother-infant dyad, for example, is sufficient in and of itself for the young child and that the opportunity for active peer interactions may be substantially delayed and then only intermittently afforded, are a consequence of this tenuous assumption, and they may have important sequelae in terms of the subsequent functioning of the individual and of the society.

SOCIAL CONSEQUENCES OF PEER RELATIONS

Most of our views of the early social needs of the child have been based on the limited perception of the contemporary Western view. Social consequences flow from these views. Stated in its most simplistic form, infants and young children will optimally thrive if and only if they are embedded in a small social structure containing adults (mother and father) with relatively few other comparably aged children. Myopically and with considerable tautology, research feeds view, which in turn feeds research.

If we remove ourselves from this familiar view and examine other cultures, other times, and other primates, the conditions that constitute optimal development become less clear. Peers may not be merely other social objects that can satisfy social-cultural goals if and when the adults are unable to function. Quite the contrary, peer relationships may be as important to social development as associations with adults—even more so. There is ample evidence of the strength of peer relations in terms of learning, imitation, and social role development. If it is reasonable to assume that peers are as important to the development of children as adults, it must also follow that the social structures based on the assumption of the adult-child relationship need rethinking. We offer three possible examples.

Peer imitation, even in infancy, has been demonstrated. Children often serve as teachers of other children. That older siblings toilet train younger children has been amply demonstrated. At present the unit of formal education is that of teacher (adult)-child. Is it now reasonable to consider a teacher (child)-child unit? Perhaps the ungraded single-room schoolhouse of the past, where teacher taught the older children who in turn taught the younger ones, was not as far-fetched as has been suggested by some. Models in which children teach other children need to be considered.

Most central to our discussion is the issue of child-rearing models. Current research tends to support adult-child models, but observation of other cultures suggests that alternative models of rearing are possible and have consequences that may not be as destructive of development as we now fear. In fact from a larger perspective, a child living the first 2 to 3 years of its life functionally separated from other peers may be more in violation of its biological-evolutionary past than the child reared in a communal peer environment.

Our ideas of childhood behavior dysfunction and its treatment are also based on the model of adult-child units. Consistent with other learning models, it is the adult who is considered to be the most capable of altering the child's behavior. Although little supporting evidence exists, it would not be inconsistent to argue for the child as therapist. (See Suomi & Harlow, chapter 6).

Once we are willing to reconsider our view of the role of peer relationships, it becomes possible to generate a variety of social consequences. We should not hesitate to do so.

CONCLUSION

The material contained in this volume examines peer relations in children and animals in a number of settings and provides an initial basis in terms of data or theory from which the social sciences can reexamine this crucial aspect of social development. Definitive answers are rare at this stage of our knowledge, and even the formulation of appropriate questions is difficult. Nonetheless, a series of specific issues must be considered if research into the origins and sequelae of peer relations and friendships is to proceed productively:

1.   What are the elements of the infant's social world and what is the sequence and chronology of the infant's differentiation of these elements?

2.   What attributes of a social partner correlate with particular elements of response in the infant? For example, toward whom is play, competition, succorance, or passivity directed?

3.   What elements of adult and subadult behavior relate to varying qualities and quantities of early peer relations, with and without concomitant levels of infant-adult interaction?

4.   What factors mediate the development of more sustained relations with specific peers (i.e., friendships)?

5.   What is the impact of specific social and physical contexts on the form and consequences of peer relations? Here the roles of culture, physical space, and physical environment enrichment are among the factors to be considered.

6.   What is the interaction effect of the infant's experience and pattern of behavior with peers and caregiver? In what ways are these complementary, competitive, and independent functions of the infant?

7.   What are the essential behaviors involved in peer relations and varying stages of growth? In what ways are they similar to or different from those behaviors involved in interactions with adults?

8.   What cognitive capacities are necessary underpinnings for various forms of peer relations?

References

Bowlby, J. *Attachment and loss,* Vol. I. *Attachment.* New York: Basic Books, 1969.

Bridges, K. A study of social development in early infancy. *Child Development,* 1933, **4,** 36–49.

Buhler, C. The social behavior of children. In C. Murchison (Ed.), *Handbook of child psychology.* Worcester, Mass.: Clark University Press, 1933. Pp. 374–416.

Maudry, M., & Nekula, M. Social relations between children of the same age during the first two years of life. *Journal of Genetic Psychology,* 1939, **54,** 193–215.

Piaget, J. *Play, dreams, and imitation in childhood.* New York: Norton, 1951.

Shatz, M., & Gelman, R. The development of communication skills: Modifications in the speech of young children as a function of listener. *Monographs of the Society for Research in Child Development,* 1973, **38** (5). Serial no. 152.

Weinraub, M., Brooks, J., & Lewis, M. The social network: A reconsideration of the concept of attachment. Educational Testing Service, Princeton, N.J., 1975.

CHAPTER 1

The Origins of Friendships[1]

WILLARD W. HARTUP
Institute of Child Development
University of Minnesota

Childhood friendships are most commonly indexed by the frequency with which individual children approach other children and make certain specific overtures to them (e.g., touching the other child, looking at him, giving things to him, taking things from him, talking to him). Both unilateral and mutual attachments are indexed by this procedure. Thus mutual friendships consist of repeated instances of two infants or children approaching each other, touching each other, manipulating each other, and giving or taking from each other. To constitute a mutual friendship, such exchanges are generally understood to occur more often between the children in question than between each individual and other children in the vicinity.

Such conceptualizations of friendship are nothing more nor less than variations on sociometry (Moreno, 1934). Friends are people who spontaneously seek the company of one another; furthermore, they seek proximity in the absence of strong social pressures to do so. Interviews are the most widely used devices to study friendships, particularly in school children and adults. It is possible, however, to identify friendships among young children by means of moving sociometrics (Hyde & York, 1948; Marshall & McCandless, 1957), based on observations of social interaction rather than verbal assessments.

For most people, friendships possess several qualities in addition to the kinds of activity displayed by two individuals in the presence of each other. First, friends evidence differentiated reactions to separation. Both instrumental activity and affect are elicited differentially by separation from friends and separation from nonfriends. Indeed, mood changes and urgent requests to be allowed to visit one's friend are defining characteristics of specific peer attachments. And friends are individuals who wish to effect proximity with each other even though there is no immediately compelling biological or social pressure to do so.

Second, people apply special conceptual and linguistic categories to their friendships. Such concepts as "friend," "to like," and "enemy" represent various dimensions of friendship. Moreover, the friendship system in adults ap-

[1] This chapter was prepared with the aid of funds from grant no. 2-PO1-HD-005027-05, National Institute of Child Health and Human Development.

pears to be embedded in a network of interpersonal constructs that is more complex than the conceptual system applied to many other social relationships (Kelley, 1955). Unfortunately, not much is known about the origins of this conceptual system, and the relation between the use of social constructs and one's behavior toward one's friends remains obscure. Nevertheless it is intuitively obvious that the individual's conceptions of friendship should have something to do with the formation, maintenance, and termination of friendship.

Thus it is possible to distinguish three components of friendship: (a) differentiated behavior by one individual in the presence of another individual, (b) differentiated activity in the absence of the same individual, and (c) conceptual activity relevant to this relationship. Indicating that "X" is one's best friend on a sociometric test may or may not validly index each of these friendship components. Therefore, a thorough accounting of the ontogeny of friendships requires reference to at least three parameters: proximity-seeking, separation reactions, and the language of interpersonal relations.

What is known about the development of friendships, beginning in infancy, as revealed by differentiated proximal activity? What is known about the differentiated reactions of infants and young children to separation from specific peers? What is known about children's early conceptions of friendship? About the role of friendship constructs in the development of the self-concept? About the development of cognitions having to do with the friendships of others? Striking lacunae are apparent with respect to the development of each of these three "faces" of friendship. Most significant is the near-total absence of information about young children's responses to separation from specific peers and the paucity of data dealing with young children's conceptions of friendship.

THE SOCIOMETRIC ANALYSIS OF FRIENDSHIP

Friendships and Amount of Social Interaction

As mentioned, friendship relations are most commonly indexed by high relative frequencies of interaction, particularly "positive" interactions that are not controlled directly by extrinsic reinforcers. Such relations have been observed in nonhuman species as various as the porpoise, the dog, and the chimpanzee (Hebb & Thompson, 1967). Although most of the existing data on peer relations among nonhuman primates deal with general responsiveness to age mates rather than with the formation of specific attachments, it appears that stable peer relationships are not uniquely human phenomena.

Current knowledge concerning the ontogeny of human friendships is almost completely limited to vicissitudes occurring after the age of 3. By that point it is apparent that best-friend relationships, as deduced from observed frequencies of associative play and friendly approach, are moderately stable across time and across situation. Marshall and McCandless (1957) reported a split-half correlation of .64 for best-friend scores across 100 2-minute observations of indoor and outdoor play. These sociometric scores also predict with modest accuracy the judgments of teachers concerning the identity of the children's best friends. Other scores, based on picture sociometric interviews with the same subjects, were stable across a 20-day interval for some groups but not others. Test-retest reliability coefficients ranged from .22 (not significant) to .74 ($p < .01$). Reliability across a 10-day interval was somewhat better; coefficients ranged from .41 (not significant) to .85 ($p < .01$).

Various other studies confirm the hypothesis that individual preschool children tend to interact with certain children more than with other children and that this differentiation is moderately stable. Nevertheless, the friendships of preschool children differ in several ways from those of older children. First, the stability of friendship choices is directly related to the age of the children in the peer group. Second, such stability is related to degree of acquaintanceship. Fluctuations in relations with specific other children are more marked during the early stages of group formation than after group structures have become established. Third, variation in best-friend scores from situation to situation is considerable, even though generalization across closely similar situations has been established (Witryol & Thompson, 1953). These trends are supported primarily by data derived from interviews. Sufficient observational material is not available to support these contentions because following older children around in their schools and neighborhoods is impractical except under extraordinary circumstances (Barker & Wright, 1951).

But when does differentiation in the social relations of children begin? Certainly it is in babyhood. Lee's (1973) beautiful observations of one small group of infants who attended a day care center provide clear evidence of differentiated social relationships. Such differentiation seemed, furthermore, to be based on both attraction and repulsion—one of the five babies (who were 8 to 10 months old at the beginning of the study) was more consistently approached than were the other members of the group and one was more consistently avoided than were the others. Individual differences in personal "style" seem to have been implicated in these early relationships. The most preferred infant was ". . . a responsive, adaptive social partner who interacted nonassertively . . . her involvements were reciprocal." The least preferred infant was ". . . almost asocial in his behavior. . . . Both the intensity and degree to which his involvements were mutual depended on whether or not he himself had initiated them." One cannot assert definitely that these behavioral differences directly produced the incipient friendships that were observed. Clearly, however, they distinguished these particular babies from other members of the group.

Are friendships, in this sense, common to all groups of infants? We do not know. The differentiation that marked the two infants described by Lee did not mark the other three infants in the group. But we should not be surprised to learn that specific peer attachments may not be a universal fact of infant social life. Such attachments, indexed by differences in amount of peer interaction, are not found universally in groups of preschool children, either. Certain children simply do not become involved in close friendships. Lee's work, however, indicates that a much closer look is needed at individual differences in the amount of approach behavior directed toward children by their peers during the first three years of life.

Friendships and the Qualitative Aspects of Social Interaction

Friendships are indexed by the qualities of social interaction as well as by its quantity. Of course there is no single configuration of social behaviors that signifies the presence of a specific peer attachment any more than specific attachments to the mother are signified universally by one behavioral configuration (see Masters & Wellman, 1974). But generally such behavior classes as altruism, sympathy, helping, empathy, and defense of the other are commonly ascribed to relationships that are labeled "friendly." Such relationships are also assumed to be "mutually regulated"; they are partnerships.

Lee's (1973) data show that reciprocity, as evidenced by reactivity and shared responsibility for the initiation or termination of social encounters, occurred in the case of her "popular" infant. Other than this, however, we know little about the role of altruism, helping, and empathy in the developing peer relationships of toddlers and young preschool children. By 4 and 5 years of age, children who are well liked by other children are more rewarding of their peers than less popular children (Hartup, Glazer, & Charlesworth, 1967) and are more cooperative and conforming to the demands of others (Lippitt, 1941; Moore, 1967). Other data reveal that such characteristics remain correlated with popularity through middle childhood and adolescence, although a strong relation between socioempathy and popularity has never been demonstrated (Hartup, 1970). But these data do not reflect on the fundamental question with which this discussion is concerned: is the interaction between mutual friends (as opposed to interaction with a popular peer) marked by high incidence of reciprocity, empathy, and helping? Is altruism the hallmark of friendship? Are primitive forms of reciprocity and empathy found in the more stable dyads that can be identified among groups of infants and toddlers?

Frequently we have assumed that cooperation and empathy are beyond the cognitive capacities of the infant (Maudry & Nekula, 1939). This may be true, but it may be that only the most mature forms of cooperation and altruism are missing from the social repertoire of the very young child. Certain altruistic "precursors," known to be common among nonhuman primates and human infants (e.g., the offering of tangible objects as "gifts" to other people) may be

distributed by children in such a way that they function significantly in the formation of early friendships. Other altruistic and sympathetic dispositions (e.g., sharing) are known to appear in the behavioral repertoire relatively early, generalizing readily toward a variety of real and surrogate objects (Aronfreed, 1970). Thus there is a need for close scrutiny of the contingencies existing in the social interaction of very young children with their peers and close examination of developmental shifts in the functioning of altruism and empathy in children's peer relations.

Such research requires extremely sophisticated observational procedures and methods of data analysis. Study of behavior sequences—both in topographic and temporal terms—is required. But when directed at the peer contacts of the infant and the very young child, these techniques would yield an improved sociometric understanding of a phenomenon about which we know very little—namely, the ontogeny of specific peer attachments.

SEPARATION FROM FRIENDS

Ordinarily the friendships of human children are not studied with respect to their disruption. Yet young children react to separation from peers in ways that are not dissimilar from their reactions to separation from adults. Parents describe their children as "moody," "depressed," or "at loose ends" when separations from peers are effected; engagement in play may be diminished; and the child's efforts may be intensified to effect reunion with the missing friend. To be sure, it is impossible to tell whether the affective response to separation inhibits play behavior or whether a diminished opportunity for play is responsible for the onset of a depressive mood. Moreover, separation from peers seldom brings on the same degree of despair that is elicited by separation from the mother. Both emotional and instrumental activity, however, are affected by peer separations.

Anecdotes from the literature of comparative anthropology support the thesis that peer attachments sometimes manifest themselves in reactions to separation. Nissen (1951) noted that chimpanzees may be upset and unhappy when a longtime friend is taken away, and Van Lawick-Goodall's (1967) records contain references to the agitation and depressionlike reactions of individual young chimpanzees to the death or absence of a specific age mate. Such reactions to separation from peers are much less well documented for other mammalian species.

Most accounts show that the reactions of young primates to separation from peers are enormously variable. In one family I know well, a 2-year-old girl attracted considerable attention from her parents and other neighborhood adults because of her close "friendship" with a 2-year-old boy. The children sought proximity with each other on a daily basis, they referred to each other as friends, and when the families became separated by 2000 miles, the little girl clearly "missed" her companion. She talked about him, evidenced concern for him, wrote him letters (with the aid of her mother), and acknowledged the separation in numerous ways. Yet neither of the child's two older sisters had ever shown these behaviors, although both are gregarious and both had been separated from close companions on numerous occasions in early childhood.

Like fear of strangers, affective reactions to separation from peers occur with sufficient regularity during the early years for the phenomenon to be regarded as commonplace. All children do not display such reactions, however; they are not universal components of the emerging peer attachment system. There is need, nevertheless, for documentary evidence concerning the incidence and persistence of children's responses to separation from peers; the incidence of depressive affective reactions, depressed engagement in play, and changes in exploratory behavior; and the occurrence of instrumental activity designed to effect reunion. Only in this way can it be determined whether separation-induced distress is as central in the ontogeny of children's relations with their peers as separation reactions appear to be in parent-child relations.

The manner in which this aspect of the child's friendship relations is articulated with the history of attachment to caretakers needs to be reviewed. Separation reactions involving peers may be more frequent and more intense when access to other attachment objects, particularly the mother, has been restricted. Data from several nonhuman primate studies are pertinent to this problem. By observing adolescents whose early rearing took place either in the wild or in the laboratory (all subjects had early access to the mother), McKinney and his associates (McKinney, Suomi, & Harlow, 1972; Bowden & McKinney, 1972) found that a period of cage experience with peers produced separation reactions marked by: (a) initial increases in exploration and locomotion, and (b) no subsequent emergence of despair. These nondepressive reactions are different from the reactions of younger subjects who are separated from most attachment objects. Note, however, that these were adolescent animals whose earlier experience had included more-or-less normal social contact with the mother.

Peer separation reactions appear to be different among monkeys who are reared together without early and unrestricted access to their mothers (Hinde, 1974). Indeed, we know that rhesus infants who have been "pair-together reared" since birth show intense proximal contact (clinging) and will choose reunion with the cage mate in preference to union with a strange peer, union with a cloth surrogate, or entrance to an empty cage (Harlow, 1969). In addition, it has been shown that peer separations in monkeys who have been reared together produce marked arrest in general social behavior and signs of depression (Suomi, Harlow, & Domek, 1970).

Such would also seem to be the case for human children, although the evidence is limited to a single case study—the classic report by Freud and Dann

(1951) concerning the social behavior of six children whose parents were killed in concentration camps during World War II and who thereafter lived in close contact with one another. As the authors described these children:

"They had no other wish than to be together and became upset when they were separated from each other, even for short moments. No child would consent to remain upstairs while the others were downstairs, or vice versa, and no child would be taken for a walk or on an errand without the others. If anything of the kind happened, the single child would constantly ask for the other children while the group would fret for the missing child" (p. 131).

Note that the unusual peer experiences of these children were confounded with early separation from parents and limited access, subsequently, to other adults. Studies of adolescent peer groups also lend support to the hypothesis that constricted parent-child relations promote intense peer attachments. Sherif and Sherif (1964) reported that the greatest solidarity among groups of adolescent boys was observed when conditions were conducive to the members' finding that their main locus of pleasurable activity consisted of the peer group. In these instances, home life was almost invariably unsatisfactory. Specifically, the Sherifs reported that:

". . . the greater the solidarity of a group, as indicated by secrecy, the greater are the personal efforts members are willing to make to associate. . . . More solidary (sic) groups of adolescents are not based primarily on proximity of the individual members, but over a period of time, a winnowing process has occurred from which a closely knit and trusted membership emerges" (p. 242).

The index of effort that was correlated with the solidarity variable in this study was the distance the boys were willing to walk between their homes and their gathering places. Members of one very cohesive group converged on foot in an area covering more than 100 city blocks, even though one member said that he had quit school because it was too far away to walk.

Thus the effort young primates will make to be together seems to be greatest when early contact with mothers and fathers is limited. This hypothesis needs close developmental and cross-species study, and its early childhood implications require detailed explanation. The evidence for such investigation is readily obtainable, however, from case records of neglected and abused children and adolescents, which can be compared with the records of children who are reared under conditions providing more benign parent-child contact. Analogues for the laboratory study of the interaction between early parent-child and peer-peer relations would also be relatively easy to devise for nonhuman primates.

As indicated, the young child's reactions to peer separations seem to lack the intensity and persistence of his reactions to separation from his mother. This difference may account for the differential attention that has been paid to these two kinds of separation—the literature dealing with separation from the mother is voluminous (e.g., Bowlby, 1973), in contrast to the literature dealing with peer separations. Note also that when a young child is brought for the first time to nursery school, both teacher and mother gird themselves for the separation experience; on the other hand, signs that a young child "misses" a friend rarely merit more than a casual word of reassurance. Yet the newer primate studies clearly show the significance of peer contact during the early years in the socialization of aggressive motivation and the development of prosocial behavior (Hartup, in press). Consequently, there is every reason to believe that a young child's separation experiences represent rare opportunities for developmental analysis. These experiences are not the trivia of the socialization process.

What problems should be studied? First, individual differences in reaction to separation should be examined in relation to both quantity and quality of prior experience with peers. Is the occurrence of distress following separation related to the child's previous interactions with the object of attachment? Are separation reactions most common when the child's experience encompasses relatively few age mates? Are such reactions qualitatively different when relatively few age mates have been encountered? Are separation reactions related to the availability of substitute attachment objects? To what extent is separation *qua* separation responsible for the child's distress? To what extent is the distress a function of the limitations placed by the separation on the child's exposure to novel stimulation (i.e., play)? How are these reactions linked to primary attachments (e.g., with the mother)?

THE LANGUAGE OF FRIENDSHIP

The language of friendship has been a neglected topic within developmental psychology even though newer data reveal that the manner in which children talk about their friendships undergoes important modifications with increasing age. In particular, the origins of children's conceptions of friendships remain obscure. Most of the empirical studies dealing with the relation between language and friendship have involved elementary school children and adolescents because it is extremely difficult to elicit appropriate speech samples from very young children. It seems appropriate, nevertheless, to call attention to the possibilities for studying the manner in which early language competencies apply to friendship relations.

Two problems have been selected for purposes of this discussion: (*a*) the nature of the conceptual system applied by the child to friendships and related developmental aspects, and (*b*) the content of children's descriptions of their friends. From a variety of sources, but particularly from Piagetian theorizing, comes a relatively clear-cut basis for expecting the language of friendship to undergo marked changes as children mature. For example, developmental changes should be produced by the increasing reciprocity involved in interpersonal relations and by the increasing ability to differentiate other persons from the environment (both phenomena being encompassed by the concept of *decentration*) (Shantz, in press).

Recent reviews of person perception research with children may be found in several places (e.g., Hill & Palmquist, 1974; Livesley & Bromley, 1973; Rosenberg & Sedlak, 1972). Although this literature is not without inconsistency, the best-documented developmental changes in children's descriptions of other persons are the following: (a) there is an increase, with age, in the number of descriptive categories used; (b) there is an increase in the flexibility and precision with which these categories are used; (c) there is an increase in the complexity and organization of information and ideas; (d) an increase occurs in the ability to analyze and interpret the other person's behavior; and (e) an increase also occurs in the use of subtle qualifying and connecting terms (Livesley & Bromley, 1973).

Perhaps the best study of these changes, as they occur within the context of friendship, has been reported by Peevers and Secord (1973). The authors examined four conceptual dimensions that appeared in "free descriptions" of liked and disliked peers by kindergarten pupils, third and seventh graders, high school juniors, and college students: (a) *descriptiveness*—the amount of information an item yielded about the person as a unique individual; (b) *personal involvement*—the degree to which the subject involved himself, in some relational capacity, in the description; (c) *evaluative consistency*—the extent to which both positive and negative descriptors were included in a single description of the same individual; and (d) *depth*—the degree to which personal characteristics were recognized as conditional on situation, time, or internal state. The findings reveal that: (a) older children and adolescents described both friends and nonfriends by more frequently using differentiated statements ("he likes basketball and so do I") and fewer undifferentiated descriptions ("he lives in a big house") than younger children; (b) higher degrees of personal involvement were manifested by the older subjects than by the younger children; (c) consistency of evaluation was greater for third- and seventh-grade subjects than for either kindergarteners or high school juniors (the former seemed unable to keep on target, and the latter were more differentiated than their younger peers); and (d) older subjects described both friends and nonfriends by recognizing situational and temporal vicissitudes rather than by citation of personality invariants. In general these results conform to other developmental studies of children's use of interpersonal constructs. However, the data are based on the subjects' descriptions of liked and disliked peers rather than persons occupying other roles.

The data of Peevers and Secord (1973) also show striking differences between the subjects' application of interpersonal concepts to friends and to nonfriends. First, significantly fewer items were used in describing disliked peers than liked peers, although there was an interaction between the subject's age and the like-dislike status of the individual described. The largest difference in number of items used to describe liked and disliked peers occurred in adolescence; a smaller difference in the same direction occurred among the kindergarten children. Except for kindergarten children, disliked peers were seen by all age groups largely in terms of simple differentiating and dispositional items ("he is mean") rather than in terms that were highly differentiated. Second, disliked peers were described more egocentrically than were liked peers. Third, there was no difference in the consistency with which liked and disliked peers were evaluated at any age level, and fourth, the general depth with which liked and disliked peers were described did not differ.

Data appearing in a recent monograph by Livesley & Bromley (1973) are mostly consistent with the results just summarized. In that investigation, 320 children between the ages of 7 and 15 years were studied, and more statements were used to describe liked as compared with disliked persons regardless of the subject's age. Among boys this difference extended to descriptions of both children and adults, but among girls it was found only in descriptions of adults. Similar results were also obtained in a study by Supnick (1964). Three groups of boys, the mean ages of which were 6.9 years, 9.2 years, and 10.9 years, were asked to describe one boy and one girl who were liked and one member of each sex who was disliked. The number of constructs used by the subjects increased with age, and there was a developmental shift from use of egocentric and concrete descriptors to use of nonegocentric and more abstract constructs. Furthermore, a greater number of constructs were used to describe boys than girls (also reported by Livesley & Bromley, 1973), although higher order interactions obscure the latter results. For example, the older two groups of subjects used more constructs to describe liked boys than disliked boys, although all groups gave more elaborate descriptions of liked girls than disliked girls. Results verifying these trends are also found in Bigelow (1974).

These data indicate that the conceptual system applied to friendships differs from the system applied to inimical relationships. It has been hypothesized that the more highly elaborated descriptions of friends than of enemies derives from the different kinds of interaction that children have had with these two types of individuals. Most investigators guess that children have more extended and varied experiences with their friends than with their enemies, a condition that would afford the child more "facts" to be used in his free descriptions of liked persons. The age differences revealed in the literature of person perception rest presumably on general cognitive development as well as on specific social learning experiences.

Very little is known about the conceptual system applied by preschool children to their emerging friendships. Flavell (e.g., Kreutzer, Leonard, & Flavell, 1975) and others are currently discovering that rudimentary social conceptual skills, previously thought to be absent in young children, may be identified by means of careful and painstaking assessment. Simply because the relevant data have been difficult to obtain, therefore, one must not assume that children under the age of 6 do not possess a distinctive language of friendship. After all, 3-year-olds frequently talk about their friends and, sometimes, about their enemies. Forced-choice interview techniques or highly structured assessment techniques (e.g., "name all the things your friend likes to do," "what does your friend look like?") may yield much-needed insights.

What terms are actually applied by children to their friendships? In one early study Austin and Thompson (1948) found that sixth-grade pupils stressed personality attributes (e.g., "brave," "kind," "loyal," and "true") to the extent that these constituted 53.3% of the reasons for considering someone to be a friend. Frequency of association and perceived similarity of tastes were the basis for 22% of these reasons; friendliness accounted for about 12% of the reasons, and ability for about 7%. Friendship terminations were ascribed by these children to a variety of circumstances, with specific attributes having to do with manners or ethics being the most commonplace.

Certain expectancy categories are used more frequently in older children's descriptions of friends than in the descriptions given by younger children, although other terms applied to friendships are age continuous. Bigelow (1974) obtained free descriptions of best friends from 960 Anglo-Canadian and Scottish children between the ages of 5 and 14 years. Eleven of the 21 categories investigated appeared more frequently in the friendship descriptions of the older children than the younger ones: friend as giver of help, duration of association, sharing of activities, positive evaluations, propinquity, admiration of character, acceptance, loyalty, genuineness, common interests, and potential for intimacy. Important categories that failed to show significant age differences cross-nationally, even though they accounted for an average of 10.8% of all descriptors employed, were: reference to the reinforcing character of the friend and reciprocity-of-liking. It is striking in these results that mutual liking, an interpersonal characteristic of considerable significance in all friendships, is not mentioned more frequently in friendship descriptions as children grow older. Perhaps age-related changes in friendship are more qualitative than affective.

Recently Livesley and Bromley (1973) reported the results of a series of content analyses applied to the interpersonal descriptions obtained in the larger study mentioned previously. First, they found no difference in the use of psychological (central) concepts in the descriptions of liked versus disliked peers. Second, they found that personality attributes, intellectual abilities, achievements, preferences/aversions, interests, social roles, frequency of association, and comparisons with self were used more frequently to describe liked than disliked persons (also see Austin & Thompson, 1948). On the other hand, references to appearance, actual incidents, specific behavior inconsistencies, self-attitudes, relations with others, and the subject's opinion of the other person were more frequently employed in descriptions of disliked than liked people.

Age differences were apparent in the use of several of these specific categories, but there was no interaction between age and friendship status of the person being described in determining the content of interpersonal descriptions. In other words, the content of friendly descriptions differed from nonfriendly descriptions at all age levels. Next, these investigators reported that there was no significant interaction between age and status of the person described, either in absolute number of trait names employed or in proportion of traits per description. As mentioned earlier, the terms employed by older children are more abstract and more differentiated than those chosen by younger children, as well as being less egocentric. Here, however, we emphasize simply that the relative difference in number of trait names referenced in free descriptions of liked peers as compared to disliked peers does not change with age. Once again, however, the lack of information concerning descriptions of friendships by children under the age of 6 is a serious problem.

The following excerpts from the study by Livesely and Bromley (1973) illustrate the major developmental trends summarized here: A girl, aged 7-6, described a boy she likes: "Max sits next to me, his eyes are hazel and he is tall. He hasn't got a very big head, he's got a big pointed nose." A girl, aged 9-8, described a boy she likes: "Charles is a sort of cousin of mine. He likes watching television and riding his bicycle. He lives in Preston. His behavior is sometimes good and sometimes it is bad. He likes watching television and eating sweets. . . ." A girl, aged 14-1, described a girl she likes: "This girl is not in my form, she is just in the same division as me. She is very quiet and only talks when she knows a person very well. She is clever in one sense, she comes top of her form. She is very reserved but once you get to know her she is exactly the opposite. . . . One of the things I admire in her is she is very tidy."

The current lack of literature on the precursors of the language of friendship is deplorable. Children talk about friends for several years before they reach the age of 6, yet we know almost nothing about how toddlers and preschool children discuss their interpersonal relationships. How do young children talk about their friends in relation to themselves, and how do they talk about themselves in the role of friend? A similar lack of information exists with respect to the conceptualizations used by young children to refer to disliked peers. Since the origins of friendship are clearly apparent within these early years, the origins of the language of friendship must also lie in this period of development.

In addition to using language to describe perceptions of liked and disliked persons, children also employ language as an instrumentality in their friendships. Consequently close attention should also be paid to developmental shifts in children's use of language in their interaction with their peers. For example, it has been known for many years that verbal aggression tends to increase, relative to physical aggression, from the preschool years through middle childhood. Only recently, however, has it been demonstrated that language serves more directly instrumental functions in aggressive interaction among young children than in such interaction among older children; on the other hand, language is used to convey person-directed, derogatory intent relatively more often among older than among younger children (Hartup, 1974). Such findings suggest that developmental changes in the functional characteristics of children's social interactions can be fully understood only by an analysis of their verbal components. Such an obvious truth, however, has been largely ignored by research workers. Gross verbal behavior (i.e., the *amount* of conversation) existing in the interchanges of children has been counted many times, and the syntax of such conversations is increasingly well understood. But a differentiated analysis of the functions of language in the ontogeny of friendships is a high-priority need.

CONCLUSIONS

Most of the current interest in children's early peer relations revolves around one problem: what is the contribution made by contact with peers to the development of basic competencies in the child? Newer studies have focused upon the impact of child-child relations on social skills, language, affects, intellectual competence, and moral development (Hartup, in press). Other investigations have treated child-child relations as a dependent variable. This presentation, however, concerns one small but significant segment of children's peer relations—friendships.

Certainly the three categories of behavior stressed here—approach behaviors, separation behaviors, and language—do not encompass every facet of children's friendships. For example, that most appealing phenomenon, the imaginary companion, has not been mentioned in the preceding pages. Manosevitz, Prentice, and Wilson (1973) reported that only six systematic studies of imaginary friends could be found prior to the publication of a study of their own. The phenomenon, however, is known to everyone and has received considerable attention both in the popular literature of child development and in fiction. The data of Manosevitz et al. suggest that preschool children who were reported by their parents to have imaginary companions were more likely than those who did not have such companions: (*a*) to be first-born children, (*b*) to self-initiate play, (*c*) to engage less frequently in "quiet play," (*d*) to engage in more different activities with adult members of the household, and (*e*) to be rated by their parents as more adept at talking and interacting with adults. Although there was no difference in the number of siblings possessed by the children in either group, the imaginary companion tended to appear at a point in development when the child had no siblings (61%). Being an only child, amount of contact with parents, and certain other familial conditions did not distinguish children who had such companions; but the general picture suggests that such surrogates are concomitants of "loneliness." The parents reported that the subjects in both groups "played well" with other children, but beyond this no mention of peer relations was made in the study. Too bad. Perhaps no direct correspondence between a child's actual friendships (or their absence) and his imaginary friendships exists, but it is unlikely that friendship relations in these two domains—fantasy and reality—are totally unrelated.

Another problem: does the subsequent social development of children who participate in friendships during infancy and very early childhood differ from that of children who do not? Existing data relate to somewhat different questions: popular children are known to be different from nonpopular children (Hartup, 1970), and sociable children are known to be different from nonsociable children (Bronson, 1966). The particulars supporting these two assertions are well known and need not be recapitulated. It is important to understand, however, that the correlates of *popularity* cannot be used as a data base for formulating assumptions concerning the ontogenetic significance of early *friendships*.

Still another related problem, which is beyond the scope of this chapter, is sibling attachments.

These final remarks serve simply to emphasize that the behavioral domain embraced by the word "friendship" is extensive. Traditional sociometric approaches, applied at any age from babyhood to adulthood, provide information about only a few facets of the phenomenon. To understand fully the origins of friendship, we must use pluralistic conceptualizations as well as ingenious methodologies. Let us hope that this volume is a harbinger of such developments.

References

Aronfreed, J. The socialization of altruistic and sympathetic behavior: Some theoretical and experimental analyses. In J. Macaulay & L. Berkowitz (Eds.), *Altruism and helping behavior*. New York: Academic Press, 1970.

Austin, M. C., & Thompson, G. G. Children's friendships: A study of the bases on which children select and reject their best friends. *Journal of Educational Psychology*, 1948, **39**, 101–116.

Barker, R. G., & Wright, H. F. *One boy's day*. New York: Harper & Row, 1951.

Bigelow, B. J. The development of children's friendship expectations: A cognitive and behavioral perspective. Unpublished doctoral dissertation. University of Dundee, 1974.

Bowden, D. M., & McKinney, W. T. Behavioral effects of peer separation, isolation, and reunion on adolescent male rhesus monkeys. *Developmental Psychobiology,* 1972, **5,** 353–362.

Bowlby, J. *Attachment and loss,* Vol. 2, *Separation.* New York: Basic Books, 1973.

Bronson, W. C. Central orientations: A study of behavior organization from childhood to adolescence. *Child Development,* 1966, **37,** 125–155.

Freud, A., & Dann, S. An experiment in group upbringing. In R. Eissler, A. Freud, H. Hartmann, & E. Kris (Eds.), *The psychoanalytic study of the child.* Vol. 6. New York: International Universities Press, 1951.

Harlow, H. F. Age-mate or peer affectional system. In D. S. Lehrman, R. A. Hinde, & E. Shaw (Eds.), *Advances in the study of behavior.* Vol. 2. New York: Academic Press, 1969.

Hartup, W. W. Peer interaction and social organization. In P. Mussen (Ed.), *Carmichael's manual of child psychology.* Vol. 2, New York: Wiley, 1970.

Hartup, W. W. Aggression in childhood: Developmental perspectives. *American Psychologist,* 1974, **5,** 336–341.

Hartup, W. W. Peer interaction and the behavioral development of the individual child. In E. Schopler (Ed.), *Proceedings of the first international Leo Kanner colloquium on child development, deviations, and treatment.* New York: Plenum Press, in press.

Hartup, W. W., Glazer, J. A., & Charlesworth, R. Peer reinforcement and sociometric status. *Child Development,* 1967, **38,** 1017–1024.

Hebb, D. O., & Thompson, W. R. The social significance of animal studies. In G. Lindzey & E. Aronson (Eds.), *Handbook of social psychology,* 2nd ed., Vol. 2. Reading, Mass.: Addison-Wesley, 1967.

Hill, J. P., & Palmquist, W. Social cognition and social relations in adolescence: A precursory view. Unpublished manuscript. Cornell University, 1974.

Hinde, R. A. *Biological bases of human social behaviour.* New York: McGraw-Hill, 1974.

Hyde, R. W., & York, R. H. A technique for investigating interpersonal relationships in a mental hospital. *Journal of Abnormal and Social Psychology,* 1948, **43,** 287–299.

Kelley, G. A. *The psychology of personal constructs,* Vol. 1. *A theory of personality.* New York: Norton, 1955.

Kreutzer, M. A., Leonard, C., & Flavell, J. H. An interview study of children's knowledge about memory. *Monographs of the Society for Research in Child Development,* 1975, **40:** (1, Serial No. 159).

Lee, L. C. Social encounters of infants: The beginnings of popularity. Paper presented at the biennial meeting of the International Society for the Study of Behavioral Development. Ann Arbor, Mich., 1973.

Lippitt, R. Popularity among preschool children. *Child Development,* 1941, **12,** 305–322.

Livesley, W. J., & Bromley, D. B. *Person perception in childhood and adolescence.* London: Wiley, 1973.

Manosevitz, M., Prentice, N. M., & Wilson, F. Individual and family correlates of imaginary companions in preschool children. *Developmental Psychology,* 1973, **8,** 72–79.

Marshall, H. R., & McCandless, B. R. A study in prediction of social behavior of preschool children. *Child Development,* 1957, **28,** 149–159.

Masters, J. C., & Wellman, H. M. The study of human infant attachment: A procedural critique. *Psychological Bulletin,* 1974, **81,** 218–237.

Maudry, M., & Nekula, M. Social relations between children of the same age during the first two years of life. *Journal of Genetic Psychology,* 1939, **54,** 193–215.

McKinney, W. T., Suomi, S. J., & Harlow, H. F. Repetitive peer separations of juvenile-age rhesus monkeys. *Archives of General Psychiatry,* 1972, **27,** 200–203.

Moore, S. G. Correlates of peer acceptance in nursery school children. In W. W. Hartup & N. L. Smothergill (Eds.), *The young child.* Washington, D.C.: National Association for the Education of Young Children, 1967.

Moreno, J. L. *Who shall survive?* Washington, D.C.: Nervous and Mental Disease Publishing Company, 1934.

Nissen, H. W. Social behavior in primates. In C. P. Stone (Ed.), *Comparative psychology,* 3rd ed. Englewood Cliffs, N.J.: Prentice-Hall, 1951.

Peevers, B. H., & Secord, P. F. Developmental changes in attribution of descriptive concepts to persons. *Journal of Personality and Social Psychology,* 1973, **27,** 120–128.

Rosenberg, S., & Sedlak, A. Structural representations of implicit personality theory. In L. Berkowitz (Ed.), *Advances in experimental social psychology.* Vol. 6. New York: Academic Press, 1972.

Shantz, C. U. The development of social cognition. In E. M. Hetherington (Ed.), *Review of child development research.* Vol. 5. Chicago: University of Chicago Press. In press.

Sherif, M., & Sherif, C. W. *Reference groups.* New York: Harper & Row, 1964.

Suomi, S. J., Harlow, H. F., & Domek, C. J. Effect of repetitive infant-infant separations of young monkeys. *Journal of Abnormal Psychology,* 1970, **76,** 161–172.

Supnick, J. Unpublished senior honors thesis. Clark University, 1964. (Cited by: Livesley, W. J., & Bromley, D. B., 1973.)

Van Lawick-Goodall, J. *My friends the wild chimpanzees.* Washington, D.C.: National Geographic Society, 1967.

Witryol, S. L., & Thompson, G. G. A critical review of the stability of social acceptability scores obtained with partial-rank-order and the paired-comparison scales. *Genetic Psychology Monographs,* 1953, **48,** 221–260.

CHAPTER 2

The Beginning of Friendship[1]

MICHAEL LEWIS, GERALD YOUNG, JEANNE BROOKS, AND
LINDA MICHALSON

Infant Laboratory
Educational Testing Service

THE SOCIAL NETWORK

Consider three examples of children's social behavior:

1.   Two 4-year-olds are busily engaged in playing with "Playdoh." The
room echoes with their glee as they roll out long "snakes." Each child is trying
to roll a longer snake than the other. The 1-year-old sibling of one of the
children, hearing the joyful cries, waddles into the room. She reaches for the
Playdoh being used by her sibling. The older child hands the 1-year-old some
Playdoh, and the child tries to roll her own snake. Unable to carry out the task
and frustrated, the 1-year-old becomes fussy, at which point the older sibling
gives the child a knife. The 4-year-old then shows the sibling how to cut the
snakes the other children have made.

2.   A mother discovers that her 24-month-old daughter along with the
child's best friend and next door neighbor have not been heard from in at least
30 minutes. The mother quietly goes upstairs to her daughter's room and
listens at the door. Muffled chattering and laughing can be heard from the
room. Opening the door, the mother discovers the two children sitting in bed
together under the blankets, both without clothes. Since they have not heard
her, the mother listens to their chatter and watches the game. The activity is
not clear to the adult; it appears to be specific and knowable only to the two
children under the blanket.

3.   Coming home from work a father engages in the following conversation
with his 4-year-old son. Son: "Did you know God is a woman with many
arms?" Father: "There is no such thing as God. Who told you such a story?"
Son: "There is too a God. Linda told me." (Linda has been the child's best
friend for the last 2½ years. They live next door to each other and are

[1] The research of this paper was supported by a National Institute of Education grant number 3-
0708 and a National Institute of Mental Health grant number 1 RO1 MH24849-02. In addition,
Gerald Young had a postdoctoral fellowship grant from the National Research Council of Canada.
Appreciation is given to Susan Lee-Painter, Gina Rhea, Pam Ritter, and Eileen Scott for data
collection and to Christine Brim and Sherry Lord for help in data analysis.

27

constantly together.) Father: "Linda is wrong." Son: "Linda is older than me and she knows better." (She is 6 years old.) Father: "But I'm older than Linda, right?" (long pause) Son: "It doesn't matter—she told me."

These examples of children's social behavior illustrate the obvious: siblings play together at very early ages. Indeed, in most cultures older siblings do much caregiving to their younger brothers and sisters.

Children establish contacts that have all the aspects of a personal and intense friendship.

Parents discover quite soon that their children engage in meaningful social relationships that may challenge the intellectual and social dominance of the parent-child relationship.

Man is by nature a social animal. From the beginning, he enters into a social network. This network becomes the context in which his personality, his cognition, and his social development are embedded. Assimilation and accommodation and the growth of structures must take place within this context. Although we can specify the cognitive features of this network (in fact, Piaget has done this), it is to the social features that we now turn our attention. We wish to consider the network of people who from the moment of the child's birth are the most important features of his world. Even within the cognitive realm, this social embedding is vital. Although all children learn the formal features of a language, it must be remembered that it is the language of the social features that surround him. Moreover, the symbols of his intellectual activity, if not the activity itself, will be common to—or will form a social contract between—the members of this network (Lévi-Strauss, 1966). Thus not only will the child's social and personality development be affected by this network, but his intellect—the qualities of his mind—will to a large degree be a function of this contract.

From birth, the social relationships of the child are rich and varied; they may be long-lasting or shortlived, may be highly ritualized or creative, characterized by intense feelings or little feeling at all. These social relationships change in form, function, and feeling over ontogenetic development, but the social network they constitute is an essential part of life from the very beginning. Unfortunately the rich tapestry of this network has been all but ignored in the very young. Instead, social intimacy is thought to center on one relationship—that of the infant and his mother. (Recently some studies of fathers and infants have been undertaken; however, the disproportionate number of infant-mother to infant-other studies still reflects the bias noted.) The infant's dealings with other members of his family, and with friends and acquaintances, are treated as though they do not exist or at least as though they are relatively unimportant.

Let us consider this network a bit more in detail. Figure 1 shows a typical

FIGURE 1. An 18-month-old infant (S no. 108) and her mother in a laboratory play-room setting. Mother has just entered the room after separating herself from the infant. The infant is moving quickly toward her.

laboratory scene—a mother with her young child. Here is one part of the social network of this child. In the case illustrated the entrance of the mother into the experimental room after a brief separation has resulted in the child's seeking proximity and physical contact with her. However, this is not the only social relationship of this child. In Figure 2, other social contacts are seen, as the child watches two 2-year-olds at play. Notice that although there is no physical approach, the little girl is deeply engrossed in the activities of her peers. Look at the positive nature and the intensity of her regard. A moment later the child will join the others in the game of putting the blocks into the pail. How can such a relationship be excluded from any relevant discussion of the young child's social network?

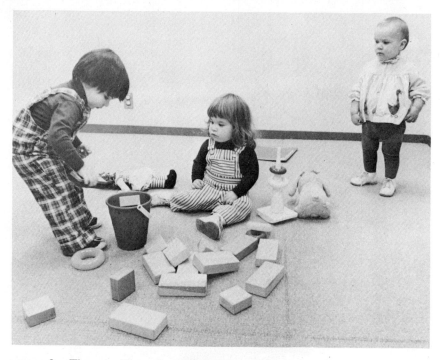

FIGURE 2.   The same 18-month-old infant watching two 2-year-old children playing in a laboratory playroom setting. At this moment the subject is intently watching the play of the other children. A moment later she will join in the play.

Lest we think this behavior unusual or not present before 2 years of age, observe the 1-year-old boy in the next set of pictures. Again we see the close physical contact between a child and his mother (Figure 3). However, this does not preclude a close and meaningful relationship between the 1-year-old and a peer. In Figure 4 the child and a peer are playing with the same toy, and in Figure 5 they are playing a follow-the-leader tag game. Thus even by 1 year of age the fabric of the social network is rich and varied.

It is clear that adults, as parents, as educators, or as scientists, have failed for the most part to take note of these circumstances. In the first study to be discussed (Peers, Parents, and People), we inquired about how many infants participated in a play group, either an informal one as in visits to one another's homes or more formal ones such as those organized by the YWCA or some other social agency. To our surprise, only 22% of the 32 1-year-old children and 28% of the 32 subjects who were 18 months old were so involved. Moreover, while soliciting subjects for study II (Friends and Strangers), we

asked mothers if their 1-year-old infants had any consistent play friends.
"Consistent" was defined as playing with another child at least once per week
in the preceding two months and twice per week in the past two weeks—certainly a minimum contact. Only 15 to 20% of the approximately 70 mothers
queried reported that their infants had this minimum social contact. This becomes especially important when we emphasize that these were mothers of
firstborns who have no siblings.

Apparently a large number of parents of children 18 months or younger do

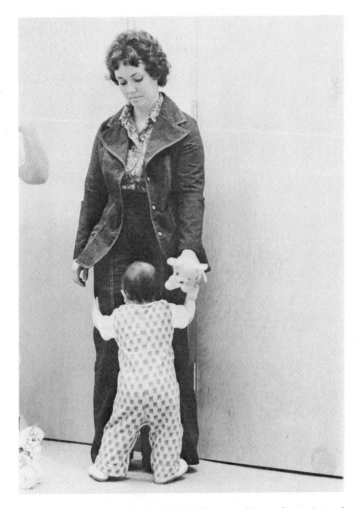

FIGURE 3.   A 1-year-old infant (S no. 121) holding onto his mother prior to her departure from the laboratory play setting.

FIGURE 4.   The same 1-year-old infant engaged in play behavior with another 1-year-old in a laboratory setting. Observe that both children are playing with a wooden puzzle piece, and the play involves sharing behavior.

not encourage or initiate peer social contact for their infants. Likewise, the research literature abounds with studies of parent-child relationships, but it includes few studies of child-child relationships in the opening two years of life. Exactly why this state of affairs exists is not clear. Harlow (Harlow & Harlow, 1969) has provided ample evidence that nonhuman primates engage in intense and meaningful peer relationships that can *at least* substitute for a relationship to an adult. Freud and Dann (1951) have likewise demonstrated a close and intense relationship between human children who had no adult parentlike figure. The reluctance of others to consider the child's peer relationships and the meaningfulness of these relationships may be attributable to hesitation to credit young children with the capability of loving or forming friendships. The expression "puppy love" reflects this attitude with regard to young children, just as the dearth of research information reflects the same bias toward infants.

The cause of this reluctance may be based on two dominant traditions: the psychoanalytic and the Piagetian. The psychoanalytic movement stresses the child's relationship with its parents as the underlying source of social-emotional development. Furthermore, it proposes that the child's other social relationships are a function of this first and prototypic interaction (Parens & Saul, 1971; Spitz, 1965). Bowlby's (1958) ethological theory, stressing attachment and the bonding of the parent and child, perpetuates this theme. Piaget (1951) is also influential in that his formulations stress the egocentricity of the child's cognitive structure, which can be interpreted as a restriction of the child's ability to interact meaningfully with others.

Early studies on peer relations in infants under 2 years of age, although seminal, were marked by a lack of experimental rigor. The investigations of Bridges (1933), Buhler (e.g., 1933), and Maudry and Nekula (1939) showed that young infants are not especially interactive with their peers, and when they do interact, their behavior is more negative than positive. In these studies, however, subjects were from institutions and were generally placed in artificial situations. Moreover, the studies suffered from poorly defined behavior cate-

FIGURE 5.   The 1-year-old target infant of Figures 3 and 4 playing a follow-the-leader tag game. This also took place in a laboratory play setting. Both children had had prior play experience and were considered friends.

gories and a lack of interobserver reliability. Shirley's (1933) results pointed to the same conclusions, despite her use of family-reared infants; however, her study is subject to the other methodological criticisms just raised. Washburn's (1932) results are inconclusive, for although she observed family-reared infants in a nursery-school setting, nowhere in her behavior checklist was there a provision for negative-type behaviors. Thus a review of these early studies reveals an asocial or antisocial infant. This is unfortunate, for this body of work was probably influential in depicting the infant as asocial and without need for peers.

The data on cultures with a high incidence of group-reared infants of working parents provide an ambiguous picture of peer relationships. The importance of peer relationships in nursery and preschool children raised in these environments is well documented (see Hartup, 1970). Marcus' (1971) review of the studies on early child development and group care on kibbutzim does not support peer interaction in infants; however, little experimental evidence exists. Only the incidental observations of Spiro (1958) show a kibbutz infant interacting positively with his peers as early as 10 months of age.

There has been renewed interest in infant-peer interactions in the last few years (Bronson, 1974; Eckerman, 1973; Lee, 1973; Lenssen, 1973; Mueller & Rich, in press; Vincze, 1971). Unlike earlier investigations, contemporary ones are methodologically more sophisticated. Generally, family-reared infants placed in free-play, naturalistic situations are observed using precise, operationally defined, reliability-checked behaviors. These studies have altered our conception of the infant with respect to his interaction with peers.

From the overall impression of these investigations, we can portray the infant as a nonaggressive (e.g., Vincze, 1971), socially inquisitive organism who prefers infants to adults (e.g., Lenssen, 1973). Infants exhibit some developing social competencies (Eckerman, 1973), although they are thought to lag behind the nonsocial object/cognitive competencies (Bronson, 1974). Moreover, consistent contact or familiarity with the same peer affects their behavior (Mueller & Rich, in press), and individual differences in consistencies in behavior or personality are evident in peer interaction (Lee, 1973).

However, certain discrepancies of opinion and empirical results in these studies do not appear to be readily resolvable. For example, Bronson (1974) reports a higher incidence of agonistic encounters than do others (e.g., Eckerman, 1973). Dragsten and Lee (1973) found that familiarity with peers and situation reduced social contact, reflected in a decrease in watching and friendly behavior as well as an increase in aggression. This contrasts with Mueller and Rich's (in press) position about peers profiting from consistent contact. Durfee and Lee (1973) report high negative affect in response to peer-initiated behaviors, contrasting with Eckerman's (1973) emphasis on the positive tone of peer interactions. The latter's data indicate little difference in mother and peer contact at 12 months of age, in contrast to Lenssen's (1973) finding of peer preference relative to the mother at 10 months of age.

Differences in such factors as theoretical orientation, subjects used (e.g., age, sex, peer, experience), environmental contexts, and observation systems, may account for the divergent results, but these considerations are beyond the scope of the present chapter. Nevertheless, the discrepant data suggest that infant-peer relations are still a relatively undeciphered area of inquiry and that infants interacting with peers are subject to the influences of demographic, environmental, and other variables. Given the increasing knowledge of peer relations in early childhood (Blurton Jones, 1972; Brindley, et al., 1973; McGrew, 1972; Smith, 1974) and in nonhuman primate infants and juveniles (Harlow, 1969; Hinde, 1971; Suomi & Harlow, 1972), infant-peer interactions should be studied to trace their developmental and comparative sources.

In the following discourse we want to cast light on the child's ability to form peer relationships and to investigate the nature of the peer in the child's social network. In the first study four children, each with its mother, were seen in a playroom. In this way the child's relationships with its mother, with strange adults, and with peers could be simultaneously assessed. In the second study we explored the child's peer relationships by observing the child separately with a friend-peer and with a stranger-peer. Finally, the growth of friendship was studied by observing children's changing relationships toward peers over 2 weeks of playing together at home.

STUDY I: PEERS, PARENTS, AND PEOPLE

The first study was initiated to permit observation of the child's social relationships with a variety of social objects in a laboratory playroom setting. Unlike most studies, a relatively large number of people and classes of social objects were present (mother, unfamiliar female adults, same-sex and opposite-sex peers). Since four child-mother dyads were used in each observation, it was possible to observe the child's relationship to its mother, to three unfamiliar female adults, and to three peers.

Sixteen groups of four infants and mothers were observed. In eight groups the infants were 12 to 13 months old; in the other eight they were 18 to 19 months old. The age range within each group was always less than 4 weeks. Two males and two females were included in each group. The infants were relatively heterogeneous with respect to social class.

The infant-mother pairs were placed in separate waiting rooms within the laboratory to eliminate interaction preceding the experimental procedure. The following instructions were given to the mothers to read:

"One of us will accompany you and your child to the playroom when all the mothers and children have arrived and we are ready to begin. Please read these instructions while you are waiting to enter the playroom.

"We would like you to carry your child to the playroom and to sit in the chair marked with 'your' color, holding the child in your lap. When you are all seated, we will knock on the mirror. This is your signal to put the child on the floor in front of your chair.

"Please *do not initiate* any action toward any of the children, but you may respond to them if they initiate the interaction. For example, if a child talks to you, you may answer, or if a child brings you a toy, you may play with it, but do not speak to the child or hand the child a toy first. We would prefer that you not leave your chair.

"However, it is possible that the children will start to hit each other or that one child will take a toy away from another. This is normal for children at this age, and again we would like you *not* to intervene until you feel the safety of your child is at stake. At that point you should go to your child and carry him or her back to your chair. Sit down and then place the child on the floor in front of you.

"The play session will last 15 minutes, and we will tell you when we are finished."

Then each mother was asked to pin two colored felt squares on her infant's shoulders. Each infant in the group was given a different color. Colors were assigned as a means of identifying the infants when they were together in the playroom.

An experimenter led the infants and mothers to a 3.7 × 4.3 meter carpeted playroom with two one-way observation mirrors. The playroom contained two sets of blocks, two pails, two sets of stacked rings, and two stuffed animals. Each mother sat in a preassigned chair marked with a piece of felt, the same color that had been assigned to her infant. The chairs were placed such that for each infant, a child of the same sex and a child of the opposite sex were equally distant. The experimenter introduced the mothers and infants before she left the room. When the experimenter tapped from behind a one-way mirror, each infant was placed on the floor in front of its mother, free to move around the room. Each play group was observed for 15 minutes.

Four observers, one assigned to each infant, coded the infants' behaviors from behind the one-way mirrors. A checklist of behaviors, which was marked every 10 seconds, is presented in Table 1 along with the operational definitions. Eight behaviors were coded: look, touch, proximity, smile, offer toy, take toy, hit, and share. The first four are considered affiliative, the remainder are called "toy play." The coding of the toy behaviors was done in a way that indicated whether a child initiated the behavior (I) or was the recipient of the behavior (R). Thus it was possible to separate out two instances of "take toy"—those in

TABLE 1. List of Behaviors for Study I

Affiliative Behaviors

Touch	A touch must result in physical contact with any part of the body.
Proximity	A person is considered to be in proximity to the target infant if he or she is within 3 feet of the target.
Look	A look is said to occur if the target baby is focused on the face or the head of a person. If the target baby is looking across the room, the head must be turned toward a person.
Smile	A smile is coded when the target baby's head is turned toward a person across the room or when the target baby's gaze is focused on a person's face or head and the corners of the mouth are turned upward.

Toy Behaviors

Offer toy	"Offer toy" is coded in four instances: (1) the target baby extends his arm with a toy in his hand toward a person, (2) the toy touches a part of the recipient's body, (3) the toy is pointed in the direction of a recipient who is across the room, and (4) the toy is put in another's lap, hand, or arm.
Take toy	There are two categories of "take toy." The first involves taking a toy that has been offered. The second is grabbing or attempting to grab a toy from the hands of another person. Physical contact with the toy is necessary for a score in either category.
Hit	"Hit" is generally defined as any aggressive act directed toward another person, including such behaviors as hit, scratch, and bite.
Share	"Share" is considered to be any cooperative interaction centering around a common toy. Examples include putting blocks in the same pail, stacking rings on one pole, examining and touching one toy.

which a child accepted a toy offered by another child (referred to as *accept toy*) and those in which the child grabbed a toy from another child (referred to as *take toy*). In addition to coding behaviors, the observers coded the person (social object) to whom the behavior was directed—whether mother, adult, or peer. In addition, it was noted to which of the three infants the behavior was directed. The frequency with which each of the coded behaviors was directed toward the mother, adult female strangers, and unfamiliar peers was examined.

A fifth observer, who was present for 12 of the play groups, made reliability checks three times for each of the four observers. Reliabilities based on (total number of agreements)/(total number of agreements plus disagreements) were calculated. In general the reliabilities were quite high, both within and across observers (ranging from .76 to .99). No observer was consistently low, and

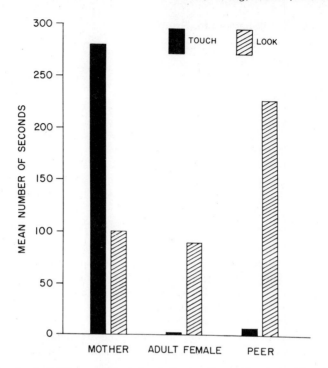

FIGURE 6.   Study I. Mean number of seconds the 12- to 18-month-old children spent touching and looking at strange adult females, peers, and mother. The maximum amount of time spent in the playroom was 900 seconds or 15 minutes.

agreement across behaviors was also good, with the most disagreements occurring with the adult- and peer-directed looks (.76 and .81, respectively).

Differences in Social Stimuli

Not surprisingly, children 12 and 18 months of age behave differentially toward their mothers, adult females, and peers.[2] Table 2 presents the four affiliative behaviors, the mean number of seconds each behavior occurred, the percentage of time out of the 15 minutes of observation that each behavior occurred, and the number of subjects who exhibited each behavior. Observe the

---

[2] Since there were very few differences between the age groups, the data have been combined in the following analyses. To make the scores for the three social objects comparable (there were three unfamiliar adults and three peers but only one mother), the adult and peer data were divided by 3. An additional adjustment was made for two of the behaviors—touch and proximity, which were double scored during the data collection (i.e., the behavior was coded regardless of whether the child initiated it or was the recipient of it). These data were further divided by 2.

two proximal behaviors, touching and proximity seeking, and the two distal behaviors, looking and smiling (Figure 6). It is obvious that although the behavior represents only 31% of the time, infants touch their mothers significantly more than either the strange adults or peers. Moreover, they touch the peers significantly more often than they touch the strange adults ($F_{(2,126)} = 62.25$, $p < .001$). The same pattern was true for proximity, although 56% of the infants' time was spent in proximity maintenance with the mother ($F_{(2,126)} = 134.41$, $p < .001$). Looking behavior shows a different pattern, with the infants looking significantly more at their peers than at either their mothers or the strange adults ($F_{(2,126)} = 140.76$, $p < .001$). Infants also tended to smile at the mother and peer more than at the adult female ($F_{(2,126)} = 4.09$, $p < .02$). The data in Figure 6 are for touch and look because the two modes (proximal and distal) are best characterized by these behaviors.

In general, the data on affiliative behaviors indicate that the three adult females (the mothers of the other infants) received little attention relative to

TABLE 2. **Affiliative Behaviors Directed Toward the Mother, Adult Female Strangers, and Unfamiliar Peers**

		Stimulus Condition	
Behavior	Mother	Adult Female	Unfamiliar Peer
Touch			
Mean number of 10-second periods	28.02	0.19	0.63
Percentage of total time	31	0	1
Number of Ss	57	9	45
Proximity			
Mean number of 10-second periods	50.38	1.29	5.62
Percentage of total time	56	1	6
Number of Ss	62	33	60
Smile			
Mean number of 10-second periods	1.12	0.50	0.69
Percentage of total time	1	1	1
Number of Ss	28	33	36
Look			
Mean number of 10-second periods	10.14	9.14	23.56
Percentage of total time	11	10	26
Number of Ss	64	64	64

either mothers or peers. The relationship toward the mother was proximal in pattern, whereas the relationship toward the peer was distal. In fact, the infants tended to touch their mothers and look at their peers equal amounts of time.

The play behavior of the infants (Figure 7) is also characterized by differential responding. Only two play categories occurred across all three social objects. The others are omitted from the figure, since they were directed only toward peers. In the first case, offer toy, we can see that approximately 50% of the infants were as likely to offer a toy to either mother or peers, whereas only 15% offered toys to the adult females (Cochran Q test: $Q_{(2)} = 19.68$, $p < .001$). However, more than 67% were likely to take toys from peers compared to 25% from mother and only 11% from the adult females ($Q_{(2)} = 45.86$, $p < .01$). (We recognize that this comparison is tenuous, since a toy could not be taken from either the mother or an adult female without first having been offered.) These play data indicate that while the adult females were still being relatively ignored, the peers were engaging in as much or more social interaction with one another than with their mothers. Sharing, a behavior exhibited only to other peers, occurred in 58% of the children, thus supporting this interpretation. In contrast, hitting occurred in only 22% of the children.

The results make clear that unfamiliar adults are for the most part ignored by the child. The young child's relationships with its mother and strange peers indicate a complex interaction. The child seeks proximal contact with its mother while engaging in distal contact with its peers. Moreover, the child engages in as much if not more toy play with its peers as with its mother. We found that 67% of the infants showed taking-a-toy-from-another-peer behavior, but 58% showed sharing behavior, and more than half exhibited offering-a-toy behavior. Thus there is some toy play by the age of 12–18 months with relatively little hitting or aggressive behavior.

These results are generally consistent with those reported in the recent literature. For example, no recent studies named the absence of toy interaction. Bronson (1974) mentions a high proportion of agonistic encounters, but she cautions against interpreting them as hostile. The high incidence of distal behaviors manifested to peers is especially supported by Eckerman et al. (in press) and Lenssen (1973). Thus the high incidence of distal behaviors, the lack of aggressive activities, and the large number of infant subjects showing some type of play behavior toward peers in this study find support in many of the previously reported investigations.

Although the data seem to be clear enough, there were large individual differences. To understand them more fully, we examined some of the demographic characteristics of the child and family. We obtained data on the mother's educational level, the family's socioeconomic status (SES), the number of siblings in the family, and the reported number of hours per week the subject

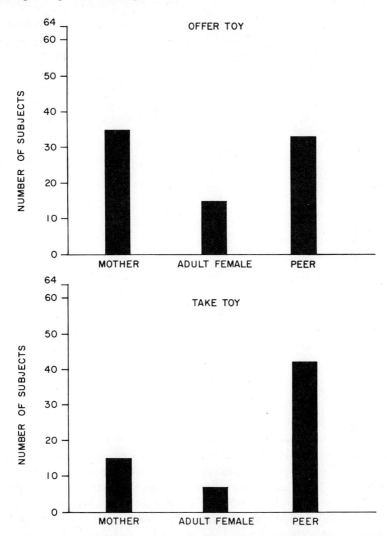

FIGURE 7.   Study I. Number of subjects (out of a possible 64) who either offered a toy (top) or took a toy (bottom) to either the mother, strange adult females, or peers.

spends interacting with other infants (hours—infants) and children older than 2 years of age (hours—child) who are not siblings. The correlational data (Spearman rank order rhos) are presented in Table 3. The SES of the family and the educational level of the mother seem to be related to the child's social behavior. For the affiliative behaviors, the higher the SES or maternal education, the more the child engaged the adult females and peers, and the less it en-

TABLE 3.   Relationships Between Demographic and Social Behavior

Behavior	Demographic Variables				
	Socio-economic Status	Mother's Education	Number of Sibs	Time (hours)	
				Infant	Child
Look at mother	− .31**	− .31**	.17	− .08	.08
Look at adult	− .08	.09	.15	− .10	− .02
Look at peer	.06	.08	− .32**	− .17	− .13
Proximity to mother	− .26*	− .22*	.11	− .08	.10
Proximity to adult	.31**	.17	− .03	.13	− .10
Proximity to peer	.26*	.20	− .10	.11	− .21*
Touch mother	− .30**	− .25*	.09	− .09	.05
Touch adult	.05	.01	.07	− .03	.11
Touch peer	.13	.22*	.05	.17	− .13
Offer toy	.25*	.02	− .17	.12	− .15
Take toy	.11	.08	− .30**	.02	− .25*
Hit	.18	.04	− .02	.13	.07
Share	.20	.18	− .14	.04	− .22*

* $p < .05$.
** $p < .01$.

gaged the mother. Likewise, play behavior seems to be positively related to these educational variables: the higher the mother's educational level, the more play activity with the peer. Interestingly, having other siblings in the family did not seem to facilitate peer relationships. The more siblings in a family, the less peer-directed behavior, both affiliative and play behavior. Likewise, amount of experience playing with older children did not facilitate play or affiliative interaction with a strange peer! Thus neither having older siblings nor having older children as playmates facilitated playing with other infants. It is interesting to note that play with other infants is not negatively related to the amount of time these infants played with strangers. Thus, although play with older children (including siblings) seemed to inhibit interaction with strange infants, play with infants did not.

The situation we have described had the young child embedded in a social context consisting of the target child, the mother, three unfamiliar female adults, and three unfamiliar peers. We wished to determine whether and in what ways a child within the first 18 months of life would manifest social behaviors indicative of a varied and complex social network. The results of this study show that the child is indeed aware of and responsive to the social network. Moreover, these results parallel the findings that have been obtained in a stress-producing situation. In several studies on infants' responses to strangers (Lewis & Brooks, 1974; Brooks & Lewis, 1974), we have repeatedly found more positive and less negative behaviors directed by infants toward peers as opposed to adults. That the same result has now been observed in a low-stress situation seems to confirm the infant's unique relationship to peers. The data, taken together with data reported in the literature, argue for the existence of a rich and varied social network in the life of children as young as 1 year old. Moreover, these relationships vary with the infant's past experience and the nature of the social object.

STUDY II: FRIENDS AND STRANGERS

That unfamiliar peers should have a very important effect, rivaling in certain respects that of the young child's mother, surely reflects the child's early and powerful relations with peers. In most studies peers differ from the infant's mother in at least two regards: (1) peers are unfamiliar, whereas the mother is familiar, and (2) peers are more "childlike." Let us consider the first condition. If the child can engage in meaningful and important peer relationships, it would be important to investigate his behavior to peer friends and to see how it might differ from behavior to unfamiliar peers. No studies thus far have examined peer interaction without confounding peer relationship with familiarity. It might well be that part of the relatively low level as well as the type of interaction between young peers is a function of strangeness rather than of age. Indeed, one would expect interactions with unfamiliar adults to be less frequent than and different from interactions with familiar adults.

Seven 12-month-old infants were observed in a playroom in two different sessions two days apart, once with a friend and once with a stranger. The target infants were 1-year-old (±15 days), firstborn, middle-class infants of both sexes. Their friends were 7- to 20-month-old infants of varying SES backgrounds who had one or no siblings and were not necessarily of the same sex as their respective targets. Each friend met the criteria of having been with his respective target twice per week in the two weeks preceding the initial contact and of having been together at least once per week in the preceding two months. The stranger peers were matched with the friend peers according to sex, age (±14 days), SES, and number of siblings. It is interesting to note, given Konner's view (see Chapter 4), that the selection of friends by the mothers included two children who were the same age as the target, one who was younger (a 7-month-old), and four who were older (15- to 20-month-olds). However, since the major analysis was concerned with friend and stranger dif-

ferences, the ages and sexes were matched; any differences as a function of age
are discussed in a later section.

It was randomly decided whether a target would see his friend or a stranger
first. When the mothers and infants arrived in the laboratory, they were placed
in separate waiting rooms filled with toys different from those in the experimental playroom. The mothers were given written instructions which an experimenter helped explain. Once the mothers were prepared and the infants
appeared calm and/or enthused, they were led to the playroom.

A 3.7 × 4.3 meter carpeted playroom containing two corn poppers, two pull
toys, and a stuffed dog was the setting of this study. Mothers were instructed to
sit on the floor 0.6 meter from one another in the center of the room with their
infants on their laps. When everyone was in position, a signal was given and
the mothers placed their infants on the floor, facing each other as well as the
others in the room. The mothers were instructed to remain seated and
unresponsive and to let their infants do what they wanted, in an effort to create
a "free-play" situation. The mothers talked minimally and did not respond at
length to their infants except when the children were upset or needed caretaking. Nevertheless, the situation seemed analogous to what might naturally occur in the home when infants are left to their own devices.

The playroom session was divided into two successive situations, lasting 42
minutes in all. In the first 30 minutes, the mothers and infants were observed
in a free-play setting; in the last 12 minutes, the mothers moved to a corner
and pretended to be busy.

Each session was videotaped and a 5-second timer was activated. The video
tapes were decoded later onto audio tapes. Then the audio tape recordings were
transcribed onto score sheets. For each 5-second period, two experimenters
coded what person(s) or social object(s) the infants were directing behavior
toward. Thus for the first 30 minutes of observation, 360 observations were
made for each infant.

There were three possible social objects—mother, adult, and peer (stranger
or friend)—to which the target infant could orient. Using a predetermined list
of behaviors, the experimenter also noted the specific behaviors directed to each
social object. If the same behavior occurred continuously or several times in
succession within a 5-second period, it was coded only once. The list contained
20 behaviors that an infant could direct to another infant. Table 4 presents the
defined behaviors and their interobserver agreements, based on five pairs of infants. Since agreements were calculated for both infants on the five tapes, they
are based on a total of 7 hours of observation. Reliabilities were based on the
(total number of agreements)/(total number of agreements plus disagreements).
All reliabilities were above 80% and most were above 85%.

Although analysis of the data in terms of complex interactions is possible (see
Lewis & Lee-Painter, 1974), the data presented in this discussion consist of the

mean number of 5-second periods in which a particular behavior occurred. Figure 8 plots the behaviors of the target child as directed toward either the friend or the stranger peer.

Target children were much more likely to engage in positive proximal activities—body contact, proximity, touch, and lean-lie—with their friends than with the stranger peers. Whereas proximity occurred approximately 11% of the 30 minutes of play, the other proximal behaviors were somewhat more infrequent. For example, body contact occurred 1% of the time for the friends and less than 0.33% for strangers. A similar picture exists for touch. Although

FIGURE 8.   Study II. Mean number of 5-second periods during which target 1-year-old infants exhibited the various behaviors. Each target infant played with both a friend and a stranger peer. The friend data are represented by the open bars; the stranger data are represented by the solid bars.

It is important to note that except for proximity and looking, most peer-directed behaviors were relatively infrequent even though there were significant differences between friends and strangers. Out of 360 possible 5-second periods, the present frequencies represent a small amount of peer interaction.

TABLE 4.   Peer-Directed Behaviors in Studies II and III

Behavior	Interobserver Agreement (percent)	Definition
Proximal		
Bounce-rock	100.0	Rhythmic repetitive movement of at least upper torso and head
Body contact	89.0	Any part of body (except hand) contacts peer in nonforceful manner
Proximity	97.6	Any part of body within body's length of peer; no contact mother
Touch	88.2	Hand or toy in hand placed on peer nonforcefully
Lean-lie	88.8	Forcefully placing at least part of upper portion of body on peer
Avert[a]	—	Sudden movement away from peer who is within body's length distance
Push-pull	92.3	Forceful extension and/or retraction of arm(s) with contact of peer
Strike	100.0	Forceful rapid arm movement contacting peer
Distal		
Look	95.7	Peer and/or his activities are visually observed
Vocalization	98.3	Single, staccato, or single vowel and/or consonant sound neither negative or positive
Gesture	84.4	Nonforceful arm movement directed to peer (e.g., wave, point, flap)
Duplicate	92.3	Duplication of specific motor action within seconds of its visual and/or auditory perception

these positive proximal behaviors occurred infrequently, the negative proximal behaviors of strike, push-pull, and avert occurred rarely or not at all. Interestingly, although not significant because of the low frequency of occurrence, there was more avert behavior toward the stranger than toward the friend peer.

In terms of the number of target subjects, five out of six[3] showed more body contact to friend than stranger (83%). Similar results were found for the positive proximal behaviors: six out of seven (87%) for proximity, four out of six (67%) for touch, three out of four (75%) for lean-lie. Interestingly, two out of three infants directed more push-pull behavior toward strangers than friends.

[3] There were seven pairs in all; some target subjects showed no difference between stranger and peer. This was because there were no data available; that is, the target subject did not exhibit that behavior toward either stranger or friend.

TABLE 4.   (continued).

Behavior	Interobserver Agreement (percent)	Definition
Affect		
Affection[a]	—	Hug with one or both arms and/or kiss with slightly protruded lips
Negative affect	83.4	Negative face (brow and forehead pucker) and/or negative sound(s) (rhythmic wail)
Positive affect	80.3	Laugh, smile, and/or positive vocalization
Play		
Offer	100.0	Object held out by arm(s) extending to peer. Includes give, show
Share	94.1	Hand nonforcefully placed on object concurrently contacted by peer. Includes accept
Take	88.2	(Try to) remove nonoffered object by extending and retracting arm(s)
Resist take	87.5	Forceful hand and/or arm movement to (try to) stop peer's apparent take
Game-play	100.0	Peek-a-boo or lead-chase

[a] Affection and avert were not scored by either observer during the 7 hours of interobserver agreement calculation; thus no percentages are offered.

The distal behaviors—look at, vocalize, gesture, and duplicate (imitate)—tended to occur more frequently than the proximal behaviors (see Figure 8). Looking occurred approximately 24% of the time. There was no difference in looking time or in vocalization between strangers and friends (three out of seven target children looked more and vocalized more at friend). Gesture is rather interesting, for whereas four out of four target boys showed more gesturing toward the friend than to the stranger, the reverse was true for the girls (three out of three target girls gestured more to the stranger peer than to the friend). Of particular theoretical importance is the duplicate or imitate category. In terms of mean data, friends were imitated more than twice as often as were strangers. In addition, five out of seven target children (71%) showed more imitation toward friend than stranger.

The affect behaviors yield a rather interesting pattern. First, there was only one instance of hugging or kissing, and that was toward a friend. Second, to both friend and stranger there was more positive than negative affect expressed.

Third, more negative affect was expressed toward the stranger than the friend. Indeed, there was nearly three times as much negative affect directed toward the stranger than friend, although only three out of five target children (60%) showed more negative affect toward the stranger than the friend. Finally, there was almost no difference in the amount of positive affect expressed toward friend and stranger peer, but there were interesting individual differences. Five out of seven target children (71%) were more likely to express positive affect toward the stranger than toward the friend.

The final set of social interaction behaviors centers around a toy object. First it should be noted that toy play as a class of social interaction behaviors occurs rather infrequently. Interaction between infants usually did not take the form of play around a toy. Indeed, sharing, offering, and taking a toy generally occurred less than 1% of the time, to either friend or stranger, although all target children showed at least one incident of these behaviors. Thus compared with proximal contact and distal behaviors, toy playing was a relatively infrequent form of social interaction.

Under these circumstances, it is rather interesting to observe that although both offering and sharing (positive social activities) occurred more often in the presence of friends than strangers, take and resist (more negative social activities) occurred at about the same frequency for both friend and stranger. More subjects took toys from strangers than friends (5 out of 7 targets—71%), and similar results were observed for resisting (4 out of 6 targets—67%). In contrast, toys were offered more to friends than strangers (5 out of 7 targets—71%).

We have been considering the target child's behavior toward stranger and friend peers. Now let us examine how the stranger and friend peers acted toward the target child. Table 5 presents these data. Viewed from the perspective of how the stranger and friend peer behaved toward the target child, the data are quite similar to those of the target child's behavior toward the peers. The friend peer directed more positive behavior toward the child than did the stranger peer. This can be seen in the three most frequent behaviors (body contact, proximity, touch). The distal behaviors—look, vocalize, and gesture—showed little or no peer differences. However, imitation was again more prevalent for friends than strangers. Interestingly, more affect, whether positive or negative, was directed toward the target child by the friend than by the stranger, with girls being more likely than boys to direct positive affect to a friend than to a stranger. This result is in contrast to that found for the target child's affective expression to his peers. Finally, the toy activities were again more often observed toward friend than toward stranger.

Thus the stranger versus friend peer difference is expressed both in the difference between the target child's behavior toward friend and stranger (a within-subject comparison) and in the friend and stranger peers' behavior

TABLE 5. Behavior of the Stranger and
the Friend Peer Toward the Target Child

Behavior	Number of 5-second Periods	
	Friend	Stranger
Proximal		
Bounce-rock	2.9	0.9
Body contact	17.6	3.6
Proximity	185.3	171.6
Touch	8.0	2.9
Lean-lie	0.1	0.6
Avert	1.3	0.0
Push-pull	0.0	0.0
Strike	0.1	0.0
Distal		
Look	224.6	223.7
Vocalization	15.6	19.0
Gesture	14.6	11.4
Duplicate	12.7	5.4
Affect		
Affection	1.3	0.0
Negative affect	9.4	5.0
Positive affect	22.0	9.0
Play		
Offer	2.9	1.4
Share	3.1	2.4
Take	10.7	6.3
Resist	1.0	2.1
Game-play	0.3	0.3

toward the target child (a between-subject comparison). We recognize that these comparisons are not independent, yet the behavior of all three infants makes clear that there is more interaction between 1-year-olds who are friends than between 1-year-olds who are strangers.

The data reflect this difference even though "friend" was minimally defined. One visit per week over the last two months can hardly be considered a strict criterion of "friendship," as the term is usually defined. In the final study to be discussed, we "created" friendship by having mothers bring their children together in their homes and again in the laboratory over a 2-week period. This creation of friendship should give us a somewhat better picture of children's differential behaviors toward peers as a function of familiarity, although long-term observations of infants in settings with other infants—as in group living or in well-staffed institutions—would tell us more about peer relationships. The description by Freud and Dann (1951) of children raised together during the war gives the impression that young peers have the potential to engage in much more contact and interaction than laboratory studies suggest. Likewise, Harlow (Harlow & Harlow, 1969) makes clear that in the absence of adult interaction, nonhuman primate peer relationships tend to be considerably more complex, intense, and frequent. These kinds of data lend support to the belief that parental contact with the child may inhibit or interfere with peer contact. Whether this is a natural condition, whether it is facilitated by the Western view of the family, or whether it is influenced by our physical surroundings (e.g., the architecture of our homes—single units) are considerations for discussion.

In any event, the contact between infants seems to center more on social dimensions of signaling and face-to-face behaviors (proximal, distal, and affect behaviors) than on toy and play behaviors, at least play behavior as engaged in by older children and adults. Although toy and play data indicate that interactions are rare, they do occur. Exactly what might facilitate them is not clear—two possibilities are prolonged exposure in different settings and a larger age mix. In short, although toy and play interactions are infrequent, the social interactions reflected in proximity seeking, visual regard, and imitation all point to a social involvement based on dimensions other than play. To restrict the dimension of peer behavior to toy play behavior would be to do a disservice to the fabric of the 1-year-old's social network. It is clear that infants interact with other infants in a rich behavioral context. Moreover, the differences in the infants' behavior toward familiar and unfamiliar peers point to the necessity of including peer relationships in any discussion of the infant's social world.

STUDY III: THE GROWTH OF FRIENDSHIP

In the last study we observed the relationship between peers who were natural friends, their mothers having brought them together because the women were friends or because they wanted their children to be friends. These children behaved differently from the children who were strangers to each other.

To extend these results, we thought it important to investigate the growth of friendship. This was accomplished first by selecting two stranger peers and their mothers and then having them to meet in each other's homes. Through repeated observations in the laboratory before, during, and after these home

visits, we could observe the changes in behavior that might be related to the beginnings of friendship. Thus, for example, in study II we found that friend
peers engaged in more proximal behaviors than stranger peers. In the final
study to be presented, we wondered whether the evolution of these behaviors
would be observable over repeated exposures in a developing friendship. Could
the origins of friendship be discerned in the very young?

Eight dyads of 1-year-olds ($\pm$ 28 days), four male and female pairs, were
selected for study from families who had not previously met. All infants were
second born. The mothers were informed that the experiment involved home
participation; that is, the children would be brought to each other's homes to
play together. Two to three home visits per week were arranged with play
sessions lasting 30 to 45 minutes. Scheduling and location were left up to the
mothers, with the strong suggestion that they hold the play sessions in alternating homes. This reportedly was done. In addition to the home visits, the
mothers were informed that there would be several laboratory visits during
which their children's play would be observed.

On the first visit to the laboratory, the infants in each dyad were strangers.
The laboratory procedures were identical to those in study II. Between visits
one and two, all eight dyads saw each other for the required two or three home
play sessions. The second visit to the laboratory playroom occurred one week
after the first. Following this visit, there was an additional week in which there
were two or three home visits. In the third laboratory visit, six of eight target
infants saw a stranger peer, and two target infants saw their friends. In the
design of this study each friend served as a stranger for another target infant.

Figure 9 presents data for some of the observed behaviors for the target infants seen in the laboratory play session. The data represent the mean number
of 5-second periods in which the various behaviors occurred. Remember that on
the first laboratory visit both infants were strangers, but prior to the second
visit both had been exposed to each other during two or three home visits.
Clearly there were increases in the proximal behaviors as a function of exposure. Seven out of eight target children showed increased proximity from
laboratory visit one to two. Likewise, there were increases in touch and lean-lie
across the two laboratory visits (7 out of 7, and 2 out of 2 target children,
respectively).

For the distal behaviors, for example, we find that looking declined over
visits one and two (3 out of 5 target children). Interestingly, these findings
agree with the results of study II, where friends were looked at less than were
strangers. On the other hand, gesturing increased across the visits (6 out of 7
target infants), and imitating remained about the same. (Although the mean
frequency data declined, 5 out of 7 target infants showed increased imitation
over the visits.)

The negative affect data indicate no change; however there is an interesting

FIGURE 9.   Study III. Mean number of 5-second periods during which target 1-year-old infants exhibited the various behaviors. Each target infant was seen on two different occasions in the laboratory playroom setting, one week apart. During that week, each infant had two or three home visits with a peer.

sex difference. Four out of the four target males showed a decrease in negative affect, but four out of the four target females showed an increase. In terms of positive affect, there was a decline over visits (6 out of 8 target children). Finally, offer, share, and take toys all showed small increases from laboratory visit one to two (4 out of 4, 3 out of 5, and 4 out of 7 target children, respectively).

It appears that increased exposure to the same peer results in interactive behavior similar to the kind found in study II. It was of considerable concern whether these behavioral increases, modest as they are, were the result of the time spent playing together in the home play sessions or whether they might be due to the child's acclimation to the playroom situation. Were these behavioral changes a function of a changing peer relationship or of a physical situation change? To determine which was the case, we observed the infants a third time in the laboratory. Recall that for the third visit two targets once again interacted with the same peer as on visits one and two, while the other infants

FIGURE 9. (Continued)

interacted with stranger peers. The strangers were not strangers to the laboratory playroom but only to the other child.

A comparison of laboratory visits two and three for the two familiar dyads revealed the same trends that were found between visits one and two. If a behavior declined between visits one and two, it either continued to decline or remained constant on visit three; if it increased over visits, it continued to increase or remained the same. In Figure 10 we compare data for the six infants who were paired with a friend on visit two and a stranger on visit three (F → S) with the data for the two infants who were paired with friends on visit two and three (F → F). Because of the small number of subjects, no statistical tests were conducted on these data; however, several trends are apparent. For example, proximity decreased when the other infant was a stranger but increased if the peer remained the friend. Thus the increase in proximity to a peer from visit one to visit two was maintained or increased on visit three if the

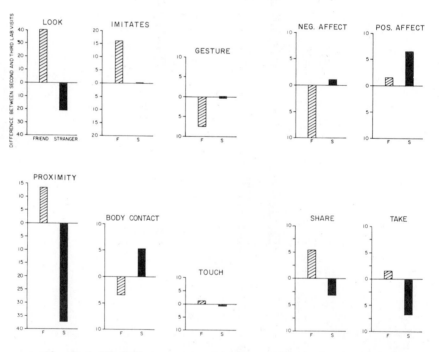

FIGURE 10. Study III. Difference scores of the target child as a function of stranger or friend, determined by obtaining mean number of 5 seconds of occurrence for a specific behavior during laboratory visit two with a friend and laboratory visit three with a stranger. For two target subjects, visits two and three were with the same friend; for six target subjects visit two was with a friend and visit three was with a stranger. A positive score indicates an increase in the behavior from visit two to three; a negative score indicates a decline.

peer was the friend but not if the peer was a stranger. Body contact provides another example. Body contact decreased from laboratory visit one to two for friends; across visits two and three it continued to decline for friends, whereas for strangers, body contact increased. Thus the general statement can be made that when a behavior increased in frequency from visit one to two, it was likely to continue increasing on visit three as long as the peer remained a friend, but it would decrease when the peer was a stranger. Likewise, a decreasing function from visit one to two could be expected to continue to decrease in the presence of a friend but to increase in the presence of a stranger.

These slope changes strongly support the view that increased exposure of 1-year-olds to other infants in home and laboratory playrooms strengthens the behaviors usually associated with long-term social contact. Moreover, although repeated exposure to the same physical surroundings (laboratory playroom) should cause changes in social interactive behavior (i.e., infants are more relaxed within familiar surroundings), this acclimation to the physical environment cannot be used to explain changes in the social relationships between these children. Rather, increased mutual social exposure must be called on to account for the change. The data provide continuing support for our belief that 1-year-old children are capable of forming and engaging in complex social interactions. The social network is affected by past experience with social objects as well as by expectations. That even a short familiarization produced the changes in mutual social interaction argues for the depiction of an organism capable of entering early into a social interaction with a variety of social objects in distinct ways. Furthermore, that the relationships themselves can be easily altered suggests that the organism is finely attuned to its social world.

A DESCRIPTION OF PEER RELATIONSHIPS

The results of the three studies can be summarized into a more global description of peer relationships as depicted in laboratory playroom studies. It is important to note that this description does not reflect the maximum potential of the child's peer behavior. Rather, the picture obtained from these studies probably reflects only a small portion of the infant's peer competence.

Our description is limited by several factors. First and most important, the data on natural peer involvement, obtained from interviewing the mothers, make abundantly clear that at least for our sample (middle- to upper-middle-class Northeasterners), infants have little opportunity to engage in peer contact. Mothers in general do not feel any obligation to ensure that their infants have extensive peer contacts, and only 20% of the mothers actively provided their infants with consistent peer exposure. Thus before the age of 2, infants in our culture (at least in the described subculture) have little opportunity for peer contact. Unlike many societies, our society presents to the infant an adult-dominated social world. Whether this is necessary or desirable is not clear (e.g., Freud & Dann, 1951; Harlow & Harlow, 1969). It is our strong belief that the emphasis on adult- as opposed to peer-dominated social experience in our culture is not based on the child's capacities but rather on a very specific ideology. For example, there is much evidence of a more highly peer-dominated social experience in the poorer social classes of this country (e.g., Brown, 1971). Moreover, although we do not have sufficient data to verify the assumption, it appears that infants in many other cultures also have intensive contacts with peers. We suspect that when the social behavior of children raised in peer-dominated cultures is more fully examined, we will find our conception of the social capacities of infants and young children considerably expanded. Thus one limitation in our description of infants' peer behavior resides in the population considered for our study. It is clear from our comments that this group, although typical of Northeastern, middle-class Americans, must represent a fairly narrow portion of the continuum of social experience.

The second limitation of the following global description of infant-peer interaction has to do with the problems inherent in laboratory studies. The ecology of the laboratory cannot reflect the more familiar settings of home, backyard, or playground. Moreover, the relatively limited amounts of observation time do not allow for the proper development of an adequate picture of the child's behavior. Nevertheless, in the laboratory studies we have discussed, the infants were observed for relatively long periods of time (40 to 50 minutes). Moreover, a laboratory setting allows for the use of elaborate recording equipment, which may contribute to our knowledge of what to look for in the more familiar settings of the infant. The laboratory setting clearly produces a situation different from that obtained in the home, but it is no less real, and it allows us to begin with a fairly reasonable picture of an unstressed 1-year-old in its relation to a peer.

With these restrictions in mind, let us turn to the 1- to 2-year-old infant. Given the choice, the infant will spend more time in proximity with its mother than other social objects—in this case, adult females and peers. This does not mean that this would hold for all social objects; rather, it may be a function of the nature of the caregiver and the roles that others assume in the care of the child. In any event, infants stay closer to their mothers than to peers and adult strangers. Seeking and maintaining of proximity serve the infant's need for caretaking and protection; however, its other activities suggest that it has a strong desire to direct a substantial proportion of its energy away from the mother (Rheingold, 1973). The data from study I show that although infants seek proximity with their mothers, many other exploratory and affiliative behaviors are directed not to her but toward other social objects. These other social objects are not other adults, but peers! There is a low level of social exchange between the infant and adult stranger. In a number of studies it has become clear that among strangers, adults are never preferred, whereas peers are almost always positively received (Brooks & Lewis, 1974; Greenberg, Hillman, & Grice, 1973; Lewis & Brooks, 1972, 1974).

Thus the mothers receive much proximity, but the infant directs other behaviors, such as visual regard, toward the peers. Mothers are good for protection, peers for watching and playing with. It is true that the mothers were somewhat restricted in terms of initiating social interaction with their infants; yet infants did not show any more play behaviors, such as toy offering, to their mothers than to other peers.

When we examine the infants' differential peer behavior, we have the opportunity to consider not only the relationship between parent and peer, but more important, the relationship between different peers (study II). A failure to demonstrate differential behavior between peer friends and stranger peers could be used to argue for the lack of truly interactive social experiences in these infants. That this is not the case—that infants do show clear differentiation—indicates their capacity to sustain long-term social interactions (what we often refer to as friendships) and that such relationships in fact exist.

We can describe the infant's peer relationships by contrasting the infant's behavior toward friend and stranger. When we do this, we find that infant friends engage each other more proximally, imitate one another more often, and show more positive affect and less negative affect to one another. Finally, friends are more likely to share with and to offer toys to each other, at the same time, being less likely to take toys away from each other. Thus 1-year-old friends exhibit the behaviors that bring them in physical proximity, and once in proximity they demonstrate the behaviors typical of close relationships.

Observation of the growth of friendship confirms the findings on peers who are already friends (study III). Proximity, sharing, and offering increase with repeated exposure to the same infant. The quality of the behavior expressed by infants to peers appears to be a function of their specific social relationship. The types of behavior we would associate with friendship were differentially exhibited to the stranger and friend in the final study.

The picture portrays infants as capable of establishing and maintaining peer relationships containing features we usually think of as indicative of friendship. At least one major difference between the description of friendship of 1- and 2-year-olds and that of older children pertains to the relatively low levels of mutual toy play behavior in the younger children. The data from all three studies indicate that a large majority of infants engage in at least one instance of mutual toy play behavior. We recognize, however, that although the infants show some capacity to engage in this behavior, it occurs less frequently than other playroom behaviors. Its low frequency can probably be accounted for by the infant's early stages of cognitive development (Piaget, 1951). However, a concept of friendship does not have to be restricted to toy play behavior.

Friendship, which may be defined in infancy as a cluster of specific and particular interactions with familiar infants, probably exists early in the developing human; however, the forms and content of that interaction are limited by the cognitive development of the child.

Before ending our description of the friendships of 1-year-olds, let us consider one last issue—namely, what facilitates or inhibits peer relationships. Unfortunately, we know very little about the precipitating conditions. We have already hinted that the milieu in which the child lives probably plays an important role in facilitating infant friendships. Clearly, in this culture, the infant needs adult assistance to arrive in a setting at which peers are present. Where this occurs naturally, we would anticipate more peer interaction. Surprisingly, our own data do not seem to support this conclusion, since like Eckerman et al. (in press), we found that having older siblings or playing with older children did not facilitate peer interaction (see study I). However, we did find that playing with other infants, although the correlation was not significant, did not have the same inhibiting effect as play with older siblings and children. This suggests that play with older children might be too threatening for infants, whereas play with those who have more equal capacities and skills is less threatening, hence is more facilitating for subsequent peer interactions.

THE MEANING OF PEER

The issue of the playmate's age raises the more general question of what constitutes a peer. Peership is usually characterized by equality of chronological age. Thus agemate and peer are used synonymously. This has important implications because the meaning of peer—from the point of view of the infant—may be quite different from the currently used age-mate criterion. We maintain that "peer" should have a meaning related to *function* rather than *age*. That is, a peer would be on one occasion all the children who could climb a tree, while on another occasion it would be those able to sing songs. In this example peers are defined functionally rather than in terms of age.

In the second study, we obtained data on seven target 12-month-olds and their natural friends. Recall that of the seven infants, two had friends who were the same age, one had a 7-month-old friend, and four had 15- to 20-month-old friends. We were interested in whether the dyadic interactions would differ with respect to the age differences in the pair. The proximal behaviors—proximity, touch, lean-lie, body contact—showed that the same-age peers received and directed more of these behaviors to each other than did unequal age peers. For example, body contact between same-age peers was 40.0, whereas for unequal age peers it was only 12.1 5-second periods.

The distal behaviors of look and gesture showed a similar pattern. However, there was a different pattern for duplicate or imitation. Imitation occurred most frequently between the 12-month-olds and their older peers, rather than between equal age peers (18.0 vs. 9.5 5-second periods, respectively).

We found that the expression of positive affect was more likely to occur between unequal age peers (22.1 5-second periods) than between equal age peers (6.0 5-second periods). Interestingly there were no differences for negative affect.

Equal age peers were more likely to share, take, and resist than unequal age peers (12.5 vs. 0.7 5-second periods for share; 22.5 vs. 3.5 for take; 3.5 vs. 0.5 for resist). However, the infants were more likely to offer toys to younger infants than to same-age peers.

The data, albeit limited by the small number of dyads, suggest that certain types of behavior are more likely to occur between equal age peers and other behaviors are more likely to occur between unequal age peers. For example, imitation occurs more frequently with unequal age mates; body contact is more frequent between age mates. This suggests that different behaviors are in the service of various functions, which are at this point unexplicated. However, that various functions are facilitated or retarded by the age composition of peer relationships cannot be denied. Therefore the function as well as the age composition of relationships must be considered.

FUNCTIONAL ASPECTS OF PEER RELATIONSHIPS

The functional aspects of the infant's social interaction with its caregiver are unquestioned. The infant's very survival is dependent on its relationship with adults who are willing to assume the care of the helpless infant. Thus for the human infant, a social relationship between an adult and the infant is vital.

Yet we should not forget that in phylogenetically older forms of man (e.g., early hunter-gatherer), our best estimates are that infants and young children within the adult group were always raised together; this may have been customary because of a functional value in early social relationships for the young child. Such assumptions of functionality, however, were always made with the provisions that the adult relationship preceded peer relationships both in importance and ontogeny and that the adult-infant relationship strongly influenced the course of all subsequent social relationships. Thus a positive adult-infant relationship was thought to be the key to a positive peer relationship. This may be only partially true. It would not be unreasonable to assume an alternative model in which peer relationships are not a derivative of the adult-infant relationship, but rather are a separate and parallel phenomenon.

To support such a theory we argue that the functions of social objects are varied and that social objects have at least two important functions in the social life of the infant. First, as already stated, the infant needs a social relationship with someone who will care for it and protect it from harm. Adults serve this function best, and a specific consistent adult may be optimal.

In addition, however, the infant has need for social relationships characterized as friendships, out of which first social play and later sexual reproduction develop. This second need is no less important and functional for the survival of the species than the first—individual survival to allow for reproductive survival. The infant must learn early to form and maintain peer social relationships to develop social skills, which will provide for its reproductive success.

Finally, peer interaction provides an excellent milieu for the development of the infant's capacities. The peer social context is quite different from the more pervasive caregiver milieu where the adult guides, directs, controls, and plays. In contrast, peers are relatively equal in terms of their social skills, the capacity to formulate and carry out their goals, and the extent of their socialization. In this social context, the infants not only mutually socialize one another, they have a better chance at successfully affecting one another. In this process the development of social competence can be observed.

This view of the function of peers, together with the more traditional view of parental relations, is schematized in Figure 11. Model A reflects the traditional view in which the parental functions are care and protection as well as all others. Explicit in this model is the belief that subsequent peer relationships (as all other social relations) are derived from the child-parent relationship. The function of peers does not emerge until childhood. The alternative view, that of the functional value of peers in infancy as well as early childhood, is presented in model B. Note that the functional value of peers exists in infancy and is not derived from the child's relationship with its parents.

Finally, one might approach this issue from a phylogenetic viewpoint. Primacy of peer over adult social interactions decreases as we move higher up the phylogenetic tree. Lower organisms' social interactions are between peers of the species. We can verify this most readily by observing that at the lower end of the tree, most responses the organism needs for survival are prewired into this system. All that is necessary for the developing species is to practice the skills as they unfold. It would be more logical to practice these skills with someone also less proficient, since the skills of the adult would be too overwhelming. Moreover, since the adult has little or nothing to teach the infant, there needs to be relatively little social interaction with adults. This would suggest that among birds, for example, the young could as easily or more easily be imprinted on a peer than on an adult member. Whom are the ducklings imprinted on as they swim single file on the pond? The "mother" or the young duckling in front?

As we proceed along the phylogenetic scale, learning becomes more im-

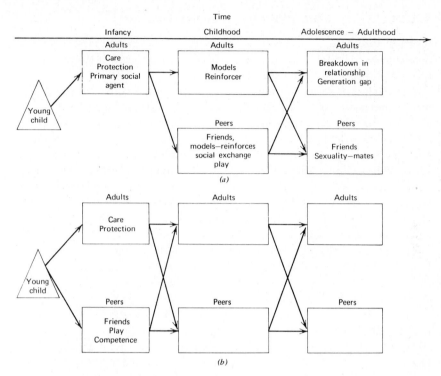

FIGURE 11. Schematic representations of the young child's social organization: (*a*) the one-track, traditional parents → peer relationship, model A; (*b*) the dual-track system where parents and peers occupy different but immediately similar tracks, model B.

portant for the survival of the organism. As such, peers who are good for practicing present skills are no longer sufficient, and adults who are good in teaching new skills are needed. Thus social interaction with adults, in addition to peers, becomes increasingly important. Single births and long periods of relative helplessness facilitate the infant-adult relationship; the primate data suggest, however, that if infant-peer relationships can be sustained (as in laboratory colonies, e.g.), these relationships satisfy many of the basic socioemotional requirements (Harlow & Harlow, 1965, 1969; Harlow, Harlow, & Suomi, 1971). The implication for a theory of social behavior is vast. We might argue that peers are not substitutes for infant-adult relationships, but rather are just as basic and maybe even older in a phylogenetic sense. Small families isolated from one another may constitute historically a rather unique and new experience, not only for the caregivers but for the infants themselves.

MECHANISMS FOR PEER RELATIONSHIPS

It seems reasonable at this point to state that infants engage in meaningful peer relationships that form an important part of their social network and are necessary for their social development.

Peer interaction in infancy must have an important cognitive basis that is not now understood. Without elaborating on the various cognitive functions necessary for this social behavior (other chapters in this book have undertaken this task), we would like to suggest that cognitive activities involving imitation, modeling, contingent response learning, object permanence, self-concept, and person differentiation are all important. The relationship between the developing cognitive and social skills is not clear. At one level the cognitive skills are the mechanisms by which the social skills emerge and are applied, yet at another level the social interactions themselves necessitate and push the development of the cognitive skills.

The results of the studies reported here as well as other work (Brooks & Lewis, 1974; Greenberg et al., 1973; Lenssen, 1973; Lewis & Brooks, 1974) reveal that infants have differential relationships between adults and other children. Infants respond with concentration, concern, and some negative affect to strange adults, yet with great interest and positive affect to strange peers. Infants are also more likely to share a toy with a peer rather than with an adult stranger, and they prefer to interact with a friend than with a strange peer. One theoretical construct that may explain the adult-child and the peer friend-stranger social differentiation is the concept of self (Lewis & Brooks, 1974; Lewis & Brooks, in press).

We have argued that the use of a categorical self as a referent for social comparisons can be used in a partial explanation of peer relationships, assuming that the infant within the first year of life has the capacity to form and maintain a schema of self-reference. This schema in its earliest form makes possible differentiation of self from other social objects. In the development of the schema, categories of self, such as gender, are added. Another such category involves the concept of self as child. That is, the infant is cognizant of his "child-ness." This knowledge might be based on size comparisons or even facial cues (Brooks & Lewis, 1974). These categories of self are used by the child to determine "likeness"; that is, the child uses self as a referent to determine its social behavior. "Like me" is a positive evaluation, and "not like me" is negative. Organisms tend to approach objects like self, tending to avoid objects classified as not like self. Approach and avoidance are used here in their broadest sense to imply such diverse activities as physical approach or imitation. Thus one factor influencing the child's social interactions with others is its use of self as a referent.

Based on this information and recalling that objects "like me" are valued, we suggest that the infant is likely to prefer to interact with peer rather than adult strangers. "Like me" may also facilitate the growth of friendship with peers, since a familiar peer's actions are more likely to be similar to one's own than those of an unfamiliar peer by virtue of the first pair's common play experience. The concept of self may also be applied to the formation of specific peer friendships. Specific friendships are formed when the infant becomes attracted to peers more like himself. That is, infants may be attracted to other infants who are "like self."

The use of such a theoretical perspective allows the organism to be an active participant rather than a passive recipient in terms of ordering and interacting with its social world. It also serves the previously discussed function of encouraging interaction between organisms with similar competencies, which may facilitate the growth of social competencies.

THE SOCIAL WORLD OF THE YOUNG CHILD

Even the very young child has a complex social network, composed of friends and strangers, adults and peers. Its complexity both requires and facilitates cognitive growth. A variety of social objects constitutes the social world of the infant and the objects have diverse social functions—namely, the protection of the young and the promotion of social competency. Unfortunately for a theory of social network, people and functions are not always constant. Adults can be played with and other children can protect. Thus when we talk of the child's social world we must consider social objects and functions independently. (A full discussion of social network theory is given in Weinraub, Brooks, & Lewis, 1975.)

When we conceptualize the child's social world, therefore, we must include the social objects and functions and the cognitive processes of the child itself. In addition, the changing needs and capacities of the organism must be considered. The structure of the social world is highly complex, and it has a fabric of tightly interwoven objects, functions, and needs.

References

Blurton Jones, N. Characteristics of ethological studies of human behavior. In N. Blurton Jones (Ed.), *Ethological studies of child behavior.* Cambridge: Cambridge University Press, 1972. Pp. 3–33.

Bowlby, J. The nature of the child's tie to his mother. *International Journal of Psychoanalysis,* 1958, **39,** 350–373.

Bridges, K. A study of social development in eary infancy. *Child Development,* 1933, **4,** 36–49.

Brindley, C., Clarke, P., Hutt, C., Robinson, I., & Wethli, E. Sex differences in the activities and social interactions of nursery school children. In R. Michael & J. Crook (Eds.), *Comparative ecology and behavior of primates.* New York: Academic Press, 1973. Pp. 799–828.

Bronson, W. Competence and the growth of personality. In J. Bruner & K. Connolly (Eds.), *The development of competence in early childhood.* New York: Academic Press, 1974.

Brooks, J., & Lewis, M. Social responses to social events. Educational Testing Service, unpublished manuscript, 1974.

Brown, C. *Manchild in the promised land.* New York: Signet, 1971.

Buhler, C. The social behavior of children. In C. Murchison (Ed.), *Handbook of child psychology.* Worcester, Mass.: Clark University Press, 1933. Pp. 374–416.

Dragsten, S., & Lee, L. Infants' social behavior in a naturalistic vs. experimental setting. Paper presented at the meeting of the American Psychological Association, Montreal, August 1973.

Durfee, J., & Lee, L. Infant-infant interaction in a day care setting. Paper presented at the meeting of the American Psychological Association, Montreal, August 1973.

Eckerman, C. Competence in early social relations. Paper presented at the Symposium on Early Competence: Data and Concepts, American Psychological Association meetings, Montreal, August 1973.

Eckerman, C., Whatley, J., & Kutz, S. Growth of social play with peers during the second year of life. *Developmental Psychology,* in press.

Freud, A., & Dann, S. An experiment in group upbringing. In R. Eisler (Ed.), *The psychoanalytic study of the child.* Vol. 6. New York: International Universities Press, 1951. Pp. 127–163.

Greenberg, D. J., Hillman, D., & Grice, D. Infant and stranger variables related to stranger anxiety in the first year of life. *Developmental Psychology,* 1973, **9,** 207–212.

Harlow, H. Age-mate or peer affectional system. In D. Lehrman, R. Hinde, & E. Shaw (Eds.), *Advances in the study of behavior.* Vol. 2. New York: Academic Press, 1969. Pp. 333–383.

Harlow, H., & Harlow, M. The affectional systems. In A. Schrier, H. Harlow, & F. Stollnitz (Eds.), *Behavior of nonhuman primates.* Vol. 2. New York: Academic Press, 1965. Pp. 287–334.

Harlow, H. F., & Harlow, M. K. Effects of various mother-infant relationships on rhesus monkey behaviors. In B. M. Foss (Ed.), *Determinants of infant behavior.* Vol. IV. London: Methuen, 1969. Pp. 15–36.

Harlow, H. F., Harlow, M. K., & Suomi, S. J. From thought to therapy: Lessons from a primate laboratory. *American Scientist,* 1971, **59,** 538–549.

Hartup, W. W. Peer interaction and social organization. In P. Mussen (Ed.), *Carmichael's manual of child psychology.* Vol. 2. New York: Wiley, 1970. Pp. 361–456.

Hinde, R. Development of social behavior. In A. Schrier & F. Stollnitz (Eds.), *Be-*

havior of nonhuman primates: Modern research trends. Vol. 3. New York: Academic Press, 1971. Pp. 1–68.

Lee, L. Social encounters of infants: The beginnings of popularity. Paper presented at the International Society for the Study of Behavioral Development, Ann Arbor, Mich., August 1973.

Lenssen, B. Infants' reactions to peer strangers. Unpublished doctoral dissertation, Stanford University, 1973.

Lévi-Strauss, C. *The savage mind.* Chicago: University of Chicago Press, 1966.

Lewis, M., & Brooks, J. Self, other and fear: The reaction of infants to people. Paper presented at Eastern Psychological Association meetings, Symposium on Infants' Fear of the Strange, Boston, April 1972.

Lewis, M., & Brooks, J. Self, other and fear: Infants' reactions to people. In M. Lewis & L. Rosenblum (Eds.), *The origins of fear: The origins of behavior.* Vol. II. New York: Wiley, 1974.

Lewis, M., & Brooks, J. Infants' social perception: A constructivist view. In L. Cohen & P. Salapatek (Eds.), *Infant perception.* New York: Academic Press, in press.

Lewis, M., & Lee-Painter, S. An interactional approach to the mother-infant dyad. In M. Lewis & L. Rosenblum (Eds.), *The effect of the infant on its caregiver: The origins of behavior.* Vol. I. New York: Wiley, 1974. Pp. 21–48.

Marcus, J. Early child development in kibbutz group care. *Early Child Development and Care,* 1971, **1,** 67–98.

Maudry, M., & Nekula, M. Social relations between children of the same age during the first two years of life. *Journal of Genetic Psychology,* 1939, **54,** 193–215.

McGrew, W. *An ethological study of children's behavior.* New York: Academic Press, 1972.

Mueller, E., & Rich, A. Clustering and socially-directed behaviors in a play group of one-year-old boys. *Early Child Development and Care,* in press.

Parens, H., & Saul, L. *Dependence in man: A psychoanalytic study.* New York: International Universities Press, 1971.

Piaget, J. *Play, dreams, and imitation in childhood.* New York: Norton, 1951.

Rheingold, H. The independent behavior of the human infant. In A. Pick (Ed.), *Minnesota Symposia on Child Development,* Vol. VII. Minneapolis: University of Minnesota Press, 1973. Pp. 178–203.

Shirley, M. *The first two years.* Vol. II. Minneapolis: University of Minnesota Press, 1933.

Smith, P. Social and situational determinants of fear. In M. Lewis & L. Rosenblum (Eds.), *The origins of fear: The origins of behavior.* Vol. II. New York: Wiley, 1974. Pp. 107–129.

Spiro, M. *Children of the kibbutz.* Cambridge, Mass.: Harvard University Press, 1958.

Spitz, R. *The first year of life: A psychoanalytic study of normal and deviant development of object relations.* New York: International Universities Press, 1965.

Suomi, S., & Harlow, H. Social rehabilitation of isolate-reared monkeys. *Developmental Psychology,* 1972, **6,** 487–496.

Vincze, M. The social contacts of infants and young children reared together. *Early Child Development and Care,* 1971, **1,** 99–109.

Washburn, R. A scheme for grading the reactions of children in a new social situation. *Journal of Genetic Psychology,* 1932, **40,** 84–99.

Weinraub, M., Brooks, J., & Lewis, M. The social network: A reconsideration of the concept of attachment. Unpublished manuscript, 1975.

CHAPTER 3

Peer Relations in Monkeys: The Influence of Social Structure, Gender, and Familiarity[1]

LEONARD A. ROSENBLUM, CHRISTOPHER L. COE, AND LYN J. BROMLEY[2]

Primate Behavior Laboratory
Downstate Medical Center

"A friend may well be reckoned the masterpiece of nature!" Although Emerson expressed that thought 100 years ago, and poets forever have crafted their exaltations of friendship, only recently have the social sciences taken firm notice of the significance of such relationships in shaping the patterns of human behavior from early infancy onward. The challenging experimental work on development and social deprivation in animals during the last two decades has dramatized the behavioral devastation caused by inadequate social contacts during rearing. The range and diversity of social encounters that constitute adequate social experience is, of course, among the most critical issues currently being considered. However, the opportunity for some degree of sustained interaction and relationships with partners at similar maturational levels (i.e., peers) clearly represents a fundamental dimension of such experience.

In this chapter we examine a number of the most salient features of peer relations and the foundations of these companionships during early and later infancy and adolescence, as investigated by the authors not in man, but in number of nonhuman primate species. The primary foci of these comparative laboratory studies of peer relations have been the role of species differences and the likely impact of species-characteristic social structures, the role of gender in shaping the form and selectivity of peer relations, the influence of familiarity between peers, and ultimately, the complex interactions of these factors in molding the course of peer relations. By providing a glimpse of the evolutionary continuity of such patterns across several primate species, we hope to suggest

[1] This research was supported by grants MH 22640 and MH 15965 from the National Institute of Mental Health.

[2] Ms. Bromley is also affiliated with the Graduate Center of the City University of New York. The authors wish to express their appreciation to Ms. Barbara Turner for her invaluable assistance.

67

the general significance of congruent features of peer relations within the primate order.

THE SOCIAL MILIEU: PIGTAIL AND BONNET MACAQUE GROUP STRUCTURE

Like the human child, the monkey infant enters into a distinct social relationship with its caregiver at birth; the infant's limited functioning and consequent dependency makes such a relationship necessary for survival. However, it is not merely physical survival that the infant derives from this initial relationship with the primary caregiver. The entire course of the infant's subsequent social development is enacted within the social arena in which the mother functions and which in large measure molds her own behavior as well as that of the infant.

The major focus of our research has been the development of social behavior in two species of macaques, the pigtail (*M. nemestrina*) and the bonnet (*M. radiata*). To place the progression of behaviors described below into a broad developmental context, several basic phylogenetic and ontogenetic factors should be brought to the reader's attention. The macaque genus includes at least a dozen species and many subspecies, and these range in habitat across more than 50 degrees of latitude, from seashore, swamp, and cliff to city, farm, and mountain. Mature body weight in males and females ranges rather broadly across the genus. A relatively narrow range of gestational periods averaging approximately 165 to 170 days seems to be characteristic of all macaques. Similarly, sexual maturity is reached in most macaque males at about 4 years and in females about 1 year earlier. These general parameters of development, however, are often influenced by the conditions of rearing, with maturation progressing somewhat more rapidly in the laboratory than in the field.

During the last 13 years, our studies in the laboratory on pigtails and bonnets have allowed us to study two primates that present quite contrasting social milieus within which infants develop. When a group of wild-born pigtail macaques are placed in a relatively large laboratory pen, adults disperse themselves throughout the available space, coming into close physical contact with one another only intermittently. On the other hand, when a similarly constituted group of bonnet macaques is placed in the same physical area, long periods of the day and evening are spent with numbers of individuals, often the whole group, in close physical contact with one another (Rosenblum, Kaufman, & Stynes, 1964). This species difference in individual distance patterning is quite stable over a variety of changes in environmental conditions (Rosenblum, Kaufman, & Stynes, 1969). Inasmuch as these patterns are also maintained following the birth of offspring, during development, infants of the two species are confronted with social structures strikingly different in their interactive characteristics.

EARLY PEER RELATIONS AS A FUNCTION OF SOCIAL MILIEU

Bonnet mothers, within moments of delivering their young, generally reestablish close contact with their associates and allow other members of the group to touch, explore, and even handle, the newborn. The pigtail mother on the other hand continues to remain relatively aloof and separated from other members of the group and often attacks vigorously or flees from others in the group who attempt to establish some form of exploratory contact with her newborn. As a consequence of the difference in spacing patterns, and the less frequent restrictive and protective behavior of bonnet mothers, bonnet infants from birth onward consistently engage in more positive interaction with other members of the social group than do equivalently aged pigtail infants (see Figure 1). It is particularly important in the current context, to realize that young bonnet infants not only have relatively more access to and interactions with other adults in the group but also obtain consistently higher levels of peer interaction beginning quite early in life.

In our normative studies (Rosenblum, 1971a) we found that during the first year of life bonnet infants almost continuously engaged in more social play than did their pigtail counterparts. This difference between the species was attributable in part to the continuing contact patterns of the mothers within the group. It was not unusual to see bonnet infants very early in life engage in play bouts, with each partner maintaining some degree of ventral and occasionally nipple contact with its respective mother (see Figure 2). Our data suggest that the difference in the degree of social play between peers in the two species is not the result of a different propensity toward playfulness in bonnet and pigtail infants; rather, it is tentatively attributed to the difference in the focus of such playfulness. When all forms of play, both social and nonsocial, become extremely prominent in both species (i.e., after the first 4 months of life), total engagement in all forms of play does not differ substantially between the two species—each is observed to play during about 10 to 11% of daylight observation time. Perhaps as a product of the bonnets' greater opportunities for peer contact during early development, as well as the generally greater facilitation of social interaction afforded by the bonnet group structure, play in bonnet infants tends to become primarily socially directed. In pigtail infants of the same age, for whom dispersal and related dominance patterns may interfere with free expression of close social interactions, infants primarily engage in nonsocial inanimate object and "exercise" play activities (Rosenblum, 1971a) (see Figure 3). Thus the potential for peer interaction, and the facility with which infantile propensities toward response to peers are expressed, are influenced by the protective envelope with which the mother surrounds her infant and the consequent degree to which she restricts or allows social interaction early in life. As with all complex behavior in higher organisms, these maternal patterns are

FIGURE 1.   Characteristic huddling pattern of bonnet group. Note the interactive potential for young infants.

subject to wide individual differences in each species, yet they are determined and constrained consistently by the social structure of the larger group of which the mother is a part (see Table 1).

THE FAMILY UNIT: SIBLING AND PEER RELATIONS DURING MATURATION

The impact of differences in social structure and maternal patterns in the two species is by no means restricted to an influence on *early* peer interactions. Observations made across a span of years indicate that differences in the pattern of peer relationships may continue throughout the life span of individuals in these groups. To understand this one must be aware that in addition to our

observations of differences in early peer relations, a number of studies have indicated parallel differences in the intensity and endurance of infant attachment
to mother in the two species. It has been demonstrated that pigtails are
consistently more disturbed following experimental separation from the
mother; they are generally unable to redirect filial behavior toward others in
the group, and there is pronounced regression and intensification of attachment
behavior following reunion with the mother. Bonnet infants on the other hand
rarely evidence sustained disturbance following removal of mother. They
readily transfer their attachment behavior to others and are frequently adopted
by others; after reunion, bonnet infants unlike pigtails do not show enhanced attachment to mother and occasionally may even fail to return to her at all
(Kaufman & Rosenblum, 1967). In keeping with their reactions to separation,
pigtail infants often show a marked disruption in their ongoing behavior when a
sibling is born. These pigtail infants often manifest a sharp increase in self-

FIGURE 2.   Young bonnet infant engaged in social exploration of another infant while
each clings to its mother.

FIGURE 3.   Pigtail infants independently gathering to explore the environment, under the watchful gaze of their mothers.

orality, as well as striking decreases in play and general activity in the weeks following the mother's next parturition. Bonnet infants on the other hand generally exhibit only brief disruptions in behavior and no sustained or pronounced emotional reaction to the birth of a sibling.

To assess the coalescent impact of the species difference in early peer relations and in the relative intensity of infant-mother attachment, we made a long-term follow-up study of multigenerational pigtail and bonnet groups (Rosenblum, 1971b). A pigtail group and a bonnet group served as subjects; each group had been formed with a breeding male and five breeding females. When the observations began, 6 years after group formation, the pigtail group contained eighteen subjects including the breeding male, four mothers and twelve offspring, and one unattached pubescent male. The uterine kinship groupings each contained one to four offspring and their mother. The mean age of the progeny was approximately 32 months at the start of this set of observations. The bonnet group contained nineteen subjects, including the adult male, five mothers, their twelve offspring, and one unattached pubescent male. The size of the bonnet kinship units ranged from two to four; progeny were at a mean age of about 30 months. There was no statistically significant difference in the ages of progeny in the pigtail and bonnet groups. Each species group contained three subjects under 1 year of age, four subjects from 1 to 3 years, and five subjects older than 3 years of age. Eighteen months following initial observations, a second set of follow-up data was obtained on each group. During the interval between observations eight new bonnet and five new pigtail infants were born, thus enlarging group sizes to 27 and 23 subjects, respectively. Inasmuch as kinship groups and total group size differed in the two species, all scores were transformed into percentages of expected interaction levels based on a random probability model.

TABLE 1. Salient Characteristics of Pigtails, Bonnets, and Squirrel Monkeys Used in Comparative Studies of Peer Relations

Characteristics	Pigtail Macaque	Bonnet Macaque	Squirrel Monkey
Origin	Asia	Asia	South America
Adult size (kg), male/female	9–15/6–9	6–9/5–8	0.7–1.1/0.6–0.8
Gestation (months)	5.5	5.5	5.5
Interbirth interval (years)	1	1	1
Age when weaning completed (months)	9–12	9–12	4–6
Age (years) at sexual maturity, male/female	4/3	4/3	4/3
Social structure (in laboratory)	Dispersed Aggressive Strong kinship bonds	Aggregative Infrequent aggression	Aggregative within sex (sex segregation) Very rare aggression
Maternal patterns	Very protective Restricts social contacts	Minimally protective Facilitates social contacts	Minimally protective Facilitates social contact (plus "aunting")

FIGURE 4. A yearling pigtail initiating play with its younger sibling while an older sibling sits nearby.

Initial observations carried out over a 3-month period indicated a striking difference between the species in the relative cohesiveness of the uterine kinship units. In each of the major social categories evaluated (i.e., physical contact, the initiation and receipt of social grooming, and social play), pigtails' scores were significantly higher than those of their bonnet counterparts in terms of the proportion of their behaviors directed along kinship lines. Thus in the 1- to 3-year age group, more than 60% of all contact and grooming interaction in pigtails was confined to the uterine kinship group, whereas less than 20% of contact and initiation of grooming was directed in this fashion by bonnets of the same age. Particularly important in the current context, even social play—nominally a behavior primarily engaged in by age mates—was similarly influenced by the kinship group cohesiveness in pigtails as compared to bonnets. Thus despite the ready availability of nonsibling age mates for pigtails, nearly 40% of all social play in pigtail infants between 1 and 3 years of age involved older and younger siblings (see Figure 4). Bonnet infants in this age group chose siblings as play partners less than 10% of the time. Follow-up data on these groups supported and underlined further the significance of the initial findings. Given the opportunities for continued interaction within a confined space, both male and female pigtail offspring continued to maintain significantly higher levels of social interaction along kinship lines than was true of bonnets. This trend was maintained even after puberty and, in the case of females, even after the birth of their own offspring (see Figure 5). In contrast, by the end of the first year of life, bonnet interactions with uterine kin in terms of contact, grooming, and play, all fell to levels at or below those to be expected by chance. Although a gradual reduction in kinship involvement occurred as offspring grew older, at every age range tested the preference for involvement with uterine kin was greater in pigtails than in bonnets. In terms of the ontogeny and continuity of group structure, it is also significant to note that the same distinction held for mothers of the two species as well. Based on these findings, it seems likely that as an outgrowth of a relatively intense early attachment to the mother and constrained opportunities for peer interaction, there occurred in pigtails facilitation of the growth of related attachments and interactional preferences for siblings, both older and younger. Thus the characteristic group structure, working in concert with congruent maternal patterns, influences the form of peer and sibling relations in a manner that serves to perpetuate that structure.

FIGURE 5.   A pigtail matrilineal family group, including the matriarch and three of her offspring, as well as the infant of the former's mature daughter.

SPECIES DIFFERENCES IN JUVENILE PEER RELATIONS

By the second year of life the impact of species-characteristic group and maternal patterns can be seen in the behavior of the young, even in the absence of
adults. To examine this development, we placed seven juvenile pigtails and
seven juvenile bonnets in a large social pen in the absence of adults of either
species. These juveniles, all born in our laboratory and raised within complex
conspecific groups of the types already described, were between 14 and 30
months of age when placed into this large heterospecific juvenile group. As
Figure 6 indicates, the bonnet juveniles quickly established and maintained the
characteristic group contact huddles, whereas pigtail juveniles were more
frequently found alone. As reflected in Figure 7, there was virtually no overlap
in the distribution of contact scores for the bonnet and pigtail juveniles. Even

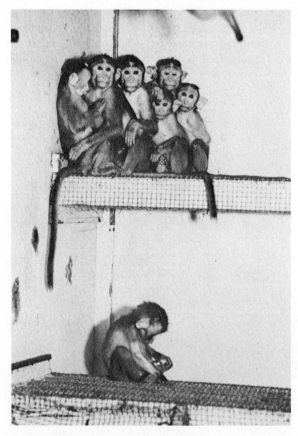

FIGURE 6.   Bonnet juveniles in a characteristic contact huddle; a pigtail juvenile sits
alone.

more striking, and also evident from the figure, was the almost exclusive confinement of contact behavior to members of the same species, even though most conspecifics were strange to one another, having been drawn from several separate groups. Throughout the 14 weeks of observations, interspecific contacts averaged only about 10% of the total contact behavior observed. Although contact and huddling appeared quite rapidly in this group because the juveniles had just been removed from their mothers and social groups, social play initiation did not appear for some weeks. Figure 8 reveals, nonetheless, that after about 6 weeks social play in both species increased considerably. However the social separation of the juveniles of these two species was virtually complete. Despite the ready availability of heterospecific age mates, initiation of play with members of the opposite species was rarely observed in either bonnets or pigtails.

It is worth noting that whereas bonnet juveniles established high levels of contact and sustained interaction with conspecifics from the very start of the group formation, pigtails spent much greater portions of their day engaged in activities directed toward inanimate objects. Thus during the first half of the study pigtails engaged in more than twice as much inanimate-object exploration and play than bonnets. Pigtails maintained this high level of object activity during the second half of the study, whereas bonnet juveniles increased their scores to about two-thirds those of their pigtail counterparts. Thus the relative propensity toward socially directed activity in bonnets as compared to pigtails was conspicuous throughout the study.

At present we can only suggest the likely impact of ontogenetic as opposed to phylogenetic factors in influencing the differences in behavior in the juveniles of these two species. It is clear nonetheless that when reared in conspecific groups, bonnet and pigtail juveniles have incorporated many of the most cogent features of their species-typical social patterns, even in the absence of an adult structure.

GENDER AND FAMILIARITY IN JUVENILE PEER RELATIONS

In a study nearing completion, a group of bonnet juveniles has been observed, to assess more fully the factors influencing peer interaction. The group consisted of four male and four female subjects, approximately 1½ years old. Previous data from our laboratory indicate that the males were 2½ to 3 years from puberty and the females were 1½ to 2 years from menarche. The subjects were reared in one of two social groups, each consisting of four mothers and their two male and two female offspring. Therefore, each juvenile was familiar with one member of the same sex and two members of the opposite sex prior to the formation of the study group. The observations on which our data are based began one month after group formation, allowing for habituation to the new home pen and new peers.

FIGURE 7.   Contact scores of interspecific group of bonnet and pigtail juveniles.

FIGURE 8.   Social play scores of interspecific group of bonnet and pigtail juveniles.

During the initial phase of this study, consisting of 7 weeks of observation, several significant features of peer interaction emerged. These features are best illustrated by considering two important affiliative behaviors: play and huddling (close physical contact in which one partner holds another with its hand or arm). Figure 9 reveals that males engaged in significantly more social play than did females. Indeed, males displayed more than twice as much social play as was observed between females. However, when considering play as a combination of three categories (i.e., social, exercise, and object-directed behavior), there was no significant difference between male and female scores. Moreover, male and female general activity levels were the same, in spite of the males' higher levels of social interaction (i.e., social play).

The overwhelming proportion of social play occurred between members of the same sex. Heterosexual play occurred only when the socially more playful males initiated brief play bouts with females; females rarely initiated play with males.

Figure 9 also indicates that huddling behavior was even more dramatically restricted along homosexual lines. Although male and female homosexual huddling scores were approximately equal, heterosexual huddling was almost never observed (see Figure 10). Thus in spite of each subject's previous familiarity with two members of the other-sex subgroup, partner choice was primarily restricted to members of the subject's own sex. This homosexual preference was also evident in other behavior scores, such as passive contact and grooming.

A second factor in partner choice, familiarity during prior rearing, played a more important role within the female subgroup than within the male

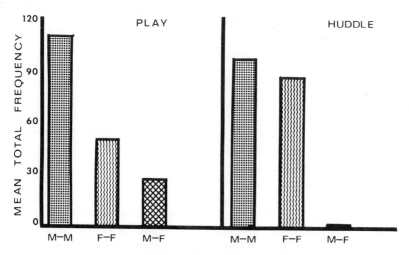

FIGURE 9. Social play and huddling frequencies for the group of bonnet juveniles (M–M = males with males; F–F = females with females; M–F = males with females).

FIGURE 10. Sexually segregated huddling of male and female bonnet juveniles (males on right, females on left).

subgroup. As reflected in Figure 11, females huddled exclusively with the previously familiar female partner. Males, however, exhibited no consistent preference for huddling with the previously familiar partner. In social play interactions both males and females preferred to play with the previously familiar partner, albeit not exclusively. It is noteworthy, however, that play initiated across sex was not preferentially directed toward previously familiar partners.

This study has not been completed, and we have yet to determine the *sustained* role of gender and familiarity factors in shaping the course of peer relations in juveniles in the absence of an adult structure. Nonetheless, it appears reasonable to suggest the following hypotheses on the basis of this and the previously reported mixed-species studies, as well as related investigations of other species reported in the literature (Burton, 1972; Erwin et al., 1974; Sackett, 1970; Simonds, 1974): (*a*) monkey infants generally show a preference for peer interactions with members of their own species, (*b*) within-species interactions among juveniles are likely to be markedly restricted to members of the same sex, and (*c*) for both males and females, prior familiarity with partners will increase the likelihood of interaction to some degree, with females being less likely to engage in sustained interaction with unfamiliar peers than are males.

ABNORMAL EFFECTS OF EXCLUSIVE PEER RELATIONS IN INFANCY

Before we close this discussion on the effects of social milieu gender, and familiarity in shaping the form of peer relations in macaques, it is instructive to examine briefly a very special experimental circumstance for the study of peer relations (Chamove et al., 1973). In an experiment conducted by the senior author and colleagues at the University of Wisconsin Primate Laboratories a number of years ago, newborn rhesus infants were removed from their mothers at birth and shortly thereafter placed with a single peer, with whom they lived continuously during the first half-year of life. Two so-called together-together pairs of this type were created, using four infant females. From the first days of life onward, the strong clinging patterns normally maintained with the mother were directed with great intensity toward each other (see Figure 12). Unlike the clinging patterns observed in infants raised with real or even artificial mother surrogates, the clinging of together-together animals failed to decline during the first half-year of life. Indeed, 6-month-old together-together animals manifested protracted periods of clinging at levels that were unusual even for 1- or 2-month-old infants raised with a more normal maternal attachment figure. As one concomitant of the aberrant levels of clinging in together-together infants, the subjects were significantly retarded in the development of social play as compared with infants having more normal opportunities for peer interaction.

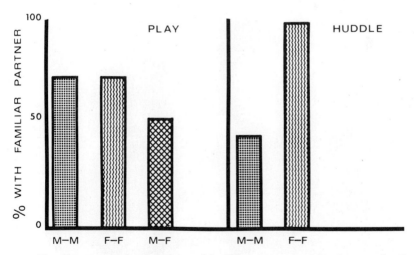

FIGURE 11.   Percentage of social play and huddling scores occurring between familiar partners (M–M = males with males; F–F = females with females; heterosexual huddling did not occur).

During the first 6 months of life, we housed each of the original together-together pairs as a dyad, permitting only brief daily exposure to the other together-together dyad in a social test situation. As reflected in Figure 13, social interactions during this period were almost entirely limited to clinging with the original together-together partner. Early in the second half-year of life, however, the two original together-together dyads were crossed, such that each animal was now paired with a member of the other dyad. Both newly constituted dyads lived alone for 2 weeks prior to the renewal of social testing. As indicated in Figure 13, when the subjects were tested in the playroom for 2 weeks, clinging with the original partner disappeared completely, whereas extremely high levels of mutual clinging between the members of the newly constituted dyads prevailed. Thus despite the prolonged and extremely intense relationship between the original together-together partners, these subjects showed a great readiness to transfer clinging behavior to a relatively strange peer after only 2 weeks of living together.

To assess further the relative endurance of the initial bond, each of the four subjects was then housed individually for an additional 2-week period; all four subjects then received 2 further weeks of social testing while individual housing continued. Under conditions of individual housing, there was a marked though incomplete reassertion of clinging with the original partner and a very dramatic though not complete disappearance of clinging with the new partner (third portion of Figure 13). Throughout the study no clinging whatsoever appeared with

FIGURE 12.   Mutual clinging of a young together-together pair.

FIGURE 13. Clinging levels of together-together partners during social tests following three living conditions.

the so-called indifferent partner (i.e., between together-together subjects that never lived together).

This study points to two significant dimensions of the development of peer relations, neither of them well understood at present. First, it is evident that exclusive interaction with a single peer is not a substitute for such a relationship with a maternal figure; nor does it provide the stimulation for normal social development afforded by opportunities for even limited social interaction with numerous peers (Rosenblum, 1961). Second, when reared with only a single partner and with relatively limited access to others, subjects may remain quite ready to transfer their intense attachment behavior to other appropriate partners. A possible explanation for this finding may be found in current work in our laboratory on the recognition of mother and the response to strangers in macaque infants. This work suggests that during restricted rearing an infant may have inadequate opportunity to learn to differentiate its primary attachment figure from other conspecifics. This deficiency in social discrimination may facilitate a readiness to move toward strangers, to a degree not seen in infants raised in more complex social environments (Rosenblum & Alpert, in press).

THE SOCIAL MILIEU: SQUIRREL MONKEY GROUPS

We turn our attention now to a series of related studies carried out on the squirrel monkey (*Saimiri sciureus*), a common South American primate.

FIGURE 14.   A group of squirrel monkey mothers and their dorsally clinging infants in a characteristic aggregation.

Several salient features of the behavior and development of this small New World primate are pertinent to the material presented next (see Table 1). Although the animals weigh about 100 grams at birth and less than a kilogram at adulthood, length of gestation in squirrel monkeys is quite similar to that of the larger macaques, lasting about 5½ months. Similarly, sexual maturation is achieved at about the same age as in macaques, females becoming reproductively active during their third year and males about a year later. Despite these similarities, infant squirrel monkeys progress substantially more rapidly toward independent functioning than do their macaque counterparts. Thus by about 5 months of age, when macaques still spend much of their time clinging to mother, the squirrel monkey infant is rarely observed on the dorsal surface of the mother (in squirrel monkeys, this position corresponds to the ventral clinging of the macaque infant). Similarly, after about the third month nipple contact declines rapidly in squirrel monkeys and weaning is virtually complete by the end of the first half-year (Rosenblum, 1968). Squirrel monkey adults are extremely gregarious, although not indiscriminately so, as discussed below, and contact huddles and close proximity between many individuals is frequently observed (see Figure 14). Similarly, the squirrel monkey mother usually allows ready access to her young infant by other females in the group, and under appropriate group conditions such infants generally receive frequent and prolonged care from one or more other members of the group who act as "aunts" (Rosenblum, 1973).

EARLY PEER RELATIONS: THE ROLES OF SOCIAL MILIEU AND GENDER

In squirrel monkeys, as in bonnets, the first elements of peer interaction often emerge while infants still maintain contact with their mother. The close huddling of squirrel monkey mothers, each with an infant perched on her back, facilitates such early peer interaction. Initial forms of rudimentary contact play involve tugging, clasping, and pushing of partners, but also a good deal of mutual, frequently competitive exploration and play with inanimate objects in the environment. As infants continue to move away from the mother, play patterns including elaborate chasing and wrestling bouts are more prolonged and frequent and involve an increasing diversity of behavioral elements (see Figure 15). Observations made in a number of complex group settings suggest that play develops more rapidly and reaches higher levels in male squirrel monkey infants as compared with females. As a result of what appear to be the complementary effects of generally higher levels of play in males and a developing

FIGURE 15. The initiation of play by a young squirrel monkey juvenile.

preference of males to play among themselves, social play between pairs and larger groupings of young males are observed most frequently. After about 2 months of age, when observed in sexually balanced groups of at least four males and four females, males increasingly engage in homosexually oriented play; thus by 5 months of age, two-thirds of all male play involves other males (see Figure 16). The tendency of females to initiate play was maintained at relatively lower levels. As a result, they do not play among themselves as often as males, but an increasing proportion of female play occurs when bouts are initiated with them by male infants of the group.

These differences in male and female peer interactions are further enhanced when there is increased complexity of the social and physical environment within which infants are raised. After about 3 months of life, male squirrel monkey infants have been found to move more readily from their mother and to engage more frequently in autonomous activity and social interaction than do female infants under conditions designed to enhance general arousal (Rosenblum, 1974).

FAMILIARITY AND JUVENILE PEER RELATIONS

In addition to the effects of the gender of infants on the form of peer interaction in squirrel monkeys, the element of familiarity between peers plays an im-

FIGURE 16. The percentage of social play involving partners of the same sex in male and female squirrel monkeys during the first 20 weeks of life.

portant role (Rosenblum & Lowe, 1971). To assess the role of familiarity in squirrel monkey peer interaction, we composed a group of eight male and seven female laboratory-born juveniles. Prior to this study the infants had been reared by their mothers in four separate groups containing five, four, four, and two infants, respectively. All subjects were removed from their mothers before being brought together for this study. To allow for whatever degree of segregation the subgroups sought to maintain, the investigators used a specially constructed chamber that contained six individual compartments each about 46 cm wide along the back wall of the pen.

Agonistic behavior between these subjects, although present to some degree in the first week of observations, rapidly declined to very low levels. Social play showed a rapid, five-fold increase during the first 6 weeks of observation. As this play increased, it became evident that although there was a preference for play with members of the same rearing subgroup, play did not exclude participation of relatively strange peers. Even in the first week 26% of play was between members of different subgroups. Play scores varied from week to week, but by the end of the first month of group formation, nearly half of all play observed involved members of different subgroups.

The readiness to interact with strange peers, manifest in the play scores, was not in evidence in other forms of interaction that were recorded. At first huddle groups were virtually exclusively comprised of members of the same subgroup, with one interesting exception. Almost immediately following group formation, the smallest subgroup, which contained only two subjects, fused with one of the subgroups of four. Little overt agonism emerged, and by the end of the first day of testing, huddling and contact between the new subgroup of six showed little that distinguished it from the other rearing subgroups. The six subjects of this new subgroup interacted frequently between themselves and in general avoided all but play interactions with the members of the other remaining subgroups. We have no information to explain this rapid subgroup fusion, but it seems likely that a subgroup of two may be unable to establish and maintain the protection of a given huddling area, or to provide its members with the degree of positive social stimulation found in the larger group huddles that usually characterize the behavior of this species.

The formation of group huddles and the contact patterns of individuals within them were quite rigidly restricted during the first several weeks of the study. During the six weeks of observation, fewer than 20% of the huddling scores involved partners not of the individual's own subgroup. Physical contact between adjacent animals within the huddles was even more exclusive. In addition to their preferences regarding contact and huddle composition, the subgroup members initially were quite active in preventing members of other subgroups from occupying the same chamber with them. Initially 92.5% of same-chamber scores were within subgroups. However these scores declined significantly during the 6 weeks of initial observation, and only 58.8% of the same-chamber scores were between members of the same subgroup at the end of the 6 weeks.

The initial observations of this study demonstrated no clear sexual differentiations. Except for the unexplained fusion of a small group to one of the larger subgroups, prior familiarity played the primary role in organizing peer interactions with these animals. A partial though progressive decrease in the exclusiveness of interaction was observed in the course of the initial 6-week observation. Almost immediately, subjects showed some degree of readiness to play with nonfamiliar peers. Next, members of separate subgroups gradually spent more time within the same enclosed areas of the chamber. Finally, some degree of huddling, albeit on infrequent occasions, occurred between members of distinct subgroups.

Fourteen months after the initial observations, follow-up data on the remaining members of the group were obtained. Unfortunately five subjects of the group died accidentally prior to follow-up observations. These follow-up observations, made when subjects were more than 2 years old, indicated that although strong subgroup preferences remained, sexual factors had begun to emerge. Females at this age now showed significantly less social play than did males. Furthermore, two of the remaining females, each a member of a different subgroup, were now spending significant periods of time in contact with each other. It is noteworthy, however, that in two of the remaining subgroups, each containing three males, more than 84% of observed physical contact was obtained between members of the same subgroups. As in the initial observations, social play was relatively nondiscriminating with regard to subgroup origins.

This study and the one discussed earlier on peer interaction and familiarity in bonnets, along with a series of related reports in the literature (Erwin & Flett, 1974; Hansen, Harlow, & Dodsworth, 1966; Suomi, Harlow, & Domek, 1970) indicate that in a variety of nonhuman primate species, familiarity between peers may be strongly influential in organizing the pattern of peer interaction prior to puberty. It also seems likely that well before puberty, at points in development not well understood at present but clearly influenced by species and environmental conditions of rearing and testing, the factors related to gender of the subjects grow increasingly important.

SOCIAL STRUCTURE AND THE DEVELOPMENT OF SEXUALLY SEGREGATED PEER RELATIONS

It comes as no surprise that prior familiarity between peers facilitates various aspects of their social interaction. Under normal conditions the entire development of social behavior occurs within a relatively constant, cohesively organized conspecific group. As we demonstrated with macaques at the beginning of the chapter, the character of the functional organization of that social group can very significantly affect infant socialization. In the course of their interaction with peers and adults, young animals must ultimately develop the species-characteristic behavior patterns and subsequently become integrated into the adult group structure. If this developmental process is to be understood in the appropriate context, we must first describe some of the structural dynamics that organize adult behavior. To determine the developmental course of the internalization of this social information, it is also necessary to study young animals both with and without adults present. During the last several years we have carried out a series of studies using the squirrel monkey as a model to study the role of adult social structure in influencing progressive changes in peer interactions and socialization of the developing young.

In the rain forests in South America, squirrel monkeys are usually found in large multimale aggregations in which the females are more numerous (Baldwin, 1968, 1971). The field observations on squirrel monkeys generally indicate that the males of the troop remain spatially separate from the females. Spatial and social segregation of the sexes among squirrel monkeys has also been demonstrated in laboratory settings, and under these conditions heterosexual interactions are relatively infrequent and often agonistic (Mason & Epple, 1968; Candland et al., 1973; Fairbanks, 1974).

Most observers agree the adult females of the troop are most active in initiating the affiliative and agonistic encounters that ultimately determine the spatial relations between adult squirrel monkeys. The relatively more passive males show strong preferences for homosexual aggregations and essentially avoid all other members of the troop. Although the extent of sexual segregation may vary at different times of the year, the males remain a distinctly separate subgroup even during the relatively well demarcated breeding season (Coe & Rosenblum, 1974).

The laboratory studies discussed below were designed to assess systematically the aggregation and dispersion tendencies of adult male and female squirrel monkeys and to determine experimentally the degree to which preadult subjects are influenced in the patterns of their interaction by the nature of this adult structure. Using a cross-sectional approach, we studied groups at specific age points, considering each age class to be divided into one subgroup of males and another of females. In light of the significance of spatial dispersion between the sexes in the adults, the spatial distribution of each age class served as a basic measure of its interactional structure as well as a variable that could be altered by interaction with a particular adult structure.

The three groups of monkeys used in these studies each contained five males and five females and were classified as adults, subadults, and juveniles, respectively. All adults were wild born and well acclimated to the laboratory prior to testing; subadults and juveniles were laboratory born and approximately 3 and 2 years of age, respectively, at the beginning of testing. As mentioned earlier, laboratory-reared females reach puberty at about 3 years, whereas males mature at about 4 years of age. Prior to testing, adult subjects were unfamiliar with others of the same sex; many of the subadults were familiar with one another, as were many of the juveniles, but none of the younger subjects were familiar with any of the adults before the experiments.

All observations were made within identical experimental living areas, which consisted of two symmetrical pens connected by a tunnel 7 in. in diameter. Each pen contained four tiers of shelves equally spaced near the back wall and a large one-way glass window in the front wall through which all observations were made. Within each pen, the arrangement of perches was designed to facilitate the recording of animal locations and the computation of interanimal distances. The simultaneous locations of all subjects within a pen were recorded on schematic spatial diagrams, completed nine times a week spread across three experimental days. Computer analysis allowed us to determine the pen location of each subject and its weekly mean distance in centimeters from each type of partner. Interanimal distances were based only on occasions when subjects were within the same pen, since the distribution of subjects between pens represented a psychological distance that was analyzed separately. In addition to the spatial diagrams completed during each observation, behavioral observations were obtained on the form of interaction between the subjects of the different sex and age groupings. These three per week samples involved 100 seconds of continuous observation of each subject in the group, in random order, during which the frequency and duration of a variety of behaviors were recorded. Inasmuch as overt aggressive behavior between subjects was rare, the two counterposed behaviors offering the most information regarding the dynamics of the spacing patterns observed were: *huddle,* which was recorded when one subject sat crouched while maintaining close contact with a partner, and *displace,* a behavior involving a subject's movement away (at least 26 cm) in immediate response to the approach or aggressive behavior of a partner.

The studies involved two discrete phases, the first on single-age groups and the second on mixed-age groups. During the first phase the adult group was observed for 3 weeks and the subadult and juvenile groups were each observed for 4 weeks. Next the subadult and juvenile groups were each merged separately with the adult group, and the social interactions of these mixed-age groups were observed for 3 weeks. In both cases the adult group was removed after the mixed-age observations, and the subadult and juvenile groups were observed for one more week, to assess any residual effects resulting from the experience of living with the adults.

When the adult subjects were observed alone, the spatial separation of the sexes emerged almost immediately and was maintained throughout the observations. Figure 17 gives the degree to which subjects were closer to (positive scores) or further from (negative scores) same-sex versus opposite-sex partners. The figure indicates that the average distance between adults of the same sex was significantly smaller than that between adults of the opposite sex. Despite the distinct separation of the sexes when within the same pen, as reflected in Figure 17, the tendency to separate did not result in consistent occupancy of different pens by the two sexes. This may be indicative of a continued motivation of males and females to remain integrated within a sphere of potential interaction, while nonetheless maintaining an appreciable degree of spatial separation. Thus the adult male and female subgroups, although spatially separate, were not functioning as independent social units.

The conclusions drawn from the spatial distribution of adult subjects were

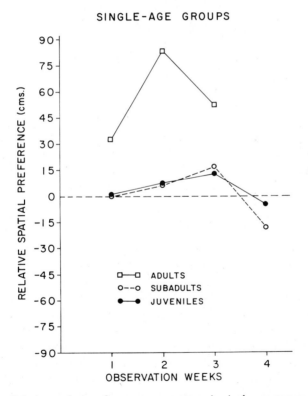

FIGURE 17. Relative preference for same-sex partners in single-age groups as indicated by differences in average distance scores. Positive scores reflect a greater proximity with same-sex animals.

supported by the behavioral observations as well. Male-male huddling occurred during 19% of the observation time; females huddled together significantly more—during 45% of the observations. Huddling between males and females, on the other hand, was totally absent. Dispersal of the males and females was also maintained and reinforced by the intermittent but consistent female displacement of the males. Each male received more displacement from females than he initiated across the 3 weeks of observation, and the displaced males usually sustained the spatial separation from the rejecting females.

Observations of the single-age groupings of subadults and then of juveniles failed to yield any evidence of the type of sexual segregation manifested by the adults. As indicated in Figure 17, the young monkeys of the same and opposite sexes were virtually equidistant from one another. On the average, subadults were 75 cm from monkeys of the same sex and 76 cm from monkeys of the opposite sex. Juveniles of the same sex were an average 93 cm apart, in fact, 3 cm further than the average distance between animals of the opposite sex.

Behavioral observations also reflected the absence of sexual segregation in the subadult and juvenile groups. Indeed, positive interactions between the sexes were common in these two groups. The total time spent in homosexual and heterosexual huddling was quite similar although rather infrequent in both groups. The amounts of hetero- and homosexual displacements were also similar. However the displacements that were observed in juvenile and subadult groups usually occurred in the course of social play and did not result in sustained increases in distances between partners. There were some indications of sex differences in the frequencies of play, but these did not result in the spatial separation of the sexes.

Following the observations of the single-age groups, the subadult group was merged with the adult group. At the conclusion of this mixed-age group observation, the subadults were removed and the juvenile group was merged with the adults. In each merger the adult monkeys continued to maintain their original, sexually segregated pattern (see Figure 18). As before, same-sex distances among the adults were less than half those recorded between subjects of the opposite sex. Displacement and huddling patterns among the adults were also similar to those observed in the single-age observations.

Despite the relative similarities between juvenile and subadult behavior when observed in single-age groups, in the presence of the adult structure the subadults responded very differently from the juveniles. Beginning in the second week of mixed-age groupings, the subadults overcame their fear of the strange adults and increasingly approached them. From this point on two factors influenced the subsequent relationship of the subadults to the adults and ultimately the pattern of interaction within the subadult group itself. First, the subadults, primarily the females, revealed a strong motivation to approach the adults. Second, the adults responded differently to the approaches of subadults

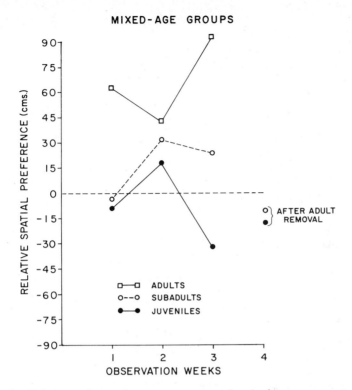

FIGURE 18.   Relative preference for same-sex partners in mixed-age groups as indicated by differences in average distance scores. Positive scores reflect a greater proximity with animals of the same sex and age. Note that the fourth-week points for subadults and juveniles are after adult removal.

of their own and opposite sex. Adult females gradually became more accepting of the approaches of subadult females than those of the young males. The adult males, though still quite reticent regarding the approaches of subadults, gradually appeared to be more accepting of the presence of the subadult males. Because of these factors, the distances between the subadults and adults of the same sex showed a significant decrease of about 50 cm after the first week of merger. At the same time there was a correspondingly significant increase of 11 cm in the distance between subadults and adults of the opposite sex (see Figure 19).

The progressive emergence of positive interaction between adults and subadults of the same sex had a dramatic impact on the interactive structure of the subadult group. As Figure 18 reveals, the spatial organization of the subadult group underwent a remarkable alteration. As the subadults became closer to same-sex adults and further from opposite-sex adults, there was a correspond-

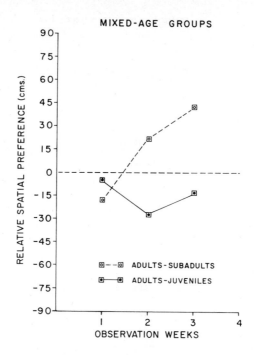

FIGURE 19.   Relative preference of younger animals for same-sex adults as indicated by differences between same-sex and opposite-sex distance scores. Positive scores reflect a greater proximity with same-sex adults.

ing increase in the distances maintained between male and female subadults. During the second and third weeks of mixed group observation, a sexually segregated subadult distribution emerged. The opposite-sex distances between the subadults reached 108 cm, which was significantly greater than the average distance of 84 cm between same-sex subjects. However, as indicated in Figure 18, when the segregated adult structure was removed, the newly emerged subadult pattern of sexual segregation immediately reverted to the undifferentiated clustering that had previously been observed.

Unlike the subadults, the juvenile group, when observed in the presence of the adult social structure, exhibited no consistent change in social orientation. Although the juveniles also began to overcome their fear of the adults after the first week of mixed-age testing, they did not sustain their approaches consistently. In addition, the adults did not have the same tolerance for juveniles of either sex as they had for subadults. As a consequence, the adults and juveniles maintained relatively large distances from one another during the 3 weeks of observation: Juveniles were an average of 132 cm from same-sex adults and an average of 121 cm from opposite-sex adults. Hence in contrast to the changes in subadult behavior when in the presence of adults, the juveniles showed no systematic change in their social organization. In addition to these spatial data, the behavioral observations gave no indication of growing affiliation with adults nor of changes in the juvenile social pattern. Furthermore, the juvenile group also continued to show an undifferentiated spatial distribution following the removal of the adult group (see Figure 18).

These findings suggest that younger squirrel monkeys initially develop the adult pattern of sexual segregation at least in part through a socialization process involving the redirection of social attachments from age peers of both sexes to animals of the same sex. The subadults were strongly attracted toward adult monkeys when available, and through a process of sexual selection by the adults, they readily associated themselves with the adult, segregated structure. The development of segregation in the brief encounter with adults in this study apparently did not create fundamental changes in the social orientation of subadults toward peers that were sustained after adult removal. However it is likely that longer periods of interaction with adults during development would produce more permanent alterations in the pattern of social affiliations. The failure of juveniles to orient in a similar manner in the presence of adults suggests that a certain level of maturation may be necessary for this aspect of socialization to occur.

In addition to the finding that age was a critical factor in the readiness for social change, there was a strong indication that males and females differed in this regard. Subadult females showed a greater readiness to develop interactive and cohesive behavior patterns with same-sex adults, and this tendency may be a precursor of the stronger attachments characteristic of the adult females.

SUMMARY

The results of these experiments support the belief that there is an evolutionary continuity of certain major determinants of peer relations within the Primate Order. The development of an infant's independence from its mother and the concomitant initiation of peer relations is markedly affected by the behavior of the mother. Her behavior can best be understood within the context of a species-specific social milieu. Moreover, the young primate's choice of partners and the varied intensity of its peer relations are also affected by other factors such as the age, species, gender, and familiarity of the animals with whom the subject has the opportunity to interact.

The normal socialization of a primate infant results in the incorporation of that individual into its conspecific social group. The late infancy and juvenile phases of development represent periods of increasing transference of specific attachment to the mother to the establishment of individual relationships of varying intensities with all other group members. The readiness to respond to this more complex array of social partners requires the maturation of appropriate response systems and the prior internalization of relevant social information regarding classes of social agents and differentiation of individuals within such classes. Alterations in the order and duration of critical socialization processes can result in devastating behavioral consequences such as those observed in isolate-reared or "together-together" infants. The attainment of appropriate maturational levels may be a necessary prerequisite for the assimilation of particular socializing events, and the normal chronology of such events may be species-specific. Thus unlike subadults, juvenile squirrel monkeys were unable to participate in a stable adult social structure, provided experimentally. Nonetheless, certain dimensions of sociability may be internalized at an early age; juvenile bonnet and pigtail macaques behave in the species-specific manner with regard to spacing and play patterns even when observed in the absence of adults.

Apparently the sexually dimorphic roles of adult male and female primates have their roots early in ontogeny and are progressively elaborated with development. Behavioral differences between the sexes begin to emerge early in life and are maintained even in the absence of adults (Rosenblum, 1961). Although a genetic-prenatal hormone basis for these differences has been suggested (Goy, 1968), there have also been experimental data to suggest that the differences can be enhanced or diminished in various environments (Sackett, 1974; Rosenblum, 1974a and b). These sexual dimorphisms may also be mediated under some circumstances through differential responses of mothers toward infants of the two sexes (Jensen & Bobbitt, 1968).

As infants grow increasingly independent of the mother, sexually dimorphic behaviors become clearer both in the frequency and intensity of various patterns. Moreover, these differences in various behaviors, such as social play, can result in transient or more sustained segregation of the sexes. Sexual segregation—for example, during the juvenile stage of development—has been observed in many monkey species. Moreover, although the formation of sexual subgroups among juveniles is potentially influenced by the adult structure, segregation can occur even in the absence of adults, as was seen in our mixed-sex group of bonnet juveniles.

Another factor that strongly influences juvenile peer relations is prior familiarity of the subjects. Particularly for females, previous association between individuals plays a significant role in the organization of primate social systems. Females reveal a strong preference for familiar associates and an aversion for strangers; such patterns may partially account for the common field report that females tend to stay within their matrilineal social group throughout life. Males, on the other hand, show a much greater readiness to interact with unfamiliar animals (Rosenblum & Alpert, in press). However it is reasonable to conclude that juveniles, whether male or female, are more willing to engage in interaction with strange conspecifics, and certainly manifest less aggression, than is true of their adult counterparts. Indeed, from our studies of both macaques and squirrel monkeys, it appears that one of the functions of the play behavior of juveniles is the mediation of new social attachments with previously unfamiliar animals. Nonetheless, as the diversity of material presented in this chapter indicates, the relative flexibility of juvenile peer relations is not unlimited but is bounded by a consistent set of social limits.

References

Baldwin, J. D. The social behavior of the adult male squirrel monkey in a seminatural environment. *Folia Primatologica,* 1968, **9,** 281–314.

Baldwin, J. D. The social organization of a semi-free-ranging troop of squirrel monkeys. *Folio Primatologica,* 1971, **14,** 23–50.

Burton, F. The integration of biology and behavior in the socialization of *Macaca sylvana* of Gibraltar. In F. E. Poirier (Ed.), *Primate socialization,* New York: Random House, 1972. Pp. 29–63.

Candland, D. K., Tyrrell, D. S., Wagner, D. S., & Wagner, N. M. Social preference of the squirrel monkey. *Folia Primatologica,* 1973, **19,** 437–449.

Chamove, A. S., Rosenblum, L. A., & Harlow, H. F. Monkeys (*Macaca mulatta*) raised only with peers. *Animal Behavior,* 1973, **21,** 316–325.

Coe, C. L., & Rosenblum, L. A. Sexual segregation and its ontogeny in squirrel monkey social structure. *Journal of Human Evolution,* 1974, **3,** 144–154.

Erwin, J., & Flett, M. Responses of rhesus monkeys to reunion after long-term separation: Cross-sexed pairings. *Psychological Reports,* 1974, **35,** 171–174.

Erwin, J., Maple, T., Willott, S., & Mitchell, G. Persistent peer attachments of rhesus monkeys: Responses to reunion after two years of separation. *Psychological Reports,* 1974, **34,** 1179–1183.

Goy, R. W. Organizing effects of androgen on the behavior of rhesus monkeys. In R. P. Michael (Ed.), *Endocrinology and human behavior.* London: Oxford University Press, 1968. Pp. 12–31.

Hansen, E. W., Harlow, H., & Dodsworth, R. Reactions of rhesus monkeys to familiar and unfamiliar peers. *Journal of Comparative and Physiological Psychology,* 1966, **61,** 274–279.

Jensen, G. D., & Bobbitt, R. A. Implications of primate research for understanding infant development. *Science and Psychoanalysis,* 1968, **12,** 55–81.

Kaufman, I. C., & Rosenblum, L. A. The reaction to separation in infant monkeys: Anaclitic depression and conservation-withdrawal. *Psychosomatic Medicine,* 1967, **29,** 648–675.

Mason, W. A., & Epple, G. Social organization in experimental groups of *Saimiri* and *Callicebus. Proceedings of the Second International Congress on Primatology,* Atlanta, Ga., Vol. 1. Basel and New York: Karger 1968. Pp. 59–65.

Rosenblum, L. A. The development of social behavior in the rhesus monkey. Unpublished doctoral dissertation, University of Wisconsin, Madison, 1961.

Rosenblum, L. A. Mother-infant relations and early behavior development in the squirrel monkey. In L. A. Rosenblum & R. W. Cooper (Eds.), *The squirrel monkey*. New York: Academic Press, 1968. Pp. 207–233.

Rosenblum, L. A. The ontogeny of mother-infant relations in macaques. In H. Moltz (Ed.), *The ontogeny of vertebrate behavior*. New York: Academic Press, 1971a. Pp. 315–367.

Rosenblum, L. A. Kinship interaction patterns in pigtail and bonnet macaques. In J. Biegert (Ed.), *Proceedings of the third International Congress of Primatology*. Basel: Karger, 1971b. Pp. 79–84.

Rosenblum, L. A. Maternal relations of infant social interactions. In C. R. Carpenter (Ed.), *Social regulatory mechanisms of primates*. Philadelphia: University of Pennsylvania Press, 1973. Pp. 195–217.

Rosenblum, L. A. Sex differences, environmental complexity and mother-infant relations. *Archives of Sexual Behavior,* 1974a, **3,** 117–128.

Rosenblum, L. A. Sex differences in mother-infant attachment in monkeys. In R. C. Friedman, R. M. Richart, & R. L. Vande Wiele (Eds.), *Sex differences in behavior*. New York: Wiley, 1974b. Pp. 123–142.

Rosenblum, L. A., & Lowe, A. C. The influence of familiarity during rearing on subsequent partner preferences in squirrel monkeys. *Psychonomic Science,* 1971, **23,** 35–37.

Rosenblum, L. A., & Alpert, S. Response to mother and stranger: a first step in socialization. In J. Chevalier-Skolnikoff & F. Poirier (Eds.), *Primate Socialization*. New York: Aldine. In press.

Rosenblum, L. A., Kaufman, I. C., & Stynes, A. J. Individual distance in two species of macaque. *Journal of Animal Behavior,* 1964, **12,** (2 & 3), 338–342.

Rosenblum, L. A., Kaufman, I. C., & Stynes, A. J. Interspecific variations in the effects of hunger on diurnally varying behavior elements in macaques. *Brain, Behavior, and Evolution,* 1969, **2,** 119–131.

Sackett, G. P. Unlearned responses, differential rearing experiences, and the development of social attachment by rhesus monkeys. In L. A. Rosenblum (Ed.), *Primate behavior: Developments in field and laboratory research*, Volume 1. New York: Academic Press, 1970. Pp. 112–140.

Sackett, G. P. Sex differences in rhesus monkeys following varied rearing experiences. In R. C. Friedman, R. M. Richart, & R. L. Vande Wiele (Eds.), *Sex differences in behavior*. New York: Wiley, 1974. Pp. 99–122.

Simonds, P. Sex differences in bonnet macaque networks and social structure. *Archives of Sexual Behavior,* 1974, **3** (2), 151–167.

Suomi, S. J., Harlow, H. F., & Domek, C. J. Effects of repetitive infant-infant separation of young monkeys. *Journal of Abnormal Psychology,* 1970, **76,** 161–172.

CHAPTER 4

Relations Among Infants and Juveniles in Comparative Perspective[1]

MELVIN KONNER

Department of Psychology and Social Relations
Harvard University

"Relations among infants and juveniles" is a somewhat more broadly conceived subject than "peer relations in infancy." The latter subject will undoubtedly prove interesting, but it can be seen from what follows that the task of this chapter—to provide a comparative perspective—could not have been attempted under the narrower subject heading. This is because species, as well as populations within species, vary in the extent to which peer relations occur. They may also vary in the extent to which relations among infants and juveniles in general are important, but this is saying something else. We need to be very much aware that even in species in which relations among infants and juveniles *are* important, the relations need not be among *peers*.

Indeed, the focus of the conference [on peer relations and friendship] is questionable. In man, the species of greatest interest for most of the participants, and in the species most closely related to man, relations between and among peers are of small importance compared with relations among nonpeer juveniles. Observations of human behavioral development in the anomalous circumstances of the advanced industrial state have given investigators an exaggerated sense of the importance of peers per se in development. In the strict sense, peers are unknown in man's environment of evolutionary adaptedness and in that of his closest relatives, the Pongidae. One has to be beyond the apes to terrestrial Old World monkeys to find prominent peer relations; and these are animals so distantly related to man that we may not have shared a common ancestor for 40 million years.

To establish adequately the comparative context for relations among infants and juveniles, four steps are necessary. First, set out the conditions under which natural selection may be expected to favor such relations, in their various

[1] This chapter was written while the author was a fellow of the Foundations Fund for Research in Psychiatry. He is grateful to Maxwell Katz, Ronnie Wenker, and Marjorie Shostak for help with data collection and analysis, and to N. G. Blurton Jones, Irven DeVore, Sarah Blaffer Hrdy, John Whiting, and Jeffrey Kurland for helpful discussion and criticism. Unfortunately for the author, these friends cannot be made to share with him the burden of his follies.

possible forms. Second, review the phylogeny of such relations among mammals. Third, consider such relations in man's environment of evolutionary adaptedness. Fourth, consider the changes such relations have undergone as the species has entered different, including anomalous, environments.

NATURAL SELECTION

Two components of natural selection are usefully separated for purposes of analysis. The one that comes most quickly to mind is differential viability. Some individuals are more likely than others to die and are said to be less well adapted. It should be noticed, as it often is not, that selection through differential viability operates at each stage of the life cycle from before conception to the end of the breeding period, not just at maturity. Consequently an immature individual is constantly balancing two forms of viability—the necessity to survive currently, and the necessity to develop toward viability at maturity. There may be tension between these forms of viability, as in an obvious case—when becoming "tied to a parent's apron strings" may improve current viability but reduce it ultimately. Much more subtle interactions are possible, and when it is considered that each life-cycle stage may affect all subsequent ones, the balance of selective effects may be very complex.

It is useful also to introduce the concept of a *selection funnel*, a stage of the life cycle in which mortality is very high and in which selection consequently may operate more intensively. A sufficiently intense selection produces optimal viability at this stage, even though in the life of the individual the adaptation necessary may result in suboptimal viability at later stages. Selection funnels may be as common as the reverse case, in which an adaptively neutral feature of the juvenile, such as play, results in improved viability in the adult.

In spite of its complexity, however, differential viability is only half the picture of natural selection. In fact, if a population were to have strictly uniform viability—if all the individuals died at the same age—evolution would still proceed apace, by means of sexual selection. Although viability were uniform, reproductive success—the number of offspring left to the subsequent generation—would vary, because sexual attractiveness and sexual effectiveness would vary. If we add to our model population the possibility of death during infancy, we have another source of variability—differential caretaking effectiveness. Thus in addition to balancing current against future viability, the immature individual must balance both factors against future sexual attractiveness, sexual effectiveness, caretaking effectiveness, and other influences on reproductive process. Again, these effects may sometimes be in opposition. An individual may die young, but leave so many offspring that selection favors his genotype in spite of his early death. To win at selection roulette means only to maximize surviving offspring, a complex sum of all these selective effects.

Three types of relations among infants and juveniles may be observed in higher primates under natural conditions: (1) juvenile or subadult alloparental behavior, (2) play relations among unrelated or distantly related juveniles, sometimes peers, and (3) play relations among sibs, half-sibs, and cousins, usually of different ages. Selection is expected to favor each of the three forms under different circumstances and for different reasons. They are discussed here in the abstract, and their natural distribution considered below in the phylogenetic review. It should be noted that many gradations among the three forms are possible.

1. Juvenile or subadult alloparental behavior will be favored by selection for several reasons (Hrdy, in press). If the juvenile caretaker is related to the infant, the caretaking behavior will be selected for precisely as parental behavior is selected for, by improving the likelihood of the spread of the genes responsible (Trivers, 1972, 1974). This follows the rule of inclusive fitness (Hamilton, 1964), by which altruistic behaviors are favored in proportion to the degree of relatedness between the altruist and the benefactor; the degree of relatedness determines the likelihood that the "altruism gene" is also located in the benefactor. From the viewpoint of selection, I may as well save my brother and sister as myself, since because each is related to me by a concordance of 0.5, the probability that one of them will have the altruism gene is unity.

If, on the other hand, the infant is unrelated to me, I may improve my status in the group (and my reproductive success) by the caretaking, through agonistic buffering. This mechanism, repeatedly observed in monkeys, results in an increase in the status of individuals carrying infants, whether their own or adopted (Itani, 1959; Hagen, 1974). If I am male and the infant is unrelated to me, I may be improving my reproductive success (RS) by grooming a future mate. This is the mechanism by which hamadryas baboons build their harems (Kummer, 1968), and it may occur in Japanese monkeys as well (Itani, 1959). It certainly occurs in a number of non-Western human groups (Marshall, 1959), and Spock's warning against boys as baby-sitters (1968, p. 568), for reasons related to their sexuality, suggests that the possibility lurks close to the surface even in Western civilizations.

Another grim possibility that may be favored by selection if infant and juvenile are unrelated, or are siblings whose births were so close together that they endanger each other's survival, is "aunting to death." In this pattern an individual adopts an infant and keeps it neglectfully but decisively until it dies. Sublethal deleterious aunting has been observed in free-ranging Indian langur monkeys (Hrdy, in press). The procedure affords the nulliparous female a chance to practice mothering and may function to reduce competition for scarce resources. As for rivalry between siblings whose births are closely spaced, there is no dearth of data (Mussen et al., 1969, p. 500; Henry & Henry, 1944). Among the !Kung San of the Kalahari Desert, a 3-year-old girl held her infant brother on her lap and played with him charmingly until she grew bored and stood up abruptly, allowing the baby to roll to the ground, a fall that could have been quite dangerous. In spontaneous speech and in doll play she gave evidence of strong violent feelings toward him. As we see later, most caretaking by !Kung infants' older siblings is quite the reverse of this, but the anecdote suggests what may happen if the normal (4-year) birth spacing is deliberately or inadvertently not observed.

Finally, regardless of whether I am related to the infant, if I am female in any mammalian species, or male in species with high male parental investment, the behavior improves my RS by affording me practice. In rats (Moltz, 1969; Herrenkohl & Sachs, 1974), mice (Noirot, 1965, 1969a, 1969b), hamsters (Richards, 1965), rhesus monkeys (Harlow & Suomi, 1971, Suomi et al., 1972), and man, experience with infants improves later parental behavior, and this is true for males as well as females (Redican & Mitchell, 1973).

2. Play relations among unrelated or distantly related individuals are favored because they afford practice not specifically of parental behaviors but of sexual and agonistic behaviors that form the basis of RS. Evolution is opportunistic and follows the path of least resistance. Selection cannot create systems that will develop independent of continuously present features of the environment of the species. It could not create a visual system in cats that would develop independently of light and pattern input, since kittens and their ancestors have never grown up in darkness. Consequently raising them without this input results in blindness or other defects (Wiesel & Hubel, 1965; Hirsch & Spinelli, 1970). Similarly, the normal development of the sexual, agonistic, and parental behavior neuroendocrine systems in higher primates was selected to permit normal growth only in the presence of play groups of other juveniles, and in the absence of play groups these systems emerge defective (Harlow & Harlow, 1965). These and other functions of play, such as exercise and "vacuum activity," have been proposed in reviews of the literature; all seem to have some merit (Loizos, 1966; Lorenz, 1965; Bekoff, 1972).

3. Relations among siblings, half-siblings, and cousins of various ages constitute the third pattern found among higher primates. Selection pressure favoring them arises from the same considerations outlined in relation to play groups and juvenile alloparental behavior, with two additional refinements. First, since the juvenile is not "saddled" with the infant but is merely part of a play group that includes the infant, the cost to the juvenile is less, while the benefit to the infant, who is protected from harm by the group as a whole, is the same. So is the benefit the juvenile derives from practicing parental behavior. Second, the benefit to any play group member for whom there are older individuals around is greater than that which would accrue to him in a peer group, since the things that need to be learned are learned more easily from those a little ahead of oneself than from those, so to speak, in the same

quagmire. On this ground only the oldest members of the group would be selected to resist, and one may expect this tendency to be more than balanced, for females, by the chance to practice parental behavior. One would have to predict that such groups will consist of younger juveniles and infants of both sexes and older juveniles who are mainly females, with the males exhibiting earlier centrifugal tendencies. This, we learn, is in fact the case.

For these reasons natural selection will be expected to favor the multiage play group over the peer group and over full-blown juvenile caretaking wherever other factors make this possible.

ECOLOGY AND PHYLOGENY

Given the general forces provided by selection, the specific nature and the extent of early social relations depend on ecological factors and on the animal's phylogeny. The ecological factors affect population density, demographic structure, fertility and consequent birth spacing, seasonality of breeding, time available for social interaction, and danger to infants and juveniles. Phylogeny affects litter size, speed of growth, and complexity and lability of the nervous system. These effects are illustrated by reviewing the natural history of these early behaviors in mammals. Allusion is made at the same time to laboratory investigations pointing to probable function.

Rodents

Rodents are born in litters and consequently are selected for dependency of normal development on a peer group of siblings. In spite of the rapidity of their attainment of sexual maturity (usually on the order of a number of weeks), a substantial experimental literature shows rodent neural and endocrine systems to be labile with respect to early social contact and other forms of early stimulation. In rats, social isolation after weaning results in reduced weight and thickness of the neocortex, reduced density of dendritic branching, reduced activity of cholinesterase (Rosensweig, 1966; Krech et al., 1966), complex changes in brain monoamine level and turnover (Stolk et al., 1974; Konner, unpublished), and increased susceptibility to induction of stereotyped behaviors by certain drugs (Sahakian, 1974; Konner, unpublished). It also affects gregariousness (Booth, 1973), reduces adult activity and increases defecation in the open-field test (Warren & Ivinskis, 1973), reduces problem-solving ability (Denenberg et al., 1968), and, with later social experience, increases shock-induced fighting (Hutchinson et al., 1965). In mice, such isolation reliably increases aggressiveness in males paired after the isolation (Welch & Welch, 1965; review in Valzelli, 1973), which it does not do in rats; it increases locomotor activity (Essman, 1968), the opposite of its effect in rats, increases stress-induced gastric erosions (Essman, 1966; Essman & Frisone, 1966; Caputo et al., 1968), and decreases the turnover of the neurotransmitters norepinephrine and serotonin in the brain (Essman, 1968; Welch & Welch, 1965). In view of the species differences in behavioral effects of isolation, it is not surprising that recent findings suggest an *increase* in turnover of these transmitters in rats (Stolk et al., 1974; Konner, unpublished). Isolation rearing causes a deficit in sexual behavior in male guinea pigs (Valenstein et al., 1955).

It is clear that although rodent species may share dependency on the sibling group for normal brain and behavior development, there are species-specific patterns of response to deprivation, and it is often difficult to see why. Even subspecies may differ in such effects, as has been shown for two subspecies of the wild deermouse, *Peromysaus maniculatus* (Rosen & Hart, 1963). The subspecies *bairdii* inhabits open fields, exhibits more agonistic behavior, is in greater danger from predators, and develops rapidly. The forest-living subspecies *gracilis* is less excitable and develops more slowly. Normal dominance behavior in *bairdii* is precluded by isolation rearing, whereas the behavior in *gracilis* is little affected. This difference is not surprising insofar as groups are generally less important in forest-living animals free from predation. But it is surprising if one expects more rapidly developing nervous systems to be less input-dependent. This idea is evidently an oversimplification; specific ecologies evidently are important.

Ungulates

Although the ungulates are the most precocial of large mammals, their locomotor systems maturing within a few days of birth, play among infants and juveniles figures in most species. Isolation experiments do not seem to have been done, but observation of sheep and goats (Collias, 1956) suggests that normal adult sexual and dominance behavior emerge gradually from the motor patterns of play among juveniles. (This does not, of course, prove that their emergence is play-dependent.) These ungulates have litters of one, but like most wild ungulates they breed seasonally, assuring that infants and juveniles always have a number of peers available. Extensive juvenile play is observed in elk, bison, chamois, and boar; the only exception among wild ungulates is moose (Altmann, 1958). Moose are unique in being solitary in adulthood. No play among juveniles is possible, although calves do play with their mothers. Since adults are solitary, the necessity for relations among juveniles may be obviated. One would have to predict that isolation would have smaller effects in moose than in other ungulate species. Also, since juveniles in the ungulate peer play groups are more distantly related than siblings in litters, one would have to predict on theoretical grounds (Popp & DeVore, in press) a higher incidence of aggressive play in the former. Aggressive play, such as head-butting, is fairly common, but it is difficult to compare frequencies with those of the occasional aggressive encounters one observes in rodent litters.

Terrestrial Carnivores

Since canids and felines reproduce in litters, sibling peers are always present, and play among the siblings is observed in wolves, coyotes, foxes (Seton, 1953; Bekoff, 1974), dogs (Scott, 1964, 1965), kittens (West, 1974), bears (Henry & Herrero, 1974), and lions (Schenkel, 1966; Schaller, 1972). Such relations are necessary for normal social behavior development in dogs (Scott, 1964, 1965). The mother lioness (Schenkel, 1966) typically participates in and facilitates play-fighting among her offspring. This suggests that simple practice by trial, error, and exercise is not all that is involved and that the mother's participation promotes transmission of information. This hypothesis is supported by the observation that lionesses teach their offspring to hunt (Schenkel, 1966; Schaller, 1972).

Aquatic Carnivores

Good information is available for the Alaska fur seal (Bartholomew, 1959). Mothers abandon their pups about 6 days after birth, which is strictly seasonal, leaving the rookery to return to sea and coming back to the rookery only once a week or so for the rest of the summer. After the mother's departure, pups aggregate into "pods" of dozens or hundreds of age mates (not litter mates), and these groupings persist into adulthood. Early social activities include play-fighting, grooming, and copulatory play, all of which gradually approach adult form. The extremes of aggressiveness and competition among males observed in another seal species (Le Boeuf & Peterson, 1969) may depend on the pattern of socialization in very large peer play groups of unrelated individuals, in which selection can be expected to allow high levels of aggressive interaction. Social behavior in the Steller sea lion also appears to emerge gradually through practice in play group relations (Gentry, 1974).

Primates

Seasonal breeding is characteristic of monkeys (Lancaster & Lee, 1965) and of a number of prosimian species (Martin, 1973; Jolly, 1967). All higher primates breed in litters of one, with the exception of the Callithricidae (South American marmosets and tamarinds), which breed twins. This family, in which males and females pair-bond for life and in which males exhibit an exceptional degree of parental investment (much greater, e.g., than males in our own species) has been very little studied. Most monkeys breed every year or every second year and, depending on group size and population density, there are from a few to a large number of same-age peers who have formed a yearling play group when their mothers are ready to next give birth. Such groups have been described for many species (Table 1). Since in all species in which genealogies are known, the matrilineage has proved to be the core of the higher primate group (Sade, 1967; Koford, 1963; Kawai, 1958; Kawamura, 1958; Goodall, 1967), it is

TABLE 1

Species	Juvenile Alloparental Behavior		Play Group Age Structure		Play Group Sex Structure		Play Group Kin Structure		References
	Female	Male	Non-peer	Peer	Mixed	One only	Sibs only	Non-relative	
Squirrel monkey (*Saimiri sciureus*)	+	−	−	+	+	−	−	+	Baldwin & Baldwin, 1974
Patas monkey (*Erythrocebus patas*)	?	−	+	−	+	−	+	−	Hall, 1968
Hanuman langur (*Presbytis entellus*)	+	−	+	+	+	−	−	+	Jay, 1963; Hrdy, in press
Vervet monkey (*Cercopithecus aethiops*)	+	−	+	+	+	−	−	+	Strusaker, 1967; Lancaster, 1971
Barbary macaque (*Macaca sylvana*)	−	+	+	+	+	−	−	+	Burton, 1971; Deag & Crook, 1971
Hamadryas baboon (*Papio hamadryas*)	−	+	+	+	−	Male	+	−	Kummer, 1968
Savannah baboon (*Papio anubis*)	−	−	(+)	+	+	(Male)	−	+	DeVore, 1963; Hall & DeVore, 1965

Species				Male		Male			Reference
Forest baboon (*Papio anubis*)	−	+	+	+	+	+	+	+	Ransom & Rowell, 1971
Bonnet macaque (*Macaca radiata*)	?	?	+	?	−	+	−	+	Simonds, 1965
Japanese monkey (*Macaca fuscata*)	+	+	+	(+)	−	+	−	+	Itani, 1959; Kurland, unpublished
Rhesus monkey (*Macaca mulatta*)	−	−	−	+	?	+	−	+	Southwick et al., 1965
Howler monkey (*Alouatta villosa*)	−	−	+	−	−	+	−	+	Gaulin, unpublished
White-handed gibbon (*Hylobates lar*)	(+)	?	+	−	−	+	+	−	Ellefson, 1965
Chimpanzee (*Pan troglodytes*)	+	+	+	−	−	+	+	(+)	Goodall, 1967; Nicolson, unpublished
Gorilla (*Pan gorilla*)	?	?	+	−	−	+	+	(+)	Schaller, 1963
Orangutan (*Pongo pygmaeus*)	?	?	(+)	(−)	(−)	(+)	(+)	(−)	Rodman, 1973

107

likely that this pattern will prove to be universal (except in sections of our own species). Because of this pattern, if the total group size is small, most of the juveniles in the play group will be fairly close cousins. As group size increases, however, the likelihood of associations among unrelated juveniles increases correspondingly, and demographic features have been described as determining the observed variations in juvenile play behavior in squirrel monkeys (Baldwin & Baldwin, 1974). Nowhere among primates, except in the Callithricidae and in rare cases of twinning in other species, is same-age sibling relations possible; thus litter mate peer play groups characteristic of rodents and of terrestrial carnivores never appear. Also absent, except for certain populations of our own species, are the large "pods" of dozens of unrelated same-age peers that characterize seal and sea lion rookeries.

Indeed, only the three basic patterns set out previously—juvenile alloparental behavior, nonsibling play groups, and multiage sibling groups—are found. Juvenile alloparental behavior is typically female, males playing the role in only three species—the ground-living cercopithecines, hamadryas baboons, barbary macaques, and Japanese macaques. Male hamadryas baboons are clearly adopting females to groom them as future harem members (Kummer, 1968). In one study (Itani, 1959) 20 of 25 infant Japanese macaques adopted by males were female; this points to a similar possibility, although the preponderance of female adoptees was not found in a subsequent study (J. Kurland, personal communication). Japanese macaques also show considerable female juvenile alloparental behavior (Kurland, personal communication), these juveniles being typically younger than male caretakers. Through "agonistic buffering," the males clearly gain a status advantage by carrying infants (Itani, 1959). The latter mechanism seems also to provide the selective advantage for male caretakers in barbary macaques, who occupy about 8% of the burden, in time, of caretaking (Burton, 1971; Deag & Crook, 1971).

In other species juvenile alloparental behavior, if any, is carried out by females. In some species (savannah baboons, bonnet macaques) mothers are very retentive, completely forbidding baby-sitting, whereas in others (Nilgiri and Hanuman langurs, vervets) infants are handed around quite freely. The subjects of juvenile alloparental behavior and primate alloparental behavior more generally have been comprehensively reviewed (Hrdy, in press) and have been interpreted plausibly in the context of natural selection theory. On the whole, the higher primates vary considerably with respect to the behavior, and many exhibit little or none of it. In positive cases, it is predominantly a female activity, but several dramatic instances of juvenile or subadult male caretaking indicate that it is not exclusive female, even in the wild. These facts are consistent with the laboratory finding that naive juvenile (prepubertal) female rhesus behave more nurturantly toward strange infants than do males (Chamove et al., 1967). Moreover, males will behave nurturantly toward infants if left alone with them, and they will improve with practice (Redican & Mitchell, 1973). Varieties of male behavior toward infants among primates have also been recently reviewed (Mitchell & Brandt, 1971).

The second pattern, the play group of unrelated or distantly related infants and juveniles, is the dominant form among monkeys, both New and Old World, excepting the Callithricidae (marmosets and tamarinds). This form grades into the sibling group and should not be taken to exclude siblings. (Indeed, all three forms grade into one another and should be thought of as a triangular continuum.) However, it is characteristic of monkeys living in large groups that many play group members are unrelated or distantly related. It is also characteristic of such monkeys that because of seasonality of births and group size, several members of the play group are same-age peers. However Table 1 shows that restriction to same age peers is not the common pattern. Indeed, the multiage play group is overwhelmingly predominant even among monkeys. Same-age peer groups are found only in rhesus monkeys and squirrel monkeys, play groups in all other cases being composed of 1-, 2-, and 3-year-olds (corresponding, in man, to a range from late infancy to puberty) and even, in many cases, adolescents and adults.

The third pattern, the sibling play group, is found in all the apes, including gibbons, and in a number of monkeys, particularly those with dispersed populations. In the apes it is found to the exclusion of the second pattern, which is demographically impossible. Except in rare instances, there are no relations among ape peers in infancy or childhood, because there are no peers. The sibling group grades into juvenile alloparental behavior, but there are important differences, the latter being closer to the human institutions of child nurse or baby-sitter and the former being typically in the group context and mainly play. On this continuum, as well, the apes lie decisively at the sibling group end.

With the sole exception of hamadryas baboons, all play groups of both the second and third patterns are mixed-sex groups. [Hamadryas play groups are restricted to males (though not to same-age males). Yearling and 2-year-old females are already, by this age, being adopted by older males in the process of harem-building.] This mixing of sexes is later seen to have functional importance.

RELATIONS AMONG INFANTS AND JUVENILES IN HUMAN HUNTER–GATHERERS

Prior demographic considerations indicate that peer groups will be unlikely in the extreme in human groups engaged in the hunting and gathering form of subsistence, the original mode of human subsistence, and the only one for more than 99% of the genus Homo's tenure on the planet. Modal band size is 30 among hunter-gatherers of all types in a wide range of environments (Lee & DeVore, 1968). Taking the population structure of the !Kung San (Bushmen) of the Kalahari Desert as exemplary (this is the only hunter-gatherer group for whom good demographic work is available: Howell, 1973; in press), the proportion of women between the age of first birth (19.5) and the end of the reproductive period (about age 45) is 40%, or six women in each band of 30 people. Infertility resulting from gonorrhea can be corrected for by subtracting the proportion of women who report having had it (35/165) times their fertility relative to women who have not had it (2.4/5.1). The resulting mean number of fertile women per band of 30 will be

$$\bar{x} = 6 - 6\left(\frac{35}{165} \times \frac{2.4}{5.1}\right) = 5.4$$

The modal intersibling birth spacing is 4 years. If women are giving birth one year in four and if, when I am born, there is a mean of 4.4 reproducing women (other than my mother) in the band, the likelihood of another giving birth in the same year is 4.4/4 or 1.1. Since mortality in the first year is 20% (most of this in the first week), the chance of my having a peer in the band on my first birthday is 88%, quite high. The chance of my having two peers is 4.4/16 × 80%, or 22%. The chance of my having three is one-fourth of this, 5.5%.

Because of continuing mortality, all these figures will continue to decline as I grow older. The chance of my being a member of a peer group of three 2-year-olds is something less than 20%.

All these estimates also define my peers as infants born in the same year as I. Thus they may be as much as 6 months older or younger, quite an age difference at age 1. If we adopt a more restrictive definition of peers, requiring them to be no more than 3 months older or younger, the corresponding figures for the end of my first year will be 44% for one peer, 11% for two, and 2.75% for three.

However, hunter-gatherer bands are characteristically nomadic and fluid (Lee & DeVore, 1968), the !Kung being no exception (Lee & DeVore, in press). This means that the band I belong to will probably split into subgroups, which will recoalesce to form new bands with other subgroups one or more times during my first few years. Although continuity of relationships will be preserved with some of the children in the band, my peer, if any, may not be among them. Furthermore, my peer's mother and my mother may dislike each other (as happened in one !Kung band with two infants of the same age), making my relationship with the other child improbable. Finally, still other children are vying with my peer for my attention, and they are both fascinating and very interested in babies.

Thus from purely demographic considerations, arising from the carrying capacity of land for hunters-gatherers, relations among peers—and, more especially, peer groups—were rare during the entire course of human evolution, during, indeed, 99% of anything that might be called human history.

What, then, does characterize relations among infants and juveniles in the human environment of evolutionary adaptedness? Infant care, behavior, and development (Konner, various works) and the social behavior of 2- to 5-year-olds (Blurton Jones & Konner, 1973) among the !Kung San of the Kalahari Desert have been extensively described. The findings need not be reviewed here, but it is useful to note that the infant care pattern is among the most indulgent and responsive, with respect both to the infant's dependent demands and to its nondemand signaling, ever described for a human population. In a number of respects the pattern resembles that found in nonhuman higher primates, departing in these respects from the pattern observed in advanced industrial states.

Of the three higher primate patterns of relations among infants and juveniles, only the multiage play group occurs with any frequency in !Kung bands, and it is ubiquitous. It is made up mostly of siblings and cousins and is completely mixed with respect to sex; a band may consist of six or eight children ranging in age from late infancy to adolescence, or it may divide into two or three smaller groups with correspondingly smaller age range.

Infants begin to participate from the time they can walk, and the sight of a toddler edging away from his mother to more or less throw himself on a pile of wrestling 2- to 5-year-olds was not uncommon. Two-year-olds who are better walkers will follow the group around, and if the children have wandered from the village camp, the infants will be carried when they tire.

The principal concern of the group is always play, although this may and typically does include the following: observation of adult subsistence activity; play at subsistence, which, however playful, may produce food; "pretend" subsistence play, which does not produce food but assumes some semblance of adult subsistence forms; rough-and-tumble play; and sex play (Draper, 1971, in press; Konner, 1972; Blurton Jones & Konner, 1973; Shostak, in press). It invariably includes also, though incidentally, protection and care and teaching of infants and children by older children. There is no "child nurse" comparable to that found in middle-level agricultural societies (Whiting, 1963). That is, children are not *expected* to take care of infants; and mothers are always within shouting (or crying) distance, receptive to infant needs. But there is care, protection, and teaching nonetheless, for all its inadvertent character; and of course older children are learning infant and child care. These relations arise from the older children's own volition; remember that they too will have few or no peers.

The relations may be viewed quantitatively in Figures 1 and 2, which are based on infant behavior observations that have already been described (Kon-

FIGURE 1. (*a*) Percentage of 5-second time blocks during continuous time-sequence observations in which infant and caretaker were observed to be in physical contact, with standard error of the mean. For San each dot represents six infants; for Boston girls, *N* = 60. (*b*) Percentage of physical contact time blocks accounted for by various categories of individuals among San and in the Boston professional and working classes: solid dots = mother; triangles = individuals other than mother, including children; open dots = children alone. Mean and standard error. (*c*) Percentage of 5-second time blocks during continuous time-sequence observations in which infant and children were observed to be in physical contact, as distributed among four categories of children. Mean and standard error.

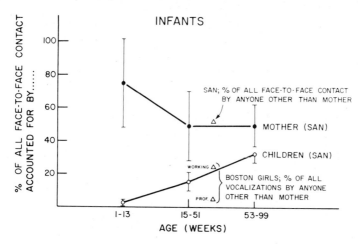

FIGURE 2. Distribution of certain nonphysical contact behaviors across different categories of individuals. For San children, face-to-face contact is represented; for Boston girls, vocalizations are represented. Mean and standard error. Symbols as in Figure 1*b*.

ner, in press). Briefly, they follow a method developed by Tulkin and Kagan (1971). Observations were 15 minutes long, divided into 5-second units, and continuous rather than time-sampling. Thirty-three infants were observed (21 male and 13 female) at from one to four age points between birth and 20 months. Six 15-minute observations were made at each age point, on at least three separate days. Conditions for onset of the observations were: infant within 10 feet of mother, awake, and not suckling. Data for different age points were average for an infant only if the repeat observations were made within 2 months of each other. Thus the data are 54 age points for 33 infants. The age points are treated as independent in this analysis.

Figure 1*a* shows total time in physical contact with anyone, expressed as a percentage of total possible 5-second time blocks, for San of various ages and for 10-month-old Boston girls (Tulkin, 1970). Physical contact is very high, declining through the 20 months.

Figure 1*b* breaks down this percentage according to who accounts for it. Thus mothers account for 75 or 80% of all physical contact, and this figure does not change significantly through the 20 months. We also see that among san the percentage of all physical contacts with anyone *other* than the mother (20 to 25%) is higher than that of either class in Boston. This means that in spite of the extremely close relation to the mother, the infant also has a closer relation to others, getting proportionately more contact with others than do Boston infants. Indeed children alone, who account for less than half of non-mother contact among San, account for as large a proportion of physical contact there as *anyone* other than the mother does in Boston. (One might predict that this would counteract an otherwise strong "apron string" tendency arising from intense mother-infant contact and indulgence. The prediction seems to be confirmed by observations of San and English 2- to 6-year-olds.)

Figure 1c simply shows that following the predictions of natural selection theory, girls account for more physical contact than do boys, and girl siblings more than anyone, over all ages. However, there seems to be an interaction between sex and relatedness, the sex difference being significant only for siblings. This situation, which is more complicated than predicted by natural selection theory, as presented earlier, may reflect a more extensive (relative) preparation of males for parental investment than occurs in most higher primates. It is in keeping, however, with the fact that San fathers account for a greater proportion of vocalizations to infants during the first 3 months (10%) than do American fathers (Konner, unpublished; Rebelsky & Hanks, 1971).

Questions will be raised about the nature of infants' relations with children, particularly the claim that it is not of the "child nurse" or baby-sitter character. These may be answered by reference to Figure 2, which gives the breakdown of all face-to-face interactions according to who accounted for them. Here the standard errors are much larger than for physical contact, but mothers do account for a smaller proportion of face-to-face than of physical contact. Children account for a larger proportion of face-to-face than of physical contact and, more important, proportionate face-to-face contact with children increases through the 20 months, and physical contact does not. Finally, compared with mother-infant physical contact, children-infant physical contact is low. All this conspires to persuade us that we are not dealing with a "child nurse" relation in which a young girl is saddled with her infant sibling to carry around all day; but rather, we seem to have a social play relation that increases in interactive complexity throughout the course of infancy. Incidentally, face-to-face contact with *peers* per se accounts for 5.7% of all face-to-face contact with *children* in the oldest group of infants (53 to 99 weeks).

The next step in this developmental process may be viewed by examining the behavior of 2- to 6-year-olds (Figures 3 and 4). The method used, which has been described at length (Blurton Jones & Konner, 1973), consisted of observing San and English children in similar social contexts, outdoors in good weather with the mothers nearby and other (familiar) children available. Twenty-six San (15 girls and 11 boys) and 21 English children (11 girls and 10 boys) were observed for one hour each, using a time-sampling procedure (30-second periods separated by 2 minutes for writing); both facial expressions (Blurton Jones) and other behaviors (Konner) were recorded.

All comparisons were made with the Mann-Whitney U test, two-tailed (Siegel, 1956). The results show that San 2- to 6-year-olds range a greater maximum distance from the mother (Figure 3), have more face-to-face interac-

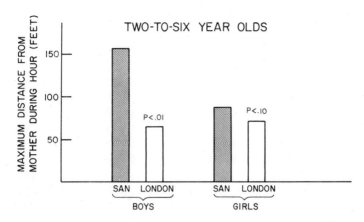

FIGURE 3. Mean maximum distance from mother during an hour of observation: 2- to 6-year-old children in London and among San, observed under similar conditions.

FIGURE 4. Mean of incidence of several behaviors during an hour of observation. (*a*) San and London 2- to 6-year-olds, face-to-face with child; (*b*) children face-to-face with mother; (*c*) caretaker (mother) nurtures; (*d*) caretaker (anyone) nurtures. All comparisons by Mann-Whitney *U* test, two-tailed.

tions with children (Figure 4*a*), fewer face-to-face interactions with mother (Figure 4*b*), and are less frequently nurtured by either the mother or anyone else (Figures 4*c* and *d*) than is the case for London children. This creates some difficulty for "apron-strings" and "spoiling" theories, which would predict that the extreme indulgence and mother contact experienced by San infants would produce overdependent children in the age range studied.

This discrepancy may be accounted for in two ways. The first, which has been discussed at length (Konner, in press), involves a version of the notion that initial indulgence of dependent demands leads somehow to greater independence later. This is plausible but difficult to demonstrate.

The other relies on the fact that proportionate contact of infants with children is greater among the San than in Boston. That is, in spite of intense contact with the mother, infants are gradually being lured from her by the attractions of a multiaged child group. This group, since it contains older children, can be approached by the infant using many of the same behaviors and signals that were appropriate for mother, and the group will care for, protect, and teach the infant, in the bargain, during the course of play. This makes for a relatively easy transition from mother-dependency to wider sociality. We return to this point later.

RELATIONS AMONG INFANTS AND JUVENILES SINCE THE END OF THE PLEISTOCENE ERA

Two questions now arise. First, are the San representative of hunter-gatherers in general? Second, what happened after hunter-gatherer life passed from existence? Both may be approached through analysis of cross-cultural samples of mutually independent societies living various ways of life. The sample used here consisted of 182 of the 186 societies in the current World Ethnographic Sample taken from the Human Relations Area Files (Murdock & White, 1969). Four were omitted because they were mounted hunters, a special and historically brief adaptation of the American Great Plains population not properly included with other hunter-gatherers. The sample had been coded for societal complexity and subsistence variables (Murdock & White, 1969) and for infant and child care variables (Barry & Paxson, 1971). The data were recoded and reanalyzed for this investigation by Maxwell Katz of the Harvard School of Education.

The results appear in Figure 5. Amount of nonmaternal care (actual *care*, not *contact*) in infancy increases with increasing societal complexity (Figure 5*a*). Nonmaternal *care* in early childhood is less in hunters, gatherers, and fishers than in other subsistence types (Figure 5*b*). The percentage of societies using children as infant caretakers is smaller for hunters, gatherers, and fishers than for other subsistence types (Figure 5*c*). This is consistent with an earlier finding on another cross-cultural sample, that pressure for nurturance, or parents' efforts to induce children to care for infants, was greater in societies whose economics involved more accumulation (Barry, Child, & Bacon, 1959). This percentage, multiplied by the amount of nonmaternal care (the "children as caretakers" index) shows the same pattern, as indicated in Figure 5d. Taking only those societies for which nonmaternal care in early childhood is rated as high, and considering who the principal early childhood companions are, hunting, gathering, and fishing societies favor the play group over the child nurse or adult nurse, whereas other societies show no preference (Figure 5e). Where the principal early childhood companion or caretaker is the play group, hunting, gathering, and fishing societies show the largest amount of contact with it, though only shifting agriculture societies are (nearly) significantly lower (Figure 5f).

To summarize: the "farming out" of the infant and young child to adult or child nurses is less frequent in hunting, gathering, and fishing societies, the basic human subsistence type. Where nonmaternal contact in these societies is high, it is most likely to be with a play group. And such societies have more play group contact than at least some more advanced subsistence types.

The question of peers is more difficult to approach using available cross-cultural data. Good data are available only for adolescence (Harley, 1963), and they show that societies that hunt and gather, societies without social stratification, and societies with population units smaller than 1500, are significantly less likely to have peer groups in adolescence than more complex societies. A more theoretical comparative study (Tiger & Fox, 1972) has attributed to adolescent male peer groups a primarily agonistic and political function. John Whiting (unpublished) has recently found that "fraternal associations" of adolescent males are significantly more likely to occur in societies where a high emphasis is placed on military glory—martial prowess, heroism, death in battle, and the like. His view is that such peer groups function to separate boys from girls and women and from their identification with women, the better to make them warriors. Our only longitudinal information about how hunter-gatherer peer relations change when they become settled is in Lewis Binford's (personal communication) description of adolescents in Eskimo band society. It seems that a number of Eskimo bands who until then had lived a nomadic hunting life, were settled about 15 years ago into large permanent villages. Adolescents aggregated into destructive roving peer gangs who have evidently come to present a serious social problem.

In this anecdote, as well as in the more parametric measures of adolescent peer group variation described earlier, one cannot help noticing at least a superficial similarity to the large "pods" of unrelated same-age peers characteristic of sea lions, careering through juvenile violence toward a violent adulthood.

d. CHILDREN AS INFANT CARETAKERS INDEX

HUNTING, FISHING GATHERING (26)

HERDING HORTICULTURE

SHIFTING AGRIC. (28) (12)

ADV. AGRIC. (30)

(6)

e. % OF SOCIETIES

H, G, F : N = 10
H, A : N = 47
(Only those for which nonmaternal care in early childhood is high)

HUNTING GATHERING FISHING

HERDING AGRICUL-TURE

PLAYGROUP CHILD NURSE ADULT

PRINCIPAL EARLY CHILDHOOD COMPANIONS OR CARETAKERS

f. AMT. OF PLAYGROUP CONTACT

(Only those for which the principal playgroup is the principal early childhood companion or caretaker)

HUNTING GATHERING FISHING (5)

SHIFTING AGRIC. (3)

HORTICULTURE (7)

ADV. AGRIC. (9)

t-test P~.07

a. NON-MATERNAL CARE, INFANCY

LOW N=29

MIDDLE N=59

HIGH N=16

COMPLEXITY

b. NON-MATERNAL CARE, EARLY CHILDHOOD

P<.001 (CHI-SQUARE)

HUNTING GATHERING 4 8 6

FISHING HERDING 5

SHIFTING AGRIC. HORTICULTURE 20 13

ADV. AGRIC. 25

c. % USING CHILDREN AS INFANT CARETAKERS

P = .018 (CHI-SQUARE)

HUNTING GATHERING FISHING HERDING SHIFTING HORTICULTURE ADV. AGRIC.

SUBSISTENCE TYPE

118

FIGURE 5. Various measures of caretaking practices of different cultures in the Standard Ethnographic Sample of the Human Relations Area Files, in relation to societal complexity or subsistence strategy. (*a*) Mean and standard error of the Barry and Paxson scale score for care by individuals other than the mother during infancy, in relation to societal complexity. Differences not significant. (*b*) Mean and standard error of the Barry and Paxson scale score for care by individuals other than the mother during early childhood, in relation to subsistence type. (*c*) Percentage of societies in each subsistence category using children as infant caretakers. (*d*) Percentage in Figure 5*c* multiplied by Barry and Paxson scale score for care by individuals other than the mother during infancy, in relation to subsistence type. (*e*) Of the societies for which nonmaternal care in early childhood is high, a two-way tabulation: three types of principal early childhood companions or caretakers by two types of subsistence strategy (food collection vs. food production). (*f*) For the societies in which the play group is the principal early childhood companion or caretaker, mean and standard error of the Barry and Paxson scale score for care by individuals other than the mother during early childhood.

119

FUNCTIONAL CONSIDERATIONS

Laboratory investigations of the functions of relations among infants and juveniles have been quite extensive, though as we shall see, in a quite limited
range. Briefly, they reveal that depriving developing rhesus monkeys (Harlow,
1969) and chimpanzees (Mason, 1960, 1965; Davenport, in press) of contact
with other developing conspecifics results in impairment of adult male sexual
behavior and also in modulation of adult agonistic behavior. Rough-and-tumble
play and sex play, moreover, are universal components of juvenile play behavior in higher primates. The only noticeable exception to this is the near
absence of childhood sex play in so-called advanced human societies. Among all
higher primates, and among human hunter-gatherers, adult sexual behaviors
are acquired gradually through observation of adults copulating (De Benedictis,
1973; Struhsaker, 1967; Goodall, 1967; Shostak, in press) and practice with
other juveniles and adolescents (Goy & Goldfoot, 1974; Tutin & McGrew,
1973; Shostak, in press; Money et al., 1970; and all works cited in Table 1).

Deficits in caretaking behavior resulting from peer deprivation do not seem
to have been studied. Observation in the wild, however, suggests that this too is
a nearly universal component of juvenile play in higher primates. Except in advanced industrial states and (perhaps) in squirrel monkeys (Baldwin &
Baldwin, 1974) and rhesus monkeys (Southwick et al., 1965), opportunity for
practicing play-caretaking with infants is always available to juveniles, and in
some species play-mothering (Lancaster, 1971) and play-"fathering" (Burton,
1971) are very important indeed.

Now that some studies have uncovered deficits of various kinds in social behavior arising from rearing *only* with peers (Chamove, 1973; Chamove et al.,
1973), one might not be going too far out on a limb by predicting that further
investigation of the behavior of these monkeys may be rewarded with the finding of a deficit in parental behavior.

Finally, it is of interest to consider more cognitive aspects of the developmental process by which an infant comes to have relationships with other juveniles. Several chapters (2, 5, 7, 9) reporting laboratory investigations of peer
interactions in human infants and toddlers arrived by different routes at the
conclusion that cognitive developmental events, perhaps of a maturational nature, taking place during the second year of life, make possible a quantum advance in the infant's ability to interact with peers. It was noted in one very useful conference discussion that this process is analogous to, and perhaps homolo-
gous with, the process by which an infant comes to be able to control or
manipulate the behavior of its mother at around 3 months of age (Watson,
1972; Stern, 1974), using various vocal and visual signals.

In this view, one of the 3-month-old's major cognitive functions is the
manipulation of active objects, with the proviso that the object's actions are

contingent on some action of the infant's. Although mechanical objects may be made to behave in this way (Watson, 1972), the ideal "contingent responsive" object is a successful caretaker, since he or she will be likely to vary the level and nature of stimulation and even the degree of contingency itself to optimize the infant's level of arousal, thus maximize its level of attention (Lewis & Goldberg, 1969; Stern, 1974).

Peers, however, exhibit *non*contingent behaviors—actions that are egocentric, not tied to the infant's own actions, and, from the infant's point of view, random. They thus present a much less manipulable set of stimulus events. Consequently acquisition of the ability to manipulate them will proceed much more slowly than for highly contingent-responsive caretakers and will require cognitive abilities not destined to mature until after the end of the first year.

Without explicitly stating it, several conference participants seemed to hold a two-stage cognitive maturation theory of the development of social relations. At about 3 months of age, the infant develops the ability to manipulate highly contingent-responsive social objects (i.e., easily manipulable adult caretakers), and for the rest of the first year, occupies itself with the elaboration of this schema and the assimilation of various new adults to it. After 12 months of age the infant develops the ability to manipulate noncontingent-responsive social objects (i.e., random, egocentric peers), an at least equally arduous accommodation, enabling it to enter the wider social world. This outlook (which, we must hasten to add, may not be explicitly espoused by anyone), is represented by the graph in Figure 6a.

From the data considered in this chapter—especially the San hunter-gatherer data, but also the comparative higher primate data—this model appears to have certain inadequacies. It is based on observations of infants interacting with essentially two classes of individuals (adult caretakers and same-age peers) representing the extremes of the continuum of contingent-responsiveness. The model may thus be an artifact of the absence, in the studies to date, of several classes of target social objects intermediate in manipulability—namely, juveniles of various ages older than the infant. San infants may be seen to develop the ability to manipulate children of various ages (and various degrees of contingent-responsiveness) throughout the first year, with increasing frequency, culminating in the emergence of some ability to manipulate same-age peers (though still at a low level of frequency) during the second year. These observations are best represented by a nonstage model showing gradual growth of the noncontingent-responsiveness (randomness) of the social objects the infant will be able to manipulate, as in Figure 6b.

Any number of research designs varying age of target social object under laboratory conditions would begin to produce data enabling us to discriminate between the two models. No such data are presently available.

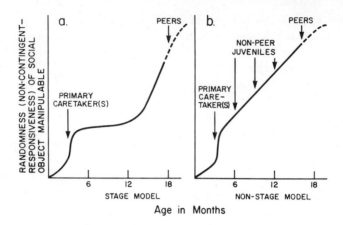

FIGURE 6.   Two models of the development of the infant's relations with nonadult individuals. The variable represented is the inverse of Watson's "contingent responsiveness," a characteristic of the infant's social target. (*a*) Infant is held to make an accommodatory quantum step during the first half of the second year while learning to handle relations with same-age peers. (*b*) Infant is held to gradually assimilate to an early developed schema for handling highly contingent-responsive social objects, social objects of less and less contingent responsiveness.

CONCLUSIONS

It was the task of this review to present the comparative perspective on peer relations in infancy. The comparative perspective is that peer relations do not exist—not in the human environment of evolutionary adaptedness nor in societies of animals most closely related to man. Ranging beyond the apes to monkeys, one does find peer relations and peer groups in a number of cases, but in almost every instance these are mitigated by nonpeer participation. In human hunter-gatherers, in all apes, in almost all monkeys that have been studied, the nearly ubiquitous play group is a nonpeer, multiage group of juveniles. The advantages of the multiage composition of play groups for transmitting nongenetic aspects of behavior in higher animals, for protecting younger children, and for facilitating smooth integration of infants into a wider social world, are clear.

Peer relations in human infancy are almost entirely an artifact of laboratory investigations and of child care conditions in advanced industrial states. In this context we can begin to understand the bizarrely inept forms of social behavior which we know in the laboratory and nursery as "parallel play" and "collective monologue." Infants are inept in relating to one another for the simple reason that they were never called on to do so during millions of years of evolution; consequently they could not have been selected for an ability to do this.

They were selected instead for an ability to become integrated into a multiage child group, quite a different matter. Indeed, they may have been selected for a specific dependency of normal developmental process on the input from such a multiage child group.

Excellent laboratory investigations have been done on relations among peers and deprivation of contact with peers in rhesus monkeys, for whom they are natural, and in humans and chimpanzees, for whom they are not. In general same-age blinders affect the research addressed in this volume. Lewis et al., (Chapter 2) investigated this problem. Twelve-month-old infants were observed with friends ranging in age from 7 ½ to 22 months. Although the number of pairs (7) was too small to permit us to rely on the differences, they do suggest that same-age and different-age pairs behave differently, even within the age range of 12 to 24 months.

Similarly, the rhesus social deprivation experiments continue to vary time with peers, "sensitive period" experience with peers, number of peers, every kind of variation of peer contact, even though after years of failed efforts to rehabilitate autistic socially isolated monkeys by placing them with *peers*, normal or abnormal, successful therapy was not achieved until the isolates were placed with normal monkeys half their age (Harlow & Suomi, 1971; Suomi et al., 1972).

The comparative perspective urges an end to this bias in our investigations. It urges a consideration of relations of nonpeer juveniles as a separate "affectional system," having unique characteristics and, perhaps, unique functional importance. It urges us to wonder a little what may be the cost to our children of our keeping them so much of the time with children precisely their own age.

It is possible that whether child groups in a species are peer groups or nonpeer groups is no more than a demographic matter. That is, there may be a general primate biogram that can fare perfectly well in ontogeny with either, depending only on population concentration. On the other hand, we must be very thoughtful in making inferences about human childhood from studies of laboratory rhesus monkeys, where the importance of peers *qua* peers is concerned. The apes and protohominids went to considerable trouble to evolve for us a successful childhood in nonpeer play groups. Perhaps we should be a bit more cautious before we abandon the nonpeer pattern. The latter course is the one we have more or less followed for some centuries.

References

Altmann, M. Social integration of the moose calf. *Animal Behavior,* 1958, **6,** 155–159.

Baldwin, J. P., & Baldwin, J. I. Exploration and social play in squirrel monkeys (*Saimiri*). *American Zoologist*, 1974, **14** (1), 303.

Barry, H., Child, I., & Bacon, M. Relation of child training to subsistence economy. *American Anthropologist,* 1959, **61,** 51–63.

Barry, H., & Paxson, L. Infancy and early childhood: Cross-cultural codes. *Ethnology,* 1971, **10,** (4).

Bartholomew, G. Mother-young relations and the maturation of pup behavior in the Alaska fur seal. *Animal Behavior,* 1959, **7,** 163–171.

Bekoff, M. The development of social interaction, play and metacommunication in mammals: An ethological perspective. *Quarterly Review of Biology,* 1972, **47,** 412–433.

Bekoff, M. Social play and play-soliciting by infant canids. *American Zoologist,* 1974, **14,** 323.

Blurton Jones, N., & Konner, M. Sex differences in the behavior of bushman and London two-to-five year olds. In R. Michael and J. Crook (Eds.), *Comparative ecology and behavior of primates.* New York: Academic Press, 1973.

Booth, C. Early social experience and gregariousness in the rat. *Developmental Psychology,* 1973, **8** (3), 360–368.

Burton, F. The integration of biology and behavior in the socialization of *Macaca sylvana* of Gibraltar. In F. Poirier (Ed.), *Primate socialization.* New York: Random House, 1971.

Caputo, D., Essman, W., Teitler, R., Lowie, G., & Frisone, J. Housing modification as a variable in fasting-induced ulcerogenesis. *Journal of Psychosomatic Research,* 1968, **12,** 129–135.

Chamove, A., Harlow, H., & Mitchell, G. Sex differences in the infant-directed behavior of preadolescent rhesus monkeys. *Child Development,* 1967, **38** (2), 329–335.

Chamove, A. Rearing infant rhesus together. *Behaviour,* 1973, **47** (1–2), 48–66.

Chamove, A., Rosenblum, L., & Harlow, H. Monkeys (*Macaca mulatta*) raised only with peers: A pilot study. *Animal Behavior,* 1973, **21,** 316–325.

Collias, N. The analysis of socialization in sheep and goats. *Ecology,* 1956, **37,** 228–239.

Davenport, R. Some behavioral disturbances of great apes in captivity. Manuscript prepared for Burg Wartenstein Symposium No. 62, "The Behavior of Great Apes," 1974.

Deag, J., & Crook, J. Social behavior and agonistic buffering in the wild barbary macaque *Macaca sylvana. Folia Primatologica,* 1971, **15,** 183–200.

De Benedictis, T. The behavior of young primates during adult copulation. *American Anthropologist,* 1973, **75** (5), 1469–1485.

Denenberg, V., Woodcock, J., & Rosenberg, K. Long-term effects of preweaning and postweaning. Free environment experience on rats' problem-solving behavior. *Journal of Comparative and Physiological Psychology,* 1968, **66,** 533–535.

DeVore, I. Mother-infant relations in free-ranging baboons. In H. Rheingold (Ed.), *Maternal behavior in mammals.* New York: Wiley, 1963.

Draper, P. "!Kung Bushman childhood." Paper presented at the Northeastern Anthropological Association Meetings, Albany, New York, April 1971.

Draper, P. Social ecology of !Kung childhood. In R. Lee & I. DeVore (Eds.), *Kalahari hunter-gatherers*. Cambridge, Mass.: Harvard University Press, in press.

Ellefson, J. A natural history of gibbons in the Malayan peninsula. Unpublished Ph.D. thesis, University of California at Berkeley, 1965.

Essman, W. Gastric ulceration in differentially housed mice. *Psychological Reports,* 1966, **19,** 173–174.

Essman, W., & Frisone, J. Isolation-induced facilitation of gastric ulcerogenesis in mice. *Journal of Psychosomatic Research,* 1966, **10,** 183–188.

Essman, W. "Free" and motivated behavior and amine metabolism in isolated mice. In Garattini and Sigg (Eds.), *Aggressive behaviour,* Amsterdam: Excerpta Medica, 1968a.

Essman, W. Differences in locomotor activity and brain serotonin metabolism in differentially housed mice. *Journal of Comparative and Physiological Psychology,* 1968b, **66,** (1), 244–246.

Gentry, R. The development of social behavior through play in the Steller sea lion. *American Zoologist,* 1974, **14,** 391.

Goodall, J. Mother-offspring relationships in chimpanzees. In D. Morris (Ed.), *Primate ethology.* Chicago: Aldine Press, 1967.

Goy, R., & Goldfoot, D. Experiential and hormonal factors influencing the development of sexual behavior in the male rhesus monkey. In Schmitt & Worden (Eds.), *The neurosciences: Third study program.* Cambridge, Mass.: Massachusetts Institute of Technology, 1974.

Hagen, S. Stumptail troop shows high regard for motherhood. *Primate Record,* 1974, **5·** (1), 3–7.

Hall, K., & DeVore, I. Baboon social behavior. In I. DeVore (Ed.), *Primate behavior.* New York: Holt, Rinehart & Winston, 1965.

Hall, K. Behavior and ecology of the wild patas monkey. In P. Jay (Ed.), *Primates.* New York: Holt, Rinehart & Winston, 1968. Also: *Journal of Zoology,* 1965, **148,** 15–87.

Hamilton, W. The genetical evolution of social behavior. *Journal of Theoretical Biology,* 1964, **7,** 1–52.

Harley, J. Adolescent youths in peer groups: A cross-cultural study. Unpublished Ph.D. thesis, Department of Anthropology, Harvard University, Cambridge, Mass., 1963.

Harlow, H. Age-mate or peer affectional systems. In D. S. Lehrman, R. A. Hinde, & E. Shaw (Eds.), *Advances in the study of behavior,* Vol. 2. New York: Academic Press, 1969.

Harlow, H., & Harlow, M. The affectional systems. In H. Harlow & F. Stollnitz (Eds.), *Behavior of non-human primates,* Vol. 2. New York: Academic Press, 1965.

Harlow, H., & Suomi, S. Social recovery by isolation-reared monkeys. *Proceedings of the National Academy of Sciences (U.S.),* 1971, **68** (7), 1534–1538.

Henry, J., & Henry, Z. The doll play of Pilaga Indian children. In C. Kluckhohn, H.

Murray, & R. Schneider (Eds.), *Personality in nature, society and culture.* New York: Knopf, 1944.

Henry, J., & Herrero, S. Social play in the American black bear. *American Zoologist,* 1974, **14,** 371.

Herrenkohl, L., & Sachs, B. Sensory regulation of maternal behavior in mammals. *Physiology and Behavior,* 1974, **9** (4), 689–692.

Hirsch, H., & Spinelli, D. Visual experience modifies distribution of horizontally and vertically oriented receptive fields in cats. *Science,* 1970, **168,** 869–871.

Howell, N. The population of the Dobe area !Kung. In R. Lee (Ed.), *Kalahari hunter gatherers.* Cambridge, Mass.: Harvard University Press, in press.

Hrdy, S. The care and exploitation of non-human primate infants by conspecifics other than the mother. *Primates,* 1974. In press.

Hutchinson, R., Ulrich, R., & Azrin, N. Effects of age and related factors on the pain-aggression reaction. *Journal of Comparative and Physiological Psychology,* 1965, **59,** (3), 365–369.

Itani, J. Paternal care in the wild Japanese monkey, *Macaca fuscata fuscata. Primates,* 1959, **2,** (1), 61–93.

Jay, P. Mother-infant relations in langurs. In H. Rheingold (Ed.), *Maternal behavior in mammals.* New York: Wiley, 1963.

Jolly, A. Breeding synchrony in wild *Lemur catta.* In S. Altmann (Ed.), *Social communication among primates.* Chicago: University of Chicago Press, 1967. Pp. 3–14.

Kawai, M. On the system of social ranks in a natural troop of Japanese monkeys: I. Basic rank and dependent rank. Translated in *Japanese monkeys,* S. Altmann. Edmonton: The Editor, 1958.

Kawamura, S. Matriarchal social ranks in the Minoo-B troop: A study of the rank system of Japanese monkeys. Translated in *Japanese monkeys,* S. A. Altmann. Edmonton: The Editor, 1958.

Koford, C. Rank of mothers and sons in bands of rhesus monkeys. *Science,* 1963, **141,** 356–357.

Konner, M. Infants of a foraging people. Ph.D. Dissertation, Department of Anthropology, Harvard University, Cambridge, Mass., 1973.

Konner, M. Aspects of the developmental ethology of a foraging people. In N. Blurton Jones (Ed.), *Ethological studies of child behavior.* Cambridge: Cambridge University Press, 1972.

Konner, M. Maternal care, infant behavior and development among the Zhun/twa (!Kung) Bushmen. In R. Lee & I. DeVore (Eds.), *Kalahari hunter-gatherers.* Cambridge, Mass.: Harvard University Press. In press.

Krech, D., Rosensweig, M., & Bennett, E. Environmental impoverishment, social isolation and changes in brain chemistry and anatomy. *Physiology and Behavior,* 1966, **1,** 99–109.

Kummer, H. *Social organization of hamadryas baboons.* Chicago: University of Chicago Press, 1968.

Kurland, J. Personal communication, 1974.

Lancaster, J., & Lee, R. The annual reproductive cycle in monkeys and apes. In I. DeVore (Ed.), *Primate behavior,* New York: Holt, Rinehart, & Winston, 1965.

Lancaster, J. Play-mothering: The relations between juvenile females and young infants among free-ranging vervet monkeys (*Cercopithecus aethiops*). *Folia Primatologica,* 1971, **15,** 161–182.

Le Boeuf, B., & Peterson, R. Social status and mating activity in elephant seals. *Science,* 1969, **163,** 91–93.

Lee, R., & DeVore, I. (Eds.) *Man the hunter.* Chicago: Aldine Press, 1968.

Lee, R., & DeVore, I. (Eds.) *Kalahari hunter-gatherers.* Cambridge, Mass.: Harvard University Press, In press.

Lewis, M., & Goldberg, S. The acquisition and violation of expectancy: an experimental paradigm. *Journal of Experimental Child Psychology,* 1969, **1,** 70–80.

Loizos, C. Play in mammals. In P. Jewell & C. Loizos, *Play, territoriality and exploration in mammals.* New York: Academic Press, 1966.

Lorenz, K. *Evolution and modification of behavior.* Chicago: University of Chicago Press, 1965.

Marshall, L. Marriage among !Kung Bushmen. *Africa,* 1959, **29** (4), 335–365.

Martin, R. A review of the behaviour and ecology of the lesser mouse lemur. In R. Michael & J. Crook (Eds.), *Comparative ecology and behaviour of primates.* New York: Academic Press, 1973. Pp. 2–68.

Mason, W. The effects of social restriction on the behavior of rhesus monkeys. *Journal of Comparative and Physiological Psychology,* 1960, **53,** 582–589.

Mason, W. The social development of monkeys and apes. In I. DeVore (Ed.), *Primate behavior.* New York: Holt, Rinehart, & Winston, 1965.

Mitchell, G., & Brandt, E. Paternal behavior in primates. In F. Poirier (Ed.), *Primate socialization.* New York: Random House, 1971.

Moltz, H. Some effects of previous breeding experience on the maternal behavior of the laboratory rat. In E. Aronson et al. (Eds.), *Development and evolution of behavior.* San Francisco: Freeman Press, 1969. Pp. 481–488.

Money, J., Cawte, J., Bianchi, G., & Nurcombe, B. Sex training and traditions in Arnhem Land. *British Journal of Medical Psychology,* 1970, **47,** 383–399.

Murdock, G., & White, D. Standard cross-cultural sample. *Ethnology,* 1969, **8** (4), 329–369.

Mussen, P., Conger, J., & Kagan, J. *Child development and personality.* New York: Harper & Row, 1964.

Noirot, E. Changes in responsiveness to young in the adult mouse, III. The effect of immediately preceding performances. *Behaviour,* 1965, **24,** 318–325.

Noirot, E. Changes in responsiveness to young in the adult mouse, V. Priming. *Animal Behavior,* 1969a, **17** (3), 542–546.

Noirot, E. Selective priming of maternal responses by auditory and olfactory cues from mouse pups. *Developmental Psychobiology,* 1969b, **2** (4), 273–276.

Popp, J., & DeVore, I. Aggressive competition and social dominance theory. Paper presented at the "Behavior of great apes" symposium of the Wenner-Gren Foundation, 1974.

Ransom, T., & Rowell, T. Early social development of feral baboons. In F. Poirier (Ed.), *Primate socialization,* New York: Random House, 1971.

Rebelsky, F., & Hanks, S. Fathers' verbal interaction with infants in the first three months of life. *Child Development,* 1971, **42,** 63–68.

Redican, W., & Mitchell, G. A longitudinal study of paternal behavior in adult male rhesus monkeys. *Developmental Psychology,* 1973, **8** (1), 135–136.

Richards, M. Some effects of experience on maternal behavior in rodents. In B. Foss (Ed.), *Determinants of infant behavior,* Vol. 4. London: Methuen, 1965.

Rodman, P. Population composition and adaptive organization among orang-utans of the Kutai Reserve. In R. Michael & J. Crook (Eds.), *Comparative ecology and behaviour of primates.* New York: Academic Press, 1973.

Rosen, J., & Hart, F. Effects of early social isolation upon adult timidity and dominance in Peromyscus. *Psychological Reports,* 1963, **13,** 47–50.

Rosensweig, M. Environmental complexity, cerebral change, and behavior. *American Psychologist,* 1966, **21,** 321–332.

Sade, D. Determinants of dominance in a group of free-ranging rhesus monkeys. In S. A. Altmann (Ed.), *Social communication among primates.* Chicago: University of Chicago Press, 1967.

Sahakian, B. Social isolation rearing and drug-induced stereotypy. Paper presented at the meeting of the International Society for the Study of Brain and Behavior, Paris, 1974.

Schaller, G. *The mountain gorilla: Ecology and behavior.* Chicago: University of Chicago Press, 1963.

Schaller, G. *The Serengeti lion.* Chicago: University of Chicago Press, 1972.

Schenkel, R. Play, exploration and territoriality in the wild lion. In P. Jewell and C. Liozos, *Play, exploration and territory in mammals.* Symposia of the Zoological Society of London, no. 18, 1966.

Scott, J. The effects of early experience on social behavior and organization. In W. Etkin (Ed.), *Social behavior and organization among vertebrates.* Chicago: University of Chicago Press, 1964.

Seton, E. *Lives of game animals.* Newton, Mass.: Branford, 1953.

Shostak, M. A !Kung woman's memories of childhood. In R. Lee & I. DeVore (Eds.), *Kalahari hunter-gatherers,* Cambridge, Mass.: Harvard University Press. In press.

Siegel, B. *Non-parametric statistics for the behavioral sciences.* New York: McGraw-Hill, 1956.

Simonds, P. The bonnet macaque in South India. In I. DeVore (Ed.), *Primate behavior.* New York: Holt, Rinehart & Winston, 1965.

Southwick, C., Beg, M., & Siddiqi, M. Rhesus monkeys in North India. In I. DeVore (Ed.), *Primate behavior.* New York: Holt, Rinehart & Winston, 1965.

Spock, B. *Baby and child care.* New York: Pocket Books, 1968.

Stern, D. Mother and infant at play; The dyadic interaction involving facial, vocal, and gaze behavior In M. Lewis & L. Rosenblum (Eds.), *The effect of the infant on its caregiver:* The origins of behavior, Volume I, New York: Wiley, 1974. Pp. 187–213.

Stolk, J., Conner, R., & Barchas, J. Social environment and brain biogenic amine metabolism in rats. *Journal of Comparative and Physiological Psychology,* 1974, **87** (2), 203–207.

Struhsaker, T. Behavior of vervet monkeys (*Cercopithecus aethiops*). University of California Publication in Zoology, no. 82, 1967.

Suomi, S., Harlow, H., & McKinney, W. Monkey psychiatrists. *American Journal of Psychiatry,* 1972, **128** (8), 927–932.

Tiger, L., & Fox, R. *The imperial animal.* New York: Dell, 1972.

Trivers, R. Parental investment and sexual selection. In B. Campbell (Ed.), *Sexual selection and the descent of man, 1871–1971.* Chicago: Aldine Press, 1972.

Trivers, R. Parent-offspring conflict. *American Zoology,* 1974, **14,** 249–264.

Tulkin, S. Mother-infant interaction in the first year of life: An inquiry into the influences of social class. Unpublished Ph.D. thesis, Department of Psychology, Harvard University, Cambridge, Mass., 1970.

Tulkin, S., & Kagan, J. Mother-child interaction in the first year of life. *Child Development,* 1972, **43,** 31–41.

Tutin, L., & McGrew, W. Sexual behavior of group-living adolescent chimpanzees. *American Journal of Physical Anthropology,* 1973, **38** (2), 195–199.

Valenstein, E., Riss, W., & Young, W. Experimental and genetic factors in the organization of sexual behavior in male guinea pigs. *Journal of Comparative and Physiological Psychology,* 1955, **48,** 397–403.

Valzelli, L. *Psychopharmacology.* New York: Wiley, 1973.

Warren, W., & Ivinskis, A. Isolation-rearing effects on emotionality of hooded rats. *Psychological Reports,* 1973, **32,** 1011–1014.

Watson, J. Smiling, cooing, and "The Game." *Merrill-Palmer Quarterly,* 1972, **18** (4), 323–339.

Welch, B., & Welch, A. Effect of grouping on the level of brain norepinephrine in white Swiss mice. *Life Sciences,* 1965, **4,** 1011.

West, M. Social play in the domestic cat. *American Zoologist,* 1974, **14,** 427.

Whiting, B. *Six cultures: Studies of child rearing.* New Haven, Conn.: Yale University Press, 1963.

Wiesel, T., & Hubel, D. Extent of recovery from the effects of visual deprivation in kittens. *Journal of Neurophysiology,* 1965, **28,** 1060–1072.

CHAPTER 5

Developments in Behavior with Age Mates During the Second Year of Life[1]

WANDA C. BRONSON
Institute of Human Development
University of California

Starting with the unoriginal proposition that development evolves through a process of interaction between the organism and various facets of his environment, this chapter probes the role that may be played by early experience with age mates in the overall scheme of developmental progressions. It is intuitively fairly obvious that by virtue of being human, the age mate represents an object of unrivalled complexity; that being developmentally a peer, his own tenuous social capacities can do little to contribute to successful handling of the complexities he represents; that being immature, he is unlikely to have been predisposed to serve at this stage the same functions he will fulfill at later ages—yet that being a conspecific, he may nevertheless provide a necessary early link in the progressive development of social behavior. Far less obvious, however, is what the nature of such a developmental link may be and what combination of research strategies might be effective in trying to tease out relationships that may span the artificial boundaries between affective, cognitive, and social development.

In the present instance the springboard for inquiry is the behavior of unacquainted toddlers who are repeatedly brought into small, informal play groups as they progress through their second year of life. The method relies on comprehensive and detailed observations, organized and analyzed to ask why the toddlers' specific behaviors occurred and what functions they might serve. This report deals with a beginning segment of work still in progress; although it cannot yet answer many of the questions that it raises, it should serve to

[1] The research project from which this report derives is supported under National Institute of Mental Health grant MH 17312. I am deeply indebted to Susan Swanson, whose thoughtful criticisms, consistent support, and unstinting work made an essential contribution to this study, and I am grateful to the participants in the conference for comments that helped clarify my thinking on this topic.

131

expand the perspective for their pursuit while adding to the limited pool of information about what toddlers actually do when they are together.

METHODS AND PROCEDURES

The Setting

As part of an intensive longitudinal study of development in the second year of life, the behavior of each of the 40 participating toddlers was observed in a setting of 10 evenly spaced play groups. Mother-toddler pairs were assembled from among those for whom a play session was scheduled by the overall program of observations in different settings, and on each occasion four, three (or rarely two) pairs met in the same 12 × 15 foot room, which was gaily decorated, equipped with a variety of toys, and supplied with light refreshments. All participants were introduced before the session; in nearly all instances entry into the playroom was preceded by a period of informal exchanges in the waiting room, with me and with one another. During the sessions (in which all were encouraged to act in whatever way they chose) the mothers generally remained seated in a chatting group at one end of the room while the toddlers, at will, stayed by them or moved about the area. The explicit intent was to sustain an informal atmosphere as similar as possible to that which prevails in spontaneously formed mother-toddler groups. Although the degree to which this intent was achieved differed somewhat in different sessions, the mothers' mutually interactive behavior typically set the kind of sociable context for their babies' activities that is usually missing in investigator-guided play group studies. The sessions lasted between half and three-quarters of an hour, and each was videotaped from an adjacent room.

A total of 107 play groups was conducted during the project; video records of the 33 that have been analyzed constitute the data base for this report. The choice of these records was guided by selection for homogeneity of age *within* groups and age differences *between* groups; thus second-year peer behavior of first, second, and third trimester age mates could become a focus of developmental comparisons. The 33 play sessions varied with respect to group size, sex composition, and length of session; randomly distributed across the three trimesters, the possible effects of these sources of variability are examined and controlled for as necessary in the data manipulations to be reported.[2]

---

[2] Specifically, 21 sessions include four, 11 include three, and 1 includes two toddlers; eight groups have equal sex representation, girls predominate in twelve and boys in eleven, one is an all-male and one an all-female group. Twenty-four sessions record about 45 minutes of observation, the other nine about 35 minutes. The trimester breakdown of the groups is 12, 9, and 12, respectively.

The Sample

The full project sample of 40 toddlers (20 boys and 20 girls) participated in one or more of the 33 play sessions coded to date. Their families resided in and around Berkeley, California, and were predominantly Caucasian, middle-class, well-educated volunteers for a longitudinal study of early development.

In the present pool of data repeated observations of the same toddler in different play groups are available for all but five children; the majority were seen on two, three, or four separate occasions, some in adjacent sessions and some in play groups separated by a number of months. The resulting individual differences in frequency and exact age of observation are handled here by recourse to summary *trimester* scores: thus peer behavior seen in one or more of a given toddler's first four play sessions (ages 13 to 16 months) yields his single or averaged trimester I assessment; sessions 5 through 7 (ages 17 to 20 months) trimester II scores, and sessions 8 through 10 (ages 21 to 24 months) trimester III data. Although there are large individual differences in the number of play group observations that determine a given child's trimester score, these are randomly distributed among the three trimesters and introduce no artifact in the present analyses. Twelve toddlers were observed at all three trimester ages; the numbers that generate each trimester data and any two-trimester combination are supplied as relevant in the forthcoming analyses.

The Coding and Classification Systems

The process of generating data for these analyses required that a trained coder view the full video record of each session starting from the group's entry into the playroom. Every subsequent instance in which one of the toddlers directed any behavior other than mere visual regard toward his age mates was marked as denoting the initiation of a peer encounter. Using a set of predetermined categories, the coder systematically characterized the sequences of visual, gestural, vocal, and affective behaviors of both the initiator and the target of the particular encounter, as well as the antecedent circumstances and the consequences of the incident. The set of specific codes descriptive of each encounter was then classified as one of the mutually exclusive types of peer events defined by the criteria of the classificatory system. A comprehensive, sequential record of all play group peer activities—from the beginning to the end of the play session—was thus generated.

The decision to exclude instances of purely visual behavior from the coding system was dictated primarily by the nature of the material: with the constantly shifting movement of the children within the playroom it is nearly impossible to assess reliably just which of his peers the toddler is glancing or gazing at. As a background for the following analyses, however, it must be stressed that visual monitoring of the peer social scene—be it through intermittent scanning, glancing, or "checking out"—is consistently prevalent throughout every session. Characteristically, whether engaged in some toy activity or merely standing by, observation of what others around him are doing claims a large share of the toddler's visual attention.

The system for classifying peer incidents was imposed on the behaviorally precise descriptions of what babies do in interacting with one another as a heuristic organizational device to facilitate emergence of effective guidelines for investigation of the intent and function of their activities. Precise and comprehensive detail is essential in the study of little-explored domains of functioning; in the complex area of interpersonal behavior, however, it can often dead-end in the seductive trap of sheer taxonomy or lose its power in a process of reduction based on purely statistical models. In an attempt to avoid both these pitfalls, the system devised for this first set in a planned process of hierarchical analyses highlights certain behaviors for criterial distinctions while provisionally lumping others; the risk-taking process of a priori decisions was shaped as much by intuition and experience of extensive observation as by considerations of various theoretical positions.

In essence, the classificatory system relies on the nature of the communicative signal that the toddler directs to his peer to determine the *class* to which the incident is assigned; the nature of other co-occurring behaviors or antecedent circumstances serve to define the *type* within the given class. Earlier work on peer behavior in the playroom setting (Bronson, 1974a) suggested that most peer incidents took the form of a brief signal-response exchange immediately followed by the dyad (or triad) splitting up to divert to other concerns. The second and much rarer form of encounters consisted of periods, be they periods of chained signal-response exchanges or periods in which both participants are joined in sustaining a common focus of attention on some toy or event with various degrees of concurrent social exchange. The system for assigning the set of codes that define each encounter to its appropriate event class and type had to be designed to permit accommodation of both these different encounter forms within the same analytic framework.

The system defines three classes. The first, named *"Disagreements,"* represents a grouping of various brief exchanges and periods which on face value suggest that some kind of agonistic event was experienced by at least one of the members participating in the encounter. Co-occurring vocal-affective behaviors emitted by either participant in the exchange determine one of three event types (1, 2, or 3), which reflect the progressively greater intensity of disaffection that characterized the incident. The attempt here is to provide a distinction among events that although formally agonistic may nevertheless be quite distinct in the phenomenological experience of the toddlers involved in the encounter. The second major class—named provisionally *"Affiliative"*—groups brief encounters and periods whose nature gives a prosocial flavor to the event. Determination of one of the four types within this class depends on the presence of different kinds of specified behaviors or circumstances that co-occur with emission of the initiating signal. Whereas the three types of "Disagreements" could be differentiated by the single parameter of level of disaffection, no single dimension could adequately reflect the distinctions experienced in observing many of the formally similar "Affiliative" encounters. The four types, denoted by letters *A* through *D,* represent a suggested ranking of the intentionality of the behavior but by no means are to be taken as suggestive of the intensity of affilia- tion. The third minor class named "*?*" incorporates incidents that were clearly not agonistic, yet involved behaviors that could not—at face value—be deemed in any sense affiliative. Increasingly rare as the year progressed this category has provisionally been placed between the two main classes of events. Table 1 sum- marizes the main behavioral criteria selected for assigning peer encounters to their event class and type.

To assess the reliability of this system, portions of the video records of twelve different sessions (totaling 165 minutes of observation) were viewed inde- pendently by two coders. A total of 140 events was recorded, and events of all types were represented. Complete agreement in the full set of encounter codes was found in 105 instances (75% of all the events). In 23 instances (16%) only one of the coders recorded the presence of an encounter; these cases invariably involved a brief signal reacted to by a look or an ignore. In the twelve instances (9%) in which the two coders disagreed, it was on issues such as (*a*) the precise nature of a gesture (e.g., a "touch object" vs. an "attempted take"), (*b*) the presence or absence of a concurrent brief vocalization, or (*c*) whether the tem- poral separation in a succession of brief encounters required coding of a series of events or should be expressed as a period of low-level play or dispute. There was no instance of omission or disagreement in encounters that involved strong, sustained, or complex peer-to-peer behavior.

Four encounters could not be classified by this system. All these have a flavor of "teasing": for example, a toddler offers a toy, but as the peer reaches for it he withdraws the object while gazing into the peer's face; or he takes the peer's toy, moves back, and immediately shows it to him with a smile. In these rare instances both a "Disagreement" and an "Affiliative" signal are integrated into the toddler's communication: it is hoped that when coding of all remaining sessions is completed, the pool of such events will be large enough to permit some study of this unusual and intriguing phenomenon.

ANALYSES AND FINDINGS

The analyses center around two issues. The first concerns the sheer quantity of peer interaction: the frequency and possible determinants of initiating acts are

TABLE 1. Classification of Peer Encounters into Types of Peer Events Based on 335, 258, and 340 Trimesters I, II, and III Encounters

| Class | Form of Event | | Type Within Class |
	Signal/Response	Period	
"Disagreements"[a]			
Percentage at Trimester I = 42% II = 46% III = 48%	*Take gesture*: successful get of toy, or unsuccessful get of toy	*Dispute*: chain of signal/response patterns all belonging to disagreement class	1 With no or minimal protest, frustration, distress
	Neutral approach gesture: withdrawal of toy or withdrawal of self by peer "*Assault*" on person *Vocal protest* at peer behavior not directed to *B* *Vocal "Mine"* or equivalent at peer behavior not directed to *B*	*Edgy play*: parallel play that borders on low-level dispute	2 With moderate protest, distress, or frustration 3 With strong protest, distress, frustration
"?"[b]			
Percentage at Trimester I = 25% II = 19% III = 15%	*Imitate*: (not to peer) action or vocalization *Touch body* *Reach toward* peer or his toy *Touch toy* in peer's possession	*Proximity*: proximity with attentional focus maintained on same toy or event *Parallel play*: noninteractive play on same toy	? *Signal*: always brief, never elaborated; response always "look at" or ignore. *Period*: no visual regard of peer
"Affiliative"[c]			
Percentage at Trimester I = 33% II = 34% III = 37%	*Offer* toy or cookie *Feed* (put food to peer's mouth) *Show* or "*Do at*" *Vocalize to* or *greet* ("Hi")	*Proximity*: shared focus of attention *Parallel play*: noninteractive toy action	A *Signal*: brief, "en passant." *Period*: at least occasional mutual visual regard

TABLE 1.   **(continued)**

Class	Form of Event		Type Within Class
	Signal/Response	Period	
	Name or *comment* on toy in peer's possession *Smile, "embrace";* *move to gaze at* *Engage in play:* (throw ball, bring book to peer)	*Joint play:* evidence of some paced turn-taking in play actions	*B* *Signal:* sustained, repeated, or done with an attention-getting vocalization. *Period:* repeated regard or vocalizations *C* *Signal or period:* accompanied by inviting or warm vocalizations or smiles
	Offer food to peer who has none and has been watching *B* eat *Offer toy* that has been dropped, is being reached for, is part of what peer is playing with *Invite peer* to join in play *Request peer's help*	*Work together:* social and/or play actions paced contingently to peer's behavior	*D* *Signal or period:* circumstantial evidence of premeditation or of contingency of actions

[a] Incidents with an agonistic flavor.
[b] Incidents whose flavor is neither affiliative nor agonistic.
[c] Incidents with a prosocial component.

examined irrespective of the signal or of the event that ensues. The second focuses on the quality of peer behavior, seeking to describe and understand the developmental change in the types of events that characterize second-year play group activities.

Initiation of Peer Encounters

Frequency • The average incidence of initiations of peer encounters by first-, second-, and third-trimester toddlers is presented in Table 2. Incidence of initiations toward the three other potential foci for interaction present in the playroom—mothers of peers, toys, and own mother—is supplied to set a standard of comparison. (Data on behavior to own mothers and to toys are drawn from independent but coordinated analyses of playroom behavior currently under preparation.) It is clear that at all three trimesters peers are noticeably infrequent targets of approach, ranking higher only than the unfamiliar adults who, seated in one place and engaged in conversation can hardly be expected to appear as inviting of potential interest.

A preference by the toddlers for activities that do not involve an age mate—a preference that remains surprisingly unchanged throughout the year—appears to be reflected in these data. It is relevant to ask here whether the wide differences in individual play group composition may have had some systematic effects that could confound or negate the inference suggested by the average trimester scores. The 33 groups indeed varied in degree of peer activity, ranging from three to as many as fifteen events recorded per average 10 minutes of observation. However none of the following parameters showed any significant differences in the observed frequency of peer encounters: group

TABLE 2.   Mean Number of Initiations to Peers, Mother, Toys, and Unfamiliar Adults per 10 Minutes of Observation[a]

	Trimester I		Trimester II		Trimester III	
	$\bar{X}$	N	$\bar{X}$	N	$\bar{X}$	N
Peers	2.2	(30)	2.6	(26)	2.0	(26)
Mother	7.2	(38)	10.6	(38)	12.5	(38)
Toys	10.9	(38)	12.9	(38)	12.5	(38)
Unfamiliar adults[b]	.32	(30)	.39	(26)	.34	(26)

[a] Excludes all initiations by solely visual regard.
[b] At each trimester about 50% of the toddlers made no such initiations at any time during the session.

size (three vs. four toddlers), sex composition (equal; predominance of boys; predominance of girls), or trimester age of participants (I, II, or III). Grouped by any of these criteria, the range of encounter frequencies remains wide, and statistical tests do not come close to suggesting a level of nonchance variation.

In the absence of definite evidence that wariness of unfamiliar age mates was a phenomenon prevalent in the play groups, the low incidence of initiations to peers is conceived here as a general preference for other activities rather than as an active avoidance of peer encounters. Within the current pool of 933 events, "withdrawal of self" in response to a neutral peer approach—a form of encounter that would support a wariness hypothesis—was observed on only three occasions. Pursuing this issue further, the frequencies of peer encounters in consecutive 5-minute segments of each of the 33 sessions were compared to see whether through decreasing potential effects of unfamiliarity, longer exposure to each other's presence may facilitate the amount of interaction. No evidence of such effects could be obtained: an overall F-test failed to show any significant differences in amount of interaction at different times of the session, and the mean frequency of encounters recorded in the first 5 minutes is no different from that seen in any subsequent 5-minute period. It remains quite possible, however, that active avoidance of peers is a relevant factor in the case of some of the babies. Suggestive evidence of such an individual characteristic can be adduced from observation of behaviors affected by, though not directed to peers (e.g., the pathways chosen by the toddler in moving between mother and toy repositories). However, since evidence of an active avoidance is the exception rather than the rule, I look to a preferential attraction to other targets in accounting for the characteristically low incidence of peer approaches observed in the playroom.

Individual Differences in Initiation Rates ● The data indicate that on the average, initiation of a peer encounter is an infrequent event. The average, of course, can obscure a wide range of individual differences: indeed, trimester initiation scores vary between an average rate of 0 to 7 per 10 minutes of observation. Do such individual differences reflect a stable orientation on the part of the given child vis-à-vis the world of his peers? Correlations between rate of initiation scores obtained in assessments increasingly distant in time (see Table 3) suggest that this indeed is a tenable hypothesis. The number of pairs currently available for continuity analyses is small, and the consequently large standard error of the correlation coefficients makes it unwise to speculate prematurely on the true strength of the association. Nevertheless, the data show that even under these highly heterogeneous conditions of individual assessments, a toddler's relative tendency to engage in peer contacts remains relatively consistent over the second year and is predictive of his subsequent behavior in nursery school.

Just what is reflected in the phenomenon of a differential proclivity to initiate peer contacts cannot be thoroughly examined until coding of all ten observa-

TABLE 3. Correlations of Rates of Initiation to Peers: (I) Within the Second Year; (II) Between 2 and 3½ Years of Age

Time Span	r	Number of Pairs	ρ
I. Adjacent play groups within any trimester (4 to 6 weeks)	.76	21	.01
Trimester I by trimester II scores	.41	21	.05
Trimester II by trimester III scores	.58	17	.05
Trimester I by trimester III scores	.73	16	.01
II. Average second-year scores by "sociability" cluster score at age 3½[a]	.42	33	.02

[a] Age 3½ behavior assessed in 5 weeks of observation in nursery school. The "sociability" cluster is defined by four Q-sort items summarized at the high end as "relates easily and frequently to others; takes every opportunity to join his peers in social activities; does not hesitate to initiate play with another child, to suggest activities, or ask for something he wants" and at the low end as "most often alone or in parallel rather than interactive play; remains on the outskirts of the group, watching others as they play; hesitates to ask for something he needs and generally talks little to others."

tions of each toddler establishes a data base sufficiently firm to permit analyses of relationships between quantity and qualities of peer interaction. However two immediately obvious potential factors—sex and sibs—can be dismissed as insufficient, even with this limited set of data. Overall second-year initiation scores (i.e., the average of all a child's play session assessments) of the 21 toddlers who had older sibs, compared with those of the 19 singleton 2-year-olds show a complete overlap of distribution: presence or absence of a sib in the home has no systematic effect. Boys' versus girls' initiation scores were compared at each trimester; no evidence of significant sex differences emerged at any age (U tests: $N = 16 \times 14$ or 14×12). By mothers' reports, nearly all the participating toddlers were having some experience with peers during this period, in child care centers, regular informal play groups, neighbor age mate exchanges, consistent playground outings, and so on. An informal survey of differences in amount of exposure to peers in these various settings makes it appear most unlikely that any systematic relations should emerge.

Targets of Contact Initiation • Analyses to date have failed to suggest any generalizations concerning proneness to be the target of a peer's contact initiation. Whatever the trimester age of the play group, the number of initiations made to other group members gives no significant correlation with the number of instances the particular toddler is selected by others as a target for contact (all three r's are about .2). Thus toddlers who are active within the peer scene apparently do not consistently attract more peer approaches than those who do not actively seek contact with their age mates. Furthermore, being selected as a target of peer initiations at one trimester age is not predictive of selection at subsequent trimester ages; correlations of individual selection rates in immediately adjacent play groups point to a similar lack of relationship (all insignificant, the four r's range from .2 to $-$ .3). The factors that make a toddler attractive to his age mates in any particular group vary widely: observation of these sessions suggests that both the qualities of his own play and the characteristics of those present act to contribute to his selection.

Since at somewhat older ages the factor of same-sex peer preference looms large in the research literature (Haskett, 1971), the possibility of sex as a determinant of target attractiveness was examined in the present pool of data. The probabilities of chance selection for either sex in each of the 33 play groups was established on the basis of the individual group's sex composition. Each toddler's number of initiations to boys and to girls in each play group was then computed as a deviation from the appropriate chance expectation and expressed in terms of a z-score. Figure 1 presents the resulting distributions of scores for boys and for girls. Given the small number of initiations a toddler is likely to emit over the full period of observation, the absolute value of these z-scores

FIGURE 1. Sex preferential behavior: distribution of initiation scores expressed as deviations from chance expectations for sex selection. Cross-hatched areas of the boys' bar represent the scores of a single toddler sampled on nine different occasions.

should not be taken as firmly established. However, the nearly normal shape of the two distributions is rather strong evidence that neither same- nor opposite-sex preference is a relevant factor in determining initiation of a peer approach in this setting and at this age. The sex selection scores obtained by the single boy whose consistently active peer behavior has been coded in all his play sessions appear in the figure; their spread reflects the degree to which factors other than sex must act to particularize an age mate as a target of preferred approach.

In summary, I wish to underscore three points made by the rate of initiation analyses. First, given the options of the playroom, toddlers of this age devote a great deal of visual attention to their peers but do not elect them as a major target for contact or active engagement. This is as true after 40 minutes of group participation as at the outset of the sessions, and in the final, end-of-second-year play groups as in the early first-trimester meetings. Interaction with age mates remains difficult for toddlers of this age who appear to find that toys and their own mothers—and particularly the combination of both—provide more effective arenas for exploration of their own capacities. Second, a large variety of factors, many of them presumably situation specific, must combine to trigger the initiation of a peer encounter by an initiation-prone toddler. More than any other, a characteristic readiness to engage with the peer world may be the single most important, though not sufficient, contributing factor. Thus far observations not yet made systematic suggest that such a readiness may be suppressed under particular group conditions, although the obverse phenomenon—initiation by a characteristically nonpeer-oriented toddler—appears unlikely to be elicited even under what seem to be the most favorable circumstances. Finally, obvious but not to be overlooked, is the evidence of apparently characteristic individual differences in readiness to engage a peer which should act as a caution to any generalized proscriptions concerning the effects of exposure to age mates.

Developmental Changes in Peer Events

From quantity and its determinants to quality and its developmental change: what occurs in playroom peer encounters, and what differences can be detected as age mates grow older?

Characteristic Forms of Peer Encounters • The most typical peer encounter involved only two participants (all but 29 of the total of 933 events were dyadic) coming together in a brief signal-response exchange (772 instances).[3] Nondis-

---

[3] In about 10% of instances two or even sometimes three consecutive signal-response exchanges between a pair followed in quick succession. Denoted as "clusters," they either lack evidence of any kind of mutually responsive interrelationship or reflect no more than a deterioration of the interaction, as when a play event is followed by a dispute over the toy. For present purposes they are handled as separate single exchange events.

putatious periods of joining in any form of what is conventionally thought of as play accounted for no more than about one-tenth of all peer activities; in the vast majority of cases such periods were brief, very few being sustained for as long as one minute.

In each trimester encounters reflecting some form of "Disagreements" prevailed in about 45% of playroom peer activities (cf. Table 1). Within this class, events centering around *takes, attempted takes,* and *disputes* (characteristically, sustained tugs-of-war) accounted for about 70% of the encounters: the issue of who is to possess some playroom object lies at the heart of what contributed to the agonistic flavor of these sessions. Within the grouping of encounters classed as "Affiliative," which reflect about a third of each trimester events, *offers*—some accepted, some ignored—were the defining criterial signal in about 40% of all instances. Adding the clearly related *show* gesture, about half of all observed "prosocial" signal-response exchanges also revolved around an age mate–toy combination: whether agonistic or prosocial, the central role of objects in mediating peer playroom interaction is made clearly evident.

At this gross level of descriptive analysis, and given the unchangingly low incidence of playroom peer encounters, the relative *lack* of developmental change comes to the fore—a point somewhat uncomfortably discussed in a preliminary report on peer playroom behavior (Bronson, 1974a). When the unit of study moves to consider the encounter as a gestalt that differentially highlights some among its specified behavioral qualities and the focus turns to analyses of thus derived *types* of peer events, a rather different picture emerges.

Developmental Changes in Types of Peer Events • Figure 2 records the average rate of initiation of different types of events for toddlers in trimesters I, II, and III. Trimester rate of initiation profiles are based on all incidents observed for the given age (335, 258, and 340, respectively); the significance of age changes was assessed by the Wilcoxon Sign Test on data generated by whichever subsample of toddlers was represented at any two ages (for sample N's cf. Table 3). Before proceeding with any analyses, we compared the frequency of initiation of all types of events by males and by females: no sex differences were found at any age on any type of event (U-tests, with N either 16×14 or 14×12).

Given this system of organizing the data, the change over the three trimesters is quite marked and clear. Without any notable changes in the relative frequency of the class of events, "Disagreements" become significantly more often more intense; concurrently, the class of "Affiliative" encounters is increasingly represented by initiations of the more sociable (C) and complex (D) types of events. Incidents classed as "?" decrease markedly after the first trimester, at which time close to three-quarters were by "touches" of a peer's toy or person. It is tempting to speculate that the tailing off of an earlier, more purely investigatory mode of peer interaction may be reflected here—a transition from the

FIGURE 2.   Rate of initiation of different types of peer events: significance of age differences and profiles within each trimester.

perception of a peer *qua* object to that of a peer *qua* a unique kind of object. In any case, whatever their class, all types of events that seem from a social perspective to be haphazard become noticeably less frequent over the year; although no more frequent, peer encounters nevertheless take on a progressively more intentional guise.

The pattern of developmental change is plausible and thus requires little in the way of exposition; more difficult to tease out is evidence that can generate hypotheses concerning possible mediating factors that promote these developments.

Disagreement Incidents ● Neither "aggression" nor "hostility" seems to be necessary or appropriate to invoke as a significant determinant of the relatively high frequency or the increased intensity of "Disagreement" events. First, recall that at all ages the majority of such events center around issues of toy

takes: the more intense anger or frustration that comes to accompany these encounters seems to be reasonably understood by reference to the concurrent
changes in the toddlers' involvement with playroom objects. From an early
prevalence of undifferentiated manipulations or exercises of discrete schemas
(frequently devoid of concurrent visual attention), toy contacts typically progress
through more focused explorations of the potential use of the particular toy to the
emergence of third-trimester events in which the toy becomes the means for
achieving a goal imposed by the child himself on the structure of his play. (Very
sketchy evidence for this statement has appeared in Bronson, 1974a; far more extensive but incomplete subsequent analyses give me the confidence to repeat it
here.) The inference is simple: as the qualities of the *particular* toy become more
important to the toddler's own scheme of things, his willingess to relinquish the
toy to another becomes less likely. I believe this to be reflected in the current peer
data not only in the decrease of events in which a toy casually changes hands, but
also in the decrease of the proportion of successful to unsuccessful takes (i.e., of
submission vs. withdrawal of object in response to a take gesture) from a ratio of
2:1 in the first trimester to 1:1 in the two subsequent periods.

A detailed analysis of all toy disagreement encounters is planned when the
available material has been completely coded. These data—which include
details of the behavioral sequence as well as its antecedents and consequences—should serve to illuminate both normative and individual differences
in the probable intent of behaviors that so easily can be misconstrued as reflecting the currently diffuse construct of "aggression." In a large number of observed playroom "takes" the initiator's direction of visual regard—focused on
the toy with nary a glance at the possessor's face—suggests that the peer is being relegated to the role of an obstacle, nothing more. In a similar vein, note
that Bates et al. (1973) describe a 7-month-old girl's take of an object from an
adult, stating that "the striking aspect . . . is that the child treats the adult exclusively as an obstacle or handle that is involved in reaching objects and not as
an agent that could satisfy her needs" (p. 22). Whether the capacity to perceive a
peer as an agent that can satisfy—and thereby also prevent—fulfillment of one's
needs may be a cognitive-social development that emerges both gradually and
later raises an issue as relevant to understanding the function of early peer-
directed behavior as it is to permitting assessment of individual differences in the
intent underlying a given toddler's agonistic act.

A second factor of potentially great interest may be examined from the
viewpoint of the increased incidence of the more intense types of
"Disagreements": it revolves around the toddler's emergent concept of
possession and his evolving notions of the concept of self. This can be expressed
as a subjective summary of impressions gained over endless hours of observation: whatever intrinsic value an object may have for the toddler, its loss, of itself, becomes increasingly experienced as a very personal affront. It is as if "I"

was being partly defined by exploration of the notion of what is "mine" or under "my" control. The objective substantiation for this impression is still diffuse. One of the threads comes from peer events of "protest" and "assertion" (essentially "Don't" and "Mine") directed toward a peer whose behavior is in no adult-observable way interfering with the initiator's interests. Occasionally the assertion may have a quasi-challenging or inviting flavor: for example, in a period of play session lull during which all toddlers have been quietly standing or sitting by their mothers, Sylvia steps out toward the middle of the room, extends the toy she has been holding toward the others, and loudly states "Mine!" (Achieving no effect, she returns to her own play.) More often, however, the circumstances surrounding such behavior at least suggestively support the notion that "mine" is being used to determine the boundaries between the alienable and inalienable "me": for example, a few moments after entry Linda—not yet engaged in anything beyond a thorough survey of the scene—mutters repeatedly "Mine! Mine!" and remains where she is, continuing her survey. Protests and assertions are frequent accompaniments of tug-of-war disputes: the unique flavor of these "pure" instances which were rare but increasingly frequent over the year is attributable to the absence of any possessive or defensive action following the statement. (Over the three trimesters, the N's of protest and assertion events are 6, 9, and 28, accounting for, respectively, 4, 7, and 14% of all "Disagreement" incidents observed at each age.) A second suggestive thread comes from instances of very intensive disputes in which neither participant has any previous investment in the toy at stake and neither pays any attention to it subsequent to the encounter in which both expended so much effort. Contradictory of the first line of argument presented, these events remain to ask insistently why the sheer fact of possession should have the power to activate the behavior of the participants in such an encounter. A final line of suggestive evidence is adduced from study of mother-toddler communication in the playroom setting. With increasing frequency, loss of a toy—even in a very brief and mild take-submit exchange—tends to be brought to the mother's attention in a manner strongly suggestive of an indignant "look at what happened to me!" communication. In this group and setting the mothers tend to be reluctant to intervene when the behavior of another person's child is at issue (cf. Bronson, 1974b): sharing an experience of personal affront rather than asking for help seems to be what underlies the toddlers' behavior in such instances.[4]

The discussion has centered on intuitions that emerge from consideration of salient or prevalent patterns; from this perspective most "Disagreement" events

---

[4] Two incidents are offered for those who find illustrative anecdotes illuminating. (1) Max pulls Diana away from the pegbanger with which she was involved in intensive play and takes over. She stands by, mute and gazing at him. Runs over to mother: with one hand on mother's lap, she orients to point toward the now totally involved Max and, looking directly at him, produces a long string of inflected and indignant vocalizations. The mother smiles at her behavior and diverts to

are social only in the very limited sense of incidentally including an age mate within their configuration. In some very rare instances a toddler is seen to focus directly on the peer, appearing to explore the effect of his agonistic behaviors on the other. Very truly social, the occasional early existence of this form of relating to age mates demands study of individual differences to pinpoint its antecedents and determine its consequences.

Affiliative Incidents • Regardless of whether they involve a toy, by definition the affiliative class of peer events has the age mate as the central focus of at least some level of attention. Examination of what such encounters involve and how they change over the year has brought out three main points.

The first concerns the offer gesture and the role it plays in the restricted social communicative repertoire of the young toddler. Its prevalence as a social signal cannot be doubted, not only as it relates to peers (where it defines an average of about 40% of all types of "Affiliative" events) but in relation to other social targets as well: about one-third of the 134 instances in which an unfamiliar adult was contacted during the 33 sessions took the form of "offer"; in the close to 3000 initiations to mothers coded for analysis of toddler-mother playroom communication, the frequency of simple offer gestures (i.e., unadorned by requests for help or play) was second only to that of purely visual checks.

What is the function of this gesture? How does it originate? Is its use restricted (as my observations of this age group suggest) only to animate targets or their play representations? The Bates et al. (1973) exploratory study of the emergence of the offer gesture and of its position in the full developmental sequence of communicative intentions is one of the beginnings of work that will be needed before such questions can be answered. At present I can merely issue strong cautions against a presumption that "offer" implies "share." Many of the gives (i.e., accepted offers) have a "deposit and move off" quality; a number of the brief offer gestures to peers seem to be near-reflexive reactions sparked by the age mate moving by, whereas in some instances of highly sustained or repeated offer incidents, the flavor is one of "I want you to *react*" rather than "I want you to *have* this." Although I shall question later whether even the seemingly facilitative type D offers are activated by the altruism that "sharing" implies, in no way do I intend any denigration of the offer gesture as a significant event in the development of prosocial communication. On the contrary: although a "take" reaction to a toy held by a peer is easily subsumed within the

---

speak to an adult. (2) In passing by Candy, Sylvia takes the flyswatter from the former's hands and moves on. Candy gazes at her retreating back: in finally turning away, she comes to face a peer's mother who is sitting nearby. Glancing at her, Candy flips her arms, spreading them in a downward gesture with a strong "Hunh!" vocalization—the echo of a perfectly adult "will you just look at that!" is experienced by the observer. The adult says nothing, Candy diverts.

well-studied tendency to reach for that which captures visual attention, the offer action, with its inherent potential to evoke a different kind of feedback both
from the target and the adults in charge, remains to be investigated as perhaps
representing an early behavioral proclivity quite significant among the
processes that contribute to the final emergence of intentional affiliation.

The possible role of the feedback a toddler receives from the age mate following an affiliative action generates the second point to be discussed. It should be
recalled that classification of a signal-response incident as "Affiliative" depended solely on the presence of one of the several predetermined kinds of
signals within the exchange (cf. Table 1); the response to such a signal was irrelevant to its classification. It clearly is pertinent to ask whether acts that are
warmly social or facilitative of the peer's interests (types C and D) may not
evoke a response from the age mate different from that elicited by the other two
less sophisticated types, thus serving to reinforce the occurrence of types C and
D and contribute to their increasing incidence. To examine this question, the
responses of the targets of affiliative events were classified into one of the three
levels. (1) *Ignore:* either no reaction or "looks only" to an offer. (2) *Limited
reaction:* look at initiator, accept an offer; or shake head, move back, and in
essence say "no." (3) *Respond with social behavior:* any affiliative response
involving behaviors beyond a limited reaction.

The results of this double categorization of events by type of affiliative initiation and level of social response are given in Table 4. Clearly the proportion of
events in which an affiliative communication evokes anything beyond a limited
reaction is very small and, more important, no evidence of greater social
responsiveness to type C and D signals can be suggested. Moreover, the higher
level of social responsiveness implicit in instances of "Respond with social behavior" shows no relation to the respondent's age: a survey of the 28 occur-
rences of such responses reveals them to be near evenly split among toddlers of

**TABLE 4. Type of Affiliative Signal by Level of Response: Percentage and
Number of Signal-Response Patterns Recorded Over All Sessions**

Level of Response	Type of Affiliative Signal			
	A: Brief, "en passant"	B: Sustained, repeated	C: Warm, inviting	D: Evidence of pre-meditation, contingency
Ignore	13% (5)	22% (21)	6% (3)	17% (9)
Limited reaction	72% (28)	68% (64)	78% (41)	73% (39)
Respond with social behavior	15% (6)	10% (9)	15% (8)	9% (5)

the three trimester ages. The significant developmental change in the complexity of initiating signals is *not* paralleled by a similar development in level of social responsiveness. Indeed, the few toddlers who at one point or another had been observed as both initiators and targets of a type *D* act gave clear evidence that a child capable of a highly sophisticated peer approach will nevertheless more often than not react in a most limited fashion when he finds himself the target of a near-replica of his own sophisticated initiation. Whatever may be the reason, it appears that the readiness to initiate what have been classed as complex types of social peer events surpasses the readiness to respond in a manner conducive to a sustained affiliative interaction. Since in this situation at least, age mates do not act to train one another to more complex social behaviors by supplying differential feedback matched to the level of the signal, the increased incidence of more sophisticated social approaches does not appear to be primarily a consequence of immediately contingent peer reinforcement. In a series of analyses, the available material has been further examined in search of any evidence of within-pair reciprocities that although delayed in time, may serve as agents reinforcing a particular type of approach. None have been revealed: within any play group, who selects whom and for what type of interaction appears to be a function of many factors in which the qualities of the age mate's own social behavior play a very minor role.

The final point takes the form of a question: given the preceding observation, what factor(s) may be operating to bring about the increased incidence of playroom encounters classed as type *D* events? Two different kinds of incident comprised the bulk of the total of only 79 recorded to date: about half these were seemingly facilitative offers of toys and cookies (cf. Table 1), and a further third consisted of periods of contingent exchanges referred to as "work together." The latter encounters by definition join the toddlers in actions that are mutually responsive and thus require both perception of what the other is doing and use of this information in shaping one's own actions. In the majority of instances there is a commonly perceived goal to be jointly achieved: sometimes mediated by the toy (putting the pieces of the segmented ball together; filling a container and getting it closed), sometimes by the reenactment of commonly experienced events (pretend feeding of each other; hide and seek). In a few instances these periods involve sustained exchanges of vocalizations or words; to date all these prototypic "conversations" have been marked by a lack of communication of meaning.[5] The factor of contingency, or of role alternation—"you do, then I do"—seems to operate rarely but increasingly in bring-

---

[5] An example: carrying a cookie, Gwen passes by Dwight who is drinking apple juice. She stops, they look at each other. In the subsequent period of exchanges Gwen repeatedly comments "juice," "cookie," "apple"; to each Dwight responds with "huh?" (All of Gwen's words have been heard to be used appropriately by Dwight on previous occasions.) Later in the session, in an unusual rejoin event, Dwight shows Gwen the flyswatter with which he has been playing and vocalizes "fly." She smiles broadly and responds "apple?" Both look at each other briefly, then divert.

ing age mates together in periods of shared social interaction. These periods are generally brief, however, and most pairs split at their conclusion not to rejoin in any later repetition of such an incident. Thus "do" rather than "be" together seems to be the crucial mediating factor, a factor closely linked to the toddler's growing interest in introducing complex sequences of different elements into his play. Nevertheless, even if they are triggered by a personal rather than social intent, such occasional experiences surely must operate to expand the dawning perception of the age mate as similar to oneself, particularly if (as sometimes occurs) each toddler additionally sees the reflection of his own pleasure at successful completion of the goal in the peer's concurrent grin or excited vocalization.

Offers of objects that on circumstantial evidence are just what the peer needs or wants at the moment contribute most to the increase in type D events thus far observed. Achievement of a cognitive capacity to perceive the relationship between the object and the age mate, and to make an inference about the peer's intent, seem to be prerequisites in initiating such an offer: a development in the toddler's ability to take the role of the other is implied by such an occurrence. What may motivate such an act? The possible contribution of parental socialization for sharing cannot be discounted: to me it seems unlikely to be significant in view of the concomitant evidence of the mothers' failure to have achieved the socializing effect they openly state as being the one they most desire—no grabbing and fighting over toys. The peer's behavior afford no immediate or subsequent rewards for the facilitative act of the toddler, who himself seldom remains to observe the consequences of his actions on the other. Adding the observation that at all ages hearing a peer in distress tends to evoke little reaction beyond checking out the source of the noise, I lean against the notion that sympathy or an altruistic intent to share play much part in activating such offers. Rather, I tend to subsume them as another example of what increasingly characterizes the toddler's behavior with all playroom objects: having learned what belongs with what, the toddler seems moved to bring together the separate pieces with no more than an end state of completion being the goal. However one aspect of such events may contribute much to the emergence of intentional sharing: the mother of the target of a facilitative offer frequently encourages him to say "thank you" or comments on how "nice" the initiator is being. Although if my analysis is correct, the mother is misinterpreting the motivational factors of the situation, she nevertheless is serving one of her most valuable functions: that of expanding the baby's view of what is happening and providing labels with which he can develop new categories for interaction.

CONCLUDING REMARKS

To reach a reasonable basis for making statements about the role of early peer experiences will require many more investigations of concurrent developments and subsequent effects than have been accomplished to date. These concluding remarks merely reflect the views my work has led me to develop and to which it will continue to be addressed.

Given a setting that allows toddlers the freedom of many choices, the data I reported unequivocally show that unacquainted second-year age mates characteristically engage in much looking but in little active seeking of social contact with one another. In this stage of development the main attraction seems to be to those social and nonsocial targets that either through direct control and exploration or through responsive feedback, afford the toddler means for expanding his ability to comprehend his environment. Having established the first attachment bond and thus achieved a secure base from which to explore the use of increasingly competent motor and cognitive capacities, mastery becomes the issue, and the age mate at this stage has little to contribute. Indeed, contrary to the main thrust of my data, in some of our earliest groups very young non-walkers—only sporadically involved in manipulating a toy—were observed intermittently echoing each other's vocalizations or reflecting each other's gestural patterns. Soon after, too sophisticated by now to find glee in achieving a mere reaction but seeking rather a response that might further the structure of a plan and too experienced not to be aware of the unpredictability that results from the age mates' own self-direction, second-year toddlers still lack the means to express and understand intents clearly enough to permit them the kind of reciprocally supportive engagement in a common goal that could lay a basis for true social mutuality. Through most of the second year the peer's most prevalent function becomes neither more nor less than to serve as a special object whose reactions contribute but one strand in the toddler's developing cognitive network. With the emergence of linguistic competence, the ability to both explain and to share experience permits the meshing so difficult to achieve earlier.

This interpretation—which goes quite beyond the data presented here—leads me to continue investigating with focus on two issues. The first is the matter of individual differences in how young age mates use one another. The material already at hand gives strong indications that characteristic and widely different styles of relating to peers will be evident from quite early in the second year. Study of the concomitants of such styles and of their relation to social behavior at nursery school age—when age mates begin to take an increasingly firm place within the child's network of social relations—represents to me the most central problem for investigation of the development of human affiliative systems.

The second issue derives from a belief in the crucial need to establish a firm base of behavioral details of what happens in early peer encounters. Seeing that such encounters emerge as a low-frequency phenomenon, heuristic organizational devices such as the classificatory system used in this study are necessary to evolve analyses aimed at genotypical phenomena. The dangers of adult-based preconceptions of what is criterial, coupled with the tendency to reify labels into inferential mediating constructs are difficult to avoid and only careful and precise attention to exactly what happens under just what circumstances can circumvent fruitless controversies and perhaps seriously misleading conclusions.

Finally, the emergent interest in early peer behavior must be finely attuned to considerations of the possible practical consequences of an investigator's intellectual excitement on social policy. The product of the years of carefully controlled and sequential work with other species (such as reported by different authors in this volume) is eloquent evidence of complex developmental interactions and tradeoffs. For the young of our own species, the question of how much experience of peers, attained at what ages and under what conditions may be facilitative, and when perhaps detrimental for their development is an issue that deserves to retain our central and sustained concern.

References

Bates, E., Camaioni, L., & Volterra, V. The acquisition of performatives prior to speech. Laboratory technical report no. 129 of the Consiglio Nazionale delle Ricerche, Rome, 1973.

Bronson, W. C. Competence and the growth of personality. In Kevin J. Connolly & Jerome Bruner (Eds.), *The growth of competence.* Academic Press: New York, 1974a.

Bronson, W. C. Mother-toddler interaction: A perspective on studying the development of competence. *Merrill-Palmer Quarterly,* 1974b, **20,** 4, 275–301.

Haskett, G. J. Modification of peer preferences of first grade children. *Developmental Psychology,* 1971, **4,** 3, 429–433.

CHAPTER 6

The Role and Reason of Peer Relationships in Rhesus Monkeys[1]

STEPHEN J. SUOMI

AND

HARRY F. HARLOW
Department of Psychology
University of Wisconsin

The importance of peer friendships has traditionally been underemphasized by developmental researchers and theorists. A number of studies have examined the social interactions of the younger members of macaque species with each other (Rosenblum, 1961; Hansen, 1966; Harlow, 1969; Rosevear, 1974; Ruppenthal et al., 1974; Norikoshi, 1974). But without question, both research and theory in the area of social development have focused mainly on the mother-infant dyad as the basis and standard for subsequent social behavior. Such a bias is understandable; mother love was sacred long before Freud discovered orality and its implications, and it is hardly surprising that learning theorists, their eyes open for primal sources of reinforcement, fixated on mother-infant affection as the alpha and omega of social learning.

In our research at Wisconsin we have not ignored mothers, be they real or surrogate. The search for primary determinants of infant affection naturally began with the mother, even though the major source was found to lie in contact comfort, not in nutrition as most theorists had previously maintained. In the process of investigating the developmental consequences of mother love, however, we found that other affectional relationships readily developed in infant monkeys. Most prominent of these were the interactions of young monkeys with age-mates or peers. It soon became apparent that the peer system, being one of affection, was a major component in the development and maintenance

[1] This research was supported by United States Public Health Service grants MH-11894 and MH-18070 to the University of Wisconsin Primate Laboratory and by the Grant Foundation.

of social activities in rhesus monkeys (Harlow & Harlow, 1965; Harlow, 1969; Suomi & Harlow, 1971a).

NORMATIVE DEVELOPMENT OF PEER INTERACTIONS

To understand the normative pattern of social development in the rhesus monkey, one must be familiar with the ontology of peer affection, as exhibited by monkeys reared both in feral and in socially complex laboratory environments (e.g., nuclear families: Harlow, 1971; Ruppenthal et al., 1974). Most investigators agree that rhesus monkeys mature at a rate four to five times that of human infants.

FIGURE 1.   Mother and infant monkey in close physical contact.

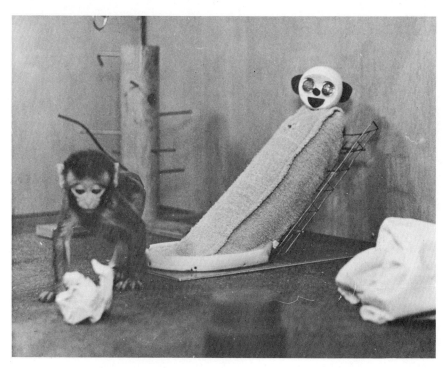

FIGURE 2.   Early exploration by infant monkey.

The rhesus monkey infant typically spends most of its first month in ventral contact with its mother (Figure 1). Initial behaviors, chiefly clinging and sucking, are primarily reflexive and are directed toward maintenance of close physical contact with the mother. The infant monkey acquires voluntary control over most of its behaviors gradually, and by 1 month of age it begins to leave its mother for brief periods to explore the surrounding environment (Figure 2). During the second month of life the infant rhesus spends an increasing proportion of time away from its mother, being exposed for the first time to other monkeys, including those its own age. Initially it does not differentiate between social and nonsocial objects in its environment, exploring each with equal frequency, both tactually and orally (Baldwin & Suomi, 1974; see Figures 3 and 4). As the baby monkey acquires greater sensory-motor integration, however, it begins to prefer mobile, animate playmates to static, inanimate playthings (Harlow & Harlow, 1965). By 3 months of age it is initiating contact and elementary play behaviors and is actively reciprocating similar initiations from other monkeys. By 4 months of age it has developed remarkable agility, ingenuity, and versatility in its repertoire of social activities.

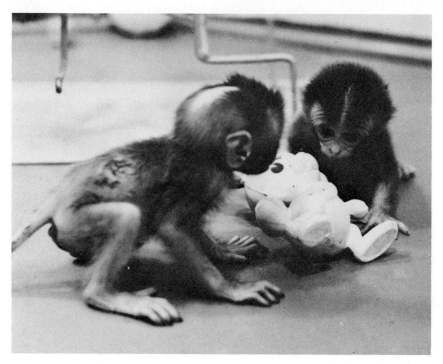

<small>FIGURE 3.</small>   Simultaneous social and nonsocial exploration by infant monkey.

Between the fourth and eighth months of life the monkey's waking hours are dominated by play activity, primarily of two forms. The first, termed "rough-and-tumble play," can accurately be described as a monkey wrestling match. Such play involves much physical contact, including vigorous rolling, scrapping, clawing, and biting; but at this age, at least when the rough-and-tumble activity is among friends, physical injury rarely results. The other distinctive play form has been denoted "approach-avoidance play," and it resembles the child's game of tag—a great deal of purposeful pursuit among play partners, but little actual physical contact. Although both sexes exhibit both forms of play at some time, rough-and-tumble play is predominantly a male activity (see, e.g., Figure 5), whereas approach-avoidance activity is mostly for the girls.

Recently, Mears and Harlow (1975) have described a third form of play which they call "self-motion play." It is practiced by both sexes and can be expressed either socially or individually; moreover, its emergence clearly predates the development of the conventional modes of play just described. Self-motion play is illustrated in Figure 6 and its development is plotted in Figure 7. Its distinguishing feature is the use of physical movement as a reinforcement in its own right

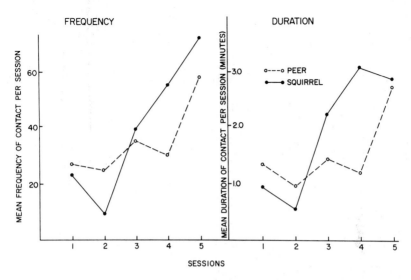

FIGURE 4. Frequency and duration of contact with inanimate object (toy squirrel) and peer during initial exposure to each.

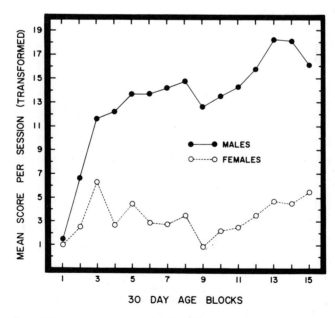

FIGURE 5. Sex differences in development of rough-and-tumble play.

157

FIGURE 6. Infant monkey engaging in self-motion play.

FIGURE 7. Development of self-motion play in young rhesus monkeys.

158

rather than as a means to approach or interact with a reinforcing object such as a play partner. It is conceivable that self-motion play, along with curiosity, is a primary motivational factor in the development of complex play and more advanced social behaviors, but at present this is an untested hypothesis.

Throughout the second 4 months of life play is the predominant social activity of monkeys, but that does not mean it is the sole social activity. Other behavior patterns that eventually develop into adult forms are discernible, but often masked in play interchange. For example, aggression matures during this chronological period, and among familiar peers it appears primarily in the form of exceedingly vigorous rough-and-tumble play that may result in bumps and bruises but rarely in open wounds. However, 8-month-old monkeys will readily and repeatedly attack a stranger placed in their familiar group, even if the stranger is older and larger (Harlow, 1969, see Figure 8). Thus by 8 months of life the capability for aggression is well-developed, even though it is seldom exhibited in interactions with familiar playmates. Clearly monkeys of

FIGURE 8. Young monkeys aggressing against an older stranger.

FIGURE 9.   Male and female play initiations among monkeys reared in nuclear family environments.

this age develop affectional relationships of varying intensities with specific peers, and although no individual relationship may be as strong as earlier mother-infant bonds, cumulatively they account for a greater proportion of infant activity than does interaction with the mother. Early in life, then, a monkey typically develops a strong attachment to a single adult female and loose attachments to numerous peers.

FIGURE 10.   Sex differences in development of male mounting behavior.

FIGURE 11. Sex differences in development of female presenting behavior.

We would be remiss if we did not point out that there exist significant differences in quantity, if not in quality, of peer-directed behaviors between male and female monkeys during the second 4 months of life. At the risk of offending many and pleasing few, we maintain that such differences are biological rather than cultural, both in their source and in their significance (Harlow & Lauersdorf, 1974). Alternative hypotheses obviously can be entertained by nonbeliev-

021

FIGURE 12. Sex differences in aggressive behavior.

ers. Yet the data themselves are unambiguous. There are clear-cut differences in the behaviors of male and female monkeys, and such differences are apparent early in life, long before reproductive capability is attained by either sex at approximately 3½ to 4 years of age in females and 4 to 4½ years in males.

For example, as mentioned previously, males show higher levels of rough-and-tumble play than females, and the reverse is true of approach-avoidance play. In general, males show higher levels of total play activity than females. However, various investigators have attributed this to different tendencies. Rosenblum (1961) reported that male rhesus monkey infants initiated play bouts with members of both sexes equally often, whereas females were more likely to interact with female rather than male partners. In contrast, Ruppenthal et al. (1974) found that males showed higher levels of play interaction with males than females, and females tended to spend equal time with male and female peers (Figure 9).

Sex differences are apparent in behaviors other than play. Although members of both sexes exhibit mounting and presenting, mounts are more common in males and presents are more typically female, as indicated in Figures 10 and 11. Mounting and presenting are the appropriate adult sexual patterns of male and female monkeys, respectively. Both sexes exhibit increasing amounts of aggressive behavior after 6 months of age, but males display much higher levels of aggression than females (Figure 12). Conversely, females exhibit higher levels of affiliative behavior, including grooming and other modes of social exploration (see Figure 13). In sum, major sex differences in behavior

FIGURE 13. Sex differences in affiliative behavior among monkeys reared in nuclear family environments.

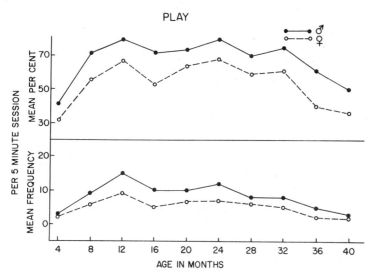

FIGURE 14. Proportion of total behavior exhibited in play interactions among monkeys reared in the nuclear family.

directed toward peers develop between 4 and 8 months of age in well-socialized monkeys, and these differences persist largely unchanged in form through adulthood.

High levels of social interaction with peers are observed well beyond 8 months of age, but the form of the interaction appears to be dependent on the sex of the monkey and on its social environment. In most feral and laboratory environments, for example, play activity begins to decline precipitously after the first year of life. It is superseded by more aggression and nonsocial explora-tion in males and by increased affiliative behavior in females. Interestingly enough, males seem to prefer to interact with monkeys their own age or older, whereas females spend much of their time with both adult females and with neonates and infants of both sexes. An exception can be found among monkeys raised in a laboratory-formed nuclear family environment (Harlow, 1971), where offspring have access to both parents, other adult male-female pairs, and siblings and peers of disparate ages. Here, monkeys continue to play at exceed-ingly high levels throughout the third year of life, as can be seen in Figure 14. However, the pattern of sex differences in forms of behavior appears to be com-parable to that found in other complex social environments (Ruppenthal et al., 1974).

To summarize, monkey infants rapidly develop extensive and complicated patterns of social interactions with peers. These activities supersede interactions with the mother soon after the third month of life and dominate monkey activity through adulthood. In the course of behavioral development the rhesus monkey maintains loose affectional ties with a large number of its peers, rather than strong ties with a single age-mate or parent.

FACTORS AFFECTING THE DEVELOPMENT OF PEER FRIENDSHIPS

Many experiments performed under controlled laboratory settings have disclosed a number of manipulations that influence the development of peer friendships. These include various forms of social deprivations early in life, breaking of specific attachment bonds by social separation, and traumatic manipulations of the environment, such as repeated presentation of fear-inducing stimuli.

Social Deprivation Early in Life

Perhaps the most well-documented finding regarding social development of primates has been that monkeys reared in impoverished social environments fail to develop species-appropriate social, sexual, aggressive, and maternal behavior patterns and instead exhibit varying degrees of psychopathology. Research at the Wisconsin Primate Laboratory has more specifically demonstrated that monkeys denied the opportunity to interact with and ultimately form affectional relationships with peers fail to develop adequate social repertoires, independent of the availability of other monkeys such as fathers and mothers.

For example, monkey infants reared for the first 6 months of life in total or partial social isolation exhibit severe deficits in locomotive, exploratory, and social behaviors when they emerge from isolation. The appropriate responses of grooming, play, and other social interactions are minimal; instead these subjects spend the majority of their time engaging in autistic-like self-clasping, stereotypic rocking and huddling, and self-mouthing behaviors (see Figures 15 and 16). Sexual responses are inadequate and inappropriate among isolate-reared monkeys, and females who have been artificially inseminated ("motherless mothers," as Arling & Harlow, 1967, termed them) typically display poor maternal behavior. Aggressive behavior is primarily self-directed or, in social situations, inappropriately directed. For example, a mature social isolate may repeatedly attack a dominant adult male, a blunder that few socially sophisticated monkeys are foolish enough to make. In summary, total or partial isolation initiated at birth has a devastating effect on the development of appropriate monkey peer relationships (Harlow, Dodsworth, & Harlow, 1965).

However, isolation from all conspecifics is not necessary to ensure inadequate formation of affectional bonds with peers. We have found that monkeys reared with biological mothers but denied the opportunity to interact with

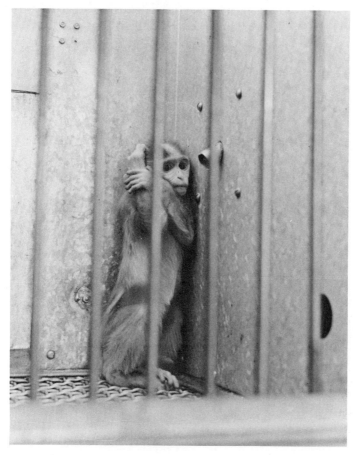

FIGURE 15.   Self-clasping behavior by isolate-reared monkey.

peers early in life also fail to develop appropriate patterns of interactive behavior when finally exposed to peers. Although such mother-reared infants do
not usually exhibit the range of aberrant self-directed behaviors—self-clasping,
stereotypic rocking, and excessive self-orality—commonly displayed by total
isolates, their social behaviors are often far from satisfactory. These monkeys
are generally contact-shy. They tend to avoid most play interactions, and they
engage in activity associated with grooming far less often than normal monkeys
of comparable age. Furthermore, infants reared by mother only (MOs) are likely
to be hyperaggressive when they do contact peers. In short, they do not make
good playmates. We have found that the longer such monkeys are chronologi-

FIGURE 16.   Self-mouthing behavior by isolate-reared monkey.

cally denied the opportunity to interact with peers, the more gross are their social inadequacies (Alexander & Harlow, 1965; see, e.g., Figure 17).

When infant monkeys are separated from their mothers at birth and permitted continual exposure to peers only, we observe a different aberration in social development. Here the problem is not failure to establish contact and affectional bonds with age-mates; it is the opposite. "Together-together-reared" monkeys (Harlow, 1969) become hyperattached to one another.

Recall that monkeys reared in adequate social environments with their mothers begin life exhibiting high levels of maternal clinging but eventually wander away from their mothers to explore the world. Many investigators have suggested that the infants are actively encouraged by their mothers to leave (Hansen, 1966; Hinde & Spencer-Booth, 1967; Hinde & White, 1974). Monkey infants housed together from birth without their mothers cling, as do all other monkey infants; but having no mothers with whom to make contact, they cling to one another, as is illustrated in Figure 18. With mothers who actively reject them later in life, clinging is an adaptive, functional response. With peers who themselves reciprocate the behavior, it is maladaptive and detrimental to social development. It is somewhat difficult for a baby monkey to explore its environment with another monkey hanging on for dear life, and even the most enthusiastic attempts at play are effectively terminated by a big bearhug.

Hence it is not surprising that together-together-reared monkeys are retarded in terms of social development. Eventually clinging subsides, and adequate development of play and associated behaviors generally follows. However, certain anomalies persist through adulthood. Together-together-reared monkeys are disturbed by the mildest of stresses. Moreover, later in life they are unusually aggressive toward monkeys outside their own specific rearing groups.

Interestingly enough, monkeys raised alone (Rosenblum, 1961) or with surrogates (Suomi & Harlow, 1974) but permitted *limited* (e.g., less than 2 hours per day) interaction with the same group of peers, show essentially normal patterns of social development and are socially adequate as adults. These data suggest that too much exposure to a given class of social partners can have deleterious consequences for social development, although the consequences are probably not as severe or as long-lasting as those of extreme social deprivation.

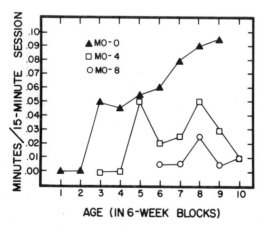

FIGURE 17. Differences in peer-directed contact among monkeys deprived of peer interactions for the first 8 (MO-8), 4 (MO-4), or 0 (MO-0) months of life.

FIGURE 18.   Peer clinging in together-together-reared monkeys.

Overexposure to the same group of friends can affect adolescent and adult peer relationships as well. We have found that monkeys housed in small (fewer than six animals) intact groups for months or years stagnate in social activity. Most socially active behaviors such as play and sex decline to levels of virtual nonoccurrence. These monkeys are not particularly exciting subjects to observe (see Figure 19).

Finally, we have found that the degree and rate of peer development is in part a function of the number of peers available in the rearing environment. For example, monkeys reared in together-together groups of four display far less retardation of social development than monkeys reared as together-together pairs (Chamove, Rosenblum, & Harlow, 1973). At the other end of the scale, third-born offspring in our nuclear family environments show more rapid and complete development of social behaviors than do second-borns, who are more sophisticated than firstborns. These birth-order deficits seem to be less a function of the parents' behaviors than of the infants' behavior (Figures 20 and 21). We believe this results because firstborns have only parents, other adults, and age-mates with whom to interact during the first year of life, whereas later-borns have not only parents, other adults, and age-mates but also older siblings (Suomi, 1972).

Social Separations Early in Life

Numerous investigators at several laboratories have examined the consequences of separating monkey mothers from their infants when the infants are 3 to 9 months of age (e.g., Seay, Hansen, & Harlow, 1962; Hinde, Spencer-Booth, & Bruce, 1966; Kaufman & Rosenblum, 1967; Preston, Baker, & Seay, 1970; Schlottmann & Seay, 1972). Also, recent work at Wisconsin has focused on the effects of peer separations on infant behavior (Suomi, Harlow, & Domek,

FIGURE 19. Monkey boredom.

FIGURE 20. Rejections initiated by mothers toward first-, second-, and third-born offspring in nuclear family environments.

FIGURE 21. Total activity directed toward mother by first-, second-, and third-born offspring in nuclear family environments.

170

1970; Suomi, 1973; Suomi & Harlow, 1975). Although the variables determining the nature and severity of an individual's reaction to a specific separation have been examined in detail elsewhere (Hinde & Spencer-Booth, 1971; Suomi, 1974), several findings pertinent to the present discussion should be pointed out.

First, even though considerable variation can be attributed to species studied, strength and form of attachment involved, and precise nature of the separation environment, almost all young monkeys have their peer friendships disrupted by social separation from mother and/or specific peers. For example, peer play activity is literally wiped out for at least the initial stages of separation from mother (e.g., Seay & Harlow, 1965; Suomi, Collins, & Harlow, 1973, see Figure 22). We have seen little evidence of increased aggression directed toward friends following separation—depression and social withdrawal are more common consequences.

Second, it has been found in some studies that even long after reunion, residual effects of separation can be detected in the subjects' activity, particularly in interactions with peers. Hinde and co-workers have reported behavioral abnormalities attributable to a 6-day period of infant separation from mother to persist up to 6 months after mother and infant had been permanently reunited. Mitchell, Harlow, Griffin, & Møller (1967) found that monkeys subjected to

FIGURE 22. Effect of maternal separation on approach-avoidance play with peers.

brief maternal separations during the first 8 months of life displayed higher levels of coo vocalizations, fear grimaces, and social withdrawal, and lower levels of assertive behaviors, such as threats, than nonseparated controls a full year after the separations.

Finally, we have learned that repetitive peer separations can have a severe stifling effect on the normative development of peer-related social activities. Monkey infants reared together from birth, then subjected to a series of 4-day-long peer separations, do not display even the retarded social development characteristic of together-together-reared monkeys. Instead, social maturation is arrested at the point of the initial separation (Suomi, Harlow, & Domek, 1970; Suomi, 1973). For example, as Figure 23 reveals, monkeys repetitively separated for 20 times beginning at 3 months of age continued to behave like 3-month-olds even when they were more than 9 months of age, in marked contrast to a nonseparated control group which displayed adequate development over a comparable chronological span.

To summarize, social separations can markedly affect the ontogeny of peer interactions. During separation itself, ongoing peer activity is usually disrupted because the separated infants are typically exhibiting depression. Following reunion, development of peer relationships is hampered primarily because the

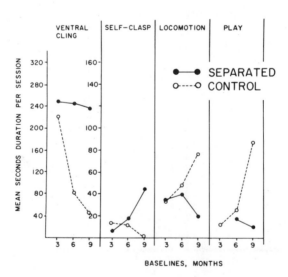

FIGURE 23. Maturational arrest in repetitively separated infant monkeys. Separations occurred between 3 and 9 months of age.

infants become hyperattached to the attachment objects temporarily lost because of the separation. In short, separation tends to enhance existing attachment bonds and to discourage development of new friendships.

Exposure to Fear-Inducing Stimuli

Two studies recently completed at Wisconsin have examined the effects of repeated presentation of fear-evoking stimuli on peer attachment formation and maintenance in young monkeys. A large body of previous research has established that fear emerges as an identifiable response in rhesus monkeys between 70 and 90 days of age, independent of rearing environment (Sackett, 1966; Mitchell, 1970; Suomi & Harlow, 1971b). The present researches focused on infant contact and disturbance behavior resulting from repeated exposure to mechanical monsters.

In the first experiment, performed by Sidowski, Harlow, and Suomi (1972), monkeys were raised either on surrogates or with partners. Beginning at 60 days of age they were exposed each week to a mechanical monster, evoking both visual and auditory action, advancing down a long tunnel (Suomi & Harlow, 1969). Control exposure to an empty tunnel was also given to each subject on a weekly basis. Subject behavior was measured before, during, and after both monster and control exposure periods every week, until subjects were 6 months of age.

In the second study Novak (1973) reared groups of monkeys for the first year of life under each of three conditions: with mothers only, with surrogates and peers, and in together-together groups. Once per week each subject was exposed, with its rearing attachment object (mother, surrogate, or peer), to an exceedingly fearful mechanical monster, complete with flashing eyes, flapping wings, and a speaker capable of emitting 13 different, prolonged, noxious noises. The apparatus was quite effective as a fear-inducing device. The subjects did not adapt to the presence of the monster, as had been the case in some previous studies. Novak recorded subject behavior in the subjects' home cage as well as during the periods of exposure to the fear stimulus. Also, she measured cortisol level periodically in all subjects. Informal observations continued for several months following the final exposure to the monster at 1 year of age.

Results were highly similar in both experiments, even though the rearing conditions and fear-invoking situations were slightly different in each. All subjects exposed to the monsters along with their attachment objects increased their contact with the objects and decreased locomotive and exploratory behaviors, both during and shortly following each exposure period. Subjects also exhibited higher levels of disturbance activity both during monster sessions and on return to their home environment.

Of equal interest were the cumulative and long-term effects of repeated exposure to the fear stimuli. Generally, these were not positive. Existing attach-

ment bonds became exaggerated in all subjects. Contact remained high, and as
a result the development of play and other advanced social behaviors was
retarded. Moreover, the exposed subjects had relative difficulty establishing
new relationships with other peers. They generally avoided contact and often
broke away prematurely from a play bout, shaking and screaming in fear.
Interestingly enough, the subjects least affected by exposure to the fear stimuli
were the monkeys reared on surrogates and given peer exposure. These subjects
spent less time on their surrogates following exposure to the monsters than
mother-reared subjects spent contacting their mothers or peer-reared subjects
spent contacting peers, as can be seen in Figure 24.

To summarize the findings regarding social manipulations early in life, virtually all the studies described produced effects detrimental to the normative
development of peer friendships. Only among animals reared in laboratory nuclear families was there any indication of enhancement of peer social capability,
in comparison with that found in most feral environments. The deleterious consequences of these manipulations were usually expressed as inability to form
social attachments of even moderate strength with any peer or, at the opposite
extreme, a tendency to form attachments to specific peers with such intensity
that other social and behavioral development was impaired. The deficiencies
were most often apparent in play behavior or lack of it, in immature patterns of
sexual behavior, and in inappropriate reactions to dominance situations. In
severe cases (e.g., among monkeys reared in total social isolation) abnormal behavior persisted throughout adulthood, resulting in totally incompetent sexual

FIGURE 24.   Rearing condition differences in reaction to fear stimuli.

and maternal behavior. However, most anomalies acquired through less traumatic early social experience produced limited impairment in adult life, providing the monkeys had adequate subsequent exposure to peers (Suomi & Harlow, 1971b).

THE ROLE OF PEER FRIENDSHIPS IN MONKEY SOCIAL LIFE

Thus far we have traced the ontogeny of monkey social interactions with peers as exhibited by subjects reared in feral or socially adequate laboratory environments. We have noted that it follows an orderly developmental sequence of behavior patterns, with some evidence of individual differences attributable to inherited factors, such as sex and dominance status of the parents (Koyama, 1970). We have also discussed how environmental events early in life can alter such development, usually in a deleterious fashion. It is now appropriate to consider what function peer friendships serve in the development and maintenance of socially adaptive behavior in monkey subjects.

One way to approach this question is to examine what is required on the part of individual monkeys to maintain the type of social group structure that characterizes the species in feral environments and to determine to what extent peer interactions fulfill the requirements. First and foremost, an individual member of any rhesus monkey group must be able to differentiate other monkeys as belonging to, or not belonging to, its own specific troop. In other words, it must be able to tell friends from strangers. If members of a given social group did not make such a differentiation, logic tells us that the group could not be maintained intact for any period of time if it overlapped in territory with nongroup conspecifics, as is often the case (Lindburg, 1972). An enormous body of field literature tells us that relatively intact social groups are the rule, rather than the exception, in monkey societies.

For an individual monkey, the ability to differentiate friends from strangers has another function. If for some reason a given monkey becomes separated from its own social group and encounters a second group of monkeys, it is in deep trouble if it behaves as if it were in its familiar social territory. Monkey groups can spot a stranger a mile away, and if the stranger does not recognize its predicament and display the appropriate submissive behaviors, it is almost certain to be threatened, repeatedly attacked, repelled, and perhaps even killed. Knowing one's friends has enormous adaptive import, even among nonhuman primates.

Second, for any social group to survive without destroying itself, each individual member must be able to recognize his own social position and behave accordingly. No group can be composed exclusively of leaders; some members must be followers. Someone must be responsible for raising infants; otherwise the group would die off. Someone must be responsible for group protection; otherwise the group might be eliminated, one by one, by predators. In short, social groups have intragroup social requirements, and in monkeys these requirements are met by various group members assuming certain social roles (Lindburg, 1972). Such roles must be learned in part. Monkeys are not honey bees; their society transcends behavioral interactions limited to preprogrammed response patterns.

These are the very factors that differentiate a social species from a nonsocial species of mammal. All mammals require some exposure to conspecifics. In every mammalian species, mating must occur and the young must be cared for, at least for a short time, if the species is to be propagated. Thus the minimal social requirements of any mammalian species are appropriate sexual congress and adequate maternal behavior. But animals such as rhesus monkeys, which are complex and gregarious socially, require far more from individual members in terms of a social behavioral repertoire, as already delineated. It is this additional behavioral capability that allows us to describe a species as being social as opposed to solitary, examples of the latter being shrews and weasels. One might appropriately ask where this capability comes from and how it is developed.

It is our contention that the primary vehicle for shaping genetically acquired potential into competent and adaptive social activity lies in the development and maintenance of peer friendships. We do not claim that this is the case for all mammalian species, but it definitely holds for the rhesus monkey, and we suspect it is also true for most of the higher primates, including man.

Although we believe development of peer relationships to be the most important cog in the socialization process of rhesus monkeys, we do not underestimate the importance of other social relationships, particularly those between mother and offspring and those falling under what Harlow (1962) has termed the "heterosexual affectional system." The development of mother-infant affection has been described in detail elsewhere (Hansen, 1966); it is clear that under normal circumstances the mother is the first individual with whom an infant develops affectional ties. Moreover, extremes in mothering (e.g., too much or too little) can have effects that influence the offspring's behavior for some time to come. But it is also clear that except in the most unusual cases, the mother-infant bond diminishes in strength, and eventually the infant directs most of its attention toward other social objects.

In a similar fashion, we are not about to dismiss the importance of heterosexual congress among monkeys or any other species; indeed, it is necessary for ensuring the occurrence of succeeding generations. Yet the data clearly demonstrate that if antecedent attachments are not developed in monkeys, there will be no sexual congress. In solitary species perhaps this may occur, but in social species such as rhesus monkeys, peer interactions must take place prior to physiological maturation if adequate sexual behavior is to be developed and performed (Harlow, 1962).

In short, we believe that development and maintenance of peer friendships are essential for monkey socialization and survival. We base this belief on two sets of data—those gathered in socially normative situations and those obtained under conditions that have been demonstrated to have deleterious effects on peer interaction patterns. In normal environments monkeys initially establish strong ties to their mothers, but within 4 months the infants are spending considerably more time interacting with friends than with parents. In interactions with friends, play is the dominant behavior, and through play, social roles perhaps predetermined by biology are established and maintained.

We say "predetermined by biology" because sex differences in developing behavior patterns are clear-cut, and they are detectable even among socially unsophisticated subjects. Partial isolate males are more aggressive than partial isolate females (Cross & Harlow, 1965), and the sex preferences of socially sophisticated infants for play partners are mirrored by sex preferences of monkeys never given the opportunity to interact physically with peers (see Figure 25; Suomi, Sackett, & Harlow, 1970). Such data do not occur by chance—certainly biological influences determine to a given extent a particular subject's be-

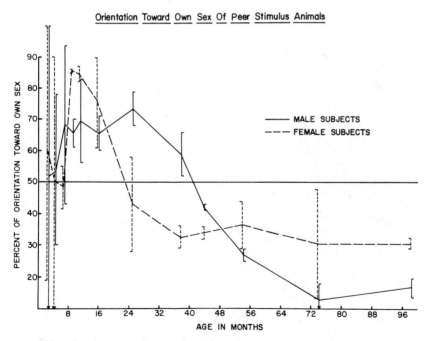

FIGURE 25.   Development of sex preferences among socially unsophisticated monkeys.

SOCIAL AND NONSOCIAL INTERACTION TIME

FIGURE 26. Proportion of time spent in interaction with age-mates, in interaction with adults, and in nonsocial activity, among monkeys reared in nuclear families.

FIGURE 27. Initial response of isolate to therapist.

havioral repertoire. Thus well-socialized adolescent female monkeys are far more interested in babies than are males, whereas juvenile males tend to prefer playmates who are age-mates of the same sex (Chamove, Harlow, & Mitchell, 081 1967; Lawick-Goodall, 1973).

Yet the rearing-condition studies clearly indicate, for example, that being born a female does not necessarily ensure that adequate child-caring behaviors will emerge spontaneously with the birth of an infant. Rather, role-appropriate behavior emerges ontogenetically, but initially in crude form. Through reinforcements incurred in the social environment, chiefly from peers, it is practiced and perfected. Rhesus monkeys are born with behavioral predispositions, but 082 they have to learn where, when, and how to exhibit them. The learning occurs in social situations—and young monkeys spend most of their social time with age-mates (Figure 26). When monkeys are denied the opportunity to interact with peers, the learning does not take place and their adult behavior is unacceptable. One's friends determine in large part one's social standing; without any friends one has no social standing other than age and gender.

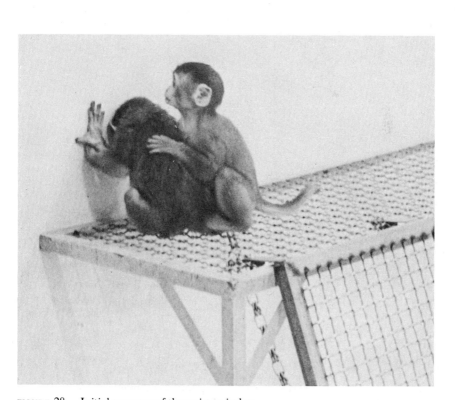

FIGURE 28. Initial response of therapist to isolate.

PERSPECTIVES

The position we have outlined is based largely on empirical data, but is also dependent on certain theoretical assumptions that by now should be obvious. To this point we have used these principles to describe the course of normative social development and to explain why specific behavioral anomalies emerge in friendship relationships following certain environmental manipulations. We are attempting to use some of this knowledge gleaned from study of normal and abnormal monkeys to reverse psychopathology produced in some of our laboratory-reared subjects. We offer the following data as an example illustrating one application of these principles.

As was previously pointed out, monkeys reared in total social isolation for at

FIGURE 29.   Isolate (above) reciprocating contact initiations from therapist.

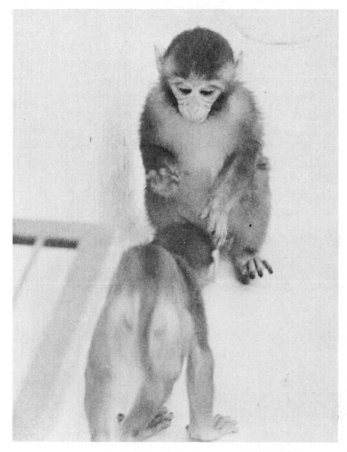

FIGURE 30.　Isolate (right) initiating play bout with therapist.

least the first 6 months of life invariably exhibit psychopathology when finally exposed to the real world. There have been various theoretical positions to explain why isolates behave in this way. Some invoke critical period notions; others speak of "emergence trauma." We have preferred to view isolate behavior as primarily reflecting a social learning deficit. Isolate-reared monkeys have no opportunity to learn that conspecific contact is soft and warm, naturally reinforcing; they have, however, acquired a fear of the unfamiliar. Hence when exposed to age-mates, they withdraw. A monkey which avoids peers is unlikely to develop complex patterns of play and other social behaviors.

　　Thus we attempted to rehabilitate isolate-reared monkeys by attacking these postulated learning deficits. We exposed 6- and 12-month isolates to other monkeys—social "therapists" chosen on the basis of behaviors they exhibited which we felt would correct the learning deficits. The rationale underlying the specific choice of therapists and the exact procedure have been described in detail elsewhere (Suomi & Harlow, 1972), but basically the results were as follows. Isolates initially withdrew from their therapists (Figure 27) but were pursued and contacted repeatedly by the normal monkeys (Figure 28). Soon the isolates began reciprocating the contact (Figure 29). Eventually they actively initiated contact both with their therapists (Figure 30) and with each other. Development of play behavior followed, and after 6 months of therapy the isolates and their normal friends were indistinguishable in levels of almost all behaviors, including play (Figure 31). Today, as late adolescents, they exhibit perfectly appropriate social behavior in their current setting.

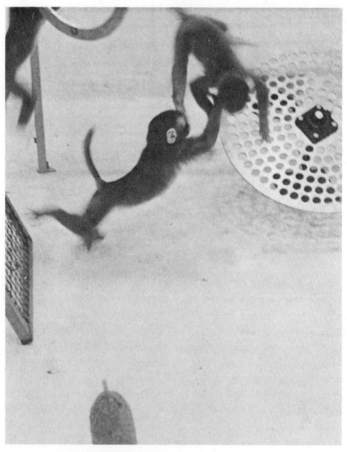

FIGURE 31.   Isolates (left, center) and therapist (right) in play bout.

We present these studies as examples of an approach designed to rectify social deficiencies expressed as a result of early inadequate or traumatic social experience. We are presently attempting to reverse monkey psychopathologies produced by manipulations other than that of social isolation initiated at birth. Specifically chosen peers are employed as therapists because we feel that peers are the most salient influence in a monkey's everyday social life, once infancy has passed.

We have discussed the role and reason of peer friendships in rhesus monkeys. We base our position on a large body of empirical data, much of it gathered at the Wisconsin Primate Laboratory. We are the first to admit that relevant data remain to be gathered and that much of our theory is incomplete and undeveloped. Still, we are curious about the degree to which our position generalizes to man. We have our suspicions, but at present these suspicions rest largely on faith—the relevant human data do not now exist. It is our hope that they will be gathered, and soon. At worst they will amplify our knowledge concerning species differences in social behavioral mechanisms. At best they will expand our understanding of the roles and reasons of our own social world.

REFERENCES

Alexander, B. K., & Harlow, H. F. Social behavior of juvenile rhesus monkeys subjected to different rearing conditions during the first 6 months of life. *Zoologische Jahrbuche Physiologie,* 1965, **60,** 167–174.

Arling, G. L., & Harlow, H. F. Effects of social deprivation on maternal behavior of rhesus monkeys. *Journal of Comparative and Physiological Psychology,* 1967, **64,** 371–377.

Baldwin, D. V., & Suomi, S. J. Reactions of infant rhesus monkeys to social and nonsocial stimuli. *Folia Primatologica,* 1974, **22,** 307–314.

Chamove, A. S., Rosenblum, L. A., & Harlow, H. F. Monkeys (*Macaca mulatta*) raised only with peers. A pilot study. *Animal Behaviour,* 1973, **21,** 316–325.

Chamove, A. S., Harlow, H. F., & Mitchell, G. Sex differences in the infant-directed behavior of preadolescent rhesus monkeys. *Child Development,* 1967, **38,** 329–335.

Cross, H. A., & Harlow, H. F. Prolonged and progressive effects of partial isolation on the behavior of macaque monkeys. *Journal of Experimental Research in Personality,* 1965, **1,** 39–49.

Hansen, E. W. The development of maternal and infant behavior in the rhesus monkey. *Behaviour,* 1966, **27,** 107–149.

Harlow, H. F. The heterosexual affectional system in monkeys. *American Psychologist,* 1962, **17,** 1–9.

Harlow, H. F. Age-mate or peer affectional system. In D. S. Lehrman, R. A. Hinde, & E. Shaw (Eds.), *Advances in the study of behavior.* Vol. 2. New York: Academic Press, 1969. Pp. 333–383.

Harlow, H. F., Dodsworth, R. O., & Harlow, M. K. Total social isolation in monkeys. *Proceedings of the National Academy of Sciences (U.S.),* 1965, **54,** 90–97.

Harlow, H. F., & Harlow, M. K. The affectional systems. In A. M. Schrier, H. F. Harlow, & F. Stollnitz (Eds.), *Behavior of nonhuman primates.* Vol. 2. New York: Academic Press, 1965. Pp. 287–334.

Harlow, H. F., & Lauersdorf, H. E. Sex differences in passion and play. *Perspectives in Biology and Medicine,* 1974, **17,** 348–359.

Harlow, M. K. Nuclear family apparatus. *Behavior Research Methods and Instrumentation,* 1971, **3,** 301–304.

Hinde, R. A., & Spencer-Booth, Y. The behavior of socially living rhesus monkeys in their first two and a half years. *Animal Behaviour,* 1967, **15,** 169–196.

Hinde, R. A., & Spencer-Booth, Y. Effects of brief separation from mother on rhesus monkeys. *Science,* 1971, **173,** 111–118.

Hinde, R. A., Spencer-Booth, Y., & Bruce, M. Effects of 6-day maternal deprivation on rhesus monkey infants. *Nature,* 1966, **210,** 1021–1033.

Hinde, R. A., & White, L. E. Dynamics of a relationship: Rhesus mother-infant ventro-ventral contact. *Journal of Comparative and Physiological Psychology,* 1974, **86,** 8–23.

Kaufman, I. C., & Rosenblum, L. A. Depression in infant monkeys separated from their mothers. *Science,* 1967, **155,** 1030–1031.

Koyama, N. Changes in dominance rank and division of a wild Japanese monkey troop in Arashiyama. *Primates,* 1970, **11,** 555–590.

Lawick-Goodall, J. van. Cultural elements in a chimpanzee community. In E. W. Menzel (Ed.), *Symposia of the fourth international congress of primatology.* Vol. 1. Basel, Switzerland: Karger, 1973. Pp. 144–184.

Lindburg, D. G. The rhesus monkey in North India: An ecological and behavioral study. In L. A. Rosenblum (Ed.), *Primate behavior.* Vol. 2. New York: Academic Press, 1972. Pp. 1–105.

Mears, C. E., & Harlow, H. F. Play: Early and eternal. *Proceedings of the National Academy of Sciences* (U.S.), 1975, **72,** 1878–1882.

Mitchell, G. Abnormal behavior in primates. In L. A. Rosenblum (Ed.), *Primate behavior.* Vol. 1. New York: Academic Press, 1970. Pp. 195–249.

Mitchell, G. D., Harlow, H. F., Griffin, G. A., & Møller, G. W. Repeated maternal separation in the monkey. *Psychonomic Science,* 1967, **8,** 197–198.

Norikoshi, K. The development of peer-mate relationships in Japanese macaque infants. *Primates,* 1974, **15,** 39–46.

Novak, M. A. Fear-attachment relationships in infant and juvenile rhesus monkeys. Unpublished Ph.D. dissertation, University of Wisconsin, 1973.

Preston, D. G., Baker, R. P., & Seay, B. Mother-infant separation in the patas monkey. *Developmental Psychology,* 1970, **3,** 298–306.

Rosenblum, L. A. The development of social behavior in the rhesus monkey. Unpublished Ph.D. dissertation, University of Wisconsin, 1961.

Rosevear, J. Y. Social and environmental influences on the maternal-infant relationship of the rhesus monkey. Unpublished Ph.D. dissertation, University of Wisconsin, 1974.

Ruppenthal, G. C., Harlow, M. K., Eisele, C. D., Harlow, H. F., & Suomi, S. J. Development of peer interactions of monkeys reared in a nuclear-family environment. *Child Development,* 1974, **45,** 670–682.

Sackett, G. P. Monkeys reared in visual isolation with pictures as visual input: Evidence for an innate releasing mechanism. *Science,* 1966, **154,** 1468–1472.

Schlottmann, R. S., & Seay, B. Mother-infant separation in the Java monkey (*Macaca irus*). *Journal of Comparative and Physiological Psychology,* 1972, **79,** 334–340.

Seay, B., Hansen, E. W., & Harlow, H. F. Mother-infant separation in monkeys. *Journal of Child Psychology and Psychiatry,* 1962, **3,** 123–132.

Seay, B., & Harlow, H. F. Maternal separation in the rhesus monkey. *Journal of Nervous and Mental Diseases,* 1965, **140,** 434–441.

Sidowski, J. B., Harlow, H. F., & Suomi, S. J. Enhancing social attachment through fear: A study of infant monkeys. *Psychonomic Science,* 1972, **29,** 323.

Suomi, S. J. Social development of rhesus monkeys reared in an enriched laboratory environment. *Twentieth International Congress of Psychology.* Tokyo: Sasaki, 1972. Pp. 173–174.

Suomi, S. J. Repetitive peer separation of young monkeys: Effects of vertical chamber confinement during separations. *Journal of Abnormal Psychology,* 1973, **83,** 1–10.

Suomi, S. J. Factors affecting response to separation in rhesus monkeys. *Proceedings of the Kittay Scientific Foundation Second International Symposium.* In press.

Suomi, S. J., Collins, M. L., & Harlow, H. F. Effect of permanent separation from mother on infant monkeys. *Developmental Psychology,* 1973, **9,** 376–384.

Suomi, S. J., & Harlow, H. F. Apparatus conceptualization for psychopathological research in monkeys. *Behavior Research Methods and Instrumentation,* 1969, **1,** 247–250.

Suomi, S. J., & Harlow, H. F. Monkeys at play. *Natural History,* 1971a, **80,** 72–76.

Suomi, S. J., & Harlow, H. F. Abnormal social behavior in young monkeys. In J. Hellmuth (Ed.), *Exceptional infant: Studies in abnormalities.* Vol. 2. New York: Brunner/Mazel, 1971b. Pp. 483–529.

Suomi, S. J., & Harlow, H. F. Social rehabilitation of isolate-reared monkeys. *Developmental Psychology,* 1972, **6,** 487–496.

Suomi, S. J., & Harlow, H. F. Effects of differential removal from group on social development of rhesus monkeys. *Journal of Child Psychology and Psychiatry,* 1975, **16,** 149–164.

Suomi, S. J., Harlow, H. F., & Domek, C. J. Effect of repetitive infant-infant separation of young monkeys. *Journal of Abnormal Psychology,* 1970, **76,** 161–172.

Suomi, S. J., Sackett, G. P., & Harlow, H. F. Development of sex preference in rhesus monkeys. *Developmental Psychology,* 1970, **3,** 326–336.

CHAPTER 7

The Emergence
of Initial Apprehension
to Unfamiliar Peers[1]

JEROME KAGAN

Department of Psychology and Social Relations
Harvard University

RICHARD B. KEARSLEY AND PHILIP R. ZELAZO

Department of Pediatrics
Tufts University Medical Center

Interpretation of the early forms of social behavior with age mates is occasionally hampered by two tacit presuppositions. The first is that people are qualitatively different from inanimate objects. The second is that past experiences with familiar adults and children are the major determinants of future reactions to unfamiliar persons, presumably as a result of the operation of the mechanism of generalization.

An alternative view, which is emerging as Piaget's attitudes toward cognition spill over into discussions of social phenomena, is that level of cognitive maturity exerts some control over social behavior. An unfamiliar child presents a different problem to 1- and 3-year-olds, even though past experience with other children may exert some influence on initial reactivity. This posture, which is implicit in several chapters in this book, implies that during the first two or three years of life peers are best regarded as a class of objects. They differ from rattles, blankets, and balls in their stimulus variety, potential for change, less reliable reactions to the child's overtures, and finally, in their special capacity to make initiations toward the agent. Thus as events, young children should be viewed as atomic-powered, mobile toys with an internal program that makes their actions difficult to predict and control, not unlike the complex machines Charles Chaplin had to cope with in the film classic *Modern Times.*

This conception of early peer interaction tempts us to place the phenomenon of early social interaction in a cognitive context. Every young child has a puz-

[1] This research was supported by National Institute of Child Health and Human Development grant no. HD-42-99, the Office of Child Development, and the Spencer Foundation.

187

zle; namely, to figure out how to behave toward and react to an age mate. Although 1- and 2-year-olds in our society have ample opportunity to learn initial schemes for adults and simple objects (as a result of contingent interaction with them), they ordinarily have little opportunity to gain familiarity, that is, to acquire schemes, for other young children. If peers are just more varied and less predictable objects, there should be maturational change in the quality of behavioral interaction with peers, from initial unfamiliarity and unsureness of what actions to initiate to later periods of sophistication and certainty in interaction. Since there is an obvious maturational sequence in the quality and form of interactions with inanimate objects over the first 36 months, there should also be a lawful growth pattern that describes interaction with peers. The 6-month-old infant examines, mouths, and bangs small objects; a 26-month-old treats them symbolically. Each phase of development is marked by changing clusters of dominant actions toward objects. As cognitive and motor systems mature, early behaviors are replaced by more mature patterns. For example, Rosenblum et al. (Chapter 3) note that mouthing is the dominant action displayed by macaques toward other young monkeys during the early weeks of life. But by 4 months rough-and-tumble play has replaced this first class of simpler actions. This sequence is analogous to the human progression from the display of crying to distress seen at 3 months to the child's asking for help at 18 months, as speech replaces fretting in a frustrating context. We do not know why the new behavior appears. Some assume, perhaps gratuitously, that greater variety, efficiency, and pleasantness accompany display of the new form. But a motivational interpretation may not be theoretically helpful. Although the butterfly inevitably follows the caterpillar, each form seems to be equally efficient and equally happy or distressed. It is not obvious that adding a statement about pleasantness or reward to explain the emergent response enhances understanding, especially since after his first birthday the macaque exhibits a decrease in rough-and-tumble play—an act that appears to be such great fun—and begins to spend more time sitting and grooming—acts that to a human observer appear to have less variety, vigor, and excitement.

The new observations of early development in monkey and child, some of which are summarized in this volume, imply that during the early years the rapidly changing hierarchies of response classes are based in part on changing cognitive and motor competences. A useful metaphor for early development is a series of waves of emerging, plateauing, and declining behavioral systems, which hold the stage for a brief era until they are displaced by a new set of actors. This view implies that at any one age there will be two important sources of individual differences in behavior. One source will be due to individual variation in rates of development; the other to factors of experience plus temperament that make one class of action toward a peer prepotent over another. To illustrate, the data from several studies suggest that there is little initiation of contact or sustained reciprocal play with a peer prior to the second birthday, regardless of past experience. Hence a 20-month-old who was low in initiation of play with a peer could be developmentally behind a 20-month-old who was precocious and already displaying more mature actions. However, in a few months the former child will show the same degree of initiation of reciprocal play exhibited by the latter several months earlier. But among 4-year-olds, all of whom are mature enough to initiate reciprocal play, some will be low and some high in the tendency to initiate interactions with others. We assume—correctly, we think—that this difference is due to patterns of past experience interacting with the child's temperament.

In general, the older the child, the longer the period between the emergence of new cognitive competences; hence the more likely it is that individual differences will be experiential in origin. But during the first two to three years, when there are more frequent changes in basic competences, individual differences are just as likely to be the result of differences in rates of development as they are to be a product of experience. Perhaps that is why there is so little intraindividual stability of patterns of social behavior from the first three years of life to later childhood, but better predictive continuity from age 10 to early adulthood (Kagan & Moss, 1962).

REACTION TO UNASSIMILABLE EVENTS

In this chapter we are less concerned with peer interaction, in the popular sense of that term, than with the cognitive basis for the child's initial reaction to an unfamiliar child of the same age and sex. We believe that during the first three years, initial encounter with an unfamiliar peer is to be viewed as a puzzle, hence a special class of uncertainty. The likelihood of solving the puzzle is a function of level of cognitive maturity and past opportunities to deal with the problem. Since reactions to all initially unfamiliar events change with age—stranger and separation anxiety are examples—the child's reactions to this event should also reveal a lawful developmental sequence.

In another volume in this series we suggested that the two major fears of infancy—stranger and separation distress—are the result of an inability to deal with a cognitive problem (Kagan, 1974). The apprehension provoked by a strange person typically emerges between 7 and 9 months; the apprehension generated by watching one's caretaker leave emerges a few months later.[2] Ex-

---

[2] Some infants do not show either or both of these fears if crying is considered as the criterion of fear. Similarly, all infants do not cry or tighten their faces in wariness every time a stranger looks at them or a caretaker leaves. But a phenomenon that is regarded as universal does not need to occur consistently. The distinction between universality and consistency holds for many natural phenomena. Smiling is universal in all societies, but there is no guarantee that a 3-hour observation of 20 children will reveal a single instance of a child smiling. Anger is a universal reaction to coercion or loss of a favorite object, but all children do not become angry every time an adult takes a toy from them. Indeed, if parents were more clever and removed toys from their children with gentleness and greater patience, they could avoid most emotional displays.

periments by Kotelchuck (1972), Spelke et al. (1973), Lester et al. (1974), and Ross et al. (1975) suggest that occurrence of "separation fear" increases most rapidly between 12 and 18 months of age and reaches a peak during the last third of the second year (see also Fleener & Cairns, 1970).

We also suggested that separation protest was dependent on the development of a new maturational competence that emerges during the last third of the first year. We called that competence "activation of hypotheses." The 5-month-old detects his mother leaving him alone or with a stranger but is not mature enough to generate hypotheses about the relation between that discrepant event and a relevant schema. Five months later the child shows apprehension to the same separation event because he actively attempts, but is temporarily unable, to relate his perception of the event "caretaker leaving" with his available knowledge. He cannot generate a representation of what might happen in the immediate future. Hence he becomes uncertain, inhibited, and may even cry. We now believe, albeit tentatively, that "stranger anxiety" may be mediated by the same mechanism. Indeed, stranger anxiety may be the first indication of this new competence.

This chapter summarizes data on another source of apprehension that emerges and peaks at about the same time as separation distress—initial encounter with a strange child of the same age and sex. We believe that this phenomenon may be based on the same mechanism that mediates separation protest. Since the situations that provoke these two distress states are so different phenotypically, any parallel in their developmental course would imply, although it would not prove, a common mechanism.

During the first two years of life infants in all societies are in frequent, reciprocal contact with adults and older children. But with the exception of twins and children in day care centers, most do not have much contact with infants their own age. Eight-month-olds do not vocalize to or play with other 8-month-olds; they neither feed, clean, rock, nor carry other 8-month-olds, nor do they praise, punish, or react contingently toward them. Hence an unfamiliar 1-year-old should be a more discrepant event to another 1-year-old than a strange 3-year-old would be to another 3-year-old. If inability to assimilate a discrepancy were the primary factor eliciting apprehension to a peer, a 1-year-old should show more apprehension to an unfamiliar peer than a 2- or 3-year-old. But if activation of hypotheses were a factor mediating apprehension to peers, as we believe it is for separation, there should be greater fear during the second and third years than during the first year.

Since the infant under one year does not develop structures that represent the possible reactions of peers toward him nor representations of how he should behave toward another child, he is less uncertain with a peer than is the child who is older than one year. The data to be presented suggest that the ability of a 1½- to 2-year-old to generate hypotheses about potential peer reactions toward him, although he is unable to resolve those questions, produces uncertainty and, as behavioral consequences, retreat to the mother, inhibition of play, and attentiveness to the unfamiliar child. But as with separation fear, apprehension to peers begins to wane as the child becomes capable of answering the questions he poses. Hence by the third year of life the child should begin to show less inhibition and less wariness in the presence of a strange peer than he displayed earlier.

An added element of interest in this report derives from the comparison of a group of children reared at home with a group reared in a day care center with 30 other infants and toddlers from 3½ to 30 months old. If daily interactions with other young children are the primary determinant of initial reaction to a strange peer, there should be major differences between the two groups. On the other hand, if cognitive maturation are an influential determinant, the two groups should behave more similarly, reflecting the interaction of level of cognitive functioning and past experience.

The data to be summarized are not concerned with the behavior of "friends," but rather with a more limited phenomenon—the initial reaction to an unfamiliar child. Moreover, the period under study clearly precedes the period of identification with role models and is just prior to the time when the child realizes that of all the objects in his world, he is most similar to the category called people, an insight that disposes him to watch, imitate, anticipate, and empathize with children and adults in preference to birds, balls, or dogs.

METHOD

Subjects and Setting

The subjects were a maximum of 62 children who are participating in a longitudinal study inquiring into the effects of group care on psychological development during the first 30 months of life. The design includes pairs of children matched on sex, ethnicity (Chinese or Caucasian), and social class. One member of the pair was reared at home by the family; the other member of the pair attended a day care center 5 days a week from 8:30 A.M. to 4:30 P.M. from 3½ until 30 months of age.

Located in a working-class area in Boston's South End, the day care center was created and administered by our research team. The parents were primarily working-class residents of the South End and paid no fee for the day care service. The center consists of a large room (approximately 2500 square feet) furnished with a large number of varied and age-appropriate toys. The caretaker ratio is three infants to one caretaker from 3½ until 14 months, and five toddlers to one caretaker during the period 14 to 30 months. During each age period, infancy and toddlerhood, each child was assigned to a primary caretaker who was responsible for the child's needs, although the child experienced ministrations from others in an environment that encouraged exploratory behavior.

The caretakers were primarily mature, working-class mothers with no special college training in psychology or education. Each caretaker was trained by our staff in a philosophy that emphasized one-to-one reciprocal interaction with and stimulation of the infants. During the second and third years the training emphasized speech and language as well as one-to-one interaction. We believe, but cannot document, that the caretakers in the center were probably more attentive and affectionate than those found in a randomly selected fee-for-service day care center for infants. The amount of one-to-one contact and stimulation of cognitive development was probably within the range of that experienced by the majority of middle-class American infants cared for at home.

Procedures

Our data came from three pairs of play sessions administered when the children were 13½, 20, and 29 months of age. The two play sessions (solo and peer play) were part of a larger test battery. During the solo play session, which always occurred first, the child was with his mother and a set of interesting, age-appropriate toys. During the peer play session that followed, a strange peer of the same sex, age, and ethnicity, and the peer's mother, were in the room with the subject and his mother. In all cases the peer play session began by having the subject and his mother enter the room in which the peer and the strange peer's mother had been for several minutes. Different sets of toys were always used for the two sessions.

Solo and Peer Play Sessions at 13½ Months

The room for the solo play session was 7 × 14 feet. The mother sat in a chair in a corner reading a magazine, and ten toys were placed in the center of the room. The child was observed for 15 minutes. Observers coded the following variables by pressing buttons attached to a recorder: time looking at mother, time proximal to mother (a circle, 29 in. in diameter, was drawn around the chair in which the mother sat, and proximity to the mother was coded whenever the child was within the circumference of that circle), vocalization to mother, smiling, fretting, and duration of each attentional-play involvement with a toy.

The 25-minute peer play session occurred in a different room (14 × 13 feet) in the same building, with nine different toys. The observers coded the following variables: look at strange peer; look at peer's mother; look at own mother; vocalize to mother, peer, or other mother; fret; proximity to stranger; proximity to mother; and time playing.

Solo and Peer Play Sessions at 20 Months

At 20 months the solo and peer play sessions did not occur in the same building used at 13½ months. Moreover, one week before the solo and peer play sessions each child was observed in the new room for an hour, while different sets of observations were made. Thus when the child returned a week later, he was partially familiar with the setting. This 16 × 24 foot room was used for solo and peer play at both 20 and 29 months. The solo play session lasted 21 minutes and included ten toys. Observers coded the following variables: look at mother, fret, vocalize to mother, proximity to mother, and time playing. Immediately following the solo play episode the child and mother left, a strange mother and peer entered the room, and a new set of ten toys was brought in. During the peer play session, which also lasted 21 minutes, the following variables were coded: proximity to mother, look at peer, look at mother, vocalization, fretting, time playing, initiating cooperative play with the peer, initiating aggressive play with the peer, and occasions of the child resisting, withdrawing or staying when the peer approached him.

Solo and Peer Play Sessions at 29 Months

The 29-month solo play session, which lasted 21 minutes, involved eight toys. The following variables were coded: look at mother, fret, vocalization to mother, proximity to mother, and time playing. Following the solo play session the child and mother left, the strange peer and mother came in, and a new set of nine toys was placed on the floor for the 28-minute peer play session. The following variables were coded: proximity to mother, look at strange mother, look at peer, look at mother, vocalization, time playing, imitation of the peer, initiating aggressive play with the peer, initiating cooperative play with the peer, reciprocal play with the peer, and occasions of the child resisting, withdrawing, or staying when the peer approached him.

RESULTS

This report deals primarily with three dependent variables that we believe are sensitive indexes of uncertainty or apprehension; namely, time in active play, time during which the child was proximal to his mother, and time spent looking at the unfamiliar peer.

Let us defend this view. Like others, we have noted that when a discrepant event occurs while a child is playing, he usually stops his play. He may show a vigilant attitude toward the event and some motor inhibition; if his caretaker is available, he may retreat to her. Inhibition of play, by which we mean that the child is neither actively examining nor manipulating an object, is likely to occur when a parent leaves a child in a room with a stranger, even though facial wariness or crying do not occur. Since the room in which we tested the children was large and the toys attractive, the child was drawn to the center of the room rather than to his mother. When he went to his mother, it was usually to stand by her, to touch her, to bring her a toy, or to get up on her lap. Rarely did the child and mother play together because we instructed the mother to assume a passive role and to discourage play with the child. Hence under these circumstances "proximity to mother" during the first 10 to 15 minutes of the session seems to be a reaction to uncertainty and apprehension, although toward the end of the play session boredom could have influenced this variable.

Age Differences in Play and Proximity to Mother

Tables 1 and 2 show the values for play and proximity to mother for solo and peer play for the first 5 and 15 minutes of each session at each of the three ages, as well as the difference scores between solo and peer play for 29 children who were seen at all three ages. The values represent the mean number of seconds of play or proximity per minute of observation.

An analysis of variance on these values revealed significant F values for session (solo vs. peer) and age for both variables, as well as a significant age-by-session interaction for time spent playing. The greatest inhibition of play during the peer session occurred when the children were 20 months old. As Figure 1 indicates, this curvilinear pattern held for day care and home-reared girls as well as home-reared boys. However the boys in day care showed a

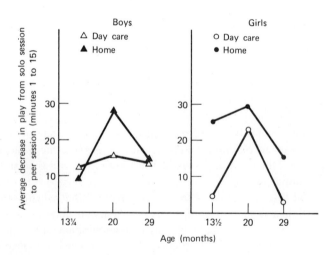

FIGURE 1. Average decrease in play for minutes 1 to 15 from solo to peer session (values are average number of seconds per minute).

TABLE 1. Mean Time Proximal to Mother for Solo and Peer Sessions for First 5 and First 15 Minutes (values are average number of seconds per minute) ($N = 29$)

		Minutes 1–15	
Age (months)	Solo	Peer	Peer Minus Solo Difference (high positive score means inhibition)
13½	20.2	20.2	0.0
20	12.3	19.0	+6.7
29	6.9	18.8	+11.9

Effects: Age, $F = 3.19$ (2, 56), $p < .05$
Session, $F = 20.50$ (1, 28), $p < .001$
Age $\times$ session, $F = 3.63$ (2, 56), $p < .05$

		Minutes 1–5	
Age (months)	Solo	Peer	Peer Minus Solo Difference (high positive score means inhibition)
13½	14.4	20.1	+5.7
20	9.3	19.9	+10.6
29	7.5	22.8	+15.3

Effects: Age, $F < 1.0$
Session, $F = 23.97$ (1, 28), $p < .001$
Age $\times$ session, $F = 2.33$ (2, 56), $p < .10$

more linear function, with no large increase in inhibition to the peer at 20 months.

Individual age comparisons revealed that inhibition of play was greater at 20 than at 13 months ($p < .05$) or 29 months ($p < .05$). We know that these differences are not due to a small number of subjects who had an unusually large amount of inhibition because at 20 months, 89% of the subjects played less during the peer than the solo session, and 77% were more proximal to the mother during peer than the solo session. At 29 months the comparable values were 72% and 83%, respectively. In general the older children were more likely than the 13-month-olds to behave as if the unfamiliar peer were a source of uncertainty.

Since there was generally greater inhibition of play and proximity to mother during the peer than during the solo play sessions, the inhibition is probably

TABLE 2. Mean Time Playing for Solo and Peer Sessions for First 5 and First 15 Minutes (values are average number of seconds per minute) ($N = 28$)

		Minutes 1–15	
Age			Peer Minus Solo Difference
(months)	Solo	Peer	(high negative score means inhibition)
13½	42.9	31.1	−11.8
20	47.5	24.8	−22.7
29	50.5	38.9	−11.6

Effects: Age, $F = 5.88$ (2, 54), $p < .01$
Session, $F = 61.06$ (1, 27), $p < .001$
Age × session, $F = 4.23$ (2, 54), $p < .05$

		Minutes 1–5	
Age			Peer Minus Solo Difference
(months)	Solo	Peer	(high negative score means inhibition)
13½	44.0	27.9	−16.1
20	49.6	20.1	−29.5
29	49.6	38.1	−11.5

Effects: Age, $F = 5.79$ (2, 54), $p < .01$
Session, $F = 58.48$ (1, 27), $p < .001$
Age × session, $F = 5.35$ (2, 54), $p < .01$

not due to the unfamiliarity of the room, since the initial anxiety to the setting should have been greatest during the first solo session. Moreover, at 20 months the child had been seen a week earlier in the same room for an hour or more. Hence the greater signs of inhibition during the peer session must be attributed to the peer, to the peer's mother, or to both. We believe the inhibition is due to the presence of the peer and not to the peer's mother because of the difference between times spent looking at the strange peer versus the peer's mother, which were coded at 13 and 29 months. The child stared at the strange peer significantly more than he stared at the strange woman at both 13½ months (mean difference = 14.0 seconds, $t = 7.00$, $p < .01$) and 29 months (mean difference = 8.1 seconds, $t = 8.90$, $p < .01$). These data suggest that the strange child was the incentive for the inhibition. Additional data gathered from the first session at 20 months, when the child was in the same room with his mother, a familiar

woman, and a totally unfamiliar woman, revealed very little looking at the unfamiliar woman, far less than occurred toward the strange peer a week later.

Age of Greatest Inhibition

We determined how many children showed their maximal apprehension at
each age (as indexed by increased proximity to mother and decrease in play) for
the children who were seen for all three observations at 13½, 20, and 29
months (see Table 3). For proximity most children showed their greatest inhibition at 29 months (48% of the group). For play most children showed their
greatest inhibition at 20 months (52% of the group). Moreover, there was the
suggestion that girls reached their peak apprehension earlier than boys. Four
boys and no girls displayed their greatest inhibition at 29 months for play. For
proximity to mother, nine boys and only five girls showed their greatest inhibition at the oldest age. However for six girls and only three boys peak inhibition
on both proximity to mother and play occurred at 20 months. This slight sex
difference is in accord with the increasingly popular view that girls'
psychological and physical development proceeds precociously to boys', and supports the basic hypothesis of this chapter—namely, that apprehension to peers is
partly controlled by maturational factors associated with the cognitive capacity to
resolve hypotheses about potential future events.

Looking at the Unfamiliar Peer

Table 4 contains the values for total time looking at the unfamiliar peer for day
care and home-reared boys and girls for the first 15 minutes of the peer play
session.

Looking at the peer decreased with age ($F = 3.10$, $\rho < .05$), and day care
children were less attentive to the peer than the home-reared infants at all three

**TABLE 3.   Frequency Distribution for the Age of the Greatest Increase in
Inhibition from the Solo to the Peer Session (numbers refer to number
of children)**

	Boys				Girls			
	Age (months)			No Change in Fear	Age (months)			No Change in Fear
Change in	13½	20	29		13½	20	29	
Play	5	5	4	—	3	10	0	2
Proximity	1	3	9	1	3	7	5	—
Play and proximity	1	3	3	—	2	6	0	—

ages ($F = 9.22$, $p < .01$ for rearing condition). Total time looking at the unfamiliar peer was separated into two components—time looking while proximal to mother and time looking when not proximal to mother. We assume that the former was indicative of greater uncertainty than the latter. Figure 2 plots the age change in time looking at the unfamiliar peer while not proximal to mother for day care and home-reared boys and girls.

Both day care and home-reared boys showed a linear decrease in this variable. The home-reared girls maintained high values through 20 months, followed by a sharp decline at 29 months. For day care girls there was little change in looking with age, but by 29 months all four groups showed similar low values for this measure.

Yet the data for looking at the unfamiliar peer while proximal to mother, which we believe to be a more sensitive index of uncertainty, revealed that two of the four groups (home-reared boys and day care girls) showed their greatest uncertainty at 20 months—the same result illustrated in Figure 1 for inhibition of play (see Figure 3). However, the analysis of variance just missed revealing a significant effect for age, sex, or rearing.

That the day care boys produced low values at all three ages, as was true for play, suggests that the experience of day care may have had an alleviating effect on the degree of uncertainty among boys. It is not clear why this did not hold for girls. One hypothesis, offered tentatively, is that boys are more interactive in the day care center than girls (not unlike rhesus monkeys—see Suomi & Harlow, Chapter 6, this volume). Hence the presence of peers in the day care center may have had a more substantial influence on reducing uncertainty with peers for boys than for the less interactive girls.

TABLE 4. Mean Time Looking at Unfamiliar Peer for Day Care and Home-Reared Boys and Girls During First 15 Minutes of Peer Play (values are average number of seconds per minute)

Children	Age (months)		
	13½	20	29
Boys			
Day care	16.4	11.8	10.5
Home reared	22.8	20.4	13.4
Girls			
Day care	14.5	16.9	9.9
Home reared	23.3	19.8	14.8

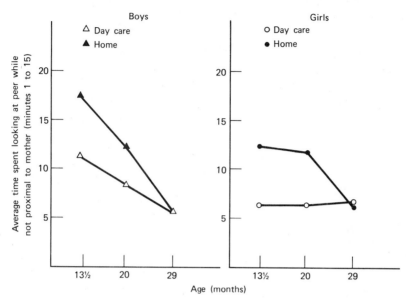

FIGURE 2.   Average time looking at strange peer while not proximal to mother (values are mean number of seconds per minute).

Detailed Analyses at 20 Months of Home Care Versus Day Care Children

Since 20 months was the age at which uncertainty and inhibition of play were maximal, as well as the age for which we had gathered the largest number of observations, we performed a detailed analysis of proximity and play at 20 months for the 62 children seen at that age (28 girls and 34 boys, 32 Caucasian and 30 Chinese, 23 day care and 39 home control children). We analyzed the differences between home control and day care treatment for the four subgroups separately. There were 14 Caucasian females, 18 Caucasian males, 16 Chinese males, 14 Chinese females, and we compared day care versus home rearing within each sex-ethnic group.

For three of the four groups, the home control children showed more inhibition than the day care children (see Table 5). A 2 × 2 chi-square analysis for all children for both variables (proximity and play) was significant ($p < .05$). The differences are based on a median split for proximity to mother and play during the peer session at 20 months. The median values were based on the scores generated within each sex-ethnic group.

Table 5 indicates a tendency, especially among Caucasian boys and Chinese girls, for the day care children to be less inhibited during the peer session at 20 months. The absence of this effect for Chinese males suggests an interaction

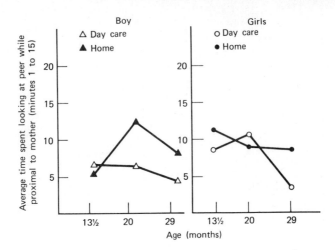

FIGURE 3.   Average time looking at strange peer while proximal to mother (values are mean number of seconds per minute).

among ethnic background (which is assumed to represent both temperamental and home rearing differences), sex, and the day care experience.

An Independent Study of Sex Differences in Apprehension

The suggestion that girls may reach their peak inhibition to peers earlier than boys is supported by an independent study from our laboratory which was not directed at this hypothesis (Shapiro, 1969). Shapiro observed 40 pairs of Caucasian middle-class children, matched on sex and age, in an unfamiliar apartment in a large building complex in which the children lived. The younger children were 18 to 20 months of age, the older children were 28 to 30 months of age. The children were observed on three different occasions one week apart, but we are now concerned only with the first two sessions. On the first session the mother of one of the children remained while the second mother left. On the second session the mothers alternated, and the mother who had departed on the first session remained. The observer watched each of the two children alternately for 10-second epochs. Hence each child was observed for 60 different 10-second sessions; each 20-minute session had a total of 120 observations derived from both children. A single attractive toy was placed in a room with the two children. There was no important effect on the child's behavior of the presence or absence of the child's own mother. This is probably because great care was taken not to initiate the experiment (by asking one of the mothers to leave) until both children were happy and unafraid. Hence the differences to be reported are likely to be a function of the presence of the strange peer. The

TABLE 5. Number of Children High or Low on Inhibition (Based on Median Split) for Each Variable at 20 Months Within Each Subgroup (minutes 1 through 15, $N = 62$)

Degree of Inhibition	Caucasian Girls		Chinese Girls		Caucasian Boys		Chinese Boys		All Children	
	DC^a	HC^b	DC^a	HC^b	DC^a	HC^b	DC^a	HC^b	DC^a	HC^b
Proximity										
High	1	6	3	4	0	9	3	4	7	23
Low	3	4	4	3	5	4	4	5	16	16
Play										
High	1	5	2	5	1	8	4	3	8	21
Low	3	5	5	2	4	5	3	6	15	18
Both variables										
High	1	3	2	3	1	10	2	2	6	18
Low	3	2	4	1	4	3	2	3	13	9

^{a} DC = day care.
^{b} HC = home control.

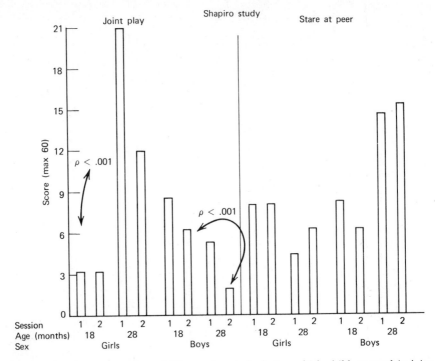

FIGURE 4. Average number of 10-second periods during which child engaged in joint play with peer or stared at peer.

most interesting result in this context is that the girls were precocious to the boys in overcoming signs of apprehension to the strange peer, as revealed by staring and joint reciprocal play with the peer. Among girls, the 18-month-olds stared more and played less than did the 28-month-old subjects, suggesting that 28-month-old girls had become less apprehensive. But among boys, the older ones played less and stared more than the younger boys (see Figure 4).

The age difference for joint play was significant for girls for both sessions. The older boys showed significantly more staring at the strange peer than the older girls on the first session ($p < .05$) and played less than the girls on both sessions ($p < .001$).

DISCUSSION

Most children behaved with greater inhibition of play at the introduction of a strange peer at 20 than at 13½ or 29 months. Although this curvilinear developmental function characterized children in two rearing conditions, the day care children were a little less uncertain than those reared at home, suggesting that the group experience had the theoretically anticipated effects. It seems that maturational forces determine the developmental function for initial inhibition with unfamiliar peers, while experience monitors the intensity of that inhibition.

This discussion is addressed to the implications of these simple facts. One possible interpretation of the data rests on the assumption that a schema for the event "peer in a strange context" does not develop until the second year of life because infants do not encounter peers very often. Hence the inhibition is due to encounter with an event that is discrepant from the child's existing schema. That explanation does not account for all the data. The day care children encounter many peers daily, some of them unfamiliar, and they had been with infants and young children ever since they were 3½ months of age; yet these subjects, like the home controls, showed greater inhibition of play at 20 than at 13½ months. We do not believe that the source of the uncertainty is the unfamiliarity of the peer as a physical event. Although it is neither parsimonious nor an obvious inference from the data, we offer the following explanation, with appropriate tentativeness.

Apprehension to the peer does not peak until late in the second year because the primary source of the apprehension is the inability to resolve activated hypotheses pertaining to questions of several types. "What action do I initiate with that person?" "What will that person do to me?" "Can I still play with toys?" "What can I expect from that child?" This interpretation resembles the one we have offered for separation anxiety—namely, that separation anxiety peaks during the second year because the source of fear is the ability to activate hypotheses but the inability to resolve them. Both proximity and inhibition of play were generally greater at 20 than at 13½ months because the older children were mature enough to attempt to generate questions about possible acts of the strange peer toward them or actions they might initiate toward the peer, whereas some of the younger children may not have reached that stage. The uncertainty that results from the inability to resolve those questions differs from the uncertainty that is a product of an unassimilated discrepancy. We might call the former *unpredictability*. Bronson (1972) also suggests that predictability of an event may contribute to its ability to provoke "distress." During our observations we have noted that if the peer made a move toward the child and offered him a toy, the latter quickly overcame his inhibition. The offering of the toy functioned as a "peace gesture." Soon the child left his mother and went off to play with the other as if the friendly act had answered the question "what will happen?" with the reply "nothing dangerous."

Other Data

The present interpretation of the results is supported by the results of investigations with different original aims. Dragsten and Lee (1973) observed 22 infants ranging in age from 6 to 18 months. Half were attending day care and half were being reared at home. The day care children were observed in their day care setting, as well as in a special experimental setting in which each day care infant was paired with another infant of the same age being reared at home. Each day care child was paired with an unfamiliar, home-reared child for three 15-minute observation periods separated by a week. The eleven children in day care were divided into three age groups: 6 to 10 months, 11 to 14 months, and 15 to 18 months. The older children (11 to 18 months) stared at the peer significantly more in the experimental setting than in the day care setting, but this difference did not occur for the 6- to 10-month-olds (see also Greenberg, Hillman, & Grice, 1973, for comparable results for stranger anxiety).

Cox and Campbell (1968) compared the behavior of children 14 and 30 months old during a 4-minute period when the mothers left them in contrast to their behavior during the previous 4 minutes when the mothers were present. The 14-month-olds showed a greater decrease in play than the 30-month-old children, suggesting that the older children had matured enough to be able to understand the discrepant event. More relevant is an investigation by Gershaw and Schwarz (1971), who saw 23- and 38-month-old children. The procedure involved an initial 4-minute baseline observation with mother present. The examiner then asked the child to leave his mother and go with the examiner to get some candy. The examiner and the child left accordingly and then returned to the room. For half the subjects the mother was present, for the other half she was absent. Only the younger 23-month-olds were distressed when the mother was absent, and they played less when the mother was gone. The older children were not distressed and did not show serious inhibition of play. Moreover, there was no relation between display of distress displayed when the examiner took the child away from his mother to get candy and display of distress when the child returned to the empty room. We interpret this result to mean that when the child understands why he is away from his mother (in this case, to get candy), there is no uncertainty, therefore, no apprehension. When the experimental child returned to the empty room and did not know why his mother was gone, he attempted to explain it. The 23-month-olds could not and became anxious. The older children, we assume, could explain the absence and did not become distressed. This difference between the 23- and 38-month-olds resembles the difference in inhibition of play to the strange peer at 20 and at 29 months.

It is interesting to note that Mary Shirley, in her classic 1933 monograph summarizing a longitudinal investigation of 25 Minneapolis children, reported a wave of "timidity" at 18 months which lasted about 3 months and was displayed by more than three-quarters of her subjects. Shirley argued that this fear seemed to be qualitatively different from the one displayed to strangers at 6 months of age. This phenomenon may have a comparable analogue in macaque monkeys, which exhibit a generally fearful posture in a variety of contexts around 5 months of age. Since development in macaques proceeds at a rate approximately four times that of the human child, the expected age of peak apprehension for the human infant is about 20 months—the time when inhibition of play was greatest in our study (Suomi, personal communication).

Implications

The emergence of the competence we call "activation of hypotheses" has implications for other processes emerging during the second year of life. The appearance of questions in the child's overt speech (where, what, why), which do not generally occur until late in the second or early in the third year, implies rather directly hypotheses about a potential quality of a future event. This is also the time when the child becomes "sensitive" to verbal reproof and signs of potential rejection. The second year seems to mark the first fragile appearance of the capacity to think about the immediate future—a capacity that will grow until the person is able to consider millennia rather than moments. But during the middle of the second year we see it in fresh form. Here is another instance of the general principle that basic competences first emerge in very narrow contexts and are applied to an increasing number of situations over the course of many years. Not until preadolescence does the child show a generalized, reliable tendency to accommodate to the future and its demands (see Rogoff, Newcombe, & Kagan, 1974).

References

Bronson, G. W. Infants' reactions to unfamiliar persons and novel objects. *Monograph of the Society for Research in Child Development,* 1972, **37**, serial no. 148.

Cox, F. M., & Campbell, D. Young children in a new situation with and without their mothers. *Child Development,* 1968, **39**, 123–131.

Dragsten, S. S., & Lee, L. C. Infants' social behavior in a naturalistic versus experimental setting. *Proceedings of 81st Annual Convention of the American Psychological Association,* 1973. Pp. 65–66.

Fleener, D. E., & Cairns, R. B. Attachment behaviors in human infants. *Developmental Psychology,* 1970, **2**, 215–223.

Gershaw, N. J., & Schwarz, J. C. The effects of a familiar toy and mother's presence on exploratory and attachment behaviors in young children. *Child Development,* 1971, **42**, 1662–1666.

Greenberg, D. J., Hillman, D., & Grice, D. Infant and stranger variables related to stranger anxiety in the first year of life. *Developmental Psychology,* 1973, **9**, 207–212.

Kagan, J. Discrepancy, temperament and infant distress. In M. Lewis & L. Rosenblum (Eds.) *The origins of fear.* New York: Wiley, 1974. Pp. 229–248.

Kagan, J., & Moss, H. A. *Birth to maturity*. New York: Wiley, 1962.

Kotelchuck, M. The nature of a child's tie to his father. Unpublished doctoral dissertation, Harvard University, 1972.

Lester, B. M., Kotelchuck, M., Spelke, E., Sellers, M. J., & Klein, R. E. Separation protest in Guatemalan infants: Cross-cultural and cognitive findings. *Developmental Psychology,* 1974, **10,** 79–85.

Rogoff, B., Newcombe, N., & Kagan, J. Planfulness and recognition memory. *Child Development,* 1974, **45,** 972–977.

Ross, G., Kotelchuck, M., Zelazo, P. R., & Kagan, J. Separation distress in home and laboratory. *Developmental Psychology,* 1975, **11,** 256–257.

Shapiro, L. N. Study of peer group interaction in 18 and 28 month old children. Unpublished doctoral dissertation, Harvard University, 1969.

Shirley, M. M. The first two years: A study of 25 babies. Vol. 2. *Institute of Child Welfare Monograph Series,* no. VII. Minneapolis: University of Minnesota Press, 1933.

Spelke, E., Zelazo, P., Kagan, J., & Kotelchuck, M. Father interaction and separation protest. *Developmental Psychology,* 1973, **9,** 83–90.

Suomi, S. Personal communication.

CHAPTER 8

Toward a Cognitive Theory of Interpersonal Development: Importance of Peers

LEE C. LEE

Department of Human Development
Cornell University

Although developmental psychologists have spent the last two decades in exploring how the child learns about the world around him, the major emphasis of this effort has been on how the child acquires knowledge of the physical or objective world. Some researchers have attempted to study the social development of the child, but they have not been concerned primarily with the *processes* through which a child acquires knowledge of the social world. Thus very little is known about how or what the young child learns as he develops abilities to initiate and react to interpersonal contacts. Not only is there sparse empirical knowledge in this area, there is no cohesive developmental theory about how the child acquires knowledge and skills in the interpersonal realm.

The importance of understanding interpersonal relations is beyond question, for our ability to interact with others affects our lives at every point. On the personal level, for example, the quality of interpersonal skills determines the success of any individual in relating to those who share his social world. And with regard to society as a whole, the orderly use of these skills among individuals or among groups of individuals renders communication among men and women possible.

In this chapter we select ideas from existent theories and empirical findings, to generate some hypotheses concerning how the child acquires interpersonal competence, assuming that interpersonal competence can be viewed as a logical extension of the frame of reference used to understand cognitive competence. Although the conditions that influence their development are different, structures and schemes are common to both. We attempt here to explain how social schemes are constructed that lead to competence in the interpersonal realm, and to elaborate on this process. We focus mainly on the period when the child moves from sensory-motor to operational thinking, which is a period when peers become a significant part of his life. Because these ideas are in their most primitive form, it would be premature and presumptuous to make comparisons with other theories; therefore no reference is made to models proposed by others.

PHYSICAL AND SOCIAL SCHEME CONSTRUCTION

Peer relations are primarily social relations, falling under the rubric of social interaction, the psychology of interpersonal encounters. Thus an examination of the social exchange process may help us to understand the developmental aspects of interpersonal competence. Since social encounters inevitably involve such processes as decision making, problem solving, information processing, and role taking, it is apparent that cognition plays an important role in the social process. One may assume that cognitive and social processes are intertwined or inextricably bound in some manner. Hence we might choose to view the developmental course of interpersonal competence in terms of structures, much as Piaget has viewed cognitive capabilities.

Commonalities of Physical and Social Scheme Construction

Given the viewpoint just suggested, as psychological structures, the cognitive and interpersonal facets of development would share a number of features: each could be seen as stemming from or manifesting a common process and undergoing similar transformations with development; moreover each could be characterized by the same functional invariants (e.g., the adaptive processes of assimilation and accommodation, which progress toward equilibrium). Only their elements would vary. Whereas cognitive development concerns the child's relations to objects, social development concerns the child's relations to persons.

From this basic assumption of the similar development of cognitive and social processes, how can social or interpersonal development be explained within this conceptual framework?

In the child's acquisition of knowledge of the world, he constructs schemes consisting of three components: the intellective, the affective, and the enactive. The *intellective* component deals with knowledge about the properties of objects. This includes perceptual and substantive information concerning these objects. The *affective* component deals with feelings and emotions evoked by the individual's interaction with external objects. In a sense, this affective component is the "personal meaning" an individual attaches to objects. The *enactive* component deals with how the individual relates to and acts on the external world. These may be behavior sequences or, more abstractly, the styles and strategies used by the individual in his interactions. All schemes, be they social or cognitive, thus include a knowledge component, a meaning component, and an action style component.

Let us explore the role played by these components in the construction of objective and social schemes, keeping in mind that the process of scheme construction always entails adaptation of the individual's existing schemes through assimilation and accommodation. Also, it is important to note that an individual assimilates his "perceptions of reality," which may or may not resemble "external reality." Thus in discussing the construction of schemes, a distinction must be made between these two classes of "reality." Although one's perception of reality cannot be separated from the external reality, in the discussion on scheme construction to follow we minimize the perceptual role, to allow for a clearer treatment of the basic issues at hand.

Physical Scheme Construction

The construction of schemes in the objective world entails the individual acting on or manipulating objects that are relatively stable. The feedback (information output) of these objects is usually constant across space and time. That is, most objects in the objective world do not change from one instance to another. Furthermore, the probability of feedback and the quality of the reactions from the objects are also relatively constant; that is, there is usually some consistent feedback from the object with each encounter. From these constancies, the child identifies and extracts the invariant features of the object, assimilates them into his existing scheme, and accommodates when the situation demands it. Let us use a yellow rubber ball as an example. How does an individual learn about the yellow rubber ball? He looks at it, manipulates it, and finds that it is round, soft, and yellow (intellective component). He throws the ball and it bounces and rolls (enactive component), and he has fun (or may not) while manipulating and throwing it (affective component). The ball will be the same the next time he interacts with it. If he encounters another ball, the feature of roundness will again (still) exist and his actions of throwing will also elicit a consistent response from the ball, that of rolling. Whether the ball is soft or whether it bounces may vary; but certain features (i.e., roundness and rollability) are properties of all balls. Thus certain features of the object ball are invariant. Whether the child will interact with the ball depends on his own initiative of enactment; thus in the individual's interaction with the objective world, he is the controller of the interaction. Also, whether he obtains information about the ball depends on his own actions; and the feedback he receives is consistent across time and space.

Social Scheme and Construction

The child's acquisition of knowledge of the social world is quite different. What is entailed in the construction of social schemes? Let us examine the simplest of all social encounters, the dyadic interaction. When two adults meet for the first time, each individual assesses the other on various dimensions (physical characteristics, emotional state, role relationships, setting, etc.). Through this assessment, each imputes certain characteristics to the social partner (intellective component). Drawing from personal past experiences of these perceived assessments certain feelings are evoked (affective component) and each individual acts accordingly (enactive component). Therefore each person enters the interaction with a "preconceived" social scheme of the social partner. Through the interactive process, each one assimilates new information that may or may not coincide with his preconceptions. If it does not coincide with the preconceived assessment, and if he wishes to continue the interchange, the individual must attempt to adjust his actions appropriately, thus accommodating to the new knowledge of the social partner. This new knowledge may also lead to an adjustment of the strategy or style of interacting. Throughout this interchange, each builds up feelings about the other.

During the next encounter each will have a specific scheme of the other, but new assessments must also be made. Although the physical characteristics may not change, the emotional state of the individual may be quite different. In addition, if the setting for this meeting is different from the last, or if this encounter involves a third social partner, the role relationship may change also. Thus the intellective component of a social scheme can change from one encounter to another. Given this change in the intellective component of a constructed social scheme, the individual must accommodate his own actions to secure a mutual exchange that results in a change in the enactive component of the social scheme as well. Furthermore, since social exchanges are actions and reactions, this enactive component may shift throughout the interaction process.

Differences of Physical and Social Scheme Construction

These brief sketches of physical and social scheme construction point out the variableness of external reality of the social world as compared with the objective world. That is, social partners differ from one situation to another according to mood, setting, and so on, and they differ from one another according to age, sex, race, and other variables.

Another important difference between objects of the objective and social worlds concerns the objects' reaction potential (i.e., the responsiveness of objects). We have seen the consistency of response from objects in the objective world: if an individual acts on those objects, the objects almost always "react"; thus feedback is attained. However, objects in the social world—that is, social partners—must act or react if the individual is to receive information for assimilation. In other words, although an individual may take the initiative to act on the social environment, he has no control over the attainment of the information, since the control rests in his social partner's desire to interact.

These differences have consequences in the child's acquisition of knowledge of the world and in the course of his interactions with the environment. That is, if the responses to the child's enactments to the external world are regularly too inconsistent, too unpleasant, or too discrepant from his already existing schemes, the child will stop acting on the environment. Or if he continues to act on the environment, he may develop "nonreality" oriented schemes that render his interactions with the environment ineffective or bizarre. The possibility that these events will occur during the child's interaction with the objective world is minimal, but the probability that they will occur during his interactions with the social world is much higher.

Such variabilities in social encounters render social schemes more difficult to construct than physical schemes. (Keep in mind that scheme development entails the construction of all three components of a scheme, i.e., intellective, enactive, and affective.) Each time the child makes an assessment of a social situation, the equilibrium he has previously established may be shattered because of new and often different or conflicting knowledge he gains with each new encounter. Thus although the child may have the necessary operations to act on the world of physical objects, he probably will not use these operations appropriately on social objects until he has acquired many more interactions within the social world. The social schemes he develops will reflect the quality and kind of social encounters he experiences. These schemes are essential in the development of interpersonal competence.

INTERPERSONAL COMPETENCE AND SOCIAL SCHEME DEVELOPMENT

What does the notion of competence mean in the social domain? The ultimate aim of social scheme construction, as of physical scheme construction, is to attain a set of logically consistent structures and operations through which one can view and act on the world. Thus in the social domain the child must acquire a knowledge that interpersonal relations are social exchanges involving processes of continual reaction, mutual exchanges in which each partner continually affects the other. He must be able to develop consistent strategies of interaction through which this reciprocity of mutual exchange can be maintained. These strategies can be effectively used only if the child has some enduring notion of the invariant features of social partners and social settings, despite their transformations in space and time. With this knowledge of the properties of the social exchange, he must make predictions concerning the social encounter and interact accordingly. Thus he must conserve the social situation and the social partner. To do this he must be able to decenter attention from himself to other people.

Quality of a Child's Thought as Baseline for Social Scheme Construction

Before we can understand the development of interpersonal competence, we must assess the child's quality of thought. During the period between the ap-proximate ages of 2 through 7, the child is in a state of transition from sensory-motor to operational thought. Very briefly, the transformation from sensory-motor to operational thought requires two main processes. First, the child must be able to coordinate rapidly and simultaneously to unify discrete independent experiences, which was beyond his capability during the sensory-motor stage. Second, he must become conscious of the nature of his own thought processes rather than the results he wishes to obtain. He must not only be able to do something, he must be able to know that he can do it. Thus operations, unlike sensory-motor acts, are liberated from action sequences and from the concrete objects in the world. In addition, they can encompass a wide range of events simultaneously.

During the preoperational period, the child begins to acquire the ability to represent events that are not immediately present to his senses. At the same time, language begins to emerge through which communication is attained. Another important developmental process takes place at this time also: there emerges in the child a sense of his own causality and efficacy with reference to the world.

In spite of all these developing mental abilities, the preoperational child is primarily self-centered. That is, he cannot see objects or events from the perspective of someone else. Also, the preoperational child attends to states rather than to transformations of these states. His thought is static and immobile; he cannot conceptualize an object in transition, but rather, only its two end points. In addition, the preoperational child cannot solve a problem requiring him to perform an operation of reversibility in his head, mentally reversing the sequence of his perceptions.

As the child matures and gains knowledge through interactions with the external environment, his actions gradually become interiorized and reversible. External motor reactions are no longer essential prerequisites for assimilating information into a scheme. Thus operative thinking emerges. With operativity, schemes increase in their range of potential application and are no longer centered on any one dimension or on the child himself. With this liberation of his thought processes, the child begins to be able to expand and reflect on his own activities in a self-regulatory and self-initiating manner.

Thus the child at this period not only can act efficiently on objects but *knows* that he can act efficiently. This knowledge entails the realization that the self and other people exist independently of each other in a permanent, continuous way, despite transformations in these entities over space or time. The realization that a self exists which can act on objects (i.e., a consciousness on the part of the child of his own causality) is part of the development of operative thinking. The child thus learns to actively structure reality.

While all these internal changes are taking place, an important external event is occurring: the demands and restrictions of the parents become salient at this transitional period. The primary tool for socialization is language, the primary vehicle for socialization is the interpersonal exchanges.

Thus the "success" of socialization depends on the child's understanding of the interpersonal situation.

Given this brief account of the child's quality of thought and the context in which the child is functioning at this period, let us explore the course of interpersonal development more explicitly. We now want to know what elements or properties of social phenomena the child must acquire. In other words, how does the child construct the intellective component of the social scheme?

Construction of the Intellective Component of Social Schemes

We have said that competence in the social domain involves the child's ability to conserve the social partner and situation. But what does "conservation" mean in the social domain, or what is it that the child conserves? The child must identify the invariant features of social encounters, that is, the important features that are necessary in assessing all social situations.

How does the preoperational child achieve this immense feat? Our earlier analysis of the social situation indicated that certain invariant features are inherent in all social situations. They include properties of the social partner and context as presented in Figure 1. Thus for social partner, the child must assess: (1) physical characteristics of the partner (sex, age, race, etc.), (2) behavioral state (reading, jumping, eating, etc.), (3) emotional state (happy, sad, angry, etc.), and (4) role relationship (father, sister, teacher, etc.). Also he must assess the context of the social encounter, which consists of: (1) setting (home, school, restaurant, etc.) and (2) group configuration (size of group, status relation of participants, homogeneity of its participants in relation to age, sex, race, social class, education, etc.). The child must evaluate these invariant features of the social partner and context at each social encounter. To achieve this, the child is obliged to learn the cues that will aid him in identifying the variants of the social exchange. Some possible variants also appear in Figure 1. For

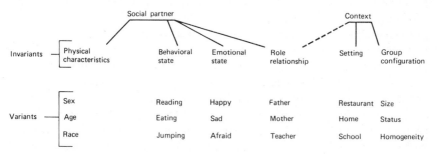

FIGURE 1.   Features of social encounters.

example, when a person smiles with delight (cue), there is a high probability that the individual is happy (variant), which is an element of the emotional state (invariant). Or if an individual is crying, the probability is high that he is sad, but there is a slight probability that he is happy. In addition, the child must learn the socially shared, imputed values of each variant. For example, the role (invariant) of father (variant) implies particular status and position in relation to the child.

How does the child acquire knowledge of these invariant features of the social encounter? During the early preoperational period when he acquires language, the child begins to label objects and events. Since labels are arbitrary designations, the child must attach personal meaning to the social partner and situation if he is to assimilate them. Initially these identifications are quite global and diffuse, and lacking real defining properties (e.g., daddy is daddy, is daddy!). As the child gains more experience with social exchanges, be begins to differentiate elements of the social partner and context. This ability to differentiate helps the child to associate certain cues (behavioral and/or perceptual) with certain variants. For example, he begins to be aware of certain unique qualities and characteristics of daddy; that is, daddy possesses some distinctive features (daddy is big, daddy is funny, etc.). This association between cues and variants aids the child in delineating the properties of each variant, thus giving definition to each variant. This delimitation of variants permits the child to gradually bring order out of a somewhat chaotic situation, by systematizing the perceived information (cues) through classification of the cues within each variant. He also develops a "cue system" that indicates a particular variant. Although he has a notion of the importance of a certain cue in defining a particular variant, his thought processes now permit him to center on only one dimension at a time, which limits his use of those cues. That is, since he uses one cue at a time in defining the social encounter, he has difficulty in comprehending class inclusion relations. Specifically, he does not see how the cues within each variant relate to one another, how the variant relates to the cues, and how one variant relates to another variant. This difficulty of perceiving each property or element of the social encounter as isolated from each other leads the child to make superficial assessments of the social situation. The element the child selects for his assessments depends on the salience of that particular element within a particular social encounter. For example, witness the nursery school child who sees his teacher in the grocery store and does not recognize her. However, recognition is immediate when he is told that she is his teacher. The initial nonrecognition was not due to the child's inability to identify the teacher from other adults whom he knows; rather, he had focused his social encounters in regard to the teacher on the school setting element alone. Thus this element has salience over other specific characteristics of the teacher. For the young child who enters school for the first time, the school context has greater salience than other environment features.

As the child moves into operativity, his thought processes cease to consist of exclusive preoccupation with one element of the social encounter at a time. He begins to notice transformation of events rather than end states; thus he is able to perceive relationships between specific behaviors and between certain behavior sequences and their outcomes. This increased flexibility of thought allows him to use class inclusion relationships and to construct a realistic hierarchy system of probability of cues. Furthermore, since operative thought is liberated from action sequence and objects, he can relate various encounters across time and space, gaining the ability to identify the invariant features of social exchanges; hence conservation of social partner and context occurs. The acquisition of abilities to conserve and to understand class inclusion relationships is accompanied by the ability to create new complex elements by regrouping elements within a class. These complex elements increase the probability of accurate assessment of the properties of the social exchange. For example, in our previous illustration of crying as a cue, the preoperational child assesses whether crying is a happy or sad state without any additional index because he centers on one dimension at a time. With greater flexibility of thought, the operational child can more accurately predict its referent by doing the following: if the individual is crying (cue_1) and is also slouching (cue_2) and everyone else present is pouting (cue_3), one can accurately conclude that the individual is sad (variant of emotional state). However, if the individual is crying (cue_1) and also jumping (cue_2) and everyone else is laughing or smiling (cue_3), one can accurately assess that the individual is happy (variant of emotional state). Thus the child takes into account other cues that are present in the immediate environment (i.e., other participants). In doing so, he is combining elements to form supraordinate classes. Likewise, with the onset of conservation, he is able to combine variants and form superordinate classes of invariants. He learns that at each social encounter he must make an assessment of the invariant features. Although the operational child has mobility of thought that permits him to compose or decompose classes in a hierarchy, he lacks the mobility of abstract thinking that is hypothetical. Such mobility of abstract thought is required to reach the next stage of social competence. Since our present interest is in the preoperational-operational period, however, we do not deal with the more advanced stages.

Construction of Enactive and Affective Components of Social Schemes

We have examined only the child's acquisition of *knowledge* of the social situation, that is, the construction of the intellective component of social schemes. Let us proceed to explore the interactive style or strategy of interaction—the construction of the enactive and affective components of the social scheme.

Although the child enters the preoperational period with the ability to present events symbolically, these mental representations differ in structural quality for the two facets of development. This difference is attributable to the differential nature of the child's interaction with objects of the two worlds. During the preoperational period when the child has a mature sense of causality, the nature of the external environment becomes extremely important. Because this is the period of intense socialization when the child is barraged with "no's" and "don't" from his social partner, who is usually an adult, the child usually reacts to the social environment rather than acting on it. This is not to say that the child has no effect on how the objects of the social world will relate to him; rather, his interactions usually consist of reacting and accommodating to the initiation or demands of elders. Thus in the child's early social exchanges, accommodation plays a salient role; opportunities for assimilation in social exchanges are minimal. It is important to remember that the meaning of external reality for the child is not the event or object itself, but the assimilation of it to his existing scheme. Since the child's opportunity to accommodate far exceeds his opportunity to assimilate, his construction of social reality during this early period is through the eyes of the elders. Also, because most of these interpersonal exchanges are accommodative, the child's sense of competence in the social realm may be less advanced than in the objective realm.

Does this mean that the child's interactions are totally inappropriate during the beginning of the preoperational period? No, that is not the case. During the early preoperational period, through accommodating to adult demands, the child develops certain interactive patterns or action sequences that are related to certain cues in the environment. Therefore, given a certain condition, he can reproduce appropriate interactive behaviors. However, he cannot *anticipate* how he should behave or why he should behave in a certain way. Thus he has imitated the appropriate behaviors that are invoked, given the presence of certain environmental cues. These cues, as we have stated in the discussion of intellective schemes, are diffused. We know very little about these early links. However, it is through these basic imitative behaviors that strategies of social interaction evolve.

How do imitative behaviors take on a personal reality for the child? Since the child during this period can retain images of absent objects and events, he reenacts past events in the absence of a model. These reenactments could be exact copies of previous behaviors and emotions of the model, or they could be distorted events of the past. Exact reenactments are typical early in the child's development, perhaps filling an important role in setting down appropriate action sequences for the child. This is evidenced in the high instances of ritualistic behaviors at around the age of 2. Distorted reenactments occur later and take place in the context of symbolic play. It is through symbolic play, when the child can do as he wishes, that he can create a personal reality. This reality may have only partial resemblance to external reality, or it may be only a slight distortion of external reality. For example, consider the fantasy play of preschoolers. In a sense, during symbolic play the child practices or experiments with his repertoire of imitative behaviors.

Furthermore, it is through symbolic play that he takes on the role of others. Through role playing he reenacts scenes from the past that include both emotions and actions of significant others (daddy, mommy, baby, etc.), until these actions and emotions become encoded into mental images. He acquires a crude sense of how others feel and act which is the beginning of role-taking ability and perhaps the precursor for genuine empathy.

Another important function of symbolic play is that it acts as a vehicle through which self-sufficiency is developed. Recall that during this period the child's control of his own social reality has been at a minimum because he is required to adapt to adult demands. In symbolic play he creates his own reality; hence in this context he is controller of reality; even if this reality is somewhat distorted, the important factor is that the child *is* effecting change in his environment.

What external events aid the child in using these internal changes to increase his interpersonal competence? During the early preoperational period the child begins to spend time with peers. Peer exchanges are a vehicle to test these personally evolved social schemes. Until this time, of course, most of his acquired behaviors are imitative. For the child to achieve competence in the social domain, these enactive social schemes must take on some personal meaning in relation to external reality. Thus in his initial encounters with peers, he is testing the new interactive scheme against an external reality, a reality that is very real. This is possible because peer exchanges, especially during initial encounters, are authority free; neither child has a previously defined rigid view of social reality. Thus each is free to create and construct his own reality. Young children, unlike adults, are not yet able to accommodate appropriately to each other's initiations because neither has attained the notion of reciprocity. Furthermore, each child is centered on himself; that is, his interests are almost exclusively focused on himself. These nonaccommodating abilities of social partners force the child to develop reality-oriented strategies. Successful strategies enable him to assimilate his social partner's reactions and force him to accommodate to them as well, thus leading to eventual construction of useful perceptions of social reality. Since this process is simultaneously occurring in both children, the social situation becomes an area for mutual struggle.

ILLUSTRATIVE EXAMPLES OF PEER INFLUENCE

Thus far the attempt to hypothesize about how the child acquires competence in the social world during the early childhood years has been on a rather abstract level. The following concrete examples should serve only as illustrations, however, since these observations have not been systematically verified as yet. These illustrative examples were derived from the dyadic play of a group of 2-year-olds seen at 6-month intervals until they reached the age of 4.

The observations of the children revealed what appears to be an interesting progression in the patterns of social exchanges. The progression is by no means monotonically related to age, but it seems that certain patterns occur more frequently at particular ages.

Two-year-olds' communications with each other appear to be in the form of one-unit exchanges (i.e., child A initiates and child B responds). (For convenience sake, we refer to these one-unit exchanges as interacts). However, often these interacts are chained into a sequence. For example,

Molly (M) and Jennifer (J), both age 2, are wandering around the playroom. J stops, looks at the mirror, smiles, pats the mirror, says, "Hi, Jennifer," and laughs. M having been watching J closely, approaches the mirror, smiles, pats the mirror, says, "Hi, Jennifer," and laughs.

J and M repeat this interact identically for six consecutive sequences. These repetitions were identical in verbal and behavioral content, inflection and volume level, and emotional tone; thus there was a rhythmic quality to these interchanges.

Another example occurred when Molly was watching Jennifer playing with the telephone:

M: Let me have a turn.	J: No. (laughs)
M: Let me have a turn.	J: No. (laughs)
M: Let me have a turn.	J: No. (laughs)
M: Let me have a turn.	J: No. (laughs)
M: Let me have a turn. (laughs)	J: Dadadadadada.

The repetition of each other's behavior or exchanges can be viewed as a chaining of identical interacts. As can be seen, the chaining of interacts can be imitative or nonimitative. Such chaining of action sequence requires that each child act and wait for the social partner to react. Because these sequences of chained interacts are rigid and unvarying in content or format, very little is required of the children cognitively except that they delay their own actions while waiting for the end of the social partner's actions if they are to act at the appropriate time. The rhythmic quality of these exchanges appear to help the child in noting the end of social partner's actions. These action sequences seem to serve the function of aiding the child in learning to restrain his or her actions until the appropriate time. It is as if they were practicing to "take turns."

The next level of interchange is a slight variation of this rigid, chained sequence. Here the ending of each child's act vary each time. For example, Molly and Jennifer (still at age 2), using separate telephones simultaneously, have the following conversation.

J: Hello Mommy.	M: Hello Daddy.
J: Hello Johnny.	M: Hello Douggy.
J: Hello Do-Do.	M: Hello Po-Po.

This type of chaining, where the interacts contain variations requires greater concentration by the child than the previous global, identical repetitions, since the child must pay attention to variation of end states to know when the other child's action ends and he can act.

As the child grows older, such interact-chainings are replaced by sequential exchanges of ideas. However, because of the child's inability to take the social partner's perspective, his speech is often noncommunicative. In the social arena the children appear to be helping each other in improving their communicative abilities. The listener is required to attend with greater effort and to learn to vary strategies of inquiry if he is to understand the message from the speaker. Also, the speaker has to repeat the message so that it has meaning for the listener. For example Morgan (M) and Kathy (K) have been playing separately. M is on the floor playing with trucks while K is at the table making Play-doh cakes.

K: There's a sink too. (While continuing to manipulate the Play-doh)
M: What? (softly)
K: There's a sink here and a bathroom.
M: What? (raised voice)
K: There's a sink here and a bathroom in case you want to go.
M: What? (shouts, indicating some annoyance)
K: There's a bathroom with two sinks so you and me can go wash.

Thus we see Morgan attempting to assimilate Kathy's message; unable to do so, he makes demands on Kathy by varying his strategy (intonation modified without changing the content of his question). Kathy, on the other hand, attempts to accommodate with difficulty. Finally, Morgan's persistent demands aid Kathy in clearly conveying her message.

Role playing appears to be the richest source of learning for the child because it contains many informative variations and many opportunities for testing strategies and learning communicative skills. Here are two examples of role play; the first involves a pair of 4-year-old girls and the second is a pair of 4-year-old boys.

Kathy and Karen

Karen looks on as Kathy irons. Kathy turns and says, "This time you can be the father." "What?" asks Karen from down on the floor. "I'll be the father and you be the mother, okay?" repeats Kathy. "But mothers should iron the clothes," adds Karen, smiling. "But fathers sometimes iron the clothes," replies Kathy. "You put 'em out to hang, okay?" suggests Kathy. . . . Kathy finishes dressing the doll. "There's, now the baby's all in her pajamies," says Kathy. "In her pajamies?" asks Karen, smiling. "Yeah," answers Kathy. "Does she have anything on her bottom?" asks Karen. "Yeah," replies Kathy. "She went potty on her pants," admits Kathy, taking the doll and sitting at the table with it. "What are you gonna do?" asks Karen, looking at Kathy holding the baby and taking a crayon out of the can. "Feed her her bottle," explains Kathy. "Feed her her bottle? That's not a bottle," smiles Karen. Kathy goes about her business and Karen looks on. . . . "Why don't you sit down and watch TV, Daddy?" suggests Karen. "Wait, gotta put the baby in her cradle . . . on her pillow . . . and drink her bottle," explains Kathy as she sets the doll down into the toy box. "Where, where's the crib?" asks Karen, going to see. "Is that a crib?" "No, that's her bottle," says Kathy to Karen. Then to the baby, Kathy says, "Now go to sleep. Mother and Daddy are going out for supper tonight." "You and me, right?" asks Karen from the table. "Yup," replies Kathy, carrying a pair of hi-heels to Karen and saying "Here Mother." "Thank you," says Karen, accepting the shoes. "We're taking the baby with us, aren't we?" mumbles Kathy. "What?" asks Karen. "We're taking the baby with us," repeats Kathy.

Later

Kathy rises from the table with the doll in her arms and says, "Thank you wife. That was a good supper." . . . Karen clears off the table, Kathy emerges from her book and says, "Mother, plug the iron in and iron your clothes." "Oh, I can't," replies Karen, "I gotta do the dishes."

Jeff and Morgan

"This will be my coffee cup; you don't be the daddy, you be the little boy . . . " contends Morgan, interrupting Jeff as he pours out the coffee. He then proceeds to explain, "But you, an' you, an' you, an' you could. . . . "I'll, I'll be the mommy," interjects Jeff. "No, you won't; I'll be the mommy," argues Morgan. "Then you're the . . . , then I'm the daddy," concludes Jeff (finding his place in the scheme of things), and adding, "Hey, where's my coffee cup?" Remembering where the argument began, Morgan firmly protests, saying, "I'm the daddy; you're the mommy. . . . " "No. No, I was gonna be . . . you were gonna be the mommy," protests Jeff. "No, I was gonna be the *daddy*," reaffirms Morgan, sure now. "But, but you took my . . . " says Jeff, exasperated, referring to the tea kettle but as a coffee cup." "This is my coffee cup. *I'm* the daddy. It says, '*Daddy Fleishner*,'" indicating where on the "cup" the name is supposedly printed. And he looks at Jeff with a very threatening expression and says, "an' your name is Jeff; yours says 'Jeff'. . . . "

Later

"I'll be cooking and you telephone, okay?" suggests Morgan. "I'll be the daddy," he adds, "okay?" "No, no—*mommies* cook," protests Jeff, walking over to the counter beside Morgan. "Oh," says Morgan, then reconsidering, "I'll cook; I'll be the mommy." "Uh?" asks Jeff. "I'll be the mommy," repeats Morgan. "And I'll be the daddy," says Jeff, walking toward the cabinet, "'cause I'm the. . . . Good." "You'll be ironing," says Morgan. "Yes, Daddy'll be ironing," confirms Jeff. "Mommies iron, mommies iron. Not boys . . . not daddies," remembers Morgan. "Oh," says Jeff, "an' you can cook," as he turns back to the ironing board in spite of what Morgan has just told him. "No, no, mommies, daddies don't iron," says Morgan, walking over to the ironing board and holding the iron flat against the ironing board to prevent Jeff from ironing. "But," says Jeff, "when the mommies are gone, daddies iron?" asks Morgan. "Yeah," states Jeff. "Oh," says Morgan, releasing his hold on the iron and returning to the counter.

Still later

Morgan identifies himself as the daddy: "I'm the daddy; I'll work for a while, in my office." "And I'm the mommy, and I'll be in there (indicating the "office") and I'll help you, okay?" asks Jeff. "No," replies Morgan, explaining. "No, you're the mommy. You help David (the baby), okay?"

Thus we see the richness of the role-playing phenomenon and the variety of demands it places on the child. It requires that the children be at a cognitive and communicative level so that they can agree on a shared goal. They must agree on who will take what role and both must abide by that decision during play. The decision often requires one child to forfeit his own desires to start playing. Each must then act out a certain role that is appropriate in the context of their play. This means that the child needs some knowledge of the imputed values of that particular role. It requires each to concentrate on the other's behaviors and ideas to carry out an interchange successfully. Often the content of social partner's behavior or message is imaginary, which necessitates viewing certain events from the social partner's perspective. In attending to a certain partner's actions, the child is essentially focusing on transformations or events between his social partner and himself. This focusing on transformation aids him in decentering attention from himself, thus learning how his actions affect his partner and how his partner's actions affect him. He learns that certain acts are effective in certain situations, thereby attaining some crude notion of reciprocity. Also frequent discussions of the imputed values of the play role, aid the child in understanding the role relationship of its participants. In this way we see that the child's play with peers serves many varied functions in aiding him toward social competence.

SUMMARY

This chapter was based on the view that the process by which a child acquires interpersonal competence is no different from that of acquiring cognitive competence, although the conditions influencing the development of each competence are not the same. Thus, it was proposed that interpersonal competence be viewed in terms of the construction of social schemes much in the same way that cognitive schemes are constructed. Using this framework, social competence was defined as the attainment of a set of logically consistent structures and operations through which a person can view and act on the world. Because of the variableness of the features and reaction potentials of social objects, social schemes are assumed to be more difficult to construct. The interface of cognitive structures and interpersonal experiences was outlined to explain a child's development of interpersonal skills, and illustrative examples were presented to show the important role played by peers in aiding the child toward social competence.

CHAPTER 9

A Developmental Analysis of
Peer Interaction Among Toddlers[1]

EDWARD MUELLER
Boston University

THOMAS LUCAS
Clark University

Although the growth of peer interaction has received considerable attention in recent years, little is known about its structural development. This chapter represents a first attempt to plot major landmarks in the ontogeny of social interaction between 1-year-old children. The observations are primarily from longitudinal videotape records of contacts between a pair of firstborn boys. These boys and three others participated twice weekly in a play group, and parts of these sessions were also videotaped. The final source of observation was a set of fraternal triplets who were videotaped once each month.

The empirical literature on early peer contacts can be divided into two parts: (1) studies in which unacquainted children were placed together either a single time (Bühler, 1927; Maudry & Nekula, 1939) or many times across a year of growth (Bronson, 1972) to assess their "peer social skill"; (2) studies in which a group of children remained in contact for an extended period and were assessed either a single time (Bridges, 1933) or longitudinally (Vincze, 1971). Studies of the former type reported little achievement of peer interaction before the age of 2. Indeed, they found that the dominant activities among 1-year-olds were fighting or engaging in disputes over toys. By contrast, studies in which toddlers had extended contact reported large amounts of both affiliative and agonistic interactions (Bridges, 1933) or a large predominance of pleasurable interchanges (Vincze, 1971). Thus there is reason to expect that social progress can be made between children permitted long-term contact. There is also basis

[1] This work was supported by a grant from the National Institute of Mental Health. A film documenting the observations in this chapter, together with a summary of research in progress seeking to verify the work, was presented at the meetings of the American Psychological Association, New Orleans, August 1974. Charles DeStefano contributed to these ideas and Mark Bleier improved the clarity and consistency of an earlier draft. We extend thanks to Dr. and Mrs. John M. Kennedy who inspired our participation in the play group and participated in the research. Finally, we thank the toddlers' parents for permitting us to study a cooperative venture in early child care.

for predicting that children placed in group care settings where the caretakers are highly controlling or too many children are together, will merely take toys from one another and not interact.

None of the investigations cited attempts to abstract the general nature of contacts between very young children. Indeed, the theoretical literature on early social development was produced by thinkers who either did not watch young children systematically, or at all (Baldwin, 1906; Mead, 1934), or discounted the possibility of early peer interaction because of the child's egocentrism (Piaget, 1952a). Nevertheless the conceptualizations of these individuals, probably more than any others, still dominate beliefs about early peer interaction and social development in general (Kohlberg, 1969). A few words about the position of each theorist serves to put this chapter in context.

It is unfortunate that Piaget's *Language and Thought of the Child,* with its stress on "egocentrism," has had such a heavy impact on beliefs about early social development. There is another significant tradition in Piaget's work, concerning the emergence of cognitive structure in infancy but recognizing that the social environment has an important role in early development (Piaget, 1951, 1952b, 1954). As will become evident, these works of the early 1950s have had a profound influence on the conceptualization presented here. A theme of this chapter is that early interactions with peers are similar in structure to early interactions with things. However, it is also true that concepts such as "role reversal," which are not needed to describe interaction with things, become crucial in describing the increasingly differentiated structure of peer contacts in the second year of life.

Mead takes "language" as the starting point of social development. Language is defined broadly and includes gestures, such as shaking one's fist in anger rather than striking out directly at another person. Mead distinguishes between two types of gesture. The dog gestures anger yet, according to Mead, it is the merest expression of emotion, in the instinctual sense. By contrast, the man who shakes his fist in anger shares the meaning of his action with the person to whom he communicates. His gesture is a "significant symbol." One man takes the perspective of the other in the sense of attributing to the other the same meaning he himself attaches to the gesture:

"When, in any given social act or situation, one individual indicates by a gesture to another individual what this other individual is to do, the first individual is conscious of the meaning of his own gesture—or the meaning of his gesture appears in his own experience— insofar as he takes the attitude of the second individual toward that gesture, and tends to respond to it implicitly as the second individual responds to it explicitly" (Mead, 1934, p. 47).

Yet as Kohlberg (1969) argues, significant symbols cannot serve as the origin of social development because the toddler strives to imitate other persons before he is capable of the representational feats necessary for making use of significant symbols. Instead Kohlberg accepts Baldwin's (1904) thesis that imitation is the basis of all social knowledge and discourse. Yet Baldwin does not define imitation in the familiar sense, connoting a reproduction of the actions of one person by another person. He considers imitation to include the reproduction of one's own actions as well. In this sense there is little doubt that imitation is fundamental in infant development (Piaget, 1951). For clarity, however, it seems better to label the tendency to repeat one's own actions as "functional assimilation" (Piaget, 1952b) or simply "repetition." Imitation refers to interpersonal copying.

Our developmental approach uses imitation, representational skills, and role-taking concepts, yet accepts none as the unique basis of peer social development. To the contrary, skill with the social environment and skill with things are seen to emerge from the same bases. These have been most thoroughly articulated by Piaget (1952b); they include: (1) the infant's active exploration of novel aspects of the environment, and (2) his use of overt action as the means of understanding. The specific form of overt action is repetition. The child repeats his action to reinstate the interesting consequence in the world (secondary circular reaction). He understands the environment in the sense that he makes its behavior contingent on his own behavior, and vice versa. He comprehends his world in the sense that he can control it and make it predictable.

Mead and Baldwin, who held that the self is a social product, explained the existence of social systems from a base in the skills of individuals (e.g., imitation, role taking). Our study also makes central assumptions about the skills of infants and how very young children interact with their world. In addition, it is recognized that infants' physical and social environments are well structured (Gibson, 1950). Social interaction is explored here as the product of structured children in repeated contact with a structured environment that constrains the children's action and leads them down the path to "peer interaction." Peer interaction emerges because two children, each capable of secondary circular reactions, contact each other at a light switch whose physical structure itself constrains the type of contact that can occur between the children.

NOMENCLATURE

The term "social" is understood in so many ways that it is almost useless, and we avoid it here. However, it is possible to define behavior as "socially directed" by reference to a person's visual gaze (see Becker, 1974; Bronson, 1973). A socially directed behavior (SDB) is one accompanied by, or immediately preceded or followed by, looking at another child. If the children are close together, looking must be directed to the face or head area. If they are far apart, it is usually not possible to distinguish the part of the person looked at; thus any look in the direction of the other person is considered. Note that an SDB always coordinates two acts. One is the act of looking at another child and the other is the act of smiling, vocalizing, manipulating a toy, or performing some other gross motor pattern. This coordination, which is absent in the first contacts between peers, is seen as a necessary advance in the development of peer interaction. Vocalizing, smiling or crying, and simply looking at the peer, are not by themselves SDBs. At first infants watch, vocalize, and smile at anything that moves about or is otherwise interesting. Only later does the SDB increase in frequency as it becomes differentiated for use with persons (Mueller & Rich, in press).

A second major concept is interpersonal "contingency" of actions. The acts of two children are defined as *contingent* whenever the acts are contiguous in time and space. The children must be physically close enough to allow their behaviors to exert mutual influence. Their actions must occur within a few seconds of each other. One may object that children's contingent actions may occur across a much longer time span, thus being missed by observers with an adult orientation to interpersonal response times. However Watson (1967) found that if a response is to act as a reinforcer during the infancy period, immediacy is especially important. Also, although some long-delayed imitative responses between children were observed in a play group, the child who was belatedly imitated had long since moved to other activities. Thus delayed imitation does not appear to play a direct role in establishing peer interaction.

We use several terms to describe encounters between children. The term "*contact*" has reference to shared direction of visual gaze. Periods of contact are times during which two children look at the same toy or play material and/or directly at each other. Contacts of three or more children are called "*clusters*" (Mueller & Rich, in press). In research based on continuous video records of a play group, contacts provide a manageable subsample of tape during which social interaction is at least possible, regardless of whether it actually occurs.

Two terms describe social interaction. An *interact* is a contingency between the mutually directed SDBs of two (or more) children. For example, child A looks at B and holds out a block (SDB 1). Observing this, child B picks up another block, looks at A, and holds out his block also (SDB 2). A opens the interact and B closes it. Since interacts involve sequential or simultaneous looking at peer, all interacts occur during times of contact. An *interchange* is a contingency between two (or more) interacts. Child A says "hi" again to B (interact 2). Interchanges involve more than the chain of interacts. It follows from their definition that they represent a higher order contingency, a contingency between interacts that are themselves contingencies between behaviors. Also, during interchanges, internal SDBs take on a dual directionality. They both close one interact and open the next one. Finally, interchanges are cyclic or iterative. They follow a back-and-forth, ping-pong ball model of interaction. They have the same form as adult conversations.

Except in stage I, where interchanges are absent, all the protocol examples in this chapter are interchanges. Indeed, one of the functions of this chapter is to demonstrate the existence of interchanges in the contacts of toddlers.

USE OF THE STAGE CONCEPT

The term "stage" as used here derives from Werner's (1948) principle of orthogenesis and from Piaget's (1952b) stages of infant sensory-motor intelligence. Both these theorists were influenced by biological usage, where stage change usually involved differentiation and structural reorganization of what had come earlier. "Stage change" means the reorganization of a system of relationships between elements.

Cognitive theorists have discussed the role of the stage concept in relation to the pervasive problems of decalage or asynchrony. Flavell (1972) shifts his attention away from stages, focusing instead on the vertical or sequential organization of elements. Wohlwill (1973) retains the stage concept for describing interrelationships "among two or more qualitatively defined variables developing apace . . ." (p. 192). In other words, stages define the relations between different yet related invariant sequences. Given the prevalence of decalages, neither theorist retains the use of stages as well-structured systems, capable of undergoing differentiation. In the light of such problems and methodological conclusions, why have we chosen to remain faithful to the classic view of stages?

The basis of our approach is in not defining the individual child as the primary structured system. As long as the structure of interacting systems is seen to reside in the child, decalage may remain the dominant result. The solution is to recognize stage-defining structures as residing in the interface between the child and his environment. To understand peer interaction, it has proved necessary to understand the skills of two children at once, as well as the structure of the physical milieu in which they meet. Then the stage of interaction is a consequent structure, a product constrained by inputs from both children and their physical environment.

At present, data are being gathered from a new play group to test the ordinality of the proposed stages. For each of the 15 dyads under study, it is hypothesized that (1) no stages are omitted and (2) contact types appear in the order predicted, although contacts of lower stage type are not expected to drop out when those of a higher stage type appear.

Subjects and Procedures

Larry and Bernie, the primary subjects of observation, were the firstborn boys. They started playing together at home two days per week when 12 and 10 months old, respectively. The first videotape was made at ages 15 and 13 months. One month later, Larry and Bernie joined three other similarly aged firstborn boys in forming a play group, which met for 2½ hours two mornings per week for three months. With one exception, the children were from academic families. The parents rotated the task of supervising the play group. The room was 20 × 35 feet, and it contained a variety of toys and play equipment. Often the parent-in-charge would bring materials for special activities such as finger paints or dress-up clothes. Even during these special activities, however, there was little effort to guide the children's play.

The play group was videotaped for one hour each week. It was important to tape early in the morning, before the children became tired and were given their snack, a very adult-oriented situation. The camera was in the room behind a cabinet. After discovering that they could not gain access, the children generally ignored it. The ideas developed in this chapter and all the specific protocols reported are based on repeated viewings of the videotapes. Slow-motion playback was frequently helpful in discerning direction of visual gaze and sequence of motor patterns.

Once each month the free play of a set of fraternal boy triplets was videotaped. The sessions were recorded in the children's home playroom. Since the boys were 1½ months premature, their ages as reported here are adjusted to "gestational" age. The tapes studied showed the progression in their contacts from 5½ to 12 months.

STAGES OF PEER SOCIAL CONTACTS

Three stages were recognized in the ontogeny of peer interaction. These stages may best be viewed as ideal prototypes in the development of peer interactions rather than as pigeonholes into which the behavior of a social unit may always be classified at any point in its development. One finding applies equally well to all the stages: the social interaction observed in these 1-year-olds was *dyadic*. The first three-person interaction we were able to record occurred when the play group reconvened after the children had passed their second birthday. In the following sections we outline the type of evolution that permitted some dyads, but not others, to progress from very simple object-centered contacts to relatively peer-oriented and complex-sustained interchanges.

Stage I: Object-Centered Contacts

One-year-olds have at their disposal a wide variety of schemes of action on objects, affording them a suitable mechanism for the systematic exploration of their inanimate environment (Piaget, 1952b). They are also versed in the rules that obtain in the interactive system between mother and infant (Lewis & Goldberg, 1969; Watson, 1972). However, the strategies derived from these two domains are not readily applicable to interaction with their peers. Despite their expertise in both the exploration of objects and the regulation of adult behavior, toddlers are at a loss when confronted with potential playmates their own age. They are unfamiliar with the properties that define their peers and with the ground rules that regulate successful interaction with other children.

The prevalence of object-centered contacts during the initial meetings of a play group of 1-year-olds may be explained by this relative deficiency in peer-appropriate strategies. Having had experience with objects, 1-year-olds with no peer experience are far better prepared to act effectively on objects than on their age mates. Whereas object-centered contacts reflect the toddler's lack of peer-appropriate strategies, the simultaneous exploration of common objects by two or more children provides opportunities to gain more understanding of their peers.

As indicated, the formation of object-centered contacts is attributed more to the interest each child has invested in some activity with an object than to his curiosity concerning the behavior of his age mates. For example, the engagement of child A with an object creates an interesting display that attracts the attention of another child and prompts his approach. Both children focus their attention on the same object and both act on it in nearly identical fashion. Yet because each one's interest is invested in the object itself, neither child recognizes the effects of his own actions on the behavior of the other child.

A cluster at the play group's toy train engine exemplifies an object-centered contact. The actions of each child are presented in detail in Figure 1. Basically one child discovers the engine, squats down, and makes the engine's whistle sound repeatedly. All other children in the room immediately toddle over to the engine and either sound the whistle or manipulate the steering handle, an action introduced by a second child. During the 68 seconds that several children are at the train, three children never look at their peers' faces and the other two children look only once or twice, and get no responses to their looks.

Contacts like this one do not include interacts. The children act unilaterally on a common object. Each child is more concerned with his own effectiveness in re-creating the interesting display of tooting the horn and turning the steering wheel than with the possible contingencies that may exist between his own efforts and those of his peers. Visual attention is focused mainly on the train, and the few glances directed toward other children go unheeded. Once the contact has been established, the power of attraction exerted by the object is clearly responsible for its maintenance. The behavior of those already engaged with the toy is unaffected by the arrival or departure of the others. It would be a mistake, however, to say that nothing interpersonal was taking place despite the apparent absence of interest in social contingencies.

A toy train may be manipulated in numerous ways: it may be pushed, pulled, or sat on; it may be banged to produce an interesting noise; its wheels

Time (seconds)	Noah (14½ months)	Larry (16 months)	Jacob (14½ months)	Bernie (14½ months)	Don (14 months)
0	At engine alone, toots horn once				Approaches
		Approaches Hits engine with toy	Approaches	Approaches	
	Toots horn once				
		Grasps steering handle Looks at Jacob's face	Toots horn, 3 times	Grasps steering handle Vocalizes at engine	
		Steps backward	Departs		
17	Toots horn, 4 times	Grasps steering handle Steps back again		Places second hand on handle Looks at Larry's face	Toots horn once
	Grasps steering handle	Grasps steering handle		Looks at Larry's face	Toots horn, 3 times loud

34   Reaches for horn, withdraws at Bernie's hand   Holds plunger 5 seconds, then toots horn once   Toots horn, 2 times and departs

66   Looks at Bernie's face   VOCALIZES AT NOAH'S FACE / Departs   Manipulates horn plunger, turns to different toy

84   Toots horn, 12 times, then departs

FIGURE 1. Illustration of a stage I object-centered contact: simultaneous events appear on the same line; socially directed behaviors are in capital letters.

may be rotated by hand. In short, the toy lends itself to many fruitful explorations. It is significant, therefore, that the participants in the contact just described are primarily concerned with re-creating approximately the same displays originally produced by the first and second children acting on the train. Of the twenty actions produced on the train during the course of the contact, twelve were replications of Noah's tooting the horn, and another six were reproductions of Larry's grasping the steering wheel. As 1-year-olds seek to reproduce an interesting environmental display, the initial action (or actions) on the object acts as a behavioral constraint on the subsequent actions of the other children in the object-centered contact. The term "constraint," rather than "imitation," is used because in these early contacts it remains unclear whether the original actions serve merely to set in motion an already acquired scheme or whether the reproduction represents a deliberate accommodation to the specific actions of the model. In either case, the resulting similarity between the participants' responses indicates that, at least initially, their curiosity was aroused not by the object alone but by the *action on the object* performed by the initiating children.

Such behaviorally constrained contacts stand in marked contrast to the object-centered contacts of *younger* boys. Consider a contact at a rattle observed in the play of two of the triplets at age 7 months:

Sandy lies supine on his playroom floor. He watches a rattle, alternately shaken and mouthed by his brother Rip. Rip is seated in an infant seat but faces at right angles to Sandy. He could have seen Sandy by turning his neck to his right but never does so during his 4½ minutes of rattle shaking. Neither does he pay much attention to the rattle, focusing instead to his left or directly forward at the camera. Sandy, on the other hand, is intent on the rattle, looking away from it only once late in the period. His gaze follows the rattle both during shaking and when the object is brought up to Rip's mouth. At one point Rip lowers the rattle to his knee. While holding the toy in its new position, Rip looks at it for the first and only time. Sandy has followed the trajectory of the rattle downward and watches it held motionless in its new position. When Rip lifts the rattle again and resumes shaking it, Sandy laughs aloud. This is the fourth time Sandy has laughed at the behavior of the rattle, and the second time the laughing has been contingent on the resumption of shaking.

As is most clearly shown at the point when both boys watch the rattle at Rip's knee, this is an object-centered contact in its purest form. Neither child displays any understanding of the other's presence or activity. Sandy laughs at the rattle, not at his brother. Rip never responds to Sandy's laughter or movements. In marked contrast to the early contacts of the 1-year-olds, there is a complete absence of behavioral similarity in the children's actions. Sandy may believe that he controls the rattle by waving his hands and by laughing. Efficacy

(Piaget, 1954) dominates his action, and laughing has not yet become specialized as a social gesture, recognized as ineffective in controlling the behavior of rattles.

Thus behavioral or "imitative" constraint is one major step toward peer interaction in the play group boys. A second major advance comes from the nonsimultaneous performance of actions by participants in an object-centered contact. Although the actions of the children in a stage I contact may be unilateral, they are seldom simultaneous, especially if the contact revolves around a single object to which all the children demand access. For example, Figure 1 reveals that the actions performed on the train are, for the most part, nonsimultaneous. Even though the children repeatedly produce two different acts on different parts of the train (i.e., tooting the horn and grasping the wheel), the timing of these acts overlaps only twice during the entire contact. No child is continuously active in his manipulation of the toy. The actions of each are bounded by brief periods of inactivity and are performed repeatedly. However, the sequencing of actions in this contact does not follow an alternating or A–B–A–B pattern. Some children toot the horn or grasp the steering wheel several times in succession before relinquishing their hold on the toy, and it is not at all clear that they do so with the intent of yielding access to another child. This may be the case, but the sequencing of actions resulting from the discontinuity in the child's manipulation of objects figures centrally in further peer-social development.

Two vectors can be identified, one organismic and one environmental, which in conjunction may generate alternating or A–B–A–B sequencing. On the organismic side, the circular reactions described by Piaget (1952b) are clearly marked by an act/watch rhythm of interaction with objects. The same rhythm seems to be even more central to the infant's successful regulation of his interaction with adults (Watson, 1972). In both these systems of interaction the infant is seldom continuously active in his exploration. Instead his actions are punctuated by pauses during which he appears to process the feedback deriving from the actions. This act/watch rhythm, when performed concurrently by more than one child around an object of common interest, is one factor that may contribute to sequencing. Of course the act/watch rhythm cannot be identified as a property of the organism in any exclusive way. We chose to place it toward the organismic end of an organism-environment continuum because however it emerged, it has become a regulatory pattern that the infant imposes on his interaction with various aspects of his environment.

The other vector whose point of origin we have localized in the environment is the demand characteristic (Koffka, 1935) of the object on which the contact centers. In Figure 1, for example, the train horn (more than the steering wheel) does not permit simultaneous manipulation by more than one child. Limited access to the horn demands that only one child act on it at a time, if he is to be

Time (seconds)	Bernie (13 months)		Larry (15 months)
0	Pushes light switch		Looks at Bernie
	Looks at Larry	(MUTUAL EYE CONTACT)	
			Pushes light switch
	Pushes light switch		Pushes light switch
	Pushes light switch		
	Pushes light switch		Pushes light switch
			STEPS BACK FROM LIGHT SWITCH WHILE LOOKING AT BERNIE
19	Pushes light switch		
	Pushes light switch		VOCALIZES WHILE LOOKING AT BERNIE

Pushes light switch

VOCALIZES WHILE LOOKING
AT BERNIE
Pushes light switch
STEPS BACK FROM LIGHT
SWITCH WHILE LOOKING
AT BERNIE

Pushes light switch

Pushes light switch

34   Looks at Larry   (MUTUAL   VOCALIZES WHILE LOOKING
EYE   AT BERNIE
CONTACT)

Pushes light switch

57   Pushes light switch,
then turns and leaves

63   Turns to adult, pushes light
switch while looking at Bernie,
then leaves

FIGURE 2.   Illustration of a stage I–II transitional contact with A–B–A–B structure (events designated as in Figure 1).

235

successful in his manipulation. Note that Noah is forced to withdraw his hand when, reaching for the horn, he discovers that Bernie already has possession of it. The importance of contacts centered around objects affording limited access should not be underestimated (Mueller & DeStefano, in press). It may be that their contribution to the production of social accommodation greatly exceeds their relative frequency of occurrence.

The joint product of these vectors is object-centered contacts in which the participants seem to be "taking turns." But the alternating structure is the fortuitous result of environmental constraints imposed by limited access to toys. The existence of such contacts shows that children need not invent turn-taking or even learn it from their parents. It is available to be extracted from certain of their early object-centered peer contacts.

Figure 2 provides an example of an object-centered contact with alternating structure. Briefly, the contact consists of alternating pushing of a household two-button light switch by Bernie and Larry. The children press the switch a total of fifteen times, and thirteen of these presses are in a perfect alternating sequence. Larry always removed his hand before Bernie pressed, but twice Larry did not wait for Bernie to remove his hand.

This contact was not entirely object-centered, since both Larry and Bernie are socially directed on occasion. The mutual eye contact at the start of the sequence is similar to that often seen at the start of adult exchanges (Argyle, 1969). However, none of the SDBs accompany either child's manipulation of the light switch and, save Larry's second gesture allowing Bernie access, none has any observable effect on the behavior of the other child. For these reasons the contact does not meet the criteria established for stage II interchanges. Aside from the problem of social directedness, the contact is a good example of the joint workings of several forces operative in the achievement of alternating structure in stage I. The imitative constraint is evidenced in each child's concern with re-creating the same action. The environmental demand is in the construction of the light switch. In pushing the switch, each child effectively excludes the other from gaining access. The result is a sequencing of actions that unlike the contact around the toy train follows an alternating pattern for much of the contact.

In summary, we have identified three features of object-centered contacts which facilitate the transition to stage II peer-social interaction: (1) the behavioral or imitative constraint produced by the tendency of 1-year-olds to reproduce an interesting action, (2) the discontinuous act/watch pattern that children employ in the exploration of their environment, and (3) the "limited access" afforded by certain objects. The element still lacking is an orientation toward influencing the behavior of peers themselves, an interest in re-creating interpersonal contingency—for example, in causing another child to repeat his action on an object rather than merely reproducing that action oneself. Interchanges are possible only when interpersonal contingencies are actively sought.

Before closing this discussion of object-centered contacts, it should be noted that stage I contacts are not a transitory phenomenon in the development of peer interaction. That is, later developing modes of interaction do not cause object-centered contacts to disappear. Novel objects retain their effectiveness as powerful elicitors of the toddler's curiosity and determinants of his behavior. Any contact may become object-centered when interest in social contingencies is subordinated to the interest invested in the object itself.

Stage II: Simple and Complex Contingency Interchanges

In stage I children were effective in interacting with things but not peers. Sometimes, however, they inadvertently controlled their peers' behaviors, as in the example of Figure 2. By contrast, in stage II they actively seek and receive "contingencies" from one another. Formerly they hit a mobile repeatedly in a secondary circular reaction (Piaget, 1952b). Now they vocalize repeatedly if the peer regularly responds. Both types of contact are circular. When the mobile stops moving, it "controls" the child's behavior, stimulating him to hit it again. The child who laughs is equally effective in controlling the initiator's behavior. He produces a repetition of the vocalization by laughing. In the child-child circular reaction, each participant adjusts the timing of his own acts to those of his partner. In this sense one could modify Piaget's terminology and call such contacts "intercoordinated secondary circular reactions." This is a rather cumbersome term, however, and "simple interchanges" was chosen instead.

Several important properties of object-centered contacts were described as emerging in stage I: the sequencing of actions on a limited-access object and the behavioral or imitative constraint on the actions of the participants. The contribution to the formation of a peer interaction system made by stage I contacts is that they combine both these features in a single contact between two children. Under these circumstances interpersonal contingencies between the actions of the children are particularly apparent. As these contingencies become increasingly apparent to the children themselves, both may seek the social consequences of their actions, thereby transforming the contact to a stage II interchange.

However, the role of imitation in producing stage II is different from its role during stage II. Behavioral imitation appears to be catalytic in leading to stage II, but imitation is not a necessary structural component of stage II interchanges. Imitation is a content rather than structural concept. Although most stage II interchanges are imitative in content, the structural relationship between SDBs is simply one of contingency. When one child bangs a stick on a table and looks at his peer, no constraint is placed on the peer's contingent behavior. He may also bang with a stick, or he may laugh or vocalize. A further constraining of the relation between the children's activities is the defining property of stage III.

There is no reason to suppose that both children in a given contact will si-

Time (seconds)	Don (14 months)	Noah (15 months)
0	Lies supine, attends to toy telephone in hands	Squats down beside Don; looks at phone
7	LOOKS AT NOAH AND OFFERS PHONE BASE, 1st time, AND LOOKS AT NOAH	Grasps base of phone, looking only at it
	Does not release base and withdraws it from Noah	Looks at phone
16	OFFERS BASE, 2nd time, AND LOOKS AT NOAH	Grasps base, looking only at it
	Releases base but hand travels back along cord and holds receiver	Sits down from squat and manipulates base, looking only at it
	Using cord, pulls base from Noah's hands.	Watches phone in Don's hands, not his face

32	Manipulates phone, then OFFERS BASE, 3rd time, AND LOOKS AT NOAH.	
		Touches base, looking only at it
	Withdraws base from Noah and manipulates it.	
		Looks only at base, then briefly Don's face
42	OFFERS BASE, 4th time, AND LOOKS AT NOAH.	
		Looks at base, just managing to touch it
	Withdraws base from Noah and manipulates it.	
		Looks at base only, then looks at Don's face again very briefly as Don begins fifth offer
50	OFFERS BASE, 5th time, AND LOOKS AT NOAH	
		Grasps top of base, looking only at it
	WITHDRAWS BASE WHILE STILL LOOKING AT NOAH.	
		Adjusts seating posture, rubs ear, and pulls at jumpsuit under Don

FIGURE 3. Illustration of stage I–II transitional contact with "puppetlike" control (events designated as in Figure 1).

Time (seconds)	Don (14 months)	Noah (15 months)
66	OFFERS BASE, 6th time, LOOKING AT NOAH'S HAND	Reaches, looking only at phone base
	WITHDRAWS BASE, LOOKING AT NOAH	Looks at Don's head, approaches and touches Don's hair
83	Don turns away from Noah and stands up	Continues watching Don's head; both toddle away.

FIGURE 3. (Continued)

multaneously see the potential for producing interpersonal contingencies. In reality, puppetlike sequences are observed in which one child's behavior is peer-directed and the other child's behavior is object-centered. Such contacts can be classified as intermediate between stages I and II. The form of such a contact is represented in Figure 3, and its content may be summarized here:

Don, on the floor having his diapers changed, notes Noah beside him. Noah has squatted down and is focused entirely on the toy telephone that Don holds in his hands. Don proceeds to offer the phone five times in succession to Noah. Each time Noah reaches out, but looks only at the phone. Four of the five times, Don pulls the phone back, and Noah still focuses only on the toy. The other times, Noah does take the phone base and begins to play with it. However, Don, still holding the receiver, pulls in the base by the cord connecting the two. Noah does not understand why the toy pops out of his hands!

There is no doubt that such contacts provide one child the means for the effective regulation of another child's behavior. Don is in clear control of Noah's responses in this example. Because Noah is interested only in the toy that Don holds, Don is restricted to repeated offerings and withdrawals of the desired object to regulate Noah's actions. If Noah, too, were seeking the social consequences of his actions, the range of options open to the pair would greatly increase. For example, Noah might imitate Don's offer of the toy with an offering of his own, or he might greet each of Don's offers with a laugh or an excited vocalization. In either case the sequence would be transformed into a simple interchange.

The dynamics but not the form of this contact contrasts with one evidencing mutuality of social attention or orientation. Here is an example of a simple interchange (Figure 4):

Larry sits on the floor and Bernie turns and looks toward him. Bernie waves his hand and says "da," still looking at Larry. He repeats the vocalization three more times before Larry laughs. Bernie vocalizes again and Larry laughs again. Then the same sequence of one child saying "da" and the other laughing is repeated twelve more times before Bernie turns away from Larry and walks off. Bernie and Larry become distracted at times during the interchange. Yet when this happens the partner reattracts attention either by repeating his socially directed action or by modifying it, as when Bernie both waves and says "da," reengaging Larry.

Simple interchanges afford each member of the dyad the opportunity to regulate the other's behavior. Responsibility for the maintenance of an interchange as well as its form is shared jointly by both children, and once an interchange has begun, no single controlling agent can be identified. Each action embedded in an interchange occupies a key pivot position in that it is both a response to

Time (seconds)	Bernie (13 months)	Larry (15 months)
	Stands about 6 feet from Larry; looks at ceiling light	Sits on floor, mouthing toy and watching Bernie
0	TURNS HEAD TO LOOK AT LARRY AND VOCALIZES "DA"	
2½	VOCALIZES "DA," LOOKING AT LARRY	
		LAUGHS (VERY SLIGHTLY), LOOKING AT BERNIE
6	VOCALIZES "DA," LOOKING AT LARRY	
		LAUGHS, LOOKING AT BERNIE
12	VOCALIZES "DA," LOOKING AT LARRY	
		LAUGHS, LOOKING AT BERNIE
14	VOCALIZES "DA," LOOKING AT LARRY	
		LAUGHS, LOOKING AT BERNIE
17	VOCALIZES "DA," LOOKING AT LARRY	
		LAUGHS, LOOKING AT BERNIE
	Looks away at something off camera	
		LAUGHS, LOOKING AT BERNIE
23	VOCALIZES "DA" AND LOOKS AT LARRY	
		LAUGHS, LOOKING AT BERNIE
28	VOCALIZES "DA," LOOKING AT LARRY	LAUGHS, LOOKING AT BERNIE
32½	VOCALIZES "DA," LOOKING AT LARRY WAVES, LOOKING AT LARRY	Looks at adult and offers object to adult
		LAUGHS AND LOOKS BACK AT BERNIE

FIGURE 4. Illustration of a stage II simple interchange (events designated as in Figure 1).

Time (seconds)	Bernie (13 months)	Larry (15 months)
34	VOCALIZES "DA," LOOKING AT LARRY	
		LAUGHS, LOOKING AT BERNIE
40	VOCALIZES "DA," LOOKING AT LARRY	
		LAUGHS, LOOKING AT BERNIE
43	VOCALIZES "DA," LOOKING AT LARRY	
		LAUGHS, LOOKING AT BERNIE
47½	VOCALIZES "DA," LOOKING AT LARRY	
		LAUGHS, LOOKING AT BERNIE
50	VOCALIZES "DA," LOOKING AT LARRY	
		LAUGHS, LOOKING AT BERNIE LAUGHS (IN FORCED WAY) 3 MORE TIMES, LOOKING AT BERNIE
54	VOCALIZES "DA," LOOKING AT LARRY	LAUGHS, LOOKING AT BERNIE
59	VOCALIZES "DA," LOOKING AT LARRY	LAUGHS, LOOKING AT BERNIE
62½	VOCALIZES "DA," LOOKING AT LARRY	
		LAUGHS, LOOKING AT BERNIE
66	VOCALIZES "DA," LOOKING AT LARRY	
		LAUGHS, LOOKING AT BERNIE
69	Turns and walks away	LAUGHS (IN FORCED WAY), LOOKING AT BERNIE, AND WATCHES HIM LEAVE ROOM

FIGURE 4. (Continued)

the previous action of the other child and a stimulus for the other to perform the act again. That is, every action produced by one child in an interchange brings to closure the interpersonal contingency begun by the preceding action of his partner. At the same time, the same act opens another interpersonal contingency, which, in turn, brings yet another contingent response from the other child. Interchanges cycle in this manner until either child tires or is distracted.

To summarize, stage II ushers in contacts that come close to most observers' conception of sustained social interaction. The remarkable observation is that children attain the turn-taking form of interaction, and even the behavioral imitation so common in interchanges, *before* they begin directing behavior to their peers. Toys pull them together, and imitation affords an unwitting control over each partner's behavior. But seeking and obtaining contingencies from one's peers is the advance in stage II. Furthermore, it is not sufficient for only one child to be socially directed. Simple interchanges await mutual social interest. Thus they require more than the presence of socially directed behavior: there must be links or contingencies between the socially directed actions of two children in contact with each other.

What do early stage II interchanges lack? They are limited to simple actions such as saying "da," laughing, or performing imitatively and with social orientation an act such as sticking one's head in a basket. The children do not yet know how to form a whole series of socially directed behaviors in which some serve the function of attaining the other child's attention and others define the interchange.

Complex Contingency Interchanges ● The vast majority of interchanges observed among the toddlers were of the stage II variety. Yet there were clear differences within interchanges characteristic of this stage. It was difficult to decide whether certain of the more complex interchanges merited recognition as a unique stage. However, it was felt that all the interchanges to be discussed here still retain the fundamental stage II property of unrestricted content. The action of one child does not constrain the contingent act of his partner.

Two kinds of change were observed. In the first type the number of SDBs used by both participants in an interchange increased. In the second type interchanges themselves were combined, either sequentially in time or simultaneously, by becoming nested.

As the children became accustomed to directing behavior to their peers, they were no longer limited to simple SDBs. Instead they combined several different actions with looking at a peer, thus forming a "complex" SDB. When Bernie waved at Larry as he vocalized "da," he produced a complex SDB. Mueller and Rich (in press) found that the proportion of complex SDBs in play group clusters increased from 7% in month one to 22% in month three.

In Larry-Bernie interaction, running-following interchanges were characterized by complex SDBs. The core of the interchange involved one child running and looking over his shoulder and the other child following him. The path the children described depended on which objects were used. In running-following at the box tunnel, the pair followed a circular path, entering the tunnel from the same end on each "round." Running between a curtain and a table followed a back-and-forth trajectory. At times a participant would appear confused, running to the table in the middle of box-tunnel running. This effectively aborted the interchange. There are several examples of these interchanges on the videotape as the behaviors were repeated day after day.

Here the crucial point is that the children did not simply run and look at each other. As they ran and looked, they also vocalized and laughed to each other over and over. In the middle of one such interchange the following interaction occurred: Larry, starting at the table, approached Bernie, who was standing at the curtain. Larry laughed as he approached. Contingently on the arrival, Bernie smiled at Larry and at the same time ran toward the table.

Just what function does this laughing serve? Is it simply responsive, that is, an "involuntary" explosion of pleasure at the continuing contingent interchange? Indeed, many times laughter in the play group had just this quality. But even in such cases laughter and vocalization seem to be preadapted, serving as a kind of social glue, keeping the children's attention together even in the distraction-filled play group milieu.

One other modification of SDBs merits notice even though it was observed in only one dyad and was limited to a single SDB. Larry and Bernie developed the ability to use the vocalization "da?" as a specialized communication routine, signifying desire to initiate an interchange. After the peer's attention was secured, the initiating child showed which particular "game" he wished to play by performing the appropriate action. Lucas and Mueller (1973) contend that the "da?" game delimiter is a precursor to the summons-answer routine and the rhetorical gambit of adult and child verbal communication (Garvey & Hogan, 1973). For Loren and Robert, the phrase "da?" served to open a sensory-motor interchange, just as the phrase "You know what?" serves to open an adult verbal-symbolic interchange.

There are two ways of handling the advent of a specialized summons: (1) It can be treated as a "marker," a device that reflects two individual children's awareness of underlying structure. Structurally, the interchange introduced by "da" is no different from one without it. (2) Alternately, the interchange can be seen as having undergone further differentiation into functionally separate "initiation" and "alternation" or "turn-sharing" component interchanges. This is analogous to the coordination of means and ends schemes in Piaget's "coordination of secondary circular reactions" (1952b) and would merit recognition as a unique stage. However, the data available are insufficient to support recognition of a separate stage.

Combinations of interchanges, the second modification of the basic stage II pattern, were rare and appeared late in the play group. It will be recalled that contacts were times of continuously shared or even reciprocal direction of visual gaze. Early contacts were limited to single toys—for example, the chalkboard, a truck, or the box tunnel. But later the dyad was able to remain in contact while moving smoothly from an interchange at the chalkboard to a second interchange at the rocking boat. Contact did not have to be reestablished at the new object because it was not lost during the transition. The children visually checked each other as they switched from one object to another. At this point social interaction has attained new flexibility; its continued existence is no longer tied to a specific set of actions on specific toys.

Nested interchanges were not observed in play group; as Larry and Bernie continued to play with each other after play group ended, however, a few additional videotapes were recorded. At 18 months Bernie was observed to imitate 20-month-old Larry's actions on a push toy. In fact, Larry had recently given the toy to Bernie when Bernie showed an interest in Larry's activity with it. Both children were aware of who possessed the toy and how each was manipulating it. Each looked alternately at the toy and at the other child. But at this point, while Bernie played with the push toy, he also engaged Larry in an imitative verbal interchange. First the children imitated a sound made by moving their tongues. This cycled back and forth five times. Then the vocalization changed to the old familiar "da," and this was imitated and repeated twice. Yet all this time interest in the imitative actions on the push toy was retained. The children were engaged with each other in two interchanges at once. The verbal interchange was nested inside the interchange involving the push toy.

Limitations of Stage II Interchanges • Stage II interchanges are either role diffuse or role rigid, and to speak of roles is somewhat misleading, since most stage II interchanges are simply imitative, not role complementary. The interchange of Figure 4 was role diffuse. When Bernie said "da," Larry was at liberty to respond in any way he chose. Instead of laughing he could have replied imitatively, or he could have appeared from behind a piece of furniture. Any contingent action would have been as appropriate as any other in maintaining the interchange. By contrast, the running-following interchange was role rigid. The child who started as the "follower" remained in that role for the duration of the interchange, even when the "leader" reversed the direction of the chase. In short, during stage II the children can exchange turns, but they cannot exchange roles.

In stage III these limitations are overcome. The child no longer simply seeks contingencies from his peer. He tries to elicit a response that is both complementary to and different from his own action. He focuses on an act and its complement simultaneously.

Stage III: Complementary Interchanges

The defining characteristic of stage III interchanges is role complementarity: the participants in a complementary interchange do different but intercoordinated or reciprocal things. Some examples include offering and receiving a toy, throwing and receiving a ball, playing the roles of "chaser" and "the one being chased." In each example there are two different actions, and each action derives its meaning from the reciprocal act. The child offers because he wants to have an object received. The child chases because he understands the idea of "being chased." Yet at first it is most difficult to be sure that each child understands and tries to elicit the complementary role. Perhaps he is not offering at all but merely holding the object toward the other child. Perhaps he is not chasing at all but merely imitating the running action of the other child. The only method for ascertaining complementarity is role reversal. For example, if the child who receives immediately offers back, and the child who previously offered now receives, it is possible to infer that each child comprehends both roles and that the children seek to elicit the complementary role when they act. Role reversal serves to measure complementarity. However, the measure should not be equated with complementarity itself. Reversal is a sufficient condition to establish complementarity only when the necessary condition of reciprocally dependent actions is present. Thus even if the interchange shown in Figure 4 were role reversed, with Larry saying "da" and Bernie laughing, it would not qualify as stage III. "Da" and laughing are not reciprocally connected. At any point either child could substitute a different action and the interchange could continue. But when a child offers or chases, he attempts to place narrow constraints on the social responses of the other child.

It should be noted that these constraints go beyond what the other child can do and include when he can do it. The child who offers does not hold his arm out endlessly waiting for the other child to receive. The actions of grasping and releasing must be exactly intercoordinated or the object will fall. The child who throws a ball to another child does not have unlimited patience, waiting motionless for the other child to retrieve and throw back. As these examples show, stage III interchanges require replacing the act/watch rhythm of earlier stages. In its place comes simultaneous and synchronous activity.

The constraints of reciprocity and timing must be mastered before stage III interchanges appear. Other problems also face children seeking to engage in complementary interchanges. The difficulties arise both from the interest in the object of stage I and the interest in the child of stage II. To exchange an object, a child must yield an object he possesses. At first his chance of getting the object back through role reversal is very small. Figure 3 illustrated one such encounter between an object-directed child and a socially directed child. Even when both children are socially directed, an offer is as likely to result in a tug-of-war as in an exchange.

Another difficulty arises directly from the interest in the peer developed in stage II, when the way to sustain a contact with another child was to keep in close physical proximity to him, often imitating his actions, and acknowledging the pleasure of the joint activity. Yet stage III interchanges require that the children not imitate, and sometimes remain at a distance from each other, as in the game of "catch" or "run in opposite directions."

Running in opposite directions is of particular interest, since its emergence from a stage II interchange is relatively clear. Larry and Bernie frequently chased back and forth between a curtain and table at the respective corners of one end of the playroom. The contact was classified as a complex contingency interchange, incorporating as it did both running-following and hiding-appearing interacts. At times, however, the children would get out of phase, one waiting too long at the curtain or table. Then they would find themselves not chasing each other but approaching and starting to pass each other. In month one of the play group, the passing was not completed. One or sometimes both children would wheel around, presumably to maintain the visual contact necessary to the interchange. But in month two we observed Larry and Bernie pass each other, hesitate but continue on to the opposite walls, only there to turn around and acknowledge the continuing contact with each other. In so doing, they appear to show the first halting recognition that the running interchange can be sustained when the partners physically separate from each other. Presumably this recognition has its origin in the children's own performance of the complementary action in previous rounds or in previous performances of two-point chasing contacts.

The temporal constraint, the nonimitative requirement, the necessity for action at a distance, the complete subordination of interest in the object, and the narrow limitation on possible complementary actions—all these problems stabilize contacts at stage II and delay the emergence of stage III.

Despite the factors making for delay, the foundations of stage III are present in stage II and even in stage I. Just as the imitation of stage II emerges from the psychic or self-imitation of stage I, role complementarity emerges from the act/watch pattern of stages I and II. The infant coordinates periods of motor activity on his environment with periods of perceptual processing. The toddler coordinates these two activities into one—producing an action and simultaneously processing its complement from another child. Stage II interchanges may foster stage III in another way. They provide experience with the component parts of complementary patterns. At one time a child repeatedly offers objects to his peer. At a second time he repeatedly receives them. One day a child may be the follower and on another day he may be the one followed. During such occasions he practices one side of a differentiated contact and gains practice at comprehending the other side, as it is performed by his peer.

The best example of a stage III interchange occurred one morning after adults had been putting up posters on the playroom walls. Because it contains aspects of each previous stage, as well as including a new gestural development, the interchange is detailed in Figure 5. It can serve as a review of earlier progress, as well as illustrating a complementary interchange with a piece of paper.

The sequence began when Bernie took a piece of paper from a toy box and placed it on a wall himself, seemingly unaware of the role of adhesive tape. Larry watched him perform this novel sequence and joined Bernie at the wall. Of course the paper fell when Bernie released it. After picking the paper up, however, Bernie gave it to Larry, who proceeded to imitate the entire sequence except for picking up the paper from the floor. Instead Larry backed away, watching Bernie and opening access. This action, less clear as an offering gesture, did not succeed. Thus Larry stepped forward again and repeated the whole sequence. This time he backed up much further, and Bernie responded, stepping forward and picking up the paper. As Figure 5 shows, the interchange then repeated, Bernie offering and Bernie backing away at the completion of the turns. However this time Bernie responded differently to Larry's gesture of backing away. Instead of approaching the paper, Bernie merely pointed at it and looked up at Larry. Larry responded to this turn of events by approaching again and picking up the paper. Before he completed his turn, however, Bernie had become distracted and had turned his attention to someone hammering on a table elsewhere in the room.

Consider the elements of earlier stages present in this interchange. In stage I fashion, a child by his own activity re-creates a spectacle he observes another child produce. Indeed at times it appears that interest is totally invested in the action on the paper. Yet in stage II fashion it is clear that even putting the paper to the wall is done partly for its effect on the other child, as when Larry looks at Bernie while holding the paper against the wall. As in complex contingency interchanges, there is a coordination of two simple interchanges—namely, an imitative interchange with the paper, and sequence of mutual object exchange. However the sequence of object exchanges is role complementary and role reversed, thus qualifying as a stage III interchange. The role reversal is less obvious than it would have been if Larry had used the accepted adult pattern of offering, as Bernie did. Yet Larry's intent is no less clear when he exaggerates his gesture to open access after an initial failure to obtain the reciprocal response from Bernie.

It is difficult to tell what Bernie had in mind when he pointed at the paper and looked at Larry just at the juncture when his turn had begun twice previously. On the other hand, the effect of his action on Larry was clear

Time (seconds)	Bernie (16 months)	Larry (18 months)
0	Puts paper to wall Releases paper Picks paper up from floor OFFERS PAPER TO LARRY	
11		RECEIVES PAPER FROM BERNIE Puts paper to wall Releases paper BACKS AWAY A FEW STEPS AND LOOKS AT BERNIE Puts paper to wall HOLDS PAPER AGAINST WALL AND LOOKS AT BERNIE Releases paper BACKS AWAY FURTHER AND LOOKS AT BERNIE
32	LOOKS AT LARRY AND PICKS UP PAPER Puts paper to wall Releases paper Picks up paper from floor OFFERS PAPER AND VOCALIZES TO LARRY	

51		RECEIVES PAPER FROM BERNIE
		Puts paper to wall
		Releases paper
		BACKS AWAY AND LOOKS AT BERNIE
65	POINTS AT PAPER AND LOOKS AT LARRY	
67		LOOKS AT BERNIE AND PICKS UP PAPER
		Puts paper to wall
		Releases paper
		BACKS AWAY AND LOOKS AT BERNIE
72	Departs	
81		LOOKS AT BERNIE AND PICKS UP PAPER
		Puts paper to wall
		Releases paper and departs,
		following BERNIE

FIGURE 5. Illustration of a stage III role-complementary interchange (events designated as in Figure 1).

enough. His gesture produced the same reaction from Larry as did Bernie's complete performance of a turn. Clearly Bernie was in a good position to discover the efficiency of gestural as opposed to enactive turn-taking. But Bernie was only 16 months old and Larry was 18 months. The advent of gestural interchanges with words was still several months away.

DISCUSSION

Three structurally different stages of toddler interaction were described. Each stage was understood to evolve from some modification of the prior stage. Figure 6 symbolically illustrates the mature or most complex organization of each stage. This diagram is useful in summarizing the structural changes that allow movement between stages.

Contacts during stage I are object-centered. If SDBs are present, they are never contingent on SDBs from other children. Despite the lack of social orientation, stage I contacts are sometimes very well structured. The actions of child A are contingent on those of child B. A and B can imitate each other. Occasionally the contact even follows an alternating or "turn-taking" pattern represented in the diagram by a looping arrow. The structure of stage I is fortuitous, but it is there. Therefore it is available for perception and comprehension by the contact participants. In stage II the children substitute (Flavell, 1972) each other for the objects of stage I. Although objects disappear from Figure 6, they remain important in supporting most interchanges. The interchange is fragile at first and must be supported by having just the right pair of toddlers (peer specificity) in just the right ecology (place and object specificity). In stage III the system has differentiated (Flavell, 1972), with pairs of complementary SDBs occurring in a coordinated fashion between peers. Furthermore, interchanges require a role switching or reversal, absent in stage II.

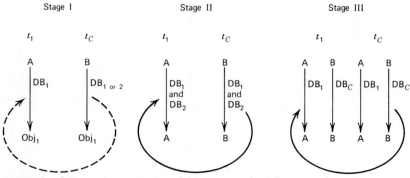

FIGURE 6.   Structural organization of three stages of toddler contacts.

TABLE 1. Summary of Stage Characteristics

	Stage I	Stage II		Stage III
	Object-centered Contacts	Simple Contingency Interchanges	Complex Contingency Interchanges	Complementary Interchanges
Dyad achievement	Contingency of actions on things	Contingencies of SDBs	Markers	Complementary and reversible "roles"
	Behavioral or imitative constraint Looping or turn-taking form		Coordination among SDBs	
Necessary mental operations	Assimilation of act/watch rhythm to actions of peers on objects	Assimilation of peers to secondary circular reactions	Sequential and simultaneous co-ordination of SDBs	Simultaneous coordination of an action and its complement
Nonstructural contact properties				
Demand on peer-directed visual attention	Absent	High	Low	Low
Tolerance for/resistance to distraction and interruptions	Absent	Low	High	High
Unit in recombination (modularization)	Absent	Absent	Present	Present

Terms such as "substitution" and "differentiation" are formally necessary to describe relationships between stages of social organization. However they do not capture the concomitant changes of participating individuals. These too have been discussed and are summarized in Table 1. The table employs Piaget's terminology (e.g., assimilation), although the terminology of learning theory (e.g., generalization) would have served equally well.

The relationship between individual change and stage change is bidirectional. Contacts at a given stage cause individuals to change. Parallel change in both members of dyad allows them to interact in a new manner. Social organization generates individual changes, which in turn generate new social organization. To illustrate, object-centered contacts afford participants the opportunity for observing contingencies between their own actions and those of other children. When both members of a dyad have assimilated peers to secondary circular reactions and have accommodated secondary circular reactions for use with peers, the structure of their contacts shifts to stage II. They assimilate peers to the act of banging on the table. But they accommodate the act itself, looking at the peer rather than at the table as they bang, and waiting for their peer to bang before they bang again.

This chapter concentrates on structural or organizational change across stages. Yet other more quantitative changes in the children's contacts also were observed. They were not the subject of detailed observation, yet they deserve further study because they help in describing the "flavor" or "style" of given contacts. The changes noted are listed in Table 1. Notice how much change of these types is observed between the simple and complex interchanges of stage II.

This chapter organizes a set of observations of contacts between a small number of toddlers. Yet it also puts some order into the seemingly contradictory literature on the origins of sociability. Previous theories described sections of what is treated here as a developmental progression. Bühler (1927), Maudry and Nekula (1939), and many other workers in the 1930s stressed the parallel or peer-ignoring quality of early peer contacts. In the present view, they were describing stage I contacts. Baldwin (1906) was the first to see the role of self-imitation in facilitating social interaction. Yet he did not realize that some of the earliest peer contacts are nonimitative. While recognizing the importance of imitation in the genesis of stage II interaction, we also suggest the roles of the act/watch rhythm, toy affordances, and peer's comprehension of SDBs. Mead (1934) argued that significant symbols formed the basis of uniquely human social interaction. Yet significant symbols were defined as requiring a person to take the perspective or role of the other, as in the present stage III. The obvious fact that children play together imitatively before role taking appears has troubled contemporary theorists (Kohlberg, 1969). The present approach views perspective taking in developmental context, treating it as emergent from earlier peer interactions of some complexity. Role taking may or may not be uniquely human; but in either case it is the product of a developmental progression.

Developmental psychology has focused much more attention on the infant-parent relationship than on the infant-infant relationship. This chapter suggests that the peer contacts are analytically useful in understanding early social development. The advantage of peer-peer interaction is that all participants use a sensory-motor level of intelligence. In parent-child contacts the parent may be holding up both ends of the "interaction."

Piaget understood that parents (1954) and peers (1948, 1951) play special roles in children's intellectual development. Peer contact permits thought to become socialized and autonomous. However he thought that the role of peers in development did not begin until the emergence of signs, at the termination of the sensory-motor period (Piaget, 1951, p. 239). The present observations support a different thesis: that peer-peer interaction occurs and even undergoes a developmental progression during the sensory-motor period.

Garvey (1974) has suggested a progression in the verbal communication tures of older preschool children. In this progression early interactions are imitative and cyclical. For example, A says "bye mommy" and B says "bye mommy," and they continue back and forth in this fashion. In later interactions children reveal that they comprehend a role and its complement: "I'll be the dragon and you be St. George that killed him." One is struck by the structural similarity between Garvey's progression of verbal interaction formats and the present stages of sensory-motor interactions. The analogy even extends to the changes developed here as internal to stage II. Why should Garvey's subjects follow an analogous progression when they are several years older than Larry and Bernie? Perhaps children must rely on the simplest communication system (simple contingency interchanges) as they master language. Perhaps Garvey's subjects never had the opportunity to advance through the progression suggested here during sensory-motor growth. Whatever the reason, the parallel in the two progressions—each the result of video-assisted observation of spontaneous play between children—suggests the promise of further work in these areas.

References

Argyle, M. *Social interaction.* Chicago: Aldine Press, 1969.

Baldwin, J. M. *Social and ethical interpretations in mental development,* 4th ed. New York: Macmillan, 1906.

Becker, J. A social learning analysis of the peer directed behaviors of nine month old infants. Unpublished doctoral dissertation, University of California, 1974.

Bridges, K. M. B. A study of social development in early infancy. *Child Development,* 1933, **4**, 36–49.

Bronson, W. C. Competence and the growth of personality. Paper presented at the Developmental Sciences Trust/Ciba Foundation, London, January 1972.

Bronson, W. C. Mother-toddler interaction: A perspective on studying the development of competence. Paper read at the Merrill-Palmer Conference on Research and Teaching of Infant Development, Detroit, February 1973.

Bühler, C. *Die ersten soczialen Verhaltungsweisen des Kindes.* Jena: Fisher Verlag, 1927.

Flavell, J. M. An analysis of cognitive-developmental sequences. *Genetic Psychology Monographs,* 1972, **86**, 279–350.

Garvey, C. Some properties of social play. *Merrill-Palmer Quarterly,* 1974, **20**, 163–180.

Garvey, C., & Hogan, R. Social speech and social interaction: Egocentrism revisited. *Child Development,* 1973, **44**, 562–568.

Gibson, J. J. *The perception of the visual world.* Boston: Houghton Mifflin, 1950.

Koffka, K. *Principles of gestalt psychology.* New York: Harcourt, 1935.

Kohlberg, L. Stage and sequence: The cognitive-developmental approach to socialization. In D. A. Goslin (Ed.), *Handbook of socialization theory and research.* Skokie, Ill.: Rand McNally, 1969.

Lewis, M., & Goldberg, S. Perceptual-cognitive development in infancy: a generalized expectancy model as a function of the mother-infant interaction. *Merrill-Palmer Quarterly,* 1969, **15**(1), 81–100.

Lucas, T., & Mueller, E. The "da" game-delimiter: Precursor to the summons-answer routine and the rhetorical gambit. *Current research résumé,* Stanford Child Language Research Forum, April 1973. (Abstract.)

Maudry, M., & Nekula, M. Social relations between children of the same age during the first two years of life. *Journal of Genetic Psychology,* 1939, **54**, 193–215.

Mead, G. H. *Mind, self and society.* Chicago: University of Chicago Press, 1934.

Mueller, E., & DeStefano, C. Sources of toddlers' peer interaction in a playgroup setting. *Early Child Development and Care,* in press.

Mueller, E., & Rich, A. Clustering and socially-directed behaviors in a playgroup of one-year-old boys. *Early Child Development and Care,* in press.

Piaget, J. *The moral judgment of the child.* New York: Free Press, 1948.

Piaget, J. *Play, dreams, and imitation in childhood.* New York: Norton, 1951.

Piaget, J. *The language and thought of the child.* London: Routledge & Kegan Paul, 1952a.

Piaget, J. *The origins of intelligence in children.* New York: International Universities Press, 1952b.

Piaget, J. *The construction of reality in the child.* New York: Basic Books, 1954.

Vincze, M. The social contacts of infants and young children reared together. *Early Child Development and Care,* 1971, **1**, 99–109.

Watson, J. S. Memory and "contingency analysis" in infant learning. *Merrill Palmer Quarterly,* 1967, **13,** 55–76.

Watson, J. S. Smiling, cooing and "the game." *Merrill Palmer Quarterly,* 1972, **18,** 323–340.

Werner, H. *Comparative psychology of mental development.* New York: International Universities Press, 1948.

Wohlwill, J. F. *The study of behavioral development.* New York: Academic Press, 1973.

CHAPTER 10

Peer Relations and the
Acquisition of Language

ELIZABETH BATES

Department of Psychology
University of Colorado

The front pages of American newspapers were filled rather recently with selected transcripts from conversations among a group of adult "peers" in Washington, D.C. Many were struck by the seeming discontinuities and distractions, and by the general difficulty of following such bits of conversations when taken out of context (*The Whitehouse Transcripts,* 1973). Because samples of real dialogue are often if not always incomplete and distorted, Chomsky (1965) suggests that the proper subject matter of linguistic theory is not "performance," or language as it is actually used by speakers and hearers, but "competence," the speaker's abstract and presumably perfect knowledge of his language. In *Aspects of a Theory of Syntax* (1965), Chomsky states that

"Linguistic theory is concerned primarily with an ideal speaker-listener, in a completely homogeneous speech community, who knows its language perfectly and is unaffected by such grammatically irrelevant conditions as memory limitations, distractions, shifts of attention and interest, and errors (random or characteristic) in applying his knowledge of the language" (p. 3).

The emphasis on "competence" in linguistic theory has carried over into child language research as well. In the past 10 to 15 years research has been aimed primarily at inferring the development of linguistic "competence" from various kinds of performance data by children. In turn, there has been much less emphasis on the nature of "real" speech by children or adults.

This state of affairs makes it rather difficult to answer some of the questions we are asking today. By Chomsky's definition, "the nature of peer language and the effects of peers on language acquisition" is a "performance" topic; indeed, it would be hard to imagine an area of study farther removed from the concept of an ideal speaker-hearer who knows his language perfectly. First of all, children are even more prone than adults to interference from memory limitations, shifts of attention and interest, and both random and characteristic "errors." Second, evidence indicates that speech among children has certain unique characteristics that are rarely if ever found in adult conversations. Even in the darkest moments of the Watergate crisis, no one was recorded saying anything quite like

"Up a lup a dup, up a lup I go."

"Nolly lolly, nolly lolly, nilly lolly, sillie Billie, nolly Lolly."

[These vocalizations are quoted by Cazden (1974, p. 12) from Johnson (1972, pp. 255–256).]

The belief that adult speech to children is distorted and ungrammatical has even led some researchers (e.g., McNeill, 1966) to conclude that children could not possibly construct a competence model of their language from the data of adult speech alone. Imagine, then, how much more difficult the situation must be for the child who must learn his language from other children. And yet in a survey of cross-cultural literature on language acquisition, Slobin (1972) reports that children in many cultures must depend primarily on peers and older children for most of their linguistic experience. Slobin mentions three studies of language development in such cultures (Blount, 1969; Kernan, 1969; Mitchell-Kernan, 1971). Chiefly qualitative analyses of small groups of children, these studies do not permit statistical comparisons. However the data indicate that at least the onset time and the general course of language development are roughly the same, regardless of the child's source of speech input.

How shall we interpret such data? Is this further evidence that children need very little input to learn language—as Humboldt says, "the thread along which language develops on its own?" Or is it possible that linguistic input to children—from adults and/or from peers—is not quite as distorted and ungrammatical as we have assumed?

In the last few years some psycholinguists have turned their attention away from strict competence models toward a more precise analysis of situational variables in language learning. In particular, there is now a rather substantial literature on the structural characteristics of adult speech to children, or "motherese" (Drach, 1969; Snow, 1972; Phillips, 1970; Broen, 1972; Farwell, 1973; Sachs, Brown, & Salerno, in press). These studies uniformly report that speech addressed by adults to children differs in important ways from speech to other adults. Fragmentary or ungrammatical utterances are extremely rare in speech to children. Utterances are shorter and syntactically less complex, and vocabularies are more restricted. Intonation contours are exaggerated in pitch and range. In short, adults provide a clear and simplified model of their language to the child listener.

Of course few parents modify their speech with a grammar textbook in hand. As Wertsch (1974) suggests, the tendency to simplify speech for children is part of a natural process that follows whenever an adult speaker assumes that he cannot trust his listener to uncover subtle or implied meanings. Whenever messages fail, speakers will increase redundancy and make the next message more explicit. Precisely the same process occurs in speaking to listeners who betray strong foreign accents and to people suspected of poor hearing. Fortunately for children, when an adult more or less unconsciously follows his linguistic "instincts" to increase redundancy, he also economizes by shortening and simplifying the message. The result, for children, is a clear and manageable model of their language.

These "instincts" can occasionally backfire, however. In a study of language development in Italy (Bates, 1974), I noted that Italian adults use a special subject–final word order about 50% of the time in speech to young children. They use the same form only 8% of the time in speech to adults. This subject–final form (e.g., verb-object-subject, or VOS) contrasts with the standard order in Italian (subject-verb-object) and is used to emphasize or stress the subject. This is the same process that we carry out in English with intonation, as in the sentences: Are *you* going to play with it? Shall *I* play with it? Hence by using a high proportion of subject–final word sentences, Italian parents are probably trying to be especially clear and emphatic with their children. Like English, however, Italian is a subject-verb-object language. By overweighting the corpus in favor of VOS, parents essentially end by giving their children the wrong model for standard syntax. And in fact, Italian children—unlike their English counterparts—do not seem to figure out the standard word order for their language for quite some time (Bates, 1974).

In most cases, however, an adult who follows his linguistic instincts will present child listeners with some fairly good data for constructing a theory of their language. But what about the child who learns his language primarily from other children? Does he receive a clear and simplified model—or merely an impoverished one? Does peer language differ in any important ways from adult speech to children? Unfortunately, there are too few data comparing the two kinds of input to permit any clear answers. Putting together research from some rather disparate sources, we must be satisfied with some very tentative answers to the following three questions:

1. Is the child who learns his language from peers at a disadvantage on some language measures? Or does peer language actually help more than adult input on certain aspects of language acquisition?

2. If there is a differential effect, what structural characteristics of peer versus adult language might be responsible for the difference?

3. Finally, what are the most promising lines for future research on language between children?

THE EFFECTS OF PEER VERSUS ADULT INPUT

Most children grow up with exposure to a variety of speakers and listeners. Hence it is difficult to determine the differential effect of one kind of linguistic partner. However a general idea of the effect of peers on language development can be obtained from data on birth order, twins, and children raised in institutions.

Perhaps the most extreme case of peer language is language between twins—two children who start off as evenly as possible on all characteristics, grow up in roughly the same environment, and spend a great deal of time together. There is a certain amount of folklore about the unique or "secret" languages shared by twins, none of it borne out by systematic research. Yet we do have evidence that, at least at some stages of development, language spoken by twins is impoverished when compared with the language of singletons of the same age and social class.

Dales (1969) studied fourteen pairs of like-sex twins (seven male and seven female), arriving at a total of 206 Gesell language and motor development scores across a 4-year longitudinal period. These findings were compared with a cross-sectional sample of 206 singletons matched by sex and age level to the twins at various stages of development. Twins were retarded in both motor and language development until between 33 and 36 months. From that point on there were no significant differences, although the twins tended to obtain lower scores overall beyond 33 months. Day (1932) compared 80 pairs of twins on a large variety of measures, including mean length of utterance (MLU), sentence complexity, and "linguistic egocentrism" (see below). Again twins were inferior to singletons on virtually all measures, although the discrepancy lessened by school age. Davis (1937) studied language development in twins from 5 to 10 years of age and found far fewer differences between twins and singletons than reported by Day or Dales. This supports the finding that the "twin effect" on language disappears by school age. Howard (1946) reports a greater retardation in the speech of triplets than that observed for twins, also citing evidence that the Dionne quintuplets were even more retarded in language. Like all the twin studies, Howard's findings are confounded by evidence from other sources that multiple births correlate with a large number of what might be termed "biological weaknesses." We cannot necessarily attribute the language retardation to the effect of the twins on each other. It is interesting, however, that the language differences disappear when the children begin school and are exposed to a larger range of speakers and listeners. It is at least clear that the full-time company of a twin in no way enhances language development.

Svenka Savic & Jocic (1972) have carried out a rather interesting analysis of twin dialogues, suggesting that the seemingly impoverished nature of individual twin utterances is deceptive. If successive utterances in dialogue are analyzed for *shared* deep structures (e.g., Twin 1: "The wolf wants to . . ."; Twin 2: ". . . bite the bird"), the twins demonstrate an underlying capacity for all the linguistic forms expressed in single phrases by single children. However Scollon (1973) has applied a similar analysis to dialogues and successive utterances by a single Hawaiian-American child. He too finds that much richer structures underlie what he terms "vertical" or successive constructions. Hence Svenka Savic and Jocic's notion of "shared deep structure" may not be typical of twins alone.

The birth-order literature also indicates that the company of other children in no way enhances language development (Davis, 1937; Koch, 1968; Zazzo, 1969; Luria & Yadovitch, 1959; Moore, 1968; Rubin et al., 1971; Sampson, 1965; Clausen, 1966). In most birth-order studies firstborns and only children score higher on language measures than later borns. Some exceptions are reported in Thurstone and Jenkins (1929), McFadden (1929), and Hsiao (1931). Most of these authors attribute the birth-order effect to the fact that firstborns and only children receive a greater share of adult attention during language acquisition than do later borns. This interpretation points up a problem that is inherent to all the studies examined in this section—twin studies, birth order, and effects of institutionalization. Whenever we can point to a high proportion of input from peers, there is also a lower proportion of input from adults. Do later borns, twins, and institutionalized children do more poorly on language measures because they have had less stimulation from adults, or because there is something inherent in the quality of speech from peers that retards the development of children exposed to peers? The most we can conclude, at least from the birth-order studies, is that older siblings are not adequate substitutes for parents in terms of linguistic stimulation. However, this research is also confounded by a number of other variables. First of all, birth order has been found to affect a large set of abilities beyond language. Moore (1968) states that "There is no evidence that language is more dependent on ordinal position than are other aspects of intelligence" (p. 104).

Second, the birth-order effect interacts in complex ways with sex of siblings and size of family. For example, Moore (1968) reports that the ordinal-position effect on language is strongest for firstborn females, particularly at age 3. Rosenberg and Sutton-Smith (1964) also note that although both male and female firstborns are linguistically superior in two-child families, only female firstborns have the advantage in three-child families. Furthermore, the presence of a female sibling tends to increase language scores in boys, whereas girls with male siblings score higher than other females on quantitative tasks. Finally, Moore (1968) reports that the arrival of a new sibling tends to lower the language scores of firstborn males, although it may enhance the scores of females.

Putting these findings together, we might infer that girls make better use of a variety of family configurations in language development; little boys in turn will obtain higher scores on language measures if they have had a sister around to talk to. Cicirelli (1972) has studied male-female and sibling-nonsibling dyads in an explicit "teaching" situation. He finds that of all the possible pairings, female siblings make the best teachers, and male siblings in particular show the greatest increment in learning when taught by female siblings. It may well be that the interactions between sex and ordinal position in language reflect that degree to which female siblings learn to do whatever it is that adults do to help their child listeners. Perhaps, in short, females become more competent speakers of "motherese." It would be interesting to learn whether the differential effect of siblings, like the twin effect, tends to equal out with the effect of schooling. It is not clear from the birth-order literature whether that is the case.

Another source of data on the effects of peer input comes from the literature on children raised in institutions. Here too the results overwhelmingly indicate that the constant company of other children correlates negatively with performance on language measures (McCarthy, 1954). But it is also true that these results, like those just mentioned, are affected by a wide range of other factors. Institutionalized children are often at a disadvantage on measures of almost anything. A study by Tizard et al. (1972) indicates that this need not always happen if children are raised in more enlightened institutions. Tizard et al. studied 85 children from 2 to 5 years of age, in thirteen residential nurseries in Great Britain. They found no evidence of so-called institutional retardation: children scored near the mean for the general population on a variety of verbal and nonverbal measures. However the nurseries had also been selected to reflect several different kinds of organization and philosophies of child care, (e.g., "free form" vs. highly structured play periods), as well as quantity and quality of interaction between staff and children. These organizational differences were in turn reflected in the children's linguistic performance. First of all, with regard to the topic of peer effects, there was no relationship between the number of hours children spend with other children (older children or peers) and the performance on linguistic tasks. However there were high correlations between types of *adult* speech to children and linguistic performance. For example, a high rate of negative commands by the staff to children correlated negatively with performance on a linguistic production task ($-.61$, $\rho <$ .05). The amount of "informative talk" and command with explanations correlated positively with language performance (.75 and .57, respectively). Interestingly these same variables also distinguish lower-class and middle-class mothers in a study by Hess and Shipman (1965), and they have the same effect on linguistic performance by lower-class versus middle-class children. For present purposes, however, the most interesting finding is that the quality of verbal input from the *staff* has a strong effect on verbal scores, whereas the amount of interaction with other *children* does not correlate with any of the verbal or nonverbal measures.

McCarthy (1954) collapsed across a number of family configurations, school settings, and other variables, to examine the effect of time spent with adults, with older children, and with younger children, on mean length of utterance.

She found that MLU is highest in children who associated primarily with adults. Children who spend most of their time with younger children score higher than children who spend time primarily with older children. The second finding is probably an artifact of the birth-order effect, since firstborns spend more time with younger children than later borns. Nelson (1973) also examined the effect of amount of time spent with other children on the earliest stages of language development, from 10 to 12 months through 24 months. She reports that there is a significant negative correlation between amount of time with other children and several measures of language comprehension and production in this critical age period. Again, however, it is difficult to determine whether this effect is due to the actual nature of peer language or to the tendency of high exposure to other children to correlate with lower exposure to adult input.

One of the problems with such data, besides the confounding with other variables, lies with the types of measures used by most researchers. The dependent variable is generally a quantitative measure, like amount of talking, vocabulary counts, or performance on verbal IQ tests. An exception is the Nelson study, which used several more qualitative measures of language development. For the most part, however, little is revealed about the kinds of linguistic knowledge that children obtain from adults, twins, siblings, peers, and others. Does "peer" versus "adult" input affect the general rate of development, the relative amount of linguistic input and output, or does it have a specific effect on certain aspects of communication? From the information presented thus far, we can only conclude that the children who spend time with peers are at a disadvantage when compared with children who spend most of their time with adults. Yet the cross-cultural findings mentioned by Slobin (1972) indicate that children who learn language from peers begin and end language acquisition within the same time as children from Western nuclear families. Let us now go on to examine the structural characteristics of child-child versus child-adult speech, to try to determine the reasons for these findings.

STRUCTURAL CHARACTERISTICS OF CHILD–CHILD SPEECH

To understand the different structural effects of adult versus child input on language learning, the best source of data would be samples of speech by the same child with peers and with adults. Unfortunately very few studies of that kind have been carried out. In the period prior to what has been called post-Chomskian psycholinguistics, researchers were more interested in quantitative measures than in structural analyses of speech samples. Hence most of the data are in the form just reviewed. In the 1960s, on the other hand, the emphasis on particular grammatical rules (or "competence," as defined by Chomsky) was accompanied by a lack of interest in the effect of situational variables on development.

A few studies are available directly comparing child-child and child-adult speech, although the measures tend to be the quantitative type discussed earlier. Smith (1933) reported that speech from children to adults is longer, richer in vocabulary, and syntactically more complex than speech between children. Comparing child-child speech in free play with child-adult speech, Hahn (1948) also found that children use more varied and complex forms with adults. However Hahn discovered that child speech to the entire peer group in school "show and tell" sessions is still more complex and varied than child-adult speech. Julia Kadar (1969) has studied the speech of Hungarian children in (1) free play with other children, (2) a structured set of tasks with adults, and (3) prolonged conversation with adults on an assigned topic. She found that utterances in the third situation in particular were syntactically more complex (e.g., more subordinate clauses, transformations, etc.) and contained more vocabulary items within all the grammatical classes but verbs. This suggests not only that adult conversation enhances the child's performance when compared with child-child speech but that there are differences between kinds of child-adult interaction (e.g., conversation on an assigned topic produces more complex and interesting speech than discussion of a task-centered situation).

Let us examine briefly Kadar's small finding that child-child speech contains fewer examples of all the parts of speech except verbs. This detail is particularly interesting, since Parisi and Genelli (in press) have discovered that the lexicon of lower-class versus middle-class Italian children from 1½ to 2½ years of age differs in numbers of nouns but not in numbers of verbs. In fact, children from both classes used almost exactly the same verbs. Parisi and Genelli suggest that this is a nascent version of what Bernstein (1966) describes as the elaborated versus restricted code. The restricted code, which is supposedly the only one used by lower-class speakers of English, is more context-based, relying more heavily, for example, on deictic devices like pronouns (e.g., "Give me that" instead of "Give me the ball"). Parisi and Genelli suggest that nouns do not develop as rapidly as a class of lexical items among children learning the restricted code because nouns can often be substituted by pronouns and other deictic devices (e.g., pointing). The small class of verbs found in the speech of very young children cannot be easily substituted by deictic devices; hence children must master them regardless of whether they are learning the elaborated (explicit) or restricted (implicit) code. If Parisi and Genelli are correct, Kadar's evidence indicates that children also rely more on deictic substitutes for nouns in speech with other children, whereas speech with adults in some way encourages them to use fewer context-based devices. In other words, adults, unlike other children, may draw the child toward a more explicit, elaborated code. This small but provocative bit of evidence may make more sense later on, when we discuss the problem of egocentrism in speech.

In summary, it is fair to say that the speech of one child to another tends to be shorter, syntactically simpler, and more restricted lexically than speech by the same child to an adult. What are adults doing to pull more complex speech from a child? We have already established that adults also speak a shorter and more simple version of their language to children. All the studies on "motherese" concluded that this phenomenon is very advantageous for the child. By extension, we should also be able to demonstrate that a child will benefit greatly from exposure to the speech of children only slightly more advanced than he is, since they would presumably use grammatical forms for which the child is "ready." Yet evidence indicates that peers do not "inspire" the child to his best linguistic efforts. In fact, children who spend most of their time with peers are at something of a disadvantage. There must be something about child-child speech—other than its grammatical simplicity—that is qualitatively different from conversations between children and adults, rendering peer input less useful for the child acquiring his native language.

With very few exceptions, virtually all qualitative analyses of peer language have dealt with the issue of egocentrism. "Egocentric speech" has been defined in varied and sometimes conflicting ways, but it generally refers to speech that does not take the listener's perspective into account. The problem was first discussed by Piaget (1926) in one of his earliest works, *The Language and Thought of the Child*. Piaget pointed out that in the dialogues of preschool children, the messages offered by the two interlocutors often bear little relationship to each other. The speaker does not make an effort to respond adequately to previous statements, nor to tailor his speech to fit the expectations of his partner. In addition to these "collective monologues," children may also engage in long soliloquies or monologues without waiting for any reaction from a listener. Or they may pick up a phrase uttered by another child and repeat or play with that phrase (i.e., "echolalia") without actually responding to it. In a study of six preschool children in Geneva, Piaget reports that anywhere from 40 to 70% of utterances may be classified as "egocentric." This report has been quite controversial. One reason for the controversy involves the failure of all researchers to find the same levels of egocentrism in child speech (cf. Mueller, 1972). But another, perhaps more important reason has to do with the widespread misunderstanding of what is meant by "egocentrism." The choice of terms is unfortunate, at least in its English translation, since it brings to mind an image of children as selfish little sociopaths. Some authors have read Piaget as suggesting that children have no social motivation whatsoever. Others have concentrated on measuring the phenomena that Piaget describes as egocentric (e.g., echolalia) without adequately considering the cognitive definition of egocentrism as failure to take the perspective of the listener.

A great deal of conflicting literature has grown around the topics of egocentrism, private speech, and taking the perspective of the listener. Excellent reviews of this literature are available by Flavell et al. (1968), Looft (1972), and Kohlberg, Yaeger, and Hjertholm (1968), and I recommend these to readers interested in pursuing the topic. For the purposes of this chapter, I would like to restrict myself to an analysis of five rather different concepts that are often confused in the literature on egocentrism. These factors may, in turn, have very different effects on the language children speak to one another.

The issues are (1) social intent and empathy in small children, (2) private or nonsocial speech and its function in problem solving, (3) repetition or play with the surface forms of speech, (4) role taking, or the ability to take the listener's perspective, and (5) the ability to produce and to understand the "listener cues" required by conversational rules. I examine these five issues separately, in the hope of arriving at a clearer definition of egocentrism and a more precise picture of peer language.

Egocentric Speech Versus Social Intentions

The most heated critiques of the concept of egocentrism revolve around Piaget's (1926) claim that the listener "is expected neither to attend nor to understand" (p. 33). Some critics, particularly Vygotsky (1962), have interpreted this to mean that children do not intend to communicate at all—they are asocial beings who speak simply to hear themselves talk. Vygotsky went to great pains to demonstrate, for example, that child "monologues" decrease greatly in frequency and length when no listeners are present and when the listener is deaf or otherwise unresponsive. In a rejoinder published after Vygotsky's death, Piaget (1962) clarified what had been regarded as a classic "debate" between the two authors, by explaining that the egocentric child may indeed be very socially motivated during most of his speech. He is "egocentric" only insofar as he is unable to adapt his speech *successfully* for his intended listener.

It is clear, however, that Piaget connected the decline in egocentrism with an increase in both social success and empathy, or an ability to consider the feelings of others. Several studies have supported his claim that by about 7 years of age, popularity among peers is inversely related to degree of egocentrism.

For example, Rubin (1972) found that popularity (assessed by sociometric techniques) correlated negatively with egocentrism measures with the Krauss and Glucksberg task (discussed below), even when IQ is held constant.

However, the correlation between popularity and egocentrism seems to vary according to the age of the child and the kinds of measures used. For example, several authors report that the correlation between egocentrism and "interpersonal competence" is weak or nonexistent among children older than 8, as compared with younger children (Deutsch, 1974; Rubin, 1972; Rothenberg, 1970; Silvern, in preparation). Deutsch (1974) suggests that these findings may reflect the difference between observational measures of popularity (e.g., teacher ratings, playground observation) and sociometric measures (e.g., "Who are the children in your class that you like most?"). The only consistent relations between popularity and egocentrism have been found with observational methods, whereas the studies reporting significant age differences tend to use sociometric measures. Silvern (in preparation) also suggests that the inconsistent findings may be due to a failure to analyze sex differences. Using both observational and sociometric measures of interpersonal competence, Silvern discovered that egocentrism and popularity were negatively related in second graders but not in fourth graders. However there were powerful sex differences among the fourth-grade children. Among fourth-grade boys, egocentrism was *positively* related to measures of popularity. Among fourth-grade girls, egocentrism was negatively related to social measures indicating compliance and cooperation, but unrelated to popularity. We might interpret these findings by suggesting that the cognitive ability to consider the expectations and feelings of others is used differently by girls and by boys. Since girls are expected by the culture to be more compliant, cooperative, and "nice," they use their cognitive role-taking abilities to predict situations in which such behavior is appropriate. Fourth-grade boys may be under less pressure to play cooperative and compliant roles. Thus they may have the same cognitive role-taking ability as the girls but use it differently to conform with different social expectations. As Silvern suggests, such hypotheses will require much more research. But it seems fair to conclude that studies of the effect of egocentrism on various social behaviors should include more careful analysis of sex differences and of the kinds of social pressure to which different children are exposed.

Although Piaget insisted in his 1962 rejoinder that young children are indeed socially motivated, he made a rather strong claim that children are not capable of a truly empathic understanding of others until almost 13 years of age. This claim should be restricted to some sophisticated kinds of insights into the motives and feelings of others, since younger children are not totally incapable of insight or compassion. Borke (1971), for example, has demonstrated convincingly that small children (3 to 5 years) can recognize the facial expressions of others as "happy," "sad," "afraid," and "angry." Garvey and Hogan (1973) examined 15-minute interactions by eighteen dyads of 3½- to 5-year-olds. They learned that although the phenomena described by Piaget as "egocentric speech" are present, children also engage in a great deal of answering and questioning about motives and so forth. Garvey and Hogan recall that in a separate work on the development of causality, Piaget himself (1964) states that children in the "precausal" era around 4 years of age tend to ask a great many questions about psychological motives. Finally, Borke (1972) offers some particularly eloquent examples of social insight in children from 1½ to 3 years of age. In one observation, a 15-month-old tries to comfort a weeping 13-

month-old playmate, first by trying to pick him up, then by locating the playmate's bottle and giving it to him. In another instance a 3-year-old explained his older brother's negative behavior to a puzzled mother by reminding her that the brother had been spanked earlier in the day. Borke (1972) concludes that

"My findings are more consistent with Piaget's general theory than his actual conclusions concerning egocentrism in the social area. If mental representation at [1½ to 2 years] is the first step toward symbolic thought, then it seems likely that conscious awareness that another person's experience is different from one's own, is the first step in the development of empathy" (p. 108).

In conclusion, no one—including Piaget—ever meant that the egocentric child has no social-communicative goals at all. Nor is he entirely incapable of insight into the feelings and reactions of others. But both his social goals and his insight will change as his cognitive capacities change. The phenomenon of egocentric speech is a result not of the child's communicative goals but of his inability to predict the perspective of others and tailor his speech to fit that perspective.

Egocentric Speech Versus Private, Task-Centered Speech

In his critique of *Language and Thought of the Child,* Vygotsky (1962) offered an alternative model to explain why children often talk to themselves, with little regard for a listener's reaction. He suggests that early speech is indeed sociocentric, but during the preschool years language begins to take on a separate, noncommunicative function in the control of motor behavior and thought processes. Hence the child begins to "talk to himself" in trying to work through difficult problems. This kind of speech gradually becomes inhibited in its external manifestations, to become "inner speech," controlling other mental processes. If task difficulty is increased, however, the child may again cease to inhibit the vocal portion of inner speech and start to "talk to himself" once again.

Several researchers have replicated Vygotsky's finding that "private speech" is a function of task difficulty (reviewed in Kohlberg, 1968). In fact, there are many situations, such as working out income tax or repairing a stubborn apparatus, when adults' lips begin moving and "inner speech" comes very close to the surface. These findings indicate that some of the child's monologues are not really "egocentric" in the same sense as his socially directed unsuccessful speech. Instead, these monologues are really "private speech," designed to serve a different kind of cognitive function. Rubin (1973) has carried out a factor analysis on a variety of measures postulated to relate to egocentrism and the inverse process, "decentration." Although IQ and performance on a nonsocial conservation task did load with most of the egocentrism measures on a single "decentration" factor, private speech was not related to this cluster of variables. This is further evidence that private, task-centered speech is functionally quite separate from other measures of egocentrism and should not be taken to indicate that the child is unable to take his listener's perspective.

From the point of view of a child listener playing somewhere nearby, however, such task-centered monologues probably provide very little useful experience in language comprehension. The fact that some of the input from peers will come from such private mutterings may in part explain the finding that peers are less efficient language models than adults.

Egocentric Speech and Language Play

In addition to the task-oriented monologues just described, Piaget extended the term "egocentric speech" to include repetitions or play with the words of other children. Such instances cannot be considered to be "responses" to another child's meaning. Instead, the child seems to pick up the speaker's words and play with them as he would any other interesting object or event in the room. Weir (1962) has recorded a large collection of bedtime monologues by her 2-year-old son which indicate that the child's pleasure with word play can go on equally well alone, without stimulation by other children. An example is the following:

> "Look at those pineapple
> In a pretty box
> And cake
> What a sticks for cakes
> For the click"[1]

Cazden (1974) gives a number of examples of repetitions, word-substitution games, and chants, in a paper entitled "Play with Language and Metalinguistic Awareness." Her results indicate that although language play changes across developmental levels, children apparently enjoy playing with language from babbling onward. Gleason (1973) also notes that games with language are a common characteristic of peer conversations at different age levels.

Both repetition, or "echolalia," and word play like the "nolly lolly . . ." example given earlier, seem, like private speech, to serve a separate, noncommunicative function. In this case the child is interested in speech and speech sounds for their own sake, not as vehicles for the communication of thoughts. I mentioned earlier that task-centered, private speech probably should not be classified with socially oriented egocentric speech, since it serves a very different function. The same can probably be said for language play. There is a great

---

[1] Cited in Cazden (1974), from R. Weir, *Language in the crib*. The Hague: Mouton, 1962.

deal of difference between an unsuccessful but well-intentioned message and phrases like "up a lup a dup I go."

Just as private speech is unlikely to facilitate the language development of one's peers, however, echolalia and language play are probably not ideal input for constructing a grammar. Language play is undoubtedly useful to the *speaker* in some way. But a high proportion of "up a lup" in the speech environment is probably of minimal use in the acquisition of language by child *listeners*.

Egocentric Speech and Role Taking

As indicated in the section on social motives, the most crucial factor in Piaget's definition of egocentric speech is the child's failure to "role take," or take the listener's perspective into account. This phenomenon operates only indirectly in such phenomena as private speech and word play, insofar as the child may ignore potential listeners altogether in both kinds of performance. Role taking may also be relevant to the question of empathy, if the feelings or motives of the listener conflict in some way with the child's own (Chandler & Greenspan, 1972). But role taking is more directly involved in speech when the child fully intends to communicate some information but fails because what is obvious to him is not at all obvious to his listener.

Role taking is the ability to take perspectives other than one's own. More precisely, it is the cognitive ability to "transform" or reverse one's own perspective. This ability has been studied with a variety of measures, including a number of nonverbal cognitive tasks. The paradigmatic experiment is Piaget's mountain task (Piaget & Inhelder, 1956). The child is seated before a fairly complex array, with trees and houses, animals and people, and so on. He is first asked to draw or to describe the mountain as he sees it. Then he is asked to indicate what the same array looks like to someone on the other side of the mountain. Piaget finds that, on this task, the ability to shift perspectives is not mastered until 7 to 9 years of age.

This experiment has been heavily criticized as entirely too complex a measure of role taking. Viewed as a mental transformation, role taking on the mountain task involves the internal or mental "rotation" of a very complex perceptual array. Also, the array is so complex that even if he could perform the transformation, a child may be unable to draw or verbalize successfully about the resulting perspective shift. Much simpler experiments have been designed by Flavell and associates (1968), Selman (1971), Marvin (1972), and DeVries (1970). In all this research, when the number of mental transformations is reduced, children demonstrate some kind of role-taking ability at a much earlier age than indicated by Piaget's original studies. For example, Marvin (1972) asked 2-, 3-, and 4-year-olds to draw a picture. When they had finished, they were told "Hold the picture up so I can take a picture of it."

Most 3-year-olds unhesitatingly picked up the drawing and rotated it to face the camera. However, if the child was asked to do the same thing with the picture "upside down," many subjects who were unable to carry out the first task reverted to the previous strategy of holding the drawing up so that only they could see it. If such a small increment in task complexity can delay performance, consider the effect of being asked to draw a complex mountain array from another person's perspective.

It seems clear that the ability to role take varies with the nature of the task. Such findings have led some psychologists (e.g., Selman, 1971; Masangkay et al., 1974) to conclude that role taking is not a unitary ability. Selman in particular has developed a stage theory of role taking in which certain kinds of perspective shifts come in as early as 2½ to 3; whereas others are delayed by several years. For example, Selman suggests that perceptual role taking, or the ability to reverse a simple, visible, visual array, is a much earlier development than conceptual role taking, which involves transformation on a conceptual framework. Irwin and Ambron (1973) agree with Selman's overall approach but find that certain kinds of conceptual role taking precede role taking on some perceptual tasks.

If role taking is narrowly defined as a mental "reversal" of perspective on some kind of content (perceptual, conceptual, etc.) clearly performance should vary with the nature and difficulty or "resistance" of a particular material under transformation, and with the number of recursions or "loops" of the role-taking operation that are required. In an article entitled "People thinking about people thinking about people . . . ," Miller, Kessel, and Flavell (1970) observe that the role-taking capacity can indeed be applied recursively, and the number of "loops" that a child can carry out on other people's thoughts will increase with age. Looft (1972) and Elkind (1967) stress that the failure to role take may recur throughout the life cycle, on different kinds of material, at different levels of complexity. R. D. Laing's little book *Knots* (1970) describes in quasi-poetic form the kinds of complex role-taking loops that frequently entangle adults, for example:

> *Jack can see that he sees*
> *What Jill can't see*
> *And that Jill can't see Jill can't see it* . . . (p. 57).

Returning to the question of egocentrism in peer speech, Rubin et al., (1971) has compared the speech of the same children alone, with adults, and with peers, on several measures of egocentrism in speech. Of the three conditions, child-child speech was higher on most measures of egocentrism. Hence regardless of the cause of egocentrism in speech, it seems to occur more frequently in the speech that children address to one another.

If a general difficulty with role taking is partially responsible for egocentric speech, what kind of specific effect should it have on the syntactic-semantic structure of child-child speech? It is likely that egocentrism will have its greatest effect on aspects of speech requiring mastery of "presuppositions," information necessary for a sentence to be understood. A typical example of failure to role take in speech would be the use of a pronoun (e.g., "He hit me!" when the antecedent (e.g., who is "he"?) is unknown to anyone but the speaker. Also, Antinucci and Volterra (1973) give examples of negations in which presupposed information is not made available to the child's adult listeners. For example, an 18-month-old subject looked at a tower on a hospital and said "No bells." Now there is no a priori reason for a tower to have bells, and a listener (e.g., another child) who did not understand how negation *should* work might be unable to retrieve the child's meaning. Adults do have a detailed knowledge of how negation works and can reconstruct the information that the boy, who had previously had experience only with church towers, had mistakenly assumed that all towers have bells. This assumption in turn formed the presupposition for the child's sentence. Antinucci and Volterra report that the most important changes in the nature of negative sentences spoken by children involve a growing ability to adapt their presuppositions to fit those of the listener. Hence a more sophisticated speaker might make the same point by providing both the presupposition and the assertion with, for example, "Gee, I thought towers were supposed to have bells, but this one doesn't."

There is a growing literature in linguistic theory regarding the nature and difficulty of different kinds of presupposition in speech, all of which must presumably be mastered by a child before adulthood. Furthermore, as Antinucci and Volterra point out, proper use of presupposition requires an ability to role take concerning the point of view of the listener. If, as the literature indicates, role taking develops in stages corresponding to different kinds of material, it should also be the case that different kinds of presuppositions in speech should also be mastered at different developmental stages. One of the more interesting lines of future research on egocentrism in speech may involve correlations between successive levels of role taking and an increasingly complex use of presupposition in speech.

Egocentric Speech and Listener Cues

The role-taking issue pertains to the child's ability to *predict* whether his listener can understand a given piece of information. Sometimes adults also fail to role take sufficiently in conversation. Assuming that the listener has more background information than he actually has, we create sentences whose presuppositions misfire. When this occurs, however, we are sensitive to a variety of cues from the listener, indicating his degree of comprehension. Such cues permit us to "redesign" an utterance that has failed, bringing it back into line with the listener's presuppositions. If we did not have such communicative devices, it is likely that adult speech would have a much higher "egocentrism quotient" than it actually does. (Soskin & John, 1963, report that the egocentrism quotient in adult speech is virtually zero.) It is possible that egocentrism is more common in child speech not only because of general failure to predict the listener's knowledge but because of insensitivity to cues from the listener indicating misunderstanding.

A study by Peterson, Danner, and Flavell (1972) tends to confirm the foregoing hypothesis. Four- and 7-year-olds conversing with adults were exposed to three different kinds of "listener feedback" indicating that the speakers were not being understood. In the first condition they were explicitly asked to repeat their message. All the children were able to augment or alter their message in some way in response to this kind of feedback. In the second condition children received an implicit verbal message indicating that the adult had not understood, but there was no explicit request to repeat. Only 7-year-olds were able to alter their speech to account for such feedback. In a third condition nonverbal facial cues were offered as feedback that a message had failed (e.g., raised eyebrows, frown, questioning look). Neither the 4-year-olds nor the 7-year-olds responded by changing or repeating their message when such nonverbal listener cues were available.

There is also evidence that young children are not particularly good at *producing* such listener cues. Dittman (1972) looked for a variety of feedback cues in conversations with first, third, and fifth graders. These included nonverbal cues like nods and smiles at the speaker, and verbal cues like "yeah" and "mm-hmm" at appropriate speech intervals. The rate at which children produced such cues was compared with adult production levels in similar settings, at similar conversational junctures. The videotape records indicate that production rates are much lower for children and occur only at points that are maximally likely to "pull" such cues from adults. Bates (1971) examined mother-child conversations with 2-, 3-, and 4-year-olds. There were no development differences in the number of messages, nor in the frequency of most speech-act categories (e.g., questions, commands, statements). The only major category that increased significantly from ages 2 to 4 was "Acknowledgments," a class of utterances offering no content other than the information "message received." This included verbal confirmations like "uh-huh" and "yeah" and nonverbal cues like nods and headshakes. Even among the oldest children, such cues were fairly infrequent. Among the twelve 2-year-olds in the study, this category was virtually nonexistent.

Hence we see that young children rarely produce the standard listener cues that characterize adult conversations and do not comprehend many such cues when they happen to be produced. If peer language tends to be more egocentric—hence less easily understood—then children not only misunderstand one another, but do not possess sufficient tools to recover or force repetition of misfired messages. The greater competency of adults in both giving and receiving listener cues may account in part for the fact that children are pulled into more explicit, less egocentric speech in their conversations with adults.

There is some evidence that the egocentrism quotients reported in certain laboratory tasks may be much higher than the proportions found in natural speech, because the child is unable to produce or respond to information about message misfire. The classic experiment for the assessment of efficiency versus egocentrism in peer communication is the Krauss-Glucksberg task (Krauss & Glucksberg, 1967, 1969). Children are seated at a table on opposite sides of a screen, enabling them to hear but not see each other. In one version of the experiment each has before him a peg and a set of three-dimensional blocks in nonsense forms. In another version each has nine two-dimensional drawings with the same nonsense forms. In both tasks one child is asked to pick up one of the forms and describe it to the other child so that the latter can locate the same form on his side. Egocentrism versus efficiency in communication are operationalized as the number of distinctive form cues (e.g., "The small red one with the points on it . . . ") that the child offers to the listener on the other side of the screen. These studies generally demonstrate that children under 7 fail to give enough cues to the listener to permit him to select the right form.

Fishbein (1971) notes that performance on the Krauss-Glucksberg task improves when the child receives more corrective feedback than another child usually provides. Shantz and Wilson (1972) also report that performance on such tasks improves when the child is trained explicitly to focus on the listener's needs.[2] In another kind of task situation Kaplan and Yonas (1967) have reported that children show more competence with "relational words" (e.g., spatial locatives) when listeners provide probes indicating that they have not understood.

These findings do not invalidate the Krauss-Glucksberg task, since it was not designed to tap responsiveness to feedback by children. Insofar as role taking involves *predicting* the amount of knowledge the speaker has in the absence of feedback, the task measures precisely what it set out to measure. However it would be dangerous to generalize from this laboratory situation to more natural settings, in which children have help from their listeners and information from the visual context to offset their communicative inefficiency.

It should also be stressed that the failure to communicate efficiently, although high in the Krauss-Glucksberg task, does not indicate a total failure to role take. Maratsos (1973) reports that 3-year-olds will inhibit their usual pointing gestures when asked to pick out toys with a listener who cannot see. Hence we are once again faced with a situation in which the failure to role take

---

[2] Fry, 1966 and 1969, reports that attempts to train the child to focus on listener feedback failed in his studies.

is largely a function of the difficulty of the perspective shift involved. Also Hoy (in press) suggests that even in the absence of complete and explicit messages from their partner in the Krauss-Glucksberg task, very young child listeners are often able to use what little context is available to figure out just which block the speaker meant. Hoy replicated the original findings in that her subjects also gave incomplete and highly subjective descriptions of the nonsense forms. She too found that the ability to make messages complete and explicit increases significantly between 5 and 9 years. However the children's competence as listeners is far better than the original studies might lead one to assume. The tape-recorded messages (e.g., "Put four sticks *in*, then put *that thing on top*," as quoted by Hoy, in press) were impossible to decode when presented out of context to adult listeners. But the child on the other side of the screen was able to connect the ambiguous message to information presented earlier. Hence "on top" is interpreted to mean "on top of the last piece mentioned." More often than not, such guesses are correct. Hoy stresses that such findings do not invalidate inferences about the child speaker's inability to role take. However when the two children share a similar scheme of referents—a far more common situation in natural settings—they display skills for deciding between alternative interpretations of an ambiguous statement by another child.

I would like to conclude that both egocentrism in creating utterances and inability to produce and use listener cues may be responsible for the difference between adult and peer input in the acquisition of language. Children playing together may often be in the position of the adult reading the Watergate transcripts. Since a child listener is not in possession of all the speaker's presuppositions, he does not always have sufficient context for deriving all the meaning in peer messages. This difference between adults and children is a relative difference, however, not an absolute one. Some authors choose to emphasize the percentage of children's messages that fail. Others stress the successful ones. One is reminded of the old philosophical question "Is this glass half-full or half-empty?"

Among researchers emphasizing the successive aspects of child-child communication are Garvey and Hogan (1973), Hoy (in press), Maratsos (1973), and Mueller (1972). Mueller is particularly critical of the egocentrism literature, insisting that egocentric speech as defined by Piaget accounts for an extremely small proportion of the utterances in his sample of 3½- to 5½-year-olds. He also examines another observation of Piaget concerning "collective monologues" in children—namely, that child conversations contain a high proportion of initiation of new topics, with much less answering or following up on statements by the other. Although Mueller admits that child conversations tend to wander off topics far more than adult dialogues, he notes that more than 50% of utterances by children are responded to appropriately by their partners. Mueller has also investigated exhaustively the factors related to

TABLE 1. Observed Probability of Occurrence of Each Category and Observed Probability of Success or Failure[a] When Predicted by Each Category (from Mueller, 1972)

Category Name	Observed Probability of Occurrence of Specified Category	Observed Probability of Predicted Outcome if Category Occurs
Categories predicting success		
Listener attention: watching speaker	.19	.89
Context: direct reply	.17	.78
Form: command or question	.43	.68
Speaker attention: looks at listener	.42	.66
Content: about listener's activity	.46	.65
Attention-getting techniques: present	.27	.61
Distance: within 4 feet	.72	.53
Clarity: words are clear	.95	.53
Fragments: grammar is clear and complete	.94	.52
Categories predicting failure		
Clarity: words unclear	.05	.83
Fragments: grammar unclear or incomplete	.07	.79
Content: about speaker's activity	.21	.64
Speaker attention: never looks at listener	.55	.61
Form: declarative	.49	.60
Listener attention: not watching speaker	.71	.57
Distance: more than 4 feet apart	.28	.57
Context: not a reply	.83	.56
Attention-getting techniques: absent	.73	.53

[a] "Success of message" refers to the eliciting of a response from the listener; "failure" refers to messages not responded to by the listener.

probability of verbal response, in conversations between 24 pairs of 3½- to 5½-year-olds during videotaped free play. The variables are presented in Table 1, ordered from the most to least effective in pulling a response. These variables are additive; that is, the probability of obtaining a verbal response from a child increases with each addition of a variable. Fragmentary or unclear utterances are the most likely to discourage response from a child partner. Of the child-child utterances that Mueller studied, however, only 12% could be classified as fragmentary or unclear.

One qualification should be added to Mueller's findings concerning children's communicative skill. It is not always possible to determine from production data alone whether children are actually predicting the listener's viewpoint and/or understanding the speaker's statements. A somewhat appropriate response, picking up on some aspect of the speaker's statement, may not necessarily mean that the listener has retrieved all the speaker's presuppositions. Everyone has had the experience of "conversing" with a thoroughly uninteresting conversationalist and allowing his mind to wander completely from the conversation. It is possible to "respond" to utterances that are not fully understood without "giving away" our rather superficial understanding of the speaker. The data from free speech are useful and interesting in assessing child competence, but it will also be neccessary to carry out experiments that test the child's comprehension of some of the presuppositions used by both child and adult speakers.

So far we have stressed the negative aspects of peer language as compared with adult input, to account for evidence that children who are exposed to a high proportion of child speech perform at a lower level on several language measures. These findings should not distract us from the findings that children raised in the constant company of peers do indeed learn to talk, mastering the essentials of their native grammar in more or less the same time period as children exposed primarily to adult speech. This achievement may be attained partly because children need not derive all their knowledge of language from the speech input presented by the environment. Perhaps, as McNeill (1966) suggests, children bring certain innate linguistic strategies to bear on the language-learning situation. Alternatively, they may derive hypotheses about the nature of language from some of their other perceptual-cognitive systems, as Sinclair (1974) has proposed. In either case the small differences between adult and child input are not sufficient to upset the workings of the language-acquisition device in any critical way.

There are some further reasons for optimism about the effects of peers on language acquisition. We mentioned earlier that adults adjust their speech to young children in a way that simplifies the language-learning task for the child. There is now a certain amount of evidence to suggest that children also speak a version of "motherese" with younger listeners.

In an interesting and important monograph, Shatz and Gelman (1973) report three studies comparing the speech of 4-year-olds to adults, to peers, and to 2-year-olds. In the first study, 4-year-old subjects were shown a new toy. They discussed the toy first with an adult, and then with a 2-year-old child. Half of the sixteen subjects had 2-year-old siblings and half did not. The subjects with siblings were run twice on the task, once with their own brother or sister and again with a nonsibling, as a control for experience in talking with 2-year-olds. In addition, all 4-year-olds were given a series of tests of egocentrism. The children performed poorly on the egocentrism tasks, as predicted by the literature. Yet all the 4-year-olds adjusted their speech for 2-year-olds, making it shorter, syntactically simpler, with more "attentional utterances" (e.g., "Hey, look . . . "). Children without siblings also adjusted their speech, and the 4-year-olds with sibs performed similarly for both their own sibling and the nonsib. Hence lengthy experience with a 2-year-old child is not solely responsible for the tendency to simplify input.

In a second study spontaneous speech by the same children with adults was compared with the 4-year-olds' spontaneous speech to 2-year-olds. Again the subjects simplified their utterances for the younger listener. A third study compared child-adult conversations with speech between two 4-year-olds. The same phenomenon of speech adjustment did not occur with children the same age. Hence, at least in this study, "motherese" is reserved for the 2-year-old listeners.

Andersen and Johnson (1973) reported the same kind of speech adjustment in a study of an 8-year-old girl conversing with adults, peers, and younger children at 5, 3, and 1½ years of age. The subject's mean length of utterance (MLU) increased directly with the age of listener. The number of utterances used to explain a block-stringing task decreased directly with age, from 125 instructions to the 1½-year-old to 14 instructions to an adult. In free play and task situations (but not in a storytelling task), vocabulary was also more limited for the younger listeners. Finally, on the basis of sound spectographic analyses, the authors reported that the child's prosodic contours are more exaggerated in utterances addressed to younger children. (Note that in this study, as compared with the work of Shatz and Gelman, speech to an 8-year-old peer differs from speech to adults.)

Both the studies just cited confirm anecdotal reports by Slobin (1972) and Gleason (1973) that children use another speech "register" when addressing very young children. We can conclude that children do indeed receive a simplified model of their language from older children as well as from adults. Hence in cultures where children spend most of their time in peer groups, they are also exposed to the advantages of "motherese."

These studies raise another question concerning the process whereby older children learn to speak this special dialect. It is possible that they do not speak a dialect at all but are simply adjusting their speech reactively throughout an interaction, on the basis of feedback from the listener. This would not be at all surprising if we consider evidence from Bates, Camaioni, and Volterra (1973) that infants from 11 to 16 months are able to augment and/or recombine their preverbal signals if adults fail to understand their commands. Consider the following example:

"Marta (16 months) is unable to open a small purse, and places it in front of her father's hand which is resting on the floor. F does nothing, so M puts the purse in his hand and utters a series of small sounds, looking at F. F still does not react, and M insists, pointing to the purse and whining. F asks 'What do I have to do?' M again points to the purse, looks at F, and makes a series of small sounds. Finally, F touches the purse clasp and simultaneously says 'Should I open it?' Marta nods sharply. . . . " (p. 29).

Hence one might view "motherese" as a trial-and-error discovery by children who are trying to communicate with a rather incompetent speaker of their language. Sachs and Devin (1974) recently carried out a study to determine whether children know a priori how to adjust their speech or whether they react on the basis of feedback. They examined the conversations of six 2- to 5-year-olds with peers and with younger children, and generally replicated the results of Shatz and Gelman. But they also added two conditions: in one the child was asked to pretend to talk with a baby doll "who is just learning to talk"; in another the subject role-played speech to a doll representing a child the subject's own age. These last two conditions of course preclude the possibility that the child adjusts his speech on the basis of cues from the listener. In the role-playing situation with the baby doll, children also adjusted their speech in the predicted directions. Sachs and Devin conclude that 2- to 5-year-olds have a separate register for speaking with younger children and will use that register even in the absence of listener feedback.

Sachs and Devin also suggest that since children in many cultures must depend on the peer group for most of their linguistic input, the ability to tailor speech to younger children may be part of the human "specialization" for language acquisition. This does not mean, however, that such an ability is specific to humans. Gardner and Gardner (personal communication) report that Washoe, the chimpanzee who has mastered part of American Sign Language, also uses two different "registers" for two classes of listeners. When communicating with one of the familiar laboratory assistants or experimenters, Washoe signs rapidly with abbreviated forms of the original signals. When trying to communicate with a new laboratory assistant or other outsiders, she signs slowly, using the complete version of each sign. It is not clear from this evidence whether Washoe is responding to listener feedback or whether she begins from the outset to assign the "slow" register to a new listener. It is clear, however, that this nonhuman speaker possesses as part of her communicative competence different mechanisms for different listeners.

To summarize thus far, it appears that children who receive most of their linguistic input from peers are at a relative disadvantage when compared with children who learn primarily from adults. Since both mothers and children use syntactically simpler, shorter utterances for younger children, it is unlikely that this difference is due to the relative grammaticality or complexity of adult versus child speech. Instead the differential effect may be attributable to the relative egocentrism of child-child speech. This would include the socially undirected input from private, task-centered speech and from word play. However the most crucial variable may be the failure of speakers to take the listener into account in socially motivated utterances. As a result, children talking with one another are often in the same position as adults reading the Watergate transcripts. Without sufficient understanding of the speaker's presuppositions and the situational context, linguistic input loses a great deal of its meaning. Also, small children fail to produce and/or react to nonverbal or implicit verbal cues from the listener that a message has failed. Thus child partners do not always force each other into confronting the failure of egocentric messages. Peers are not entirely unresponsive to their listeners' needs, however. They know enough to tailor their utterances in some ways to the limited capacities of a much younger listener.

One final point concerning peer language has not been covered at all in this chapter. So far I have treated peer versus adult language as variants within a single language code. For many children, this statement is applicable. For other children, particularly in large urban centers, peers may speak a very different dialect from adults, or at least from such relevant adult figures as teachers. In such cases the relative merits of peer versus adult input is also heavily influenced by sociological factors.

Labov (1973) has spent many years studying dialects in northern urban centers, particularly what has come to be known as Black English. One important contribution of his work has been the establishment of Black English as a separate dialect, a language with grammatical rules that differ systematically from the standard English dialect. Hence the black ghetto child taught by middle-class teachers (including middle-class blacks) must master a second language to get along well in school. A related contribution by Labov regards the effect of different speaking situations on the use of Black English, standard American, and a number of variants in between. As the formality of the situation increases, speakers are more likely to shift toward the standard dialect accepted by the white society. In many cases a speaker who is not fluent in the standard dialect may overgeneralize the rules that he does know, resulting in characteristic "hypercorrections." Labov has eloquent documentation of the discomfort some black speakers feel in situations requiring a shift toward formal speech. Many children simply restrict speech altogether, answering in monosyllables or not at all, thus fueling the interpretation by some researchers that they are "nonverbal" beings. By reducing the formality of the situation and carrying on interviews that include one or more of the subject's peers, Labov obtained long, rich samples of the black dialect from these supposedly "nonverbal" children. Hence we see that verbal expression is greatly facilitated by the presence of peers and by other factors indicating that the child's own dialect is acceptable.

Some of the same factors may influence comprehension as well as production. Peisach (1965) presented samples of peer versus teacher utterances to children from varied social backgrounds. The utterances had words deleted, and children were asked to supply the missing words. Although social class correlated significantly with performance (i.e., middle-class children performed better than lower-class children on both types of utterance), lower-class whites and blacks alike were penalized less by speech samples drawn from the speech of children from similar backgrounds.

These circumstances present school boards with political problems that have no easy solutions. Should children be forced into speaking the dialect accepted by the larger society? Or should they be encouraged to use the speech register in which they are most fluent? This is not a uniquely American problem. Cremona and Bates (in preparation) have investigated knowledge of linguistic "inferiority" in lower-class, rural children in Italy. They presented pairs of sentences in dialect and in standard Italian, asking children to decide which one was "better." Both phonological and lexical variants were used. First graders in the first months of school selected the standard variant as "better" more than 80% of the time. By grade 5, discrimination had reached 100%. Yet on a series of production tasks, Cremona and Bates found that the same children clearly spoke the dialect that they themselves had learned to scorn. By grade 5, children had shifted only slightly toward the standard dialect, primarily on lexical items. The implications of these findings for the child's sense of self-esteem are clear. The child has somehow learned to place a negative value on the form of speech that he himself uses.

In the cases presented, we can presume that the language the child speaks with peers is shared by at least some of the adults in the child's environment. There are more extreme situations, particularly in immigrant communities, in which the language of the parents is altogether different from that of the child's peer group. Such settings provide an ideal natural experiment on the effect of peers versus adults on language acquisition. However there are a number of powerful political questions involved in such research. Labov has suggested that in such circumstances the child will generally adopt the dialect of the peer group. Kazakis (1970) obtained very different results in a study of Turkish children in a Greek urban community, where a strong positive value is placed by parents on the dialect spoken in the home. In these circumstances, despite pressure from peers, the children retain their dialect through adolescence. Both Labov and Cremona and Bates have reported on situations in which the peer group influences the child's linguistic productions, whereas certain adults (e.g., teachers) influence the child's evaluation of his own productions. In the case reported by Kazakis, on the other hand, adults (in this case parents) determine both the dialect that the child speaks and his evaluation of that dialect, despite negative pressure by peers. Hence the effect of peers versus adults on language may involve not only the structural conditions discussed earlier but the emotional value that the child attaches to his speech. When peers and adults speak versions of the same linguistic code (e.g., among middle-class American speakers of English), we may feel free to investigate the cognitive and structural aspects of peer versus adult speech without asking a great many subtle political and sociological questions. When adults and peers speak different codes or even different languages, however, it is essential that we also investigate factors that may contribute to the emotional value attached by the child to one of those two codes.

SUGGESTIONS FOR FUTURE RESEARCH

Tentative answers have been provided for some of the questions raised at the outset. It seems fair to conclude that peer language is a somewhat less efficient model for language learning than input from adults. The reasons for this difference are less clear. The data on "motherese" indicate that adults speak a simplified version of their language to children. Some recent studies reveal that older children (including 4-year-olds addressing 2-year-olds) also speak a version of "motherese." It is probably not true that the adults are better partners for language acquisition simply because they "talk better."

I have put forth the hypothesis that a high proportion of speech with other children is less useful in language acquisition because of the relative egocentrism of messages from other children and because children are less competent in giving and receiving "listener cues." Some of the investigators mentioned in this chapter insist that the problem of egocentrism versus role taking has been greatly exaggerated. In some cases this is probably true. There are studies that have treated role taking as a single operation, an all-or-none capacity that may be absent in child speech until as late as 8 or even 13 years of age. However more recent studies of role taking (e.g., Selman, 1971) propose instead that there is more than one level of role taking, differing in the number of recursive operations and in the kinds of perspective shifts required by a given task. This theory has important implications for language acquisition, particularly the area of language referred to as "pragmatics," or rules involving speakers, listeners, and the context of speech.

To illustrate, the class of possible presuppositions that a speaker can use in trying to convey information is potentially infinite. It should not be surprising that children can predict their listener's knowledge on some presuppositions with great ease, although they fail to account adequately for others. A child may know perfectly well, for example, that listener A has witnessed event X and listener B has not. Halliday (1973) observes that his 1½-year-old son used two different intonation patterns in describing an event that the listener had seen, versus an event that the listener had not seen. Other more subtle presuppositions may not be so manageable. For example, a child narrating a long story may use the pronoun "he" to refer to two different characters, without being aware that the listener has confused the two antecedents.

There has been a great deal of recent linguistic research on the nature and role of presuppositions in language and on different classes of presuppositions. Just as transformational grammar provided useful heuristics for investigations of child syntax, recent pragmatic research in linguistics may be of great value in investigations of egocentrism versus role taking in child speech. In particular, it would be possible to view the mastery of different kinds of presuppositions as a subset of the kinds of material that children handle at different stages in the development of role taking. Future research on what has previously been viewed as homogeneous "egocentric speech" should include an evaluation of the different kinds of presuppositions and conversational rules violated by children at different stages of development.

Second, there may be similar developmental shifts in the kinds of information that children can draw from listener feedback *after* a presupposition has misfired. In fact, the whole area of production and comprehension of listener cues deserves a great deal of further research, including both verbal and non-verbal conversational rules.

Third, further comparisons of peer versus adult input may indicate, as Piaget (1926) predicted, that for some kinds of presuppositions adults may be *too* helpful. Adults are so good at retrieving the child's presuppositions that they may fail to force him to confront his communicative inefficiency. A doting mother who second-guesses all her child's needs, acting on even the most minimal requests, may retard the child's progress toward greater explicitness in speech. At the same time, peers, by failing to retrieve information from requests or other matters that are important to the speaker, may pressure the egocentric child toward a greater mastery of conversational principles. The role of peers versus adults may also be related to the child's developmental level. For some acquisitions input from peers could be particularly useful. For others the child may profit more from conversation with adults. In short, we need a more structured, qualitative theory of linguistic pragmatics as it affects language acquisition.

A particularly fruitful area for research on peer versus adult language is the bilingual community, where peers and adults speak altogether different codes. With regard to structural aspects of language development, it would be interesting to note whether a given grammatical structure (e.g., request forms, spatial and temporal locatives) is acquired first in the language spoken by the child's peers or first in the language he hears from his parents. However a great deal of caution is necessary in interpreting such results. Whenever a child is exposed to more than one linguistic code, it is necessary to take into account the emotional or social value that he places on each language.

It is no easy matter to determine the role of the school or other adult interventions in any of these situations. Often there are sensitive political questions involved that psychologists cannot answer, at least not in their roles as psychologists. If the child is tormented by his peers because of the language he speaks, should we intervene? Does the school have a right or a responsibility to teach a child one code when his peer group and his parents place a high value on another? These are often ethical questions without easy answers. But we should at least have a better grasp of the processes by which peer versus adult codes are acquired, in case we are ever called on to help.

References

Alvy, K. Relationship of age to children's egocentric and cooperative communication. *Journal of Genetic Psychology,* 1968, **112** (2), 225–286.

Andersen, E., & Johnson, C. Modifications in the speech of an 8 year old as a reflection of age of listener. *Stanford Occasional Papers,* Spring 1973.

Antinucci, F., & Volterra, V. Lo sviluppo della negazione nel linguaggio infantile: Uno studio pragmatico. In *Studi per un modello del linguaggio: Quaderni della Ricerca Scientifica.* Rome: CNR, Istituto di Psicologia, 1973.

Baldwin, T., McFarlane, P., & Garvey, C. Children's communicative accuracy as related to race and socioeconomic status. *Child Development,* 1971, **42,** 345–357.

Bates, E. The development of conversational skills in 2, 3 and 4 year olds. Unpublished master's thesis, University of Chicago, 1971.

Bates, E. *Language and context: Studies in the acquisition of pragmatics.* Unpublished doctoral thesis, University of Chicago, 1974.

Bates, E., Camaioni, L., & Volterra, V. The acquisition of performatives prior to speech. Laboratory technical report no. 129, Istituto di Psicologia, Rome, 1973.

Beeker, G. Ability to differentiate message from source and birth order and subject-sex interaction. *Psychological Reports,* 1968, **23,** 658.

Bernstein, B. Elaborated and restricted codes: Their social origins and some consequences. In A. G. Smith (Ed.), *Communication and culture.* New York: Holt, Rinehart & Winston, 1966.

Blount, B. G. The acquisition of language by Luo children. Unpublished doctoral thesis, University of California at Berkeley, 1969.

Borke, H. Interpersonal perception of young children. *Developmental Psychology,* 1971, **5,** 263–269.

Borke, H. Chandler and Greenspan's "ersatz egocentrism": A rejoinder. *Developmental Psychology,* 1972, **7** (2), 107–109.

Bragg, B., Ostrowski, M., & Finley, G. The effects of birth order and age of target on the use of persuasive techniques. *Child Development,* 1973, **44,** 351–354.

Breland, H. Birth order effects: A reply to Schooler. *Psychological Bulletin,* 1973, **80,** 210–212.

Broen, P. The verbal environment of the language learning child. *ASHA Monographs,* no. 17. Washington, D.C., 1972.

Bruggemann, C. Twins: Early grammatical development. *Folia Phoniatica,* 1970, **22** (3), 197–215.

Cazden, C. The neglected situation in child language research and education. In F. Williams (Ed.), *Language and poverty.* Chicago: Markham, 1970.

Cazden, C. Play with language and metalinguistic awareness: One dimension of language experience. *Urban Review,* 1974, **7** (1), 23–39.

Chandler, M., & Greenspan, S. Ersatz egocentrism: A reply to H. Borke. *Developmental Psychology,* 1972, **7,** 104–106.

Chomsky, N. *Aspects of a theory of syntax.* Cambridge, Mass.: MIT Press, 1965.

Cicirelli, V. The effect of sibling relationship on concept learning of young children taught by child teacher. *Child Development,* 1972, **43,** 282–287.

Cicirelli, V. Effect of sibling structure and interaction on children's categorization style. *Developmental Psychology,* 1973, **9** (1), 132–139.

Clausen, J. Family structure, socialization, and personality. In L. W. Hoffman and M. L. Hoffman (Eds.), *Review of child development research.* New York: Russell Sage Foundation, 1966.

Cremona, C., & Bates, E. Preference for dialect and standard Italian in rural Italian children. In preparation.

Dales, R. J. Motor and language development of twins during the first 3 years. *Journal of Genetic Psychology,* 1969, **114** (2), 263–271.

Davis, E. A. The development of linguistic skill in twins, singletons with siblings and only children from age five to ten years. *Institute of Child Welfare Monographs,* no. 14, 1937.

Day, E. The development of language in twins: I. A comparison of twins, and single children. *Child Development,* 1932, **3,** 179–199.

Deutsch, F. Observational and sociometric measures of peer popularity and their relationship to egocentric communication in female pre-schoolers. *Developmental Psychology,* 1974, **10,** 745–747.

DeVries, R. The development of role-taking as reflected by behavior of bright, average and retarded children in a social guessing game. *Child Development,* 1970, **41,** 759–771.

Dittman, A. Developmental factors in conversational behavior. *Journal of Communication,* 1972, **22** (4), 404–433.

Drach, K. The language of the parent: A pilot study. In Working Paper no. 14, *The structure of linguistic input to children.* Language Behavior Research Laboratory, University of California at Berkeley, 1969.

Elkind, D. Egocentrism in adolescence. *Child Development,* 1967, **38,** 1025–1034.

Ervin-Tripp, E. An analysis of the interaction between subject, topic and listener. In J. A. Fishman (Ed.), *Readings in the sociology of language.* The Hague: Mouton, 1968.

Farwell, C. The language spoken to children. In *Papers and reports on child language development*, Vols. 5 & 6, Stanford University, April 1973.

Fay, W. H. Marathon monologues of a 3 year old. *Journal of Communication Disorders*, 1967, **1** (1), 41–45.

Feffer, M. H., & Gourevitch, V. Cognitive aspects of role-taking in children. *Journal of Personality*, 1960, **28**, 383–396.

Feitelson, D., Weintraub, S., & Michali, O. Social interactions in heterogeneous preschools in Israel. *Child Development*, 1972, **43**, 1249–1259.

Fishbein, H. D. The effects of feedback variation on referential communication of children. *Merrill-Palmer Quarterly*, 1971, **17** (3), 243–250.

Flavell, J. H., Botkin, P. T., Fry, C. L., Jr., Wright, J. W., & Jarvis, P. E. *The development of role-taking and communicative skills in children.* New York: Wiley, 1968.

Fry, C. L. Training children to communicate with listeners. *Child Development*, 1966, **37**, 675–685.

Fry, C. L. Training children to communicate with listeners who have varying listener requirements. *Journal of Genetic Psychology*, 1969, **114**, 155–166.

Gardner, R., & Gardner, B. Personal communication.

Garvey, C., & Hogan, R. Social speech and social interaction: Egocentrism revisited. *Child Development*, 1973, **44**, 562–568.

Gleason, J. Code-switching in children's language. In T. E. Moore (Ed.), *Cognitive development and the acquisition of language*. New York: Academic Press, 1973.

Glucksberg, S., & Krauss, R. What do people say after they have learned to talk? *Merrill-Palmer Quarterly*, 1967, **13**, 309–316.

Hahn, E. Analyses of the content and form of the speech of first grade children. *Quarterly Journal of Speech*, 1948, **34**, 361–366.

Halliday, M. A. K. Early language learning: A sociolinguistic approach. Paper prepared for the Ninth International Congress of Anthropological and Ethnological Sciences, Chicago, 1973.

Hanlon, C. The effects of social isolation and characteristics of the model on accent imitation in 4th grade children. *Journal of Experimental Child Psychology*, 1971, **11** (2), 322–336.

Hess, R., & Shipman, V. Early experience and the socialization of cognitive modes in children. *Child Development*, 1965, **36**, 869–888.

Hoemann, H. The development of communicative skills in deaf and hearing children. *Child Development*, 1972, **43** (3), 990–1003.

Howard, R. W. The language development of a group of triplets. *Journal of Genetic Psychology*, 1946, **69**, 181–188.

Hoy, E. The measurement of egocentrism in children's communications. In press.

Hsiao, H. The status of the first born with specific reference to intelligence. *Genetic Psychology Monographs*, 1931, **9**, 1–118.

Johnson, H. M. *Children in "The Nursery School."* New York: Agathon Press, 1972. (First published 1928.)

Kadar, J. Vocabulary and the development of the frequency of word types in the speech of 3–6 year old children in the course of the solving of verbal tasks and communication (in Hungarian). *Altalanos Nyelveszeti Tanulmanyok,* 1969, **2,** 149–159.

Kaplan, E., & Yonas, P. Communicative requirements and children's production of relational words. *Journal of Experimental Child Psychology,* 1967, **5,** 142–151.

Kazakis, K. The relative importance of parents and peers in first language acquisition: The case of some Constantinopolitan families in Athens. *General Linguistics,* 1970, **10** (2), 111–120.

Kernan, K. The acquisition of language by Samoan children. Unpublished doctoral dissertation, University of California at Berkeley, 1969.

Kim, C. C., Dales, R. J., Connor, R., Wallins, J., & Witherspoon, R. Social interaction of like-sex twins and singletons in relation to intelligence, language and physical development. *Journal of Genetic Psychology,* 1969, **114,** 203–214.

Koch, H. L. Twins and only children. *Psychologische Beitrage,* 1968, **16** (3), 431–445.

Kohlberg, L., Yaeger, J., & Hjertholm, E. Private speech: Four studies and a review of theories. *Child Development,* 1968, **39,** 691–736.

Krauss, R., & Glucksberg, S. The development of communication: Competence as a function of age. *Child Development,* 1969, **40,** 255–266.

Labov, W. The logic of non-standard English. In F. Williams (Ed.), *Language and poverty.* Chicago: Markham, 1970.

Laing, R. D. *Knots.* New York: Pantheon Books, 1970.

Langlois, J., Gottfried, N., & Sear, B. The influence of sex of peer on the social behavior of preschool children. *Developmental Psychology,* 1973, **8,** 93–98.

Longhurst, T., & Turnure, J. Perceptual inadequacy and communicative ineffectiveness in interpersonal communication. *Child Development,* 1971, **42** (6), 2084–2088.

Looft, W. Egocentrism and social interaction across the lifespan. *Psychological Bulletin,* 1972, **78** (2), 73–92.

Luria, A., & Yadovitch, F. *Speech and the development of mental processes in the child.* London: Staples, 1959.

Maratsos, M. Non-egocentric communicative abilities in preschool children. *Child Development,* 1973, **44,** 697–700.

Marvin, R. Attachment behavior, cooperation and communication skills in 2, 3 and 4 year olds. Unpublished doctoral thesis, University of Chicago, 1972.

Masangkay, Z., McCluskey, K., McIntyre, C., Sims-Knight, J., Vaughn, B., & Flavell, J. The early development of inferences about the visual percepts of others. *Child Development,* 1974, **45,** 357–366.

McCarthy, D. Research in language development. In L. Carmichael (Ed.), *Manual of child psychology.* New York: Wiley, 1954.·

McFadden, J. A further note on the differential IQ of siblings. *Journal of Applied Psychology,* 1929, **13,** 86–91.

McNeill, D. Developmental psycholinguistics. In F. Smith & G. A. Miller (Eds.), *The genesis of language.* Cambridge, Mass.: MIT Press, 1966.

Miller, P., Kessel, F., & Flavell, J. Thinking about people thinking about people thinking about people . . . A study of cognitive-social development. *Child Development,* 1970, **41,** 613–625.

Mitchell-Kernan, C. Language behavior in a black urban community. *Monographs of the Language Behavior Research Laboratory* no. 2, University of California at Berkeley, 1971.

Mittler, P. Genetic aspects of psycholinguistic abilities. *Journal of Child Psychology and Psychiatry,* 1969, **10,** 165–176.

Moore, T. Language and intelligence: A longitudinal study of the first 8 years. Part II: Environmental correlates of mental growth. *Human Development,* 1968, **11,** 1–24.

Mueller, E. The maintenance of verbal exchanges between young children. *Child Development,* 1972, **43** (3), 930–938.

Nelson, K. Structure and strategy in learning to talk. *SRCD Monographs,* 1973, Vol. 38 (1 & 2).

Parisi, D., & Genelli, W. In preparation.

Peisach, C. Children's comprehension of teacher and peer speech. *Child Development,* 1965, **36,** 467–481.

Peterson, C., Danner, F., & Flavell, J. Developmental changes in children's response to three indications of communicative failure. *Child Development,* 1972, **43,** 1463–1468.

Phillips, J. Formal characteristics of speech which mothers address to their young children. Unpublished doctoral dissertation, Johns Hopkins University, 1970.

Piaget, J. *The language and thought of the child.* London: Routledge & Kegan Paul, 1926.

Piaget, J. *The construction of reality by the child.* New York: Basic Books, 1954.

Piaget, J. Comments on Vygotsky's critical remarks. In L. Vygotsky, *Thought and language.* Cambridge, Mass.: MIT Press, 1962.

Piaget, J. *The moral judgment of the child.* New York: Free Press, 1964.

Piaget, J., & Inhelder, B. *The child's conception of space.* London: Routledge & Kegan Paul, 1956.

Rosenberg, B., & Sutton-Smith, B. The relation of ordinal position and sibling sex status to cognitive abilities. *Psychonomic Science,* 1964, **1,** 81–82.

Rosenberg, B., & Sutton-Smith, B. Siblings' association, family size, and cognitive abilities. *Journal of Genetic Psychology,* 1966, **109,** 271–279.

Rothenberg, B. Children's social sensitivity. *Developmental Psychology,* 1970, **2,** 335–350.

Rubin, K. Relationship between egocentric communication and popularity among peers. *Developmental Psychology,* 1972, **3,** 364.

Rubin, K. Egocentrism in childhood: A unitary concept? *Child Development,* 1973, **44,** 102–111.

Rubin, K., Hultsch, D., & Peters, D. Non-social speech in 4 year old children as a function of birth order and interpersonal situation. *Merrill-Palmer Quarterly,* 1971, **17,** 41–51.

Sachs, J., Brown, R., & Salerno, R. Adults' speech to children. In W. von Raffler Engel (Ed.), *Proceedings of the International Conference on First Language Acquisition.* The Hague: Mouton. In press.

Sachs, J., & Devin, J. Young children's knowledge of age-appropriate speech styles. Paper presented to the Linguistic Society of America, December 1973.

Sampson, E. E. The study of ordinal position: Antecedents and outcomes. In B. Maher (Ed.), *Progress in experimental personality research.* Vol. II. New York: Academic Press, 1965.

Scarlett, H., Press, A., & Crockett, W. Children's descriptions of peers: A Wernerian developmental analysis. *Child Development,* 1971, **42,** 439–453.

Schooler, C. Birth order effects: Not here, not now! *Psychological Bulletin,* 1972, **78,** 161–175.

Scollon, R. The acquisition of discourse. Unpublished doctoral thesis, University of Hawaii, 1973.

Selman, R. Taking another's perspective: Role-taking development in early childhood. *Child Development,* 1971, **42,** 1721–1734.

Shantz, C., & Watson, J. Spatial abilities and spatial egocentrism in the young child. *Child Development,* 1971, **42,** 171–183.

Shantz, C., & Wilson, K. Training communication skills in young children. *Child Development,* 1972, **43,** 693–698.

Shatz, M., & Gelman, R. The development of communication skills: Modifications in the speech of young children as a function of the listener. *SRCD Monographs,* 1973, no. 5, Vol. 38.

Silvern, L. Cognitive role-taking and social development. In preparation.

Sinclair, H. On pre-speech. In *Papers and reports on Child Language Development.* Stanford University Committee on Linguistics, 1974.

Slobin, D. On the nature of talk to children. In E. & E. Lenneberg (Eds.), *Foundations of language development: A multidisciplinary approach.* In press; manuscript circulated 1972.

Smith, M. E. The influence of sex, age and situation of the frequency, form and function of questions asked by preschool children. *Child Development,* 1933, **4,** 201–213.

Snow, C. E. Mothers' speech to children learning language. *Child Development,* 1972, **43,** 549–565.

Soskin, W., & John, V. The study of spontaneous talk. In R. Barker (Ed.), *The stream of behavior.* New York: Appleton-Century-Crofts, 1963.

Sutton-Smith, B., & Rosenberg, B. G. *The sibling.* New York: Holt, Rinehart & Winston, 1970.

Svenka Savic, M. A., & Jocic, M. Some features of the dialogue of twins. Unpublished paper, Institute for Linguistics, Novi Sad, 1972.

Thurstone, L., & Jenkins, R. Birth order and intelligence. *Journal of Educational Research,* 1929, **20,** 641–651.

Tizard, B., Cooperman, O., Joseph, A., & Tizard, J. Environmental effects on language development: A study of children in long-stay residential nurseries. *Child Development,* 1972, **43,** (2), 337–358.

Vygotsky, L. S. *Thought and language.* Cambridge, Mass.: MIT Press, 1962.

Weeks, T. Speech registers in young children. *Child Development,* 1971, **41,** 1119–1131.

Weinheimer, S. Egocentrism and social influence in children. *Child Development,* 1972, **43,** 567–578.

Weir, R. *Language in the crib.* The Hague: Mouton, 1962.

Wertsch, J. Simply speaking. *Papers from the Tenth Regional Meetings of the Chicago Linguistic Society,* Chicago, April 1974.

The Whitehouse Transcripts. Published by *The New York Times,* 1973.

Zazzo, R. Les jumeaux: Le couple et la personne. Paris: Presses Universitaires de France, 1960.

CHAPTER 11

General Issues in the Study of Peer Relations

SOME PROPOSALS FOR UNIFYING THE STUDY OF SOCIAL DEVELOPMENT

Harriet L. Rheingold
Department of Psychology
University of North Carolina

Carol O. Eckerman
Department of Psychology
Duke University

The opportunity to participate in this volume stimulated us to try to set forth some proposals that might integrate what we know about the behavior of the infant and the young child with mother and father and what we are finding out about their behavior with peers. It will be recalled that in reviewing the data on peer relations, Hartup (1970) pointed to the need for integrating theory about the development of peer relations with more general principles of behavioral development. Peers are people too, and one set of proposals encompassing all the people in the child's life would be desirable.

In formulating these proposals we realized that the diversity of the infant's social encounters is largely neglected in our study of early social development. We lack even descriptions of his social encounters with the majority of the people composing his social world. Rather, separate lines of study have evolved, each based on the infant's encounters with a single kind of social object. One line of study, attachment, typically treats the infant's interactions with only his mother, although recently we have begun to include fathers. A second line, fear of strangers, focuses on unfamiliar adults who in most studies force their actions on the infant with little attention to his behavior. A third line, peer relations, studies the actions of young children together, usually at play in nursery schools, kindergarten, or the primary grades. To limit a study of early social development to attachment to mother ignores the infant's many experiences with others. To consider other adults only as strangers who evoke fear or wariness ignores the variety of pleasant encounters an infant may have with adults outside the immediate family. To begin the study of peer relations when the child is 3, 4, or 5 years of age, as is usual, ignores his earliest experiences with

293

other children, including those with siblings. (We note with appreciation that the contributors to this book did study younger children.)

The proposals, then, seek to account for the infant's and young child's behavior with the people in his environment, regardless of the age or particular roles of these people. The statement is still in a preliminary form and perhaps naive in its claims, but to us it carries the promise of a framework for a fuller exposition.

The infant is the subject of the proposals that follow, but they apply as well to the older child. Although the *human* infant is the focal point, the proposals can be extended, at least in part, to the young of other mammalian species. And some of the proposals are general enough to include the infant's behavior with nonsocial as well as social objects.

Proposal 1.   The infant from a very early age not only responds to the people in his environment but also initiates interactions with them.

This proposal only sets the stage for the other proposals. It warrants full documentation at some time; but for the present, since its meaning is clear and noncontroversial, we refer to some previous although still partial statements (Rheingold, 1966, 1969).

Proposal 2.   The environment of the average infant and young child contains many persons—specifically, others besides the mother.

Every mammalian infant is social by biological origin and is born into a social environment. At the least he is a member of a dyad, his mother being the other. The number and characteristics of other members vary by species, but for the modal human infant the social environment is composed of a larger group—a family of mother, father, and often one or more siblings. He is, at the same time, a member of a larger family group including aunts, uncles, cousins, and grandparents. Still other groups of persons are also members of his social environment: doctors and nurses, baby-sitters, friends of the family, and neighbors, both adults and children. Thus from a very early age most infants are exposed to and have encounters with many other members of their species—with people of all ages.

Proposal 3.   Both the initiating and responsive behaviors of the infant to these persons are a function of the stimulus properties of the persons. Their behavioral repertoires, and their experiences with him, as well as his with them, are subsumed under their stimulus properties.

This proposal has proved the hardest to state but only because it encompasses so much. It means that each person in the infant's environment combines a set of physical attributes, the set of responses of which he is capable, and a history of past encounters with the infant. The infant responds to each person (and also initiates interactions with that person) in terms of the person's individual combination of these three classes of attributes. Each person's past encounters with the infant are also a function of the infant's similar combination of physical attributes, his behavioral repertoire, and his past encounters with that person. The infant of course early acquires the ability to perceive similarities and differences among the various persons in his environment.

Proposal 4.   The stimulus properties of people (as inclusive as set forth in Proposal 3) can be specified; they are knowable.

This proposal may seem like idle fancy, but people after all belong to the real, not the mystical, world, and their properties, behaviors, and encounters with the infant, as well as his with them, can be named. It is to the specification of these classes of events that we all bend our efforts.

One stimulus property could spell the difference between social objects and all others. For example, people are more often active and present stimulus change as they behave. They come and go; they initiate and respond. In contrast to nonsocial objects, they behave in more variable ways and more often in apparently unpredictable ways.

Next we could specify a factor previously mentioned, the powerful stimulus dimension of the child's history of experiences with a person, or the lack thereof—a history of exposure and interaction with that person. Of course we are speaking first of *familiarity* and second of the nature of the *interchanges* between the person and child during the periods of familiarization.

Familiarity by itself is probably a weak stimulus dimension of social objects, although it cannot be completely written off. But familiar stimulus objects, if they are people, are not static. The stimulus change they normally provide as they move and speak may enhance sheer familiarity within a framework of sameness. Thus the social object may be at once familiar and yet always changing, providing inconsistency within consistency, and variety within sameness. This is stimulus change par excellence.

The next steps entail setting forth the stimulus properties of different *classes* of persons (e.g., caretakers, adults, peers) and of different *persons* within each class, such as mother, father, baby-sitter, and sibling, within the class of caretaker. A model is provided by Bijou and Baer's (1965) analysis of the stimulus components of the mother. Peers, for example, possess stimulus properties in many ways different from those of older children and adults. Their activity is often faster paced, and their voices are higher in pitch. In appearance and actions they are more similar to the infant himself than are adults. Their responses may well be more variable, hence less predictable. They may imitate and elaborate on the child's own actions more frequently than do adults.

Proposal 5.   Different persons present different sets of stimulus properties, but the sets possess some common elements; that is, the sets are not mutually exclusive.

We come now to the three proposals that constitute the heart of the matter. Although at one level of analysis every person in the child's environment possesses a unique set of stimulus properties and behavioral repertoires, as well as a unique history of prior encounters, at a more molar level no set is unique in all its elements. The sets are not mutually exclusive but share common elements. In particular, the set presented by the mother possesses some elements in common with that presented by the father or even by a sibling or peer.

The recent advances in classificatory theory hold promise here (Sokal, 1974). We are now ready to move from a monothetic classification of people—that is, establishing classes of people that differ by at least one property that is uniform among the members of each class (here, mothers in one class, peers in another)—to polythetic classifications that establish taxa of people in terms of the extent to which they share a large proportion of their properties but do not necessarily agree in any one property. If we adopt polythetic principles of classification, we eschew the concept of an essence or type of any taxon (e.g., the mother), since no single uniform property is required for defining a given group.

One way to develop the classification of persons in the child's life might be for students of the child's behavior to set them forth, based on observation and present knowledge and theory. Another—probably better, even if much more time-consuming—would be to use the child's behavior itself to organize the many persons in his life into classifications.

Proposal 6.   The infant responds to different persons with different sets of responses from the universe of responses at his command at any time. These sets also are not mutually exclusive but contain varying combinations of common elements.

As the characteristics of people can be organized into sets possessing some common elements—into clusters that may overlap—so the social behaviors of the child can be organized into sets possessing some common elements. At any one time in the life of the developing child he has in his repertoire a specifiable number of responses; that is, he is capable of a finite number of behaviors. The number increases with time and all that time brings; they are roughly age-dependent but they are also experience-dependent. From this population of responses he accords the different social objects in his environment different sets of responses. Thus as he distinguishes among people on the basis of their characteristics, including his history of experience with them, he responds with different sets of behaviors. In particular, he has not one set reserved exclusively for the mother, another for the father, and different sets for a peer, the neighbor, and so on; rather, each set shares some behaviors with others.

Just as the characteristics of people are specifiable, so are the infant's responses. They differ in kind, latency, frequency, duration, and sequence.

Some of his behaviors are initiating, some are responsive. Some are in response to a person's appearing, some to a person's departing, and some are elicited by other behaviors of the person. But the combinations or sets of responses to different persons overlap and even intersect. They can be classified into clusters, just like the stimulus properties of people.

Proposal 7.   The infant's responses to the people in his environment change continuously with maturity and experience.

That the infant's early experiences with those who care for him during the first year of life determine his later behavior toward all other people is still a hypothesis in need of examination. The statement is true only in the sense that every social encounter with any person modifies the next encounter with that or any other person, but not in the sense of any social encounter or even set of encounters persisting over time in an unmodified form with the power or energy to modify later encounters with new and varied persons. In particular, relations with a father do not develop out of relations with a mother; they develop concurrently. Relations with a peer or peers do not develop out of relations with a father; rather, relations with peers develop concurrently with relations with a mother and a father.

CONCLUSIONS

The proposals outlined here bear more verisimilitude to what happens in the life of the infant and the young child than the concepts we have used until now. The infant encounters more people than his mother in the first year of life, and more even than his father. Later when his behavior with peers begins to interest investigators, he still has a mother and a father. These proposals then allow for a smooth progression of social development, of changing responses to people of all kinds; thus they correct the discontinuous account now common in the literature.

These proposals also force an examination of the properties of social objects to discover their commonalities and differences, a more useful procedure than studying a social object (e.g., mother, stranger, peer) by itself. At the same time the proposals direct attention to the *interaction* between the infant's behavior and that of another person, advancing our efforts to a stage beyond the study of the effect of the caretaker's behavior on the infant, or even the effect of the infant's behavior on the caretaker.

The proposals, furthermore, bypass the constructs of attachment to the mother, with its attendant concepts of fear of the stranger and separation anxiety, and such other constructs as dependency and even the notion of separate affectional systems. We think these constructs have unnecessarily confined the study of social development. The proposals eliminate especially the current disjunctive approach that separates the concepts of peer relations and attachment.

We have but one subject, a child, who has social encounters with many different people. To be sure, the diversity of his behavior—its variety, complexity, and richness—becomes greater as he matures. Yet this diversity can be accounted for within our single set of proposals. The proposals thus offer a statement at once more parsimonious and more inclusive than we have had heretofore. Our proposals are truly developmental ones. Their commitment is to the study of the ontogeny of social behavior. The focus is on an adapting, not an adapted, organism.

References

Bijou, S. W., & Baer, D. M. *Child development.* Vol. 2. *Universal stage of infancy.* New York: Appleton-Century-Crofts, 1965.

Hartup, W. W. Peer interaction and social organization. In P. H. Mussen (Ed.), *Carmichael's manual of child psychology,* 3rd ed. Vol. 2. New York: Wiley, 1970.

Rheingold, H. L. The development of social behavior in the human infant. In H. W. Stevenson (Ed.), Concept of development. *Monograph of the Society for Research in Child Development,* 1966, **31,** No. 5 (serial no. 107).

Rheingold, H. L. The social and socializing infant. In D. A. Goslin (Ed.), *Handbook of socialization theory and research.* Chicago, Ill.: Rand McNally, 1969.

Sokal, R. R. Classification: Purposes, principles, progress, prospects. *Science,* 1974, **185,** 1115–1123.

SOME PERSPECTIVES ON RESEARCH ON PEER RELATIONS

Marian Radke Yarrow
Laboratory of Developmental Psychology
National Institute of Mental Health

In 1974 the subject of peer relations is frontier research. We are well aware that this volume was written to awaken or reawaken interest in this territory. Indeed it has been a long time since major research issues in developmental psychology have been joined with concern regarding peer attachments and peer relations. Only a few investigators have shown a steady interest in this area. The chapters in this book reflect the "newness" and uncertainty that most of us feel in formulating research and theory about peers in relation to child development. Most of the chapters are "tentative" and suggestive, posing more than solving problems and proposing rather than adopting established conceptualizations and theories.

At such a stage of knowledge a treatise of this type should be a forum in which ideas and data are exposed as much to "incite" interest and criticism as to present fully documented reports. My comments, therefore, are directed to the general conceptualizations, strategies, and problem interests. If a volume like this one affects the larger research community, it is likely to affect not only the density of research but also the characteristic directions and choices in research relating to peers. I should like, first, to think about the chapters in the context of the discipline of developmental psychology—historically and contemporaneously.

Peers are the life of people—not only of children. With the exception of the brief infancy and toddler years, the individual is likely to be with near-age mates for very considerable portions of his time and for very widely varying relationships. Closeness to some peer(s) and acceptance by one's peers are potent factors in the well-being of the individual. Why, then, has there been so little developmental study? Why is the interest appearing now? Why has it surfaced in the study of infants and very young children, periods of life when peers (in our society at least) are least prominent in the child's habitat? It takes only short reflection to arrive at some speculations.

The overriding influence of psychoanalytic theory and its derivatives (placing heavy emphasis on the caretaker relationship) is one. Unlike the mother-child attachment and relationship, the peer relationship is virtually barren of theory. Reinforcement theory, too, at least in the laboratory, has focused attention on the adult as the social reinforcer and determiner of child behavior. Furthermore, most efficient strategies and designs and techniques for investigating peer relationships have yet to be worked out. Studying peers in interaction presses the necessity for dealing with problems in dyadic or reciprocal terms, not as one-way influences, and this is difficult research.

Why is there now more interest in problems involving peers? Parenthetically, the present "discovery" of peers as a significant element of development and socialization can be overemphasized. The insightful and experienced educator has a wealth of data on peer influences and could undoubtedly supply us with a long list of hypotheses and questions. Likewise, as is true of most topics of development, the scholars of the 1930s were cognizant of peer influences, and their careful, though atheoretical, accounts provide groundwork for our return to the peer. Fortunately, a few investigators (Hartup, see Chapter 1) have not been deflected from research on peer interaction when the stronger tides in developmental studies have taken other courses. Is present interest a side-effect of some of the skeptical questions appearing in many quarters about the ultimate power and irreversibility of the early mother-child relationship? Have some of the attachment issues reached a kind of static level in research? Is it also conceivable that the great societal phenomenon of "peer culture" has fed questions to developmentalists, leading them to search for additional transmitters and pathways of development outside the traditional ones of parent-child relations? It seems quite probable, too, that the monumental work of the Harlows (see, e.g., Harlow & Harlow, 1965), which fired interest in the study of love (mother love), has likewise given impetus to the study of peer contacts and influences of peers on other juveniles.

We have indications of certain strong continuities between the research on peers and the research on infant-mother attachment and relations. The parallels are striking—in conceptualizations, variables, and designs. Thus in Hartup's formulation of friendship, the components of the relationship are: (a) seeking out each other, (b) reacting to separation, and (c) wishing to effect proximity. The variables in the experimental and observational studies of Mueller (Chapter 9), Lewis et al. (Chapter 2), Kagan et al. (Chapter 7), and Bronson (Chapter 5), are direct transfers from other-infant studies: proximity, touching, looking, smiling, offering a toy, and so on. Comparisons of reactions to the strange and the familiar peer are replicas of stranger-anxiety studies. In many of the research settings investigators have brought together the familiar configuration, child–other person–toy, with a peer substituted for mother. Analysis units tend to be subject child's responses directed to a peer, rather than units of interaction.

The continuity is a welcome state of affairs in some respects, a cause for concern in others. Among the strong positive aspects of continuity is the possibility of establishing replicating evidence and broadened bases of understanding of the very young child's comprehension, mastery, and effects in his social world. In this sense, Kagan's chapter is a good example. Tied directly to earlier evidence of separation anxiety involving mother and child are his data on the child's apprehension in the presence of a peer and his attempts to puzzle out this social object. Here, as in the other contexts, the experimenter derives evidence on the child's initial competencies in dealing with uncertainties and future events. Lee's statement (Chapter 8) of a cognitive framework for viewing and analyzing peer-peer behavior is another instance of good continuity with the body of data and theory on developmental processes. It is altogether likely that from such studies featuring the *peer* as subject matter, investigators will acquire sensitivities to different aspects of the developmental process, thus becoming able to provide feedback to research on infancy and infant-mother relations.

On a more critical note, one may raise the question of whether the research we described here is too heavily bound to the existing frameworks and interests in early development—locked to the problems and issues of mother-child research. We need also to consider the possibility that we may be confined to a comfortable, productive, but nonetheless restricted range of research problems and variables. We need to balance continuity in research with investigations that are born out of the uniqueness of the peer as a social object in the child's environment.

Because we are most concerned in this book with very young subjects, many issues worthy of inquiry revolve around *emerging* capabilities. Investigations could benefit by extending horizons in a number of ways. It would be illuminating, for example, to examine the differential responses to social peer objects and to impersonal objects in the environment—when both pose similar frustrations or satisfactions to the child (e.g., the infant is prevented from getting his toy by a peer's resistance or because the toy is wedged between two barriers). Likewise, it would be important to identify the distinctions in infants' and toddlers' responses toward peers and toward older humans (see Lewis et al., Chapter 2).

Sensitivities to the psychological qualities of peer objects are another realm in which developmentalists should investigate emergents. In the literature there are many assumptions about what the young child is aware of regarding the psychological states of others, and about when he has a sense of the Other and a sense of causality. These capabilities are, of course, very relevant for social exchange with peers and caretakers and for the child's sense of self as an effecter in his social environment.

In general, I think we have underestimated the "sensing" capacities of the tiny ones of the species. There are reasons for this: strongly held theoretical positions about developmental stages, few data and hard-to-obtain data, reliance on language development. What we are likely to conclude in our theoretical treatises about early sensitivities tends to be at variance with our anecdotal funds from our own or our friends' toddlers who, at least on one occasion, appear to have manifested remarkable psychological "insight" or compelling empathic ability. Somewhere between the treatise and the anecdote is a territory much in need of research.

My colleagues Carolyn Waxler and Robert King and I have been concerned with some of the problems posed here. My own yearnings to study these problems go back to a conviction of Kurt Lewin's regarding the child's early sensitivity to the social aspects of his environment (Lewin, 1942). Lewin cites an event of two 18-month-old children sitting opposite each other on a sandy beach. They are yelling for a banana that an adult is holding. When the banana is given to one child, she immediately feeds the open mouth of the other, then takes a big bite herself. Lewin was convinced that young children are often better able than adults to see through (or feel through) a social surface to the underlying condition. His provocative speculations, along with his discerning observations of children in support of his belief, provided a historical stimulant.

In our research we have chosen to get as close as possible to the beginnings of children's awareness and responsiveness to the affective qualities of social objects—peers and others. Three cohorts of children, beginning at ages 10, 15, and 20 months, were followed for 9 months. Through trained mothers we obtained systematic descriptions of day-to-day affective events (a parent's anger, a peer's fright, pain, joy, etc.). In addition, there were regular supplements of experimental, simulated, affective episodes.

The data with which one works in this domain are subject to multiple interpretations, and one must proceed temperately. In the context of this discussion I can relate only a small sampling of data and some beginnings of analysis. Brief anecdotes may convey the nature of the observations. A 15-month-old boy walks over to a 5-year-old who has been yelling at him, swats the older child and then ducks. A 10-month-old girl stares fixedly and solemnly as two 2-year-olds are hitting each other. A 22-month-old rubs his elbow after his mother responds to the pain from hurting her own elbow. When tears stream down a woman's face as she peels onions, her 25-month-old daughter looks up at her and says anxiously, "Mommy sad." At 12 months, S tries hard to protect mother from having her throat swabbed by the doctor. At 16 months, S comes into the living room and finds a friend (same age) sobbing; S becomes suddenly sober, walks over to friend, pats him, then picks up a toy and gives it to him. Father embraces mother; the 17-month-old begins to whine and tries to get between her parents. The dog sneezes, and S (18 months) gets a tissue to wipe the dog's nose.

Certainly children in the second year of life show many intriguing reactions to affect or inferred states in others. The children are not always responsive; they sometimes make errors in their assessments; they also get involved in sequences of responses and communications that would appear to imply a series of sensitive inferences regarding Other, Self, Other. Not infrequently the child "tries on" or reflects the affect he observes in the Other, then looks to the mother as if asking for confirmation: has he sized it up correctly? Sometimes it appears that events themselves propel the child into the activity with the Other (e.g., a peer is tugging hard to move something; a mother is singing to quiet a crying baby). Once the child is *in* the activity, the structure of the activity makes it interactive, with tones of affect. Although the child may not have initiated sympathy or help, he ends up feeling that way—or so it seems. This kind of event, which transforms the impersonal into the personal, would appear to be a significant route of learning.

From our data on children's interventions in events involving another person being hurt or angry or excited or feeling sad, we are looking for what may be identifiable maturational courses. At this stage of study, however, individualistic responses are more easily seen. Sadness in Other, for example, arouses very different reactions in these children. Some proceed with calm management of the situation; others show no response at all. In others one observes agitation, tender affection, approach-avoidance, keeping a wide physical distance but (from this safe position) trying to bring comfort. The analyses have only begun.

The contributors to this volume have legitimately concentrated their research on early development. I should like to express a strong feeling, however, about the relative emphases that now exist in developmental psychology regarding very young versus older children. In developmental psychology one hears little about human juveniles—until they are "delinquent." It is not that we need less study of infants, toddlers, and preschoolers, but that we need more investigation of the child from 6 years on. This is particularly important in the realm of peer relations. The discipline has been seriously injured by continuing to think in terms of "the latency period." Children are not dormant once they pass through preschool. Psychological processes continue to develop. Researchers studying cognitive development have, of course, been studying development through all of childhood. In learning experiments, too, older children are often the subjects. But data on the attachments, the affects, the broad domain of social development are relatively sparse and nonsystematic. From a theoretical point of view, it would seem to me a great advantage to have some investigators with knowledge and expertise about young children move up the age scale, thus guaranteeing developmental continuities. This appears highly preferable to, let us say, a transplantation of research problems based on the perspectives and orientations of experts in adult social psychology.

It seems of utmost importance that research into the functions and formations of peer relations be extended beyond the very early years. If and as we initiate research on peership in older children, we are likely to turn to the kinds of research problems that are already familiar. Our interests in adult effects—such as the effects of the adult model and the adult social reinforcer on the child behavior—are likely to reappear, with peers replacing adults. It is reasonable to investigate learning from age mates or adjacent age mates through imitation and reinforcement. At the same time we can be more penetrating in our questions. Yes, peers are models and reinforcers for peers. Can we also turn this kind of "process" question toward a number of important substantive social psychological aspects of development? One such mode of inquiry would involve investigation of developmentally changing potencies of adults and peers as models and reinforcers. We are reminded of Lewis' example of the preschooler who preferred the peer's description of God over the father's. Questions of parents versus peers as carriers of norms and values have a long history of interest, but the area could profit now from theoretically and methodologically more sophisticated approaches.

It is interesting to note that embedded in child development research over the years are many data on relations among peers: there are many studies of child-to-child aggression, cooperation, sociability, submission, and so on, but more often than not these behaviors have been studied as "outcomes" of maternal variables (which, of course, need not be denied). Less often have the peer interactions been granted a life of their own and studied in terms of their formation and the perpetuation of relatively stable configurations. For that matter it would probably be difficult for developmental psychologists to give even appropriate descriptions of typical behavior configurations of peer interaction under varying circumstances—no data, for example, paralleling the descriptions of typical clustering by bonnet juvenile monkeys and distancing by pigtail monkeys (Rosenblum et al., Chapter 3). To satisfy myself on this point, I went back to observational data on nursery school children in one of our studies at the National Institute of Mental Health. What is peer life composed of (within the constraints of the preschool setting with adult supervision)? Interestingly, rather stable (by age and sex) compositions appeared for peer interaction in free-play settings. About half the time children were noninteractive; for about 12% of the time they were engaged in cooperative exchanges, for about 1% in helping-sympathetic interaction, 1% in competitiveness or possessiveness, 5% in physical aggression, and 5% in verbal blaming, accusing, or threatening. This is not a complete catalog; other dimensions obviously exist: joking, informing, and dramatic play, to mention a few. Using these data only as a crude starting point, it would be most revealing to observe what happens to this configuration under differing stimulus conditions: adults are absent; a "problem" child is present; the industry in which the parents are employed lays off its workers; the amount of pressure for achievement by the teachers is increased; the play space or play facilities are increased or decreased. Surely a great many unthought-of research questions exist in this "latency" area of study.

One final issue in peer research, whether our subject peers are 12 months or 12 years, needs to be discussed. This is a set of issues involving research procedures. The first concerns the setting that we invariably construct for experiments or turn to in naturalistic observation. With a long tradition behind us, we tend to investigate children in play: a child with a toy, a group in free play with many toys and apparatuses for play. Even our testing of children is presented as "games for you to play." A student of cultures might draw some conclusions about our own. I am more concerned, for the moment, with what we learn about children and development if our predominant source of data is from play.

One comparison of play versus nonplay data from a study of nursery school children by my colleague Charles Halverson illustrates the issue nicely. He observed social interactions in the usual free-play periods, also in the "quiet room" without toys during a period of presumed rest. Not only did interaction not cease, its character changed considerably: the ratios of affiliative to negative contacts changed; the nature of sex differences changed. If this instance is a fair indicator of setting effects, we will want to pay close attention to it in research on peer relations. We may learn and conclude quite different things from research settings of child-toy-child and settings of child-child-child. We may want to investigate play as but one of the many contexts of peer interaction. Peers also work, study, "suffer," explore, "meditate," and love. Children need also to be studied vis-à-vis one another in roles we have reserved for ourselves, in roles of caretakers.

As the focus of investigation turns to peership, a new and methodologically complicated configuration follows: the research reported on juvenile monkey behavior demonstrates the effects of adult presence on peer sex groupings and peer interaction. This strongly suggests that research problems and designs are likely to involve child-peer and adult interactions—at least a triadic interaction and more likely more.

Research on peer relationships, formation of friendships, influences of peers on the individual psyche, adult-peer-child triads, all add up to a critical imperative—namely, facing the serious problems of studying interactions, not only in the momentary sense. It is encouraging that a number of studies in this volume evidence very serious commitments to methodological problems. We are all well aware that there are difficulties: how to conceptualize interactions as distinguished from socially directed responses of one subject toward one or more others; how to obtain records of interaction that are truly replicable by more than one observer, and really replicable in the form and at the level of detail that the given research question requires; how to construct experimental conditions involving interactions that are not trivial; how to gain access to interaction; how to design studies in which we can examine the formation or development of relationships, such as friendship. Furthermore, how does one analyze interaction?

There is enough challenging substantive and methodological research to predict considerable activity and advance in this domain of child development.

References

Halverson, C. Cognitive, social, and emotional behavior in the preschool child: Longitudinal and cross-sectional analyses. National Institute of Mental Health Annual Report, 1974–75.

Harlow, H., & Harlow, M. K. The affectional systems. In A. Schrier, H. Harlow, & F. Stollnitz (Eds.), *Behavior of nonhuman primates*. Vol. 2. New York: Academic Press, 1965. Pp. 287–334.

Lewin, K. Changes in social sensitivity in children and adults. *Childhood Education,* 1942, **19** (2), 53–57.

Author Index

Italicized pages indicate full reference.

Subject Index

Italicized pages indicate illustrative material.